# SOUTH AMERICAN INDIAN LANGUAGES

# SOUTH AMERICAN INDIAN LANGUAGES

## *Retrospect and Prospect*

Edited by Harriet E. Manelis Klein and Louisa R. Stark

 University of Texas Press, Austin

International Standard Book Number 0-292-77592-X
Library of Congress Catalog Card Number 85-51429
Copyright © 1985 by the University of Texas Press
All rights reserved
Printed in the United States of America
First Edition, 1985
Requests for permission to reproduce materials from this work
should be sent to Permissions, University of Texas Press,
Box 7819, Austin, Texas 78713.

For reasons of economy and speed this volume
has been printed from camera-ready copy furnished
by the editors, who assume full responsibility for its contents.

# Contents

vi    *Contents*

# SOUTH AMERICAN INDIAN LANGUAGES

# Introduction
## Harriet E. Manelis Klein and Louisa R. Stark

This book had its inception as a two-part symposium
held in conjunction with the annual meetings of the
American Anthropological Association in 1977 and
1978. Given the interest engendered by these se-
ssions, the editors decided to solicit additional
articles and materials, the result of which after
several years of further effort is this collection
of essays.

The current state of knowledge of South American
Indian languages has advanced considerably since
the last major study by J. Alden Mason which appeared in 1950 in volume VI of the Handbook of
South American Indian Languages. At that time,
Mason described South America as "...the region of
greatest linguistic diversity in the world, and of
the greatest ignorance concerning the native languages (1950:163)." Since then there have been published several classifications of South American
Indian languages (Greenberg 1960; Ibarra Grasso
1958; Key 1979; Loukotka 1968 [original 1935];
McQuown 1955; Swadesh 1964; Tovar 1961; Voegelin
and Voegelin 1977), one volume of broad comparative
studies (Matteson et al. 1972), a useful overview
(Suarez 1974), a brief summary of descriptive studies on the native languages of Latin America

(Grimes 1968), and a yearly bibliography
(Bibliographie Américaniste: Linguistique
Amérindienne). However, these publications do not
provide the reader with detailed data on the
current status of the Indian languages of South
America, that is, the region south of the present
republican boundaries of Panama. It is our
purpose, therefore, to provide the general as well
as the specialized reader with this information.
This volume complements in many ways The Languages
of Native America: Historical and Comparative
Assessment edited by L. Campbell and M. Mithun
(1979) which focuses on Canada, North America and
Mexico, and J. Suárez's The Mesoamerican Indian
Languages (1983).

The articles included in this volume, both synchronic and diachronic, are organized into three
sections which follow roughly a geographic division: Lowland, Highland, and the Southern Cone.
The divisions adopted are those which have become
traditional among area specialists and are based on
geographic rather than cultural distinctions. This
classification thereby avoids arguments over typo-
logies of culture. Furthermore, since linguistic
research still has not grouped individual languages
or language families according to any consistently
agreed upon criteria, we have decided to utilize an
area model despite its obvious inadequacies.

In Part I of this volume we present papers which
reflect the diversity of languages and language
families to be found in Lowland South America. The
Northern Amazon, a culture area defined by Galvão

(1960) and Steward (1948), is a region which has
been characterized by a high degree of intertribal acculturation. This process has come about
largely from continuing contact, sometimes hostile
but frequently friendly, which resulted in language spread or language death. This large degree
of linguistic adaptation, and concomitant absorption of individual languages, has had a major impact on the contemporary linguistic picture. There
is a massive presence of Arawakan, Cariban, and
Tupí-Geral in this region, as well as many
languages with a more restricted distribution, but
which are generally exclusively Amazonian.

The Western Amazon, defined by Galvão for Brazil
as the Juruá-Purus culture area, is linguistically
more diverse than the Northern Amazon. In this
region Arawakan and Panoan, two major language
groups, are found as well as a large variety of
unrelated large and small language families.

Historically, the indigenous languages spoken in
Lowland South America were even more numerous in
the 15th century than they are today. But such
factors as disease, warfare, slavery and the
assimilation of native groups by other indigenous
groups or into the national society have resulted
in the extinction of many Indian languages. For
example, over a century ago there were more than 35
tribes and languages in the Rio-Branco Rio-Orinoco
region of Venezuela; today there are only 20. There
were 85 ethnic groups at the beginning of the
century in lowland Peru; today there are 63. And at
the time of the Spanish conquest of Ecuador there

were 30 Indian languages; today there are twelve.
However, even with the loss of so many languages in
the Lowland area, there are still 170 native
languages currently spoken in Brazil.

Part II of this volume focuses on the indigenous
languages spoken in Highland South America. This
area is noted for its multilingualism. Under the
settlement program of the Incas, the evangeliza-
tion of the Catholic clergy, and the forced dispersal of Indian groups as a result of economic
policies of the Spaniards, many of the indigenous
peoples of the Andes became bilingual or multilingual. In fact, during the colonial period the
Andean region was characterized by three "lenguas
generales" -- Puquina, Quechua and Aymara -- and
Jesuit priests were required to learn all three
early in the sixteenth century. Given that Quechua
had been the language spoken by the Inca, and thus
carried more prestige, it was the language chosen
by the Spaniards as their most important contact
language, thus reinforcing its dominance. Thus by
the late 1500's Quechua became the most important
language and has remained so. Today Puquina is
probably extinct.

In the Andean region, then, there have been for
the past five hundred years two major indigenous
languages, Quechua and Aymara. There were, of
course, historically far more languages. Even into
our own times there are some languages with a limited number of speakers still to be found in the
Andean area. Related to Aymara are Kawki and Jaqaru, both spoken in the central highlands of Peru.

Unrelated to any of the languages mentioned above
are Uru, spoken in the Lake Titicaca district and
Chipaya in the Carrangas district, both in Bolivia. There indeed may be other Andean languages
but their discovery or re-discovery has still to be
accomplished.

Quechua or Quichua is still the largest autochthonous language of the Americas, today numbering
anywhere between seven and eleven million speakers. It is a very dispersed language and has resulted in many dialects. But, whether there is any
advantage to defining certain of these dialects as
separate languages is not clear and in spite of the
fact that mutual intelligibility is sometimes
difficult, especially between Quechua I [also called Quechua B] and Quechua II [also called Quechua
A], most linguists prefer to refer to Quechua as a
single language. Although much work has been done
on Quechua, this volume has certain lacunae in the
coverage of the language in regional terms due to
the absence of syntheses of northern Peruvian Quechua and Inga [Colombian Quechua], which in turn
precludes a general overview of the language.

Both Quechua and Aymara have always attracted
the attention of many linguists, be they American
or European and this is especially the case during
the past twenty years. In Quechua there has been
much interest in advancing the work of Alfredo Torero (1964) and Gary Parker (1963). They proposed
that the origin of Quechua was not in the zone of
Cuzco, but in the northern part of the Central
Highlands of Peru. More recently, Torero proposed

that the origin of the language was on the Peruvian
coast, from which it was carried to the northern
Highlands (1974).  In this volume articles discussing the nature, intensity, duration, direction and
spread of contacts within the Andean region take
the argument even further.

Aymara, a Jaqí language, is the second most
widely spoken indigenous language of South America,
with between 1.5 million and 2 million speakers.
Dialect studies in Aymara indicate that there are
basically two dialect areas, and that recent language innovations seem to be spreading outward from
La Paz, Bolivia.

Most of the indigenous languages discussed in
Part III do not belong to any of the major language
families of the Andean or Amazon areas.  Rather,
the distinguishing feature of the languages of the
Southern Cone is the relatively large number of
language groupings, some of which are little known
or which can be classified as language isolates.
Additionally, both languages and isolates are
characterized by a paucity of speakers.  Research
on the indigenous languages of this region is not
as detailed nor as well known as studies of those
languages located in Lowland and Highland South
America.

In addition to the multiplicity and size of language families the Southern Cone is rather unusual
in having an indigenous language - Guaraní - which
has spread to encompass an entire nation (Paraguay)
and large segments of its contiguous borders (Brazil, Bolivia and Argentina).  In Paraguay, both

Guaraní and Spanish are recognized as national languages and bilingualism is officially sanctioned.
Spanish is predominant in urban areas, whereas
Guaraní is the predominant language in the rural
regions.    In Argentina, Guaraní is now considered
the most widely spoken indigenous language due to
the large migrant population from Paraguay; Brazil
is now also receiving large numbers of these Guaraní speaking migrant workers.    In fact, a recent estimate places one million Guaraní speakers in these
two countries (Albó 1979: 15).  Other Guaranian
languages are also spoken in Paraguay and in neighboring regions of Bolivia, Brazil and Argentina.

At the outset, it was hoped that some kind of
regional balance could be maintained in the organization of this volume.  Our hope was to include all
of the languages of South America.  We have found,
however, that there is simply not sufficient contemporary material written on certain areas, languages and families, whereas for others far more
research has been done.  For example, the Andes and
certain parts of the Amazon are more heavily represented, indeed there is even some overlap in information.  On the other hand, many of the languages
of Colombia, Bolivia, the Guyanas and parts of
Brazil as well as entire families such as Chibchan
receive scant attention or are slighted.

The majority of works which we have included are
based on fieldwork and research carried out during
the past decade by specialists in their respective
fields.  The heterogeneity of contributions represent the particular interests and theoretical bia-

ses of their authors and do not fit into any a
priori framework. Nevertheless, there are certain
overall patterns that are evident in the book. In
particular the articles may be classified by the
following themes:

(1) Those that focus on the current state of a
particular linguistic area (Rodrigues pp. 405-439,
Klein pp. 691-731, Clairis pp. 753-783, Klein and
Stark pp. 802-845) or language family (Sorensen
pp. 140-156, Davis pp. 286-303, Durbin pp. 325-
303, Briggs pp. 595-616).

(2) Those that are concerned with the history of
one or more language families (Rodrigues pp. 371-
404, Hardman pp. 617-643, Mannheim pp. 644-688).

(3) Those that focus on the history and current
status of (a) the languages of a particular geographical area (Migliazza pp. 17-139, Stark pp. 157-
193, Wise pp. 194-223), or (b) a particular language family (Price pp. 304-324, Stark pp. 443-
480, 516-545, 732-752, Mannheim pp. 481-515,
Croese pp. 784-801).

(4) Those which focus on the current state of
research on a particular language group (Kensinger
pp. 224-285, Briggs pp. 546-594).

Considerable work has been accomplished, but
there is still much to be done for each of the
regions we have discussed. By taking stock of our
present state of knowledge, revealing its deficien-
cies and suggesting areas for future investigation,
it is hoped that research will be stimulated both
in the field and in the library. With the Indian

languages of South America dying off at an alar-
ming rate, it is imperative that research be carried out before they become extinct.   If we can
promote interest in this field through this book,
just as the Handbook of South American Indians
inspired our own generation of linguists and
anthropologists, then we will feel that its preparation and publication will have been more than
justified.

In the organization and planning of such a general volume a number of people have given us of
their time and assistance.   In particular, we would
like to thank Javier Albó, Kathy Bork, Suzanne
Comer, Gertrude Dole, Susan Sherer Goscinski, Pam
Hunte, Robert Pergolizzi, Janet Starkweather, Joel
Sherzer, and Katherine Young.   Our special thanks
go to Jonathan Brezin and Herbert S. Klein for
their highly appreciated technical assistance.   We
would also like to thank the editors of the various
journals who have allowed us to reprint contributions which originally appeared in their publications.   Finally, we gratefully acknowledge support
from the Montclair State College Faculty Development Fund and the Social Science Research Council.

REFERENCES
Albó, Xavier. 1979.   Panorama Sociolingüístico de
    Centro y Sud America. In Linguistic Composi-
    tion of the Nations of the World, vol. III, H.
    Kloss and G. McConnell, eds., pp. 9-34. Quebec:
    Les Presses de l'Université Laval.

Bibliographie Linguistique. Linguistique Amérindienne. Journal of the Société des Americanistes (Paris).

Campbell, Lyle and Marianne Mithun, eds. 1979. The Languages of Native America: Historical and Comparative Assessment. Austin: University of Texas Press.

Galvão, Eduardo Eneas. 1960. Áreas culturais indígenas do Brasil: 1900-1959. Boletim do Museu Paraense Emílio Goeldi, Nova Série 8, 1-41. Belém: Conselho Nacional de Pesquisas, Instituto Nacional de Pesquisas da Amazonia.

Greenberg, Joseph H. 1960. The General Classification of Central and South American Languages. In Men and Cultures: Selected Papers of the Fifth International Congress of Anthropological and Ethnological Sciences, Anthony E.C. Wallace, ed. Philadelphia: University of Pennsylvania Press.

Grimes, Joseph. 1968. Ibero-American and Caribbean Linguistics. In Current Trends in Linguistics, vol. 4, Thomas Sebeok, ed., pp. 302-309. The Hague: Mouton.

Ibarra Grasso, Dick Edgar. 1958. Lenguas Indígenas Americanas. Buenos Aires.

Key, Mary Ritchie. 1979. The Grouping of South American Indian Languages. Tübingen: Gunter Narr.

Loukotka, Čestmír. 1968 [original 1935]. Classification of South American Indian Languages. Johannes Wilbert, ed. Los Angeles: Latin American Center, University of California.

McQuown, Norman A. 1955. The Indigenous Languages of Latin America. American Anthropologist 57.3: 501-570.

Mason, J. Alden. 1950. The Languages of South American Indians. Handbook of South American Indians, VI:157-317. Bureau of American Ethnology Bulletin 143. Washington, D.C.: U.S. Government Printing Office.

Matteson, Esther et al. 1972. Comparative Studies in Amerindian Languages. The Hague: Mouton.

Parker, Gary. 1963. La clasificación genética de los dialectos quechuas. Revista del Museo Nacional (Lima) 32: 241-52.

Steward, Julian. 1948. Handbook of South American Indians III. Bureau of American Ethnology Bulletin 143. Washington, D.C.: U.S. Government Printing Office.

Suárez, Jorge A. 1974. South American Indian Languages. In Encyclopaedia Brittanica.

------. 1983. The Mesoamerican Indian Languages. Cambridge Language Surveys. Cambridge: Cambridge University Press.

Swadesh, Maurice. 1963. Discussion and criticism. Current Anthropology 4.3: 317-318.

Torero, Alfredo. 1964. Los dialectos quechuas. Anales Científicos de la Universidad Agraria 2: 466-78.

------. 1974. El quechua y la historia social andina. Lima: Universidad Ricardo Palma.

Tovar, Antonio. 1961. Catálogo de las lenguas de América del Sur. Buenos Aires: Editorial Sudamericana.

Voegelin, C.F. and F.M. Voegelin. 1977. Classification and Index of the World's Languages. New York: Elsevier.

# PART I
# Indigenous Languages of Lowland South America

# 1. Languages of the Orinoco-Amazon Region: Current Status

## Ernest C. Migliazza

INTRODUCTION

Published surveys, linguistic maps and culture area classifications[1] of South America fail, in one way or another, to present the current status of indigenous languages. In part this is due to: the profusion and confusion of tribal and language designations; conjectured genetic affiliations which have not been proven; the incorporation within the same taxonomy of different historical periods covering several hundred years;[2] failure to take into account cultural change, migration and extinction. This paper endeavors to present an up-to-date assessment of twenty-three Indian languages still spoken in the region surrounding the Amazon-Orinoco watershed.[3]

Most of this area is covered with tropical rain forest; there are, however, natural savannas where Brazil, Venezuela and Guyana meet (see Map 1). The indigenous populations, though frequently spread across several national boundaries, are similar in that all are undergoing, in different degrees, socio-cultural change due to the rapid penetration of the various national societies into their territories. Such penetration, as evidenced in other circumstances, not only creates an irreversible

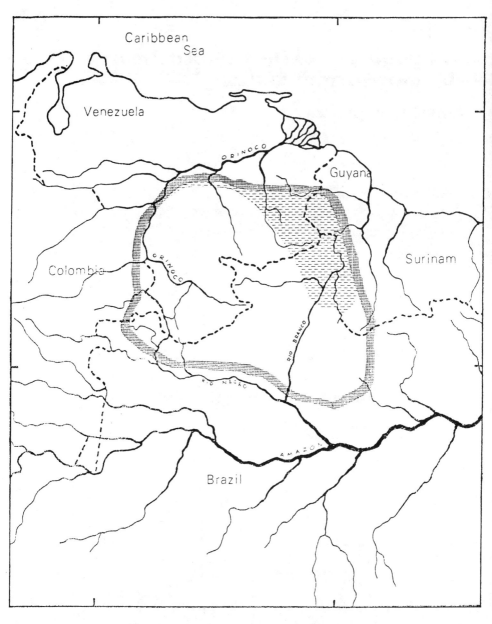

RIO BRANCO—RIO ORINOCO REGION   BOUNDARY

SAVANNAH

RAINFOREST

**MAP 1.**

state of interdependence between the "pioneering" and indigenous populations, but also adversely affects the continued usage of local Indian languages.

The tribes of this region, classified by Galvão (1960) as part of the "Northern Amazon" culture area, are of diverse origin, yet they show remarkable cultural homogeneity. This is suggestive of contact and also of the fact that the apparently diverse local features are somehow manifestations of basic adaptive systems shared by all tropical forest tribes. Their subsistence economy is essentially based on slash-and-burn horticulture, supplemented by gathering, hunting and fishing. The technological level of the groups is fairly uniform with the exception of the Yanomama, where pottery is less used. Division of labor is according to sex and age. Cremation of the dead and endocannibalism are not uncommon. Traditional socio-political systems, except for highly acculturated communities, are still active, with the matrilocal extended family as a basic unit and the village as the politically autonomous unit.

The last one hundred years of European colonization has brought about a "leveling" of dialect differences within the languages of this area. However, there are still tribes and segments of tribes in relative isolation who are not as much "village" endogamous as they are "dialect" endogamous. While observing their tribal marriage rules, local people tend to marry among those who speak their own dialect. Only when the community comes into permanent contact with, or is integrated into, the national society, do dialect boundaries cease to be barriers to gene flow. In other words, among the aborigines of this area there is still evidence supporting the hypothesis suggested by Hill (1972:314) that "dialect tribe" may have been a significant unit of the demographic organization of ancient man.

There are noticeable linguistic features shared, in various degrees, by the languages of this region which stem from diffusion and centuries of contact rather than genetic relationship. These common features constitute areal patterns suggesting that these languages are part of a <u>linguistic area</u>.[4] There are also traits of typological interest:

1. There is a common pattern of discourse redundancy similar to that described by Derbyshire (1977a) for Hishkaryana.

2. Except for a few Arawak languages, all others are ergative languages and have a transitive verb phrase pattern in which the nominal Object precedes the Verb, (O-V). The Subject can either precede the Object or follow the Verb (S-O-V or O-V-S).

3. A lack of active-passive formal distinction is also noticeable in these languages, and the equivalent to a relative clause formation is by apposition and nominalization rather than embedding.

At the time of discovery, the indigenous languages spoken in this region were indeed numerous; over a century ago, there were still about fifty tribes and languages (see Map 3). Today, only twenty-three indigenous languages are still spoken (see Map 2). One of these has only two surviving speakers, and three others have fewer than twenty speakers each.

A comparison between Map 2 and Map 3 reveals a lack of noticeable tribal migrations during the last 150 years, except for an expansion of the Yanomama from the south to the north and north-west, and a marked decrease of Carib and Arawak tribes. Nevertheless, many local groups have ap-parently become extinct or assimilated into other local groups during this time period. Today, the languages of the surviving indigenous people may be genetically grouped into four major linguistic families; Yanomama, Saliban, Arawak and Carib. In addition, a few languages are still labeled "inde-pendent" or better "unclassified" because of their uncertain or yet unknown genetic affiliation. In-formation on the current status of the extant lin-guistic groups will be presented in accord with the following pattern:

1. Name. This section begins with the most com-monly accepted designation. The number preceding the name of each language refers to its location on Map 2. Whenever possible other designations are presented by comparing external, internal or auto-designations. External designations are names gi-ven by outsiders or people who are not members of the Indian tribe in question. Often these names are the result of misinterpretation or lack of knowledge of the local language. Internal desig-nations are those given by one village to another village of the same tribe, but which are not always

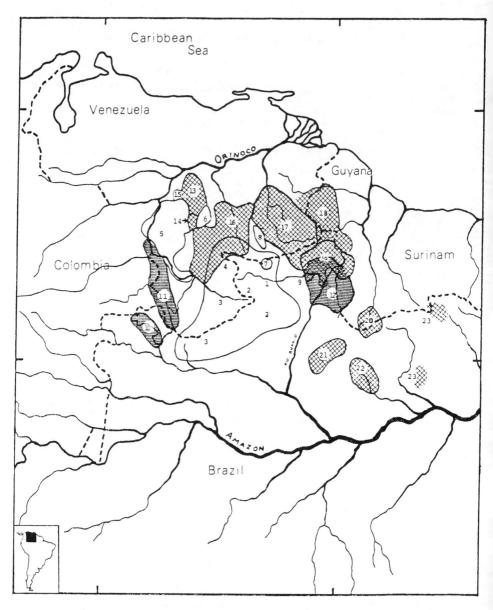

LANGUAGES OF THE ORINOCO - Amazon Region: 1977

| Yanomama | Saliban | Independent | Arawak | Carib | |
|----------|---------|-------------|--------|-------|--|
| 1. Yanam | 5. Piaroa | 6. Hoti | 10. Baniwa | 13. Panare | 19. Makushi |
| 2. Yanomam | | 7. Uruak | 11. Bare, etc.* | 14. Yabarana | 20. Waiwai |
| 3. Yanomamɨ | | 8. Sape | 12. Wapishana | 15. Mapoyo | 21. Waimiri |
| 4. Sanɨma | | 9. Maku | | 16. Yekuana | 22. Hishkaryana |
| | | | | 17. Pemon | 23. Warikyana |
| | | | | 18. Kapon | |

* Mandawaka, Guarekena, Baniva (Yavitero).

## MAP 2.

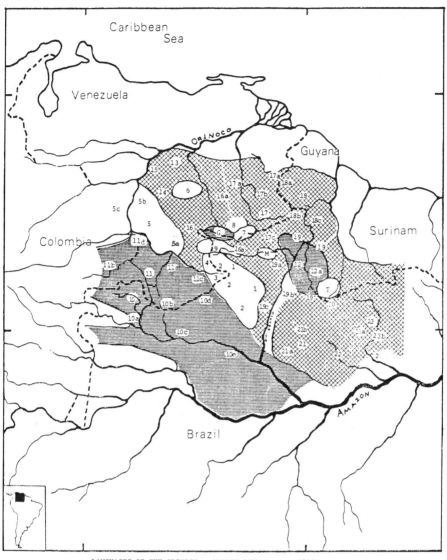

LANGUAGES OF THE ORINOCO – AMAZON REGION:  c. 1800

| Yanomama | Saliban | Independent | Arawak | Carib | |
|---|---|---|---|---|---|
| 1. Yanam | 5. Piaroa | 6. Hoti | 10. Baniwa | 13. Panare | 19. Makushi |
| 2. Yanomam | 5a. Maco | 7. Uruak | 10a. Tariana | 14. Yabarana | 19a. Sapara |
| 3. Yanomamɨ | 5b. Ature | 8. Sape | 10b. Mandawaca | 15. Mapoyo | 19b. Parauiana |
| 4. Sanɨma | 5c. Saliva | 9. Maku | 10c. Jabaana | 16. Yekuana | 19c. Paushiana |
| | | M. Maracana | 10d. Baruana | 16a. Mayongong | 20. Waiwai |
| | | T. Taruma | 10e. Manao | 17. Pemon | 21. Waimiri |
| | | | 11. Bare | 17a. Arekuna | 21a. Atroari |
| | | | 11a. Kuriobana | 17b. Kamarakoto | 21b. Jawaperi |
| | | | 11b. Piapoco | 17c. Taurepang | 22. Hishkaryana |
| | | | 11c. Mawaca | 18. Kapon | 23. Warikyana |
| | | | 11d. Saniva | 18a. Akawaio | 23a. Kashuyana |
| | | | 12. Wapishana | 18b. Ingariko | 23b. Kahuyana |
| | | | 12a. Atorai | 18c. Patamona | 23c. Pawiyana |
| | | | G. Guinau | | |

**MAP 3.**

accepted as a self-designation. Auto-designations are those names which the people use to refer to themselves.

2. <u>Location, Population and Number of Speakers</u>. Only the present general location of the tribe is given in this section. Estimates of population and actual speakers are based on census data gathered by a variety of persons (e.g. the author, government officials, local school teachers, missionaries, Malaria Service Personnel and field anthropologists). The number of speakers of a language is often less than the population number, especially in cases where the Indians are in permanent contact with the national society and/or there are local elementary schools where instruction is in the national language.

3. <u>Ethnolinguistic situation</u>. In this section the general language situation is presented as much as possible within the socio/cultural context and in terms of external contact pressure. Where known, a summary of the recent history of the group is given. Types of external contact recognized in this work are derived from Ribeiro (1957): A tribe may be in <u>permanent</u> contact with the local pioneering national society, or in <u>intermittent</u> contact, or <u>isolated</u>, i.e. only accidental outside contacts.

4. <u>Prognosis and Suggestions</u>. Based on the present socio-cultural situation it is often feasible to foretell the possibilities for the survival of a particular language. Recent published linguistic studies or ongoing research are inclu-

ded, but bibliographical references already given
in O'Leary's 1963 Ethnographic Bibliography of
South America are not necessarily included here.

YANOMAMA FAMILY
   1. Yanam
   2. Yanomam
   3. Yanomamɨ
   4. Sanɨma

The term Yanomama was first introduced into the
anthropological and genetic literature by J.V. Neel
(Arends et al. 1967), and at first it referred
only to the Yanomamɨ language. Migliazza (1972)
has argued that the term should be used to designate the whole family because it is understood by
the majority of Yanomama speakers and, although
pronounced with local phonetic variation, it is
used as a general name, meaning "a native Yanomama
person", by all speakers to designate all other
speakers of Yanomama. In recent years this term
has been used in an increasing number of scholarly
papers in human genetics, anthropological linguistics and cultural anthropology. However in Brazil
and Venezuela the term Yanomami, which was first
introduced by Migliazza (1967), has been officially
adopted. In the past, other terms such as Shirianan, Xiriana (especially in Brazil), Waikan,
Guaika, Yanoama, and Yanomamo were also used to
refer to the same family.
   It is only after the year 1800 that Europeans
reported actual encounters with the Yanomama Indi-

ans.  However,  from  the  middle  of  the  16th  century,
lists  of  tribal  names  contain  some  designations
which  could  be  identified  as  Yanomama  local  groups
on  the  tributaries  of  the  Orinoco,  Negro,  and  Branco  Rivers.   Maps  of  this  period  report  names  of
tributaries  of  the  middle  and  lower  Río  Branco
which  can  be  interpreted  in  the  Yanomama  language
and  possibly  indicate  an  area  occupied  by  them  in
prehistoric  times.

The  Yanomama,  in  spite  of  being  constantly  engaged  in  intervillage  warfare,  are  one  of  the  largest
groups  of  yet  unacculturated  tropical  forest  Indians  in  South  America.   They  are  distributed  over  an
area  of  100,000  square  miles  (see  Map  4)  in  just
over  200  villages  averaging  seventy  people  per  village  and  totalling  in  1970  about  15,000  people.   In
past  estimates  the  total  number  was  as  high  as
50,000,  but  as  surveys  were  taken  from  1950  to  1970
and  more  villages  were  visited  it  became  clear  that
the  number  was  not  over  15,000,  with  a  demographic
density  of  about  1.5  inhabitants  per  10  square
miles.   However,  the  distribution  is  not  uniform;
villages  located  at  the  center  of  the  Yanomama  area
(i.e.  the  Yanomam  and  Yanomamɨ)  and  engaged  in
warfare  have  a  much  higher  population  (at  times  as
high  as  200  people)  than  those  located  in  areas
where  warfare  is  not  so  intense  (usually  below  40
people).

The  heaviest  concentration  of  Yanomama  people  is
in  the  Parima  Mountain  range  where  there  are  at
least  four  known  centers  of  concentration  in  which
the  demographic  density  is  as  high  as  6  inhabitants

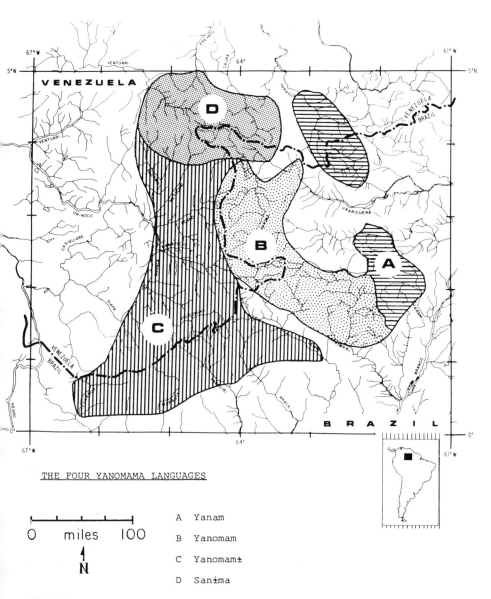

THE FOUR YANOMAMA LANGUAGES

0   miles   100

N

MAP 4.

A   Yanam

B   Yanomam

C   Yanomamɨ

D   Sanɨma

to one square mile. Toward the periphery the population is more scarce. In six specific peripheral
river areas, where village people have been counted, the ratio ranges from one inhabitant per 5
square miles to one per 9.6 square miles. Considering historical records, population density and
occupied areas, at the beginning of the last century the Yanomama could not have numbered more than
7,000 people. Until 1968 they were an expanding
tribe. Unfortunately during the last ten years
their number has diminished. Various epidemics
have in some areas reduced the population by half.
Today their total number is not over 14,000. The
estimation of 8,400 Yanomama in Brazil alone given
by Ramos and Taylor (1979) seems to us too high
considering the epidemics of the last 10 years.

For the first twenty years of outside contact
(1950-1970) only non-Indian settlers in Yanomama
territory were missionaries. The first mission
station was established in 1950 on the upper Orinoco. In 1970 there were twenty-one mission stations located on almost every major river of their
territory; yet no more than ten Yanomama adults
could read and write in their own language.

Until recently it was uncertain as to whether
Yanomama was one language with several dialects or
a family of languages. Migliazza (1972) has offered linguistic evidence to show that Yanomama is a
family with four major languages: Yanam, Yanomam,
Yanomamɨ, and Sanɨma (see Map 4). Each of these
languages has several dialects.

In relation to other South American languages,

Yanomama was at first classified as independent or
isolated by Koch-Grünberg (1913, 1923), Mason
(1950), McQuown (1955), and Loukotka (1968). In
recent classifications by Greenberg (1960), Wilbert
(1963), and Voegelin and Voegelin (1977), it was
considered, without putting forward any linguistic
evidence, to be a family of the Macro-Chibcha phylum. Migliazza (1978b), using regular sound correspondences, has shown that Yanomama exhibits a
genetic relationship with the Panoan languages
(about 40% cognates), as well as with Guaymi (Chibcha), although to a much lower degree (20% cognates). Pano and Chibcha have traditionally been
classified within different phyla. This points to
the need for more comparative research and a revision of the present phylogenetic classification of
South American languages.

Recent anthrolinguistic publications concerning
the Yanomama family include Borgman et al. (1965);
Migliazza (1967, 1970, 1972, 1973); Spielman,
Migliazza and Neel (1974).

The common surface word order of the Yanomama
languages is Subject-Object-Verb. In narratives
the sequence Object-Verb-Subject also occurs. Case
is overtly marked with suffixes except for the direct object, which is unmarked.

1. Yanam: Ninam and Yanam, meaning "person", are
general auto-designations in the Yanam language.
Village people identify themselves also with the
name of a place or river plus a suffix [-theri]
meaning "dwellers of" or "inhabitants of", or [-p]

or [pɨk] "plural" for people. For example
[parawap] or [parawapɨk] "people of the Paragua
River"; [parawautheri] "inhabitants of the Paragua
River". Internal designations: Shiriana or Shiri-
shiana; Casapare [kasrapai] "long lips" (a derogatory term) for the Uraricaá and Mucajaí River villages. External designations: Jawaperi, Crichana,
Jawari, names given by Carib, Makú, Arawak and
local Brazilians to the Yanam.

Location and Population. Yanam has three dialects, a northern one on the upper Uraricaá and
Paragua Rivers with 200 speakers; and a southern
variant on the Apiaú and Ajaraní Rivers (see Map 4)
with 400 speakers. In 1970 the total population,
as well as the number of speakers of Yanam was
about 700 people; today there are about 400.

Ethnolinguistic situation. During the last 400
years the Yanam have moved in different stages from
the Ajaraní and the southern part of the Parima
mountain range to the Mucajaí and Uraricaá-Paragua
Rivers, i.e. to the east and northeast part of the
present Yanomama area (see Map 4). In their expansion, probably due to village fissioning caused by
internal strife, they have contributed to the extinction, or caused the migration of, the Carib and
other tribes (Paushiana, Mayongong, Purukoto, Mara-
caná, Makú). In the north they also intermarried
with some Makú, Mayongong, Uruak and Sapé. As a
result of contacts with these other tribes, the
northern and central Yanam have borrowed sets of
specialized vocabulary related to bitter manioc

processing, fermented drink and "Hallelujah" songs from the Carib.

Yanam speakers are generally monolingual. The first sustained contact with non-Indians was in 1958 with Protestant missionaries, first on the upper Uraricaá, then on the Mucajaí River. Before that time the Yanam had only sporadic encounters once every five or more years with outsiders. Notable were those with the explorer Schomburgk during the last century, and with Koch-Grünberg at the beginning of this century (Schomburgk 1841, Koch-Grünberg 1913, 1922, 1923). In the 60's diamond miners started working seasonally in the upper Paragua and Uraricaá Rivers, and the Yanam population in that area diminished 20% due to "civilized" diseases. As a result of these inter- mittent contacts a few Yanam young people learned some Spanish and Portuguese.

In the Apiaú and Ajaraní Rivers Catholic missio- naries started regular visits in 1960. During the past ten years a road (the Northern Perimeter high- way or "Perimetral") that will eventually join the Rio Branco with the Rio Negro has been built in the Ajaraní River area. As a consequence of three years of contact with the road workers, the Yanam of the area contracted "civilized" epidemics and about three-fourths of the population died.

Today some Yanam are in intermittent and some are in permanent contact with the national so- ciety. Their young people are starting to acquire needs which can be met only by the "civilized"

people; this, in turn, has made them eager to learn
some Portuguese and Spanish.  In two villages (Uraricaá and Mucajaí) an elementary school was started
in the 60's; it is not very well attended, but a
few children are starting to learn Portuguese.

<u>Prognosis and Suggestions</u>.  The drastic changes in
their contact situation and mortality during the
last ten years could bring about the extinction of
the Yanam language within the next two generations.  Already the population has been reduced to
almost half of what it was in 1970. The national
society is rapidly penetrating the area and the
younger generation of Yanam males, instead of sta-
ying within their group to ensure cultural autonomy, is tending to leave to become cheap laborers
in a different "civilized" economy.  Once outside
they become ashamed of being Yanam, rejecting their
own language and refusing to teach it to their
children.

Linguistic work in Yanam includes that of Migliazza and Grimes (1961), Albright (1965), and Migliazza (1972).  These studies deal with phonological
and syntactic aspects of the southern and central
dialects.  In the southern dialect, which is quite
different from the other two, no linguistic research has yet been undertaken.[5]  Considering the
rapid rate of extinction of this dialect, it is
urgent that it be studied, in part because of its
importance for the reconstruction of proto-
Yanomama.

2. Yanomam. The auto-designation of village residents are geographical names plus [-theri], while
the word for "people" is Yanomam or Yanoam according to the dialect. External designations which
have appeared in the literature are: Surara (from
Tupi of the Rio Negro, meaning "soldier"), a misinterpretation of Becher (1960) who thought it was
the name of a particular village; Guadema, Wadema,
Warema, misinterpretation of [warima] "inlaw" by
Gheerbrandt (1954) and Vinci (1956) who thought it
was a name for a local Yanomama group. Another
similar term is Xurima [šorima] from the Rio Negro. Internal designations: Waika, and Parahuri,
are derogatory terms but not auto-designations.
Location and Population. Yanomam has two main dialects: a central one spoken in the headwaters of
the upper Parima and Orinoco River area (2,800
speakers) and a peripheral one spoken in the upper
Demeni, Catrimani and the Upper Uraricuera areas
(1,500 speakers). The total number, population and
speakers, in 1970 was 4,300. Because of contact and
epidemics, today there are less than 3,800
Yanomam.
Ethnolinguistic situation. In their expansion the
Yanomam have taken over the territory of the
Paushiana (Carib) of the Catrimani River. From the
upper Catrimani, they have moved north to the upper
Uraricuera River and expelled the Makú and Mayon-
gong (Makiritare) living in that area.
    The Yanomam are monolingual and only a few of

them, located on the lower Catrimani and Demeni River, can speak a few words of Portuguese. In the 1960s missionary work was started on the Demeni, Catrimani, Parima and Uraricuera Rivers. The "Perimetral" (the Northern Perimeter Highway) mentioned above, is also passing through the southern part of the Yanomam territory. Contact between Indians and roadworkers was inevitable and major flu, measles and malaria epidemics are taking their toll. In only one year, from Fall 1976 to Summer 1977, half of the Yanomam of the Catrimani died.

Another recent point of contact with non-Indians is on the upper Parima area, one of the most populated Yanomam areas, where in the early 60's the Brazilian Air Force and the Unevangelized Field Mission missionaries opened airstrips on the tops of the Surucucu and Parima mountains. A few years ago the Surucucu mountain area was invaded by miners prospecting for cassiterite. In less than two years the Yanomam of the area contracted venereal diseases and epidemics which decimated their population. A few years ago a uranium field, discovered in the same region, brought over one hundred field geologists. Just south of that region, gold was also found and soon the actual road building and mining is expected to start.

Due to the recent penetration of the national society into their territory the Yanomam are in the process of changing from an isolated society to one with intermittent contact with the outside world. This change will probably mark the beginning of a slow extinction process for the Yanomam language.

The Indians themselves are still monolingual and
there are four mission stations in their territory,
three Protestant (upper Parima, upper Demeni in
Brazil, and the headwaters of Butau River in the
Parima Mountain of Venezuela) and one Catholic
(Catrimani River). These mission stations operate
schools to teach the natives to read and write in
their own language as a preliminary step to learning the national language. Their teaching success
has been mostly limited to the children; the Yanomam adults do not see the point nor the advantage,
as yet, in learning to write or to read in their
own language, and even less in becoming Christians,
except for gaining the friendship of the missionaries and obtaining their goods.

Prognosis and Suggestions. The Yanomam language is
not in immediate danger of extinction. But unless
its speakers are helped in their adaptation to the
oncoming contact situation with the rapidly penetrating national society, chances for survival beyond the next two generations are not good.

Recently another disease, onchocerciasis, has
been added to the flu, malaria, and measles that
have plagued the Yanomam in their fight for survival. Onchocerciasis, commonly known as African
river blindness, has reached the Yanomam of the
Demeni River as well as the Yanomamɨ further west,
where entire villages have been infected.

Recent linguistic studies of Yanomam include:
Borgman and Cue (1963), Tracy (1966) and Migliazza
(1972). Primers and translations of portions of
the Bible were completed in the 1960's by the New

Tribes Mission (Demeni River), Unevangelized Field
Mission (Parima area) and Consolata Fathers (Catrimani). Current linguistic field research is in
progress in the Parima area (Sandra Cue) and on the
Catrimani River (John Saffirio). French anthropologist Bruce Albert has conducted field work in the
Catrimani area.

3. Yanomamɨ. Auto-designation: Yanomamɨ, Yanoama.
The same term, spelled as Yãnomamö appeared in
Bible translations in Venezuela as well as in some
of the ethnographic literature (Chagnon, 1968,
1974). Designations for residents of a village are
usually composed of a geographical term plus
[-theri] as shown above. Internal designations
are: Waika, used in a derogatory sense with the
general meaning of "bad people", Shamathari,
designating a group of villages descended from a
common ancestor, probably called Shama "tapir".
External designations: Guaica, Waicá, Guaharibo
(meaning "howler monkey" in Brazil), Xurima
[šorima].

Location and Population. Yanomamɨ, mostly spoken
in southern Venezuela (see Map 4), has two main
dialects: an eastern one spoken in the Parima
mountains with about 3,000 speakers, and a western
one with 5,000 speakers. The latter is subdivided
into three mutually intelligible varieties, one of
which is spoken in the valley of the Padamo River,
another on the Ocamo and upper Orinoco Rivers and a
third, internally designated as [šamathari], is
spoken south of the Orinoco River and in adjacent

Brazil. In 1970 the approximate number of speakers was 8,000. Today the number has been reduced to about 7,500.

Ethnolinguistic Situation. Yamomamɨ is the largest language of the Yanomama family; its speakers are monolingual. The majority of them are still isolated with only accidental outside contact. However, a few of the villages are in intermittent contact with mission stations while ten villages are in permanent contact with these outposts of "civilization."

The first published report about the language of the Yanomamɨ dates back to 1838 when Codazzi recorded a "Guaharibo" word list on the upper Orinoco (Codazzi 1841). However, the first sustained contact with the Yanomamɨ was started in 1950, on the upper Orinoco near the Mahekoto-theri village, by missionaries of the New Tribes Mission. In 1954 the Salesian missionaries also settled on the upper Orinoco. Today there are about eight mission stations among the Yanomamɨ, two of which are on the Brazilian side of the border. The Ministry of Health in Venezuela has employed Yekuana Indians as nurses and has medical posts on the upper Orinoco at Platanal and Mavaca adjacent to mission stations. In spite of missionary efforts to educate and "convert" them, the Yanomamɨ remain attached to their language and culture, and fairly detached from the outside world. However, they have started trading for outside goods such as axes, machetes, knives, pots, and in some cases they have acquired shotguns.

Their area is now being explored and plans are being made for development mostly on the Brazilian side of the border. During the last ten years, measles, malaria and colds have taken the life of about five hundred Yanomamɨ. Recently onchocerciasis has spread to almost all villages of the Brazilian Yanomamɨ, and is also affecting many Venezuelan Yanomamɨ.

Prognosis and Suggestions. The survival of the Yanomamɨ language is not yet seriously threatened; it will be a variety of Yanomama which will outlast the others. No one knows how soon the planned development and penetration by the national society will take place. At present, "missionary schools" are monolingual in Yanomamɨ and have had little success in getting the Yanomamɨ to attend.

A small number of recent language studies is limited to partial grammars and dictionaries: Barker (1956, 1971); Berno (1969); Lizot (1970, 1973, 1975); Migliazza (1972); and Spielman, et al. (1974). The Yanomamɨ are also well known in the ethnographic literature, especially through the work of Chagnon (1968, 1974), Lizot (1975b, 1976, 1977), and Zerries (1964). A linguistic analysis of their formal chanted language is much needed.

4. Sanɨma. Self-designation is [tsanɨma] or [Sanɨma]. Village designation is either the name of the headman's lineage (Ramos 1972) or a geographical name. People of the village are referred to as [-dili] or [-dubu] suffixed to the village

location name. Suffix [-dili] means "inhabitant
of", and [-dubu] or [-tɨpɨ] means "they, animate
pronoun". There are internal designations, mostly
derogatory names such as [nabadɨbɨ] "enemy" or
"aliens"; [Kobaliwa] a southern, more backward
group of Sanɨma. The most common external designations are: Shirishana [s̆iris̆ana] given by the
Yekuana Indians, and Guaharibo (from the Brazilian
term for howler monkey) applied to them in the past
by the Venezuelans.

Location and Population. There are at least three
mutually intelligible varieties of Sanɨma. One is
spoken in the Caura River area; a second is spoken
on the Erebato and Ventuari Rivers, and a third on
the upper Auaris extending west to the upper Padamo
River area. In 1970 Sanɨma speakers numbered about
2,000. The Sanɨma population has not diminished as
fast as that of the other Yanomama language speakers. The contact they have with the more acculturated Yekuana allows them access to certain "outside" medicine such as malaria preventives, measles
vaccine, etc. The current population is estimated
at 1,700.

Ethnolinguistic Situation. Historical documents
point to the fact that the Sanɨma have fought with
their northern Carib neighbors, the Yekuana (Makiritare and Mayongong), for more than 200 years.[6]
Only in the last 30 years have the Sanɨma of the
Ventuari and Erevato areas maintained relatively
peaceful and friendly relationships with their
neighbors. Often the Sanɨma villages are located

near the more prosperous and bigger Yekuana ones
and in many instances Sanɨma women have been given
to the Yekuana as wives, but not vice-versa.

Permanent contact with the Yekuana has resulted
in cultural and linguistic change. Most noticeable
are the use and processing of bitter manioc to make
cassava bread and a fermented drink; the dimini-
shing use of the chanted language in trade and
rituals; borrowing of a phonological process involving the palatalization of consonants when preceded
by a high front vowel; and the increasing number of
Sanɨma bilinguals (Sanɨma-Yekuana) which in some
areas is as high as 25% of the population.

There are at present three mission stations in
Sanɨma territory (one Catholic and two Protestant),
two in Venezuela (one on the Erebato and one on the
Caura River), and one in Brazil on the upper Auaris
River. Mission work is done both in the Sanɨma and
Yekuana languages. Except for the mission sta-
tions, most of the Sanɨma are still isolated from
the non-Indian world. In the 1960's most of the
Sanɨma of the lower Auaris River area moved across
the border into Venezuela, leaving only about 200
on the Brazilian side at the headwaters of the
Auaris.

Prognosis and Suggestions. Sanɨma is the most
unique of the Yanomama languages both in lexical
items and in structure. Given the present sustained contact with a Carib language, one can foresee
a certain number of changes in lexical items and
phonology as well as an increasing number of

bilinguals. However, the prognosis for the
survival of the language is still good.

Recent linguistic studies are scarce; to our
knowledge there is only the work of Wilbert (1962,
1963), Borgman (1969-1970), and Migliazza (1972).
Some language-related anthropological studies are
found in the works by Ramos (1972), Taylor (1972,
1974), and Ramos and Taylor (1974). British
anthropologist Marcus Colchester has conducted
field work in 1979-1980 among the Sanɨma of the
Upper Erebato and Upper Ventuari.


SALIBAN FAMILY
The Saliban (also written Salivan) family of languages had been considered independent (Loukotka
1935, 1968; Rivet (1920) until Greenberg's (1960)
classification which places it tentatively within
the Andean-Equatorial Stock. There is disagreement
in the literature on the members of this family
(see Wilbert, 1963 and Kaplan, 1975 for a good
summary of this problem). Last century this family
included three or four languages: Saliva, which
used to be spoken in the "llanos" of the Meta and
Orinoco Rivers in Colombia and, to a lesser extent,
on the Venezuela side of the Orinoco; Ature, which,
up to the last century, was spoken by a small group
near the Ature falls of the Orinoco, and was
thought by some authors to be another name for the
Piaroa (see Wilbert, 1963, for a detailed discussion); Piaroa, spoken on the west side of the
Orinoco approximately where it is spoken today

(see Map 2); <u>Maco</u>, closely related to Piaroa,
spoken by a small number of people in the southern
part of the Piaroa area (see Map 3). Of these
languages only Piaroa has survived in a substantial
way. Estimates in the 1950's give a number of
around 500 speakers of Saliva in Colombia and 250
in Venezuela, although, Morey (1972) reports that
in Colombia the Saliva population has been estimated from 1200 to 2000 individuals.[7]    While in
permanent contact with the non-indigenous population, the majority of Saliva still speak their
own language among themselves and use Spanish with
outsiders. According to Morey (1972) the Saliva
language in Colombia is in no immediate danger of
extinction, even though a few of the younger
children now speak only Spanish. Ature is
extinct. And the Maco language, with about 130
speakers, is mutually intelligible with Piaroa.

5. <u>Piaroa</u>. The auto-designations of the Piaroa are
[tɨha] "people" and [de?aruwã] "jungle's master."
Their language is referred to as [wo?tɨheh] or
better [de?aruwã thiwene] "jungle's master's
speech" (Krute-Georges, personal communication).
The name Piaroa appeared in the literature around
1760 (Kaplan, 1975) and it may have been the
Spanish pronunciation of [de?arua].[8]    External and
internal designations which appeared in print
include: Piaroa; Maco; Mako or Itoto (a name of a
subgroup); Ature or Adole.

Location, Population and Number of Speakers. Most
of the Piaroa occupy the east bank of the Orinoco
from the mouth of the Meta River in the north to
the Ventuari River in the south, i.e.    from 7° to 4°
parallels north.    The Piaroa language has at least
two mutually intelligible varieties: a southern one
called Maco (see Map 2), with about 130 speakers,
and a northern one, Piaroa proper, spoken in the
central and northern part of this territory (see
Map 2) with about 2,500 speakers.    Based on recent
estimates, the total number of Piaroa varies from
4,000 (Monod 1970) to 1,886 (Wilbert 1963).    The
most recent estimate is that of Kaplan (1975) who
estimates a population of about 2,500. Some 10% are
integrated into the Venezuelan pioneering society
and do not use Piaroa.[9]
Ethnolinguistic Situation.    Historical documents
(see Kaplan, 1975) on the Piaroa describe them as
"peaceful", not warlike people.    Their contact with
the "civilized" world goes back at least to 1700
when the Jesuits settled among them on the banks of
the Orinoco River, and the area became a center of
Indian slave trade.    It is remarkable that the
Piaroa culture and language, as well as a "chanted language", not only survived but until 1970
maintained a certain degree of autonomy in spite of
prolonged contact with the outside world.
    The Piaroa are a horticulturalist tropical fo-
rest tribe which, until 1970, was on the increase.
About 50% of them are bilingual either in Yekuana

(Carib), or Yabarana (Carib), and/or Spanish. Their type of outside contact varies from <u>isolated</u> to <u>intermittent</u> in certain areas, to <u>permanent</u> in others. Some Piaroa are integrated and live in or near the Venezuelan town of Puerto Ayacucho on the east bank of the Orinoco River. Wilbert (1963) reported that a group of Piaroa has gone to live on the upper Orinoco at "Punta Piaroa" near the New Tribes Mission center called Tama-Tama. Also, a few families are intermarried with the Yabarana and Yekuana. Apart from the common local diseases, about 48% of 406 Piaroa tested in 1950 had filariasis (Wilbert, 1963).

There are both Catholic (Salesians) and Protestant mission stations among the Piaroa, the largest being those at Coromoto and Isla Raton. In the 1970's a good number of the Piaroa were advised to move out of their jungle into the more "civilized" mission stations.

Krute-Georges (personal communication) reports that there is great variability in the degrees of bilingualism and acculturation:

> ...at Coromoto everyone uses Piaroa, the younger males tend to be functional bilinguals where Spanish is spoken in contacts with mission workers, townspeople and officials, and Piaroa in the village with other Piaroa. In Puerto Ayacucho there are three Piaroa who have progressed to secondary schooling and a dozen others to other vocational schools;

yet local people claim that there are a
number of villages up the Cuao River who
have never seen whites. There are some
Piaroa groups along the Orinoco and
nearby tributaries, who are fairly
acculturated, some to the point of
denying their Piaroa ancestry. At Isla
Ratón, they produce handicrafts for trade
and tourists. Along the Parguaza River
there are Piaroa who are somehow
culturally and linguistically distinct.[10]

Prognosis and Suggestions. Although there is a
fair percentage of bilinguals, the prognosis for
the survival of Piaroa appeared good until 1970.
Now, with the recent migrations and without a sound
bilingual program, this language is threatened by a
diglossia situation in which it will be confined to
domestic domains, while in elementary schools children use Spanish.

Most of the recent studies are ethnographic:
Wilbert (1963) (good for references to word lists
by past explorers), Monod (1970) and Kaplan
(1975). No detailed linguistic study has yet been
published. Krisólogo (1976) has published a small
dictionary (Spanish-Piaroa) and prescriptive
grammar; Boglar (1970) an article on story
telling. Laurence Krute-Georges (Columbia
University) did linguistic field research among the
Piaroa in 1979-1980. Portions of the Bible have
been translated by the New Tribes Mission and the
Salesians.

INDEPENDENT LANGUAGES
>    6. Hoti
>    7. Uruak
>    8. Sapé
>    9. Makú

In this section four languages of uncertain or unknown affiliation are presented. Except for Hoti,
these are languages on the verge of extinction. At
present there is little chance for them to be studied by linguists except for historical comparative
purposes. Uruak, Sapé and Makú show some lexical
similarity with Tucanoan and thus were
provisionally classified by Greenberg (1960) within
Macro-Tucanoan. However, they also show some
similarities with some of the Arawak languages of
the area, as well as with Warao.

6. Hoti. Various external designations have been
mistakenly applied to local groups who are now
recognized as Hoti. Some of them are: Orechicano,
Chicano, Shikana, Monteros, Waruwaru, and Yuana.
Coppens, Mitrani and Guarisma Pinto, during their
fieldwork in 1972-1973, discovered that these
designations referred to an independent group,
whose self designation is Hoti.
Location and Population. The area occupied by the
Hoti lies between the parallels 5° 20' and 6° 25'
north, and the meridians 65° 10' and 65° 40' west.
The northern Hoti maintain contact with the Panare

(Carib) on the Kaima, a tributary of the upper
Cuchivero River. The southern Hoti are located on
the Iguana (tributary of the Asita River) and
Parucito (tributary of the Manapiare Rivers).
Coppens and Mitrani (1974) in 1972 and 1973
actually counted 43 Hoti on the Kaima, 80 on the
Iguana and 18 on the Majagua (tributary of the
Parucito). However, they estimate the total number
to be between 300 and 400.

Ethnolinguistic Situation. According to Coppens
(Coppens and Mitrani 1974), no scientist had
contacted the Hoti before 1961 when the archaeologist Cruxent met them on the lower Kaima River.
Using names obtained from other Indians, Hoti
groups were mentioned by Koch-Grünberg (1913) and
Wilbert (1963), who assumed that linguistically
they were either independent or a subgroup of the
Yabarana (Carib). Guarisma Pinto and Coppens
(1975) and Coppens and Mitrani (1974) suggest that
Hoti should be considered an independent language
with some similarity to Yanomama (E.E. Mosonyi:
personal communication to Guarisma Pinto) or Piaroa
(M. Durbin: personal communication to Coppens)
until further comparative studies can be undertaken. Migliazza (1975) in a preliminary comparison of 200 Hoti words collected by Coppens, found
about 20% presumed cognates and some regular sound
correspondence with Yanomama.

The Hoti are essentially horticulturalists who
supplement their diet with hunting and gathering.

Their material culture is similar to that of their Carib neighbors, the Panare (Coppens 1975b).

Northern Hoti communicate with the Panare, as some speakers are bilingual in Hoti and Panare. The Southern Hoti are mostly monolinguals and fairly isolated except for their contacts with one mission station (New Tribes Mission) established on the Iguana River in 1969, and with one Yabarana/ Piaroa village on the Parucito River.

Prognosis and Suggestions.     There are no language studies published on Hoti.    A word list (589 entries) of Guarisma Pinto and Coppens (1978) has just been published.    Virginia Guarisma Pinto (Universidad Central de Venezuela) was engaged in 1972-1973 in carrying out a linguistic analysis of Hoti.    Missionaries of the New Tribes Mission are currently learning the language and, possibly, translating the Bible into Hoti.    The Hoti are fairly isolated from the outside world and although the number of speakers is small, the prognosis for the survival of this language seems good.    A grammatical description and a good lexicon of Hoti are the immediate needs.

7. Uruak.    There are various external and internal designations which have been used to refer to the Uruak people.    Carib speaking people call them Aru- tani or Urutani.    They were referred to as Aoaquis by Almada in 1787 (Almada, 1861) and later on by the term Oewaku.    Since the last century the Yano- mama have called them [ɨrɨak] and in the ethnogra-

phic literature they are known as Awake.  Their
self-designation is Uruak; a few of their young
people say that their other name is Urutani.  Both
Uruak and Urutani are meaningful words in the Yanomama language, which may be the origin of their
name.

Location, Population and Number of Speakers.  Their
traditional area extended from the Urutani mountain, in the Pacaraima range dividing Venezuela
from Brazil, to the island of Maracá in the Uraricuera River in Brazil.  Today they are confined to
the headwaters of the Paragua and Uraricaá Rivers
(see Map 2 and 3) except for a few individuals who
live along the mid and lower Paragua.  Most Uruak
are intermarried with the Yanam, some with the
Pemon (Carib) and a very few with the Sapé of the
Paragua River.  In 1963 we counted 17 non-mixed
Uruak on the upper Paragua and Uraricaá Rivers.
Twenty more were of mixed marriages.  Presently
there are about ten pure Uruak of which only five
can still speak their language.

Ethnolinguistic Situation.  Names of rivers and
mountains in the general area of the Uraricaá and
upper Paragua Rivers suggest that speakers of Uruak
occupied the area before the Yanomama and the
Carib.  Two hundred years ago the Purukoto (Carib),
a subgroup of the Taurepan, were their immediate
neighbors.  Probably at that time the Uruak numbered at least two or three hundred and their
subsistence pattern was similar to that of their
Carib neighbors.  There is also a possibility that

the territory occupied by the Uruak extended south
to the headwaters of the Cauamé River, just southeast of the Maracá Island in Brazil (Almada, 1861).
Genetic affiliation of Uruak is uncertain.
Traditionally the language has been classified as
the only member of an independent family called
Awake.  Greenberg (1960) suggests a relationship
between Awake and the Macro-Tucanoan group of the
Andean-Equatorial phylum.  Recent lexical comparisons show some similarities between Uruak and
Arawak.  Common word order in Uruak is Subject,
Object, Verb, in which the subject is overtly
marked by a suffix.  The verb includes personal
pronominal affixes.  The five speakers of Uruak are
bilingual in Uruak and Yanam (Yanomama).  All
others do not (or say they do not) speak Uruak
fluently.  In terms of external contacts they were,
until 1962, still isolated, having only sporadic
contact with the outside non-Indian world.  Since
then they have entered into intermittent contact
with diamond miners who have seasonally invaded
their land, with the same consequences already
pointed out for the Yanam.

Prognosis and Suggestions.  Except for two recent
word lists (Migliazza, 1964, and Coppens, 1975a) no
linguistic study has been done on the Uruak.
Considering the small number of speakers, field
study of the Uruak language is extremely urgent.
Linguistically mixed marriages and new types of
contact with the "civilized" make the maintenance
of the Uruak language impossible; in a few years it
will be displaced by Yanam.

8. Sapé. They are known in the literature as Kariana or Kaliana; however, they call themselves Sapé.

Location, Population and Number of Speakers. The Sapé are now located in three small settlements (Coppens, 1977) on the Paragua and Karun Rivers in Venezuela. The Sapé numbered about thirty in 1964, now there are less than twenty-five. Those who speak Sapé, however, number about five.

Ethnolinguistic Situation. Traditionally, Sapé is classified as an independent language. Greenberg (1960) provisionally classified Caliana (Sapé) within Macro-Tucanoan. Sapé exhibits some lexical correspondences with the now extinct Guinau (Arawak) of the Caura River area (a river nearby and parallel to the Paragua) as well as with the Warao or Guarao language of the Orinoco delta area.[11]

The Sapé have been involved in the regional trade network which put them in periodic contact with several tribes such as the Mayongong, Arekuna, Purukoto, Guinau, Uruak and Yanomama. Sapé subsistence is similar to that of their Carib neighbors. Their traditional habitat was the mid and upper Paragua, where they claim that at the turn of the century they were a small tribe of about one to two hundred people. Epidemics, and the invasion of the upper Paragua by the Yanam, decimated and caused the dispersal of their population.

Most Sapé have intermarried with the Arecuna (Pemon), and a few with the Uruak and Yanam. These linguistically-mixed marriages, especially with the

economically more powerful Pemon (Carib), have led
to a language displacement from Sapé to Pemon.
Other Sapé individuals spoke Pemon, Spanish, Uruak
and Yanam for trade purposes. In the early 1950's
the influx of diamond miners into the Paragua River
increase contact between the Sapé and the outside
world, the Indians serving first as guides and
traders, then as laborers. Today, most of the Sapé
speak Spanish and are in permanent contact with the
national pioneering society with whom they maintain
a state of economic interdependence.

Prognosis and Suggestions. The Sapé offer a good
example of language displacement, first through
linguistically-mixed marriages (Sapé-Pemon) and
secondly, through permanent contact with the national society. There is no more hope for language
maintenance and, as soon as the last five speakers
die, the language will be extinct.

There are no studies published on the Sapé language. Two recent word lists are included in Migliazza (collected in 1973 and published in 1978c)
and Coppens (1975a).

9. Makú. The auto-designation of this group is
Makú or Mako. In the literature the name Macu also
appears, which should not be confused with the
designation given to the Maco (Piaroa) of the
Orinoco, nor with the Macu (Puinave) of the Japurá
and Uaupes Rivers.

Location and Population. Around 1930 there were
two hundred Makú on the upper Uraricuera and lower
Awaris Rivers (Rice, 1937). By 1950, there was only

one family left on the lower Uraricuera. In 1960,
there were three Makú left who could speak their
language. Seven other Makú descendents, but not
speakers, had been dispersed in the Territory of
Roraima, four among the Makushi (Carib) and three
with the Yanam. In 1969 only two speakers were
left, an old man and his sister living near the Boa
Esperança farm on the Uraricuera River just below
Maracá Island.

Ethnolinguistic Situation. The Makú were rainforest horticulturalists whose language is of yet
unknown affiliation. They say that about three
centuries ago they lived at the foot of the Malu-
waka (in Spanish "Marahuaca") mountains between the
upper Padamo and Cunucunuma Rivers in Venezuela.
Reports from last century mention the Makú as regular traders traveling from the upper Orinoco to the
Rio Branco and maintaining good relations with the
Yekuana.[12]

The Makú were driven out of Venezuela into the
Auaris and Uraricuera Rivers by the Yanomama. In
the 1930's a final attack by the Yanam (Yanomama)
at the Kulekuleima rapids forced the surviving Makú
down the Uraricuera River and into contact with the
Brazilian pioneering society. There, disease decimated the remaining one hundred Makú and by the
1950's only one family was left. There are a few
Makú descendents from people kidnapped during raids
who have integrated with the Yanam of the Mucajaí
and Uraricaá Rivers.

Prognosis and Suggestions. The Makú language with
only two speakers, is practically extinct. The

only recent linguistic work consist of a phonological and syntactic sketch (Migliazza, 1965a,
1966). Tape-recorded and transcribed data of 630
words and sentences with a few texts were collected
by Migliazza in 1960 and 1963 and deposited in the
Anthropological Division of the Museu Paraense E.
Goeldi, Belem, Brazil.

ARAWAK FAMILY
 10. Baniwa
 10a. Tariana
 11. Baré, Mandawaca, Guarekena, Baniva
 12. Wapishana

Languages of the Arawak family spoken in this
region were, until the last century, represented by
a great variety of tribes and names (see Map 3).
Most of them are now extinct and, especially in the
Río Negro basin, they have been displaced by the
"Lingua Geral," a creolized Tupí language used in
the Amazon and Río Negro area. The main surviving
languages are: Tariana, Baniwa, Baré, Mandawaca,
Guarekena, Baniva (Yavitero) in the upper Río Negro
and Orinoco basins, and Wapishana in the Río Branco
and Rupununi (Map 2). Of these languages the current status of only the Baniwa and Wapishana is
available from recent publications and fieldwork.
Recent information on the other languages is either
not published or not available at present.

10. <u>Baniwa</u>. The Baniwa of the Içana River, not to
be confused with the Baniva-Yavitero of the upper

Orinoco Basin, are also known as the Corripaco, the name of one of the three mutually intelligible dialects (also referred to as languages) based on their word for "have not" [Korripako] or [Kurripako]. The other dialects are the Karry and Enhen, based on the words for "no" [karru] and "yes" [enhen] (Oliveira and Galvão, 1973). Kurripako autodenomination is Kurrim (W. Coppens, personal communication). Although Baniwa is the most widespread and popular name for the Arawak of the Içana River, other names have appeared in the recent literature. There are either different spellings of Baniwa, such as Baniua and Maniba (Matteson et al., 1972); or names of clans and dialects, such as Karutana or Carutana for Karru; Coripaco, Karupaka for Korripako; Unhun or Cadauapuritana for Enhen.

Location, Population and Number of Speakers. The Baniwa area extends from the Içana River (right-bank tributary of the Río Negro) in Brazil to the Guainía River in Colombia. The population and number of speakers is estimated at over 2,000 (Grimes, 1978) distributed in small villages of 15 to 100 people. Sixteen of these villages on the Içana have actually been contacted (Oliveira and Galvão, 1973); but there are more on the Guainía River, probably Korripako that the missionaries of the New Tribes Mission estimate at over 2,000 in Colombia and 210 in Venezuela (Grimes, 1978). Also, Romero and Antolínez (1975) estimate 212 Korripako in Venezuela. On the Içana, the two villages studied by Oliveira had, in 1971, populations in

which about 70% were below 30 years of age.  Her
estimate of the Içana on the Baniwa River is over
500 individuals (Oliveira 1975).  Most Baniwa speak
their own language and over 60% of them know some
Portuguese or Spanish.  On the lower Içana many
Baniwa also speak "Lingua Geral" or Nhengatú, a
Tupí language spoken by the mestizo population of
the Río Negro.  In Brazil the three main dialects
of Baniwa are Karru, spoken on the mid and lower
Içana River, Enhen, on the mid Içana near the mouth
of the Aiarí River, and Korripako on the upper
Içana: Cuyarí is spoken on the Guainía River in
Colombia (Oliveira and Galvão, 1973).  A few Baniwa
live along the upper Río Negro and are integrated
into the national society.

Ethnolinguistic Situation.  Noble ( 1965) and Voegelin and Voegelin (1977) classify Baniwa as a
member of the northern subgroup of Maipuran.
Matteson, in her comparative analysis shows the
close relationship of Baniwa and Curipaco (Kurripako).  She reconstructs Proto-Curipaco-Maniba,
which, together with Tariana and Palicur, form her
Eastern Newiki subgroup (Matteson, 1972).  The first
outside contact with the Baniwa dates back to 1725
when a Portuguese expedition reached the upper Río
Negro near the present Venezuelan border.  By 1763
the Fort of San Gabriel was built on the Río Negro
and contact with the Arawak tribes was established.  Today the Baniwa of the mid and lower Içana
River are in permanent contact with the Brazilian
pioneering society while the others (Korripako) are
in an intermittent type of contact which is in the

process of becoming permanent. However, most of
the Baniwa are preserving a significant number of
their tribal customs, as well as their language.

The Baniwa are horticulturalists, their basic
food being manioc. Fishing is also of prime importance while hunting and gathering supplement their
diet. A drink of fermented manioc is consumed
daily in the lower Içana villages. For trading
purposes they produce toasted manioc flower (fari-
nha), collect "sorva", a latex used in the plastic
industry, and vines for wickerwork and baskets.

They are organized into twenty exogamous patrilineal clans identified with either an animal or a
constellation. Residence is patrilocal and preferred marriage is with a patrilateral cross cousin.

On the lower Içana there is a Catholic mission
station. On the mid and upper Içana the "New Tribes Mission" has worked among them for the past
thirty years and, as a result, a good number of
Baniwa adults (about 25%) know how to read and
write in their own language.

Prognosis and Suggestions. Although outside
contact is increasing, Baniwa is still spoken at
home as well as in everyday activities. There are,
however, a few elementary schools in the area in
which the national language is taught to the
children. The prognosis for the survival of the
language is excellent. The Baniwa have shown a
strong tendency to maintain their ethnic identity,
and to see their speech (and its various styles) as
a defensive barrier to keep other local people
out. Except for the comparative study of Matteson

(1972) and a myth by Saake (1956), to our knowledge
no recent linguistic study has been published about
Baniwa. The New Tribes Mission has a type-written
dictionary for the use of its missionaries. Oliveira (1975) has published a study of Baniwa kinship terminology.

10a. <u>Tariana</u>. Also referred to as Tariano (Matteson, 1972), this language is spoken by a tribe on
the Vaupés River (Brazil and Colombia). Noble
(1965) and Voegelin and Voegelin (1977) have classified Tariana as a member of the Northern Maipuran
subgroup, and Matteson (1972) locates them within
the East Newiki branch of Arawakan. Local missions
(Salesians) estimate 1583 Tariana (Grimes, 1978),
with a high degree of bilingualism in the Tucanoan
languages and Portuguese. Alva Wheeler of the
Summer Institute of Linguistics (SIL) collected
comparative data in 1963, and Matteson (1972) has
published a comparative study.

11. <u>Baré, Mandawaca, Guarekena, Baniva</u>. To these
four Arawak languages which are still spoken in
Venezuela, we could add <u>Piapoco</u> which is spoken
mainly in Colombia but which also has a few speakers in Venezuela. We do not have clear recent information on the current status of these languages
and can only cite a few references.

The traditional classification of Noble (1965)
and Voegelin and Voegelin (1977) show Baré, Mandawaca and Guarekena as closely related members
(together with the extinct Maipure and Guinao) of

the Orinoco subgroup of the Northern Maipuran group of Arawakan. Piapoco belongs to the Piapocoan subgroup of Northern Maipuran while Baniva and Yavitero form a different subgroup of Maipuran. The comparative study of Matteson (1972) shows Piapoco closely related to Cabiyari and Yucuna of Colombia, forming the Western Newiki subgroup of Newiki.

The Baré are located along the upper Rio Negro in Venezuela extending from the Brazilian border to the Casiquiare canal. E. Mosonyi (personal communication) locates them in, and around, the four communities of San Carlos, Santa Rosa, Santa Lucía, and Solano, adding that the number of Baré speakers is low and limited to old people. The Mandawaca (also Mandahuaca) are located to the east of the Baré extending from the Baria River to the Casiquiare canal (Lizarralde, 1971).

A high percentage of the Baré are either bilingual in Baré and Spanish, or just speak Spanish. Grimes (1978) estimates 238 Baré and 3000 Mandawaca. The latter figure is either an over-estimate or a mistake. A more realistic estimate seems to be that of Romero and Antolínez (1975) of the Venezuelan "Oficina Central de Asuntos Indígenas" which, for 1974, estimates the Baré at 700 and Mandawaca at 500, giving a total of 1200 individuals.

The Guarekena (or Uarekena) are located mainly on the upper Guainía River (the name given to the upper Rio Negro in Venezuela) and its tributary the San Miguel. They number 367 (Romero and Antolínez, 1975) and are bilingual in Spanish (Grimes, 1978).

There are about 3000 Piapoco speakers in Colombia (Grimes, 1978), and about 100 in Venezuela in
the area where the Guaviare and Atabapo Rivers
enter the Orinoco.

The Baniva Yavitero (Baniva or Banibo), not to
be confused with the Brazilian Baniwa of the Içana
River, are found mainly in the area of the Atabapo
River (Lizarralde, 1971). They number around 2000,
according to Romero and Antolínez (1975), but the
number of Baniva speakers is unknown.

For further information the following publications should be helpful: González-Ñáñes (1973,
1974), Mosonyi (1968), Lizarralde (1971).

12. Wapishana. The term Wapishana is used today in
Brazil and Guyana to refer to speakers of two
mutually intelligible dialects: Wapishana and Atoraí. Other names which have appeared in the literature are Wapishana, Wapityan, Wapitschana, Mati-
sana, Uapixana, Vapidiana, Attaraye, Dauri and Ato-
rayu. On the upper Tawini (State of Pará, Brazil)
and headwaters of the Essequibo (Guyana) they are
called "Wapichiyana" by the Carib-speaking people.
Location, Population and Number of Speakers. The
Wapishana are currently scattered throughout the
savanna area of the Territory of Roraima (Brazil),
and the Rupununi district of British Guyana (between latitudes 1° and 4° North, and longitudes 59°
and 61° West, see Map 2). They form an Arawak linguistic island within a predominantly Carib-speaking area. Historically, the Waphishana were first
encountered on the Tacutú River basin (Brasil-Guya-

na border) which is the approximate center of their
present-day location.

In the literature, the number of Wapishana ranges from one thousand to nine thousand.   In Guyana,
during the last forty years they seem to have been
on the increase.[13]   In 1946 government figures cited
2,200 Wapishana on the Guyana side (Butt, 1965),
while in 1968 the Unevangelized Fields Mission
estimated 4,000 people (Grimes, 1974). From our
survey in 1970, and recent reports, we estimate
from 6,500 to 7,000 people distributed among
fourteen mixed villages in Brazil (1,500 to 2,000
people), ten villages in Guyana (about 4,000 people), and the rest scattered on ranches in agricultural colonies, and in small towns.   There are also
some 50 to 100 isolated Wapishana on the Tawini
River at the head-waters of the Mapuera (State of
Pará, Brazil), and between the headwaters of the
Tacutú and Essequibo Rivers (Guyana).   The number
of Wapishana speakers is about 60% of the population, i.e.  4,200 individuals still use their
languages while the others (mostly young people)
use only Portuguese or English.

Ethnolinguistic Situation.  During the early
European contacts, there were four Arawak speaking
tribes in the area now occupied mainly by the
Wapishana: Mapidian, Amariba, Wapishana, and Atoraí
(Farabee, 1918a, 1918b; Gillin, 1948). Amariba,
said to have been spoken on the upper Tacutú River,
is considered extinct (Loukotka, 1968). Mapidian
(Maopityan), called Mawayana ("frog people") by
surrounding Carib tribes, is listed by Loukotka

(1968) as "perhaps extinct."  Frikel (1958) and
Malcher (1964) locate the Mapidian on the upper
Mapuera, Kafuini and Turunu.  Possibly other
groups, like the Shereu (Sereu, Chereu, Djereu,
Tchereu) of the Turunu River, may be the descendents of the Arawak speaking Mapidian, even if
today they speak the Charuma variety of Parukoto.
In the 1960's there were about 80 Mapidian, all
bilingual, in Mapidian and Parukoto (Waiwai).  Like
the Wapishana of the area they speak their Arawak
language and a Caríb language.  Today, about 40
Mapidian are intermarried with the Waiwai.

The Taruma language, once spoken on the upper
Essequibo (Guyana), should also be mentioned here.
Although it has traditionally been classified as
"independent," according to Butt (1965) it belongs
to the Arawak family and is closely related to Wapishana.  She reports that the Taruma have mostly
been absorbed by the Wapishana, although a few are
with the Waiwai (see also Evans and Meggers, 1960:
339).  In the 1960's, however, there were still a
few individuals who could speak Taruma.

The Wapishana dialect, spoken in Brazil on the
savannahs of the upper Río Branco area, is almost
extinct.  Brazilian farmers and cattle ranchers
have been in permanent contact with the Wapishana
for over a century.  They have taken over their
land and used the Indians as cheap labor.  The
designation "Wapishana" spread to the east of the
upper Río Branco and Tacutú Rivers to the Ataraí (a
dialect mutually intelligible with Wapishana) who
also became identified to the outsiders as Wapisha-

na.  Most of the "Wapishana" still spoken in the
villages east of the Río Branco and in Guyana is a
mixture of Wapishana and Atoraí.  A few speakers of
Wapishana proper are found on the Surumú and Amajarí Rivers on the northern part of the savanna in
the Territory of Roraima.  The last small group of
Wapishana not in permanent contact with "non-Indians" lives on the Tawini, in the State of Pará.
Within a year or so they too will be acculturated
to the national society, as a result of the "Perimetral" highway which will go through their land.

There are several government and mission schools
among 40% of the Wapishana who are considered integrated into the national society.  The rest live in
villages located within or near cattle ranches, and
are in permanent contact with the pioneering national society.  They have added to their subsistence
economy the raising of pigs and cattle.  More than
80% of the Wapishana can speak the national language, either Portuguese in Brazil or English in Guyana.  Until the beginning of this century the Makushi and the Wapishana were at war with each other.
Now the northern part of the Wapishana area overlaps with that of the Makushi and Taurepan.

Here there are many intermarriages between
Wapishana and Makushi.  As a result, there is a
certain amount of bilingualism, although it is
always the Wapishana who are bilingual; rarely does
one find a Makushi or Taurepan who can speak
Wapishana.  On the Tawini River the "isolated"
Wapishana are bilingual in Wapishana and Parukoto.

Prognosis and Suggestions.    Although the annual
population growth is 3% for the Wapishana, unless a
good language maintenance program can be started
soon the prognosis for the survival of the Wapishana language is not good.    Already a diglossia situation is present in many villages.    Many children
understand Wapishana but do not want to speak it;
for them it is a sign of backwardness.

   A basic linguistic study of the still isolated
Wapishana of the Tawini River, as well as of the
Mawayana, is indispensable.    The Taruma language is
still a puzzle for South American historical linguistics.    There are still a few speakers left on
the upper Essequibo near the Waiwai; field research
in their language should be done immediately.

   Typological features and phonemes of Wapishana
appeared in Migliazza (1967).    More recent linguistic studies have been done by Tracy (1972a, 1972b,
and 1974), including a small mimeographed English-
Wapishana dictionary, a phonemic analysis, and a
verb morphology.

CARIB FAMILY
     13. Panare
     14. Yabarana
     15. Mapoyo
     16. Yekuana (Makiritare)
     17. Pemon (Arekuna, Taurepan, Kamarakoto)
     18. Kapon (Akawaio, Ingarikó, Patamona)
     19. Makushi
     20. Waiwai
     21. Waimiri

22. Hishkaryana

23. Warikyana

There are eleven Carib languages spoken in the
region outlined in Map 2. Until 1940 they were able
to maintain a relatively isolated position
regarding the advancing "civilization". Since
then, they have been threatened in different degrees by "progress" and the incoming pioneering
society.

Akawaio, Ingarikó and Patamona are names for
three small groups geographically distinct, but
virtually speaking the same language, designated
here as Kapon. It became apparent during our survey of 1969 that there are only minor variations
between Akawaio and Patamona, and that Ingarikó is
only a local Makushi name for Akawaio and Patamona. We found no significant language differences
among their speakers to warrant the label of different languages.[14]

Pemon is closely related to Kapon and is also
the language designation for three mutually intelligible dialects spoken by the Arekuna (Venezuela),
Taurepan (Brazil-Venezuela border) and Kamarakoto
(Venezuela).

Although there is general agreement among linguists that these languages belong to the Carib
family, no historical comparative work showing
their degrees of relationship has yet been published. The most promising work towards this goal
is that of Marshall Durbin and Haydee Seijas (see
M. Durbin, 1977 and in this volume.)

Traditional classifications have grouped the
Carib languages according to geographical areas.
Loukotka (1968) classifies almost every language as
an independent group of the Karaib Stock.  His list
of languages spoken in this region includes many
names that refer to either extinct languages or
dialects, or are synonyms for the languages listed
here.  Voegelin and Voegelin (1977) classify nine
of these languages as members of the Northern
branch of the Cariban family; Hishkaryana, however,
is given as of "unknown affiliation"; Ingarikó is
listed separately from Akawaio and Patamona.

Durbin's internal classification (Durbin, 1977
and in this volume), which as he states, is based
on field research which is still incomplete, represents the results of the most recent internal
comparison of Carib languages.  No linguistic evidence is given in his paper, although probably it
will appear elsewhere.  In one of his groupings,
Yekuana (Venezuela) is included with Parukoto and
Warikyana (Northern Pará, Brazil).  This is of
interest since Frikel (1970), reporting the oral
history of the Kashuyana (collected in 1948),
states that their ancestors originally came from
mountains far to the west.

Two observations on Durbin's classification
should be noted.  First, his Table 2.2 (Durbin,
1977: 35), giving the internal relation among Carib
languages, contains more than one name for what is
actually one language.  For example Wabui is a
general name for the people of the Nhamunda River,
also known as speaking Hishkaryana.  Parukoto is a

general name for Hishkaryana, Waiwai and a few
other related groups in the same area. Other names
refer to languages now extinct, as for example,
Pauxiana (Meyer, 1956) or Paushana, Sapara[15] (spoken in Brazil and not in Venezuela) and Wayumara.
One should also note that there are many cases of
word lists collected in the past, which looked
different in the transcription and in language
designation but turned out to have been collected
from the same village but by different field
workers or explorers. Quite a few of these are
found also in Loukotka (1968) from whom Durbin
adopted his tables.

Secondly, based on data from our field work, as
well as from recent publications and reports by
students of some of these languages, we suggest
(for the Carib languages described in this paper),
the following partial modification of Durbin's
internal subgrouping:

Northern Carib:
  B. Western Guiana Carib (Same as Durbin's).
     Panare - (Venezuela)
     Yabarana - (Venezuela)
     Mapoyo - (Venezuela)

  D. East-West Guiana Carib
     Pemon (Arekuna, Taurepan, Kamarakoto) -
          (Venezuela-Brazil)
     Kapon (Akawaio, Ingariko, Patamona) -
          (Guyana-Brazil)
     Makushi - (Brazil-Guyana)

Waimiri - (Brazil)
   Extinct or mistaken languages of this group:
   Sapara and Wayumara (Brazil)
   Yawapery and Chrichana (same as Waimiri,
      Brazil)
   Pauxiana or Paushana (Brazil)
   Purukoto or Purucoto (Brazil)

Southern Carib
  C. Southern Guiana Carib
    Yekuana - (Venezuela-Brazil)
    Hishkaryana - (Parukoto) - (Brazil)
    Waiwai - (Parukoto) - (Brazil-Guyana)
    Warikyana - (Brazil)

The main change is the inclusion of Waiwai in subgroup (C) of Southern Carib, since it is more similar to Hishkaryana than is Warikyana, and it exhibits the change of Proto-Carib *p to h.   In fact, Waiwai has no phonemes /p/ but only /h/ and /f/ which correspond to proto-Carib *p.

13. Panare.   In the ethnographic literature this group has been referred to mostly by the name Panare, although their self-designation is [e?nãpa] (Muller, personal communication).   A few times the general term Mapoyo has been used to refer to sub-[16]groups of Panare.   A spelling variation,"Panari", appears in Voegelin and Voegelin (1977).   Loukotka (1968) lists two other names, "Abira" and "Eye", which were probably external designations for the southern Panare.

Location and Population. The Panare are located
mainly in the basin of the Cuchivero River and,
extending westward to the Suapure River, the tributaries of the Orinoco. On the Cuchivero there
are two groups of Panare: the northern Panare, who
live on the lower Cuchivero River and surrounding
plains of the Orinoco, where the forest gives way
to the savanna, and the southern Panare, located in
the forested mountains of the upper Cuchivero.

Most of the Panare still speak their own language, but the number of speakers and precise population size is still unknown. Layrisse and Wilbert
(1966) estimated 412 individuals, while Cruxent
(1948) estimated 1800 people. Fuchs (1967) suggests that the Panare population is increasing
slightly. Romero and Antolínez (1975) give a figure of 1300; and Grimes (1978) gives a figure of
1200. Recently Dumont (1976) located the Panare
between 6° and 8° north, 65° and 67° west, distributed in about fifty settlements averaging 40 (from
20 to 60) inhabitants each. In 1971 Dumont gave an
estimate of 1500 to 2000 individuals.

Ethnolinguistic Situation. There are at least two
language variants of Panare (Riley, 1953, 1954,
1958-1959). The southern variety is spoken by
monolingual tribal people of the upper Cuchivero.
They were "isolated", with very little (or only
sporadic) contact with the outside world, until
1970 when diamond mining spread to their area. The
northern variety is spoken in the lower Cuchivero
and the adjacent plains (llanos) of the Orinoco.
Some of the northern Panare villages are in an

intermittent contact situation, while other villages are in permanent contact with their Creole
neighbors; bauxite mining is about to start in this
northern area. Economically the Southern Panare
subsist on swidden horticulture, supplemented by
hunting and fishing; the northern Panare have added
domestic animals (chickens and pigs) borrowed from
the nearby Creole population, with whom they maintain some trading relations.[17]  As a result, many
northern Panare males can speak the Spanish based
trade-language of the Creoles.

Prognosis and Suggestions. Although the Panare
language is still far from any immediate danger of
extinction, there are indications pointing to the
fact that the process of language displacement has
started in the north of their tribal location where
a diglossia situation prevails. While a few years
ago, the government project "Conquest of the
South", would have accelerated language displacement, the situation has now changed. Coppens
(personal communication) reports:

> The so called 'Conquista del Sur'
> (President Caldera's period) is not exis-
> ting any more; the succeeding organism,
> Comisión para el Desarrollo del Sur de
> Venezuela, is basically dedicated to re-
> search and regional planification. The
> road from Caicara to San Juan de
> Manapiare, which crossed the Panare area
> (in Caldera's period), has been
> completely abandoned.

Except for word lists and some observations on the
Panare language by Riley (1958-1959), very little
has been published on the Panare language until
recently: Dumont (1974) has written a paper on
naming: Cauty (1974a, b, c, d) has published four
papers on some of the phonological and morphological aspects of the language; Muller (1974) on
possessives, and Tosantos (1977) some general notes
on Panare. Muller has completed a manuscript on
the Panare language as has Henley on Panare demo-
graphy.

14. <u>Yabarana</u>.    Quite a few names have appeared in
the literature referring to the Yabarana. Some of
them are external designations, or refer to small
related groups who are now merged with Karinuaka,
Mapoyo, Wokiare, Guawuiri. Alternate spellings for
Yabarana are Yavarana or Yauarana. Other names
that were given to the Yabarana and Hoti are
Curasikana or Kurashikana, Orechichano, Yabarana
Monteros.
<u>Location and Population</u>.    The Yabarana are pre-
sently located in the area of the Manapiare River
basin above the village of San Juan de Manapiare.
There are about twenty Yabarana who are not "mixed"
(Wilbert, 1963), while a total of fifty four include those with Piaroa and Macu admixture. Coppens
and Mitrani (1974) estimate that there are only
three Yabarana families and twenty individuals
without Piaroa admixture. Sotillo and Mosonyi
(1975) have counted a total of 62 Yabarana; this
includes 18 men, 25 women, and 19 children.

Ethnolinguistic Situation.  Historical records mention the Yabarana as a large tribe, located on the
lower and mid-Ventuari River, that has been in contact with the non-Indian world since the seventeenth century.  Through the years they have been
sought by slave traders, plantation owners, and,
during the last century, by rubber collectors.  As
a result of these contacts their population has
diminished greatly, with those who have survived
escaping their present location on the upper
Manapiare (Wilbert, 1963).

Today most Yabarana are intermarried with the
Piaroa and Macu; even the few who have no admixture
live in permanent contact with the Piaroa and the
Makiritare of the Ventuari River.

In general, the Yabarana can speak Piaroa and
understand Yekuana.  They also speak the Spanish of
the area, as they interact with the nearby Creole
settlement of San Juan de Manapiare (population,
529), where there are Salesian and New Tribes
Mission stations.  They also have intermittent
contacts with the Panare, their northern Carib
neighbor.  Sotillo and Mosonyi (1975) indicate that
of 62 Yabarana, 42 still speak their own language
fluently, while the others only understand it.
Prognosis and Suggestions.  Given the very small
number of speakers, intermarriages with speakers of
other languages and the degree of resulting
bilingualism, the prognosis for survival of the
Yabarana language is poor.  Their economic
dependency on other more numerous and powerful

groups will soon cause the displacement of their
language by Piaroa and trade-Spanish.

Except for small word lists nothing has been
published on the Yabarana language. Field study is
urgent, but even more necessary is a language maintenance program. Otherwise Yabarana will cease to
be used in the community and will remain only in
the memory of some older individuals.


15. Mapoyo. The name Mapoyo [mapwoi] is a Carib
internal designation meaning "people, Indians" as
opposed to non-Indians.[18] The same language has
appeared in the literature as Nepoye, Nepoyo, Mopoi
and Mapoye. Loukotka (1968) uses the name to
designate a group of languages (mostly extinct)
which, among others, includes both Mapoyo and
Yabarana. The Mapoyo refer to themselves as Wanai,
meaning "person".

Location, Population and Number of Speakers. There
are about 75 Mapoyo, of whom only four are less
than 15 years old, located in the savannas between
the Rivers Caripo and Villacoa, eastern tributaries
of the Orinoco (Henley, 1975). About forty others
have migrated to Venezuelan population centers on
the Orinoco and are integrated into the national
society. There, there are only two speakers of
Mapoyo (Muller, 1975): a man 68 years old and a
woman 50.

Ethnolinguistic Situation. During the 18th and
19th centuries the Mapoyo were reported to be
northern neighbors of the Piaroa, living along the

right bank of the Orinoco and from the basin of the
Parguaza to the Suapure River.  Raids, slavery and
contact with "civilization" have reduced them to a
small group, that in the last sixty years has had
to intermarry with the local creolized population
in order to survive.

Social pressure and lack of women have forced
Mapoyo men to join other neighboring Indian
groups.  At present, there are twenty adult males,
of whom seven are unmarried and having difficulties
finding wives among the surrounding population of
creole cattle farmers.  The local social contempt
and ridicule toward Indian ethnicity and the lack
of women have been major factors in the extinction
of their language.  All Mapoyo speak Spanish; the
Mapoyo language is not in use anymore.  The elementary school in their community was closed in
1971.

Prognosis and Suggestions.  The Mapoyo language is
practically extinct.  However, there are two good
speakers still living.

A basic word list of Mapoyo was published by
Muller (1975a).  A Swadesh basic list of 200 Mapoyo
words compared to Panare has also been published by
Muller (1975b).  In her comparison she found 32%
cognates with a separation of less than 3,000
years, later corrected to 42% (personal communication) and 2,000 years separation.  In our inspection of the same list, we found that for the first
100 words there were about 60% cognates, or about
1,000 years separation, and, for the 200 words
about 45% or 2,000 years separation.

16. Yekuana.  The name Yekuana [ye?kwana] is chosen
because it is the most common auto-denomination in
the recent Venezuelan ethnographic literature.
Other self-designations locally employed are: De-
kuna [de?kwana] and [soto].  Many external designations and alternative spellings of the same name
have appeared in the literature; the most common
are: Maquiritare or Makiritare, Mayongong (a Pemon
word for Yekuana), Maionggong, Maiongkong, Mas-
chongkong, Mañongon, Cunuana, Pawana.  One can also
add most of the names listed by Loukotka (1968:212)
under his Maquiritare group.
Location, Population and Number of Speakers.  The
Yekuana live mainly in southern Venezuela near the
Brazilian border in the following river areas: mid-
Paragua, Caura, Erebato, upper Ventuari, upper Auaris (Brazil), Matacuni, Cuntinamo, Padamo and Cunucunuma.
      The 1950 Census reported by Fuchs (1967) divides
the Yekuana into Makiritare and "Muñangones."  The
number of Makiritare was estimated at 7,794 of
which only 1,144 were actually counted; the Muñangones, a term referring mainly to the eastern Yekuana of the Paragua region, totalled 105. For the
1960's, Wilbert (1963) gives an estimate of 1200
Yekuana.  Coppens (1971 and 1972) tentatively estimates the total population as between 2,000 and
3,000. Arvelo-Jiménez (1973) gives an approximate
number of 1,500. Voegelin and Voegelin (1977) give
1,000 in Venezuela, and Grimes (1974) over 2,000.
      Considering their annual growth rate of about 2%
during the last ten years, the current number of

Yekuana can be estimated at about 2,000. Almost all of them still speak their tribal language.

Ethnolinguistic Situation. First contacted in the 18th century both from the Orinoco (Venezuela) and Branco (Brazil) River basins, the Yekuana have been known throughout the centuries as good workers, traders, as well as makers of the best canoes, baskets, cassava graters, hammocks and curare. Although geographically still isolated from the pioneering national society, there are historical indications that during the last two centuries, their territory and population have diminished. However, in the last 15 years their number seems to be increasing.

In 1767 the Yekunan were trading with the Spanish in the town of Angostura (Ciudad Bolívar) on the Orinoco and helping them build nineteen forts along the Orinoco up to Esmeralda. Ten years later they rebelled against the Spanish and began trading first with the Dutch, and later with the British, at the mouth of the Essequibo River in Guyana (Coppens, 1971). They also traded with the Portuguese of the Río Negro and Río Branco.

During the last century the territory occupied by the Yekuana extended further south than presently. They had villages on the Uraricuera and Auaris Rivers as well as in the Parima Mountain Range.

The Yanomama expansion from the south to the north forced the Yekuana to migrate from the Uraricuera across the border to the upper Caura as well as to the mid-Paragua River. From the Parima mountains and upper Orinoco, the Sanuma, a subgroup

of Yanomama, not only forced the Yekuana northward
to the headwaters of the Ventuari, but also settled
among them in the same area.  Today the Sanuma are
in a state of economic interdependence with the
Yekuana, yet their villages are kept separate and
there is little intermarriage.

The rubber boom at the end of last century attracted many Yekuana as laborers, with the result
that small villages were built on the lower part of
rivers.  There, sustained contact with the Creole
population caused the spreading of diseases and
epidemics from which many Yekuana died (Arvelo-
Jiménez, 1973).

Currently the Yekuana have sustained contact
with missionaries, both Catholic and Protestant,
situated mostly at the periphery of Yekuana territory.  In spite of the presence of European trade
goods for at least two centuries, the main bulk of
Yekuana are monolingual and remain faithful to
their traditional social systems and tropical forest subsistence economy.  Those living at the
periphery are usually bilingual in Spanish and Yekuana.  In 1950, only 2.5% were considered literate; now about 15% of the population is literate.
Some Yekuana have been trained by the government as
nurses and work with the Malaria Service on the
upper Orinoco and its tributaries.

The New Tribes Mission, with its main base on
the Cunucunuma, maintains a medical post, elementary school, and adult literacy training center.
It has also translated the New Testament into Yekuana, as well as preparing other reading materials

in the language. On the Erebato, the mission "Fra-
ternidad de Foucauld" maintains a medical post and
school. The same holds true for Jesuits who have a
mission in a Yekuana village on the Ventuari (Cacu-
ri). On the upper Auaris the Unevangelized Fields
Mission maintains a school with an adult literacy
program in Portuguese which serves the Sanuma as
well as the only Yekuana village left in Brazil.
Prognosis and Suggestions. Most of the Yekuana
live in an area which is still isolated and remote
from either Venezuelan or Brazilian creole centers. This situation, plus their ethnic pride,
sense of superiority, and determination to maintain their identity, has ensured and will ensure
the survival of their language for quite a few
generations.

Caldera's Venezuelan government program "Conquest of the South" which, according to Arvelo-
Jiménez (1973), was to connect the Yekuana territory to the rest of the nation as well as to promote creole colonization of the area has been eliminated by the succeeding government of Carlos Andrés Peréz. At present the area is free from creole penetration, insuring that the Yekuana language
and ethnic identity will be maintained for a long
time. The Yekuana have shown for centuries that
they are able to trade peacefully with all of their
neighbors.

No serious linguistic study of Yekuana has ever
been published. To the best of our knowledge, the
latest publications have been by Escoriaza (1959 &
1960) with language notes, and Migliazza (1967)

with a chart of the Yekuana phonemes, and a word
list (548 entries) of Schuster (1976).

17. Pemon. The word [pemoɲ] meaning person is a
self-designation for three Carib local groups known
also by the internal designations of Arekuna, Kamarakoto and Taurepan. These three names are sometimes used interchangeably to designate the same
people. The most common external and internal designations which have appeared in the literature
for the three main groups of Pemon are: Jarecuna,
Daigok (savanna people), Taulepang, Potsawugok,
Pishauco, Purucoto, and Kamaragakok. Other local
names are listed in Loukotka (1968: 210-211).
Location, Population and Number of Speakers. The
Pemon inhabit mainly the Gran Sabana of Venezuela,
which extends from the Paragua River to the Guyana
border, and includes the adjacent area in Brazil.
Traditionally, they are subdivided into three
groups with corresponding minor dialectical differences: 1) the Kamarakoto, located in the northern-
central part of the Pemon territory, in the area of
the upper Carrao River, there are also a few of
them on the Kamarang River in Guyana intermarried
with the Akawaio and Arekuna (Butt Colson, 1973);
2) the Arekuna who occupy most of the Pemon territory from the Paragua to Guyana; 3) the Taurepan
who are the southern Pemon, located on the Venezue-
lan-Brazilian border, from the Amajarí River to the
foot of Mount Roraima.

In the past, the Taurepan lived as far west as
the Uraricaá and Paragua Rivers, where they were

called Purucoto and are listed by Loukotka as
speaking a language of the Makushi group (1968:
209). Further investigation in needed here, since
the Taurepan of the upper Amajarí River maintain
that the Purucoto, who are now extinct, were their
"relatives" and spoke "almost" the same language.

Published Pemon population estimates vary from
1,000 to 12,000 (Grimes, 1974) to over 15,000 (see
Grimes, 1978, under Arekuna). Some of these figures are exaggerated and others do not include the
Kamarakoto or the Taurepan. Fuchs (1967) reports
the results of the 1950 census, giving an estimate
of 2,724 Arekuna, 523 Kamarakoto and 2,483 Taurepan, with a total of 5,605, but states that only
4,054 were counted. These figures have been criti-
cized as too high when compared to the figures reported by other field researchers: Armellada (1949)
estimated 2,500 Pemon; Layrisse and Wilbert (1966),
quoting the 1960 National Census, give a total of
2,700. The most recent and realistic estimation is
that of Thomas (1975) who notes that in 1970 there
were 4,000 Pemon in Venezuela with a growth rate of
about 3% per year. This figure included 1,500 Arekuna, 600 Kamarakoto, and 1,900 Taurepan. For
1977, including the 550 Taurepan of Brazil (Migliazza, 1978a) and the more than 100 Arekuna in Guyana (Butt, 1965), and using a 3% annual growth
rate since 1970, the total figure can be estimated
at around 5,500 Pemon. Over 90% of them speak
their tribal language.

Ethnolinguistic Situation. Although trading contacts with Europeans go back to the 17th century,

the first sustained contacts that the Pemon had
with outsiders came at the end of the 18th century
when, to the south of their territory, a Carmelite
mission station and a Portuguese military post were
established on the upper Río Branco.  At the same
time, to the north, the Capuchin missions had contact with the Pemon on the Caroni River.  Toward
the end of last century the Makushi "Hallelujah"
religious movement spread to the Pemon; currently
there are two more local religious movements, the
Chochimuh and San Miguel (Thomas, 1976).

Early this century Seventh Day Adventist missionaries entered the Pemon territory near Mount Roraima.  In the 1930's the Venezuelan authorities
expelled the foreign Adventist missionaries from
the Pemon area.  As a result, the Pemon Adventist
settlements spread to the Kamarang River in Guyana,
and, to the Amajarí and upper Surumú Rivers in Brazil.  Today, in Venezuela there are four major Pemon Catholic centers and also a number of Pemon
villages that are declared Adventist (Thomas,
1976).

Trade is very important for the Pemon and is
related to their marriage arrangements and locations of households.  It is even reflected in their
kinship terminology.  Since European contact on the
lower Orinoco and on the coast of Guyana, there has
been a marked increase in the trading activity of
all of the tribes located south of the Orinoco.
This activity, plus religious proselytizing, has
played an important role in levelling language differences that are still noticeable between the Are-

kuna, Kamarakoto, and Taurepan. Before European
penetration linguistic differences between the
three groups were probably more pronounced and intertribal marriage and trade were less frequent.
The Makushi, who are the southern neighbors of the
Pemon, think of themselves as distinct from the
Pemon, although their language is almost mutually
intelligible with Taurepan. In some villages of
the Amajarí River area the Makushi and Taurepan are
intermarried. However, the Makushi do not clearly
distinguish between Taurepan and Arekuna and often
refer to both of them as Jarekuna [žarekuna].

Today the Pemon are in permanent contact with
the pioneering national society. Only a few of
their villages, located along the upper reaches of
small rivers, have an "intermittent" type of contact. Thomas (1972) reports that traditionally
most of the Pemon were organized in households or
small clusters of households of near kin scattered
over the savannas, but not too far from gallery
forests. Even today, the population is typically
sparse, except where households have organized into
larger villages as a result of the influence of
religious groups. There are mixed settlements of
Pemon (Taurepan) with Makushi and Wapishana in
Brazil, and Pemon (Arekuna) with the local creole
population of the lower Paragua and Caroni region.
In the Paragua River area some Pemon are intermarried with the Sapé and a few with the Uruak. Cattle ranchers and diamond mines located within the
Pemon territory have employed Pemon as cheap labor
for many years. About 10% of the Pemon are integ-

rated into the national pioneering society of Brazil, Venezuela or Guyana, and 8% do not speak their
own tribal language.

At first missions, and then local governments,
have maintained elementary schools in the Pemon
area for the last thirty years. In 1950, about 9%
of the Pemon were declared literate (Fuchs, 1967).
Currently about 15% of the Pemon claim to be literate. An estimated 70% are bilingual either with
Spanish or Portuguese, and some speak English.

Prognosis and Suggestions. Although there is currently a noticeable population growth among the Pemon, the language situation is not stable. The
increasing frequency of mixed marriages with speakers of other languages, the increased penetration
of the pioneering national society, the demands for
wage laborers, as well as the effects of programs
for "development" and "integration", threaten the
survival of the Pemon "identity" and language. A
language maintenance program should be initiated as
soon as possible in all centers or villages where
there are elementary schools.

To the best of our knowledge, there has been no
published linguistic studies on Pemon since the
works of Armellada (1944, 1964) and Salazar
(1968). There are other related works by Armellada
(1972, 1973). Thomas (1971) has analyzed Pemon
kinship terminology. Lately the Amerindian Languages Project of the University of Guyana has started
linguistic field work among the Arekuna living in
Guyana which has subsequently resulted in two phonological studies, Edwards (1978b) and Gibson

(1977). There is hope that their work will stir some interest among other linguists in Venezuela, and that soon more linguistic, sociolinguistic and applied studies in Pemon will be initiated.

18. Kapon (Akawaio, Ingarikó, Patamona). These three designations, which have appeared in historical and ethnographic literature, refer to a group of Carib people who call themselves [kapoŋ] meaning people or "sky people" (Butt Colson, 1971). Akawaio, Ingarikó and Patamona are not self-designations but internal and external designations that the local people have learned and now use when talking to outsiders. Designations which appear in the literature are the following: Akawaio, Akawai, Acuway (probably from the word "Kawai" meaning tobacco juice which is drunk by a shaman[19]), Capong, Waika (name given by the Pemon). Ingarikó, Ingarico, [iŋgɨrɨko], a name given by the Makushi to the Akawaio and Patamona of Brazil. Other names are Kowatingok or Kwatingok (people of the Cotingo River), and Irengakok (Ireng River people). Patamona, Partamona, Paramuna, Eremagok or Arenakotte (Ireng River people).

Location, Population and Number of Speakers. The Kapon are concentrated in three contiguous areas: (1) a northern one on the upper Mazaruni basin of Guyana, where they are known as Akawaio; (2) a southern one near the Roraima mountain and the upper Cotingo and Wailan Rivers in Brazil, where they are called Ingarikó; and (3) a southeastern one extending from the Potaro River basin to the

Ireng River (called Mau in Brazil) where they are
known as Patamona. There are also four small villages of Ingarikó mixed with Makushi on the upper
Cotingo River area of Roraima (Brazil). Butt
(1965) reports a few settlements of mixed Akawaio
and Arekuna in Venezuela on the Kamarang headwaters.

Population estimates range from 2,000 (Butt,
1965) to 5,000 (Edwards, 1978b) for the Akawaio;
1,695 to 2,000 (Butt Colson, 1971) for the Patamona; and about 60 (Migliazza, 1967) to 150 for the
Ingarikó (Migliazza, 1972). The figure of 500 for
the Ingarikó reported by Voegelin (1977) and Durbin
(quoted by Grimes, 1974) was not confirmed in the
field and probably includes some of the Akawaio of
Guyana.

The number of Kapon speakers is equal to the
number of Kapon not integrated with the national
society. Currently the most realistic number is a
total of about 6,000 Kapon with a growth rate of 3%
per year. The rest of the Kapon, about 1,000, have
either assimilated with the Arekuna (Pemon) and Makushi, or into the national economy of Guyana, Brazil or Venezuela, and have thus lost their tribal
identity and language.

Ethnolinguistic Situation. Most of the information concerning the Akawaio and Patamona are from
the ethnographic work of A. Butt Colson (1965,
1971, 1973). Although the Kapon had contact with
the Dutch since the 18th century, they remained in
relative isolation until 1932 when the Seventh-Day-
Adventists began missionary work on the Kamarang

River.  A government station was established in
1946 on Akawaio territory, and both Anglican and
Pilgrim Holiness missions were established in 1957
on the upper Mazaruni and Kukui Rivers respectively.  These missions, along with the government agency, started schools, medical facilities and offered opportunities for wage labor.  Some of these
outposts had an airstrip and a store.  In 1959, the
penetration of diamond miners into the Mazaruni
River area increased the contact of the Akawaio
with the outside world.

The name Akawaio appeared as early as 1596.  It
was written "Wocowaios", and referred to Amerindians coming from the Mazaruni and down the Supe-
naam River to the coast for trading purposes.  In
the 19th century they were reported as making regular trading trips to Georgetown.  Thus, local items
made in the west by the Yekuana would be traded,
through a Yekuana-Pemon-Akawaio network, in Georgetown for European goods.  However, since the rapid
economic change of the past forty years brought
about mining communities, missions and a government
post established in the Mazaruni River area, the
Akawaio have stopped their regular trading trips to
the coast.  They have come into "permanent contact"
with non-Indians, have become bilingual in Akawaio
and English, and are working for a cash return in
their own territory.  Some young Akawaio have left
their land and have become "integrated" into the
pioneering national society while others have married into other tribes.  On the Kamarang River
there are Akawaio families, intermarried with Are-

kuna from the Gran Sabana of Venezuela, who can
also speak Spanish.

To the southeast of the Akawaio live the Patamona who speak practically the same language and
are culturally a segment of the same tribe (Colson,
1973: 10). They are called "Eremagok" (Ireng River
people) by the Akawaio. It seems that today there
is not much contact between the Akawaio and Patamona. Thus to the northern Akawaio of the Kamarang
River, Patamona, or "Eremagok", is just a general
name for people to the south. In the past, however, the two groups have been reported as travel-
ling together. The southern Akawaio of the upper
Kukui River and the Patamona of the upper Ireng
River are in frequent contact for trading, and they
occasionally intermarry.

The Ingarikó are Kapon living on the upper Cotingo and Wailan rivers just west of the upper
Ireng. According to the Makushi and to the Pentecostal missionary working with them, they are the
same as the Patamona in Guyana, but have always
lived on the Brazil side of the Mau (Ireng) River
and in the area of the upper Cotingo River. The
Ingariko were more numerous in the early part of
this century when they went back and forth to the
Guyana side of the Ireng River. In the 1950's,
many went to Paramakatoi, having been attracted by
jobs and schools offered by the Pilgrim Holiness
Mission. A Pentecostal mission was established on
the upper Cotingo in the mid 1960's; it had a
school and an airstrip. Their reports show that
there are currently two villages considered "pure"

Ingarikó and four more with Makushi admixture, comprising a total of not over 150 Ingariko. Butt Colson (1973) reports that Ingarikó is a nickname for the Kwatingok (Cotingo people) who are really Akawaio. They are in "permanent contact" with the local cattle ranchers, diamond miners and small trading stores, yet only a few of them speak either Portuguese or English fluently.

The Patamona in Guyana are also in a "permanent contact " situation with the pioneering society as well as with the Catholic and Protestant (Pilgrim Holiness) missions which are located at Kurakubaru and Paramakatoi respectively, two mountain villages east of the Ireng River and not too far from each other. The Patamona have worked in gold and diamond mines and even on cattle ranches as wage laborers. The Pilgrim Holiness missionaries were quite successful in the 1960's and attracted more Patamona to Paramakatoi. There are a few schools and quite a few speak, as well as read and write, English.

Prognosis and Suggestions. The Kapon language is in no immediate danger of extinction. However, the increasing rate of penetration of settlers in the last thirty years has brought considerable cultural changes affecting the language situation. Current government development projects such as the Mazaruni Dam Project (Bennett, Butt Colson and Wavell, 1978), if not accompanied by a language maintenance program, may increase language displacement as more Kapon become wage laborers in English-speaking communities.

Until recently, the only available study of the
Kapon language was that of Armellada (1943-1944)
who presented forty Carib word lists and grammati-
cal notes.  In the last few years the Amerindian
Languages Project of the University of Guyana has
begun field research on the Carib languages of
Guyana.  Some of the results concerning Kapon are:
Gibson (1977), a phonological study of Akawaio;
Edwards and Gibson (1977), a phonology of Patamona;
Edwards (1978a), some synchronic and diachronic as-
pects of Akawaio phonology.

19. <u>Makushi</u>.  The current self-designation [makuši]
used to be an "internal designation" which became
generalized after contact between this group and
the pioneering national society.  The name has appeared under different spellings: Macushi, Macuxi,
Macusi, Macussi, Makuxi.  Other names which have
appeared in the literature (Loukotka, 1968), but
referred to local groups of Makushi, are: Eliang òr
Erieng (people of the Ireng or Mau River), Teweia
and Monoico (on the Cotingo River), Keseruma, Ase-
pang and Pezaco (on the lower Tacutú River).  Some
of the descendents of speakers of related (now extinct) Carib languages spoken in Roraima, have been
absorbed by the Makushi and are also referred to as
Makushi.  Locally, the name "Caboclo" is used to
refer to all the savannah Indians in "permanent"
contact with the national society, and is widely
used in northern Brazil for "civilized" Indians.
<u>Location, Population and Number of Speakers</u>.  The
Makushi occupy the savannah area drained by the

rivers forming the headwaters of the Río Branco in
Brazil, as well as the northern Rupununi savannahs
of Guyana. Their territory partly overlaps with
that of the Wapishana (Arawak). According to Frikel (1958), there are also some scattered Makushi
further south of the Wapishana near the headwaters
of the Tauini on the boundary between the Roraima
Territory, the State of Pará and Guyana.

Population figures for the Makushi which have
been provided by government agencies, missions, and
individuals are sometimes underestimated and other
times exaggerated; they vary from 1,000 to 12,000
in Brazil and 500 to 5,000 in Guyana. Recent totals are: Abbott (1976) 10,000, Hodsdon (1976)
16,000, Neel et al. (1977) 4,000, Grimes (1974)
4,000 to 5,000.

Our field work during the past twenty years
gives the following figures which we believe to be
the most conservative and accurate estimation so
far.

TABLE 1. Makushi Population Estimate

|  | Brazil | Guyana | Total | Integrated* |
|---|---|---|---|---|
| 1900-30 | 3,000 | 2,000 | 5,000 | 2% |
| 1930-50 | 4,000 | 2,300 | 6,300 | 5% |
| 1950-60 | 3,700 | 2,000 | 5,700 | 10% |
| 1960-68 | 3,500 | 2,000 | 5,500 | 13% |
| 1968-70 | 4,000 | 900 | 4,900 | 15% |
| 1970-77 | 3,800 | 1,300 | 5,100 | 20% |

*but living near traditional area

Some of the factors responsible for population fluctuation can be summarized as follows:

1900-1950. The growth in population of over 1,100 was due mainly to the absorption of the Makushi, and their identification with (in name as well as language and cultural traits) remnants of other tribes of the area such as Sapara, Wayumara, Makú, Paraviyana, Paushana, Jarecuna, Ingarikó, Taurepang, and Wapishana. Some of these groups adopted the name Makushi as the result of intermarriage.

1950-1968. The population declined because of (1) epidemics due to increased contacts with cattle ranchers and diamond miners; (2) dispersion and integration into other parts of the country as manual laborers and through military service; (3) absorption by the Patamona (Kapon) in Guyana as a result of a religious campaign by the "Pilgrims Holiness".

1968-1977. Another decline in population, due in part to the migration of a significant number of Makushi from Guyana to Brazil after a local revolt in 1968. Beyond this, highway construction and the increased number of agricultural colonies in Brazil detribalized many Makushi who became wage laborers.

The number of Malocas (Indian village or house) in the Territory of Roraima (Brazil) is around 70. Some of them consist of just one house with one nuclear family averaging five persons. The majority have about 30 to 50 people in six or seven houses and a few villages have up to 300 people. In Guyana there are about eight large Malocas or

villages and quite a few single houses scattered
within cattle ranches. It should also be noted
that some villages have a mixed population of Makushi and Wapishana. The integrated Makushi are
dispersed in small towns, agricultural colonies,
and farms.

The current number of Makushi speakers coincides
with the number of as yet "unintegrated" Makushi,
i.e. about 85% of the population. Of these, 70%
are bilingual either in Makushi and Portuguese or
in Makushi and English.

Ethnolinguistic Situation. The Makushi were first
contacted in the 17th century in both Guyana and in
Brazil. Carmelite missionaries controlled the lower Río Branco by 1725 and had seasonal encounters
with the Makushi. However, sustained contact with
Europeans started in 1765 when the Portuguese built
the Fort of São Joaquim at the mouth of the Tacutú
River. By 1780 the fort had thirty soldiers and a
number of Indian Militia, most of them Makushi. A
few years later the first cattle farm of the territory was established near the fort.

Having been hunted for almost a century by
Dutch, Spanish and Portuguese slavers, the Indians
of the upper Río Branco rose in insurrection in
1787. They destroyed the ten Carmelite missionary
posts on the Río Branco and attacked Fort São Joaquim. This gave the Spanish in Venezuela another
opportunity to fill the vacuum left by the Portuguese and to resettle at Santa Rosa on the Uraricuera River. In 1788, the Portuguese Colonel Lobo
D'Almada, arriving from the Río Negro, defeated the

Spanish, made them retreat to the Paragua River in Venezuela, and reinforced Fort São Joaquim.

The next information we have on the Makushi is about forty years later in Guyana when a Mr. Youd, a British missionary, established the first mission among the "Macusi" on the Pirara, a left bank tributary of the Mau (Ireng) River (Brett, 1851, 1868). The post became very popular and a large number of Makushi went to live there. Nine years later soldiers from Fort São Joaquim took possession of the mission and expelled Mr. Youd, who went to the Rupununi River. A year later, Mr. Youd was again expelled by a Captain Leal of Fort São Joaquim. The Makushi of the Rupununi area were, in 1836, estimated at about 3,000 (Schomburgk, 1847-1848). Since then, missionary work among the Makushi in Guyana has been carried out by Anglican missionaries. There, the "Ariroya" cult (from the word "Hallelujah", Butt, 1960) had its origin and spread north and west to other Carib tribes as well as to the Wapishana and the Yanomama of the Uraricaá and Paragua Rivers. At the beginning of this century, Catholic missionaries had their headquarters at St. Ignatius (Butt, 1960). In the late 1950's, the Unevangelized Fields Mission started work in Guyana and later, in 1968, moved to Brazil. Catholic missionary work among the Makushi on the upper Río Branco was taken over by the Benedictines in 1909, who were replaced by the Consolata missionaries in 1948. In the 1940's the Baptist Mid-Missions established a post among the Makushi of the Surumú River. It included a school, a medical facility, a store, and later an airstrip.  In the 1960's a few other missions started working among the Makushi in Roraima; the most noticeable was that of the Seventh-Day-Adventists and the Pentecostals.

The western and northern neighbors of the Makushi were the Taurepang, Jarecuna (Arekuna) and Ingarikó-Patamona, all Carib-speaking people.  Today, many of the Taurepang and Jarecuna have moved to Venezuela near the Brazilian border.  Some villages in Brazil are Taurepang mixed with Makushi and Wapishana.  There are only two villages of Ingarikó at the headwaters of the Cotingo River (Migliazza, 1967).

The southern neighbors, and close relatives, of the Makushi were the Pariana (Paraviyana, now extinct) on the Río Branco where the town of Boa Vista was founded in 1830.  Just before that time John Natterers visited the Río Branco and collected a word list, probably the first, of the Makushi language (Martius, 1867).  Other southern neighbors, but not linguistically related, were the Wapishana (Arawak).  Makushi and Wapishana villages have been hostile to each other for centuries and local fights were common till the first quarter of this century.  However, marriages between Makushi and Wapishana families started at least two centuries ago, and have occurred with increasing frequency during the past fifty years, during the period when the pioneering national society completed the settling of the best part of the savanna for cattle raising.[20]

Since the last century, most of the Makushi have been in permanent contact with cattle ranchers; yet even today their degree of acculturation varies. About 16% of the total population are "integrated", in which case the Makushi language has been replaced by Portuguese or English. Some 10% are still in "intermittent" contact, comprising only a few villages located in the northern part of the upper Cotingo River, and a few families in the southern corner of the Territory of Roraima near the State of Pará and Guyana. The rest are in a "permanent" contact situation in which bilingualism prevails.

A religious movement in Guyana, organized by the Pilgrim Holiness missionaries, caused a Makushi migration to Guyana between the years 1950 and 1965. A local revolt in Lethem compelled about 500 Makushi to escape to the Brazilian side in 1969. In the 1970's, some returned to Guyana while others dispersed throughout the Territory of Roraima.

Within the last thirty years, missions and the Division of Education of the Territory of Roraima have established about forty elementary schools in or near Makushi villages. This has made a substantial contribution to the high number of bilinguals (Makushi-Portuguese) which represent over 75% of the present generation. The same thing has happened in Guyana where elementary school children have learned English; recent estimates give a figure of about 80% bilingualism in Makushi and English. Although Makushi and Wapishana are genetically unrelated languages, their contact over a period of 500 years and their adaptation to the same savannah and

tropical forest environment have contributed to the
development of common ethnolinguistic features.
However, in comparison to the Wapishana, the Makushi stand out as being more "conservative." Not
only did they seem to be more successful in warfare, but presently they are more resistant to
change and acculturation. They also have more
autonomous villages and and maintain a more traditional cultural identity and language than the
Wapishana. In mixed villages it is usually the
Wapishana who learn Makushi rather than the opposite. Within mixed families of Wapishana fathers
and Makushi mothers, it is the father who knows
Makushi; the children are either bilingual or speak
just Makushi.

Before 1968, the Makushi language exhibited two
mutually intelligible dialects: an eastern one spoken in the region of the Mau (Ireng) River and
eastward into Guyana, and a western one spoken in
the area of the Surumú-Cotingo Rivers and southwest
to the Uraricuera River. During the last ten years
speakers of both dialects have mixed on the Brazilian side. There are, however, about 700 Makushi
in the Mau River area, and in Guyana the eastern
dialect is also spoken.

While in the past the Makushi used to live together in extended families in large conical houses,
today some of them who are not "integrated" live in
nuclear families in small rectangular mud houses.
Sororal polygyny, although rare, is still practiced
in some isolated villages. Their traditional subsistence economy (horticulture and hunting) has

been expanded to include the raising of a few chickens, pigs, goats and sometimes a few head of cattle. In some of the most prosperous villages, the Makushi exchange garden products, such as toasted manioc flour, bananas, and in season, corn and beans, for trade goods or money. They also work occasionally as wage laborers on cattle farms and in the diamond mines. Since 1965, many Makushi have been employed by the government in road construction.

Prognosis and Suggestions. In spite of a steady population growth during the last ten years, of about 2% per year, the rapid penetration of the national society through road construction, military service, cattle farms, agricultural colonies, mines and elementary schools is threatening the survival of the language by increasing the number of "integrated" Makushi. Extinction of their language is not imminent, with 80% of tribal members still speaking Makushi; but there is a steady decline in the number of speakers. To ensure its survival, a bilingual education program should be implemented immediately. This should begin with the preparation of an adequate grammar of Makushi and the compilation of a dictionary, followed by the collection of texts and reading materials. The third phase of such a program would involve the training of bilingual teachers. The small number of Makushi who are not only bilingual, but who have also been trained in vocational schools as elementary school teachers, should be trained to teach both Makushi and the national language.

Some ethnographies and vocabularies were compiled during the first half of the century; see for example Farabee (1924), Meyer (1951). Recent linguistic work includes: Carvalho (1936), Hawkins (1950), on patterns of vowel loss; Foster (1959), a phonemic analysis; Burns (1963), on verb inflections; Migliazza (1967), contains external and typological information; R. Hodson (1974), on personal and impersonal deixis in Makushi; C. Hodson (1976), an analysis of Makushi semantic clauses; and Abbott (1976), a description of Makushi "clause" structure. A phonological study is in progress by Neusa M. Carson, a doctoral student at the University of Kansas. Bible translation is being carried out by members of the Unevangelized Fields Mission and the Summer Institute of Linguistics.

20. <u>Waiwai</u>. The internal designation Waiwai refers to a group of Parukoto speaking people of diverse origin and languages. Different spellings have appeared in recent literature: Waiwaiyi, Wayawai, Woyawai, Wayewai. Different names applied to them have been: Parukoto, Tapioca, Taruma, Mouyenna or Mapidian and lately Shereu and Catawian. Some of these are names of small groups that have intermarried with the Waiwai.
<u>Location and Population</u>. The traditional location of the Waiwai was on the Mapuera and Kafuini Rivers in the State of Pará, Brazil, which borders with Guyana. In 1950, there were about 180 Waiwai in more than seven villages extending from the head-

waters of the Essequibo River (Guyana), to the upper Mapuera River (Brazil), (Butt, 1965). In 1960,
their number was 250 (Butt, 1965); a recent report
give an estimate of 700 (Grimes, 1974).
Ethnolinguistic Situation. The Waiwai, according
to Butt (1965) are a conglomeration of Parukoto
(Carib), Mawayana (Arawak) and Taruma. Originally,
an isolated Parukoto tribe of the Mapuera River,
the Waiwai were contacted in the 1940's by American
missionaries of the Unevangelized Fields Mission,
first on the Brazil side of their territory and
then, in 1949, on the Guyana side near the headwaters of the Essequibo. The mission station,
located at Kanashen (a village with an airstrip),
provided the Waiwai with medical aid, an alphabe-
tization program and their only sustained contact
with outsiders. In 1956, the whole village, including their shaman, converted to Christianity and
the church became part of their daily life. Converted Taruma and Mapidan (Mawayana) families joined the Waiwai and their number increased to 250.
    Some Waiwai men learned to read and write in
their own language and were trained as missionaries. They then travelled in small teams to other
Carib groups of the area attempting to convert them
to Christianity. As a result, the new ideology,
ceremonial practices, feasting, taboos, etc., of
the newly converted Waiwai started spreading to
other neighboring tribes. To the southwest they
contacted the Waimirí on the Alalau River, but with
little success. To the south they contacted the
Parukoto-speaking groups of the upper Nhamundá and

Mapuera Rivers, as well as the Shereu of the upper Cachorro River. Quite a few families of these two tribes were attracted to, and joined, the Waiwai village of Kanashen. About 40 Arawak-speaking Mawayana of the upper Mapuera and Turunu Rivers also intermarried with the Waiwai. In the 1960's, the Parukoto-speaking Katuema (a derogatory Tupí name for the Mapuera River Indians; also spelled Catawian, Catuena, Katwena), who lived in eight villages around the Mapuera River area, were contacted and about 100 of them have since joined the Waiwai (Grimes, 1974).

A small group of Waiwai went to Surinam in the 1960's and evangelized the Trio as well as their neighbors, the Waiyana. As a consequence of an unsuccessful local revolt in the Rupununi district, foreign missionaries were not allowed to work in Guyana after 1969. They went, however, to the Brazilian side and were followed by most of the Waiwai who moved across the border to the upper Mapuera and Kafuini Rivers where the Brazilian Air Force has an emergency airstrip. There, local small groups joined them, thus increasing the number of the "new" Waiwai to 700.

The Waiwai are in intermittent contact with the non-Indian world. In Guyana they were making tourist items and various curios which were sold for them in Georgetown. They have, however, maintained their traditional subsistence economy as well as many other aspects of their material culture. Now most of them know how to read in their language and a few can manage a simple conversation in English.

During 1976 some families moved back north to the
Essequibo where they had been ten years ago.
Prognosis and Suggestions.  At present the Waiwai
language is in no danger of extinction.  In fact,
it has been expanding; Arawak-speaking people have
learned Waiwai and joined them.  And other closely
related Carib languages have also merged with Waiwai, probably causing some specific linguistic
changes.

There are only three not too recent linguistic
studies by Hawkins (1952, 1953 and 1962), who describes the phonology and morphology of Waiwai as it
was spoken in 1949 and 1951. Almost thirty years
have passed since then, and many speakers of other
languages have been absorbed by the original Waiwai
of the 1960's. Robert Hawkins has translated the
New Testament and part of the Old Testament in Waiwai.  Derbyshire (1961) has compared some features
of Hishkaryana to Waiwai and Kashuyana.  Soon the
"Perimetral Norte" highway will pass through the
southern part of the Waiwai area, and they will be
in permanent contact with the Brazilian pioneering
society.  When this happens, the last opportunity
to study the Waiwai language in its own traditional
social context will be lost.


21. Waimirí.  This designation is used here for
local groups living in the area between the Jatapú
and Jauaperí Rivers (Amazonas State and Territory
of Roraima, Brazil).  We are still uncertain about
the self-designations of these groups.  The various
names that have appeared in the literature either

refer to the same tribe and language, but reported
by different people and informants at different times, or they refer to dialects of the same language. Waimirí, Uaimirí, or Wahmirí, is a southern
group; Yauaperí, Jawaperí, Atroarí, Atruahí or Atroahí, is a northern group; Crixaná, Chrichaná,
Quirixaná a western group of the last century; Pa-
rikí, Anfika, Anfehhine and other names of uncertain eastern groups probably refer to the Waimirí.
Location and Population. Since the last century
the traditional territory of the Waimirí, Atroahí,
and other small related Carib groups was located to
the east of the Río Negro, especially in the basin
of the Jauaperí River toward the Guyana border.
The Crichaná, Chrichaná or Crixaná, were reported
last century to be on the Jauaperí and Curiuaú Rivers not far from the Río Negro. During this century only the names Atroahí (or Jauaperí) and Waimirí have been reported on the Jauaperí and Alalaú
Rivers. Local reports mention that these people
have also appeared to the east on the upper Uatumá
and Jatapú Rivers. The inhabitants of the upper
Nhamundá River have also known about them, although
by different names.

In 1964 and 1965, when areal surveys were made,
ten villages (each consisting of one large round
house) were found: two were located just north of
the Alalaú River and eight to the south of it, between the Santo Antonio and Uatumá Rivers. Probably there were others which were not found since
the FUNAI (Fundaçẽo Nacional do Indio) are known to
make contact with groups of Waimirí on the upper

Camananau and Curiuaú Rivers, tributaries of the
Río Negro.  In 1968, as the Manaus-Boa Vista highway (BR-174) reached their territory, the Waimirí
started to moved eastward.  In 1970 there were four
villages north of the Alalaú and five or six to the
south of it.

Recent reports on the population size of the
Waimirí varies from 200 to 2,000.  In 1943 the estimate was 500 in the Territory of Roraima, and
there were probably equally as many in the State of
Amazonas.  Expedito Arnaud (personal communications) reports a total of 1,000 Waimirí-Atroarí in
the early 1970's.  Grimes (1974), quoting S.I.L.
estimates, gives 500 Atruahí and 500 to 1,000 Waimirí.  Some agencies have raised the total number
of Waimirí to 2,000. However, based on the fact
that surveyed "isolated" Carib villages of the same
"culture area" who are neighbors of the Waimirí, as
well as the visited Waimirí villages, average no
more than 50 people per village, we estimate that
today there are no more than 200 Waimirí in the
Territory of Roraima, and about 300 to 400 in the
State of Amazonas.

Ethnolinguistic Situation.  The existence of Carib
Indians inhabiting the area of the Jauaperí and
Curiuaú Rivers (left tributaries of the lower Río
Negro) has been known for at least three centuries.  They lived not far from the Río Negro.  It
is still a mystery as to how they survived, since
in the 17th and 18th centuries various Portuguese
expeditions were conducted up the Río Negro and
Branco hunting Indians to be sold as slaves, with

the result that many local Indian groups of the
lower Rio Negro and Rio Branco became extinct.

Early last century the Waimirí were reported as
"friendly" and trading Brazil nuts and other forest
products with outsiders. It was during this time
that a trader killed some Jauaperí Indians in a
misunderstanding over payment for some Brazil
nuts. The next boat that went upriver was ignorant
of what had happened a few months earlier, and when
it arrived at the Indian village its occupants were
attacked and killed. Only one person escaped to
tell the story. Punitive expeditions were then
sent upriver, killing and destroying entire villages. In 1866, Pereira Vasconcelos went up the Jauaperí and killed many Carib Indians, burning their
villages. In revenge, the Jauaperí went downriver
and, in 1872, attacked the settlement of Moura on
the Rio Negro, forcing its inhabitants to abandon
the place. In 1873, the government sent soldiers
up to Moura and found it abandoned. They then proceeded up the Jauaperí and killed every Indian they
could find.

In 1884, Barbosa Rodrigues succeeded in making
friendly contact with the Jauaperí, using a Makushi
as an interpreter. They told him what had happened
in the past and their reasons for being afraid of
outsiders. Barbosa called them Crichanas, relating
them to the Crichaná of the Catrimani River, who
are now extinct. He also reported that early inhabitants of the Jauaperí area were "Cericuna, Kari-
puna, Atruai and Arawak." The fact that Makushi (a
Carib language of the upper Rio Branco area) could

be understood by the Carib of the Jauaperí River is
significant not only for making friendly contact
with them, since they are still isolated and hostile to outsiders, but for the classification of
the language as well.

A few other reports should be mentioned. In
1905 an adventurer named Vidal went up the Jauaperí
River for commercial exploitations and, as a result
of some misunderstanding, killed an Indian. He
then ran away to Manaus pretending that he had been
expelled by the Indians who he said had burned his
home. The Governor of Manaus, Constantino Neri,
sent a military expedition to "purge" the Jauaperí
River. Members of the expedition surrounded some
Atroarí Indian villages, burned them and left 283
Indian bodies for the vultures. They then took one
woman and eighteen male prisoners to Manaus. Explorers Hübner and Koch-Grünberg (1907) also reported these facts.

The 1925 list of Rio Branco valley tribes, recorded at the Indian Protection Service office of
Manaus, has four names for what appears to be the
same group: Atroahy, Chrichaná, Waimiry and Jauaperí. It is known now that the Atruahí or Atroarí
were also called Jauaperí after the name of the river they inhabited. The Chrichaná or Crichaná, a
variety of Paushana, were either a subgroup of the
Crichaná of the Catrimani River who joined the Atroarí, or mistakenly identified as such by Barbosa
Rodrigues (1885), who thought the Atroarí were Crichaná. Waimirí could have been a variety of the
Waimirí-Atroarí language, since the Carib living on

the Alalaú and to the south of it were referred to as Waimirí, and those to the north of it, on the Jauaperé, were referred to as Atroarí.

Throughout the years, until today, the Waimirí have maintained their isolation from the incoming pioneering society. Almost every year they came into conflict with outsiders. In spite of constant efforts to make friendly contact on the part of FUNAI personnel, the Waimirí have answered with unpredictable hostility, killing many dedicated FUNAI employees. When the Manaus-Boa Vista highway reached their territory many contacts were made, and many resulted in death. In 1968 an Italian priest and eight Brazilians (including two women) died in their first day's attempt to pacify the Indians. From that time until 1976, when the road was finished, twenty-four "civilized" people were killed. There is no record of how many Waimirí have died as a result of these contacts. There are no longer any villages on the Jauaperí River, only on the Alalaú basin. As the road was built through their territory the Waimirí moved deeper into the forest.

Today there is no longer evidence of Atroarí being a distinct language from Waimirí; now both names refer to the same people. They are still monolingual and "isolated" as to external contact. They have a typical tropical forest subsistence economy: slash-and-burn horticulture, hunting, collecting, and fishing. All we know of the Waimirí language comes from a very few word lists collected early this century.

Prognosis and Suggestions. During the last 40
years, nothing has been published about the Waimirí
language. Language study, or field research, will
be extremely useful and should be started as soon
as possible. How long their language will survive
is difficult to know. Unless the Indians are vac-
cinated and under constant medical attention, any
sudden contact with the outside world will be dan-
gerous to their health, as well as to their prolonged existence.

22. Hishkaryana. The name [hiskaru+yana] "deer
(species) + people" is a self-designation (Frikel,
1958). In the literature it has appeared also as
Hixkaryana, Hichkaruyana, Hitchkaruyana, Hishcari-
ana, Hishcariyana, Chawiyana, Tucano, Kumiyana,
Sokaka or Sakaka. The Hishkaryana have also been
designated as Wabui (Babui, Uabui, Abui) which is a
general name for all of the Indians of the Nhamundá
River. Other external designations for the Carib
people of the Nhamundá and Mapuera Rivers are: the
Tupí word Katuema "no good people"; the Carib words
Totokumu "people" and Totoimo "people-fierce".
Frikel (1958) and Malcher (1964) give a list of internal designations for groups of the Nhamundá River which appears to consist of other names for
people speaking Hishkaryana.
Location and Population. The main villages (Maloca) of the Hishkaryana are located on the upper
Nhamundá River above the fumaça rapids. The Nhamundá is a northern tributary of the Amazon, and
divides the Brazilian state of Pará from Amazonas.

The territory of the Hishkaryana extends from the
Nhamundá eastward to the Mapuera River and westward
to the Jatapú River.  In 1951 there were about 80
Hishkaryana distributed in four villages, plus five
villages of Chawiyana with 150 people; the Sekaka
had become extinct (Frikel, 1958). Most of the
Indians were monolingual, with a few men who could
also speak some Portuguese for trade purposes.  Recently the Hishkaryana have absorbed most of the
other small groups of the area, thus raising their
current estimated number to 350 (Derbyshire 1977a).
However, counting all local groups recognized as
Hishkaryana speakers (i.e., the close and mutually
intelligible varieties from the Jatapú to the Mapuera Rivers) would result in a total number of about
500.

Ethnolinguistic Situation.  Hishkaryana is spoken
by Carib Indians of the Parukoto-Charuma language
group (Frikel, 1958). Included in this same group,
according to Frikel, are the Waiwai and Katuema,
and a few other minor local subgroups such as the
Faruaru, etc., who have different local names but
speak either a close variety of Hishkaryana or Waiwai.  Derbyshire (1965, 1977a) reports that Hishkaryana is spoken by people of mixed origins, i.e.,
from diverse local tribal groups of the Nhamundá
and Mapuera River.  Frikel (1958) reports that the
Chawiyana of the upper Nhamundá in 1940 numbered
about 300-350 people, but in 1955 were only 150.
They used to be enemies of the Hishkaryana but now,
intermarried with them, are becoming a single
group.

The Faruaru, Farukoto or Parokoto, meaning "people of the Paru River", are different spellings for the same people who live on the Mapuera River. For all purposes they speak Hishkaryana.

The Hishkaryana of the Nhamundá had, in the past, different degrees of sporadic to intermittent contact with outsiders according to their location on the upper or lower part of the river. The oldest document about them is that of Friar Francisco de São Marcos who in 1725 transferred the Babui (Hishkaryana) from the Trombetas River westward to the Nhamundá where they are still found today (Frikel, 1958). Contact with Europeans may have actually occurred before 1725, probably in the 17th century, when the Franciscans were visiting the lower Trombetas River area regularly, even before the Fort of Pauichis (Pauxi) was built in 1697, near the modern town of Obidos (Frikel, 1970).

Until this century the Hishkaryana were still isolated and their language and culture was only slightly affected by the sporadic contacts they had with outsiders. During this century contact had become intermittent; there have been more frequent visits by small pioneering teams of the Creolized national society coming upriver from the Amazon seeking seasonal forest products. Catholic missionaries made annual or semiannual trips to their most accessible village. It is during this period that some Hishkaryana have learned some Portuguese.

In 1959, Desmond and Grace Derbyshire of the Summer Institute of Linguistics started linguistic

fieldwork in Hishkaryana at Cassaua. It was the
first sustained contact the Indians had had with
outsiders. The Derbyshires analyzed Hishkaryana
and taught a few Indians how to read in their own
language. After the first initial years spent in
the village they moved away, but went back perio-
dically for additional fieldwork until 1975. In the
middle 1970's, the people of Cassaua were of mixed
origin. Some of them had come, a generation earlier, from the Mapuera River; there were still regular contacts and interchange between the groups
on the Nhamundá and Mapuera Rivers.

Recently, communications between the Hishkaryana
and the non-Indian world have increased such that
they have regular intermittent contacts with the
Brazilians. One highlight was a visit they received in 1965 from Senator Robert Kennedy who, to
their amazement, swam from the bank to the little
airplane awaiting him in the middle of the Nhamundá
River in front of their village.

Prognosis and Suggestions. In spite of recent increased contacts with the pioneering society, the
Hishkaryana language is in no immediate danger, at
least not until the "Perimetral Norte" highway,
which is projected to pass through the northern
part of their territory, is built.

There are a few good language studies by Derbyshire. These include comparative notes of Hishkaryana with Waiwai and Kashuyana (1961a); a tagmemic
syntactic description (1961b); thirty texts transcribed in Hishkaryana and literally translated into
Portuguese and English (1965); an analysis of Hish-

karyana discourse redundancy (1977a); and notes
showing that Hishkaryana is an OVS (Object-Verb-
Subject) language (1977b). Most recently he has
published a full description of Hishkaryana including phonology, morphology and syntax (1979). Derbyshire has also translated the New Testament into
Hishkaryana. Gudschinsky (1973) has compared person marker prefixes of Hishkaryana with Apalai.

23. Warikyana. This designation, adopted from
Frikel (1970), refers to Carib groups who used to
live in the area of the Trombetas (Kahuwini, "sky-
water", in Arawak). The groups appear under different names but speak Warikyana, as opposed to
Parukoto and Pianokoto. The designations of local
Warikyana groups are formed by the name of the location (place or river) they inhabit plus the suffix [-yana], "people of", "inhabitant of". The
most influential group is the Kashuyana, also spelled Kaxuyana or Kachuyana, who live on the Cachorro
River, a tributary of the Trombetas. Other designations for local groups of the Trombetas basin,
who are either extinct or integrated with the
Kashuyana, are: Kahyana, Kahuyana, Yaskuriyana, and
Ingarüne. Pawiyana (Pawixi, Pawitxi) is the name
of a small group, speaking a related variety of
Warikyana.

Location and Population. At the beginning of the
last century, about 2,000 Warikyana-speaking people
were scattered along the mid and upper Trombetas
River (northern tributary of the Amazon) and its
affluents. Early in this century they were found

greatly reduced in number (1,000) by disease and internal feuds (Frikel, 1970). Between the years 1920-1950, after internal wars and epidemics, the following local groups remained (1) Kashuyana and Warikyana occupying together six or seven villages located on the Yaskuri, Trombetas and Cachorro Rivers, 180 people; (2) Kahuyana and Kahyana, four villages on the Trombetas and Kachpakura Rivers, 90 people; (3) Ingarüne, three villages at the head-waters of the Trombetas (Panama & Ponekuru creeks), 70 people; and (4) Pawiyana, two villages on the Erepekuru River, 40 people. By 1968 only the Pawiyana survived, all the others except the Kashuyana had become extinct. The Kashuyana migrated in 1968 to the upper Paru de Oeste River, near the Trio.
Ethnolinguistic Situation. The ethnohistory of the Kashuyana (as shown by Frikel, 1970) is indeed one of continuous contacts, admixtures, wars, and diseases. Their oral history, as well as mythology, say that prehistorically the Trombetas River basin was populated by people coming from the north. Then a group from the Amazon River went up the Trombetas and joined them. Later, after the whole population was decimated by natural disasters, other Carib people, coming in several waves from the high mountains to the west, appeared near the headwaters of the Mapuera River. At first they found hostility, but later they succeeded in settling along the Kuxuru (Cachorro River) and became known as the Kashuyana.

In historical times (17th and 18th centuries), the Kashuyana intermarried with the Arikyana (or

Warikyana) who came up from the lower Amazon River;
[ari-kuru] literally "Cassava bread River", is a
name for the Amazon in their language. Several
fissionings occurred soon after, giving rise to
local groups and names. Most important were: the
Kashuyana who went to live on the Mapuera and Cachorro Rivers; some Warikyana (called Yaskuriyana)
who did not mix with the original Kashuyana, and
lived on the Yaskuri River; the Kahuyana (or Kahyana) who went to live on the mid Trombetas and the
Kuha (Rio do Velho) its tributary; the Ingarüne who
lived at the headwaters of the Trombetas on the Panama branch; and the Pawiyana or Pawishi (or Pawixi
in Portuguese) located on the lower Trombetas.

Other local groups who did not speak Warikyana
were also found in the Trombetas basin: the Tuna-
yana or Xaruma (Parukoto language) on the Turunu
River, and the Marayo and Maraxo (Pianokoto-Trio
language) on upper Kaxpakuru and Panama Rivers.

During the 18th century the Warikyana diminished
considerably in number. The main causes were diseases (flu, measles, and gonorrhea) from outside
contacts and conflicts with the penetrating pioneering society, which at that time, consisted mainly
of escaped black slaves (called Moçambeiros) from
the farms of the lower Amazon. Indeed, the Moçambeiros were already well established on the Trombetas River by the beginning of the 19th century.
They became traders and some intermarried with the
Indians, especially the Warikyana.

During the last century a slow "merging" process
began among the different Warikyana groups. Those

that became too small because of disease and internal fights merged with their neighbors.  Notable is
the fusion of many Ingarüne with the Kashuyana (end
of last century) who became the strongest and most
numerous groups on the Trombetas.  Their language,
a variety of Warikyana, became dominant and, in
this century, was the only one in use.

By 1925 there were about 500 Kashuyana, according to the reports of Brazilians who traded with
them for "Brazil nuts".  In the 30's a series of
measles, flu, malaria and yellow fever epidemics
introduced by the traders killed most of them.  In
the mid-1940's there were about 80 people left of
whom only 8 were more than 30 years old.

TABLE 2.  Warikyana Population Estimates

| Subgroup | Number of People | Number of Villages | River Area |
|----------|------------------|--------------------|------------|
| Kashuyana | 80 | 5 | Cachorro, Trombetas |
| Warikyana | 30 | 2 | Ambrosio, Yaskuri |
| Kahuyana | 30 | 2 | Trombetas |
| Kahyana | 60 | 2 | Kachpakuru, Imno-humu |
| Ingarüne | 70 | 3 | Panama, Ponekuru |
| Pawiyana | 40 | 2 | Lower Erepe-kuru |

Frikel (1970, but see also Malcher, 1964) gives the above population estimates of Warikyana speaking people between 1940 and 1950.

The Kashuyana joined the Warikyana right after 1950, building their villages along the Trombetas River. Before 1960 an epidemic of malaria and yellow fever struck the Warikyana village, resulting in the survival of only two people. According to Derbyshire (1961a) who visited the Kashuyana in 1958, the number of speakers then was about 80.

By 1965 the Kahuyana were almost extinct and the few survivors joined the Kashuyana. The Kahyana of the Kachpakuru River became extinct in 1949 because of internal fighting (Frikel, 1966).

The Ingarüne who stayed in the Upper Trombetas were, in 1953, living next to a group of Trio-Maraxo and intermarried with a few of them. In 1960, most of them migrated to Surinam and the rest of the Trio village on the Upper Paru de Oeste where the Franciscans have a Mission station. There may be a few Ingarüne, isolated at the headwaters of the Trombetas on the border with Guyana, that are without contact; no information is available on them.

The Pawiyana who lived in the lower Trombetas and worked for many years at the Portuguese Fort at the mouth of the river, participated in a revolt and were massacred during the second half of the 18th century. Those who escaped went up the Erepekuru River and are still there today in a much reduced number with only intermittent contact with outsiders.

The only Warikyana-speaking people left on the Trombetas by the year 1965 were the Kashuyana, reduced to about 60 people. They were in intermittent to permanent contact with the pioneering national society of the lower Trombetas. Almost all of them knew some Portuguese, and some of the adult males could carry on a conversation for trading purposes.

In 1966, the group was small and could not provide wives for a good number of their young men. Because of their permanent contact with the Catholic mission, they would not raid other distant groups in order to obtain women. Instead, they decided to migrate to join distant relatives. One or two families went to live with the Hishkaryana (Parukoto language), but the main group decided, in 1968, to migrate by airplane (courtesy of the Brazilian Air Force) in order to take up residence near the Trio (Pianocoto-Trio language) of the upper Paru de Oeste next to the Franciscan Mission Station. There they intermarried with the Trio and settled a few miles downriver from them. Today, these Warikyana descendants are in a stable diglossia situation, speaking Warikyana and Trio.

Prognosis and Suggestions. Very little is known of the Warikyana language. The most recent works are those of Derbyshire (1961), comparing some linguistic features of Kashuyana with Waiwai and Hishkaryana; and Wallace (1970), a word phonology. Worth mentioning are the ethnohistories of Frikel (1955, 1966 and 1970), and also his classification of the Northern Pará (Carib) languages (1958).

It is recommended that the language of the Pawiyana (Pawixi) be studied thoroughly. They are the
only Warikyana speaking group (two villages) left
in the Trombetas basin who actually speak a variety
of Warikyana. It is doubtful that there are any
others left, but if there are some, they are very
isolated and soon will be "discovered" when the
"perimetral" highway is built.

The other Warikyana, those who mixed with the
Trio or with the Hishkaryana, are rapidly acquiring
the language of their more powerful neighbors with
whom they are intermarried. Their contact situation offers a good opportunity for sociolinguistic
studies.

ACKNOWLEDGEMENTS
The majority of the fieldwork necessary to this paper was undertaken as a Research Associate first
with the Museu Emilio Goeldi (Brazil), and then in
the Department of Human Genetics of the University
of Michigan, supported by a grant from the National
Science Foundation. A summarized version of it was
presented at the 76th American Anthropological Association Annual Meeting in Houston, November,
1977. W. Coppens, A. Dessaint, J. Hill, L. Stark,
D. Thomas and V. Thorne have read portions of this
paper; they all have made useful comments which I
gratefully acknowledge. I am also thankful to my
students who assisted in compiling some information
during the earlier stages of this paper. An earlier version appeared in Antropológica 53 (1980).
Their kind permission to republish is acknowledged.

NOTES

1. See for example Voegelin and Voegelin (1965, 1977). Loukotka (1968), Hopper (1967), Rowe 1974), Greenberg (1960), McQuown (1955) Nimu-endaju (1932), to mention the most recent ones. See also eight major attempts to delineate South American culture areas; the most outstanding are: Wissler (1922), Cooper (1924), Kroeber (1948), Steward (1949) and Murdock (1951).

2. Aware of these problems, Galvão (1960) proposed eleven indigenous culture areas of Brazil which, being based upon a defined and limited time span (i.e., tribes found between 1900 and 1959), are most realistic and render a truer picture of the situation within that time.

3. Although about 4,000 Guahibo and about 100 Trio are reported to be living within or near the boundary defined in Map 1, they are not included in this paper. Trio will be part of a subsequent paper dealing with all extant languages of South America.

4. This has also been the suggestion of Larry Krute-Georges (1978). According to him, there is a diffusion from west to east of nasalization, aspiration  and glottalization.

5. Migliazza (1972), based on 300 words he collected on the Ajaraní River, classifies this dialect as a southern variety of the Yanam language. However, there are many linguistic differences between this dialect and the northern one which, coupled with the fact that they were almost mutually unintelligible, may warrant the

claim that the Ajaraní Yanomama form a cultural
and linguistic island, and should be considered
a "language" of the Yanomama family and not a
dialect of Yanam.

6.  See Migliazza, 1972, Appendix B.2.  Since prehistoric times, the Carib and Arawak tribes have
practically surrounded the Yanomama.  However,
contact with Europeans has weakened and caused
the extinction of many Carib and Arawak subgroups of the Río Branco and Río Negro areas,
and, in a way, has aided Yanomama expansion.

7.  For more external information on the Saliva of
Colombia, see Morey (1972).

8.  Larry Krute-Georges (personal communication,
1978) has suggested that perhaps the word Piaroa is a hispanicization of the form [de?arua]
or [de?aruwa].

9.  Larry Krute-Georges who did preliminary fieldwork with the Piaroa during the summer of 1977,
suggests that integration to the "pioneering
society" should  be separated from integration
or cultural change due  to permanent contact
with "mission society".  Today, a sizeable number of Piaroa are involved, or in contact, with
the Salesian and New Tribes Missions.

10.  According to W. Coppens (personal communication) Isla Raton is inhabited mainly by Guahibo,
Kurripako and Criollos.

11.  Although the tribal designations Guinau and
Guarao are quite similar and may have a common
origin, they  are the names of different languages.

12. Sampaio (1825), Rodrigues (1885), Almada (1861), Macgillivary (1836), Schomburgk (1841), Koch-Grünberg (1906).

13. According to local and government estimates it seems that during the past 30 years the Amerindians of Guyana have increased disproportionately compared to the rest of the population. The Guyana government estimated that in 1946 there were about 15,000 Amerindians in the country, but this is too conservative. In 1962, the estimate was 27,840 (Butt, 1965) while the current estimate, that of Jameson (1978), is 40,000.

    Although there has been an annual growth rate of about 3% due to better health programs during the last  twenty years, the present figures seem exaggerated and  the old figures too conservative.

14. This was also the impression of Anthropologist Audrey Butt Colson (1971) who suggested their self-designation "Kapon".

15. The last two speakers of Sapara died in 1965, near the farm "Boa Esperança" on the Uraricuera River (Brazil).

16. Muller (1975) published the Swadesh word list of Panare and compared it to Mapoyo, showing that they are two different Carib languages.

17. For more recent external information on the Panare see Dumont, (1971, 1976).

18. Most of the information reported here on the Mapoyo is from Henley (1975).

19. Butt Colson (1971) explains further that the Akawaio use tobacco leaves and ashes of the

Ireng River water weed to make pellets for sucking between their lower lip and teeth. This is interesting because the Yanomama make similar use of tobacco.

20. A beneficial and positive result (among the many negative ones) of the intense settling of the savanna of Roraima by cattle farmers during the first half of this century, is the termination of large scale hostilities between the Makushi and Wapishana Indians and their subsequent intermarriage. However, both the Makushi and Wapishana are now fighting (legally or otherwise) the local farmers who have appropriated the Indian land.

REFERENCES

Abbot, Miriam. 1976. Estrutura Oracional da Língua Makuxi. Série Linguística. Brasília: Summer Institute of Linguistics.

Albright, Sue. 1965. Aykamteli Higher-level Phonology. Anthropological Linguistics 7,7.

Almada, Manoel da Gama Lobo de. 1861. Descripção Relativa ao Rio Branco e seu Territorio (1787). Revista Trimensal do Instituto Histórico, Geográphico e Ethnográphico do Brasil XXIV.

Arends, T., Brewer, C., Chagnon, N., Gallango, M., Gershowitz, H., Layrisse, M., Neel, J., Shreffler, D., Tashian, R., and Weitkamp, L. 1967. Intratribal Genetic Differentiation among the Yanomama Indians of Southern Venezuela. Proceedings of the National Academy of Sciences, 57.

Armellada, C. de. 1943-1944. Gramática y Diccionario de la Lengua Pemón. 2 vols. Caracas:
Artes Gráficas.

------. 1949. Notas históricas, geográficas y
etnográficas. Venezuela Misionera XI, 130-131.

------. 1964. Tauron Panton: Cuentos y Leyendas de
los Indios Pemón. Caracas: Universidad Católica
Andrés Bello.

------. 1972. Pemonton Taremaru: Invocaciones
Mágicas de los Indios Pemón. Caracas: Universidad Católica Andrés Bello.

------. 1973. Tauron Panton II: Así Dice el Cuento. Caracas, Universidad Católica Andrés Bello.

Arvelo-Jimenez, Nelly. 1973. The Dynamics of
Ye'cuana (Maquiritare) Political System: Stabi-
lity and Crisis. IWGIA Document 12. Copenhagen:
International Work Group for Indigenous Affairs.

Barker, James P. 1956. Dictionary and Grammar,
Yanomamo Notes. New Tribes Mission (mimeo).

------. 1971. Yanomamo Lexicon. Puerto Ayacucho,
New Tribes Mission (manuscript).

------. 1979. Una Gramática Técnica de la Lengua
Shamatari. Boletín Indigenista Venezolano XVIII,
15.

Becher, Hans. 1960. Die Surára und Pakidái; Zwei
Yanonámi-Stämme in Nordwestbrasilien. Mittei-
lungen aus dem Museum für Völkerkunde in Hamburg
XXVI.

Bennett, Gordon, Audrey Colson and Stuart Wavell.
1978. The Damned: the Plight of the Akawaio
Indians of Guyana. Survival International
Document VI. London: Survival International.

Berno, José M.  1969.  Diccionario Yanomamu-
Castellano/Castellano-Yanomamu.  Puerto
Ayacucho, Misión Salesiana Mavaca (mimeo),
n.p.

Boglar, Lajos.  1970.  Aspects of Story-telling
among the Piaroa Indians.  Acta Ethnographica
Academiae Scientiarum Hungaricae 19.

Borgman, Donald M.  1969-1970.  Sanɨma Phonemics
and Myths (manuscript).

Borgman, Donald M. and Sandra L. Cue.  1963.  Sentence and Clause Types in Central Waica (Shiriana).  International Journal of American Linguistics 29, 3.

Borgman, D. M., Cue S. L., Albright, S., Seeley, M.
and J. Grimes.  1965.  The Waican Languages.
Anthropological Linguistics 7, 7.

Brett, W. H.  1851.  Indian Missions in Guiana.
London: G. Bell.

------.  1868.  The Indian Tribes of Guiana.
London: Bell and Daldy.

Brinton, D. G.  1971.  The Arawak Language of
Guiana in its Linguistic and Ethnological
Relations.  Transactions of the American
Philosophical Society 14,3.

Burns, Harold.  1963.  Macushi (Carib) Verb
Inflection (manuscript).

Butt, Audrey J.  1960.  The Birth of a Religion.
Journal of the Royal Anthropological Institute
90,1.

------.  1965.  The Guianas.  Bulletin of the International Committee on Urgent Anthropological and
Ethnological Research 7.

124     *Ernest C. Migliazza*

Butt Colson, Audrey J. 1971. Hallelujah among the
Patamona Indians. Antropológica 28.

------. 1973. Inter-tribal Trade in the Guiana
Highlands. Antropológica 34.

Carvalho, Braulino de. 1936. Vocabulário e Modo
de Falar dos Macuchys. Boletim do Museu Nacional XII, 3 & 4.

Cauty, André. 1974a. Reflexiones sobre "las For-
mas Flexionales" del Idioma Panare. Antropológica 37.

------. 1974b. Reflexiones sobre Denominación y
Designación en el Idioma Panare. Antropológica
39.

------. 1974c. Un Criterio de Decisión sobre la
Presencia de la Oclusiva Glotal en el Idioma
Panare. Revista Colombiana de Antropología
XVII.

------. 1974d. Los Sistemas Fonológicos y Silábi-
cos de la Lengua Panare. Revista Colombiana de
Antropología XVII.

Chagnon, Napoleon. 1968. Yanomamö. The Fierce
People. New York: Holt, Rinehart and Winston.

------. 1974. Studying the Yanomamö. New York:
Holt, Rinehart and Winston.

Cocco, Luis. 1972. Iyëwei-teri. Quince Años entre
los Yanomamos. Caracas: Escuela Técnica Popular
Don Bosco.

Codazzi, Augustine. 1841. Resumen de la Geografía
de Venezuela. Paris: Imprenta H. Fournier & Cía.

Cooper, John M. 1942. Areal and Temporal Aspects
of Aboriginal South American Culture. Primitive
Man XV, 1-2.

Coppens, Walter.    1971.    Las Relaciones Comerciales
de los Yekuana del Caura-Paragua.    Antropológica
30.

------.    1972.    The Anatomy of a Land Invasion
Scheme in Yekuana Territory, Venezuela.    IWGIA
Document 9.    Copenhagen: International Work
Group for Indigenous Affairs.

------.    1975a.    Vocabulário Sapé and Vocabulário
Uruak (manuscripts).

------.    1975b.    Contribución al Estudio de las
Actividades de Subsistencia de los Hotis del Río
Kaima.    Boletín Indigenista Venezolano XVI, 12.

------.    1977.    Los Sapé (manuscript).

Coppens, Walter and Philippe Mitrani.    1974.    Les
Indiens Hoti, Compte-rendu de Missions.    L'Homme
XIV, 3-4.

Crevaux, J. N., Sagot, P., and L. Adam.    1882.
Grammaires et Vocabulaires Roucouyenne, Arrou-
ague, Piapoco et d'Autres Langues.    Bibliothèque
Linguistique Américaine VIII.    Paris: Maisonneuve
et Cie.

Cruxent, J. M.    1948.    Datos Demográficos.    Memoria
de la Sociedad de Ciencias Naturales La Salle
VIII, 21.

Derbyshire, Desmond.    1961a.    Notas Comparativas
sôbre Três Dialectos Karíbe.    Boletim do Museu
Paraense Emílio Goeldi, Antropología 14.

------.    1961b.    Hishkaryana (Carib) Syntax Structure, Parts I & II.    International Journal of
American Linguistics 27, 2.

------.    1965.    Textos Hixkaryana.    Publicações
Avulsas 3.    Belém: Museu Paraense Emílio Goeldi.

------. 1977a. Discourse Redundancy in Hixkaryana. International Journal of American Linguistics 43, 3.

------. 1977b. Word Order Universals and the Existence of OVS Languages. Linguistic Inquiry 8, 3.

------. 1979. Hixkaryana. Lingua Descriptive Studies 1. Amsterdam: North Holland.

Dumont, Jean-Paul. 1971. Compte-rendu de Mission chez les Indiens Panare. L'Homme XI, 1.

------. 1974. Of Dogs and Men: Naming among the Panare Indians. Atti del XI Congresso Internazionale degli Americanisti 2.

------. 1976. Under the Rainbow. Austin: University of Texas Press.

Durbin, Marshall. 1977. A Survey of the Carib Language Family. In E. Basso (editor), Carib Speaking Indians: Culture, Society and Language. Tucson: University of Arizona Press.

Edwards, Walter F. 1978a. Some Synchronic and Diachronic Aspects of Akawaio Phonology. Anthropological Linguistics 20, 2.

------. 1978b. A Preliminary Sketch of Arekuna (Carib) Phonology. International Journal of American Linguistics 44,3.

Edwards, W. and K. Gibson. 1977. Patamuna Phonology (manuscript).

Escoriaza, Damian de (pseud. D. de Barandiarán). 1959. Datos Lingüísticos de la Lengua Makiritare. Antropológica 6.

------. 1960. Algunos Datos Lingüísticos más sobre la Lengua Makiritare. Antropológica 10.

Evans, Clifford and Betty J. Meggers. 1960.
Archeological Investigations in British Guiana.
Bureau of American Ethnology Bulletin 177.
Washington D. C.: Smithsonian Institution.

Farabee, W. C. 1918a. The Central Arawaks. Publications in Anthropology 9. Philadelphia:
University of Pennsylvania Museum.

------. 1918b. The Arawaks of Northern Brazil and
Southern British Guiana. American Journal of
Physical Anthropology 1, 4.

------. 1924. The Central Caribs. Publications in
Anthropology 10. Philadelphia: University of
Pennsylvania Museum.

Foster, Patrick. 1959. Makuxi Phonemes (ms).

Frikel, Protasio. 1955. Tradições Histórico-
lendárias dos Kachuyana e Kahyana. Revista do
Museu Paulista 9.

------. 1958. Classificação Lingüístico-etnológica
das Tribos Indígenas do Pará Setentrional e
Zonas Adjacentes. Revista de Antropologia 6, 2.

------. 1966. Os Ultimos Kahyana. Revista do
Instituto de Estudos Brasileiros I.

------. 1970. Os Kaxuyana, Notas Etno-históricas.
Publicações Avulsas 14. Belém: Museu paraense
Emílio Goeldi.

Fuchs, Helmuth. 1967. Urgent Tasks in Eastern
Venezuela. Bulletin of the International Commit-
tee on Urgent Anthropological and Ethnological
Research 9.

Galvão, Eduardo. 1960. Areas Culturais Indígenas
do Brasil 1900-1959. Boletim do Museu Paraense
Emílio Goeldi, Nova Série, Antropologia 8.

Gheerbrant, Alain. 1954. La Expedición Orinoco-
Amazonas 1948-1950. Buenos Aires: Hachette
(Translated into English: Journey into the Far
Amazon. New York, Simon and Schuster).

Gibson, K. 1977. The Phonological Study of the
Akawaio and Arekuna Languages with Emphasis on
Arekuna (manuscript).

Gillin, John. Tribes of the Guianas. In Julian
H. Steward (editor), Handbook of South American
Indians, Vol. 3. Washington, D. C.: Smithsonian
Institution.

Gonzalez-Ñañez, Omar. 1973. Ensayo de Interpretación de la Realidad Artesanal y Otros Aspectos
de la Actividad Económica y Cultural de los Aborígenes del T.F. Amazonas, Venezuela. Boletín
Bibliográfico de Antropología Americana 36 (45).

------. 1974. El Piapoco, el Baniva y el Guare-
quena: Tres Lenguas Arahuacas del Sur de Venezuela. Boletín Bibliográfico de Antropología
Americana 37 (46).

Greenberg, Joseph. 1960. The General Classifica-
tion of Central and South American Indian Lan-
guages. In A. F. C. Wallace (editor), Selected
Papers of the Fifth International Congress of
Anthropological and Ethonographical Sciences,
Philadelphia: University of Pennsylvania Press.

Grimes, Barbara F. 1974. Ethnologue (8th ed.).
California: Wycliffe Bible Translators.

------. Ethnologue (9th ed.). California: Wycliffe
Bible Translators.

Guarisma P., Virginia and Walter Coppens. 1978.
Vocabulario Hoti. Antropológica 49.

Gudschinsky, Sarah C. 1973. Sistemas Contrastivos de Marcadores de Pessoa em Duas Línguas Carib: Apalai e Hixkaryana. Série Lingüística. Brasília: Summer Institute of Linguistics.

Hawkins, W. Neil. 1950. Patterns of Vowel Loss in Macushi (Carib). International Journal of American Linguistics 16.

------. 1952. A Fonologia da Língua Uaiuai. Boletim 157. São Paulo: Universidade de São Paulo.

------. 1962. A Morfologia do Substantivo na Língua Uaiuai. Publicações Avulsas 21. Rio de Janeiro: Museu Nacional.

Hawkins, W. Neil and Robert Hawkins. 1953. Verb Inflection in Waiwai (Carib). International Journal of American Linguistics 19.

Henley, Paul. 1975. Wanai: Aspectos del Pasado y del Presente del Grupo Indígena Mapoyo. Antropológica 42.

Hill, Jane. 1972. On the Evolutionary Foundations of Language. American Anthropologist 74, 3.

Hodsdon, Cathy A. 1976. Análise de Cláusulas Semânticas na Língua Makusi. Série Lingüística. Brasília: Summer Institute of Linguistics.

Hodsdon, Ross. 1974. Personal and Impersonal Deixis in Makusi (manuscript).

Hopper, J. (editor). 1967. Indians of Brazil in the Twentieth Century. Washington, D.C., Institute for Cross-cultural Research.

Hübner, Georg and Theodor Köch-Grunberg. 1907. Die Yauapery; kritisch bearbeitet und mit Einleitung versehen von Theodor Koch-Grünberg. Zeitschrift für Ethnologie 39.

Humboldt, Alexander von.   1956.   Viaje a las Regio-
nes Equinocciales del Nuevo Continente.   Caracas: Ministerio de Educación.

Jameson, Kenneth P.   1956.   Income and Land Distribution in Guyana (mimeo).

Kaplan, Joanna Overing.   1975.   The Piaroa: a
People of the Orinoco Basin; A Study in Kinship
and Marriage.   Oxford: Clarendon Press.

Koch-Grünberg, Theodor.   1906.   Die Makú. Anthropos
I.

------.   1913.   Abschluss meiner Reise durch Nordbrasilien zum Orinoco, mit besonderer Berück-
sichtigung der von mir besuchten Indianerstämme.
Zeitschrift für Ethnologie 45.

------.   1922.   Die Völkergruppierung zwischen Rio
Branco, Orinoco, Rio Negro und Japura.   Festschrift Eduard Seler.   Stuttgart: E. Seler.

------.   1923.   Vom Roroima zum Orinoco: Ergebnisse
einer Reise in Nordbrasilien und Venezuela in
den Jahren 1911-1913.   Vol. III: Ethnographie.
Stuttgart: Strecker und Schröder.

Krisologo, Pedro J.   1976.   Manual Glotológico del
Idioma Wo'tiheh.   Caracas: Universidad Católica
Andrés Bello.

Kroeber, Alfred L.   1948.   Anthropology.   New York:
Harcourt, Brace & Co.

Layrisse, Miguel and Johannes Wilbert.   1966.
Indian Societies of Venezuela: their Blood Group
Types.   Monografía 13. Caracas: Instituto Caribe
de Antropología y Sociología.

Lizarralde, Roberto.   1971.   Mapa Etnográfico de
Venezuela. Antropológica 29.

Lizot, Jacques.  1970.  Dictionnaire Yanõmamɨ-Fran-
çais.  Paris: Laboratoire d'Anthropologie Sociale du Collège de France.

------.  1973.  Onomastique Yanõmamɨ.  L'Homme XIII,
3.

------.  1975a.  Diccionario Yanomamɨ-Español.
Caracas: Universidad Central de Venezuela.

------.  1975b.  Le Cercle des Feux.  Paris:
Editions du Seuil.

------.  1976.  The Yanomamɨ in the Face of Ethnocide.  IWGIA Document 22.  Copenhagen: International Work Group for Indigenous Affairs.

------.  1977.  Population, Ressources et Guerre
chez les Yanomamɨ.  Libre 2.  Paris: Payot.

Loukotka, Čestmír.  1935.  Clasificación de las
Lenguas Sudamericanas.  Lingüística Sudamericana I.

------.  1944.  Klassifikation der Südamerikanischen
Sprachen.  Zeitschrift für Ethnologie 74.

------.  1968.  Classification of South American
Indian Languages.  Edited by Johannes Wilbert.
Los Angeles: Latin American Center, University
of California, Los Angeles.

Macgillivray, William.  1836.  The Travels and
Researches of Alexander von Humboldt in 1799.
Edinburgh: Oliver and Boyd.

Malcher, Gama José M.  1964.  Indios.  Publicação
1.  Rio de Janeiro: Conselho Nacional de Prote-
ção aos Indios.

Martius, K. F. P. von.  1867.  Beiträge zur Ethnographie und Sprachenkunde Amerika's zumal Brasiliens.  2 vols. Leipzig: F. Fleischer.

Mason, Alden J.  1950.  The Languages of South Ame-
    rican Indians. <u>In</u> Julian H. Steward (editor),
    Handbook of South American Indians, Vol. 6.
    Washington, D. C.: Smithsonian Institution.

Matteson, Esther, Wheeler, Alva, Jackson, Francies
    L., Waltz, Nathan E. and Diana R. Christian.
    1972.  Comparative Studies in Amerindian Lan-
    guages. The Hague: Mouton.

McQuown, Norman A.  1955.  The Indigenous Languages
    of Latin America.  American Anthropologist LVII,
    3.

Meyer, Alcuino W.  1951.  Lendas Macuxis.  Journal
    de la Société des Américanistes XL.

------.  1956.  Pauxiana.  Pequeno Ensaio sobre a
    Tribo Pauxiana e sua Língua, Comparada com a
    Língua Macuchi.  X Congresso Nacional de Geogra-
    fía, Rio de Janeiro.

Migliazza, Ernest C.  1964.  Notas sôbre a Organi-
    zação Social dos Xiriâna do Rio Uraricaá.  Bole-
    tim do Museu Paraense Emílio Goeldi, Antropolo-
    gía 22.

------.  1965a.  Fonologia Máku.  Boletim do Museu
    Paraense Emílio Goeldi, Antropología 25.

------.  1965b.  Notas Fonológicas da Língua Tiriyó.
    Boletim do  Museu Paraense Emílio Goeldi, Antro-
    pología 29.

------.  1966.  Esbôço Sintático de um Corpus da
    Língua Máku. Boletim do Museu Paraense Emílio
    Goeldi, Antropología 32.

------.  1967.  Grupos Linguísticos do Território
    Federal de Roraima.  Atas do Simposio sobre a
    Biota Amazónica 2.

------. 1970. Território de Roraima e Orinoco -
    População Indígena (Indigenous Population of
    Roraima and Orinoco) (Map and Paper). Boa
    Vista: Government of the Federal Territory of
    Roraima.

------. 1972. Yanomama Grammar and Intelligibi-
    lity. Ph.D. Dissertation, Indiana University.

------. 1975. Yanomama-Hoti Genetic Relationship
    (manuscript).

------. 1978a. The Integration of the Indigenous
    People of the Territory of Roraima. IWGIA Docu-
    ment 32. Copenhagen: International Work Group
    for Indigenous Affairs.

------. 1978b. Some Evidences for Panoan-Yanomama
    Genetic Relationship. Paper Presented at the
    LSA Summer Meeting, Urbana, Illinois.

------. 1978c. Makú, Sapé and Uruak Languages:
    Current Status and Basic Lexicon. Anthropologi-
    cal Linguistics 20, 3.

------. 1978d. Yanomama Diglossia. In: W. McCor-
    mack and S. Wurm (editors), Approaches to Lan-
    guage. World Anthropology Series, The Hague:
    Mouton.

Migliazza, Ernest C. and Joseph Grimes. 1961.
    Shiriana Phonology. Anthropological Linguistics
    3, 4.

Monod, Jean. 1970. Los Piaroa y lo Invisible:
    Ejercicio Preliminar a un Estudio sobre la
    Religión Piaroa. Boletín Informativo de Antro-
    pología VII.

Morey, Robert V. 1972. Notes on the Saliva of
    Eastern Colombia. Current Anthropology 13, 1.

Mosonyi, E. E.   1968.   Introducción al Análisis
Infraestructural del Idioma Baniva.   Economía y
Ciencias Sociales X, 3.

Muller, Marie-Claude.   1974.   El Sistema de Pose-
sión en la Lengua Panare.   Antropológica 38.

------.  1975a.   Vocabulario Básico de la Lengua
Mapoya.  Antropológica 42.

------.  1975b.   La Diferenciación Lingüística Pana-
re-Mapoya.  Antropológica 42.

------.  1979.   La Lengua Panare, Lengua Atípica de
Venezuela (manuscript).

Murdock, George P.   1951.   South American Culture
Areas.   Southwestern Journal of Anthropology VII,
4.

Neel, J.V., Tanis, R.J., Migliazza, E.C., Spielman,
R.S., Salzano, F., Oliver, W.J., Morrow, M. and
S. Bochofer.   1977.   Genetic Studies of the Macu-
shi and Wapishana Indians.   Human Genetics 36.

Nimuendaju, Curt.   1932.   Idiomas Indígenas del
Brasil.   Revista del Instituto de Etnología de
la Universidad Nacional de Tucumán 2.

Noble, Kingsley G.   1965.   Proto-Arawakan and its
Descendants.   International Journal of American
Linguistics 31, 3.

O'Leary, Timothy.   1963.   Ethnographic Bibliography
of South America.   New Haven: Human Relations
Area Files.

Oliveira, Adélia Engrácia de.   1975.   A Terminolo-
gia de Parentesco Baniwa 1971.   Boletim do Museu
Paraense Emílio Goeldi, Antropología 56.

Oliveira, Adélia Engrácia de and Eduardo Galvão.
1973.   A Situação Atual dos Baniwa (Alto Rio

Negro) - 1971. Publirações Avulsas 20, Belém,
Museu Paraense Emílio Goeldi.

Ramos, Alcida R. 1972. The Social System of the
Sanumá of Northern Brazil. Ph.D. Dissertation,
University of Wisconsin.

------. 1974. How the Sanumá Acquire their Names.
Ethnology XIII, 2.

Ramos, Alcida and Kenneth Taylor. 1979. The
Yanomama in Brazil 1979. IWGIA Document 37.
Copenhagen: International Work Group for Indi-
genous Affairs.

Ribeiro, Darcy. 1957. Culturas e Línguas Indígenas do Brasil. Educação e Ciencias Sociais 2,
6.

Rice, A. Hamilton. 1937. Exploration en Guyane
Brésilienne (1924-1925). Paris: Société d'Editions Géographiques, Maritimes et Coloniales.

Riley, C.L. 1953. Noticias sobre los Indios Panare de Venezuela. Boletín Indigenista Venezolano
1, 1, 2.

------. 1954. Notes on the Panare Indians of
Venezuela. Kroeber Anthropological Society
Papers 10.

------. 1958-1959. Some Observations on the Panare
Language. Boletín del Museo de Ciencias
Naturales IV/V, 1/4.

Rivet, Paul. 1920. Affinités du Saliba et du Piaroa. Journal de la Société des Americanistes de
Paris 12.

Rodrigues, Alexandre Ferreira. 1885. Diario de
Viagem Philosophica pela Capitania do São Joze
do Rio Negro (1785-86). Revista Trimensal do

Instituto Histórico, Geográphico e Ethnográphico do Brasil XLVIII.

Rodrigues, J. Barbosa. 1885. Rio Jauapery. Pacificação dos Crichanas. Rio de Janeiro: Imprensa Nacional.

Romero, Eddie and Gilberto Antolinez. 1975. Población Indígena de Venezuela. Gaceta Indigenista 9.

Rowe, John Howland. 1974. Tribal Distribution Map. In Patricia Lyon (editor), Native South Americans. Boston: Little, Brown and Co.

Saake, Wilhelm. 1956. Die Juruparilegende bei den Baniwa des Rio Issana. Proceedings 32nd International Congress of Americanists.

Salazar, Mariano G. 1968. Gramática Sucinia de la Lengua Pemón. Madrid: Raycar.

Sampaio, Francisco Xavier Ribeiro de. 1825. Diario da Viagem (Capitania São Joze do Rio Negro), 1774-1775. Lisboa: Tipografia da Academia.

Schomburgk, Robert H. 1841. Robert Hermann Schomburgk's Reisen in Guiana und am Orinoko während der Jahre 1835-1839. Herausgegeben von O.A. Schomburgk. Leipzig: G. Wigand.

------. 1847/1848. Reisen in Britisch Guiana in den Jahren 1840-1841. 3 vols. Leipzig: J.J. Weber.

Schuster, Meinhard. 1976. Dekuana: Beiträge zur Ethnologie der Makiritare. München: Klaus Renner Verlag.

Sotillo, Pedro J. and Jorge C. Mosonyi. 1975. Investigación en la Zona Yabarana del Territorio Federal Amazonas. Gaceta Indigenista 12, IV.

Spielman, Richard S., E.C. Migliazza, & J.V. Neel.
1974. Regional Linguistic and Genetic Differences among Yanomama Indians. Science 184.

Steward, Julian H. 1949. South American Cultures:
an Interpretive Summary. In Julian H. Steward (editor), Handbook of South American Indians, Vol. 5. Washington, D.C.: Smithsonian
Institution.

Taylor, Kenneth I. 1972. Sanumá (Yanoama) Food
Prohibition: the Multiple Classification of
Society and Fauna. Ph.D. Dissertation, Univer-
sity of Wisconsin.

------. 1974. Sanumá Fauna: Prohibitions and Classifications. Monografía 18. Caracas: Fundación
La Salle de Ciencias Naturales.

Thomas, David. 1971. Pemón Kinship Terminology.
Antropológica 30.

------. 1972. The Indigenous Trade System of
Southeast Estado Bolívar, Venezuela. Antropológica 33.

------. 1975. Demografía, Parentesco y Comercio
entre los Indios Pemón. Boletín Indigenista
Venezolano XVI, 12.

------. 1976. El Movimiento Religioso de San Miguel entre los Pemón. Antropológica 43.

Tosantos, Gonzalo. 1977. Apuntes sobre el Idioma
Panare. Cumaná: Editorial Universitaria de
Oriente.

Tracy, Frances V. 1966. The Phonology and Outline
Grammar of the Aikamtheli Dialect of Shiriana.
With Notes on Other Dialects. M.A. Thesis, Uni-
versity of Pennsylvania.

------. 1972a.   Dictionary, English-Wapishana, Wapishana-English (mimeo).

------. 1972b.   Wapishana Phonology.   In J.E. Grimes (editor), Languages of the Guianas. Summer Institute of Linguistics Publications in Linguistics and Related Fields 35.   Mexico: Summer Institute of Linguistics.

------. 1974.   An Introduction to Wapishana Verb Morphology. International Journal of American Linguistics 40, 2.

Vinci, Alfonso.   1956.   Samatari (Orinoco-Amazzoni).   Bari:   Leonardo da Vinci.

Voegelin, C. F. and F. M. Voegelin.   1965.   Languages of the World: Native American Facsicle Two. Anthropological Linguistics 7, 7.

------. 1977. Classification and Index of the World Languages.   Vol. 6.   New York: Elsevier.

Wallace, Ruth.   1970.   Notas Fonológicas da Língua Kaxuyâna. Boletim do Museu Paraense Emílio Goeldi, Antropología 43.

Wheeler, Alva.   1963.   Field Notes on the Tariano Language.   Lomalinda: Summer Institute of Linguistics.

Wilbert, Johannes.   1961.   Identificación Etnolingüística de las Tribus Indígenas del Occidente de Venezuela.   Memoria de la Sociedad de Ciencias Naturales La Salle XXI, 58.

------. 1962. Notes on a Sanema Vocabulary.   Journal de la Société des Américanistes 51.

------. 1963.   Indios de la Región Orinoco-Ventuari.   Monografía 8.   Caracas: Fundación La Salle de Ciencias Naturales.

Wissler, Clark. 1938. The American Indian. New
    York: The Macmillan Co.
Zerries, Otto. 1964. Waika: die kulturgeschicht-
    liche Stellung der Waika-Indianer des Oberen
    Orinoco im Rahmen der Völkerkunde Südamerikas.
    Band I. München: Klaus Renner Verlag.

# 2. An Emerging Tukanoan Linguistic Regionality: Policy Pressures

## Arthur P. Sorensen

INTRODUCTION

The task of this paper is to examine several co-
occurring factors which indicate that much of the
Northwest Amazon, in both Brazil and Colombia, may
well emerge as a bipartite regional area suggestive
of a mutual linguistic patria chica. Here Indian
languages will quietly but strongly persist alongside the national languages, analogous to the cases
of Guaraní and Quechua elsewhere in South America.

The geographic location of the area can be defined as the drainage system of the Vaupés River,
also called the Caiarí, and adjacent parts of two
or three other river systems, and some stretches
along the Río Negro. Roughly half of it lies in
Colombia, half in Brazil, and covers a region which
may be greater than the state of Texas. Locals
call it the Vaupés, in Spanish, or the Uaupés, in
Portuguese.

Only recently has the bulk of the area come
under effective national control. The population -
very sparse - now ranges from a few slightly acculturated communities to several highly acculturated ones, some individuals of which have had considerable experience in civilized centers outside
the Vaupés. Acculturation, as of 1976, is still

uneven and very much in transition, without having levelled off into any noticeable status quo. Nevertheless, linguistic and certain other cultural trends can be identified, and a profile of factors can be drawn. A potential "first stage" of folkway regionality can be hypothesized.

Analytically, a number of factors, which interact to form these trends, can be stated. Some factors interact minimally, some neutrally, some reinforce each other, while still others strongly conflict. Easily identifiable are four basic factors or rubrics – multilingualism, monolingualism, lingua francas, and national languages – and five corollary factors which grow out of these.

AUTOCHTHONOUS MULTILINGUALISM

The institution of multilingualism in the central Northwest Amazon, based in and maintained by exogamy among social linguistic units, may be characterized by an "easy-going," matter-of-fact attitude towards the knowledge of languages other than one's original father tongue and one's original mother tongue. Capability to learn new languages is accepted without emotion. Multilingualism in this region, moreover, consists of different patterns which vary enormously and which are linked to a large extent with geographical placement.

Linguistic exogamy is due to the pervasive insistence that marriage partners be from different originally linguistically identifiable groups or "tribes." This accounts for individuals having <u>father</u> tongues separate from their <u>mother</u> tongues.

The communities along the middle stretch of the
Vaupés River comprise the climax area of multilingualism, with an intensified focus along its tributary, the Papurí, and its tributaries.    Here are
interspersed Uanano, Desano, Tukano, Piratapuyo,
Tuyuka, Barasana, Siriano, Yurutí, and Karapana
communities.    Every individual knows several languages:  in addition to his or her father tongue and
mother tongue, everyone knows Tukano, Spanish, Portuguese, and at least two or three of some ten
other Indian languages.    Spanish is typically spoken with a slight Portuguese accent.

Some rubber-gathering areas in the headwaters
regions of the Vaupés River and adjacent parts of
the Inírida and Apaporis drainages are now being
permanently settled by Indians who used to live in
the preceding area of the Vaupés.    They represent a
second, derivative multilingual pattern, for they
are presently reconstituting their multilingual
antecedents with some modifications.    Thus Tukano,
which functions as their principal lingua franca,
is being adopted as the home and community language
in many cases.    All understand Spanish, and most,
Portuguese.

The "backbone" of this new population are now
middle-aged couples, with their oldest children already marrying.    The traditional system of "tribal"
exogamy is preserved intact.    The original tribal
identification of the individual is all-important,
even if he or she now uses Tukano as his or her
normal language of communication - almost as if he
or she were a Tukano.    Thus one retains basic

identification with his or her original, ancestral
linguistic group - Tuyuka, Desano, Tukano, Siriano,
etc. - of which he or she is a sib member (or patrilineal clan member), yet one can also be spoken
of loosely - carelessly - as belonging, again socially, to a Tukano language group.

Still a third multilingual pattern occurs among
the caboclos, in Portuguese, mestizos, in Spanish,
or "cabucos," as they are called in Vaupense Spanish. These are the families of those rubber gatherers who had taken Indian women for wives, and
who have stayed on over the years along the upper
middle Vaupés and its tributaries rather than going
back to the interior. They usually have considerable families. The interesting phenomenon here is
a realignment of language functions: the Spanish
language occurs as if it were the tribal father-
tongue, and the Kubeo language as the tribal mo-
father-tongue. The prominence of Kubeo is all the
more pronounced because it is used by all married
Indian women even if they are not Kubeo - although
most are. All cabucos (halfbreeds) understand
Kubeo. Whether they speak it unselfconsciously or
not depends on how strict their fathers were about
Spanish. Just the same, most of these patriarchs
understand Kubeo; many speak it, even natively.

In Mitu, capital of the Colombian Vaupés, a
special subvariation in this multilingual pattern
exists. Many of its residents are descendents of
the earlier Geral- and Portuguese-speaking rubber
gatherers from Brazil who stayed on in the area.
They, also, all know Kubeo; most use Spanish ins-

tead of Portuguese or Geral. The majority are
reluctant, or secretive, however, about admitting
to knowing Kubeo.

In the traditional Kubeo region, from the middle
to upper Vaupés, and in its northern tributaries,
still a fourth multilingual pattern exists, one
which is clearly the least multilingual-like. Here
a few older Kubeo may still be encountered who are
monolingual, but most Kubeo are minimally bilingual
in at least Kubeo and Spanish. Unlike the other
riverine Vaupés tribes, there are exogamous groupings of sibs within the Kubeo - as if they were
more than one "tribe" - with the result that the
Kubeo language may serve simultaneously both as the
potential father-tongue and the potential mother-
tongue for many individuals. Many Kubeo also know
considerable amounts of other languages - especially Tukano - or even Kurripaka, a language not from
the multilingual area but from just beyond.

Finally, the fifth and last multilingual pattern
comes from the area of the longest on-going acculturation - the lowest stretch of the Vaupés River,
and the middle Rio Negro. This includes some settlements of Uananos, Piratapuyos, Tukanos and Desa-
nos, and it includes all of the settlements of the
Tarianos, Arepasos and Barés. The outstanding characteristic of this area is that Tukano and, secondarily, Geral have been adopted as the language of
the home and the community by all these groups.
There are many younger individuals who can not con-
verse in their otherwise original Tariano, Arepaso
or Baré. Especially in the vicinity where the Vau-

pés River flows into the Río Negro, there is considerable Tukano-Geral bilingualism in daily conversation.  Added to this is the general knowledge of
Portuguese, making for a characteristic, trilingual
expectation.  Many individuals also know Spanish.

Beyond the truly multilingual area, on the lower
course of the Río Negro and especially on its upper
course, and on adjacent parts of the Orinoco drainage, there is prevalent bilingualism between Geral
and either Portuguese or Spanish.  There are
occasional enclaves of trilingualism, sometimes
among these three languages, but principally with
an Arawakan language as the third member.  Actually
this may be considered a sixth multilingual pattern, to the extent that the bilingualism qualita-
tively resembles central Northwest Amazonian multilingualism.

MONOLINGUALISM
The "monolingual tradition," coming from the period
of European national language consciousness at the
turn of the century, pertains to the national culture bearers entering the area.  It may be characterized by an intense, rigid, emotional view that
one's own language is superior and desirable, and
that other languages are inferior and undesirable.
The hispanic monolingual tradition is further characterized by a measure of jealousy, and by suspi-
cion towards other languages.  This "monolingual
tradition" is particularly strong in Colombia and,
in comparison to other Latin American countries,
one may speak of a Colombian chauvinism in Spa-

nish. Coupled with growing nationalism in Colombia, the promulgation of Spanish assumes crusade-
like qualities. It is overlooked that Spanish
itself is a vestige of colonialism, and is not
unique to Colombia.

## LINGUA FRANCAS AND NATIONAL LANGUAGES

There are four lingua francas in the region. In
chronological order of appearance, they are: Tukano, Geral, Portuguese, and Spanish. Since both
Portuguese and Spanish are also national languages,
factors three (lingua francas) and four (national
languages) will be discussed together.

Extensive bilingualism must have existed for a
long time before first contact with civilization,
and the use of Tukano as an aboriginal lingua franca may well have accompanied this for at least part
of that time.

Geral, as it is most commonly called, was
brought into the area during the mid- and late
nineteenth century by the balateros - the first
rubber gatherers, who formed their crude rubber in
large balls or balas. Geral is also called Tupí,
Guaraní, even Tupí-Guaraní, as well as Nheengatú,
Ienkatú, etc. Most of the place names, animal
names, and food names used in local Spanish and
Portuguese were borrowed directly from Geral and
are very much still in use: they are considered ro-
mantically to give a certain regional flavor to
Spanish and Portuguese. Outsiders coming in adopt
them, and sport them. Geral has even taken on the
aura of a "classical" language.

In the 1890s, the Brazilian government formally dismissed Geral and instituted Portuguese as the official language at Manaos. Geral has not yet been completely supplanted by Portuguese, but Portuguese has spread well up into the Vaupés. This switching from one lingua franca to another must have had an underlying effect on the ease with which lingua francas are adopted in the area.

As the rubber boom accompanying World War I developed, Spanish-speaking Colombians were also reaching the area as rubber gatherers, coming in overland to certain headwaters points to descend the rivers, carrying their language with them.

The prior presence of Geral and Portuguese in the Colombian sector of the Vaupés attests to civilizing influences coming _up_ the Rio Negro and subsequently _up_ the Vaupés. Much of the way of life in the Colombian Vaupés among non-Indians and acculturating Indians is Brazilian in tone - "cabuco." This turns out to be a sore, or at least sensitive, point for Colombian nationalizers, who presently promulgate a conscious and rather forced attitude that cultural influences are now coming from Villavicencio, which is the capital of Colombian Plains life.

Effective national control, somewhat longer underway in the Brazilian sector of the Vaupés, has extended only during the late sixties to the remotest points in the Colombian sector. Nationalization has come to be closely allied with promulgation of national languages: Portuguese and Spanish. The whole question of _intensive_ national

language policy is really only a very recent phenomenon in this area.

INTERACTION OF BASIC FACTORS

Having described each of the basic factors in some
detail - multilingualism, monolingualism, lingua
francas, national languages - the remainder of the
analysis is based on the interaction of these factors with each other.  Although some of these five
resultant corollary factors are transitory, and
some may seem inconsequential in themselves, cumu-
latively they reinforce the trend towards a special
linguistic regionality.

Monolingual Values Which Conflict With Professed
Official Policies

The bearers of national cultures (government
clerks, teachers on a one-year rural service stint,
and others), are bringing in their unconsciously
held monolingual values that vary from those multilingual values long established in the area.  Many
of these culture bearers may have strongly held
assumptions or expectations that erupt into conflict when they are exposed to the actual linguistic environment of the Vaupés.  For a Colombian
national, raised in a comfortably homogeneous linguistic environment where he already speaks what he
believes to be the world's best language, exposure
to the actual speaking of other languages, especially in his own country, comes as a real shock.

Other languages - and especially languages of
such "backward" people as Indians - are considered

inferior, childish, even anti-rational. There is
discrediting, downplaying, belittling of them, as
there also is of substandard forms of one's own
language. The pejorative connotations of labels
such as "dialectos" may be applied to them. In the
Colombian Vaupés, for instance, monolingual Spanish-speakers at times indiscriminately lump together the Indian languages in a rather sarcastic way
as simply "lengua" - or even as "inglés"!

Indian languages may be even considered as less-
than-languages: collections of child-like utteran-
ces with no real vocabularies or grammar. As a
corollary to this, the assumption is held that exposure to Spanish will lead the more intelligent
Indian automatically to abandon his Indian tongue
completely in favor of Spanish. When it is realized that this does not happen, the Indian is viewed
negatively as unnecessarily stubborn. In Colombia,
for someone to use a language other than Spanish in
public is considered to reflect something between
poor upbringing and aberration.

The Indians easily accept, and learn, Portuguese
or Spanish, or both, but as lingua francas and not
as languages of the home. This is counter to the
expectation of the monolingual nationalizer, and
much to his disappointment. There is, however, no
prejudice against anyone adopting the national
language.

A consequence of the monolingual tradition for
the monolingual speaker may be a linguistic mental
block towards the learning of other languages. In
addition, as has already been noted, the negative

reaction of the person identified with the Spanish
language in Colombia to Indian languages in the
Vaupés is a very real factor.  For him, then, to be
reminded officially that Indian languages are tolerated and protected deprives him metaphorically of
being able to take the bull by the horns and forci-
bly hispanicize the Indian--the attitude which he
otherwise feels!

A Colombian Spanish-speaker in long residence
gradually develops an opinionated tolerance for Indian languages.  Those who have resided for a long
time in the area--and usually with Indian wives--by
far and large express some shame that their half-
breed children also understand an Indian language
as well as speak Spanish.  The children usually do
not share such a feeling of shame, but they are
guarded about their linguistic knowledge.

There are important and influential individuals
who form exceptions to these statements; and, popularly, layman opinion is moderating.  With regard
to Indian languages, the official policies in both
Brazil and Colombia for several years now are that
not only are they to be tolerated but that they are
to be protected.

The Formal Schooling System

Beginning about 1920, children were gathered from
the communities along the rivers and brought into
the large mission boarding schools.  Until the
1940s, in both Brazil and Colombia, the more intel-
lectually responsive students were sent on to the
Brazilian Salesian missions at Yavareté or Uaupés

(now São Gabriel) for middle school training--for
many students this meant shifting to Portuguese.
In the 1940s a middle school was established in
Mitú, the capital of the Colombian Vaupés, to off-
set this.  Until the 1940s, both the Dutch Montfor-
tiano Fathers in Colombia, and the largely Italian
Salesian Fathers in Brazil, used Tukano, in many
cases well spoken (though inadequately described),
as the language of instruction.

In more advanced courses, students were introduced fairly successfully to Portuguese by the Salesians in Brazil, but less successfully to Spanish
by the Dutch in Colombia.  In the 1940s, the national Colombian Xaveriano Fathers as well as various
Colombian orders of Sisters were sent in, and for-
cibly removed the Dutch Fathers, largely for the
linguistic pur.pose of promulgating Spanish.  A very
harsh program ensued and continued until the mid-
1960s. It was expected that new students would take
a year or two to understand Spanish, enough to go
on to the second grade; advanced students were
assigned to translate in the lower grades, but were
kept under severe surveillance while doing so.

By the late 1960s, due to the effects of the Va-
tican II Council, as well as indirectly to a sense
of competition from North American linguistic missionaries who had just recently come into the area,
advanced students from the boarding schools were
being spread out as teachers to the Indian communities.  There they ran small bilingual schools where
children were drilled in Spanish for a year or two
prior to being sent to the same boarding schools.

By the mid 1970s, further changes had occurred.
Some big missionary boarding schools had been pha-
sed out, while some small schools in larger Indian
communities are now run for three or four grades.
Formal schooling has legally passed out of the
hands of the missionaries to the civil authorities.  At the big schools in Mitú, and at the
couple of surviving boarding schools, there is a
yearly succession of technically trained, outside,
non-Indian graduates coming into the area to do
their obligatory year of rural service.  The small
community schools are handled by Indians and the
growing body of cabuco halfbreeds, some of whom
have finished their high school training in Villavicencio, Cáqueza, or Bogotá.  Indian languages
play no formal role in the curriculum beyond the
first or second year.  However, beginning at about
the fifth grade, English is brought in!

The Brazilian schools, which up until the late
sixties had been regarded as the more tolerant,
have relaxed some, but have changed less, and now
appear as the more strict.  Their principal changes
have been a higher percentage of Brazilians, rather
than Italians, as teachers, and a more intensive
promulgation of Portuguese.

The Spanish-Portuguese Overlap

A cause for dismay and concern is found in the
overlap of Portuguese and Spanish as lingua francas, each being found well within the borders of
Colombia and Brazil, respectively.  Colombians feel
threatened in their claims for nationality within

Colombian political borders where so many Indians
know Portuguese as well as Spanish.  Between non-
Indian monolingual Brazilian Portuguese-speakers
and non-Indian monolingual Spanish-speakers there
is a rivalry over the use and pronunciation of
these two languages that are so close to being
mutually intelligible.  (For the linguist they are
on the technical borderline separating "language"
from "dialect.")  This rivalry ranges from jocula-
rity over the other's unfortunate pronunciation, to
ill-concealed disgust.  Both monolingual Brazilians
and monolingual Colombians feel that the other,
speaking his language when inside the borders of
the other's country, is ill-bred.  To make matters
worse, the fact that Indians seem to file away in
their minds both languages without much difficulty,
and then use only the appropriate one at the appropriate time, perplexes the national culture bearer,
who may go a step further to believe that the Indian is hiding the other language.  There may even
be resentment at the Indian's superior linguistic
capability - although this is rationalized away as
being vagueness or evasiveness or some other negatively charged evaluation, hence an inferior characteristic, of the Indian.

The North American Linguistic Missionaries
About twenty years ago, in the mid-1950s, the first
North American, English-speaking missionaries
entered the area; by the late 1960s, they had
spread widely to the more remote points in the
region.  It was noted that they were well received

by Indians, and that this was largely due to their
interest in indigenous languages. A point of contention has been that, when the contract that the
missionaries had with the government was presumably
in force (it was annulled retroactively in the mid-
1970's), one of their duties was to hispanicize the
Indians. (What this in effect really meant was the
improvisation of quasi-hispanic orthographies for
the Indian languages, for subsequent ease in reading Spanish.) Many Colombians, with their chauvi-
nistic feelings for Castellano, resented non-native
Spanish-speaking foreigners teaching Spanish to
Indians. Although these missionaries did not
create programs for teaching English to Indians, it
was well noted by all parties that they formed good
models for the correct pronunciation of American
English, and that the Indians were apt pupils and
could pronounce English well. The fact that it was
North Americans, and not Colombians, who maintained
contact with the least acculturated of the Indians
(as well as with many more acculturated ones) has
given rise at times to claims of a kind of de facto
North American colonialism and imperialism in the
upriver areas.

Vocal Placement

It has long been recognized that the impression of
the sound of Eastern Tukanoan languages is similar
to that of American English and, although considerably less so, to that of Brazilian Portuguese.
That is, an Eastern Tukanoan accent in Spanish is
similar to an American English accent. This im-

pression of similarity becomes all the more marked
when Indians reach the grades in middle and high
schools where English is taught (English is the
educational second language in all Colombia now).
They often mimic the Spanish-accented English of
their school teacher.  This causes conscious embar-
rassment and mixed feelings on the part of the teacher because, as he or she recognizes, the Indian
accent would have been closer to that of a native
speaker of English.

CONCLUSION
The preceding profile of factors can now be summarized in order to highlight the linguistic characteristics of picturesque side-by-side halves of
a folkloristic patria chica-like regionality likely
to emerge as the Northwest Amazon becomes incorporated into Brazilian and Colombian national cultures.  The autochthonous multilingual tradition
remains quietly pervasive, and is not seriously
challenged by the emotional stances of those nationalizers whose underlying expectation has been
monolingualism in the national language.  Ready
adoption by Indians of Portuguese and Spanish, but
as lingua francas, not as languages of the home,
further indicates persistence of Indian languages.
Overlapping lingua franca areas of Portuguese and
Spanish cause concern for border-jealous officials
(the population could "go either way"), yet too
great an attempt at corrective measures would
recognizably be inadvisable.  The distribution of
North American, English-speaking linguistic missio-

naries has prompted a defensive hispanicization in order to assure the currency of Spanish in the remoter Colombian areas. Undoubtedly there could be a corresponding lusitanicization in the Brazilian area. The formal schooling systems do not really divert attention from Indian languages so much as intensify knowledge of lingua franca national languages. Official policies are protecting Indian languages by negating coercive action against them. Public opinion at the popular level is beginning to accept national cultural pluralism. All in all, the region should emerge as linguistically rich treasures for both Brazil and Colombia.

ACKNOWLEDGEMENTS

This paper is a condensation, with some elimination of detail, of two papers read at AAA Annual Meetings: "Multilingual Patterns along the Vaupés River," in Washington, D.C. 1976; and "An Emerging Tukanoan Linguistic Regionality, and Policy Pressures," in Houston, 1977. The latter paper was read in a Symposium on South American Indian languages organized by Harriet E. M. Klein and Louisa R. Stark. Much of the funding of this stage of the research originated in a grant from NIMH. The continued field research has been done under the auspices of the national Instituto Colombiano de Antropologia. All of these are gratefully acknowledged.

# 3. Indigenous Languages of Lowland Ecuador: History and Current Status

## Louisa R. Stark

INTRODUCTION

At the time of the Spanish Conquest there were probably some thirty Indian languages spoken in Ecuador (McQuown 1955: 548,551), today there are
twelve. Of these languages, three (Colorado, Cayapa, and Coaiquer) are spoken in the western littoral, one (Quichua) is spoken in the highlands, and
nine are spoken in the eastern lowlands, or Oriente, of Ecuador (Siona, Secoya, Tetete, Cofan, Huaorani, Shuar, Achuar, Quichua, and Záparo). This
work is limited to those languages currently spoken
in the Ecuadorian lowlands, both western and eastern, with a focus on their history and current
status.

In the discussion that follows, a combination of
ethnohistorical and linguistic data will be used in
an attempt to reconstruct the history and diffusion
of each language. Some of the conclusions may differ from earlier works that have treated this subject (Jijón y Caamaño 1952; León 1974; Paz y Miño
1940-1942) because in the past few years good basic
data has been published on many of the lesser known
languages of Ecuador. This has yielded new theories as to the history and distribution of these
languages (see References).

In examining the current status of each language, the number of speakers will be estimated and the area or areas in which it is spoken will be described. The concluding section will provide a description of the social environment in which the language is currently found, and of how this environment is affecting its potential for survival. Language survival is an important question in a country such as Ecuador where two out of three native linguistic groups have disappeared during the past three hundred years.

THE WESTERN LITTORAL

1. The Barbacoan Languages (Macro-Chibchan Phylum)
Of the multitude of languages which were probably spoken on the western slopes of the Andes in Ecuador, there are only three which still exist today: Colorado, Cayapa, and Coaiquer. These languages form the Barbacoan branch of the Macro-Chibchan phylum. However, their position within the phylum is somewhat peripheral; lexical correspondences between the Barbacoan and other Chibchan languages show less than a ten percent correlation (Wheeler 1972:95).

Within the Barbacoan group of languages, however, Colorado and Cayapa are much more closely related to one another than either is to Coaiquer. Cayapa, however, shows more affiliations with Coaiquer than does Colorado.

History. Ethnohistorically it is quite probable that long before the arrival of the Incas, a language which we will call Barbacoa extended from just north of the Guaytara River in Colombia as far as the western part of the province of Tungurahua in Ecuador.  It spread down the central Cordillera almost to Quito and along the western slopes from Quito southward.  By glottochronological calculations, around 50 B.C. the Cayapa-Colorado and Coaiquer branches of Barbacoan split off from one another.  This may have come about because of the very inhospitable geographical area between the Chota Valley and the present-day town of Ibarra, an area which could have formed a barrier between the two groups.  After this split the Coaiquers seem to have occupied the area from the Chota Valley northward, and the Cayapa-Colorados the area from Ibarra southward.

The Cayapas and the Colorados seem to have spoken a single language until around 1000 A.D. when, by glottochronological calculations, the language split into two.  Quite possibly this occurred when an intrusive group moved into the valley formed by the Guaillabamba River, thus forcing the Colorado-Cayapas out of this area and placing a barrier between them.  Both Cayapas and Colorados, however, continued to live further to the east than they do today.  As late as the 1750s the Colorados were divided into two groups with one group, the Yumbos, still living just to the west of Ambato (Maldonaldo 1750) and spreading as far north as Mindo and Pacto (Costales Samaniego 1965:8).  The other group, the Tsachila, lived to the west in the general area of Santo Domingo.  During the same period the Cayapas were settled at the headwaters of the Santiago River around the community of Pueblo Viejo de Cayapas (Maldonaldo 1750). According to Cayapa ethnohistorical sources, they had come to this area from the region around Ibarra, having been driven out of their homeland by another group (Barrett 1925:31), most likely the Incas. However, further migrations of both Colorados and Cayapas towards the coast have occurred only recently, probably because of pressures from non-Indians who have been seizing their lands for agricultural purposes.

The Coaiquers have not fared much better. With the coming of the Jesuits to the Chota Valley in the seventeenth century and their establishment of large haciendas in that area, the Coaiquers began to recede northward. But in the north they also faced a squeeze from white and mestizo colonists who were invading their traditional territories in Colombia. Thus the area inhabited by the Coaiquers today represents a withdrawal from both north and south to an extremely inhospitable geographical area - one which has the sole advantage of not being coveted by land-hungry outsiders.

Present-Day Situation

Colorado. The Colorados (Tsachila) number approximately one thousand (Jara 1973) and live in the eastern part of the province of Pichincha along the Chihuepe, Baba, Tahuazo, and Poste Rivers. Today the Colorados exist primarily on subsistence agriculture, with some hunting. Until recently they have lived around the town of Santo Domingo. However, with the success of the Ecuadorian government in attracting colonists to this area, the Colorados have found themselves pushed further and further away from the Santo Domingo area and into the more inaccessible zone in which they now live. Recently the government has been persuaded to award some lands to the Colorados such that there now exist seven officially recognized Colorado comunes of 100 to 250 persons with land holdings which average approximately one hundred hectares per family (Robinson 1971:136).

Less than fifty percent of the Colorados may be classified as bilingual in Spanish and Colorado (Lindskoog 1975). However, because of increased contact with Spanish-speaking whites and mestizos there has been a good deal of pressure on the Colorados to learn that language. And through increased schooling future generations will certainly show a greater degree of bilingualism.

It also seems quite certain that with increased contact with the outside world, which is bound to intrude more and more into the area in which they now live, and the impossibility of withdrawing into less accessible areas, the Colorados will have more contact, and perhaps be tempted to acculturate to the dominant mestizo culture. On the other hand, the town of Santo Domingo de los Colorados identifies itself closely with the Colorados in its parks, dominated by statues of the Indians, and in the stores and restaurants named after them. The Colorados are also seen as an important element in the tourist trade with thousands of tourists arri-

ving weekly simply to have the opportunity of
glimpsing one of the town's "exotic red-headed"
Indians.  There are also certain tribal members who
are well known curers, serving that function not
only for their own people, but also for other Ecuadorians and even foreigners.  Thus recognition of
the Colorados as a distinctive cultural entity,
which provides the dominant mestizo culture with
certain symbolic, economic and medical benefits,
may, in the long run, aid the Colorados in their own
attempt to maintain a separate cultural identity.
Cayapa.  The Cayapas, who today prefer to call
themselves Chachis, number between 2,500 and 3,000
(Lindskoog 1975) and live in the province of Esme-
raldas along the Cayapa River and its tributaries,
but with settlements also along the Santiago, Ver-
de, Ostiones, Canande, Viche, Sucio, and Cojimes
Rivers (Lindskoog and Lindskoog 1964:3).  The Cayapas are primarily engaged in slash-and-mulch agriculture, with some hunting and fishing.  Recently
much of their territory has been invaded by Black
Ecuadorians from the coast who have lumbered on
some parts of it, and have taken over other portions for the planting of bananas.  In order to
stop these abuses the Cayapas have managed to have
some of their lands surveyed by IERAC (Instituto
Ecuatoriano de Reforma Agraria y Colonización) in
an attempt to secure legal titles to them.

Among the Cayapas perhaps 20% are bilingual, the
majority of them adult men.  There is a certain
amount of dialectal variation within the language,
with those living in more isolated areas speaking

more conservatively (Lindskoog and Lindskoog 1964: 121). The Summer Institute of Linguistics has had several bilingual schools among the Cayapa which may bring about more bilingualism in future generations. However, for the moment, because of their isolation and basic mistrust of outsiders, it seems that the Cayapas will survive as a viable linguistic and ethnic group for many years to come. Coaiquer. There are perhaps 1,000 Coaiquer (Ehrenreich 1984:47) living in the province of Carchi along the San Juan River and its tributary the Gualpi (Ponce Rubio 1975). An additional 2,500 live across the border in Colombia (Ehrenreich 1984:47) along the Guiza, Cuaiquer, and San Juan Rivers, and their tributaries (Ortiz 1965:60).

The Coaiquer, who in Ecuador call themselves Awa, migrated from Altaquier, in Colombia, some sixty years ago (Ehrenreich and Kempf 1978). They live a three day walk to the west of the community of Maldonaldo in the province of Tulcan. Economically they support themselves with subsistence agriculture and hunting. Traditionally, the Ecuadorian Coaiquer have little contact with the outside world, including the community of Maldonaldo where only occasionally a few will go to trade.

The majority of the Coaiquer are bilingual, having learned Spanish from their parents and grandparents who, in turn, had learned it in Colombia. Women and pre school-aged children know less Spanish than adult men, yet can still communicate in it. The Ecuadorian Coaiquer give the appearance of wanting very much to acculturate, both ethnically and linguistically (Ehrenreich 1984:39). This, accompanied by the recent establishment of a mission and school at Plan Grande de San Marcos, may lead eventually to the disappearance of the Coaiquers as a viable ethnic and linguistic entity.

THE ORIENTE
The largest number of Indian languages spoken in Ecuador today is found in the eastern lowlands or Oriente. While languages such as Cofan and Huaorani have yet to be classified, others such as Siona, Secoya, Tetete, Shuar, Achuar, Lowland Quichua, and Zaparo belong to long-established language families.

2. Western Tucanoan (Tucanoan)
There are three representatives of the Tucanoan languages spoken in Ecuador today: Siona, Secoya, and Tetete. Linguistically they form the western branch of the Tucanoan family. Within this family they are most closely related to Cubeo, a language classified as Middle Tucanoan, located on the Quereri, Cuduiari, and Vaupés Rivers of eastern Colombia. Cubeo and Siona share 95.1% cognates lexically (Waltz and Wheeler 1972:125). Because of the greater dialectical variation within Cubeo and the proliferation of the Tucanoan languages within the Vaupés zone, it seems quite certain that speakers of Western Tucanoan probably migrated to the south and west from that area.

History. The Siona-Secoya of Ecuador were originally two cultural and linguistic groups, the Siona

of the Aguarico and the Secoya of the Santa Maria
(Uuyoja). These groups were descendants of the
group that the early Spanish priests labeled "Enca-
bellados" because of their long hair. In 1635
there were alleged to have been 8,000 "Encabella-
dos" living at the mouth of the Aguarico River
(Steward 1948:739). The Siona (also called Coñe by
the early chroniclers) were located in 1632 along
the upper Putumayo River from which they extended
downstream from the region of Santiago and Sibundoy
to as far as the Ecuatorial line (Steward 1948:
741). From these accounts, and because of the close
linguistic affiliations of the two languages, we
can hypothesize that during the sixteenth century
the area between the Putumayo and Aguarico Rivers
was inhabited by speakers of Western Tucanoan, at
that time a single language, or dialect of Tucanoan.

The sharing of a mutually intelligible language
did not prevent Siona, Secoya, and Tetete bands
from engaging in a great deal of intertribal warfare. This often resulted in the decimation of a
dissident group, or at least in its dispersal. Later many of the small groups that survived were
further reduced in number by the rubber boom on the
upper Putumayo. Thus today there remain only small
remnants of what was once a large and very powerful
tribal group.

Present-Day Situation. While speakers of Western
Tucanoan in Peru and Colombia can still be classified as either Siona or Secoya speakers, those in

Ecuador, because of a great deal of intermarriage,
are in the process of forming an amalgamated group
called Siona-Secoya (Vickers 1976). They differ
from the Tetete which form a separate community.
Siona-Secoya. Until recently the Siona-Secoya were
located primarily along the Cuyabeno River, a tributary of the Aguarico, in the province of Napo.
They numbered approximately 200. However, in 1973
most the of Siona-Secoya from Puerto Bolivar on the
Cuyabeno migrated to San Pablo on the Aguarico,
leaving seven to eight households at the former
settlement. By 1978, a small group, composed primarily of Siona, split off from the community at
San Pablo and moved to a site known as Campo Eno
about 7 km. upriver. At about the same time another group, consisting primarily of Secoyas, moved
downriver from San Pablo where they established yet
another settlement (Vickers 1983:454). More recently, there have been reports that there are only a
few Siona-Secoya left at San Pablo, the rest having
apparently moved to new sites, albeit located near
the settlement (Vickers 1984). As of 1980, there
were 297 Siona-Secoya living in or near San Pablo
(Vickers 1983:454).

In both the Cuyabeno and Aguarico settlements,
Siona and Secoya are still spoken in the home.
However, approximately 70% of the group speaks some
Spanish as well, although less than 50% speak the
national language with any degree of fluency (Vickers 1984). Women generally have less of a command
of Spanish than men. The 30% of the population
which is still monolingual in Siona or Secoya is

made up primarily of adult women or children under
the age of six or seven.

One of the reasons that the Siona-Secoya moved
from Puerto Bolivar to San Pablo in 1973 is because
the Summer Institute of Linguistics had moved their
bilingual Secoya-Spanish school there.  Another
reason was because San Pablo had more river traf-
fic, and thus more contacts with the outside
world.  It is also located in an area which has
been attracting speakers of Secoya from neighboring
Peru, in particular from communities along the An-
gusilla River (Vickers 1984). With the arrival of
these migrants, plus the use of Secoya in the bilingual school attended by their children, speakers
of Siona are at a definite disadvantage.  Thus it
is quite possible that in Ecuador Siona will be
replaced by Secoya or, perhaps for those living at
Camp Eno, by Spanish.  On the other hand, the
stress that the Summer Institute of Linguistics has
placed on language maintenance combined with their
recognition by INCRAE (Instituto Nacional de la
Colonización de la Región Amazónica Ecuatoriana) as
a "legitimate" tribal entity may provide the Siona-
Secoya with the necessary ammunition to counteract
the potential erosion of their cultural and linguistic identity.

Tetete.  According to Siona-Secoya oral history, a
number of generations ago there was a fairly large
group of Tetete speakers living on the Cuyabeno
below the Cuyabeno Lakes.  Linguistically their
language was probably an offshoot of Siona (Langdon
1974: 17; Vickers 1977). This group of Tetetes came

into conflict with another group of Tucanoans
living on the Aguarico who decimated them in a
sneak attack.   Those that survived escaped to the
headwaters of the Cuyabeno which runs near the
Pacayacu.   In the late 1960s Orville Johnson,
working with the Summer Institute of Linguistics,
encountered three Tetetes, two old men and one old
woman, living in the Pacayacu Gorge.   It is probable that these were the total number of surviving
Tetetes; whether they are still alive today is
unknown.

## 3.  Cofan (Unclassified)

Cofan is generally considered to be unclassified,
although it shows some lexical influence in the
form of borrowings from neighboring Chibchan languages (Wheeler 1972:95).  However, for the moment
there is no evidence to regard these affinities as
showing any kind of genetic relationship.

History.   Cofan oral tradition asserts that they
migrated to the Oriente from the Sierra, from an
area somewhere to the north and west of their present location (Yost 1975).  However, they have lived in the Oriente since at least the seventeenth
century when they were described as inhabiting the
area between the Aguarico and Chamabi Rivers and
numbering some 15,000 (Ortiz 1965:71).

Present-Day Situation.   Cofan is spoken by some 400
people living along the Aguarico, San Miguel, Guamues, and Putumayo Rivers on the Ecuador-Colombia

border.  As of 1980, the Cofan were situated in
four locations in Ecuador (Vickers 1984).

(1) A small group of Cofan (between 20 and 25)
were located on the Rio Bermejo (a tributary of the
San Miguel) on the Ecuadorian side of the border.
However most of their contacts were with Indians
and non-Indians in Colombia.

(2) There were 60 Cofanes located in Dovino, on
the Aguarico.  This group is the most "isolatio-
nist."  They have not organized politically, preferring, it appears, simply to be left alone.

(3) There was a group of 42 Cofanes living on
the south-west side of the Aguarico in Sinangue, a
settlement which is located inside the Reserva Eco-
lógica Cayambe.  There has been pressure placed on
the Cofanes to leave the Reserva, presumably because Indians are not allowed to live in the park.
Ironically the Quichua park rangers who are attempting to persuade the Cofanes to move are members of
communities that are located themselves within the
boundaries of the Reserva!

(4) The largest concentration of Cofanes is to
be found at Dureno located to the east of Lago Agrio on the Aguarico.  As of 1980 there were 198
Cofanes residing at Dureno.  This group maintains a
strong political organization which has proven useful in their dealings with outside authorities.

The Cofan language is divided into two mutually
intelligible dialects.  One of them is spoken along
the Aguarico River in Ecuador, while the other is
spoken on the San Miguel, Guamues, and Putumayo Rivers in Colombia (Borman 1962:45).

Traditionally the Cofanes have lived as hunters and swidden agriculturalists. However, starting in the late 1960s, their territory became the center for oil production by the Texaco-Gulf Corporation in cooperation with the Ecuadorian government. This has encouraged migration to the area by lowland Quichuas who, as a result of being pushed out of the Quijos-Napo area by white and Mestizo colonists, have been coming into the Aguarico area to look for jobs with the oil companies, as well as the opportunity to colonize land. At the same time, the Aguarico River has been turned into a center of intense colonization by whites and Mestizos from the Ecuadorian highlands who have been aided in this endeavor by the Ecuadorian Air Force. Thus the Cofanes are undergoing pressures from two sides: from the Serranos and lowland Quichuas who have been taking away their lands, and from other lowland Quichuas who have come into the area in large numbers to work for the oil companies. These migrations have exerted pressures on traditional Cofan cultural and linguistic patterns. For although as recently as the early seventies only three "Ecuadorian" Cofanes spoke Spanish with any kind of facility (Robinson 1971:136), pressures from speakers of "prestige" languages from outside, plus the existence of a bilingual school under the auspices of the Summer Institute of Linguistics in Dureno have brought about an increased degree of bilingualism.

As of 1980, most of the Cofanes, especially those at Dureno, had abandoned hunting and turned

to other economic pursuits.  Many are now supporting themselves manufacturing "traditional" artifacts which they sell either to shop keepers or
directly to visitors in the town of Lago Agrio.
Through their business contacts in Lago Agrio the
Cofanes are learning more Spanish.  On the other
hand, as in the case of the Colorados, the locals
at Lago Agrio recognize the value of the Cofanes as
tourist attractions and, in so doing, place a pre-
mium on their cultural distinctness (Vickers 1984).
This recognition may help assure the survival, at
least for a while, of the Cofan culture and language in Ecuador.


4. Huaorani (Unclassified)
Huaorani is the name that is used today to designate the tribal and linguistic group traditionally
referred to as Auca, a Quichua word meaning "savage" or "enemy."  However, as with many of the indigenous groups of the Ecuadorian Oriente, there
have been several other language names associated
with this group.  In particular, their language has
been called Aushiri (Awishiri, Auschiri, Auishiris,
Abijiras, Avigiras, Auxiras, Abiras, Ahuishiri,
Avixiras), Sabela (Ssabela), and Huaorani (Huagra-
ni, Waorani).  Of these, the short word list that
we have for Aushiri (Tessmann 1930:486) links that
language to Záparo rather than to Auca (Peeke 1974:
4).  Sabela is the name given to a tribal group encountered by Tessmann in 1925 (Tessmann 1930:298).
From his word list it seems that he was referring
to the same tribal group and language that is known

today as Huaorani (Peeke 1974:4). The third name, Huaorani, "the people", is the name that the Aucas call themselves (Yost 1981:677). The term Huao is the adjectival form.

History. From their own ethnohistorical accounts, it appears that the Huaorani moved upriver along the Curaray, Yasuni, and Napo Rivers to the area which they occupy today. This migration probably took place some forty years ago (MacDonald 1975) and its recent occurrence is supported by the fact that Huaorani is a very uniform language, showing little dialectal variation.

Present-Day Situation. The Huaorani today live in the province of Pastaza, to the west of the Ti- hueno and Oglán Rivers, to the north of the Cura- ray, and to the south of the Napo. As such they embrace the first parallel south and extend from approximately 78 to 77 longitude. The Huaorani are divided roughly into three groups: those who live in an evangelical mission station at Tihueno (around 200), those who inhabit the Huao "Protec- torate" between the Curaray and Coca Rivers (around 500) and those who maintain a semi-nomadic life to the north and east of the "Protectorate" (around 100) (Yost 1981:679).

At the moment the majority of Huaorani are mono- linguals. However they have recently undergone a major cultural change which began when the Ecuado- rian government in collaboration with the Summer Institute of Linguistics managed to relocate the

majority of Indians on a "Protectorate," an area
which amounts to one-tenth of their original territory.  Moreover, the government is currently
completing a road through the "Protectorate" which
is bound to open up even that zone to a certain
amount of colonization by Quichuas as well as by
whites and Mestizos.  The missionaries, have attempted to isolate the "Protectorate" from the outside world on the one hand, while they have introduced economic innovations in the form of trade in
ethnographic artifacts on the other.  Through the
latter a few Huaorani began to have contact with
non-tribal members, in particular the Quichuas of
neighboring communities with whom they formed trading alliances.  Associated with these alliances
has been a certain amount of ritual kinship
(compadrazgo).  This has led, in some cases, to
Quichua-Huao marriages which have placed some of
the Huaorani under pressure to share with their new
relatives the lands that have been granted them on
the "Protectorate".  Beyond this, there has evolved
the belief, fostered by Quichua teachers in Huao
schools, that to be Huaorani is equated with being
a savage - that it is far better ("more civilized")
to identify with Quichua language and culture than
to maintain their own traditions (Yost 1981:
700-701).

There are also an increasing number of Huao men
who have joined local oil company crews; this has
necessitated the learning of some Spanish.  And
today there are young women who have migrated to
neighboring towns such as Tena and Puyo to work as

maids for white and Mestizo families there (Yost
1981:699).

For those who wish to retain their traditional
way of life, there is some optimism in that the
Ecuadorian government, in 1983, greatly increased
the geographic area that the Huaorani could use for
hunting and swidden agriculture.  This was accomplished by designating lands adjacent to the "Protectorate" as a forest preserve.  These lands form
a bridge between the "Protectorate" and the Yasuni
National Forest.  Neither the forest preserve nor
the National Forest may be colonized, yet both may
be used for traditional economic pursuits by the
Huaorani.  Essentially then, the Huao "Protectorate" of 66,000 hectares has been increased by an
additional 650,000 hectares through access to the
forest preserve and the Yasuni National Park
(MacDonald 1984).

As a result of their recent membership in
CONFENIAE (Confederación Nacional Indígena Amazónica Ecuatoriana), concern has been voiced by some
Huaorani about the importance of maintaining their
traditional cultural identity.  However, the leadership of CONFENIAE is Quichua and the Huaorani
may well find it difficult to maintain a distinct
identity within the organization if they cannot
withstand pressure to merge culturally with its
Quichua leaders.

In general, the Huaorani, since "pacification",
have experienced more and more contacts with members of other ethnic groups - missionaries, oil
company employees, representatives of the national

government and even tourists, who are now entering
the area in ever greater numbers in order to visit
"real savages". This has resulted in a split between those Huaorani who wish to retain their own
culture, language and territory and those who wish
to become Quichua or, in some rare cases, Mestizo.
Thus traditional Huao culture and its language are
coming under increasing assault from outside sources. Whether the group manages to survive as a
discrete linguistic and cultural entity is a question that only the Huaorani can answer.

## 5. The Jivaroan Languages

There are two representatives of the Jivaroan languages spoken in Ecuador today: Shuar and Achuar.
Shuar is the general term used by most writers
today when referring to the language formerly called Jivaro or Jibaro. Achuar (Atchura, Achuara) is
spoken by Indians living to the east of the Shuara
along the Rio Pastaza. Linguistically Shuar and
Achuar are related to two languages spoken in northern Peru, and in the disputed frontier area between Ecuador and Peru. These are Aguaruna, numbering around 18,000 speakers, spoken to the south
along the Rio Marañon, and Huambisa, spoken by
approximately 5,000 Indians living along the Rio
Santiago. These languages, along with Shuar and
Achuar, form the two branches of the Jivaroan family. Aguaruna, the most conservative language,
forms one branch while the other three languages,
Huambisa, Achuar, and Shuar, form the Shuaran
branch of Proto-Jivaroan.

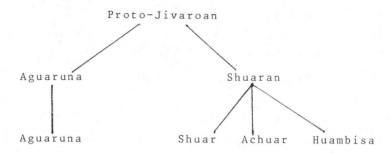

History.  Piecing together linguistic evidence with
ethnohistoric sources, we can assume that speakers
of Proto-Jivaroan were located somewhere along the
Rio Marañon.  This may have been near the area of
the Pongo de Manseriche since these rapids and the
neighboring Canusa (Cangasa) River figure impor-
tantly in the origin myths of the Shuara (Stirling
1938:125, 129).  At some point there was a split
between Aguaruna and Jivaro branches.  However,
judging from the high degree of mutual intelligibility between Aguaruna and Huambisa (Larson 1957),
this split must have occurred fairly recently.  The
Aguaruna remained on the Rio Marañon while those
who were later to become Shuaran speakers moved
northward, settling between the Pastaza in the
north, the upper Rio Zamora in the south, and from
about 1,200 meters altitude on the eastern slopes
of the Andes to the west, to the Rio Pangui in the
east.  Then at the turn of the century the western
Shuaran (the Shuara), as the consequence of head
hunting raids, forced those living in the Chiguasa
and middle Macuma areas to move eastward.  These
migrants today form the group known as the Achuara,

and are speakers of Achuar. At the same time, the western Shuaran forced the Jivaro living in the Río Yaupi region to migrate southward, forming the tribal group now known as the Huambisa (Harner 1972:. 36). However, the languages spoken by these three groups (Shuar, Achuar, and Huambisa) are very closely related. In fact, from a linguistic point of view their relationship to one another is more that of mutually intelligible dialects than of languages.

### Present-Day Situation

Shuar. There are approximately 15,000 Shuaras (Harner 1972: 211) living in the provinces of Morona-Santiago and Zamora-Chinchipe. They are divided into three groups.

   (1) The Interior Shuara live to the east of the Cutucú mountain range and number approximately 4,000. They lead a traditional life, depending on hunting and subsistence agriculture to sustain themselves. Having had only sporadic contact, at best, with outsiders, the Interior Shuara speak only Shuar. Many of the Shuara living in the "interior" do so by choice, preferring to avoid contact, when at all possible, with outsiders (Harner 1972:39), Indian or white. Thus it is quite probable that this group will continue to remain, for the time being, monolingual speakers of Shuar.

   (2) The Shuara living in the Upano Valley number approximately 9,000. They are in constant contact with both Salesian missionaries and the white and Mestizo colonists who are moving into the valley. Here the majority of the Shuara are associa-

ted with the Federation of Shuar Centers (Federa-
ción de Centros Shuar), operating out of Sucúa.
The Federation, although involved in bringing about
very fundamental economic changes among the Shuara,
has been very committed to maintaining as much of
the traditional culture as possible - in particular, the language.  For although all Shuaras living
in the Upano Valley speak Shuar, there has been the
feeling that as younger people become bilingual in
Spanish, the Shuar language will weaken and eventually disappear.  With this in mind, not only are
there daily radio broadcasts in Shuar, but also bilingual education programs in Shuar and Spanish.
Here bilingual education is seen not only as a vehicle for learning Spanish so as to gain access to
the goods and services that are available to the
country's Spanish-speaking majority, but it is also
valued as a method for reinforcing the use and
maintenance of the Shuar language, and its concomitant culture.

   (3) The group of Shuara living in the Zamora
Valley number approximately 2,000 and are in constant contact with Franciscan missionaries and
white and Mestizo colonists.  However, those living
in the Zamora Valley lack the kind of cultural reinforcement provided by the Federation in the Upano
Valley.  Beyond this, they are currently suffering
economically at the hands of colonists coming into
that area.  There is no system of bilingual education in this region; all schooling is carried out
in Spanish.  As a result, children learn Spanish in
the schools and feel negatively towards the reten-

tion of Shuar in their homes. Unless there is a drastic change in the present situation, it is doubtful that many of their own children will grow up speaking any language other than Spanish.

Achuar. There are probably between 4,000 and 5,000 Achuaras living in Ecuador, Peru, and the disputed area between the two countries (Varese 1971:185). In Ecuador between 2,000 and 3,000 are found living to the east of their traditional enemies, the Shuara. Although there is a great deal of movement among the Achuara because of feuding and warfare, the major part of this group inhabits an area extending from the Macuma River in the west to the Corrientes in the east. Their population is most concentrated in the western part of this zone, and becomes progressively more sparse as one moves towards the Corrientes.

With the exception of the few Achuara who were associated with Catholic and Protestant missionaries, and have thus learned Spanish, the majority have traditionally been monolinguals and have participated in an economy based on swidden agriculture and hunting. However, around 1973 some of the the Achuara living to the west of the Pastaza affiliated with the Federation of Shuar Centers and started to develop an economy based on cattle raising. And around 1975 the Shuar Federation began to set up bilingual schools in Shuar and Spanish among the Achuara of the area (Kelekna 1978). Thus in the western sector there are young people who have learned to speak some Spanish through education in the bilingual schools.

Between the Pastaza and Corrientes Rivers the Achuara have had more contact with Quichua speakers. In an unusual dichotomy they tend to regard the Quichuas as powerful shamans from whom they can learn secrets of shamanism, while at the same time they regard them as representatives of "modern life" from whom they can learn about the outside world. Thus there has been the tendency for Achuar men to learn Quichua. The Achuara in this area have also had the opportunity to learn Spanish through bilingual education programs sponsored by the Protestant missionaries, such that now there are younger people who speak some Spanish (Kelekna 1978).

Among the northern Achuara, especially in Pastaza Province, teachers in the Achuara-Spanish schools are often Napo Quichua trained by the Summer Institute of Linguistics. This can promote problems since the Napo Quichua rarely speak any Achuar, and very few Achuar children know Quichua (Taylor 1981:659).

However, in the general case of the Achuara, bilingual education programs in Spanish, or Spanish and Shuar, and the tendency for the eastern Achuara to want to learn Quichua, have been balanced by a strong ethnic identity which is tied closely to the speaking of Achuar. Thus it appears quite certain that in the foreseeable future neither Spanish, Shuar, or Quichua will make great inroads into the overall maintenance of Achuar as a viable linguistic entity in this part of the Ecuadorian Oriente.

## 6. Lowland Quichua (Quechumaran)

Just as highland Quichua has replaced many of the Indian languages of the Sierra, so lowland Quichua has replaced, and is still replacing, a large number of the indigenous languages of the Ecuadorian Oriente. Here Quichua is spoken by an estimated 10,000 Indians, of which 70% are monolinguals (Jara 1973). The language is diffused in a diagonal band, running from the northeast to southwest, across the provinces of Napo and Pastaza.

History. Traditionally it has been believed that in the early colonial period Quichua was introduced into the Ecuadorian Oriente by Spanish priests who used it as a lingua franca for communicating with the various linguistic groups in the area. However it seems doubtful that the presence of a few Quichua-speaking Spanish clergy can account for the rapid diffusion of Quichua throughout the Ecuadorian lowlands. It is more probable that Quichua was spoken in the Oriente long before the arrival of the Spaniards. It was most certainly used in the pre-hispanic period as a trade language (Oberem 1971:259), facilitating extensive commercial networks between the jungle and the highlands (Murra 1944:794). But beyond this there were probably migrations of highland Quichua speakers to the Oriente during the colonial period - people who fled to the lowlands to escape exploitation by their Spanish conquerors (Jaramillo Alvarado 1954:41; Murra 1944:814; Peréz 1947:335). It was these fu-

gitives who probably caused the original spread of
the Quichua language in the lowlands. And according to oral histories collected from Quichua speakers in the Oriente, these migrations have been
continuing ever since. As a result, Quichua has
spread throughout the Ecuadorian lowlands, replacing many of the languages once spoken there.

Traditionally all of lowland Quichua has been
divided into three dialects (Orr and Wrisley 1965:
iii). However, judging by the vast area in which
the language is spoken, it is quite probable that
there are other dialects to be found in more remote
parts of the Oriente. Of the areas that have been
studied linguistically, the northernmost comprises
the Limoncocha dialect which is spoken from the
community of Suno on down the Napo River. Morphologically the dialect is quite similar to the highland Quichua spoken in the province of Imbabura.
This points to the probability that after the Conquest speakers of the Imbabura dialect migrated
into the Oriente through the pass at Pimampiro, a
pass which was well-known as part of an important
pre-hispanic trade route (Juan y Ulloa 1826:343;
Wolf 1892:213). In the central Oriente the Tena
dialect is spoken by Indians living in the region
of Tena, Arajuno, and Ahuano. Morphologically this
dialect most closely resembles those dialects spoken in the central provinces of the Sierra. This
would seem to indicate that the source of migration
of Quichua speakers into the central Oriente was
from the central highlands, probably through the
passes at Papallacta and Pileleo, both of which

were also situated on two well-known pre-hispanic
trade routes (Wolf 1892:213). Finally, the southernmost, or Bobonaza, dialect is that which is
spoken along the Puyo and Bobonaza Rivers.  This
dialect shows phonological and lexical affinities
to the Quechua spoken in the Peruvian montaña (on
the Tigre, Napo, and Pastaza Rivers), which in turn
has been influenced by Peruvian highland Quechua
(as opposed to that of the Ecuadorian highlands).
From this evidence we may hypothesize that the origin of the Bobonaza dialect was probably in the Peruvian lowlands, a conclusion which is also supported by ethnographic evidence (Whitten 1976:47).

Present-Day Situation.  Today the Ecuadorian Oriente is in a state of flux.  Whereas formerly the
economy of the lowland Quichua was based on hunting
and subsistence agriculture, or on labor as peons
on haciendas, the recent rise of the oil industry
and government-sponsored colonization projects has
begun to bring the Quichua more into the mainstream
of the country's economy.  These new economic bases
have also resulted in a great deal of internal migration.  Thus where just a few years ago the Quichua that had been studied in the Oriente could be
divided into three discrete dialects, today these
dialects are becoming more and more mixed as speakers of one dialect move into areas where others
are spoken.

    Aside from this mixture of dialects, Quichua has
had a strong influence on other jungle languages.
In the case of Záparo, where there were 20,000

speakers some 125 years ago (Osculati 1850:281) today there are seven, with Quichua and Huaorani
(Auca) spoken exclusively in the area that was once
purely Záparo.  The same fate seems to have befal-
len Shimigae and Andoa.  And in the future it can
be predicted that Huaorani may perhaps suffer the
same fate.

    Thus speakers of lowland Quichua are increasing
in number.  This does not come just from supplan-
ting other Indian languages; it has also been based
on continued migrations of Quichua speakers from
the Sierra, especially from the provinces of Tungurahua, Cotopaxi, Chimborazo, and Loja.  And although these migrations have not been terribly numerous, with increased land-pressure in the Sierra,
and with the opening of the new Salcedo-Napo road,
the Oriente is experiencing, and will continue to
experience, a steady influx of Highland Indians.

    Thus the speaking of Quichua is increasing in
the lowlands.  Judging from the very limited number
of Spanish speakers in the Oriente and the newly
raised economic and social consciousness of the Indians, it seems certain that in the future, as in
the present, Quichua will be the most important
linguistic entity in the Ecuadorian lowlands.

## 7. Záparo (Zaparoan)

Záparo is a member of the Zaparoan family of languages.  At the end of the seventeenth century the
languages forming this family extended from the
headwaters of the Pastaza, Tigre, and Napo Rivers
in the north to the Marañon in the south.  Today

Zaparoan languages are spoken in scattered areas of
Colombia, Ecuador, and Peru. Those spoken in Peru
are the following: Iquitos with approximately 200
speakers is located in San Antonio de Pintoyacu
which is some 500 miles to the west of the city of
Iquitos; Cahuarana with perhaps four speakers is
located at the headwaters of the Blanco and Negro
Rivers; Arabela with perhaps fifty speakers is located on the Arabela; Andoa-Shimigae with perhaps
six speakers is located in Santo Tomás de Andoa
(Wise 1972), and Záparo with five families (Villarejo 1959:155) or less is spoken today in scattered
areas of Colombia, Ecuador and Peru.

History.   In comparing linguistic data from the Zaparoan languages, we find that Iquitos and Cahuarana, both spoken in the Iquitos area in Peru, form
the most conservative branch of the family. If we
combine this evidence with the fact that Záparo
oral history tells of the Zaparoan-speaking peoples
migrating from a place of origin along the Marañon
(Stark 1981), we may hypothesize that their homeland was in the area where Iquitos and Cahuarana
are still spoken today.

   From the Iquitos area speakers of Zaparoan seem
to have migrated northward along the Tigre until
they reached its headwaters where they settled and
formed the Arabela Andoa-Shimigae branch. At a
somewhat later date this group split into two languages, Arabela and Andoa-Shimigae, which are still
spoken in this area today. Finally, some years
later a group of speakers of Andoa-Shimigae migra-

ted northward, forming the Záparo language.  By
1850 there were an estimated 20,000 speakers of
this language (Osculati 1850:281).

During the last part of the nineteenth century
the Záparos themselves split into two groups.  One
group was established along the Bobonaza and Conambo Rivers, and the other at the headwaters of the
Curaray in settlements along the Lliguino, Nushino,
Nugano, and Supino, as well as perhaps some of the
other rivers of the area.  The two groups of Záparos were enemies, and rarely communicated with one
another.  As a result, their isolation from one
another gave rise to dialect differences within the
language.

Later a group of Zaparos split off from those
located at the headwaters of the Curaray and migrated northward, eventually settling in Colombia between Puerto Leguizamo (formerly Caucaya) and Puerto Montclar de Putumayo, on the Putumayo.  In 1940
this group numbered twelve speakers of Záparo
(Ortiz 1965:332).  It is uncertain whether any exist
today.

It is not known where the five families encountered in the Peruvian lowlands in 1959 (Villarejo
1959:155) may be today, or if indeed they are still
extant.  However, the vocabulary included in the
short word list published of their language (Villarejo 1959:182-183) indicates that it is more similar to the dialect of Záparo spoken at the headwaters of the Curaray than to that of the Bobonaza
and Conambo.

Present-Day Situation. Since the mid-nineteenth century, speakers of Záparo have decreased rapidly in number, primarily as a result of disease and forced labor. As their number diminished, they found it harder to find marriage partners within their own group and began to intermarry and be absorbed by other cultural and linguistic groups. Thus although there is the remote possibility that there may be additional speakers of Záparo in isolated areas of the lowlands, in Ecuador today there are only seven known speakers of Záparo. As of 1974 one speaker lived in Chapana, a settlement on the Curaray, one lived in the Huaorani settlement of Andaoripungo which is also on the Curaray, two lived in Montalvo on the Bobonaza, and three were living on the Conambo. Of the seven, five were over sixty years of age, and the two younger men, one at Andaoripungo and the other at Montalvo, did not speak Záparo with any fluency. Thus with the advanced age of the majority of the speakers, Ecuadorian Záparo will in all probability be extinct within a very few years.

CONCLUSION

Historically the languages of the Ecuadorian Oriente have spread as the result of fissioning, is in great part due to inter- and intra-tribal warfare. Today some of the groups speaking these languages are too small to divide any further and may find themselves eventually being absorbed both culturally and linguistically by the lowland Quichua.

The Indian languages of the coast have historically spread into new areas after being driven out
of their homelands by other cultural and linguistic
groups. However today little remains in the way of
areas which can absorb groups seeking refuge from
the linguistic and cultural pressures of the dominant Spanish-speaking culture. Thus the coastal
languages may eventually be overwhelmed and replaced by the national language.

Since the Conquest, Indian languages have disappeared in Ecuador at the rate of one every twenty-
five years. There is no reason to believe that
this rate of extinction will change in the future.
Consequently, at some point in the future the country will probably be left with two languages, Quichua and Spanish. And it will be only through re-
sidual borrowings from the languages that they have
absorbed that we will be reminded of the multi-lin-
gual situation that was once Ecuador.

ACKNOWLEDGEMENTS
I wish to thank Pam Hunte, Pita Kelekna, John
Lindskoog, Theodore E. MacDonald, Jr., Bill
Vickers, and Jim Yost for commenting on earlier
versions of this paper.

REFERENCES
Barrett, Samuel A.  1925.  The Cayapa Indians of
    Ecuador, 2 vols.  New York: Museum of the Ame-
    rican Indian.
Borman, M.B.  1962.  Cofan Phonemes.  In Ecuado-
    rian Indian Languages: I.  Benjamin Elson (ed.).

Norman, Oklahoma: Summer Institute of Linguistics. pp. 45-59.

Costales Samaniego, Alfredo. 1965. Los Indios Colorados, Llacta, 22, Quito.

Ehrenreich, Jeffrey. 1984. Isolation, Retreat and Secrecy: Dissembling Behavior among the Coaiquer Indians of Ecuador. In Jeffrey Ehrenreich (ed.), Political Anthropology in Ecuador: Perspective from Indigenous Cultures. Society for Latin American Anthropology and the Center for Caribbean and Latin American Studies,the State University of New York at Albany, Albany, New York, pp. 25-54.

Harner, Michael J. 1972. The Jivaro: People of the Sacred Waterfall. Garden City, New York: Doubleday/Natural History Press.

Jara, P. Fausto. 1973. Report to I° Seminario de Educación Bilingüe, Quito (manuscript).

Jaramillo Alvarado, Pío. 1954. El Indio Ecuatoriano. Quito: Casa de la Cultura Ecuatoriana.

Jijón y Caamaño. 1952. Antropologia Prehispánica del Ecuador, Quito.

Juan, Jorge y Antonio de Ulloa. 1826. Notícias Secretas de América, Parte II, London.

Kelekna, Pita. 1978. Personal Communication (January 1978).

Langdon, E. Jean Matteson. 1974. The Siona Medical System: Beliefs and Behavior. Ph.D. Dissertation, Tulane University.

Larson, Mildred L. 1957. Comparación de los vocabularios aguaruna y huambisa. Tradición 7: 147-168 (Cuzco).

León, Luis A. 1974. Bosquejo histórico de las lenguas vernáculas del Ecuador y la Educación Bilingüe. América Indígena XXXIV (3):745-775.

Lindskoog, John N. 1975. Personal Communication (August 1975).

Lindskoog, John N., and Carrie A. Lindskoog. 1964. Vocabulário Cayapa. Quito: Instituto Lingüístico de Verano.

MacDonald, Theodore. 1975. Personal Communication (March 1975).

------. 1984. Personal Communication (October 1984).

Maldonaldo, Pedro. 1750. Carta de la Provincia de Quito.

McQuown, Norman A. 1955. The Indigenous Languages of Latin America, American Anthropologist 57(3): 501-570.

Murra, John. 1944. The Historic Tribes of Ecuador. In Handbook of South American Indians, Vol. 2:785-821, Washington, D.C.: Smithsonian Institution.

Oberem, Udo. 1971. Los Quijos: Historia de transculturación de un grupo indígena en el Oriente ecuatoriano (1528-1956), Memorias del departamento de antropología y etnología de América I, Facultad de filosofía y letras, Universidad de Madrid.

Orr, Carolyn, and Betsy Wrisley. 1965. Vocabulario Quichua de Oriente del Ecuador. Quito: Instituto Lingüístico de Verano.

Ortiz, Sergio Elias. 1965. Lenguas y dialectos indígenas de Colombia, Vol. I, Part 3, Historia extensa de Colombia. Academia Colombiana de Historia, Bogota.

Osculati, Gaetano. 1850. Explorazione delle regioni equatoriali lungo il Napo ed il fiume delle Amazzoni, Milano.

Paz y Miño, L.T. 1940-1942. Lenguas Indígenas del Ecuador. Boletín de la Academia Nacional de Historia, Vol. XX, Nos. 57 and 58, Vol XXII, No. 59.

Peeke, M. Catherine. 1974. Preliminary Grammar of Auca. Norman, Oklahoma: Summer Institute of Linguistics.

Peréz, Aquiles R. 1947. Las Mitas en la Real Audiencia de Quito. Quito: Imprenta del Ministerio del Tesoro.

Ponce Rubio, P. Vicente. 1975. Autoridades de Carchi visitaron zona habitada por indios Coaiqueres. El Comercio, May 9, 1975.

Robinson, Scott A. 1971. Datos Geo-Demográficas y Estado Actual de los Grupos Indígenas del Litoral y la Amazonia Ecuatoriana. In La Situación del Indígena en América del Sur. Georg Grünberg (ed.), Montevideo, Uruguay, pp. 135-139.

Stark, Louisa R. 1981. La lengua zápara del Ecuador. Miscelanea Antropológica Ecuatoriana (Boletín de los Museos del Banco Central), Guayaquil, Ecuador: Vol. I, pp. 12-91.

Steward, Julian H. 1948. Western Tucanoan Tribes. In Handbook of South American Indians, Vol, 3 pp. 737-747. Washington, D.C. Bureau of American Ethnology, Bulletin 143.

Stirling, M.W.    1938.    Historical and Ethnographi-
    cal Material on the Jivaro Indians.    Bureau of
    American Ethnography, Bulletin 117, Smithsonian
    Institution, Washington, D.C.

Taylor, Anne-Christine 1981. God-Wealth: The Achuar
    and the Missions.  In Norman E. Whitten, Jr.,
    Cultural Transformations and Ethnicity in Modern
    Ecuador, pp. 647-676. Urbana, Illinois: Univer-
    sity of Illinois Press.

Tessman, Günter, 1930.    Die Indianer Nordost-Perus,
    Hamburg.

Varese, Stefano.    1971.    Grupos Etno-lingüísticos
    de la Selva Peruana.    In La Situación del Indí-
    gena en América del Sur, Georg Grünberg (ed.).
    Montevideo, Uruguay, p. 185.

Vickers, William Taylor. 1976.    Cultural Adaptation
    to Amazonian Habitats: The Siona-Secoya of Eas-
    tern Ecuador.    Ph.D. Dissertation, University of
    Florida.

------.    1977.    Personal Communication (June 1977).

------.    1983.    The Territorial Dimensions of Sio-
    na-Secoya and Encabellado Adaptation. In Raymond
    B. Hames and William T. Vickers (eds.), Adaptive
    Responses of Native Amazonians, pp. 451-478. New
    York: Academic Press.

------.  1984. Personal Communication (October
    1984).

Villarejo, P. Avencio. 1959.    La Selva y el Hombre:
    Estudio antropocosmológico del Aborigen Amazóni-
    co, Lima: Editorial Ausonia.

Waltz, Nathan E., and Alva Wheeler.    1972.    Proto
    Tucanoan.    In Comparative Studies in Amerindian

Languages.    Esther Matteson, et al. (eds.). pp.
119-149.    The Hague-Paris: Mouton.

Wheeler, Alva.    1972.    Proto Chibchan.    In Comparative Studies in Amerindian Languages,    Esther Matteson, et al. (eds).    pp. 93-108.    The
Hague-Paris: Mouton.

Whitten, Norman E., Jr.    1976.    Sacha Runa: Ethnicity and Adaptation of Ecuadorian Jungle Quichua.    Urbana: University of Illinois.

Wise, Mary Ruth.    1972.    Personal Communication
(October 10, 1972).

Wolf, Teodoro.    1892. Geografía y Geología del
Ecuador. Leipzig: Brockhaus.

Yost, Jim. 1975.    Personal Communication (July
1975).

------. 1981.    Twenty Years of Contact: The Mechanisms of Change in Wao ("Auca") Culture.    In Norman E. Whitten, Jr., Cultural Transformations
and Ethnicity in Modern Ecuador, pp. 677-704.
Urbana, Illinois: University of Illinois Press.

# 4. Indigenous Languages of Lowland Peru: History and Current Status

## Mary Ruth Wise

INTRODUCTION

Since the publication of the Handbook of South American Indians thirty years ago, extensive anthropological and linguistic research has been carried
out among forty-eight of the ethnic groups of Peruvian Amazonia, plus studies in Colombia or Ecuador
of three additional groups represented in Peru.[1]
Limited data have been collected on eleven other
languages and cultures, including four now considered extinct. Information gathered on various field
trips supports the categorization of other groups
as uncontacted or extinct. (See the right-hand
half of Table 1, i.e. 1975, for an enumeration of
groups where data have been collected.)

With these data in hand, it is possible to obtain a more accurate picture of the current situation and genetic classification of the languages of
the indigenous groups of lowland Peru - including
those living in the eastern foothills of the Andes
- than was possible when the Handbook was published. Although we are still dependent on those volumes as the major compilation of data from earlier
sources, they can now be supplemented by studies,
such as those by Lyon (1975) and Shell (1965),
which have cleared up some of the points of confu-

Degree of Integration into the National Society – 1900

| | Isolated | Sporadic Contact | Permanent Contact | Integrated |
|---|---|---|---|---|
| ARAWAKAN | Ashánínca Campa<br>Caquinte Campa<br>Pajonal Campa<br>Culina | Nomatsiguenga Campa<br>Pichis Campa<br>Ucayali Campa<br>Iñapari?<br>Machiguenga<br>Piro | Amuesha<br>Upper Perené Campa | Chamicuro |
| CAHUAPANAN | | Chayahuita | Jebero | |
| HARÁKMBET | Amarakaeri<br>Arasairi<br>Sapiteri<br>Toyoeri | Huachipaeri | | |
| HUITOTOAN | | Andoque<br>Bora<br>Meneca Huitoto<br>Muinane Huitoto<br>Murui Huitoto<br>Ocaina<br>Resígaro | | |

TABLE 1. Ethnic Groups of the Peruvian Amazon (continued)

Degree of Integration into the National Society - 1975

| Isolated | Sporadic Contact | Permanent Contact | Integrated | Extinct |
|---|---|---|---|---|
| | X Caquinte Campa | X Amuesha   -a<br>X Ashaninca Campa<br>X Nomatsiguenga Campa<br>X Pajonal Campa<br>X Upper Perene Campa<br>    -a<br>X Pichis Campa<br>X Ucayali Campa<br>X Culina<br>X Machiguenga<br>X Piro   -a | Y Chamicuro | Y Iñapari? |
| | | X Chayahuita | X Jebero | |
| | | X Amarakaeri<br>Y Arasairi  -a<br>X Huachipaeri<br>Y Sapiteri | Y Toyoeri | |
| | | X Bora   -a<br>X Murui Huitoto  -a<br>X Ocaina  -a | Z Andoque<br>  (with Huitoto)<br>Z Meneca Huitoto<br>  (with Murui)<br>X Muinane Huitoto<br>  (with Murui)<br>X Resígaro (with<br>  Ocaina & Bora) | |

| Isolated | Sporadic Contact | Permanent Contact | Integrated |
|---|---|---|---|
| **JIVAROAN** | | | |
| Candoshi | Achual | | |
| | Aguaruna | | |
| | Huambisa | | |
| | Jivaro | | |
| | | | |
| **PANOAN** | | | |
| Amahuaca | Cashibo | Atsahuaca | |
| Cashinahua | Sensi | Capanahua | |
| Cujareño | | Panobo | |
| (Masronahua?) | | Remo | |
| Isconahua | | Shetebo | |
| Mayo | | Shipibo-Conibo | |
| Mayoruna | | | |
| Morunahua | | | |
| Nocamán | | | |
| Parquenahua | | | |
| Pisabo | | | |
| Sharanahua-Marinahua | | | |
| Yaminahua? | | | |
| | | | |
| **PEBA-YAGUAN** | Yagua | Yameo | |
| | | | |
| **QUECHUA** | Pastaza Quechua | Napo Quechua | |
| | | San Martín Quechua | |
| | | Tigre Quechua | |
| | | | |
| **TACANAN** | | Ese'ejja | |

TABLE 1. Ethnic Groups of the Peruvian Amazon (conclusion)

Degree of Integration into the National Society – 1975

| Isolated | Sporadic Contact | Permanent Contact | Integrated | Extinct |
|---|---|---|---|---|
|  |  | X Achual |  |  |
|  |  | X Aguaruna |  |  |
|  |  | X Candoshi |  |  |
|  |  | X Hyambisa |  |  |
|  |  | X Jivaro |  |  |
| Cujareño | X Amahuaca | X Cashibo | X Capanahua | Atsahuaca |
| (Masronahua?) | X Mayoruna | X Cashinahua | Y Shetebo (with | Mayo? |
| Morunahua |  | X Isconahua | Shipibo) | Nocamán |
| Parquenahua |  | X Sharanahua– |  | Y Panobo |
| Pisabo |  | X Marinahua |  | Y Remo? |
|  |  | X Shipibo–Conibo |  | Sensi |
|  |  | X Yaminahua |  |  |
|  |  | X Yagua |  | Yameo |
|  |  | X Napo Quechua –a |  |  |
|  |  | X Pastaza Quechua |  |  |
|  |  | X San Martín Quechua –a |  |  |
|  |  | Y Tigre Quechua –a |  |  |
|  |  | X Ese'eija |  |  |

Degree of Integration into the National Society - 1900

| Isolated | Sporadic Contact | Permanent Contact | Integrated |
|---|---|---|---|
| TUCANOAN | Secoya | Orejón | Muniche |
| TUPI-GUARANI | | Cocama-Cocamilla | |
| | | Omagua | |
| ZAPAROAN | Aushiri | Andoa | |
| Arabela | Záparo? | Cahuarano | |
| Taushiro | | Iquito | |
| | | Omurano | |
| UNCLASSIFIED | Abishira | Cholón | Aguano |
| | Ticuna | Urarina? | Hibito? |

KEY
x indicates ethnic group where extensive research has been carried out.
y indicates ethnic group where limited data have been collected.
z indicates ethnic group where extensive research has been carried out in Colombia or Ecuador.
-a indicates acculturated.
Unmarked groups are those where the only information gathered supports their categorization as extinct or isolated.

Degree of Integration into the National Society - 1975

| Isolated | Sporadic Contact | Permanent Contact | Integrated | Extinct |
|---|---|---|---|---|
| | | X Orejón -a | Y Muniche | |
| | | X Secoya | | |
| | | | X Cocama-Cocamilla | |
| | | | Y Omagua (with Cocoma and mestizos. Prior to 1949 more extensive research was carried out.) | |
| | X Taushiro | X Arabela -a | X Andoa (with (Quechua)) | Aushiri |
| | | | X Iquito | Y Cahuarano |
| | | | | Omurano |
| | | | | Z Záparo |
| | | X Ticuna -a | Aguano | Abishira |
| | | X Urarina | | Cholón |
| | | | | Hibito |

sion in the Handbook.  The material contained in it
and other historical sources allows us to compare
the current status of the ethnic groups of today
with that of 1900 and to draw some conclusions
regarding their probable status in the next
decades.[2]

COMPARISON OF STATUS IN 1900 AND 1975
At the beginning of the twentieth century, seventy-
eight ethnic groups had survived the slavery, hostilities, smallpox epidemics and other unfavorable
factors resulting from the first centuries of contact with the western world.  Of these, sixty-three
still exist, but very few remain in the same situation as they were in 1900. For example, only four -
out of twenty-three in 1900 - remain isolated, contact with eleven having been established prior to
1948 and with eight since then.

The slave raids and enforced labor during the
rubber boom of the 1880's have ceased, but until
very recently most groups were still subject to exploitation at the hands of the patrones and to the
culture change resulting from the loss of their
traditional territories.  The indigenous groups are
faced with ever-increasing numbers of people from
different cultures: petroleum explorers, road construction crews, lumberers, hunters, thousands of
colonists from the mountains and coast, merchants,
tourists, government workers, missionaries, scholars, and many others.  It is inevitable that
change take place not only all around them, but
also in their own socio-economic systems and other

aspects of culture.  According to Varese (1972:82, my translation):

> More than 70% of the ethnic minorities
> maintain permanent relations of inter-
> action with members of the rest of the
> nation.  Some 35% (which includes a few
> local groups of the 70% above) maintain
> sporadic relations; so that directly or
> indirectly, in greater or lesser degree,
> all of the native societies are tied to
> the national economic system.

My estimate of the ethnic groups which are in permanent contact or integrated is 87%.

The degree of integration into the national society of the seventy-eight groups which survived in 1900 is compared with that of 1975 in Table 1. Criteria proposed by Ribeiro (1971) are followed in classifying ethnic groups according to degree of integration with the national society.  His definitions are summarized below:

Isolated - groups which fled after having some contact with western culture.  These groups subsist by means of their own work and maintain full cultural autonomy.

Sporadic contact - groups which maintain a fairly high degree of autonomy and gain their subsistence from traditional methods, but which have acquired other needs which can only be

satisfied through contact with the outside world.
These contacts almost always take place through a
few individuals who function as intermediaries.

Permanent contact - these groups have lost their
economic autonomy and part of their socio-political
autonomy.  Nevertheless, they maintain those traditional customs which are compatible with their new
situation.

Integrated - these groups maintain a degree of
ethnic identity.  However, it is impossible to reconstruct their traditional culture since they have
adapted to the national culture or another ethnic
group in every way possible and have lost their native language.

I have added a sub-category, permanent contact-
acculturated, which includes those groups which
have adopted many aspects of western culture and
are fairly bilingual, but for whom a reconstruction
of the traditional culture is possible from a study
of the folklore, interviews with older people,
etc.

While 94% of the seventy-eight groups maintained
at least some degree of autonomy in 1900, only 64%
are able to do so at present.  18% are now integrated with the national society or another ethnic
group, while another 18% having disappeared.
Viewed from another perspective, only 13% of the
existing groups are not in permanent contact with
the outside world.  This contrasts with 56% in
1900.

FACTORS FAVORING SURVIVAL

Population

In Table 2, 1975 population figures are compared
with those of 1900. Study of Table 2 provides some
basis for proposing a minimum population figure for
a viable group, i.e. one with the potential for
surviving and maintaining at least a degree of ethnic identity in the face of permanent contact. All
of the groups which have become extinct had a population of 200 or less at the turn of the century
with the possible exception of Hibito, which had
500 members in 1851, but was probably integrated by
1900. The Cahuarano are another possible exception: Tessman (1930) listed a population of 1000 in
1925. Since, however, his figures seem quite inex-
act (he says, for example, there were 100 Amuesha
in 1925; but according to our figures there are at
least 4000 at present), I believe that the Cahuarano population must have been much lower. Therefore, I conclude from reviewing the tables that all
of the groups which have disappeared in this century had less than viable populations and were already very near to extinction in 1900.

The only groups which began the century in isolation and are now extinct are Nocamán and Mayo.
It has been quite impossible to learn very much
about the Nocomán, who were possibly a sub-group of
the Cashibo. Wars and raids between the Mayoruna
and Mayo rather than contact with the outside world

TABLE 2. Comparison of present population of ethnic groups with the estimated population in 1900 (or the date closest to 1900 for which data are available)

| | | 1900 | 1975 Minimum | 1975 Maximum[a] |
|---|---|---|---|---|
| **ARAWAKAN** | | | | |
| Amuesha | 1881: | 2,000 | 4,000 | 5,000 |
| Campa (general) | 1896: | 20,000 | | |
| Ashaninca Campa | | | 15,000 | 18,000 |
| Caquinte Campa | | | 300 | 1,000 |
| Nomatsiguenga Campa | | | 2,500 | 4,000 |
| Pajonal Campa | | | 2,000 | 4,000 |
| Upper Perené Campa | | | 2,000 | 3,000 |
| Pichis Campa | | | 3,000 | 5,000 |
| Ucuyali Campa | | | 3,000 | 5,000 (in Peru) |
| Culina | 1930: | not in Peru | 150 | 400 (in Peru) |
| Chanicuro | | 60 | 100 | 140 |
| Iñapari | | ? | Extinct | |
| Machiguenga | 1924: | 3000–4000 | 7,000 | 10,000 |
| Piro | 1922: | 500–600 | 1,700 | 2,500 |
| **CAHUAPANAN** | | | | |
| Chayahuita | 1925: | several hundred | 6,000 | 6,000 |
| Jebero | 1925: | 600 | 2,300 | 3,000 |
| **HARAKMBET** | | | | |
| Amarakaeri | 1940: | 1800? | 400 | 500 |
| Arasairi | 1940: | 800? | 22 | 22 |
| Huachipaeri | 1940: | 1500? | 165 | 165 |
| Sapiteri | 1948: | 200 | 27 | 27 |
| Toyoeri | | | 69 | 83 |

TABLE 2. Comparison of population (continued)

| | | 1900 | 1975 Minimum | 1975 Maximum |
|---|---|---|---|---|
| **HUITOTOAN** | | | | |
| Andoque | 1910: | 10,000 | 10 | 10 (in Peru) |
| Bora | 1910: | 15,000 | 1,000 | 1,500 (in Peru) |
| Huitoto Meneca | | ? | 50 | 50 (in Peru) |
| Huitoto Muinane | 1910: | 2,000 | 60 | 60 (in Peru) |
| Huitoto Murui | 1910: | 15,000 | 600 | 800 (in Peru) |
| Ocaína | 1910: | 2,000 | 150 | 250 (in Peru) |
| Resígaro | 1910: | 1,000 | 11 | 11 |
| **JIVAROAN** | | | | |
| All the Jívaro except the Candoshi | 1900: | 20,000 | | |
| Achual | | | 2,000 | 3,000 (in Peru) |
| Aguaruna | | | 22,000 | 22,000 |
| Huambisa | | | 5,000 | 5,000 |
| Jíbaro | | | 1,000 | 2,000 |
| Candoshi | 1900: | 3,500? | 2,000 | 3,000 |
| **PEBA-YAGUAN** | | | | |
| Yagua | 1925: | 1000-1500 | 3,000 | 4,000 |
| Yameo | 1925: | 50 | Extinct | |
| **QUECHUA** | | | | |
| Napo Quechua | | ? | 6,000 | 10,000 (in Peru) |
| Pastaza Quechua | | ? | 2,000 | 4,000 |
| San Martín Quechua | 1925: | 1000 or more | 15,000 | 15,000 (in Peru) |
| Tigre Quechua | | ? | 2,000 | 2,000 (in Peru) |

TABLE 2. Comparison of population (continued)

| | | 1900 | 1975 Minimum | 1975 Maximum |
|---|---|---|---|---|
| **PANOAN** | | | | |
| Amahuaca | 1925: | 3,000 | 500 | 1,500 (in Peru) |
| Atsahuaca | 1902 | 20-25 | Extinct | 500 |
| Capanahua | 1925: | 100 | 350 | 500 |
| Cashibo | 1925: | 1500-2000 | 1,000 | 1,500 (in Peru) |
| Cashinahua | 1920 | 42 families | 850 | 1,200 (in Peru) |
| Cujareño | | | 20 | 100 |
| Isconahua | | | 28 | 50 |
| Mayo | | | Extinct | |
| Mayoruna | 1925: | ? | 550 | 1,000 (in Peru) |
| Morunahua | 1925: | ? | 150? | 150? |
| Nacóman | 1925: | | Extinct | |
| Panobo | 1925: | 3 | Extinct | |
| Parquenahua | | 100-200 | 200? | 200? |
| Pisabo | | | 100? | 100? |
| Remo | | | Extinct | |
| Sensi | 1925: | 100 | Extinct | |
| Sharanahua | 1925: | 2,000? | 1,000 | 1,500 (in Peru) |
| Shetebo | 1925: | 360 | (see Shipibo) | |
| Shipibo-Conibo | 1925: | 2,500 too low? | 11,300 | 15,000 |
| Yaminahua | | ? | 200 | 600 (in Peru) |
| **TACANAN** | | | | |
| Ese'ejja | 1905: | 700-900 | 600 | 1,000 (in Peru) |
| **TUCANOAN** | | | | |
| Muniche | 1925: | 200 | ? | |
| Orejón | 1925: | 500 | 190 | 300 |
| Secoya | 1928: | 200 | 250 | 500 (in Peru) |

TABLE 2.  Comparison of population (concluded)

|  |  | 1900 | 1975 Minimum | 1975 Maximum |
|---|---|---|---|---|
| **TUPI-GUARANI** | | | | |
| Cocama-Cocamilla | 1936: | 9500-10,500 | 15,000 | 18,000 |
| Omagua | 1925: | 125-150 | 600 | 600 |
| **ZAPAROAN** | | | | |
| Andoa | 1925: | 12 families | 5 | 5 |
| Arabela | 1954: | 40 | 150 | 200 |
| Aushiri | 1925: | 75 | Extinct | |
| Cahuarano | 1925: | 1000 inexact? | 5 | Extinct as a group |
| Iquito | 1925: | several hundred | 150 | 150 |
| Omurano | 1925: | 25 | Extinct | |
| Taushiro | 1925: | 70? | 18 | 18 |
| Záparo | 1900: | a few | Extinct | |
| **UNCLASSIFIED** | | | | |
| Abishira | 1925: | 55-75 | Extinct | |
| Aguano | 1925: | 100 | Some 40 families? | |
| Cholón | | some | Extinct | |
| Hibito | 1851: | 500 | Extinct | |
| Ticuna | | ? | 3,000 | 4,000 (in Peru) |
| Urarina | 1930: | 300 inexact? | 2,000 | 3,500 |

aThe minimum population indicated for each is the figure which seems most accurate to my colleagues in SIL who have, in most cases, done field work in the area over a period of several years. Other authors estimate a greater number in many cases and, therefore, I include a maximum population figure which is closer to their figures.

account for the disappearance of the latter. Other
groups survived the initial contact and in some
cases there is a tendency toward increasing population. The Candoshi population, for example, was
reduced to about half around 1940 due to a measles
epidemic soon after contact, but now the population
is growing rapidly, having doubled in one area in
the last twenty-five years.

Four of the groups which have a population of
200 or less are isolated, eight more are integrated
with other groups or with the national culture.
The situation of all sixteen small groups which are
in contact with western culture is very precarious;
it is at least possible that they all will have become extinct or will be almost completely integrated with other groups or mestizos within the next
quarter century. (The Culina and Yaminahua are not
included among the sixteen since there are several
hundred speakers of each of these languages in
other countries.) The Zaparoan family as a whole
is in danger of extinction or integration with Quechua both in Peru and Ecuador. Amarakaeri appears
to be the only viable population group remaining of
the Ḥarákmbet family.

The Huitotoan groups were among those who suffered the most cruel treatment at the hands of the
rubber workers and were reduced in population from
around 45,000 to several hundred. The present population seems to be stabilizing and even growing
as far as the Bora and Murui Huitoto are concerned. Probably only those two groups will continue

to maintain their ethnic identity in Peru (plus Muinane Bora and Menaca Huitoto in Colombia).

## Health Precautions

The precautions taken after contact constitute another important factor in the viability of a group. The growing Mayoruna population is in striking contrast to the decimation of the Cashibo and Candoshi populations from epidemics in the early years following contact. An intensive immunization program was begun among the Mayoruna almost immediately after contact, which was effected in September of 1969. Care is still taken to avoid carrying disease into the tribal area and an attempt is made to ensure that medical help is available. Various projects have been undertaken which should help provide an adequate protein supply for the growing population, and a reservation was established by the Peruvian Ministry of Agriculture in 1973 to help the group maintain a degree of economic and political autonomy.

## Socio-Political Organization

Other factors such as kind of socio-political organization are much harder to define, but have evidently played a part in the survival, integration or disappearance of various groups. Ribeiro (1971), on the basis of his study of the history of contact of Brazilian groups, hypothesizes that groups with strong unilineal structures are more resistant to external, destructive factors than those in which the basic social unit is the exten-

ded family. This hypothesis seems to be validated
by comparison of the Jivaroan groups with the Amuesha who have survived but are quite acculturated
and, without other counter-influences, would probably have lost most of their ethnic identity by
now. There is no evidence that the Amuesha were
ever organized in units larger than an extended
matrilocal family, although there were religious-
political leaders who had a degree of influence on
somewhat larger groupings. In contrast, the Aguaruna society is not only patrilineal but there is a
well-defined segmentary lineage system which allowed the whole tribe, or even all of the Jivaroan
groups, to unite against outside incursions
(Larson, 1979). Consequently, this group has been
able to maintain a strong sense of identity and
much of their traditional way of life in the face
of increasing outside contact.

"Law of Native Communities"
Other current, external factors in Peru favor survival of most of the groups now in sporadic or permanent contact with the national society, provided
the population is of adequate size for a viable
group. One of these factors is the Law of Native
Communities. Under the law, in effect from 1974
until May 1978 (and now replaced by a modified version), 372 native communities received official
recognition and 200 have title to their lands (sta-
tistics from Chirif and Mora, 1977). Some twenty
others probably obtained their titles in 1978, and
some more will have obtained them since the statis-

tics were compiled. There are, of course, many
others who still do not have titles and, of those
who do, the amount is often not adequate for fishing and hunting, as well as slash-and-burn agriculture. Nevertheless, many communities now have at
least some land which is respected as theirs
through the implementation of this law.

## Education

As a result of the Jungle Bilingual Education
Program of the Ministry of Education, thousands
from twenty-seven language groups have become
literate in both their own language and Spanish
during the past twenty-five years. As Ortiz (1970)
points out, control of the printed word is essential if minority groups are to obtain a just relationship with western majority cultures. At the
same time they need to acquire the majority language in order to conduct fruitful dialogue. Knowledge of arithmetic has also been important to
individuals and communities in defending themselves from unscrupulous merchants, lumber workers and
others.

Pedagogical materials in the various vernacular
languages have been based on the results of linguistic analyses so that not only have extensive
data been gathered on most languages still spoken
in the Peruvian Amazon, but efforts have been made
to use the data in ways which will contribute to
the maintenance of or revitalization of a sense of
ethnic identity and prestige of the languages and

cultures.    Publications  by  native  speakers  have
also  been  encouraged.    Native-authored  literature
is  developing  in  some  twenty  languages  which  not
only  helps  preserve  the  rich  folklore  for  future
generations  but  contributes  to  the  prestige  of  the
languages  and  a  sense  of  fulfillment  on  the  part  of
the  authors.

TYPES  AND  QUANTITY  OF  DATA  AVAILABLE
In  addition  to  research  by  the  Summer  Institute  of
Linguistics  (SIL),  members  of  the  Centro  de  Investigación  de  Lingüística  Aplicada  (CILA)  of  the  University  of  San  Marcos  have  done  fairly  extensive
research  on  the  following  languages:  Aguaruna,  Amahuaca,  Amarakaeri  (and  other  members  of  the  Harákmbet  family),  Cashinahua,  Cacataibo  (a  dialect  of
Cashibo),  Pajonal  Campa,  Ese'ejja,  Machiguenga,  and
Yaminahua.    A  few  of  those  studies  remain  unpublished,  but  the  majority  were  printed  by  CILA  as
Documentos  de  Trabajo.
        Anthropologists  of  the  Catholic  University,  San
Marcos  University,  the  Centro  Amazónico  de  Antropología  y  Aplicación  Práctica  and  the  Unidad  de  Apoyo
a  las  Comunidades  Nativas,  as  well  as  from  various
U.S.  and  European  universities,  have  gathered  data
and  in  most  cases  written  articles  and  monographs
on  at  least  twenty-four  ethnic  groups  (Amuesha,
Ashaninca  Campa,  Pajonal  Campa,  Pichis  Campa,  Perené  Campa,  Culina,  Machiguenga,  Piro,  Amarakaeri,
Huachipaeri,  Bora,  Murui  Huitoto,  Aguaruna,  Amahuaca,  Mayoruna,  Cashinahua,  Isconahua,  Sharanahua,

Shipibo, Yagua, Ese'ejja, Secoya, Ticuna, and
Urarina).

1,297 titles--linguistic, ethnographic, and
pedagogical and translated materials in the verna-
cular--were prepared by the SIL, and published in
its series, in international journals, or by the
Peruvian Ministry of Education in the period 1946-
1975. All of the unpublished data collected by the
SIL during the years 1946-1975 on fifty-six jungle
languages (in addition to several varieties of
Quechua) have been catalogued and filmed for
microfiche. The filming is still in process for
about 20,000 of a total of 80,000 pages. These
materials are available either in fiche or hard
copy from the Instituto Nacional de Investigación y
Desarrollo Educativo in Lima. Plans are to make
microfiche copies available also through the
International Linguistics Center of the SIL. These
unpublished field notes, as well as all unpublished
documents, are listed in the 1946-1976 bibliography
of the Summer Institute of Linguistics in Peru,
which numbers 2,172 entries (see Wise and Shanks
1978).


SOME QUESTIONS OF LANGUAGE CLASSIFICATION
The data now available have raised some questions
on earlier classifications of some of the languages, and have made it possible to classify others
previously considered to be isolates. Among the
first group are the Harákmbet languages, while
Amuesha is among the latter. Some earlier classifications, such as Loukotka (1968:140-141), list

Amarakaeri (Mashco) and Huachipaeri as Pre-Andine
Arawakan and Iñapari as one of the "Mashco" languages or as "Mashco-Piro." Barriales and Torralba
also list the Iñapari as one of the Mashco groups
(1970:4-5). A brief word list of Iñapari taken in
1956 shows that it is clearly Arawakan and fairly
closely related to Campa and other languages of the
Pre-Andine group. At the same time, it is clear
from comparison of the Iñapari list with any of the
Harákmbet ("Mashco") languages and dialects that it
is not closely related to those languages, if at
all. Listing of Iñapari, which does belong among
the languages commonly classified as Pre-Andine
Arawakan, as "Mashco-Piro" is perhaps the source
for inclusion of the Harákmbet languages among the
Pre-Andine group. Noble (1965) excludes the Harákmbet languages from his list of members of the Arawakan family. On the basis of Amarakaeri data I
have seen, I believe he is probably right, but
would not like to rule out the possibility that
Matteson (1972) is correct in listing it as a
separate branch of Arawakan.

The classification of Amuesha has long been in
doubt--ranging from possibly Arawakan to Pre-Andine
Arawakan; recent classifications such as Noble and
Matteson list it as an isolate within Arawakan.
The Amuesha data show clearly that it is Arawakan,
and at least as closely related to Campa and Machiguenga as are Piro and Apuriná--other languages
commonly regarded as members of the Pre-Andine
branch. The abundance of Quechua loans in Amuesha,
and resultant phonological changes, may explain why

many cognates between Amuesha and Campa have not
been recognized (see Wise, 1976, for a more detailed discussion). Furthermore, a very brief comparison with Waurá of the Xingu Park, generally considered southern Arawakan, shows that it and Amuesha
share about an equal percentage of cognates with
Campa. It is possible, then, that the notion of a
Pre-Andine group should be replaced with a different one grouping together all varieties of Campa
(including Machiguenga), Piro, Apuriná, Amuesha,
Waurá, Iñapari and possibly others.

   In the north of Peru, extensive data gathered on
Resígaro may confirm Noble's listing of that language as Arawakan. This might imply that all of
the languages classified as Huitotoan are also Arawakan. Previous classifications range from Macro-
Carib by Tax (1960) to Tupí-Guaraní by Mason
(1950). With the exception of Iñapari, there are
extensive data collections available for all of the
dubious classifications listed above. Detailed
comparative Arawakan studies using accurate, extensive data are among the list of urgent research
priorities. Matteson's "Proto-Arawakan" comes the
closest to date, but there are some errors in the
data she presents and a number of dubious reconstructions.

   The classification of Candoshi has also been in
doubt, varying from Zaparoan to Jivaroan, while in
some cases the Murato dialect has been classified
as Zaparoan and the Shapra dialect as Jivaroan.
The work of Payne (1976), while not conclusive, is
the first attempt to demonstrate systematic phono-

logical correspondences between Candoshi and other Jivaroan languages.

Although it is now possible to discount earlier suggestions that Urarina might be Panoan, it remains unclassified, as does Ticuna; Taushiro is only tentatively classified as Zaparoan. On the other hand, a number of questions have been cleared up in the last thirty years regarding the classification of Panoan languages, and the Tacanan family has been identified and subsequently classified within Macro-Panoan. Apart from Quechua, comparative studies are--to my knowledge--more advanced in Panoan than in any other language family presently represented in Peru.

Data are still lacking which would confirm the classification of Chamicuro as an isolate within Arawakan, or provide a basis for grouping it with members of some other branch. In view of the precarious state of this group, research should be carried out very soon. Other languages on which it is urgent to gather data very soon are: Cahuarano (only five speakers are known to be still living), Muniche (spoken only by a few older bilinguals), and Iñapari (if remaining speakers can be found). There are rumors from time to time that a few speakers of Panobo (Huariapano) are still living, but none have been located since some data were collected in 1958 and in 1961; this may indicate that further research will be impossible. Investigators on previous field trips have failed to locate any remaining speakers of Aguano, although there is evidently a community aware of its ethnic origin.

SUMMARY

In summary, extensive data are available on most of the contemporary languages and cultures of Peruvian Amazonia. Furthermore, these data have been used not only for scientific purposes but also to en- hance the prestige and sense of ethnic identity of the minority groups--and hence their chances for survival. There are, nevertheless, almost unlimi- ted opportunities for further research and some areas which demand top priority on the part of ethno-linguists.

NOTES

1. Both sociological and linguistic criteria have been used in distinguishing one group from an- other. For example, Meneca Huitoto, Muinane Huitoto, and Murui Huitoto are listed as sepa- rate groups since they speak different varie- ties of Huitoto. In the past they also formed distinct sociological groups but at the present time they are in the process of integrating with one another, at least those Huitoto speakers who live in Peru. On the other hand, there are very few dialectal differences between the Achual and the Jivaro (of the Corrientes River), but they are listed as separate groups since they consi- der themselves as sociologically distinct groups.

2. Los grupos étnicos de la Amazonía Peruana by Darcy Ribeiro and Mary Ruth Wise (1978), provi- des the basis for most of the summary statements in this paper. That monograph is part of a lar-

ger comparative project initiated by Ribeiro;
the 1978 edition was prepared by Wise.

## REFERENCES

Barriales, O.P., Joaquin and Adolfo Torralba, O.P.
1970. Los Mashcos: Hijos del Huanamei. Secreta-
riado de Misiones Dominicanas del Perú.

Chirif, Alberto and Carlos Mora. 1977. Atlas de
Comunidades Nativas. Sistema Nacional de Apoyo a
la Movilización Social, Dirección General de
Organizaciones Rurales.

Larson, Mildred L. 1979. Organización socio-
política de los aguaruna. Revista del Museo
Nacional. Lima.

Loukotka, Čestmír. 1968. Classification of South
American Indian Languages. Edited by Johannes
Wilbert. Reference Series, Vol 7. Los Angeles:
University of California Press.

Lyon, Patricia. 1975. Dislocación tribal y clasificaciones lingüísticas en la zona del río Madre
de Dios. XXXIX Congreso Internacional de Americanistas: Actas y Memorias, 5, 185-207.

Mason, J. Alden. 1950. The Languages of South
American Indians. In Handbook of South American Indians, edited by Julian H. Steward, 6,
157-317. Washington, D.C.

Matteson, Esther. 1972. Proto Arawakan. In Comparative Studies in Amerindian Languages, edited
by Esther Matteson et al., 160-242. The Hague:
Mouton.

Noble, G. Kingsley. 1965. Proto-Arawakan and Its
Descendants. Publications of the Indiana Univer-

sity Research Center in Anthropology, Folklore
and Linguistics, 38. Bloomington: Indiana University Press.

Ortiz, Alejandro. 1970. Lenguas aborígenes y educación nacional. Educación 1(2), 50-52. Lima.

Payne, David. 1976. Proto-Jivaro-Candoshi Phonology: A Preliminary Sketch. Información de Campo, no. 208 (microfiche) Lima.

Ribeiro, Darcy. 1971. Fronteras indígenas de la civilización. Translated by Julio Rossiello. Mexico.

Ribeiro, Darcy and Mary Ruth Wise. 1978. Los grupos étnicos de la Amazonía Peruana. In Comunidades y Culturas Peruanas, No. 13. Pucallpa, Peru: Instituto Lingüístico de Verano.

Shell, Olive. 1965. Pano Reconstruction. Ph.D. Dissertation in Linguistics, University of Pennsylvania.

------. 1976. (Spanish version) Estudios Panos III: Las lenguas pano y su reconstrucción. Serie Lingüística Peruana, no. 12, Instituto Lingüístico de Verano.

Steward, Julian H., editor. 1946-1950. Handbook of South American Indians. vols 1-6. Washington.

Tax, Sol. 1960. Aboriginal Languages of Latin America. Current Anthropology 1, no. 5-6. (Sept-Nov): 430-436.

Tessman, Gunter. 1930. Die Indianer Nordost-Perus. Hamburg.

Varese, Stefano. 1972. Las comunidades nativas de la selva: Esquema de un marco contextual. Primer Seminario Nacional de Educación Bilingüe: Algunos estudios y ponencias, 68-102. Lima.

Wise, Mary Ruth. 1976. Apuntes sobre la influencia inca entre los amuesha: Factor que oscurece la clasificación de su idioma. Revista del Museo Nacional, tomo XLII: 355-366. Lima.

Wise, Mary Ruth and Ann Shanks. 1978. Bibliografía del Instituto Lingüístico de Verano en el Perú, 1946-1976. Lima.

# INDIGENOUS GROUPS OF LOWLAND PERU

1. Aguaruna
2. Huambisa
3. Candoshi
4. Achual
5. Quechua del Pastaza
6. Jíbaro
7. Quechua del Tigre
8. Taushiro
9. Arabela
10. Urarina
11. Quechua del Napo
12. Secoya
13. Orejón
14. Huitoto Murui
15. Huitoto Muinane
16. Huitoto Meneca
17. Bora
18. Ocaina
19. Yagua
20. Ticuna
21. Chayahuita
22. Jebero
23. Chamicuro
24. Quechua de San Martín
25. Cocama-Cocamilla
26. Iquito
27. Mayoruna
28. Shipibo-Conibo
29. Capanahua
30. Piro
31. Cashibo
32. Amuesha
33. Campa del Alto Perené
34. Campa del Pichis
35. Campa Ucayalino
36. Campa Pajonalino
37. Campa Nomatsiguenga
38. Campa Ashaninca
39. Campa Caquinte
40. Machiguenga
41. Morunahua
42. Yaminahua
43. Amahuaca
44. Culina
45. Sharanahua-Marinahua
46. Cashinahua
47. Amarakaeri
48. Huachipaeri
49. Sapiteri
50. Toyoeri
51. Ese'ejja (Huarayo)
52. Isconahua
53. Cujareño
54. Parquenahua
55. Aguano
56. Andoa
57. Andoque
58. Arasairi
59. Muniche
60. Omagua
61. Pisabo
62. Resígaro
63. Shetebo

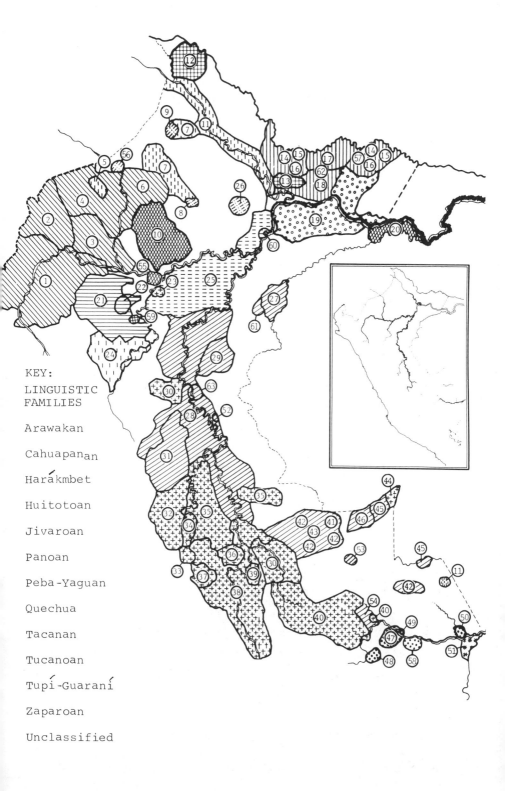

KEY:
LINGUISTIC
FAMILIES

Arawakan

Cahuapanan

Harákmbet

Huitotoan

Jivaroan

Panoan

Peba-Yaguan

Quechua

Tacanan

Tucanoan

Tupí-Guaraní

Zaparoan

Unclassified

# 5. Panoan Linguistic, Folkloristic and Ethnographic Research: Retrospect and Prospect

## Kenneth M. Kensinger

INTRODUCTION

This chapter surveys the linguistic, folkloristic, and ethnographic research conducted among the Panoan speaking tribes of eastern Peru, western Brazil and northern Bolivia in the nearly forty years since the publication of the first volume of the Handbook of South American Indians under the editorship of the late Julian Steward (1946-59), assesses what progress has been made, and indicates those areas where research is most urgently needed.[1]

Perhaps the most striking fact facing the researcher in the 1980's is the apparent reduction in the number of extant language groups from those listed by Mason (1950).[2] It is not clear just what the reasons are for this decrease. Some Panoan languages may have disappeared as the groups speaking them either died out or were assimilated into other Panoan groups or into the Mestizo societies of the region. However, I believe that many of the approximately one hundred groups listed by Mason may well be the names of constituent sub-groups or alternative appellations for a single language group.

A probable source for this confusion derives from the naming patterns of the Panoans themselves,

exacerbated by misunderstandings on the part of
both reporters and informants.  Let me illustrate
the problem by discussing the Peruvian Cashinahua
situation.  Although they acknowledge that they are
identified by others as Cashinahua (kasi 'bat',
nawa 'people') they call themselves hunikuinbu
(huni 'man', kuin 'real', bu 'generic/people').
Their society is divided into two male and two female named moieties, inubakebu (male) and banu-
bakebu (female), duabakebu, (male) and inanibakebu
(female).  The linked pairs of inubakebu-banubakebu
and duabakebu-inanibakebu are further subdivided
into alternating generation namesake groups or marriage sections, awabakebu and kanabakebu, yawabake-
bu and dunubakebu.  (For supporting evidence on
this point, see footnote 8 regarding the Marubo situation.)  They also identify local groups by place
of residence (generally a name reflecting some
floral,[3] faunal, or geological feature of the lo-
cale),[4]  by the name of the preeminent focal male,
or by reference to a group's location[5] upriver or
downriver from the speaker's village.

The Cashinahua have a large repertoire of insulting names for their Panoan neighbors, the Sharanahua, Marinahua, Mastanahua, Chandinahua, etc.[6]  I do
not know how widespread this practice is among
other Panoan groups.  I do know that the Sharanahua
refer to the Cashinahua as Sainawa (sai 'scream/
yell/shout'), a term the Cashinahua find insulting.

Furthermore, the Cashinahua gave me a multiplicity of names they use to refer to the Culina, in-

cluding Pisinawa and Chapunawa, all terms of insult (pisi means something foul smelling, chapu means rotten). Since the form of the name is clearly Panoan, an inexperienced reporter could mistakenly identify an Arawakan speaking group as one or more Panoan speaking groups.

Names for groups cited by Mason probably also resulted from misunderstanding. For example, Mason (1950:265) was probably unaware when he stated, "the Nocoman (Nokaman), recently identified by Tessman, is probably now extinct", that the term could have been the citation emphasis form of the first person plural pronoun (nukuma in Cashinahua); thus the informant could well have been responding that another group was "ours, our people" which the reporter took to be the name of that group.

Finally, confusion may also be a result of population movements over time in response to contact, population growth, raiding, etc. Words and word lists used for classifying and identifying languages and groups have been drawn from diverse sources dating to as early as the late 16th century. Lyon (1975) discusses the problems this creates for the classification of indigenous languages. The problem of which of the groups named in the Handbook correspond to either extant or extinct groups will probably never be solved.

Before examining the comparative work done on the Panoan language family, I want to discuss the work completed or in progress among eleven constituent groups, namely, the Amahuaca, Capanahua, Cashibo, Cashinahua, Chacobo, Isconahua, Marubo,

Matses/Mayoruna, Sharanahua, Shipibo/Conibo, and
Yaminahua.[7] The order of presentation will be
alphabetical.


AMAHUACA

The Amahuaca are located in small settlements scattered along the Inuya, Tamaya and Mapuya Rivers and
the headwaters of the Piedras, upper Sepahua, Jurua
and Purus Rivers, around the Catholic mission on
the Sepahua River, and on the island of Chumichinia
in the Ucayali River of eastern Peru. Dale Kietzman, Henry Osborn, Robert and Delores Russell,
Richard Hyde, Sylvia Young de Hyde, and Margarethe
Sparing, all working under the auspices of the Summer Institute of Linguistics, and Andre-Marcel
D'Ans have done linguistic research and analysis.
Ethnographic fieldwork has been carried out by Robert Carneiro, Gertrude Dole, and Joseph Woodside.
Carneiro and Dole have published and/or presented
numerous papers. Matthew Huxley has provided some
ethnographic data based on limited fieldwork and on
Carneiro's and Dole's fieldnotes. No complete ethnography has been published nor has any systematic
examination of folkloristic material appeared.


Amahuaca Sources

Alvarez, Ricardo. 1951. De médica entre los ama-
    huacas. Misiones dominicanas del Perú, XXXII:
    219-222.

------. 1961. Encuentro con los amahuacas del Ma-
    puya. Misiones dominicanas del Perú, XLII:
    16-23.

Carneiro, Robert L.   1962.   The Amahuaca Indians of
    Eastern Peru. Explorers Journal, XL (6): 26-37.
------. 1964a.   Shifting Cultivation among the Ama-
    huaca of eastern Peru.   Beiträge zur Völkerkunde
    Südamerikas: Festgabe für Herbert Baldus, 9-11.
    Hannover.
------. 1964b.   The Amahuaca and the spirit world.
    Ethnology 3: 6-11.
------. 1964c.   Logging and the patron system among
    the Amahuaca of eastern Peru.   Actas y Memorias
    of the 35th International Congress of America-
    nists,   Mexico, D.F. 1962: 323-325.
------. 1970.   Hunting and Hunting Magic Among the
    Amahuaca of the Peruvian Montana.   Ethnology 9:
    331-341.
------. 1974.   On the use of the stone ax by the
    Amahuaca Indians of eastern Peru.   Ethnologische
    Zeitschrift Zürich.   Bern: 107-122.
------. 1979.   El Cultivo de roza y quema entre los
    Amahuacas de este del Perú.   In Etnicidad y eco-
    logía, Alberto Chirif, comp., pp. 27-40. Lima:
    Centro de Investigación y Promoción Amazónica.
D'Ans, Andre-Marcel.   1972.   Repertorios etno-bo-
    tanico y etno-zoologico amahuaca (pano).   UNM-
    San Marcos, Documento de trabajo #3.
D'Ans, Andre-Marcel and Els Van Den Eynde.   1972.
    Léxico Amahuaca (Pano).   Universidad Nacional
    Mayor de San Marcos, Peru, Centro de Investiga-
    ción de Linguística Aplicada, Documento de Tra-
    bajo No. 6.
Dole, Gertrude E.   1961.   The Influence of Popula-
    tion Density on the Development of Social Orga-

nization among the Amahuaca Eastern Peru. Paper
read at the Annual Meeting of the American
Anthropological Association, Philadelphia.

------. 1962. Ethnographic Work among the Amahuaca. Middlebury College News Letter, XXXVI:60.

------.1973a. Amahuaca: A Tropical Forest Society
in Southeastern Peru. University Park, PA:
Pennsylvania State University Audiovisual Services. (An Ethnographic Film)

------. 1973b. Endocannibalism among the Amahuaca
Indians. In You and others, A. Kimball Rom-
ney and Paul I. DeVore, eds., pp. 249-256.
Cambridge, MA. (Reprinted in Lyon 1974)

------. 1974a. The Marriages of Pacho: A woman's
life among the Amahuaca. In Many Sisters:
Women in Cross-cultural Perspective, Carolyn
J.Matthiasson, ed., pp. 3-35. New York: Free
Press.

------. 1974b. Types of Amahuaca Pottery and Techniques of Its Construction. Ethnologische Zeitschrift, Zurich 1:145-159.

------. 1979a. Pattern and Variation in Amahuaca
Kin Terminology. In Social Correlates of Kin
Terminology, David J. Thomas, ed. Working Pa-
pers on South American Indians, 1: 13-36.

------. 1979b. Amahuaca Women in Social Change. In
Sex Roles in Changing Cultures, Ann McElroy and
Carolyn J. Matthiasson, eds., SUNY - Buffalo
Occasional Papers in Anthropology, 1: 111-121.

Huxley, Matthew A. and Cornell Capa. 1964. Fare-
well to Eden. New York: Harper and Row.

230    *Kenneth M. Kensinger*

Hyde, Richard and Eugene Loos. 1975. Algunas observaciones sobre el tono alto en amahuaca. In Información de Campo No. 20. Yarinacocha: Instituto de Verano.

Hyde, Sylvia (in collaboration with Robert Russell, Delores Russell, and Maria Consuela de Rivera). 1980. Diccionario Amahuaca (Edición Preliminar). Serie Lingüística Peruana 7. Yarinacocha, Peru: Instituto Linguistico de Verano.

Kietzman, Dale W. 1952. Afinidades culturales de los amahuacas del Peru. Peru Indigena, 11 (5/6): 226-233.

Osborn, Henry. 1948. Amahuaca phonemes. International Journal of American Linguistics 14: 188-190.

Russell, Robert. 1958. Algunos morfemas del Amahuaca (Pano) que equivalen a la entonación del castellano. Peru Indígena, 7, (16 y 17): 29-33.

------. 1975. Una gramatica transformacional del amahuaca. Estudios Panos IV. Serie Linguistica Peruana No. 13. Yarinacocha: Instituto Linguistico de Verano.

Russell, Robert and Delores Russell. 1958. Allophonic variation in Amahuaca. Unpublished manuscript.

------. 1959a. Vocabulario Amawaka. Serie Lingüística Especial, No. 1, Publicações do Museu Nacional, Rio de Janeiro, pp. 168-171.

------. 1959b. Syntactonemics in Amahuaca. Serie Lingüística Especial. Rio de Janeiro: Museu Nacional.

Woodside, Joseph Holt.    1980a.    Developmental Se-
    quences in Amahuaca Society.    University of
    Minnesota PhD dissertation.    Ann Arbor: Univer-
    sity microfilms  #8109532.    Abstract in Disser-
    tation Abstracts International 41/11-A: 4761.
------.  1980b.    Amahuaca Observational Astronomy.
    Bulletin of the Center for Archaeoastronomy,
    3(1): 22-26.
Young de Hyde, Sylvia.    1973.    El verbo reflexivo
    del amahuaca. In Estudios Panos, Eugene E.
    Loos, ed., 11:9-51, Serie Linguistica Peruana
    No. 11.    Yarinacocha: Instituto Linguistica de
    Verano.

CAPANAHUA
The Capanahua are located in settlements scattered
along the Tapiche and Boncuyo Rivers, eastern tributaries of the Ucayali River of eastern Peru.
Eugene and Betty Loos of the Summer Institute of
Linguistics have published materials on both the
grammar and phonology based on extensive study of
the language and a two volume set of texts.  Their
ethnographic observations have not been published.
Thelma Schoolland, also of SIL, has published a
volume of folklore, as have Romaina, et. al.

Capanahua Sources
Hall de Loos, Betty and Eugene Loos.  1973.  La
    Estructura semantica y fonologica de los pre-
    fijos verbales en capanahua.  Estudios Panos I:
    63-132. Serie Linguistica Peruana No. 10.  Yari-
    nacocha:  Instituto Linguistico de Verano.

232    *Kenneth M. Kensinger*

------. 1980. Textos Capanahua. Comunidades y
Culturas Peruanas No. 17. Vol. I, 175 pp., Vol.
II, 261 pp. Yarinacocha, Peru: Instituto Lin-
guistico de Verano.

Hall de Loos, Betty. 1981. Autocorrección en el
relato Capanahua. Revista Internacional de Estudios Etnolingüísticos 1:47-70.

Loos, Eugene E. 1960. Capanahua Patrilineality
and Matrilocality. Unpublished manuscript.

------. 1963. Capanahua narration structure. Studies in literature and language, Vol. IV, Supplement 1963. Austin, Texas: University of
Texas.

------. 1969. The phonology of Capanahua and its
grammatical basis. Summer Institute of Linguistics Publications in Linguistics and Related
Fields, No. 20. Santa Ana, CA: SIL.

Romaina, Amelia, Joaquina Romaina, y Manuel Romaina. 1976. Quimisha yohuan xeni: cuentos folkloricos de los capanahua.

Safir, Ken. 1982. Nasal Spreading in Capanahua.
Linguistic Inquiry 13 (4): 689-694.

Schoolland, Thelma. nd. Cuentos folkloricos de
los capanahua. Comunidades y culturas peruanas,
6.

## CASHIBO

The Cashibo are located in various settlements
scattered along and between the Aguaytia and Huallaga Rivers west of the Ucayali River in eastern
Peru. Wistrand Robinson (1969b) identifies several
dialect groups which are apparently mutually intel-

ligible.  Olive Shell of the Summer Institute of
Linguistics has published on both the phonology and
grammar.  Estrella and Shell have published a book
of stories.  Wistrand Robinson has also published
several papers on Cashibo grammar; her unpublished
dissertation on Cashibo folklore includes considerable ethnographic data.  She has also published
several brief papers of ethnographic interest.
Frank has published his dissertation and a paper
based on ethnographic field work.  Trujillo Ferrari
has published a paper on Cashibo economic behavior.
Emmermacher reported on a German film expedition in
1952. SIL sources indicate that representatives of
this group have informed them that they prefer to
be referred to as Cacataibo.  They also noted that
Maria Chavez, a linguist from Universidad Nacional
Mayor San Marcos is currently engaged in linguistic
field work and producing a dictionary.

## Cashibo Sources

Emmermacher, K. W.  1952.  Excursion 1952 Amazonas,
    Rio San Alejandro Cashibo Kakataibo Tribe.  Ger-
    man Film Expedition.

Estrella Odício, Gregorio and Olive Shell.  1977.
    Cuentos del hombre Cacataibo (Cashibo).  Comuni-
    dades y culturas peruanas, II. Yarinacocha: In-
    stituto Linguistico de Verano.

Frank, Erwin H. 1978.  ...y se lo comen.  (A cri-
    tical study of written sources about canniba-
    lism among Pano-speaking Indians of eastern Peru
    and Brazil.)  Unpublished MA thesis, Universi-
    tat Bonn.

------. 1983a.  Ein Leben am Rande des Weltmarkts:
Ökologie and  Ökonomie der Comunidad Nativa de
Santa Martha.  Bonner Amerikanistische Studien
10.  Bonn: Seminar für Völkerkunde, Universität
Bonn.

------. 1983b.  Mecece: La Función Psicológica, So-
cial, y Económica de un complejo ritual de los
Uni (Cashibo) de la Amazonia Peruana.  Amazónia
Peruana V (9):63-78.

------. 1983c.  Die Logik interner Organisation das
Beispiel der Comunidad Nativa de Santa Martha.
Paper read at the 1983 meeting of the Deutsche
Gesellschaft für Völkerkunde,  Freiburg/Basel,
October 13, 1983.

------. n.d.  Inca bana- Schöpfungs- und Inca-
Mythen der Uni. Unpublished manuscript.

Gray, Gloria.  1953.  Bolivar Odicio, el Cashibo
Civilizador.  Peru Indígena 4(9):146-154.

Shell, Olive A.  1950.  Cashibo I: Phonemes.
International  Journal of American Linguistics
16: 198-202.

------. 1951.  Sonidos de habla Cashibo.  Peru
Indígena 1:51-53.

------. 1953.  Pronombres Cashibos.  Peru Indígena,
IV (10/11): 111-114.

------. 1957.  Cashibo II: Grammemic analysis of
transitive and intransitive verb patterns.
International Journal of  American Linguistics
23:179-218.

------. 1959.  Vocabulario cashibo-castellano.
Yarinacocha, Peru: Instituto Linguistico de
Verano.

------. 1973. Los modos del cashibo y el analysis del performativo. In Estudios Panos, Eugene Loos, ed., I: 23-62. Serie Lingüística Peruana No. 10. Yarinacocha: Instituto Lingüístico de Verano.

------. 1975. Cashibo modals and the performance analysis. Foundations of Language 13:177-199.

Trujillo Ferrari, Alfonso. 1960. Analysis del comportamiento economico de los Kashibo frente a los efectos aculturativos. Revista de Museu Paulisto, n.s., vol. XII: 199-309.

Wistrand Robinson, Lila M. 1965. A type of Cashibo moral judgement. American Anthropologist 67:1521.

------. 1966. A Functional Analysis of Cashibo Religion. Unpublished ms.

------. 1967. Cashibo Language Contacts and Their Sociocultural Setting. Unpublished ms.

------. 1968a. Cashibo relative clause constructions. MA thesis, University of Texas, Austin.

------. 1968b. Desorganización y revitalización de los cashibo. América Indígena 29:611-18.

------. 1968c. Cashibo Kinship System and Social Relationships. Unpublished ms.

------. 1968d. Cashibo Language Variation. 15 pp. with charts. Unpublished ms. Revised under title Alternate Methods of Cashibo Dialect Description (1970).

------. 1969a. Un texto cashibo: el proceso de cremacion. America Indígena 29:1029-38.

------. 1969b. Music and Song Texts of Amazonian Indians. Ethnomusicology 13(3): 469-488.

------. 1969c. Folkloric and Linguistic Analyses of Cashibo Narrative Prose. PhD dissertation, University of Texas at Austin. Abstract published in Dissertation Abstracts International 30/12-A:5435.

------. 1970. Bilingual Indian School. Americas 22(8):2-8.

------. 1971a. Cashibo Verb Stems, Causatives, and Proposition Consolidation. Papers from the Fifth Kansas Linguistic Conference, pp. 204-213. Lawrence, Kansas: University of Kansas.

------. 1971b. Cashibo Chants. Paper read at the 1971 Meeting of Kansas Anthropologists, Washburn University, April 17, 1971.

------. 1971c. Cashibo Culture Contact. Paper read at the 1971 Meeting of Anthropologists, Washburn University, April 17, 1971.

------. 1971d. Origin of the Inca Demi-gods. Paper read at the Kansas Folklore Society, Kansas State University.

------. 1971e. Cashibo-Spanish Bilingualism and Culture Contacts. Paper read at meetings of Council on Anthropology and Education, American Anthropological Association, New York, NY, December 1971.

------. 1972a. A South American Indian Orpheus Tale. Journal of American Folklore, 85 (April-June):181-83.

------. 1972b. Cashibo Men's Rites. 6 pages with footnotes, map and ten page text, Chani Banaoti, with translations. Unpublished manuscript.

------. 1973a.  Cashibo T-shaped Stone Axes.  Journal of the Steward Anthropological Society, University of Illinois at Urbana,  Fall 1973.

------. 1973b.  Western and Mythological Influences
on More Recent Cashibo Ethnohistory.  Paper presented at the 21st annual meeting of the American Society for Ethnohistory, Edmond, OK.

------. 1973c.  Some Remarks on Cashibo Arrows and
Their Use. Unpublished manuscript; data published in Patricia J. Lyon, A Comparative Study of
the Arrows of the Peruvian Montana.

------. 1975a.  Some Generative Solutions to Problems in Cashibo Phonology.  In A. A. Hill
Festschrift volume.  Peter deRitter, Publisher,
pp. 257-295.

------. 1975b.  Cries of Anguish: Oral History of a
Minority People. Heritage of Kansas: Kansas
Folklore Society Papers, 8 (2): 17-22.

------. 1975c.  Cashibo Song Poetry.  Yearbook for
Inter-American Musical Research.  Austin: Insti-
tute of Latin American Studies, University of
Texas at Austin, Vol. XI:117-140.

------. 1976.  La poesia de las canciones cashibos.
Yarinacocha, Peru: Summer Institute of Linguistics microfiche series.

------. 1977.  Notas etnográficas sobre los cashibo.  Folklore Americano, Diciembre 1977, 23:
117-140.

------. 1978.  A Cashibo Text on Ayahuasca.  Unpublished manuscript.

------. 1983a.  Cashibo Fauna.  In revision for
Journal of Ethnobiology.

------. 1983b.  Cashibo Flora.  In revision for
Journal of Ethnobiology.
------. 1984.  The Vampire Bat People:  Myths,
Tales, and Histories of the Cashibo/Cacataibo.
Unpublished manuscript.

CASHINAHUA (Cashinawa, Kaxinawa, Kaxinaua, etc.)
The Cashinahua live in several settlements along
the Curanja River of eastern Peru and in the state
of Acre, Brazil.  Aquino (1979) states that "approximately 900 Kaxinawa Indians....in the Alto Juruá
region, primarily live along the Envira, Humaitá,
Tarauaca, Jordão, and Iboiacu rivers, but more than
two-thirds of them are concentrated along the Jordão and Humaitá rivers."  Seeger and Vogel reported
on the situation of the Brazilian Cashinahua in
1978.  Kensinger has published a brief phonological
statement.  Robert Cromack's dissertation on Cashinahua grammar has been published; Richard Montag
has added to the analysis of the grammar.  Although
Gail Cromack's text analysis and D'Ans' book aug-
ment but do not replace the splendid collection of
texts by Capistrano de Abreu (neither provides the
native language texts), a full, systematic analysis
of Cashinahua folklore remains to be done.  Kensinger has published and/or presented numerous papers
and a monograph based on his analysis of Cashinahua
semantic and/or cultural domains.  Aquino has published his dissertation and a report on current
conditions among the Brazilian Cashinahua.  Barbara
Keifenheim and Patrick Deshayes have been doing
fieldwork with the Curanja River Cashinahua for

several years, focusing on ideology and religion.
Cecilia McCallum, a graduate student at the London
School of Economics, is currently doing fieldwork
with the Brazilian Cashinahua with emphasis on
Cashinahua-Brazilian relations.

## Cashinahua Sources (Cashinawa, Kaxinawa, Kaxinaua)

Aquino, Terri Valle De. 1977. Kaxinawá: de se-
ringueiro 'caboclo' a peão 'acreano'. Disser-
tação de Mestrado apresentada ao Curso de Pós-
graduação em Antropologia da Universidade de
Brasília. 115p. (mimeo).

------. 1979. The Kaxinawa Struggle for Their
Lands. Cultural Survival, Inc., Special Report:
Brazil. Number 1, December 1979, pp. 49-54.
(Excerpted from: Nimuendaju, commissao pro-Indio
[R(io) (de) J(aneiro)], Vol. 1, No. 1, Jan.-Feb.
1979, pp. 7-9.)

Capistrano de Abreu, J. 1941. Rã-txa hu-ni-ku-ĩ:
a língua do índios Caxinauás do rio Ibuaçú, af-
fluente do Murú (Prefeitura de Tarauacá), 2a.
edição, Edição da Sociedade Capistrano de Abreu.
Rio de Janeiro: Livraria Briguiet.

Cromack, Gail Westoby. 1967. Cashinawa "Spirit"
Narratives and Their Cultural Context. MA
Thesis, The Hartford Seminary Foundation.

Cromack, Robert Earl. 1968. Language Systems and
Discourse Structure in Cashinawa. PhD Dissertation, Hartford Seminary Foundation. Abstract
published in Dissertation Abstracts International 30/02-A:705. Published as Hartford Studies

240    *Kenneth M. Kensinger*

in Linguistics 23. (Reviewed by Henry Rosers
1975, Linguistics 147:122-124.)

------. 1975. Relaciones entre el Alimento y el
Ciclo Vital en el Grupo Cashinahua. Revista
del Museo Nacional (Lima) 41:423-432.

D'Ans, Andre-Marcel. 1975. La Verdadera Biblia de
los Cashinahua. Lima, Peru: Mosca Azul Editores

------. 1978. Le dit des vrais hommes (mythes,
contes, legendes, et traditions des Indiens
Cashinahua). Paris:UGE 10/18.

------. 1983. Parentesco y Nombre. Semantica de
las denominaciones interpersonales Cashinahua
(Pano). In Educación Linguística en La Ama-
zonia Peruana, Angel Corbera, compilador. Lima:
Centro Amazónico de Antropologia y Aplicación
Práctica.

D'Ans, Andre-Marcel Y Maria Cortez Mondragon.
1973. Terminos de colores cashinahua (pano).
Lima: Universidad nacional Mayor de San Marcos,
Centro de investigacion de linguistica aplicada,
documento de trabajo no. 16.

Der Marderosian, Ara H., Kenneth M. Kensinger, Jew-
Ming Chao, and Frederick J. Goldstein. 1970.
The Use and Hallucinatory Principles of a Psy-
choactive Beverage of the Cashinahua Tribe.
Drug Dependence 5:7-14.

Kensinger, Kenneth M. 1963. The Phonological
Hierarchy of Cashinahua (Pano). In Studies
in Peruvian Indian Languages: 1. Summer Institute of Linguistics Publications in Linguistics
and Related Fields, No. 9. 207-217.

------. 1965. The Cashinahua of Southeastern Peru.
Expedition 7 (4): 4-9.

------. 1967. Change and the Cashinahua. Expedition 9 (2):4-8.

------. 1973a. Banisteriopsis Usage Among the
Peruvian Cashinahua. In Hallucinogens and
Shamanism, Michael J. Harner, ed., 9-14. New
York: Oxford University Press.

------. 1973b. Fact and Fiction in Cashinahua Marriage. Paper read at the American Anthropological Association, New Orleans. (Revised version
published under title  An Emic Model of Cashinahua Marriage, Kensinger 1984.)

------. 1974a. Cashinahua Medicine and Medicine
Men. In Native South Americans: Ethnology
of the Least Known Continent, Patricia J. Lyon,
ed., 283-288. Boston: Little Brown and Co.

------. 1974b. Leadership and Factionalism in
Cashinahua Society. In Leaders and Leadership in Lowland South America, Waud H. Kracke,
ed. In press.

------. 1975a. Studying the Cashinahua. In The
Cashinahua of Eastern Peru, The Haffenreffer
Museum, Brown University, Studies in Anthropo-
logy and Material Culture, Vol. 1, Kenneth M.
Kensinger, et. al., 9-85. (Reviewed by Dean E.
Arnold, 1977, Man 12 (3-4): 122-124.

------. 1975b. Dual Organization Reconsidered.
Paper read at the Conference on Anthropological
Research in Amazonia, Sky's Edge Environmental
Campus of Queens College, CUNY. Unpublished
manuscript.

242    *Kenneth M. Kensinger*

------. 1977.  Cashinahua Notions of Social Time
and Social Space. Actes du XLIIe Congres Internacional des Americanistes, Paris.  Vol. II:
233-244.

------. 1978.  Learning How to Behave in Cashinahua: Two Case Studies.  Unpublished paper presented to the South  American Indian Caucus, New
York.

------. 1980.  The Dialectics of Person and Self in
Cashinahua Society.  Paper read at the American
Anthropological Association annual meetings,
Washington, DC.

------. 1981.  Food Taboos as Markers of Age Categories in Cashinahua.  In Food Taboos in Lowland South America, Working Papers on South American Indians, No. 3, ed. by Kenneth M. Kensinger and Waud H. Kracke, pp. 157-176. Bennington,
VT:  Bennington College.

------. 1982.  Sex and Food:  Reciprocity in Cashi-
nahua Society?  Paper presented at the American
Anthropological Association annual meetings,
Washington, DC.

------. 1983a.  On Meat and Hunting.  Current Anthropology 24 (1):128-129.

------. 1983b.  Cashinahua Siblingship.  Paper read
at the American Anthropological Association annual meetings, Chicago.

------. 1984.  An Emic Model of Cashinahua Marriage.  In Marriage Practices in Lowland
South America, Kenneth M. Kensinger, ed.  Illinois Studies in Anthropology No. 14, pp.
221-251.  Urbana: University of Illinois Press.

Kensinger, Kenneth M. and F.E. Johnston.   1969.
    The Cashinahua and the Study of Evolution.
    Expedition 11 (1):6-9.

Montag, Richard.   1973.   La estructura semántica de
    las relaciones entre frases verbales en Cashina-
    hua.   Estudios Panos II: 107-159.   Serie Lin-
    güística Peruana No. 11.   Yarinacocha: Institu-
    to Lingüístico de Verano.

Montag, Susan Allison de.   1981.   Diccionario Ca-
    shinahua, 2° ed. Serie Lingüística Peruana 9,
    Yarinacocha, Peru: Instituto Lingüístico de Ve-
    rano.

Seeger, Anthony and Arno Vogel.   n. d.   Relatório
    da viagem do Alto Rio Juruá, Município de
    Cruzeiro do Sul, Estado do Acre, em Janeiro-
    Fevereiro de 1978.   Mimeographed. (Section 3
    deals with the Cashinahua of the Breu and Cai-
    pora Rivers.)

Shultz, Harald and Vilma Chiara.   1955.   Informa-
    ções sobre os Indios do Alto Rio Purus.   Revista
    do Museu Paulista, São Paulo, IX: 181-201.

CHACOBO

Gilbert and Marian Prost of the Summer Institute of
Linguistics did linguistic research among the
Chacobo, southeastern Panoans of Bolivia.   G. Prost
has published several papers based on his extensive
study of the language.   M. Prost has published some
observations of an ethnographic nature.   Handke and
Kelm have published papers on ethnographic topics.
No folkloristic studies have been published.

244    *Kenneth M. Kensinger*

Chacobo Sources

Handke, Wanda. 1954. The Chacobo in Bolivia.
Ethnos 23:100-126.

------. 1956. Los Indios Chacobo del Rio Benisito.
Trabajos y Conferencias 2:11-31.

Kelm, Heins. 1972. Chacobo 1970; Eine Restgruppe
der Sudost-Pano em Oriente Boliviens. Tribus
21:129-246.

Prost, Gilbert. 1960. Fonemas de la lengua Chacobo. Notas Linguisticas de Bolivia, No. 2.
Cochabamba, Bolivia:SIL.

------. 1962. Signalling of transitive and intransitive in Chacobo (Pano). International Journal
of American Linguistics 28:108-118.

------. 1965. Chacobo. In Gramáticas estructurales de lenguas bolivianas, Tomo II, pp. 1-13,
Instituto Lingüístico de Verano en colaboración
con el Ministerio de Asuntos Campesinos y el
Ministerio de Educación y Bellas Artes, Oficia-
lía Mayor de Cultura, Dirección Nacional de
Antropología. Riberalta, Beni, Bolivia.

Prost, Marian D. 1970. Costumbres, habilidades y
cuadro de la vida humana entre los Chacobos.
Riberalta, Bolivia: Instituto Lingüístico de Verano y Ministerio de Educación y Cultura de
Bolivia.

ISCONAHUA

The Isconahua are a very small remnant group who
formerly lived on the headwaters of the Calleria
River of eastern Peru; they now live among the

Shipibo.  Braun, who refers to this group as Isco-
bakebo, provides limited data, mostly ethnographic,
in his dissertation.  Additional data are provided
by Momsen and Momsen, et. al.  Loos (1976:5) ac-
knowledges receipt of linguistic data from Antonio
Rodriguez but cites no published materials.

Isconahua Sources

Braun, Robert A.  1973.  Iscobakabu Situational
    Ethnic Displays.  Paper Presented at the American
    Anthropological Association meetings, New
    Orleans.
------.  1975.  The Iscobakebu in Peru:  Culture
    Change and Regional Integration in the Central
    Oriente.  PhD dissertation, University of
    Illinois.
Momsen, Richard.  1964.  The Isconahua Indians.
    Revista Geografica (Rio de Janeiro) 32: 59-81.
Whiton, Luis, H. Bruce Green, and Richard Momsen.
    1964.  The Isonahua of the Remo.  Journal de la
    Société des Américanistes 53:84-124.

MARUBO

The Marubo are located in the headwaters of the
Itui and Curuca, tributaries of the Javari River in
the Brazilian states of Amazonas and Acre.  Delvair
Montagner Melatti and Julio Cezar Melatti have published various articles based on their ethnographic
fieldwork.  John Jansma and family, of the New Tribes Mission, have lived for many years with the Marubo at Vida Nova on the Itui River.  According to
Melatti (personal communication), Jansma "escreveu

um artigo sobre a lingua" and "tem trabalhado tambem no preparo das cartilhas de alfabetização que
os Marubo usam". Gerald Raymond Kennell, Jr. and
Paul Rich of the New Tribes Mission have also worked with the Marubo. A major summary of what is
known about the Marubo can be found in the 1981
CEDI volume; it is based on the work of Mellati and
Montagner Mellati. Delvair Montagner Mellati is
currently writing her Ph.D dissertation for the
University of Brasília on Marubo curing rituals.

## Marubo Sources

Allen, Ruth. 1963. Marubo Work. The Amazon Chal-
    lenge 9:6-8. Woodworth, WI: New Tribes Mission.
Centro Ecumênico de Documentação e Informação
    (CEDI). 1981. Marúbo. In Povos Indígenas no
    Brasil 5: Javari, 36-59. São Paulo: CEDI.
Kennell, Jr., Gerald Raymond. 1976. Descrição de
    fonémica de Marúbo (Chainawa).[8] Processo FUNAI/
    BSB 3779/76:2-5.
------. 1978. Descrição da gramatica e da fonêmica
    da língua Marúbo. Processo FUNAI 3507: 6-52.
Lucena Rodrigues, Francisco Paulo. n.d. Marúbos;
    um povo in extinção. (also texts) Processo
    FUNAI 3534/75 and 3974/75.
Melatti, Delvair Montagner. 1977. Cerâmica Marú-
    bo. Cultura, No. 25. Brasília: Ministério de
    Educação e Cultura. pp. 70-77.
Melatti, Delvair Montagner and Julio Cezar Melatti.
    1975. Relatório sobre os índios Marúbo. Traba-
    lhos de Ciências Sociais, Série Antropologia
    Social: 13. Brasília: Fundação Universidade.

------. 1977. As canções que espantam os males do corpo. Revista de Atualidade Indígena, No. 2. Brasília: FUNAI. pp. 2-7.

------. 1979. A criança Marúbo: educação e cuidados. Revista Brasileira de Estudos Pedagógicos, No. 143. Brasília: Instituto Nacional de Estudos e Pesquisas Educacionais (Ministério da Educação e Cultura). pp. 291-301. Reprinted in Soriano de Alencar, Eunice. 1982. A criança na família e na sociedade, pp. 38-51. Petrópolis: Vozes.

Melatti, Julio Cezar. 1977. Estrutura social Marúbo; um sistema autraliano na Amazônia. Anuário Antropológico/76. Rio de Janeiro: Tempo Brasileiro, pp. 83-120.

------. nd. O comerciante Marúbo e seus laços de parentesco. To appear in Anuario Antropologico/83.

Melatti, Julio Cezar and Delvair Montagner Melatti. 1985. A maloca Marúbo: organização do espaço. To appear in Revista de Antropologia 27. São Paulo: Universidade de São Paulo, FFLCH, Departamento de Ciencias Sociais.

MATSES (Mayoruna/Matís)[9]

The Matses are located in various scattered settlements along both sides of the Yavari River and its tributaries in eastern Peru and western Brazil. Harriet Fields of the Summer Institute of Linguistics has analyzed the phonology and grammar of Mayoruna, and with Merrifield has analyzed the kinship system. Harriet Kneeland has also publi-

shed a paper on an aspect of the grammar, on beliefs, and a language learning course on Mayoruna. Steven Romanoff, in a brief manuscript on
hunting, suggests that the Matses are a linguistically mixed group made up of small remnants of
once larger groups. In his dissertation, he states
"...the contribution of captives to the present-day
population (21% of females and 6% of males)....the
contribution of their fertility (45% of the population having one or both parents captive)" (1984:
44). Various kin terms in the Fields and Merrifield study clearly suggest non-Panoan additions to
the kinship vocabulary. Additional data on the
Mayoruna are provided by Vivar. CEDI (1981) summarizes what is known about the Mayoruna and
Matís.

Wallace de Garcia Paula reports on a group she
calls Matís who have been settled recently in a
village near the Posto de Atração Itui by FUNAI
personnel. The report includes a 380-term comparative vocabulary, Marubo-Matis-Mayoruna. Numerous
sets seem to indicate misunderstanding on the part
of the interpreter and/or the informant and/or the
linguist. As a result, I am reluctant to draw any
conclusions about the relationships between the several languages, and whether or not Matis and Mayoruna are one and the same language-culture.

According to Melatti (personal communication),
Silvio Cavuscens and his wife Claire are currently
working with the Matses "com objetivo mais assis-
tencial do que etnográfico", as is Luis G. Calixto
Mendez of the Asociación para el Apoyo a las Comu-

nidades Nativas (ANACONDA) and the Instituto de
Investigaciones de la Amazonía Peruana (IIAP).

Matses Sources

Alviano, Fray Fidelius de. 1957/58. Ensaios da
   Lingua dos Indios Magiorunas ou Maiorunas do Rio
   Jandiatubo (Pano). Revista do Instituto Histo-
   rico e Geografico Brasileiro 237:43-60.
Borja, Arceu Calvalho. 1980. Levantamento: Situa-
   ção Atual das Populações Indígenas no Brasil.
   Publisher unknown. Information on the Mayoruna
   of the Upper Javari and its tributaries and of
   the settlement of Lameirão by the chief of the
   FUNAI Posto Indígena de Atração Lobo.
Centro Ecumênico de Documentação e Informação
   (CEDI). 1981a. Mayorúna. Povos Indígenas no
   Brasil 5: Javari, 60-81. São Paulo: CEDI.
------. 1981b. Matís. Povos Indígenas no Brasil
   5: Javari, 82-93. São Paulo: CEDI.
Fields, Harriet. 1963. Informe sobre los 'mayoruna' o 'capanahua salvages' del rio Yaquerana.
   Información de Campo 131. Yarinacocha: Instituto Linguístico de Verano.
------. 1973. Una identificación preliminar de los
   sufijos indicadores de referencia en mayoruna.
   Estudios Panos II: 283-306. Serie Linguística
   Peruana No. 11. Yarinacocha: Instituto Linguístico de Verano.
------. n.d. Datos misceláneos sobre la cultura
   mayoruna, Información de campo 344. Yarinacocha: Instituto Linguístico de Verano.

Fields, Harriet L. and William Merrifield.  1976.
    Parentesco Mayoruna (Pano) .  Comunidades y cul-
    turas peruanas, 9.  Translated by Marlene Ballena
    D.
------.  1980.  Mayoruna (Panoan) Kinship.  Ethno-
    logy XIX (1): 1-28.
------.  1983.  The Matses literacy program.  Notes
    on Literacy 37: 8-15.
Kneeland, Harriet.  1973.  La frase nominal relati-
    va en mayoruna y la ambigüedad.  Estudios Panos
    II: 53-105.  Serie Lingüística Peruana, No. 11.
    Yarinacocha: Instituto Lingüístico de Verano.
------.  1975.  Notes on Mayoruna beliefs, Informa-
    cion de Campo 132.  Yarinacocha: Instituto Lin-
    güístico de Verano.
------.  1979.  Lecciones para el apprendizaje del
    Idioma Mayoruna.  Yarinacocha: Instituto Lin-
    güístico de Verano-Ministerio de Educación.
    Documento de Trabajo 14, 250 pp.
------.  1982.  El 'ser cómo' y el 'no ser cómo' de
    la comparación en matses.  In Mary Ruth Wise
    and Harry Boonstra, Eds., Conjunciones y otros
    nexos en tres idiomas amazónicas.  Yarinacocha:
    Serie Lingüística Peruana 19, pp. 77-126.
Mendizabal Lorack, Emilio.  1967.  La Conquista del
    Peru por los Peruanos.  Vision del Peru, Revista
    de Cultura, Vol. 2.  Lima.
Mercier, Juan Marcos.  1974.  Contacto con los ma-
    yorunas.  In Amazonía: Liberación o esclavi-
    tud? Juan Marcos Mercier and Gaston Villeneuve,
    eds., pp. 178-86.  Lima: Editores Paulinas.

Montagner Melatti, Delvair. 1980. Proposta de criação do Parque Indígena do Vale da Javari. Processo FUNAI/BSB: 1074/79.

Rich, Paul. 1981. Mayoruna - Another unreached tribe, Brown Gold, January. New Tribes Mission.

Romanoff, Steven. 1977. Informe sobre el uso de la tierra por los Matses, en la selva baja peruana. Amazonia Peruana 1(1): 97-130.

------. 1983. Women as Hunters Among the Matses of the Peruvian Amazon. Human Ecology 11 (3): 339-342.

------. 1984. Matses Adaptations in the Peruvian Amazon. PhD dissertation, Columbia University.

------. n.d. Responses to Scarcities of Game Animals by Matses Indians, Western Amazon River Basin. Unpublished ms.

Varese, Stefano. 1972. Relaciones interétnicas en la selva del Peru. In Aportes al estudio de la fricción interétnica en los indios no-andinos, Georg Grunberg, org., pp. 157-192. Montevideo: Tierra Nueva.

Vivar A., Judith E. 1975. Los mayoruna en la frontera Perú-Brasil. América Indígena, Vol. 35, No. 2.

Wallace de Garcia Paula, Ruth. 1979. Relatório de Viagem. Brasília: Ministério do Interior, Fundação Nacional do Indio. pp. 44 (mimeo).

## SHARANAHUA

The Sharanahua are located in several settlements scattered along the upper Purus River in eastern Peru. They constitute a mixed group of remnant

peoples including Marinahua, Mastanahua and Chandinahua and possibly some Yaminahua, in addition to
the Sharanahua. The Sharanahua and Marinahua languages are mutually intelligible. It is not clear
if the language spoken by the Mastanahua, Chandinahua and Yaminahua share this characteristic among
themselves or with the Sharanahua and Marinahua.
Linguistic research has been done by Eugene and
Marie Scott of the Summer Institute of Linguistics. E. Scott has published a phonological statement, co-authored by Eunice Pike, and the first
part of a grammatical analysis with Donald Frantz.
Janet Siskind did ethnographic fieldwork with the
Sharanahua and has published her results in To Hunt
in the Morning and in several papers. Torralba has
published several Sharanahua myths.

Sharanahua Sources

Frantz, Donald G. 1973. On question word move-
    ment. Linguistic Inquiry 4(4):531-534.
Pike, Eunice and Eugene Scott. 1962. The Phono-
    logical Hierarchy of Marinahua. Phonetica 8:
    1-8.
Scott, Eugene and Donald G. Frantz. 1973. La pre-
    gunta en sharanahua y constreñimientos propues-
    tos sobre la permutación de la pregunta. Estu-
    dios Panos I: 184-209. Serie Lingüística Perua-
    na No. 10. Yarinacocha, Peru: Instituto Lingüís-
    tico de Verano.
------. 1974. Sharanahua questions and proposed
    constraints on question movement. Linguistics
    132:75-86.

Siskind, Janet.  1970.  The Culina eat snakes and
never bathe: Cultural competition for an ecological niche.  Paper delivered at the 35th Annual
Meeting of the Society for American Archaeology,
Mexico, D. F.
------.  1973a.  To Hunt in the Morning.  New York:
Oxford University Press.
------.  1973b.  Tropical forest hunters and the
economy of sex.  In Peoples and cultures of
native South America, Daniel Gross, ed.  New
York: Doubleday.
------.  1973c.  It's just as easy to fall in love
with a good provider.  Paper presented at the
American Anthropological Association meetings,
New Orleans.
------.  1974.  Special Hunt of the Sharanahua.  Natural History, 83.  8:72-79.
Torralba, A.  1976a.  Leyendas saranahuas: Rohua,
el hombre bueno.  Misiones Dominicanas del Perú
Año XLVII (no. 238): 30-32.
------.  1976b.  Leyendas saranahuas: Bapa la mujer
que no espero.  Misiones Dominicanas del Perú,
Año XLVII (No. 284):23-26.

SHIPIBO-CONIBO
The Shipibo-Conibo live in many settlements scattered along the banks of the upper Ucayali and lower
Urubamba River and the oxbow lakes and tributaries
on both sides of the river north and south of Pucallpa in eastern Peru.  Although some differences
exist in the cultural practices and the speech between and among the different communities of the

Shipibo and Conibo, it seems clear that these variations are not of sufficient magnitude to require separation into cultural or linguistic sub-groups in this essay. The Shipibo live downriver and the Conibo upriver.

Intensive and extensive linguistic research has been carried out by James Loriot (aka Lauriault), who has published a phonological statement on Shipibo. His study of Shipibo paragraph structure (published with Hollenbach) opened new linguistic vistas for Panoan scholars. He has not published the voluminous collection of folkloristic and other texts on which his analysis of paragraph structure was based. Faust has published a textbook for learning to speak Shipibo-Conibo.

Considerable ethnographic research has been carried out among the Shipibo-Conibo by Behrens, Gebbart-Sayer, Hoffman, Lathrap, Roe, DeBoer, Harner, Bergman, Campos, Abelove, Chirif, Karsten, Morin, and Nissley, all of whom have published or presented various papers on miscellaneous topics. Ethnographic field work has been completed by Daniel Levy (on shamanism) and Raquel Ackerman (on social organization from the women's perspective). Bergman's dissertation is a detailed cultural geography with an ecological and dietary focus. The French chemist, J. Tournon, has investigated Shipibo-Conibo ethnobotany and ethnomedicine. J.J. Goussard has studied Conibo ethno-ornithology.

The Shipibo-Conibo are the largest and best studied Panoan group. But, considering the amount of fieldwork completed, many aspects of Shipibo-Conibo

language and culture remain to be analyzed and do-
cumented in print. The data languishing in field
notes, manuscripts, etc., were they to be published, would vastly enrich the literature on and our
knowledge of the Shipibo-Conibo.[10]

## Shipibo-Conibo Sources

Abelove, Joan M.  1978.  Preverbal learning of kin-
    ship behavior among Shipibo infants of eastern
    Peru.  Unpublished PhD dissertation, City Uni-
    versity of New York.  Abstract published in Dis-
    sertation Abstracts International  39/08-A:5011.
Abelove, Joan and Roberta Campos. 1981.  Infancy
    Related Food Taboos Among the Shipibo. In Food
    Taboos in Lowland South America, Working Papers
    on South American Indians 3, ed. by Kenneth M.
    Kensinger and Waud H. Kracke. Bennington, VT:
    Bennington College, pp. 172-176.
Behrens, Clifford A.  1981a.  Time Allocation and
    Meat Procurement Among the Shipibo Indians of
    Eastern Peru, Human Ecology 9 (2):189-220.
------. 1981b.  Report of Current Research on Shi-
    pibo Ecology and Economy.  Paper presented at
    the American Anthropological Association annual
    meetings, Los Angeles, CA.
------. 1982.  A Quantitative Analysis of Shipibo
    Protein Procurement and Consumption.  Paper pre-
    sented at the American  Anthropological Associa-
    tion annual meetings, Washington, DC.
Bergman, Roland W.  1974.  Shipibo subsistence in
    the Upper Amazon rainforest.  PhD dissertation,
    Geography, University of Wisconsin, Madison.

Abstract published in Dissertation Abstracts
International 35/01-A:341.

------. 1980. Amazon Economics: The Simplicity of
Shipibo Wealth. Dellplain Latin American Studies, Syracuse University. Ann Arbor: University
Microfilms International. Reviewed by J.E. Re-
xine, 1983. Modern Language Journal 67 (3):
295-296; by N.R. Stewart, 1982, Geographical Review 72 (4):471-472; by N.J.H. Smith, 1982, Economic Geography 58 (3):301; by T. Martin, 1982,
Americas 38 (4):544-545.

------. In press. Subsistence Agriculture in La-
tin America. In Food, Politics, and Society in
Latin America, eds. J.C. Super and T.C. Wright.
Lincoln, NE: University of Nebraska Press.

------. In press. Producción Tradicional de los
Shipibos en la Region Amazónica del Perú. Lima:
Centro Amazónico de Antropología y Aplicación
Práctica.

Bertrand-Rousseau, P. 1980. Cinco Fábulas Shipibo. Debates en Antropología, tomo 5:225-232.

------. 1983. De como los Shipibo y otras tribus
aprendieron a hacer los dibujos (típicos) y a
adornarse. Amazonia Peruana 5 (9):79-85.

Bodley, John H. 1978. Preliminary Ethnobotany of
the Peruvian Amazon. Reports of Investigations
No. 55. Laboratory of Anthropology, Washington
State University.

Bodley, John H. and Foley C. Benson. 1979. Cultural Ecology of Amazonian Palms. Reports of Investigations No. 56. Laboratory of Anthropology,
Washington State University.

Bradfield, Robert B. and James Loriot. 1961. Diet
    and food beliefs of Peruvian jungle tribes: 1.
    The Shipibo (monkey people). Journal of the
    American Dietetic Association, 39:126-128.

Campos, Roberta. 1977. Producción de pesca y caza
    de una aldea Shipibo en el rio Pisqui. Amazonia
    Peruana, Ecologia, I (2):53-74.

Chirif Tirado, Alberto, C. Mora y R. Moscoso. 1977.
    Los Shipibo-Conibo del Alto Ucayali: Diagnostico
    Socio-Economico. Lima: SINAMOS-ONAMS.

Davilos, Carlos. 1982. Etnohistoria y Artesania
    Shipiba. Lima: Seminario de Historia Rural An-
    dino, Universidad Nacional Mayor San Marcos.

DeBoer, Warren R. 1975. The Ontogeny of Shipibo
    Art: Variations on a Cross. Paper presented at
    the 74th annual meeting of the American Anthro-
    pological Association, San Francisco.

------. 1984. The Last Pottery Show: System and
    Sense in Ceramic Studies. In S.E. van der
    Leeuw, ed. Albert Egges van Giffen Instituut
    voor pre en proto historie. Amsterdam: Univer-
    sity of Amsterdam. In Press.

DeBoer, Warren R. and Donald W. Lathrap. 1979.
    The Making and Breaking of Shipibo-Conibo
    Ceramics. In Ethnoarchaeology: Implications
    of Ethnography for Archaeology. Carol Kramer,
    ed. New York: Columbia University Press.

DeBoer, Warren R. and James A. Moore. 1982. The
    measurement and Meaning of Stylistic Diversity.
    Ñawpa Pacha 20: 147-62.

Eakin, Lucy. 1973. Cuentos Shipibo. Información
    de Campo No. 178. Yarinacocha: SIL.

------. 1980. Nuevo Destino: The life story of a
Shipibo bilingual educator. SIL Museum of
Anthropology Publication No. 9. 26 pp. plus 14
pp. photographs.

Eakin, Lucille, Erwin H. Lauriault, and Harry Boon-
stra. 1980. Bosquejo etnográfico de los Shipibo-Conibo del Ucayali. (Translated by Marlene
Ballena.) Lima: Ignacio Prado Pastor.

Farrier, Robert L. 1967. The Inca tapu and the
Shipibo Indian: a discussion of the controver-
sial tupu of Incaic Peru and an attempt to define it. Journal of Société de Américanistes,
Paris ns., tome LVI, No. 2:449-458.

Faust, Norma. 1973. Lecciones para el aprendizaje
del idioma Shipibo-Conibo. Documento de Trabajo
No. 1. Yarinacocha, Peru: Instituto Linguístico
de Verano.

Garcia Blasquez, Raul, Milagro Luna Ballon y Samuel
Verastegui Serpa. 1973. El grupo étnico mino-
ritario de los Shipibo y los problemas laborales
y de formacion de mano de obra. Lima: Ministério de Trabajo, Centro Interamericano de Admini-
stración de Trabajo.

Gebhart-Sayer, Angelika. 1982. Aesthetic Therapy:
An Aspect of Shipibo-Conibo Shamanism. Paper
presented at the 44th International Congress of
Americanists, Manchester, England.

------. 1983. Aspekte der Töpferei bei den Shipibo-Conibo (Ost-Peru.) Masters thesis Eberhard-
Karls-Universitat, Tübingen.

------. 1984. Art and Shamanism Among the Shipibo-Conibo. Lecture presented at the Center for

Inter-American Relations, New York.  March 1,
1984.

Goussard, J.J.  1983.  Etude comparée de deux
peuplements aviens d'Amazonie Péruvienne.
Doctoral thesis, l'Ecole Pratique des Hautes
Etudes, Laboratoire de Biogéographie et Ecologie
des Vertébrés, Université de Montpellier II.

Griffen, Gillet G.  1984.  A 20th-Century Aesthetic
View of Shipibo-Conibo Design.  Lecture presen-
ted at the Center for Inter-American Relations,
March 22, 1984.

Guillen Aguilar, F.N.  1975.  El sistema de colores en el Idioma Shipibo.  Educación 6 (13):
27-34.

Harner, Michael J.  1974.  Waiting for Inca-God.
Paper presented at the 73rd annual meeting of
the American Anthropological Association, to
appear in Leaders and Leadership in Lowland
South America, Waud H. Kracke, Ed.

Heath, Carolyn.  1980.  El Tiempo Nos Vencio: La
Situación Actual de los Shipibos del Rio Ucayali, Boletin de Lima 5:3-14.

Hern, Warren M.  1976.  Knowledge and Use of Herbal
Contraceptives in a Peruvian Amazon Village.
Human Organization,  35(1):9-19.

------.  1977.  High Fertility in a Peruvian Amazon
Indian Village. Human Ecology 5(4):  355-368.

Hoffman, Hans.  1964.  Money, Ecology, and Acculturation among the Shipibo of Peru.  In Explora-
tions in Cultural Anthropology, Ward H. Good-
enough, ed., pp. 259-276.  New York: McGraw-Hill
Book Company.

------. 1975. Time Allocation in Shipibo Culture.
Paper presented at the American Anthropological
Association meetings, San Francisco.

Illius, Bruno. 1982. Some Observations on Shipibo-Conibo Shamanism. Paper presented at the 44th
International Congress of Americanists, Manchester, England.

Karsten, Rafael. 1955. Los indios shipibo del rio
Ucayali. Revista del Museu Nacional. Lima. 24:
154-173.

Krarup, Helge. 1981a. Shipibo-indianerne i Peru.
Arkitekten 83(8):179-183, Copenhagen.

------. 1981b. Trues af underganga pa grund af
traemangel. Forskningen & Samfundet 7(6):
11-14.

Krarup, Helge and Mette Kvist Jørgenson. 1981.
Shipibo-Coniboernes keramic. CRAS 28:25-33.
Silkeborg, Denmark.

Krarup, Mette Kvist Jørgensen. 1981a. Shipibo-
kvinder i Perus jungle. Jorden Folk 16(4):
361-371

------. 1981b. Shipibo indianerna i Perus Djungel:
Overlevnad pa Andras Vilkor. Peru Rapport
21(2):28-33, Stockholm.

------. 1982. Problemer i Forbindelse med oend-
ringe iden etniske kunet: Ved overgangen fra
lokal til global brugs-kontekst. Paper presented
at the 10th Nordic Ethnographic meeting, Copenhagen.

Lathrap, Donald W. 1970. A Formal Analysis of
Shipibo-Conibo Pottery and its Implications for
Studies of Panoan Prehistory. Paper presented

at the 35th Annual Meeting of the Society for
American archaeology, Mexico City.

------. 1976. Shipibo tourist art. In Ethnic and
tourist arts: cultural expressions from the
fourth world, Nelson H. Graburn, ed. Berkeley:  .
University of California Press.

------. 1983. Recent Shipibo-Conibo Ceramics and
their Implications for Archaeological Interpretation. In Structure and Cognition in Art,
Dorothy K. Washburn, ed., pp. 25-39. New York:
Cambridge University Press.

Lathrap, Donald W., Angelike Gebhart, and Ann M.
Mester. 1984. The roots of the Shipibo Art
Style: Three Waves on Imariacocha or There Were
"Incas" Before the Incas. In preparation.

Lauriault, Erwin H. 1952. El húshati chama. Peru
Indígena, 2(4):56-60.

Lauriault, James. 1948. Alternate-mora timing in
Shipibo. International Journal of American Linguistics. 14:22-24.

Loriot, James. 1954. An ethnophonemic alphabet
for Shipibo. Información de campo #176. Yarinacocha: Instituto Lingüístico de Verano.

------. 1958. A Set of Completion [Wh] Questions
in Conibo. Currently being revised as "A Set of
Content Questions in Conibo" Unpublished ms.

------. 1960a. Shipibo stress and intonation. Información de campo #176. Yarinacocha: Instituto
Lingüístico de Verano.

------. 1960b. A key to Shipibo Language. Información de campo #177. Yarinacocha: Instituto
Lingüístico de Verano.

------. 1980. A Bilingual Alphabet for the Shipibos. Unpublished manuscript.

Loriot, James and H. Davila. n.d. Datos para el
diccionario shipibo-conibo. Información de
campo #179. Yarinacocha: Instituto Lingüístico
de Verano.

------. 1974. Leyendas de los dioses y otros cuentos. Información de campo #183. Yarinacocha:
Instituto Lingüístico de Verano.

Loriot, James and Barbara Hollenbach. 1970. Shipibo paragraph structure. Foundations of Language, 6:43-66.

Loriot, James and Erwin H. Lauriault. 1975. Textos Shipibos. Datos Etno-Lingüísticos No. 2.
215 pp., (microfiche). Yarinacocha: Instituto
Lingüístico de Verano.

Lucas, Theodore Drexel. 1970. The Musical Style
of the Shipibo Indians of the Upper Amazon.
DMA dissertation, University of Illinois at Urbana. Abstract published in Dissertation Abstracts International 31/09-A:4820.

------. 1971. Songs of the Shipibo of the Upper
Amazon. In Yearbook of Inter-American Musical
Research 7:59-81.

Meyer, Bernhard H. 1974. Beiträge zur Ethnographie der Conibo und Shipibo. University of
Zürich dissertation.

Morin, F. 1972. Les Shipibo, trois siecle d'ethnocide. In Collectif, De L'Ethnocide, pp. 177-
187. Paris: Collection 10/18.

------. 1973. Les Shipibo de l'Ucayali: Rencontre
d'une civilization amazonienne et de la civili-

sation occidentale. Aspects psycho-sociologi-
ques des changements. Unpublished doctoral
thesis, L'Ecole Pratique des Hautes Etudes
(6eme Section) University of Paris.
------. 1976. L'attente de l'Inca ou l'example
d'un messianisme rate. In Collectif, l'Autre
et l'Ailleurs, Hommage a Roger Bastide, pp. 416-
422. Paris: Berger-Lavrault.
Nissley, Charles M. 1960. The Shipibo Indians of
the Lower Ucayali Valley of Eastern Peru. M.S.
Thesis, University of Florida.
Novati, I. Musica y Marco Temporal en los Shipibos
del Rio Maputay. Scripta Etnologica 4 (2):
7-30. Buenos Aires.
Roe, Peter G. 1975. A Componential Approach to
Art. Paper presented at the 1st Annual Conference on Anthropological Research in Amazonia,
Sky's Edge Environmental Campus of Queens College, CUNY.
------. 1976. Archaism, Form and Decoration: An
Ethnographic and Archaeological Case Study From
the Peruvian Montana. Nawpa Pacha 14:73-94.
------. 1977. Innovation and Constraint in Shipibo
Art. Paper presented at the 76th Annual Meeting
of the American Anthropological Association,
Houston.
------. 1978. Essays toward an Amazonian Cosmolo-
gical Model: Perspectives from the Shipibo. A
paper presented at the 18th annual meeting of
the Northeastern Anthropological Association as
part of the symposium "Amazon Mythology: A Jam
Session", E. Jean Langdon, organizer.

------. 1979a.  Marginal Men:  Male Artists Among
the Shipibo Indians of Peru.  Antropológica,
N.S. Vol. XXI.  No.2,  189-221.

------. 1979b.  Artistic Communication Among the
Shipibo and Pisquibo.  Paper presented in the
symposium, Trade and Transport in Lowland South
America, Warren R. DeBoer, organizer, at the
12th Annual Conference of the University of
Calgary Archaeology Association, Calgary,
Canada.

------. 1979c.  Ethnicity, Myths and Oral Tradition:  The Case of the Shipibo Indians of the
Peruvian Jungle.  Paper presented at the 19th
annual meeting of the Northeastern Anthropological Association, New England College, Henni-
ker, New Hampshire.

------. 1980.  Art and Residence Among the Shipibo
Indians of Peru: A Study in Microacculturation.
American Anthropologist  82:42-71.

------. 1982a.  Process in Amerindian Oral Narratives.  Reviews in Anthropology 9:269-285.

------. 1982b.  Ethnoaesthetics and Design Grammars:  Shipibo  Perceptions of Cognate Styles.
Paper presented in the symposium, Interaction
Processes in Archaeology and Ethnography, Dorothy K. Washburn, organizer, at the 81st annual
meetings of the American Anthropological Association, Washington, DC.

------. 1983a.  Mythic Substitution and the Stars:
Aspects of Shipibo and Quechua Ethnoastronomy
Compared.  Paper presented at the 1st Interna-
tional Conference on Ethnoastronomy, Wash., DC.

------. 1983b.  The Cosmic Zygote:  Cosmology in
the Amazon Basin.  New Brunswick:  Rutgers University Press.

------. 1984.  Many Crosses:  Shipibo Aesthetics,
Cosmology and Design.  Lecture presented at the
Center for Inter-American Relations, March 15,
1984.

Roe, Peter G. and Peter E. Siegel.  1983.  The Life
History of a Shipibo Compound: Ethnoarchaeology
in the Peruvian Montana.  Paper presented at the
82nd annual meeting of the American Anthropological Association, Chicago.

Suarez, Nicasio E.  1982.  El pueblo Shipibo se
organiza.    Geomundo 6(8):184-195.

Tournon, J.  1984a.  Plantas Medicinales. Amazonia
Peruana 10 (in press).

------. 1984b.  Plantes medicinales Shipibo-Conibo.
Journal d'Agriculture Tropicale et de Botanique
Apliquee.  In press.

Waisbard, Simone and Roger Waisbard.  1957.  Les
Indiens Shamas de l'Ucayali et du Tamaya.
L'Ethnographie, n.s. no. 53, annee 1958-1959:
19-74.

YAMINAHUA

It is still not clear whether or not Yaminahua is a
distinct language group or if it is closely related
to and/or part of the Mastanahua and Chandinahua
remnants found among the Sharanahua.  The Amahuaca,
Cashinahua, Sharanahua, and Shipibo-Conibo all refer to them as a separate group.  B. J. Kramer carried out a brief ethnographic field study with a

group identified by the Conibo and the Amahuaca as
Yaminahua but was prevented from doing more research because of a killing on the Mapuya River
involving oilmen, Amahuaca, and Yaminahua.  D'Ans
has published a brief lexicon.  Norma Faust and
Lucille Eakin of the Summer Institute of Linguistics have been engaged in linguistic fieldwork for
several years.  According to David Payne (personal
communication), "Norma is currently writing a reference grammar and Lucy a pedagogical grammar, and
together they are compiling a dictionary....Faust
and Eakin comment: Yaminahuas from Brazil have
lived on Rio Acre in Bolivia for at least 9-10
years.  Most recently returned to Brazil apparently
due to some killings."  Seeger and Vogel describe
the 1978 situation of the Jaminawa-Arara of the
Bajé, Tajo and Humaitá rivers of the state of Acre,
Brazil.  Whether or not these are culturally and
linguistically the same as the Peruvian Yaminahua
is uncertain.  Loos (1976:204-207) includes a limited number of phrases from Jambinahua del Acre and
Jaminahua de Jurua but cites no published source.
Graham Townsley has completed his PhD ethnographic
fieldwork among the Peruvian Yaminahua and is currently writing his dissertation for Cambridge University.  French ornithologist J.J. Goussard includes data on Yaminahua ethno-ornithology in his doctoral thesis.

Yaminahua Sources

D'Ans, Andre-Marcel.  1972.  Lexico Yaminahua
    (pano).  Documento de trabajo, No. 1.  Lima:

Universidad Nacional Mayor de San Marcos, Centro
de Investigación de Lingüística Aplicada.

Eakin, Lucille. n.d. Location in Yaminahua narrative. To appear in Notes on Linguistics, SIL
Dallas.

Faust, Norma. n.d.(a) Yaminahua kinship. Unpublished manuscript.

------. n.d.(b) Narrative Discourse in Yaminahua.
Unpublished manuscript.

Faust, Norma and Lucille Eakin. n.d. Yaminahua
phonology. Informacion de Campo No. 207.
Yarinacocha: Instituto Linguistico de
Verano.

Goussard, J. J. 1983. Etude comparée de deux
peuplements aviens d'Amazonie Péruvienne.
Doctoral Thesis, l'Ecole Pratique des Hautes
Etudes, Laboratoire de Biogéographie et Ecologie
des Vertébrés, Université de Montpellier II.

Kramer, Betty Jo. 1975. The Yaminahua of Southeastern Peru: Settlement Pattern and Organization of Work. Unpublished manuscript.

Seeger, Anthony and Arno Vogel. n.d. Relatório da
viagem do Alto Rio Juruá, Município de Cruzeiro
do Sul, Estado do Acre, em Janeiro-Fevereiro de
1978. Mimeographed. (Section 4 deals with the
Yaminahua -- Jaminahua - Arara -- of the Bajé,
Tejo, and Humaitá rivers.)

Townsley, Graham. 1983. Apuntes sobre la historia
de los Yaminahua en el Peru. Amazonía Indígena
(Boletín de análisis editado por COPAL, solida-
ridad con los grupos nativos) 3(6):11-14.

PANOAN

Greenberg, Key, Loukotka, McQuown, Swadesh, Rodrigues, and Tovar have published classifications of
South American Indian Languages since that of Mason
in the Handbook; not one of them provides the data
on which their classification is based. Each places the Panoans within, or organizes them into,
somewhat different clusters. These disagreements
cannot be settled except through the kind of detailed studies exemplified by the work of Shell on
Proto-Panoan phonology, of Loos whose recent publication on comparative Panoan and Proto-Panoan grammar show great promise of clarifying the relationships within the Panoan group, and of Key who has
investigated Tacanan ties with Panoan and Araucanian. Girard includes a lengthy discussion of
Proto-Panoan-Takanan in his study of Proto-Takanan.
He also provides the most complete listing of published and unpublished sources of linguistic data
on these languages as of 1971. Suarez has discussed Macro-Pano-Tacanan suggesting links to Moseten. Migliazza has suggested a relationship between Panoan-Tacanan and Yanomama. Although we are
still a long way from being able to demonstrate the
validity of the linguistic phyla proposed in any of
the classifications, we now have a solid, reliable
corpus of data on most of the Panoan languages
which make future classifications, or the refinement of old ones, less speculative.

Archaeological work has largely been limited to
the upper Ucayali and lower Urubamba river valley
Most scholars view the modern Shipibo-Conibo as the

descendants of the groups whose artifacts have been recovered. See, for example, the archaeological studies of DeBoer, Lathrap, Lathrap et. al., Myers, Raymond, and Weber. Although these studies and related ethnohistorical studies have raised interesting questions about the cultural history of the region and the role some of the Panoans have played in it, they have not as yet shed much light on the relationship between the various Panoan groups and the history of their development out of an ancestral culture.

Very little attention has been given to pan-Panoan ethnology. Lathrap has distinguished between the riverine Panoans, i.e. the Shipibo-Conibo, and the interfluvial Panoans, Braun's "backwoods Eastern Panoans," suggesting that the latter are refugee populations which experienced culture loss in their less protein-rich environments. Kensinger has suggested a two-section moiety-like social system for the Proto-Panoans, with Dravidian terminology, unilineal descent groups, and symmetrical marriage exchange. Roe has examined Panoan design systems. Italo has published a paper on material culture and subsistence activities based on published sources. Wistrand Robinson includes a discussion of Panoan folklore in her dissertation on Cashibo, in her 1975 paper, and in her 1984 manuscript. Although Roe uses Shipibo-Conibo folklore as a starting point and draws on other Panoan sources, the scope of his study is Amazonian not Panoan. Similarly, studies by Chirif, Chirif et. al., D'Ans, Figueiredo and de Amorim Folha, Calixto

Méndez, Morin, and Ribeiro and Wise, focus on the
Peruvian selva and include materials on non-Panoan
groups.

Panoan Sources

A:   Comparative and Historical Linguistic Studies

D'Ans, André-Marcel.  1970.  Materiales para el
   estudio del grupo lingüístico pano (introduc-
   ción-léxicos-bibliografia).  Série: Léxicos, 1.
   Lima:  Universidad Nacional Mayor de San Marcos, Plan de Fomento Lingüístico.

------.  1973.  Estudio Glotocronológico sobre
   Nueve Hablas Pano.  Documento de Trabajo No. 17.
   Lima:  Universidad Nacional Mayor de San Marcos,
   Centro de Investigación de Lingüística Aplicada.

Girard, Victor,  1971.  Proto-Takanan Phonology.
   University of California Publications in Linguistics, 70.  Berkeley: University of California Press.  Reviewed by Marshall Durbin, 1974,
   American Anthropologist 76 (2):458-459; by Mary
   Ritchie Key, 1974, General Linguistics 14 (1):
   55-65.

Kensinger, Kenneth M.  1981.  Recent Publications
   in Panoan Linguistics.  International Journal of
   American Linguistics 47 (1):68-75.

Key, Mary Ritchie.  1968.  Comparative Tacanan
   Phonology: with Cavinena phonology and notes on
   Pano-Tacanan relationship. The Hague:  Mouton.
   Reviewed by Victor Girard, 1970, International
   Journal of American Linguistics 36: 73-78; by
   George L. Trager, 1968, Studies in Linguistics

20:87-89; by Norman Zide, 1969, American Anthropologist 71:722-724.

------. 1971. Response to Girard on Tacanan.
International Journal of American Linguistics
37: 196-201.

------. 1978. Araucanian Genetic Relationships.
International Journal of American Linguistics 44
(4):280-293.

------. 1979. The Grouping of South American Indian Languages. Tubingen: Gunter Narr.

------. 1981. North and South American Linguistic
Connections. La Linguistique 17 (1):3-18.

Longacre, Robert. 1968. Comparative Reconstruction of Indigenous Languages. In Current
Trends in Linguistics, Vol. IV, Ibero-American
and Caribbean Linguistics, 320-360. (Discussion
of Proto-Panoan and Tacanan 349-353, of Proto-
Panoan 349-352.)

Loos, Eugene E. 1973a. La señal de transitividad
del sustantivo en los idiomas panos. In Estudios Panos I, Eugene E. Loos, ed., 133-184.

------. 1973b. La construcción del reflexivo en
los idiomas panos. In Estudios Panos II, Eugene
E. Loos, ed., 161-261.

------. 1973c. Algunas implicaciones de la reconstrucción de un fragmento de la gramática del
proto-pano. In Estudios Panos II:263-282.

------. 1976. Verbos Performativos: partículas
que tienen significado performativo o significado relacionado a los performativos en idiomas
panos. Estudios Panos V. Serie Lingüística
Peruana No. 14.

272    *Kenneth M. Kensinger*

272    *Kenneth M. Kensinger*

Loos, Eugene E., Ed. 1973a. Estudios Panos I. Série Lingüística Peruana, 10. Yarinacocha, Loreto, Peru: Instituto Lingüístico de Verano.

------. 1973b. Estudios Panos II. Série Lingüística Peruana, No. 11. Yarinacocha: Instituto Lingüístico de Verano.

Shell, Olive Alexandra. 1965. Pano Reconstruction. PhD dissertation, University of Pennsylvania. Abstract published in Dissertation Abstracts International 26/12:7307.

-----. 1975. Estudios Panos III: Las lenguas pano y su reconstrucción. Estudios Lingüísticos Peruanos No. 12.

Suarez, Jorge A. 1969. Moseten and Pano-Tacanan. Anthropological Linguistics, 11(9):255-266.

------. 1973. Macro-Pano-Tacanan. International Journal of American Linguistics 39 (3): 137-154.

Wistrand Robinson, Lila M. 1983. Sample Cognate List and Preliminary Sound Correspondences Toward a North and South American Indian Relationship. Paper read at Southeastern Conference on Linguistics, University of Maryland at College Park, April 1983. (Comparison of Panoan-Tacanan with Uto-Aztecan for a connection between North and South America.)

B:   Ethnohistorical and Archeological Studies

DeBoer, Warren R. 1974. Ceramic Longevity and Archaeological Interpretation: An Example from the Upper Ucayali, Peru. American Antiquity 39: 335-343.

------. 1975.   The River and the Forest:    Issues in
Panoan Prehistory.   Paper presented at the Ame-
rican Anthropological Association meetings, San
Francisco.

------. 1981a.   Buffer Zones in the Cultural Ecology of Aboriginal Amazonia: An Ethnohistorical
Approach.   American Antiquity 46 (2):364-377.

------. 1981b.   The Machete and the Cross:   Conibo
Trade in the Late Seventeenth Century.   In P.
Francis, S. Kense, and P. Duke, Eds., Networks
of the Past, pp. 31-49.  Proceedings of the 12th
Annual meetings of the University of Calgary
Archaeology Association.   Calgary: University of
Calgary Press.

------. 1983.   The Archaeological Record As Preserved Death Assemblage.   In Archaeological Ham-
mers and Theories, J. A. Moore and A. S. Keene,
eds., pp. 19-36.  New York: Academic Press.

DeBoer, Warren R. and Stephen Kaufman.   1977.
Developments in Ethnoarchaeology: Examples from
the Upper Amazon. Paper presented at the 42nd
Annual Meetings of the Society for American
Archaeology, New Orleans.

Lathrap, Donald W.   1958.   The Cultural Sequence at
Yarinacocha, Eastern Peru.   American Antiquity
23 (4):379-388.

------. 1962.   Yarinacocha:   Stratigraphic Excava-
tions in the Peruvian Montaña.   PhD dissertation, Harvard University.

------. 1965.   Investigaciones en la Selva Peruana,
1964-1965. Boletín del Museo Nacional de Antropología y Arqueología, Lima, 4:9-12.

274    *Kenneth M. Kensinger*

------. 1970. The Upper Amazon. New York: Praeger; London: Thames and Hudson.

Myers, Thomas P. 1972. Sarayacu: archaeological investigations at a 19th century mission site in the Peruvian montaña. Proceedings of the XXXIXth International Congress of Americanists, Vol.4: 25-37.

------. 1972-74. An Archaeological Survey of the Lower Aguaitia River, Eastern Peru. Ñawa Pacha 10-12:61-89, Plates VII-XVI.

------. 1974. Spanish Contacts and Social Change on the Ucayali River, Peru. Ethnohistory 21(2): 135-157.

------. 1975. Community Size and Tribal Movements in the Peruvian Montaña: 1577-1800. Paper read at the American Anthropological Association meetings, San Francisco.

------. 1976a. Isolation and Ceramic Change: a case from the Ucayali River, Peru. World Archaeology 7(3):333-351.

------. 1976b. Defended Territories and No-man's-lands. American Anthropologist 78(2):354-355.

------. 1977. Early Trade Networks in the Amazon Basin. Paper presented to the 42nd Annual Meetings of the Society for American Archaeology, April 28-30, 1977.

------. 1978. The Impact of Disease on the Upper Amazon. Paper read in the Symposium "Epidemics and Native American History in the Tropics", organized by David Sweet. 26th Annual Meeting of the American Society for Ethnohistory, November 2-4, 1978. Austin, Texas.

------. n.d.    Panoans of the River and of the
    Forest:    An Historical Perspective.    Unpubli-
    shed manuscript.

Raymond, J. Scott, Warren DeBoer and Peter Roe.
    1975.    Cumancaya:    A Peruvian Ceramic Tradition.
    Occasional Papers No. 2, Department of Archaeo-
    logy, University of Calgary.

Roe, Peter G.    1970.    Cumancaya, Archaeological
    Excavations on an Oxbow Lake in the Peruvian
    Montaña.    Paper presented at the 35th Annual
    Meeting of the Society for American Archaeology,
    Mexico City.

------. 1972.    The Cumancaya Culture and Its Rela-
    tionship to the Sierra.    Paper presented at the
    37th Annual Meeting of the Society for American
    Archaeology, Miami.

------. 1973.    Cumancaya:    Archaeological Excava-
    tions and Ethnographic Analogy in the Peruvian
    Montaña.    PhD    dissertation, Department of
    Anthropology, University of Illinois at Urbana-
    Champaign.

Weber, Ronald LeRoy.    1975a.    Caimito:    An Analysis
    of the late Prehistoric culture of the Central
    Ucayali, Eastern Peru. PhD dissertation, Univer-
    sity of Illinois.    Ann Arbor: University Micro-
    films No. 75-24431.

------. 1975b.    The Late Prehistory of the Tamaya
    River of Eastern Peru: A Model of Population
    Movements for Tropical Riverine Environments.
    Paper presented at the American Anthropological
    meetings, San Francisco.

C:    Ethnological Studies

Braun, Robert A.  1975.  Population Dynamics and
    Social Organization Among the Backwoods Eastern
    Panoans (Peru). Paper presented at the annual
    meetings of the American Anthropological Asso-
    ciation, San Francisco.

Calixto Méndez, Luis G.  1977.  Evolución étnica
    del Ucayali Central.  In Congreso Peruano:
    El Hombre y la Cultura Andina, 3. Lima.

Chirif, Alberto.  1975a.  La cuestión de las tier-
    ras y del desarrollo económico de las comunida-
    des nativas, en marginación y futuro.  Lima:
    SINAMOS (DGOR-UACN).

------.  1975b.  Ocupación territorial de la Amazo-
    nía y marginación de la población nátiva.  Ame-
    rica Indígena 35(2).

Chirif Tirado, Alberto.  1977.  Ley Nacional y Nor-
    ma Tradicional. Série Comunidades. Lima: Sinamos.

Chirif, Alberto, Carlos Mora, Carlos Yanez, and
    Tulio Mora.  1975.  Comunidades Nativas de Selva
    Central Diagnóstico Socio-Económico.  Lima:
    SINAMOS-ONAMS.

Chirif, A. and C. Mora.  1977.  Atlas de Comunida-
    des Nativas. Lima: Sinamos.

D'Ans, André-Marcel.  1982.  L'Amazonie Péruvienne.
    (Anthropologie, Ecologie, Ethno-histoire, Per-
    spectives contemporaines).  Paris: Payot.

Figueiredo, Napoleão y Maria Elena de Amorim Folha.
    1975. O Destino das Sociedades Tribais na Amazo-
    nia Brazileira. Revista de Cultura do Para 5 (18
    & 19): 75-110.

Italo, Signorini. 1968. La Famiglia Etno-Linguis-
tica Pano: Ecologia e Attività di Sussistenza.
Rome: Edizioni Ricerche, pp. I-XXXI.

Kensinger, Kenneth M. 1975. Proto-Panoan Social
Organization. Paper presented in the symposium,
Panoan Research, American Anthropological Asso-
ciation annual meetings, San Francisco, CA.

Morin F. 1976. L'attente de l'Inca ou l'expression d'un messianisme raté. In L'Autre et
l'Ailleurs: Hommages à Roger Bastide. Paris:
Berger-Levrault.

Ribeiro, Darcy and Mary Ruth Wise. 1978. Los Grupos Étnicos de la Amazonía Peruana. Comunidades
y Culturas Peruanas, No. 13. Yarinacocha: Instituto Lingüístico de Verano.

Roe, Peter G. 1975. Comparing Panoan Design Systems Through Componential Analysis. A paper
presented at the 74th Annual Meeting of the American Anthropological Association, December
1975, San Francisco.

Wistrand Robinson, Lila M. 1975. An Overview of
Pan-Panoan Oral Tradition and Its Implication.
Paper read at Panoan Symposium, American Anthropological Association, San Francisco, December
1975.

CONCLUSION

Table I summarizes the research and publications on
the Panoan speaking groups since publication of the
Handbook of South American Indians. Considerable
fieldwork and analysis has been done: however, considering time and manpower expended, relatively few

TABLE 1. Summary of Panoan Research

| | Field-work | Phono-logy | Grammar | Lexicon | Folk-lore | Ethno-graphy | Ethno-history | Archaeo-logy |
|---|---|---|---|---|---|---|---|---|
| Amahuaca | m | p | b.p | b,p | – | b,p a,d | – | – |
| Capanahua | m | b,p | b,p | b | b | – | – | – |
| Cashibo | c | p | p | b | p,d | b,p | p | – |
| Cashinahua | c | p | b,p | b | b | b,p a,t | – | – |
| Chacobo | l | p | p | – | – | p | – | – |
| Isconahua | l | – | – | – | – | p,d | – | – |
| Marubo | l | p | p | – | – | p | – | – |
| Matses | l | a | p | – | – | p,d | – | – |
| Sharanahua | l | p | p | – | p | b,p | – | – |
| Shipibo-Conibo | c | p | p | a | b | b,p d | p | b,p |
| Yaminahua | l | – | – | p | – | p | – | – |
| Panoan | – | b,p | b,p | – | b,p | – | p | p |

KEY:
c considerable fieldwork by one or more researchers
l limited fieldwork either in scope or number of researchers
m moderate fieldwork either in scope or number of researchers
b book and/or monograph
p published or presented papers/manuscripts
d PhD dissertation, unpublished
t MA thesis, unpublished

publications have resulted. Although we <u>have</u> made progress, there is an urgent need to get the results of the research that has been done into the public domain. Publication of books, monographs, papers, etc., is the most obvious means of doing this. But, the exigencies of publishing mitigate against a rapid flow of data and research conclusions. What we need is a more informal way of disseminating this knowledge; namely, a series of working papers, distributed to all those interested.

Although I consider publication of the knowledge already in hand, or perhaps more accurately, in mind, to be the most urgent task facing us, much research is still needed. The table points out the obvious gaps. Linguistic research is needed for the Isconahua. Despite excellent progress by Shell and Loos, much work remains to be done on the reconstruction of Proto-Panoan grammar and establishing the links between the Panoan and other language families. Ethnographic research is needed for the Capanahua and Chacobo. Most of the cultural history of the Proto-Panoans remains to be researched and written. Except for the work of Wistrand Robinson in Cashibo and to a limited extent in Pan-Panoan, Roe's book on Amazonian cosmology, and some work by D'Ans and G. Cromack in Cashinahua and Schoolland in Capanahua, modern folkloristic study of the Panoans is an open field.

Finally, it should be mentioned that a new area of research has emerged since publication of the Handbook; namely, studies of the impact of bilingual education and literacy. Literacy programs

and/or bilingual schools taught by trained native
speakers are operating in at least six of the eleven Panoan groups. Documentation is needed on the
effects on the cultures of these groups of literacy, bilingualism, and a nationally oriented curriculum.

ACKNOWLEDGMENTS

The present version of this paper benefited greatly
from the corrections, additions, comments and cri-
ticisms of the following people, none of whom are
responsible for any errors, omissions, or over-
sights: Joan Abelove, Roland Bergman, Robert Carneiro, Alberto Chirif, Warren DeBoer, Gertrude
Dole, Philippe Erickson, Erwin Frank, J.M. Hanna,
Francis E. Johnston, Mary Key, Daniel Levy, Eugene
Loos, James Loriot, Julio Cezar Melatti, Ernest
Migliazza, F. Morin, Thomas Myers, Charles Nissly,
Peter Roe, Steven Romanoff, J. Tournon, and Lila
Wistrand Robinson. Additional data were obtained
from Cecilia McCallum, Silvio Cavuscens, David
Payne, and Barbara Keifenheim. I gratefully ac-
knowledge their kind assistance.

NOTES

1. In order to make the bibliographies on the
   individual languages and groups more readily
   available to interested researchers, I have chosen to list items by society-language, plus a
   section on Panoan. Where a source deals with
   several groups, it is listed among the sources
   for each group. The general bibliography inclu-

des only those items which are not listed in one
of the "sources" lists.

2.  In citing Mason, I am implying neither a preference for nor approval of Mason's classification
over those of Greenberg (1960, and in Steward
and Faron, 1959), Key (1979), Loukotka (1968),
McQuown (1955), Swadesh (1959), Tovar (1961);
his happens to be the classification used in the
Handbook, the reference point for this essay.
(For an evaluation of the various classifications, see Lyon 1974:41-43, Rowe 1974:43-50,
Rodrigues 1974:51-58, Wistrand Robinson 1971.)

3.  For example Xumuyabu (xumu 'gourd' ya 'with/
has'), Isuyabu (isu spider monkey, etc.),
Maxayabu (maxa 'rocks' etc.).

4.  That is, the focal male deemed preeminent from
the perspective of the speaker. The nature of
Cashinahua political/social structure requires
that each local group have at least two focal
males, one of whom may be preeminent in dealings
with outsiders. Several pairs of focal males
may exist in any local group. Thus, speakers
may identify themselves or others, as being "so-
and-so's" people, selecting the focal male to
whom they have the closest ties. (For a fuller
discussion of Cashinahua social structure and
leadership see Kensinger 1974b, in the Cashinahua sources.) Thus, a village may be known by
as many names as its resident focal males.

5.  For example, I have heard frequent references
to Mananbu, those who live up the river.

6.  The difficulties I encountered while attempting
    to ascertain the language group identity of
    individuals who visited the Cashinahua village
    or whom we encountered on the river using the
    names of groups the Cashinahua had given me was
    the source of considerable perverse pleasure and
    laughter for my Cashinahua hosts.  Directly or
    indirectly insulting an "enemy" with impunity is
    a recurrent theme in Cashinahua humor.

7.  There may well be several additional extant Pa-
    noan-speaking groups.  I am holding in abeyance
    questions about the status of the Mastanahua,
    Chandinahua of the Alto Purus, and that of the
    various groups cited by Wistrand Robinson (1969)
    I do not have adequate data to discuss the Paca-
    huara (Bormida and Califano 1974), Caripuna, and
    Araona of Bolivia and the Brazilian Canamari,
    Shawanahua (Katukina), Camannahua (Huaninnahua
    or Katukina) cited by Loos (1976).  Groups from
    the Rio Quixito and from the confluence of the
    Itui and Itacoai reported by CEDI (1981:94-109)
    may also be Panoan.

8.  Regarding the term Chainawa, CEDI (1981:37,
    citing Mellati 1977:94, 107), states "Segundo os
    missionários [of the New Tribes Mission], a
    língua que os Marúbo falam é a dos extintos
    Chaináwabu.  Pelo menos um informante
    indígena confirmou essa origem.  Convém porém
    esclarecer que Chaináwabo era o nome que se
    aplicava às gerações que se alternavam com as
    chamadas Yenenáwabo, para construir um clã

matrilinear.    Para essa unidade perdurar era
necessário que mantivesse alianças matrimoniais
com pelo menos um otro clã (tambem de duas
denominações)."

9.    What to call this group, and whether or not to
even consider them one group is problematic.
The term Matses is the autodenomination of the
group with which Romanoff did his recent 18
months of fieldwork and is the term used by Cavuscens and Calixto Méndez.    If I were to be
consistent I would opt for the term Mayoruna;
most, if not all the Panoan groups (the Shipibo-
Conibo may be the exception), use autodenomina-
tions other than the tribal names used in this
paper and in the literature generally.    Because
of the uncertainty about the relationship between the Mayoruna of the early literature and
the Matses, I have chosen to follow the lead of
the scholars currently working in the area.    I
have, however, decided to include the Matís in
this cluster despite Mellati's (personal communication) advice, "Aliás, acho que V. se deve
incluir os Matís como uma sociedade distinta na
sua bibiografia, pois, a pesar de sua autodeno-
minação, "Matís", ser parecida com a autodenomi-
nação dos Mayorúna, "Matsés", são politica e
culturalmente (não sei até que ponto lingüisti-
camente) distintas."

10.    Although most of the archeological and ethnohistorical research seems to bear most directly
on the Shipibo-Conibo, I have chosen to deal
with it in the Panoan section.

GENERAL REFERENCES

Bormida, Marcelo y Mario Califano. 1974. Los ultimos Pakaware. Scripta etnologica; archivo para una fenomenologia de la cultura, No. 2:158-172. Buenos Aires.

CEDI (Centro Ecumênico de Documentação e Informação) 1981. Povos Indígenas no Brasil, Volume 5 Javari. São Paulo: Centro Ecumênico de Documentação e Informação.

Greenberg, Joseph H. 1960. The general classification of Central and South American languages. In Men and Cultures: selected papers of the Fifth International Congress of Anthropological and Ethnological Sciences, Philadelphia: University of Pennsylvania Press.

Loukotka, Cestmir. 1968. Classification of South American Indian Languages. Reference Series, V. 7. Latin American Center, University of California, Los Angeles.

Lyon, Patricia J. 1974. Native South Americans: Ethnology of the Least Known Continent. Boston: Little, Brown and Company.

------. 1975. Dislocación tribal y clasificaciones lingüísticas en la zona del Rio Madre de Dios. Proceedings of the International Congress of Americanists, 1970, 39 (5): 185-207.

Mason J. Alden. 1950. The Languages of South American Indians. In Handbook of South American Indians. Vol. 6:157-318. Julian H. Steward, ed.

McQuown, Norman A. 1955. The indigenous languages of Latin America. American Anthropologist 57: 501-570.

Rodrigues, Aryon Dall'igna. 1974. Linguistic
Groups of Amazonia, In Native South Americans,
Patricia J. Lyon, ed, pp. 51-58.

Rowe, John Howland. 1974. Linguistic Classification Problems in South America. In Native
South Americans, Patricia J. Lyon, ed., pp.
43-50.

Steward, Julian H., Ed. 1946-1959. Handbook of
South American Indians. Washington, DC: Smith-
sonian Institution, Bureau of American
Ethnology.

Steward, Julian H., and Louis C. Faron. 1959.
Native Peoples of South America. New York:
McGraw Hill.

Swadesh, Morris. 1959. Mapas de clasificación
lingüística de México y las Américas. Cuadernos
del Instituto de Historia, Serie Antropológica
no. 8. Universidad Nacional Autónoma de México,
México.

Tovar, Antonio. 1961. Catálogo de las lenguas de
América del sur: enumeración, con indicaciones
tipológicas, bibliografía, y mapas. Buenos Aires: Editorial Sudamericana.

Wistrand, Lila M. 1971. Review of Classification
of South American Indian Languages by Cestmir
Loukotka (ed. by Johannes Wilbert). Linguistics
75:106-113.

# 6. Some Macro-Jê Relationships
## Irvine Davis

INTRODUCTION

A number of closely related languages spoken in
central Brazil have been traditionally regarded as
constituting the Jê linguistic family.[1] More recently the Kaingang dialects of southern Brazil,
including Xokleng, have been included in this family. In a previous paper I examined the comparative
phonology of the Jê languages and attempted some
reconstructions of Proto Jê lexical items (Davis
1966). In the present paper I present evidence for
the relationship of the Jê languages to two other
Brazilian languages, Maxakalí and Karajá, and make
some observations regarding the composition of the
Macro-Jê stock.

THE JÊ-MAXAKALÍ-KARAJÁ RELATIONSHIP

Maxakalí has generally been included within the
Macro-Jê stock by comparativists, but its relationship to the Jê languages has not previously been
demonstrated by careful comparative techniques.
Karajá, on the other hand, has generally been placed outside of Macro-Jê in spite of the fact that
significant similarities to certain Jê languages
were noted as long ago as by nineteenth century
ethnologists (Ehrenreich 1894). The paucity of

available descriptive material for Karajá has undoubtedly prevented recent authors from following
this lead.

Evidence for the relationship of Maxakalí and
Karajá to Jê[2] is presented below. The cognate sets
have been carefully chosen and have a relatively
high degree of reliability. The possibility of
chance similarities or of similarities due to
borrowing is reduced by comparing Maxakalí and
Karajá items with forms reconstructed from divergent branches of the Jê family rather than with
items from individual Jê languages. The phonetic
content of each form is at least partly explainable
in terms of regular correspondences, and all proposed cognates are close semantic equivalents. Furthermore, use is made of basic vocabulary items
that are less likely than culture-bound references
to be affected by loans.

Items preceded by an asterisk in the following
list are Proto Jê reconstructions. Maxakalí, M,
and Karajá, K, cognates follow. The notation K(w)
indicates that the citation is from Karajá women's
speech. In general, the corresponding form in
men's speech lacks the velar stop. Parentheses en-
close portions of Maxakalí and Karajá forms which
apparently do not enter into the comparison. Hy-
phens indicate infraword morpheme divisions that
are well supported by internal evidence. English
glosses following the Proto Jê items apply also to
the Maxakalí and Karajá cognates unless otherwise
indicated.

1.  *a- your, M ?ã̃-, K ã̃-
2.  *cwa tooth, M -coc, K čuu
3.  *ka you, K kai
4.  *ka-kre, -kreñ to scratch, K ɨ-θɛ
5.  *kaŋã̃ snake, M kãñã̃(noc)
6.  *ka-zo, -zor to suck, M -cɨp, K -dʕɔ-
7.  *kə skin, bark, M -cac, K(w) (dʕə)kɨ
8.  *keckwa sky, M ñãñko(tɛ?)
9.  *-kɛ, -kec left, M -cac
10. *kɛn stone, M cap
11. *ki hair, M -cɛ?
12. *ko horn, M kɨp
13. *-kõ, -kõm to drink, M -co?op, K -õ-
14. *kok wind, K(w) kɨhɨ
15. *kõn knee, M -kopa(-cic), K (dʕi-)ɔho
16. *kra child, M kitok son
17. *krã̃, krãñ head, K ra(-dʕi)
18. *krẽ, krẽr to eat, M -cit, K (-rə)θ'-
    to swallow
19. *krɔ rotten, M -ktoc, K rɔ
20. *krɨz parrot, M konnɨ̃ŋ
21. *ku, kur to eat, K(w) -kɨ-
22. *ku-krɨt tapir, M (?i-)citta?,
    K(w) kõri
23. *kũm smoke, M -ŋõñ
24. *ku-zɨ fire, M kɨcap, K (hɛo)dʕɨ
25. *kwɨr manioc, M kon, kohot, K (ʒji)ura
26. *ma liver, K baa
27. *-ma, -mar to hear, M (-cɨ)pak
28. *mɛc good, M -mac
29. *meñ honey, K bədi

30. *mĩ, mĩñ <u>alligator</u>, M mã?ãñ
31. *mŏ, mŏr <u>to go</u>, <u>walk</u>, M mõŋ
32. *mrɔ, mrɔc <u>ashes</u>, M pitohok, K bri(bɨ)
33. *mut <u>neck</u>, K bedʕɔ <u>throat</u>
34. *na <u>rain</u>, M tɛhɛc
35. *nŏ, nŏr <u>to lie</u>, K rŏrŏ- <u>to sleep</u>
36. *nɔ <u>eye</u>, K ruɛ
37. *niw <u>new</u>, M -tip
38. *ñĩ <u>meat</u>, M (coŋ)ñĩñ, K -de
39. *ñĩ-ña-krɛ <u>nose</u>, K deãθɔ̃
40. *ñŏt <u>to sleep</u>, M -ñŏn
41. *ñõ-tɔ <u>tongue</u>, M -ñõñcŏŋ, K dɔrɔ(dʕɔ)
42. *ñĩ, ñĩr <u>to sit</u>, M -ñĩm, K -dã̃-
43. *ŋo <u>louse</u>, M -kit
44. *ŋrɛ <u>egg</u>, K θii
45. *ŋrɛ, ŋrɛr <u>to sing</u>, <u>dance</u>, M -kɨtɛc,
    K -θɛ-
46. *ŋri-rɛ <u>small</u>, M -ktŏŋnãŋ, K -riɔre
    <u>child</u>
47. *pa <u>I</u>, K -wa- <u>me</u>, <u>mine</u>
48. *par <u>foot</u>, M -pata?, K waa
49. *pat <u>anteater</u>, K wari(ri)
50. *pĩ <u>tree</u>, <u>firewood</u>, M mĩhĩm, mĩm
51. *prɨ <u>path</u>, M pɨtahat, pɨtat, K rɨɨ
52. *pɨ-ci, -cit <u>one</u>, M pɨcɛt
53. *rã <u>flower</u>, M -ta? <u>fruit</u>, K ra <u>fruit</u>
54. *rɔp <u>dog</u>, K (ijɔ)rɔ
55. *rɨ <u>long</u>, M -toc, K irɛhɛ
56. *ta, tam <u>third person</u>, K dʕabĩ <u>to him</u>
57. *tɔ, tɔr <u>to fly</u>, M -to(paha?), K -ɔ-
58. *tu, tum <u>belly</u>, M -tɛc, K -wo-
59. *tɨk <u>black</u>, M -nĩñ

60. \*twəm <u>fat</u>, <u>grease</u>, M -top, K wɛɛ
61. \*za-ra <u>wing</u>, <u>feather</u>, K Өa <u>feather</u>
    <u>ornament</u>
62. \*za-re <u>root</u>, M (-ñĩ̃p)catit, K (iru-)dʕɨ
63. \*zaz-kwa <u>mouth</u>, M -ñĩ̃-koc
64. \*zi <u>bone</u>, K dʕii
65. \*zici <u>name</u>, M -cɨcet(?ac)
66. \*zo, zoc <u>leaf</u>, M cɨc
67. \*zi <u>seed</u>, K idʕɨ

Although the data are insufficient for a thorough reconstruction of Proto Macro-Jê, it is
nevertheless possible to trace some of the major
developments in the historical phonology.

A basic feature of Jê structure which apparently
dates back to the Proto Macro-Jê horizon is the existence of parallel series of voiceless stops /p t
c k/ and of nasals /m n n ŋ/.[3] These are quite
regularly reflected, especially in nonfinal position, in the languages under consideration. The
evidence suggests that they have descended generally unchanged to Proto Jê but have undergone various
types of change in both Maxakalí and Karajá. In
Maxakalí the two series have become realigned so
that, with few exceptions, both nonfinal \*/p t c k/
and nonfinal \*/m n n ŋ/ appear as /m n n ŋ/ contiguous to a nasal vowel and as /p t c k/ in other
environments. At the same time, velars have undergone a split which has resulted in palatal reflexes, /c/ and /ñ/, under conditions that can probably be traced to the presence of a following front
or central vowel at some stage in the history of

the language. Final consonants have undergone
other kinds of change, so that it is impossible on
the basis of the present data to trace their development with any degree of certainty. Some final
consonants, however, exhibit the same reflexes as
nonfinal consonants.

The voiceless stop series and the nasal series
are partly retained in Karajá. In most cases final
consonants have been lost, although a few Karajá
forms show the retention in non-final position of
consonants that are reconstructed in final position
for Proto Jê. Apart from final zeroing, */p/ is
reflected as /w/ in prevocalic position and as zero
preceding /r/. The alveolar stop is reflected variously as /r/, /dʕ/, or zero under conditions that
are not clear. A single example indicates Karajá
/č/ as a reflex of */c/. The velar stop is retained in a number of items of women's speech but is
reflected as zero in most items of men's speech.
The Proto Macro-Jê series */m n ñ ŋ/ is reflected
in Karajá nonfinal position as /b r d zero/. It
should be noted, however, that examples are lacking
for Karajá reflexes of prevocalic */ŋ/.

In addition to the voiceless stop and the nasal
series, Proto Macro-Jê probably hd an */r/ phoneme
as well as a phoneme corresponding to Proto Jê
*/z/. Except for some final occurrences, */r/ is
reflected in Maxakalí as /n/ when it is contiguous
to a nasal vowel and as /t/ in other environments.
In Karajá the phoneme has undergone a split in
which it is retained as /r/ in some environments
and becomes /θ/ in other environments. The change

to /θ/ was probably conditioned by a following
front vowel, although the present evidence is not
entirely clear. The Proto Jê phoneme */z/ is reflected in the Jê languages by a wide variety of
sounds and its phonetic characteristics are unknown. In non-final position it corresponds quite
regularly to Maxakalí /c/, or to /ñ/ when it is
contiguous to a nasal vowel. In Karajá it corresponds regularly to the implosive /dˤ/.

Consonantal sound correspondences, except for
irregularities and loss in final position, are summarized below. Numbers refer to the cognate sets
previously listed.

| PROTO JÊ | MAXAKALÍ | |
|---|---|---|
| *p | p | 48, 51, 52 |
| | m | 50 |
| *t | t | 52, 57, 58, 60 |
| | n | 40, 59 |
| *c | c | 2, 9, 28, 52, 65, 66 |
| | ñ | 8 |
| *k | k | 5, 8, 12, 15, 16, 19, 20, 24, 25, 63 |
| | c | 7, 9-11, 13, 18, 22 |
| | ŋ | 23 |
| | ñ | 8, 59 |
| *m | p | 13, 27, 32, 60 |
| | m | 28, 30, 31 |
| *n | t | 34, 37 |
| *ñ | ñ | 30, 38, 40-42 |
| *ŋ | k | 43, 45, 46 |

|  |  |  |
|---|---|---|
|  | ñ̃ | 5 |
| *r | t | 16, 18, 19, 22, 25, 32, 45, 46, 48, 51, 53, 55, 62 |
|  | n | 20, 46 |
| *z | c | 6, 24, 62, 65, 66 |
|  | ñ̆ | 63 |

| PROTO JÊ̂ | KARAJÁ |  |
|---|---|---|
| *p | w | 47-49 |
|  | zero | 51 |
| *t | r | 41, 49 |
|  | dʕ | 33, 56 |
|  | zero | 57, 58, 60 |
| *c | č | 2 |
| *k | k | 3, 7, 14, 21, 22 |
|  | zero | 4, 13, 15, 17-19, 22, 25, 39 |
| *m | b | 26, 29, 32, 33, 56 |
| *n | r | 35, 36 |
| *ñ̃ | d | 29, 38, 39, 41, 42 |
| *ŋ | zero | 44-46 |
| *r | r | 19, 22, 25, 32, 35, 46, 51, 53-55 |
|  | θ | 4, 18, 39, 44, 45, 61 |
| *z | dʕ | 6, 24, 62, 64, 67 |

In addition to the consonants covered in the above tabulation, Proto Jê̂ */w/ has been reconstructed with a limited distribution. One cognate set (60) shows a corresponding /w/ in Karajá, while

the remaining examples of Proto Jê */wV/ correspond
to Maxakalí /o/ and to Karajá /u/ (2, 8, 25, 60,
63).

Vowel correspondences are considerably less
regular than are consonantal correspondences, and
few conclusions can be reached regarding vowel
developments. It can be noted, however, that Maxakalí sequences of the type V?V (13, 30) and VhV
(25, 32, 34, 50, 51) and Karajá sequences of the
VhV (14, 15, 55) correspond regularly to Proto Jê
single vowels.

COMPOSITION OF THE MACRO-JÊ STOCK

It is not possible on the basis of presently available evidence to arrive at a definitive classification of the Macro-Jê languages. The following is
offered as a tentative outline in which are indicated those languages that can be classified with
some degree of confidence, together with various
lesser-known languages designated as unclassified.
I. The Jê family has the following subfamilies: A.
Kaingangan subfamily (Several Kaingang dialects and
Xokleng); B. Central Jê subfamily (Several Xavante
dialects, Xerente, and extinct Akroá and Xakriabá);
C. Northwest Jê subfamily (1.   East Timbira language: Canela, Krinkatí, Gavião, Krahó, nearly extinct
Krenjê, and several extinct local dialects; 2.
Apinajé-Kayapó language: Apinajé and several Nor-
thern Kayapó dialects; 3. Suyá language).

Southern Kayapó is an unclassified Jê language.
II. The Maxakalían family consists of several Maxakalí dialects, all extinct except one; and Pataxó

and Malalí, both of which are extinct or nearly so.
III.  The Karajá family contains Karajá proper, Javahé, and Xamboiá, probably all dialects of a single language.  Unclassified Macro-Jê languages are:
Jeikó, Ofayé, Kamakanian (including Kamakan, Kuta-
xó, Masakará, and related languages or dialects),
Purían (including Purí, Coroado, and Koropó), Botocudo (including several dialects).  All of these
are either extinct or on the verge of extinction.

Maxakalí and Karajá are included in the same
stock with the Jê languages on the basis of the
fact that regular sound correspondences are detec-
table in a relatively small corpus of data and on
the basis of lexical similarity.  Lexicostatistical
comparisons based on the Swadesh 100 word-list show
about 25% shared cognates between Maxakalí or Karajá and individual Jê languages.

Languages listed as unclassified Macro-Jê are
included largely on an impressionistic basis.  Jeikó has long been extinct and is known only through
a fragmentary word list collected by Martius early
in the last century (Martius 1867).  It is placed in
the Jê family in most classifications on the basis
of some obvious similarities to the Jê languages.
The most likely cognates in the data are: Proto Jê
*krã, Jeikó grangblá head; Proto Jê *-mu, Jeikó
u(l)epu to see; Proto Jê *nã, Jeikó ná mother;
Proto Jê *nõtɔ, Jeikó aenettá tongue; Proto Jê *pa,
Jeikó aepang arm; Proto Jê *par, Jeikó aephahno
foot; and Proto Jê *zazkwa, Jeikó aingkó mouth.
Most comparable Jeikó items, however, show no similarity to reconstructed Proto Jê forms, and it is

probable that the language does not belong in the
Jê family but rather elsewhere in the Macro-Jê
stock.

Ofayé has generally been placed outside of the
Macro-Jê stock.    Until recently very little data
were available for this language formerly spoken in
southern Mato Grosso.    A few years ago considerable
data were obtained by Sarah Gudschinsky from one of
the last survivors of the tribe, and evidence presented in an unpublished paper shows this language
to be related to Jê.

In colonial times a group of non-Tupi tribes occupied a large area of what is now the state of
Bahia as well as northern Minas Gerais and Espirito
Santo.    Loukotka has examined the available linguistic data for a number of these tribes and has
concluded that they are related to Jê (1931, 1932,
1937, 1955). He groups the languages into four
families (corresponding to Maxakalían, Kamakanian,
Purían, and Botocudo in the present listing), and
cites some lexical similarities in support of their
relationship to Jê. The similarities involve a
number of items that can be reconstructed for Proto
Jê and are sufficient to establish beyond reaso-
nable doubt the fact that Kamakanian, Purían, and
Botocudo do indeed belong within Macro-Jê.    The
exact classification of these languages will require a more thorough comparative study.    In some
cases this, unfortunately, may not be possible at
this late date.    The Purían languages have been
extinct for some time and only fragmentary vocabularies exist.    Languages of the Kamakanian group

may also be extinct, but as late as in the 1930's a
vocabulary was collected by Guérios (1940).  For
Botocudo there probably remain a few individuals
who can recall some of the language.  In each case
the written data are meager and the possibilities
of field work either non-existent or fast becoming
so.

Languages within the Jê family show at least 40%
shared cognates when compared one to another in
contrast to a maximum of about 30% when compared to
other Macro-Jê languages.  Each family within the
Macro-Jê stock is furthermore characterized by
certain unique phonological developments.  Maxakalían, for example, is characterized by the splitting of velars to yield palatals in some environments and the retention of velars in other environments.  Karajá, on the other hand, is characterized
by the double reflection of */r/.

Maxakalían includes, in addition to modern Maxakalí spoken by an indigenous community in northeastern Minas Gerais, a number of languages and
dialects now extinct or practically so.  The internal classification of the Maxakalían family is a
task that involves the same difficulties as those
faced in the comparative study of Purían, Kamakanian, and Botocudo.

The Karajá family is represented by Javahé and
Xamboiá in addition to Karajá proper, although data
are available only for the latter.  It is reported
that there is a high degree of mutual intelligibility among the three tribes, but the exact nature
and extent of dialect differences is unknown.

One Jê language, Southern Kayapó, is listed as unclassified. Although the language is now extinct, there are several word lists available. A careful examination of the data may result in the assigning of Southern Kayapó to one of the known Jê subfamilies, or as itself a coordinate subfamily.

Languages within each of the Jê subfamilies yield a minimum of 70% shared cognates when compared one with another, in contrast to a maximum of about 60% when compared with languages of other subfamilies. In addition, each subfamily is characterized by unique phonological developments. Kaingangan, for example, shows /f/ or /ɖ/ as a reflex of */z/ in some initial positions. Central Jê has /h/ as reflex of */k/ before a mid central vowel, and Northwest Jê shows /s/, /h/, or /?/ as reflexes of */z/ in certain initial environments.

The internal structures of the Kaingangan and Central Jê subfamilies are not entirely clear. Further comparative study may clarify the picture and reveal whether diversity within each subfamily is merely dialect difference or whether distinct languages need to be recognized.[4] Taven and Dorin, often listed as Kaingangan languages, probably represent Kaingang subgroups that no longer exist as distinct entities.

The Northwest Jê subfamily includes three distinct languages, two of which have numerous dialects. Lexical comparisons between dialects of the same language show a minimum of 80% shared cognates in contrast to a maximum of 75% in comparisons involving dialects of different languages. Reflexes

of Proto Jê̂ */z/ also serve to distinguish the
three languages.  East Timbira shows /?/, Apinajé-
Kayapó shows /h/, and Suya shows /s/ as initial
reflexes of */z/ in certain environments.

Finally, it remains to note certain facts relating to possible wider relationships of the Macro-
Jê̂ languages--relationships of phylum order.  There
are in Brazil at least three languages or language
families not included in Macro-Jê̂ but which show
quite striking similarities to the Macro-Jê̂ languages.  These are Borôro, the Tupi languages, and
Fulnió.

Guérios has published evidence showing similarities between Borôro and certain Jê̂ languages
(1939).  Some of the similarities, particularly
those involving pronominal prefixes, are impressive, but the evidence needs to be expanded and
systemized before it can be taken as proof of genetic relationship.

The resemblances between Tupi and Jê̂ languages
involve similarities in general structure as well
as many lexical similarities.  Even a cursory examination of the available data reveals a good number of possible cognates.  The following possibilities are drawn from my Proto Jê̂ reconstructions and
the Proto Tupi forms listed by Hanke, Swadesh, and
Rodrígues (1958): Proto Jê̂ *ma, Proto Tupi *pɨa
liver; Proto Jê̂ *mzɛn, Proto Tupi *men husband;
Proto Jê̂ *ŋo, Proto Tupi *ɨgɨ water; Proto Jê̂ *ŋo,
Proto Tupi *ŋkɨv louse; Proto Jê̂ *paarm, Proto Tupi
*po hand; Proto Jê̂ *par, Proto Tupi *pɨ foot.
Comparisons with individual Tupi languages reveal

further possibilities: Proto Jê * krã, krãñ, Guajajara kaŋ- head; Proto Jê *ku, kur, Guajajara -?u to
eat; Proto Jê *prɨ, Guajajara pɛ path; Proto Jê
*pɨci, pɨcit, Guajajara pitci one.

   Fulniô is listed by Greenberg as an unclassified
Macro-Jê language, but to my knowledge no evidence
for this supposed relationship has been published.
With a good amount of Fulniô data now becoming
available it may be possible to demonstrate such a
relationship through careful comparative techniques.[5] The similarities in pronominal prefixes are
quite striking. Both Jê and Fulniô have first
person i- and second person a- prefixes. In addition, there are numerous other possible cognates,
including some that suggest a correspondence between Proto Jê */p/ and Fulniô /f/: Proto Jê *prə,
Fulniô fèlòwã ashes; Proto Jê *par, Fulniô fehe
foot; Proto Jê *pika, Fulniô f'è'ā earth.

   If these suggested relationships can be demonstrated, existing classifications of Brazilian languages will have to be radically revised. This
possibility, however, must await more extensive reconstructions within the Macro-Jê and Tupi groups,
as well as a closer examination of the Borôro and
Fulniô data.

ACKNOWLEDGEMENTS
The editors of this volume gratefully acknowledge
permission from the International Journal of American Linguistics, Irvine Davis and the University of
Chicago Press to reprint this article which originally appeared in 1968.

NOTES

1.  The spelling of language and tribal names in
    this paper closely follows current Brazilian
    usage. The symbol x indicates a voiceless al-
    veopalatal sibilant and j represents its voiced
    counterpart. Other consonantal symbols have
    their normal values. Accent marks are placed
    over stressed vowels. In addition, these marks
    distinguish stressed mid open é and ó from
    stressed mid close ê and ô.

2.  The Karajá data are from David Fortune of the
    Summer Institute of Linguistics who collabora-
    ted with the author in lining up possible Jê-
    Karajá cognates. The Maxakalí data are from
    material filed at the Museu Nacional, Rio de
    Janeiro by Harold Popovich of the Summer Insti-
    tute of Linguistics. The Jê items are my re-
    constructions based on a comparison of Canela,
    Apinajé, Suyá, Xavante, and Kaingang. The data
    for these languages were collected largely by
    members of the Summer Institute of Linguistics
    and are on file at the Museu Nacional.

3.  Members of the 'nasal' series are realized
    variously as nasal continuants, pre-nasalized or
    post-nasalized voice stops, or even as simple
    voiced stops, depending on the specific environ-
    ment and on the language involved. These are
    sometimes symbolized, as in the present Karajá
    data, by the normal voiced stop symbols.

4.  A preliminary study of Kaingangan dialects
    found in Ursula Wiesemann, Notas sôbre Proto-

Kaingang: Um Estudo de Quatro Dialetos, to be
published.
5. Fulniô data are from Douglas Meland of the
Summer Institute of Linguistics.

REFERENCES
Davis, Irvine. 1966. Comparative Jê Phonology,
Estudos Lingüísticos 1.2:10-25.
Ehrenreich, Paul. 1894. Materialen zur Sprachen-
kunde Brasiliens,II: Die Sprache der Caraya
(Goyaz). Zeitschrift für Ethnologie 26: 20-37,
49-60.
Gudschinsky, Sarah C. n.d. Ofayé-Xavante, Uma
Lingua Jê. Unpublished manuscript.
Guérios, R.F. Mansur. 1939. O Nexo Lingüístico
Bororo-Merrime-Caiapó. Revista do Circulo de
Estudos 'Bandeirantes'. Tomo 2.1 (Curitiba).
------. 1940. Estudos sôbre a língua Camacã,
Arquivos do Museu Paranaense, IV (Curitiba).
Hanke, W., M. Swadesh, and A. Rodrígues, 1958.
Notas de Fonologia Mekens, Miscellanea Paul
Rivet, 187-217 (Mexico).
Loukotka, Chestmír. 1931. La Familia Lingüística
Maŝakali. Revista del Instituto de Etnologia
(Tucumán) 2. 21-47.
------. 1932. La Familia Lingüística Kamakan del
Brasil. Revista del Instituto de Etnologia
(Tucumán) 2. 493-524.
------. 1937. La Familia Lingüística Coroado.
Journal de la Société des Américanistes (Paris)
29. 157-214.

------. 1955. Les Indiens Botocudo et leur Langue. Lingua Posnaniensis 5. 112-135.

Martius, Carl Friederich Phil. v. 1867. Beiträge zur Ethnographie und Sprachenkunde Amerikas zumal Brasiliens, II (Leipzig).

# 7. Nambiquara Languages: Linguistic and Geographical Distance between Speech Communities

## David Price

INTRODUCTION

The Nambiquara languages are spoken by American Indians living in the western part of the state of Mato Grosso and adjacent parts of the territory of Rondônia, Brazil. The area traditionally inhabited by these Indians was on the order of 50,000 km$^2$, and within this region they were divided into some 25 regional clusters of villages, usually coinciding with the drainage basins of particular streams. Social relations between villages of the same cluster were generally more intense than between villages of different clusters, owing to their geographical proximity. But the village cluster did not constitute a clearly defined ethnic unit, as described by Barth (1969). Although individuals of particular ability might come to exercise a limited hegemony over a group of neighboring villages, no leader was recognized as having authority over all the villages in the cluster. While most marriages were contracted between villages of the same cluster, there was no rule that this ought to be so. And whereas more distant neighbors found it convenient to have a name for the cluster, members of the cluster had no name for themselves.

Since representatives of Western society have been unable to cope with the idea of unlabeled so-

cial aggregates, there has been a tendency to understand all manner of spurious locutions as 'tribal names'. Many of the supposed group designations that appear in the literature are, in fact,
kin terms. Most of these erroneous designations
came into being early in this century, when Col.
Cândido Mariano da Silva Rondon built a telegraph
line through the Nambiquara area. A passage in his
Conferencias vividly describes the kind of meeting
between Brazilians and Indians in which such errors
must have arisen. In 1912, he and two companions
visited a village in the northern part of the Nambiquara region. It is clear that both parties to
the encounter were determined to show their peaceful intentions, although severely handicapped in
their ability to communicate by the fact that neither spoke the other's language. Shortly after the
Brazilians' arrival, a new group of ten Indians,
carrying their bows and arrows as if returning from
the hunt, appeared in the village. Rondon says,

> We later learned that these ten indivi-
> duals came from a village of Tagananis
> located in the same savannahs, not very
> far from where we were, and that there
> were still other villages in the region,
> belonging to groups of Tauitês, Minis and
> Tachiuvitês (1916:147, my translation).

We must suppose that when the Brazilians pointed to
the newly arrived Indians, their hosts understood
that they wanted to know who these people were, for

the terms Taganani, Tauité, Mini and Tachiuvité are
clearly decipherable as my brother, my son, father
and my grandson. However, the Brazilians did not
realize that these words referred to kin relations,
but assumed that they were names for some sort of
ethnic units. Thus much of the early literature
refers to 'bands' of Tagananis, Tauités, etc.

COMPARATIVE STUDIES

There are several published Nambiquara vocabularies
(Albuquerque 1910, Boglár 1960, Campos 1936, Lévi-
Strauss 1948a, Listas de vocábulos nambiquaras
1942, Oberg 1953, Rondon 1947, Rondon and Faria
1948, Roquette-Pinto 1913 and 1935, Schmidt 1928,
Souza 1920). Unfortunately, however, the majority
of these vocabularies are attributed to spuriously
named 'bands'. To make matters worse, many of them
were taken from Indians encountered outside the
regions where they lived, when they came to visit
and trade along the telegraph line. Thus, to pick
a typical example, a 'Taganani' vocabulary taken at
Telegraph Post José Bonifácio gives almost no clue
as to what people spoke the language in question,
or where they actually lived. We find ourselves in
the position of the boy at the end of Bergman's The
Silence, idly fingering a list of 'words in an
unknown language'.

    The same kind of misunderstanding that gave rise
to spurious names for local groups also produced
many erroneous entries in the sample vocabularies.
Albuquerque, for instance, lists a term for the
straw that a Nambiquara man wears through his upper

lip, which, however, merely means <u>mouth</u>. And for
<u>egg</u>, he gives a phrase which actually means <u>the</u>
<u>chicken</u> <u>over</u> <u>there</u> (1910:146). Many of the voca-
bularies contain a high proportion of spurious en-
tries of this type, which makes different dialects
appear more divergent than they really are. Thus,
Aytai's (1972) application of lexicostatistical methods to published material suggests considerable
time depth between dialects that are, in fact, very
similar.

A further difficulty for the comparativist is
the fact that the majority of the published vocabularies were transcribed by persons with no formal
training in linguistics, who tended to encode more
of what is distinctive in their own languages than
what is distinctive in Nambiquara. Thus, Unrazú is
hardly recognizable as a $h\tilde{u}^3$ $li^3$ $\underline{yau}^3$ $\underline{su}^3$ $\underline{water}^2$, and
Urinodzú barely passes muster as wa$^3$ $lin^3$ n'u$^3$ su$^2$
<u>manioc</u> <u>dough</u>. Some entries are even further remo-
ved from phonological reality, owing, apparently,
to a mis-reading of handwriting. Such is the case
with Aiutchú, which should have been Aintchú, for
ain$^3$ su$^2$ <u>fish</u>. These examples from Roquette-Pinto
(1935:345-6), who double-checked his material and
consciously selected his orthographic system
(1935:259, 261), show the inadequacy of such
wordlists for detailed phonological comparison.

Nevertheless, there have been at least five attempts to describe the internal structure of the
Nambiquara family. Roquette-Pinto (1935:213-14)
presents no criteria for his classification, and it
is probable that social as well as linguistic data

were utilized.  Lévi-Strauss distinguishes among
speech communities primarily on the basis of the
geographical distribution of a single verbal suffix
(1948b:7-13).  Rondon and Faria present, without
comment, three parallel columns for inspection
(1948:27-73).  Loukotka presents nine columns of 12
words each for inspection (1968:96-99); and Aytai
gives lexicostatistical results for a comparison
involving eight dialects, without presenting the
data (1972:129-145).  The results of these studies
are confusing, and leave one in doubt about the
number of different languages or dialects spoken,
their degree of similarity or difference, the regions in which they are spoken, and their relationship to the traditional social organization.

In an effort to ameliorate this confusion, I
made a formal comparison of Nambiquara phonological
reflexes,[1] using new,[2] carefully transcribed materials (Price 1978).  I used data from three speech
communities: the Kithãulhú, who live on the middle
course of the Rio Camararezinho; the Mamaindê, who
live on the Rios Cabixi and Pardo; and the Sabanê,
a group whose last survivors live intermingled with
other Nambiquara in the northern part of the region.  While a relationship has long been recognized between the languages spoken by the Kithãulhú
and the Mamaindê, the status of Sabanê has remained
in doubt.  Lévi-Strauss questions whether it really
belongs to the Nambiquara family (1948b:10), and
Mason says that it seems to have some Aruak elements (1950:284).  It also appears as Aruak on the
generally excellent Carta do Estado de Mato Grosso

(Rondon 1952:5). Loukotka classifies it as Nambiquara, but he apparently does so on the basis of
only five words (1968:98).

My own comparison shows that Kithãulhú, Mamaindê, and Sabanê are clearly members of the same linguistic family, but different enough so that they
should be considered separate languages. All previously published wordlists are close to one or
another of these three languages except for "Ta-
uitê" (Roquette-Pinto 1935:344) which may be intermediate between Kithãulhú and Mamaindê. Elsewhere
(Price and Cook 1969), I have called Kithãulhú and
allied dialects Southern Nambiquara, and Mamaindê
and allied dialects Northern Nambiquara. Lévi-
Strauss calls Southern Nambiquara, Northern Nambiquara, and Sabanê languages a, b, and c (1948:
8-12).

GEOGRAPHICAL DISTRIBUTION
The geographical areas in which these three languages are spoken remain to be defined, although
the data at hand are not adequate for a detailed
dialectic geography. In 1967-69, I recorded vocabularies in 15 Nambiquara dialects, but experience
has shown that this material does not lend itself
to careful phonological analysis, and the inclusion
of a certain number of spurious responses tends to
exaggerate dialectal differences based on lexical
measures. However, in the course of numerous trips
to various parts of the Nambiquara region, I have
developed a certain sensitivity to dialectal variation. I have an extremely deficient but pragmatic

control of the Kithãulhú dialect, and this has
helped me to perceive both range and variation in
the Southern language.  At times I have also traveled in the company of Indians whose adjustment to
differing speech communities could be observed and
discussed.

The range of the Southern language extends
northward from the Rio Sararé, down the Guaporé
Valley and across the Chapada dos Parecis as far as
the Rio Iquê (see map).  Descriptive studies have
been published by Kroeker (1982), Lowe (1972), and
Price (1976).  Four major dialects, called Campo,
Manduca, Guaporé, and Sararé, can be distinguished.  The range of the Northern language extends
northward from the Rio Piolho to the headwaters of
the Rio Roosevelt.  Excellent descriptive work by
Kingston (eg. 1970) remains unpublished.  Several
dialects can be distinguished.

No one knows exactly where the Sabanê lived
before contact with Western society.  In 1949 an
Indian agent wrote that they were living 'promis-
cuously' intermingled with the other Nambiquara
(França 1949), and today, none of the surviving
Sabanê knows where they originally came from.
Lévi-Strauss puts them on the Rio Ananaz (Tenente
Marques) (1948b:9), in accordance with Rondon's
statement that when they visited the telegraph
line, they came 'more than twenty leagues from the
north' (Rondon 1916:149). However, on the map of
Mato Grosso whose production Rondon, himself, su-
pervised, the Sabanê are shown to the west of Vil-

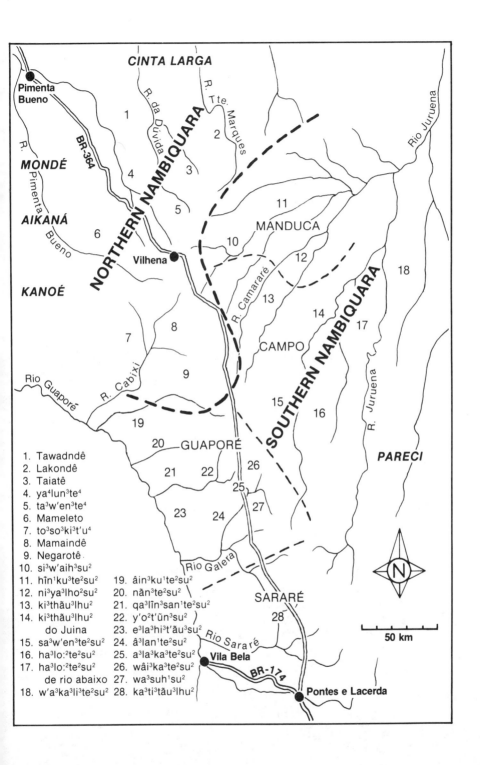

CINTA LARGA

Pimenta
Bueno

MONDÉ

AIKANÁ

KANOÉ

NORTHERN NAMBIQUARA

Vilhena

MANDUCA

SOUTHERN NAMBIQUARA

CAMPO

GUAPORÉ

PARECI

SARARÉ

Vila Bela

Pontes e Lacerda

N

50 km

1. Tawadndê
2. Lakondê
3. Taiatê
4. ya⁴lun³te⁴
5. ta³w'en³te⁴
6. Mameleto
7. to³so³ki³t'u⁴
8. Mamaindê
9. Negarotê.
10. si³w'aih³su²
11. hĩn¹ku³te²su²
12. ni³ya³lho²su²
13. ki³thãu³lhu²
14. ki³thãu³lhu²
    do Juina
15. sa³w'en³te²su²
16. ha³lo:²te²su²
17. ha³lo:²te²su²
    de rio abaixo
18. w'a³ka³li³te²su²

19. âin³ku¹te²su²
20. nãn³te²su²
21. qa³lĩn³san¹te²su²
22. y'o²t'ũn³su²
23. e³la³hi³t'ãu³su²
24. â³lan¹te²su²
25. a³la³ka³te²su²
26. wâi³ka³te²su²
27. wa³suh¹su²
28. ka³ti³tãu³lhu²

hena, on the headwaters of the Rio Pimenta Bueno
(Rondon 1952:5).

In order to decide between these alternatives, I
compared a Sabanê vocabulary with material from
three languages to the west of Vilhena (Kanoé, Aikaná, Mondé) and one to the north (Cinta Larga-
Gavião). None of these languages is supposed to be
related to the Nambiquara family (Loukotka 1968:
163, Rodrigues 1969:4035-36), so shared lexical
material should be the result of borrowing, and
thus an indication of the degree of historical proximity. The proportion of apparent cognates identified by simple inspection was 34% for Kanoé, 28%
for Aikaná, and 23% for Mondé, but only 13% for
Cinta Larga-Gavião. Comparativists such as Matteson (1972) would interpret all of these percentages
as indicating a common origin. I suspect that
Kanoé may, in fact, be distantly related to the
Nambiquara family, but the available evidence
(Becker-Donner 1955:298-321, 336-39; Bontkes 1967;
Nimuendajú 1955:196-97) does not permit a clear
determination.[3] On the other hand, neither Aikaná
nor Mondé seem related to the Nambiquara languages,
so the relatively high percentage of cognates they
share with Sabanê does appear to suggest historical
proximity.

While the Nambiquara must have numbered in the
thousands at the beginning of this century, their
population has been reduced to some 650 individuals. About 50 of these are children who are
probably more comfortable speaking Portuguese than
the languages of their parents. Of the remainder,

approximately 425 speak Southern Nambiquara, 150
speak Northern Nambiquara, and 25 speak Sabané.[4]
Despite the social upheaval consequent to massive
depopulation, it is possible to make a few observations on the correlation between ecology and
linguistic variation, and on the social manipula-
tion of this variation.

An examination of the map reveals that minor
linguistic differences are generally correlated
with different river systems. Within the Junuena
drainage, the Manduca dialect group tends to be
associated with the tributaries of the Camararé,
and the Campo dialect group with the other tributaries of the Juruena.[5] In the Guaporé Valley,
there is a clear division between the dialect of
the Rio Sararé and that of the Rio Galera. On the
headwaters of the Roosevelt, there is a distinction
between the dialect of the Rio da Dúvida and that
of the Tenente Marques. In general, the divisions
between dialects tend to lie in open savannahs.
Each village cluster, exploiting the fertile agricultural lands in the vicinity of a particular
stream, formed a speech community whose linguistic
patterns tended to drift apart from those of other
communities, on other streams.

But major linguistic differences do not correlate with the drainage basins of major rivers, as
might be expected. The Southern and Northern languages both cross over the watershed that divides
streams flowing southwest into the Rio Guaporé from
streams flowing north and east into the Ji-Paraná,
Roosevelt, and Juruena. The position of the Nambi-

quara, straddling the height of land between the farthest headwaters of major rivers, suggests that they represent the last remnants of a people who have only managed to survive in this relatively inaccessible region. But the fact that the two languages cross the height of land with only minor dialectal differences suggests that settlement on both sides of the divide has been relatively recent. Documentary and ethnohistorical evidence tends to support this hypothesis; it is probable that the Nambiquara moved out onto the Chapada after the Pareci were nearly exterminated by slaving expeditions in the eighteenth century (Price 1983).

RELATIONS BETWEEN SPEECH COMMUNITIES

The Nambiquara are very conscious of dialectal differences, and are prone to make deprecatory remarks about forms of speech that differ from their own. A 14-year-old ha$^3$ lo$^2$ te$^2$ su$^2$ was able to list, without hesitation, four words that were different in ki$^3$ thãu$^3$ lhu$^2$, illustrating a lexical substitution and two phonological reflexes. The extent of dialectal difference is sometimes exaggerated, as when I overheard a Kithãulhú doing a derogatory imitation of the Guaporé manner of speaking, in which he pronounced all occurrences of /l/ in the male interlocutor morpheme as (l), although the people imitated actually use (r) after front vowels. When recording a vocabulary with the wa$^3$ suh$^1$ su$^2$, I discovered that my informant was purposely choosing uncommon synonyms for common terms, so as to make his language appear as different as possible from

that of the w'a ka li te su [3 3 3 2 2] who accompanied me.
Dialectal differences serve as important markers of
membership in the various village clusters, streng-
thening group identity by separating the speech of
one community from that of another.

But the Nambiquara try not to let linguistic
differences interfere with communication.  I once
travelled to the Mamaindê, accompanied by a [3 3 3 2 2]
w'a ka li te su  who had never before heard Northern Nambiquara.  At first, he looked a bit puz-
zled, and seemed to be listening very intently.
Then, after a day in the village, he began to con-
verse in an ad hoc pidgin consisting of roots from
which he had dropped the inflectional affixes, and
which he was attempting to modify in the direction
of Mamaindê phonology.  Similarly, when I went to
the central Guaporé valley, the Indians adopted my
Kithãulhú way of speaking so rapidly that it was
quite some time before I realized that they used
different forms in speaking with each other than
they did with me.  Lévi-Strauss's material shows
that the w'a ka li te su [3 3 3 2 2] modified their language
enormously in an effort to make themselves understood (cf.  Price 1972:184, note 12), and there is
a suggestion that the Nambiquara were dropping inflectional affixes in an effort to communicate during their earliest contacts with Brazilian society.[6]

This linguistic adaptability is certainly facilitated by the fact that all the Nambiquara languages employ similar phonological systems.  When
people who speak one language visit speakers of

another language, they need not learn to hear and produce new sounds in order to communicate. They only need to produce familiar sounds in combinations that might have occurred in their own language. And core vocabulary that has the greatest pragmatic utility is highly cognate between all speech communities, even including, up to a point, Sabanê. Thus a quick adaptation to a new speech community can be achieved by simply narrowing the code to what is common to both the language of the visitor and the language of the hosts. Such a code, supplemented by gestures when necessary, is usually quite adequate for practical, every-day concerns. In 1912, only a short while after contact, Roquette-Pinto remarked on the linguistic adaptability of the Nambiquara. He wrote, "The Indians of [this region] speak different but related dialects. With each [person] speaking his own language, they understand each other very well" (1935:257).

Traditional Nambiquara social organization rested on a balance between factionalism and matrimonial alliance. Imminent hostility between villages was held in check by the frequent necessity to contract exogamous marriages. As the village cluster was a simple result of ecological variables and not clearly definable as an ethnic unit, the relations between villages of the same and different clusters were more a matter of degree than kind. Villages of the same cluster intermarried more frequently and fought less; villages of different clusters

intermarried less and fought more. But villages of
different clusters did sometimes intermarry; they
did maintain alliances so as to assure access to
scarce economic goods; and they probably did, as
they do now, occasionally accept each others'
dissidents. Thus, while membership in the close-
ly-knit village cluster fostered a pride in one's
own way of speaking, continued interaction with
other clusters tended to inhibit too radical a
differentiation between dialects. A situation of
dynamic tension between hostility and alliance
favors dialects that differ just enough, but not
too much.

ACKNOWLEDGEMENTS
Research among the Nambiquara was carried out under
fellowship 1-H1-MH-31,735-01A1 BEH-B from the National Institute of Mental Health and grant GS-1839
3-5631-xx-1650 from the National Science Foundation
in 1967-1970, as well as a grant from the Programa
de Pós-Graduação em Antropologia Social, Instituto
de Ciências Humanas, Universidade de Brasília, from
December 1973 through March 1974. From August 1974
through July 1976, I worked with the Nambiquara for
the Fundação Nacional do Indio.

I want to thank the editors of this volume for
giving me an opportunity to present this updated
version of Price 1978 (and to Anthropological Linguistics for their permission to do so). Readers
interested in the details of the comparison should
consult the original study.

NOTES

1.   Under pressure from Brazilians and missiona-
     ries, many Nambiquara have come to accept names
     for their village clusters.  The materials used
     in my analysis come from three groups now widely
     known as Kithãulhú, Mamaindê, and Sabanê.
Their phonological inventories are:


     Kithãulhú         Mamaindê         Sabanê


Consonants:

| p | t | k | q | ' |   | p | t | k | q | ' |   | p | t | k |   | ' |
|---|---|---|---|---|---|---|---|---|---|---|---|---|---|---|---|---|
| s |   |   | h |   |   | s |   |   | h |   |   | s |   |   |   | h |
| l |   |   |   |   |   | l |   |   |   |   |   | l |   |   |   |   |
| n |   |   |   |   |   | m | n |   |   |   |   | m | n |   |   |   |
| w | y |   |   |   |   | w | y |   |   |   |   | w | y |   |   |   |


Vowels:

| i |   | u |   | i |   | u |   | i |   | u |
|---|---|---|---|---|---|---|---|---|---|---|
| e |   | o |   | e |   | o |   | e | ə | o |
|   | a |   |   | ai |   | a |   | ai |   | a |
| ai | au |   |   | iw |   | ow |   |   |   |   |
|   |   |   |   | ew |   | aw |   |   |   |   |


Length:

    V:    V        V:    V        V:    V

Tones:

    1  2  3      1  2  3  4      3  4

Nasalization:

    $\tilde{V}$  V        $\tilde{V}$  V        $\tilde{V}$(?)  V

Laryngealization:

    $\underline{V}$  V        $\underline{V}$  V        $\underline{V}$(?)  V

In most respects the orthography used in this paper
conforms to the one approved for use in the Nambiquara literacy program (Kindell et al. 1975).
2. The Sabanê word list used in my comparison was
taken from Iracema, a woman who had married into
the Kithãulhú-speaking village of Camararé.
Since Price 1978 was published, I have transcribed and compared a vocabulary taped with Joaquim
Idalamaré, an old Sabanê man who resided with
other Sabanê speakers at Posto Pyreneus de Souza. I found a few differences, but none that
would materially change the outcome of the comparison.
3. Bontkes only found 12 surviving Kanoé in 1967.
Hopefully, someone will make a serious study of
their language before it becomes extinct.
4. These figures are for 1982. I am grateful to
Pe. António Iasi and José Eduardo F. M. Costa
for furnishing up-to-date census data.
5. I have shown the dialect boundary between Manduca and Campo as crossing the Rios Camararé and
Camararezinho. This is because I am inclined to
class ki³ thãu³ lhu² as a Campo dialect. I am
aware, however, that it is really intermediate
between the other Campo dialects and Manduca,
and the fact that I am more familiar with the
other Campo dialects than with Manduca may have
influenced my decision. Further, detailed study
might well show that ki³ thãu³ lhu² is closer
to Manduca, in which case the major dialect
boundary would run between the Camararezinho and
the tributaries of the Juina.

6.  Albuquerque understood "Ari" as meaning 'water'
    (1910:143). This form is quite different from
    the word for 'water,' but very like a li$^3$-$^1$, the
    root for 'clean.'

## REFERENCES

Albuquerque, Severiano Godofredo de. 1910. Rela-
    tório dos serviços executados em Campos-Novos da
    Serra do Norte. Relatorios Diversos; Publicação
    No. 37 da Commissão de Linhas Telegraphicas
    Estrategicas de Matto Grosso ao Amazonas, Annexo
    No. 4:135-147. N.d.; Rio de Janeiro: Papelaria
    Luiz Macedo.

Aytai, Desidério. 1972. Os cantores da floresta,
    parte IV: A origem dos índios Mamaindê, Revis-
    ta da Universidade Católica de Campinas 16:
    129-45.

Becker-Donner, Etta. 1955. Notizen über einige
    Stämme an den rechten Zuflüssen des Rio Guaporé,
    Archiv für Völkerkunde 10:275-343.

Barth, Fredrik. 1969. Introduction. In Ethnic
    Groups and Boundaries, F. Barth, ed., pp. 9-38.
    Boston: Little, Brown and Co.

Boglár, Lajos. 1960. Nambiquara vocabulary. Acta
    Ethnographica 9:89-117.

Bontkes, Willem. 1967. Formulário dos vocabulá-
    rios padrões para estudos comparativos preli-
    minares nas línguas indígenas brasileiras:
    Kanoê. Archive of the Summer Institute of
    Linguistics, Brasilia.

Campos, Murillo de Sousa. 1936. Interior do
    Brasil. Rio de Janeiro: Borsoi and Cia.

França, Afonso Mansur de.  1949.  Aviso do Posto
    Cel.  Pirineus  de Souza, março de 1949.
    Arquivo da 5a DR da FUNAI, Cuiabá, Mato Grosso.

Kindell, Gloria; Menno H. Kroeker; Barbara J. Kroe-
    ker; Ivan Lowe; Peter Kenneth Ewart Kingston and
    P. David Price.  1975.   Relatório de conferên-
    cia sobre a ortografia nambikuára - 19 a 25 de
    abril de 1975.  Typescript in the archive of the
    Summer Institute of Linguistics, Brasília.

Kingston, Peter K. E.  1970.  Mamaindê syllables.
    Unpublished manuscript in the archive of the
    Summer Institute of Linguistics, Brasília.

Kroeker, Barbara.  1982.  Aspectos da língua nambi-
    kuara. Brasília: Summer Institute of Linguis-
    tics.

Lévi-Strauss, Claude.  1948a.  Sur certaines simi-
    larités structurales des langues Chibcha et Nam-
    bikwara.  Actes du 28ᵉ Congrès International
    des Américanistes, 185-192. Paris.

------.  1948b.  La vie familiale et sociale des in-
    diens Nambikwara, Journal de la Société des Amé-
    ricanistes de Paris 37:1-32.

Listas de vocábulos nambiquaras.  1942.  Imprimatur
    Aloisius Riou, SJ.  São Paulo.

Loukotka, Cestmír.  1968.  Classification of South
    American Indian Languages.  Los Angeles: Univer-
    sity of California Press.

Lowe, Ivan.  1972.  On the relation of formal to
    semantic matrices with illustrations from Nambi-
    quara.  Foundations of Language 8:360-90.

Mason, J. Alden.  1950.  The Languages of South
    American Indians. Smithsonian Institution: BAE-B

143: Handbook of South American Indians, Julian
H. Steward, ed.  6:157-317.

Matteson, Esther.  1972.  Toward Proto-Amerindian.
In Comparative Studies in Amerindian Languages,
ed. E. Matteson, A. Wheeler, F. L. Jackson, N.E.
Waltz, and D.R. Christian, pp. 21-89.  The
Hague: Mouton.

Nimuendajú, Curt.  1955.  Vocabulários Makuší,
Wapičána, Ipurinã, e Kapišanã, Journal de la
Société des Américanistes de Paris 44:179-97.

Oberg, Kalervo.  1953.  Indian Tribes of Northern
Mato Grosso, Brazil. Smithsonian Institution:
Institute of Social Anthropology Publication No.
15.  Washington, D.C.: Government Printing
Office.

Price, P. David.  1972.  Nambiquara Society.
Unpublished PhD dissertation, Department of
Anthropology, University of Chicago.

------.  1976.  Southern Nambiquara phonology, IJAL
42:338-48.

------.  1978.  The Nambiquara linguistic family.
AL 20:14-37.

------.  1983.  Pareci, Cabixi, Nambiquara: A case
study in the Western classification of native
peoples.  Journal de la Société des Américanistes 69:129-48.

Price, P. David and Cecil E. Cook, Jr.  1969.  The
present situation of the Nambiquara, AA 71:
688-93.

[Rodrígues, Aryon D.] [1969] Língua: Línguas amerindias.  In Grande Enciclopédia Delta Larousse,
pp. 4034-36.  Rio de Janeiro: Editora Delta.

Rondon, Cândido Mariano da Silva. 1916. Conferencias realizadas nos dias 5, 7 e 9 de outubro
de 1915 pelo Sr. Coronel... no theatro Phenix
do Rio de Janeiro... Publicação n. 42 da Commissão de Linhas Telegraphicas Estrategicas de
Matto Grosso ao Amazonas. Rio de Janeiro: Typ.
Leuzinger.

------. 1947. História natural: etnografia. Publicação no. 2 da Commissão de Linhas Telegráficas
de Mato-Grosso ao Amazonas; Annexo No. 5. Rio
de Janeiro: Imprensa Nacional.

------. 1952. Carta do Estado de Mato Grosso e
regiões circunvizinhas. Escala 1:1,000.000.
Serviço de Conclusão da Carta de Mato Grosso
(Ministério da Guerra), sob a direção de Can-
dido Mariano da Silva Rondon.

Rondon, Cândido Mariano da Silva and João Barbosa
de Faria. 1948. Glossário geral das tribos sil-
vícolas de Mato-Grosso e outras da Amazonia e do
norte do Brasil. Publicação n. 76 da Comissão
Rondon, Anexo No. 5. Rio de Janeiro: Imprensa
Nacional.

Roquette-Pinto, E. 1913. Os indios Nhambiquára do
Brasil-Central. Proceedings of the 18th International Congress of Americanists, 382-387. London: Harrison and Sons.

------. 1935. Rondonia. São Paulo: Companhia Editora Nacional. 3ᵃ edição.

Schmidt, Max. 1928. Ergebnisse meiner zweijähri-
gen Forschungsreise in Matto Grosso: September
1926 bis August 1928. Zeitschrift für Ethnologie 60:85-124.

Souza, António Pyreneus de.   1920.   Notas sobre os
costumes dos índios Nhambiquaras, Revista do
Museu Paulista 12:391-410.

# 8. A Survey of the Carib Language Family

## Marshall Durbin

### INTRODUCTION

The study of Carib languages spans three centuries
and has produced commentary by observers of diverse
linguistic, national, and occupational backgrounds.
In addition to formally trained linguists, there
have been hundreds of others who have gathered Carib data--including priests, missionaries, soldiers, colonists, doctors, teachers, explorers, anthropologists, oil men, geographers, geologists,
wayfarers, farmers, and a princess.  It is often
stated that on one of Columbus's three trips, a
sailor gathered a Carib vocabulary, though if this
is so the language was probably Island Carib--an
Arawakan language that will not concern us here.

As far as we know, the first word resembling
Carib to appear in the historic literature was
Caraiba, used by the historian Petrus Martyr in his
work published in 1516, ten years after the death
of Columbus (von den Steinen 1938:217).  The first
reference to the concept of Caribs (that is,
Indians of the Caribbean area) is found in the
notes of Columbus himself, edited by de las Casas,
wherein are references to Canibales, Caniba, and
Canima (Morison 1963:100, 103).  Subsequently, the
term Carib was used to refer to this geographic
grouping.

At present, we are faced with a very difficult
and confusing situation concerning the Carib languages. In the first place, a highly varied nomenclature for dialects of the same language, and for
tribal and subtribal groups, has resulted from the
fact that linguistic observations have been made
from a variety of geographical vantage points--
including the Caribbean Sea, the Atlantic Ocean,
the Pacific coast of South America, Rio Negro, the
Amazon, Xingu, Orinoco, and Magdalena rivers, and
Lake Maracaibo, among other more local points. In
some cases, approaches to a given tribe have been
made from different geographic directions, giving
rise to commentaries on different dialects of the
same language. These different geographical approaches to the same group have also resulted in
varying sets of names for the same population or
language, since neighboring tribes have different
names for a particular group.

Other problems arise from the fact that students
of Carib have used at least 11 glossing languages
(including Dutch, English, German, Norwegian, Swe-
dish, French, Spanish, Italian, Portuguese, Czech,
and Latin). In many cases these observers gathered
their data through an intermediary language--Eng-
lish, Portuguese, Dutch, French, or a Pidgin--which
neither they nor the Indians understood very well.
Often manuscripts that were written in the authors'
own languages, or those in which they were fluent,
were cast into still a third tongue by an editor,
translator, or publisher who failed to observe the
original orthographic conventions. Original manu-

scripts have disappeared after being badly copied (sometimes many times over), and many works available to us today represent third- or fourth-hand attempts.

In addition, we must take into account the history of Carib tribes since contact. Many have become extinct, while others have been dislocated. As a result, surviving Carib languages have been influenced by other Indian tongues, including Arawakan, Tupi-Guaranian, and Chibchan dialects (among other isolated groups), to say nothing of the European, East Indian, African, Pidgin, and Creole languages with which they have been in contact.

The problems I shall confront in this paper are: (1) the location of the original homeland of the Caribs; (2) the directions of their various dispersions; (3) the location at contact time of groups that are presently extinct or dislocated, and for which we have linguistic data; (4) the number of Carib languages and dialects that have ever existed (as witnessed by linguistic material); (5) the subgroupings of these languages and other internal relations; and (6) routes of recent migrations. Although there can be no absolute solutions to these problems, they have served as the focus for the research that Haydée Seijas and I have undertaken.

ANALYSES PRIOR TO THE 19TH CENTURY
The earliest extant linguistic material is that of the missionary priest Pierre Pelleprat (1606-1667), who participated in the Jesuit intrusion into the Guianas that lasted from 1646 to 1681. His lin-

guistic works, considered by del Rey (1971,1:
210-11) to be a bibliographic rarity, are (1) Introduction à la langue des Galibis, sauvages de la
Tarre [sic] ferme de l'Amérique méridionale, à
Paris Chez Sevastian Gramiosy, and (2) Introduction à la langue des Galibis.  The first work appeared as part of Relation des Missions des Pp. de
la Compagnie de Iesus dans les isles, dans la terre
ferme de l'Amérique méridionale, Paris.  Sometimes
it appears as a separate document.  Pelleprat left
a copy of the work in Guarapiche, Venezuela, when
he left there in 1653. The work undoubtedly did not
originate with him, since he notes that Fr. Dionisio Mesland's researches had helped him considerably (del Rey 1971, 1:298-99). Dionisio Mesland
(1615-1672) was the great Jesuit intellectual who
introduced Cartesianism to America.  He apparently
studied Galibi and made notes for a grammar, together with a vocabulary of the Indians of Guiana
(Carib?)  with some conversations and pious sayings
(del Rey 1971, 1: 196). However, none of these
data, except indirectly those probably used by
Pelleprat, have survived today.  Pelleprat's grammar and vocabulary are reprinted in del Rey (1971,
2: 9-23). The grammar is inadequate since it appears to be based upon a pidgin Carib used by the
French at that time.  The vocabulary corresponds to
what is variously known today as Carib, Galibi, Kariña, Carina, or Cari'na, which was spoken from
French Guiana (near the mouth of the Amazon) to
central eastern Venezuela.

The first major attempt to solve some of the
problems of classification of Carib languages was
made by Fr. Salvatore Filippo Gilij (1721-1789; see
del Rey 1971, 1: 118). Gilij spent most of his time
at Cabruta, a central Venezuelan town on the Orinoco, though he also traveled widely up and down the
river (Gilij 1965, vols. 1-3). He had more than a
passing acquaintance with several Carib languages,
and apparently spoke Tamanaco (now extinct) with
great fluency. He was the first to recognize the
Carib (as well as the Arawak) family as a unity,
though this classification was based only upon a
portion of Venezuelan Carib; Gilij was unaware of
most Carib tribes elsewhere in South America.

The most interesting aspect of Gilij's perception of the Carib family was that he recognized
what are presently called sound correspondences and
cognates. He stated (1965, 3:137):

> Letters together form syllables. The syl-
> lables sa, se, si, etc., occurring very
> frequently in Carib [prob. Kariña], are
> never found in its daughter language Tama-
> naco, and everything that is expressed in
> Carib as sa, etc., the Tamanacos say with
> ča. Thus, for example, the little shield
> that the Caribs call saréra the Tamanacos
> call čaréra. Pareca is also a dialect
> of the Carib language. But these Indians,
> unlike the Tamanacos and Caribs, say soft-
> ly in the way Frenchmen do, šarera.

Further, Gilij took great care to point out that
these languages could not be related to or derived
from those of Europe, or from Arabic or Hebrew, as
was frequently asserted at the time.  Nor did he
consider these languages primitive in terms of expression, complexity, vocabulary, or grammar.  He
stated that they merely differed.

It should be pointed out that Gilij came to
these conclusions regarding language relationships
during his 19 years of residence in Venezuela
(1749-1767), long before Sir William Jones's famous
1786 discourse on Sanskrit, Greek, Latin, Gothic,
Celtic, and Persian.  However, in spite of Gilij's
recognition of systematic sound correspondences and
cognates as a basis for positing genetic relationships in languages, he consistently viewed Carib
(Kariña) as the mother (matriz) language of all
other Carib languages with which he was acquain-
ted.  He never recognized the possibility of a
prior parent language giving rise to all the exis-
tent daughter tongues.[1]

RESEARCH IN THE 19TH AND 20TH CENTURIES
After the publication of Gilij's work, almost 125
years passed before Lucien Adam published the next
great treatise on Carib, Materiaux pour servir à
l'établissement d'une grammaire comparée des dialects de la famille caribe (1893).  This study includes a comparative list of 329 words, plus some
comparative grammar for Akawaio, Aparai, Arekuna,
Bakairi, Bonari, Island Carib, Caraibe, Chayma,
Crichana, Cumanagoto, Galibi, Guaque, Ipurucoto,

Karibis, Karinaco and Makusi, Ye'cuana (Maquiritare), Motilon, Wayana, Palmella, Paravilhana,
Pianakoto, Pimenteira, Piritu, Roucouyene, Tamanaco, Tiverigoto, Trio, Waiwai, Wayumara, and Yao.
The value of the work lies in its bibliography and
the listing of languages, though there were many
languages with published sources that Adam did not
include. No attempts are made at internal subdivision, except for purely geographical ones. The
comparative work uses mainly inspection rather than
the comparative method (which was well established
by this time in Europe). Nevertheless, Adam's work
set the stage for later language classifiers.

Karl von den Steinen was a contemporary of
Adam's. He tended to work more with a particular
Carib language (Bakairi) than with classifying.
Nevertheless, it was he who first made the proposal
that the homeland of the Caribs was in the lower
Xingu Basin (1892)--a proposal that persists to the
day in many researchers' minds. Von den Steinen
had studied the comparative method with Dr. Georg
Wenker (the author of a German dialect atlas), but
it is doubtful that von den Steinen ever grasped
the concepts of the comparative method, if indeed
Wenker understood them himself. Specifically, von
den Steinen established a protophonology (Grund-
sprache), but only by inspection and not by establishing true correspondence sets. For example, he
established *p in Proto-Carib and showed how this
became /w,f,x/ in Bakairi and /h/ in Ye'cuana under
certain conditions, but he actually confused correspondence sets that derive from Proto-Carib *p

and *w. Von den Steinen in fact believed (for an unknown reason) that the language that had undergone the greatest amount of change represented homeland Carib, though he took great efforts to demonstrate that Bakairi and Nahukwa are not at all the same as Proto-Carib. As will be seen below, our beliefs are to the contrary.

Von den Steinen made many useful observations, despite his obviously poor training in the comparative method. To Adam's list of languages, he added data for Apiaka, Aracaju, Central American Carib, Carijona, and Carinaca, which indicates that he did not rely solely upon Adam for his comparative materials.

De Goeje was the next great classifier. His first Etudes linguistiques Caraïbes appeared in 1910 and contained a comparative grammar and a much larger vocabulary (559 words) than Adam's. Many more published sources had since appeared for the languages Adam had compiled. The bibliography is much more complete and de Goeje was able to add Arara, Mapoyo, Pauxi (Pauxiana), Yabarana, Avaricoto, Opone-Carare, Core, Guanero, Hianacoto-Umaua, Kariña, Caribi, Akuku, Nahukwa, Upurui, Pajure, Palenque, Paria, Piritu, Saluma, Tiverigoto, Trio, Yabarana, and Yauapery. De Goeje, unlike Adam, was an accomplished fieldworker and included vocabularies and short grammars of Kariña, Trio, and Wayana in his work; however, his classificatory work surpasses Adam's in quantity only and is based upon comparison by inspection, though his synchronic studies, like those of von den Steinen, are quite valuable.

Working during the same period as de Goeje was Theodor Koch-Grünberg, who compiled vocabularies of no less than 10 Carib languages: Hianacoto-Umaua, Makusi, Mapoyo, Arekuna, Wayumara, Purucoto, Tauli-pang, Yabarana, Ingariko, and Sapara (1928). Although Koch-Grünberg attempted little classification, his phonetic details are so excellent that they have contributed a great deal toward our understanding of the groupings of Carib languages.

A second work of de Goeje's with the same title as his first volume appeared in 1944. It gives information on some additional languages: Akuria, Pariri, Yaruma, Azumara, Chikena, Guayana, Ihuruana (Ye'cuana), Kamarakoto, Kumayena (Okomayana), Mocoa (Motilon), Wayarikure (Triometesen), Parechi, Paru-koto (Barokoto), Patagona (Guague), Patamona (Inga-riko), Quaca (Chayma), Sapara, Sikiyana, Urukuyana, Varrique (Chayma), and Wama (Akuriyo). As can be readily seen, many of these represent dialect names while others represent genuinely new-found langua-ges. The work also includes a short comparative grammar (morphology) and a vocabulary consisting only of a list of reconstructed Proto-Carib words. The dictionary is awkward to use because one must constantly refer to Adam's (1893) and de Goeje's (1910) works through a set of code numbers. It is not clear how de Goeje arrived at the Proto-Carib reconstruction without correspondence sets.[2] Of great value, however, are appendices containing a

grammar and vocabulary of Wayana, and vocabularies
of Triometesen and Akuriyo.

The next landmark in Carib linguistic studies
appeared in 1968, when B.J. Hoff published the most
comprehensive phonology and morphology that has yet
appeared for any Carib language, one that will
serve for a long time to come as a guide to comparativists of Carib languages.  His method is that
of the structuralist school.  The value of the work
lies in the fact that Hoff presents us with a complete morphological analysis of a Carib language.
Consequently, we now have a complete view of the
verbal affix system.

During much of the first half of the 20th century, one man had been assiduously collecting bibliographies and vocabularies (from his own fieldwork, from that of others, and from published
sources) for all South American Indian languages.
By the time of his retirement from South American
studies in the 1950s, Paul Rivet had an incredibly
large bibliography and a vast collection of vocabularies in his possession.  In his publications his
principal endeavor was to show that Panče, Pijao,
Colima, Muzo, Pantagora (all in Colombia) and Patagon in Peru were Carib languages (Rivet 1943a), and
that the Choco family in Colombia was a part of Carib (Rivet 1943b). However, in retrospect, these
conclusions almost certainly seem not to be valid,
since Rivet's work was characterized by the crudest
sort of inspection.

Rivet cannot, however, be held totally responsible for the type of methodology he employed,

since he built upon a number of early Americanists
such as Adelung and Vater (1806-17), Balbi (1826),
D'Orbigny (1839), Ludewig (1858), and von Martius
(1867), in addition to the scholars mentioned
above. With the exception of Gilij, they had shown
very little originality. The manner of comparison
of these early Americanists was to establish relationships by utilizing sources from many different
languages. That is, there were no controls or constraints placed upon the comparing process as there
are in formal linguistic comparison. Rivet also
used history, ethnohistory, racial characteristics,
geographical distributions, folk accounts, and folk
etymologies to establish relationships (as in his
well-known classifications of South American languages published in 1924 and 1952); these techniques were also much in vogue in his time, especially among Americanists.[3]

Wilbert has pointed out that only Brinton (who
attempted to establish a critical evaluation of
source materials) was able to confine himself to
linguistic material, working principally with a
lexicon. Furthermore, as Wilbert suggests, neither
Rivet (1924), Rivet and Loukotka (1952), nor Chamberlain (1903; 1913) followed the criteria set
forth by Brinton (1891).

The last major classification of Carib has been
done by Čestmir Loukotka, a student of Rivet's.
His first study appeared in 1935, and it was followed by others published in 1941, 1944, 1948, 1952
(with Rivet), and finally, 1968. It was the work of
Loukotka and Rivet that perhaps most influenced

Mason in his classification of Carib published in the <u>Handbook of South American Indians</u> (1950).

Loukotka's style is similar to Rivet's, though considerably more sophisticated. First, he includes a large number of languages for which no data exist--that is, he depends upon historical sources for part of his classification; for the other part of his classification he depends upon published and unpublished sources. Loukotka enlarged Brinton's basic vocabulary to a diagnostic word list of 45 lexical items, which he tried to compile as fully as possible for each language (Wilbert 1968: 11). Because of different methods of collection he never presents more than 14 words for any given Carib language (head, tooth, eye, water, fire, sun, moon, arrow, man, jaguar, maize, one, two, three). Some languages have as few as two entries for comparative purposes. Since Loukotka was obviously comparing by inspection, he was never able to solve the problems of what he called "mixed languages," languages that are of one structure but have borrowed lexically from another. Thus, he usually was indecisive about Island Carib (Arawakan) and finally classified it incorrectly as Carib. The great value of Loukotka's work lies in the enormous bibliography he provides (both published and unpublished) and in his internal linguistic subdivisions (which are basically correct, though he gives no evidence concerning internal relationships of subdivisions). Most of his work is based upon geographical subdivisions, which in some cases coincide with

the linguistic subdivisions and in other cases do
not. For example, Loukotka places Carib within his
Tropical Forest Division, which is also a geographical and cultural category. Johannes Wilbert,
who edited Loukotka's posthumous publication
(1968), has correctly recognized the nature of Loukotka's method and has entitled the map accompanying the author's classification of Carib "Ethno-
Linguistic Distribution of South American Indians." To our knowledge, no ethnohistorian, historian, or archaeologist has utilized Loukotka's materials, even though they represent a rich source.

Specifically, Loukotka gives us a number of
divisions of languages for which linguistic data
exist. These are shown in Table 1 which excludes
all languages for which there are no linguistic
data, as well as all subdivisions and languages
that our analyses have demonstrated to be non-
Carib. What starts out as a confusing plethora in
Loukotka can be reduced to 21 major subdivisions by
critical evaluation and analysis of the source materials. As Table 1 shows, we are dealing with
linguistic material from 52 languages rather than
the hundreds sometimes thought to be the constitu-
ents of the Carib family.

Finally, the works of Greenberg (1959), McQuown
(1955), Ortiz (1965), and Swadesh (1955;1959)
should be mentioned in reference to classification
of Carib languages. Steward and Faron (1959), Tax
(1960), and Voegelin (1965) have relied upon Greenberg's classification. Greenberg, McQuown, and

TABLE 1.  Major Subdivisions of Carib Languages for which Linguistic Material is Available

| Western Languages | Eastern Languages | Trio | Chikena | Waiwai |
|---|---|---|---|---|
| Galibi | Wayana | Trio | Chikena | Waiwai |
| Caribisi | Upuri | Wama(Akuriyo) | Saluma | Parukoto |
| Kariña | Aparai | Urukuyana | Pauxiα | Wabui |
| Cariniacoα | Roucouyeneα | Triometesen | Cachuena | Hishkaryana |
|  | Aracajuα | Kumayena |  | Bonariα |
|  |  | Fianakoto |  |  |

| Yauapery | Pauxiana | Makusi | Pemong | Maquiritare | Mapoyo |
|---|---|---|---|---|---|
| Yauapery | Pauxiana | Makusi | Taulipang | Maquiritare | Mapoyo |
| Waimiri |  | Keseruma | Arekuna | Ye'cuana | Yabarana |
| Crichanaα |  | Purucoto | Ingarico | Ihuruana |  |
|  |  | Wayumara | Patamona | Cunuana |  |
|  |  | Paravilhanaα | Kamarakoto |  |  |
|  |  | Sapara | Uaica |  |  |
|  |  |  | Akawaio |  |  |

TABLE 1. Major Subdivisions of Carib Languages for which
Linguistic Material is Available (continued)

| Panare | Tamanaco α | Yao α | Motilon | Opone α | Carijona | Arara α |
|--------|-----------|-------|---------|---------|----------|---------|
| Panare | Tamanaco α<br>Chayma α<br>Cumanagoto α<br>Tiverigoto α<br>Palenque α<br>Caraca α<br>Quirequire α<br>Guayqueria α | Yao α | Yupe<br>Chaque<br>Iroca<br>Macoa<br>Manastara<br>Maraca<br>Pariri<br>Shaparru<br>Wasama<br>Japreria<br>Coyaima α | Opone α<br>Carare α | Guaque α<br>Carijona α<br>Umaua α | Arara α<br>Apingui α<br>Pariri α |

| Palmella α | Pimenteira α | Xingu |
|------------|--------------|-------|
| Palmella α | Pimenteira α | Yaruma α<br>Bakairi<br>Nahukwa<br>Naravute α |

Key:
α extinct
{ includes dialects of one language

Source: Adapted from Loukotka 1968: 198,224.

Ortiz relied upon earlier sources based principally
upon inspection, while Swadesh's work is based upon
his lexicostatistical method.

   I would also like to mention the research of
contemporary descriptive linguists (chiefly missionaries) who are working in the area.  Notable are
Fray Cesareo de Armellada (1972); Fr. Adolfo Villamañan (1970-1974); George and Emilio Esteban Mosonyi (whose work on Carib is largely unpublished but
is long, reasoned, and thorough); and those members
of the Summer Institute of Linguistics who are working on Carib in Guyana, Surinam, Brazil, and Co-
lombia--especially Grimes (1972), Derbyshire
(1961), and Hawkins (1952).


EXTERNAL RELATIONSHIPS
The Carib family is a well-known and easily recognized entity.  Up to now there have been only three
other linguistic groups that have been proposed as
being related to Carib.  Chocó (northwestern Colombia) was proposed by Rivet (1943a), but there is no
recent or strong evidence that Carib and Chocó are
in fact related; consequently, this relationship is
generally not accepted.  Gê (also spelled Jê or Žê)
and Pano (Brazil, Peru, and Bolivia) were proposed
as related to Carib by Greenberg (1959); while this
hypothesis may eventually prove true, no data or
analyses have yet substantiated it.  Island, Black,
and Central American Carib (related languages found
in the Caribbean area) were thought to be Carib
ever since Adam proposed them as such in 1893; however, Walter Taylor's extensive work (e.g., 1969)

has clearly shown that this group belongs to the Arawak family.

In addition, Shebayo (Arawakan from Trinidad), Mutuan and Pimenteira (probably Tupi-Guarani from Brazil), Hacaritama (Arawak from Colombia), Patagon (isolated language from Peru), and Pijao, Colima, Muzo, Pantagora, and Panče (language isolates from Colombia) have been proposed as related to Carib, but they definitely are not. Most of these proposals are simply cases of misidentification, though there will probably never be enough evidence to properly identify Pantagora, Panče, Colima, Muzo, and Patagon.

RESEARCH PLAN

Seijas and I have now collected approximately 1,000 separate references on the Carib languages, some original and some not. The proliferation is such that it is not feasible to list all the sources or to include the evaluations and comments in the references to this paper; in fact, the proliferation is so great that it is not feasible to list here all the different names for each separate language and dialect—all this will have to be included in a later work. Nor can we state with certainty at this point how many separate Carib languages there are, since our survey is not yet complete; however, we do feel there are considerably fewer languages than the names that have appeared in the literature would indicate.

Our own work on Carib has consisted, first, in trying to make a complete bibliography of all references containing Carib language data (either vocabulary, grammar, or texts) that can be used for comparative purposes. By this process we have been able to eliminate many references traditionally given in Carib bibliographies (those containing ethnohistorical information but no linguistic data). Second, we have attempted to obtain copies of each reference. These two processes have consumed a great deal of time, since it can be truly said that there is no best library in the world for Carib materials or for South American Indian language materials in general. We have found the following libraries to have large collections of Carib source materials, each collection differing somewhat from the others: Arcaya Library, Caracas; Biblioteca Nacional, Caracas; Middle American Research Institute Library, Tulane University, New Orleans; Olin Library and George Meisner Rare Book Room, Washington University, St. Louis; Newberry Library, Chicago; New York Public Library, New York; Fundación La Salle Library, Caracas; Anthropology Library of the Smithsonian Institution, Washington, D.C.; Bibliothèque Nationale, Paris; Biblioteca Nacional, Madrid; and Biblioteca de Museo de Antropología e Historia, Bogota. Other libraries we would like to consult are: University of Texas Library, Austin; University of Florida Library, Gainesville; Library of Congress, Washington, D.C.; Peabody Museum Library, Cambridge; Library of the Museu Paraense Emilio Goeldi, Belem, Brazil; and the national libraries of Brazil, Surinam, Guyana, and French Guia-

na.   All of these, we suspect, may have sources not
yet noted.   Since the publication of some of our
work, we have also received notice from several
persons about word lists in their possession.
Thus, the bibliography will inevitably be expanded.

After obtaining copies of all the accessible Carib language materials from the above-mentioned
libraries, we noted for each item (whether a grammar, vocabulary, or text) its linguistic value for
comparative purposes, the number of words included,
whether a phonetic transcription was used or not,
the native language of the observer, the place and
date when the material was gathered, and information about the origin of informants, where available; in addition, we recorded bibliographic information regarding publications and later reprin-
tings.   We have noted very few unpublished manuscripts for the Carib languages.   This annotated
bibliography is nearing completion and should be
ready for publication soon.   It is our hope that
this will save future workers a great deal of
time.

Our next step was to make source cards for each
language, (1) noting all alternate language and
dialect names, (2) briefly listing all the sources
for that language, and (3) noting those to which we
had access.   We then proceeded to examine separate
geographical areas for related languages.   The mass
of Carib languages are in the Guiana region, but we
began by examining those geographical areas distant

from that region where isolated Carib-speaking peoples are found.

Our procedure was to gather as many original and secondary sources as we possessed (using as many original sources as possible). We then attempted to recast data from these earlier works into a set of contrastive phonological statements that are meaningful in light of today's knowledge of Carib. By comparing various transcriptions of related languages and dialects, by using our knowledge of the set of phonological contrasts found in the transcriber's native language, and by referring to present-day Carib languages, we were able to make statements about the phonological systems. After these interpretative statements were made for each separate publication concerning a given geographical area, we proceeded to apply the comparative method to these restated data to arrive at a reconstruction of the Carib languages in that area. The work has been slow and tedious, since we have had to acquire a great deal of knowledge of colonial history, archaeology, geography, botany, and zoology. However, we have been greatly aided by doing fieldwork ourselves on several Carib languages in Venezuela. As of 1974 we have nearly completed the analysis of all groups outside the Guiana mass of Carib languages.

It is our eventual goal to arrive at a large list of reconstructed Proto-Carib lexemes that will shed some light upon the general problems mentioned earlier. In the following sections I shall discuss our findings to date.

GEOGRAPHICAL DISTRIBUTIONS

There are at present three geographical areas of Carib speakers, smaller than they once were, but still substantial: (1) Colombia, which can be divided into two geographic units, (a) southeastern Colombia and (b) northeastern Colombia-Venezuela border; (2) an area south of the Amazon, which can be divided into (a) outlying areas of eastern and northern Brazil and (b) the Xingu River Basin; and (3) the Guiana land mass, which can be considered a single homogeneous unit.

It is well known that Carib speakers once made great incursions into the Caribbean islands as far north as Cuba--onto Hispaniola, Puerto Rico, and the Lesser Antilles (including Trinidad, Tobago, Margarita, and Cubagua off the coast of Venezuela). While the native Arawak speakers on these islands borrowed heavily from the invading Caribs, it is our contention that there was no Carib language in the islands outside of that spoken by invading Carib males for a generation or so after the invasions. As noted earlier, what are called Island, Black, and Central American Carib are certainly Arawak languages. One language identified as Carib has also been reported from northern Peru (near southern Ecuador), but we do not believe it to be Carib (Durbin and Seijas 1973b). Suggestions have been made that Carib intruded as far north as Florida and Texas, but there is no positive evidence for this. In short, we can say that the vast majority of Carib languages have always been (as they are today) in the Guianas.

INTERNAL SUBDIVISIONS

The following is a discussion of internal subgroupings found in the geographical divisions mentioned above; as will be shown, these do not always correspond with linguistic subdivisions.

## Colombia

Southeastern Colombia. In southern Colombia between the Vaupés and the Caquetá rivers we find three Carib languages that are closely related: Hianacoto-Umaua, Carijona, and Guaque. There are satisfactory published data for Hianacoto-Umaua only (Durbin and Seijas 1973c). A few speakers of Carijona still survive (Arthur Sorensen 1973: personal communication; Schindler: 1977). These languages have in common the innovation whereby Proto-Carib *p has become Proto-Hianacoto-Umaua-Carijona-Guaque *p, *b, *h (Durbin and Seijas 1973c: 30). They are not closely related to their northern Colombian neighbors but rather to languages in the southern Guianas, northern Brazil, and Brazil south of the Amazon.

Northeastern Colombia-Venezuela border. In northeastern Colombia, extending down the Sierra de Perijá over into Venezuela (almost up to Lake Maracaibo--perhaps around the lake aboriginally), are the Yukpa (also known as Yuko or Motilon). There appear to be two languages: (1) Japreria (mostly located in Venezuela, with occasional incursions into Colombia); and (2) a series of dialects of

Colombian Yukpa or Yuko (Iroka, Las Candelas, Mana-
ure, Maraca, San Genaro, Sokomba, Susa, and Yowa)
and Venezuelan Yukpa (Irapa, Macoita, Pariri, Shaparru, Viakshi, Wasama, and Rionegriño), which together constitute another language. All these languages appear to be closely related to a group of
Venezuelan Coastal Carib languages that are now extinct: Chayma, Cumanagoto, Piritu, Pariagoto, Palenque, Tamanaco, Tiverigoto, Caraca, and Yao.

While the Yukpa dialects are most closely related to the above-mentioned Venezuelan coastal languages, another group, Opone and Carare in northeastern Colombia, appear to be more closely related
to Yukpa than they are to any other languages (Durbin and Seijas 1973a). Opone and Carare are found
spoken along rivers of the same names, which are
tributaries of the Magdalena River in the Department of Santander. They appear to be dialects of
the same language, with not more than three surviving speakers, if any.

This distribution suggests to us a movement from
the Venezuela coastal area through the plains into
the southern part of the Sierra de Perijá. Our own
analyses (Durbin and Seijas 1973d; 1975) suggest
that Yukpa migration into the Sierra de Perijá came
from the south, and therefore that the area between
Lake Maracaibo and the Sierra may have been occupied by ancestors of these speakers at one time.
We surmise that they were pushed into the Sierra,
first by Barí speakers (also called Motilones;
their language is as yet unclassified), and later
by Spanish colonists. In support of this hypothe-

sis we may cite Jahn (1927: 39-73), who mentions a
group residing around Lake Maracaibo in early times
that he believes to have been Carib.   Furthermore,
Layrisse and Wilbert's blood studies indicate that
Yukpa mixed intensively during the last 700 years
with a large Diego-negative Indian population in
the area, who could have been the Barí (Layrisse
and Wilbert 1966: 65).  Finally, our sound-corres-
pondence studies indicate that Spanish has influenced some of the Venezuelan groups toward change
(Durbin and Seijas 1975: 71).  Along with or perhaps after the movement into the Sierra de Perijá
by the Yukpa (Yuko) groups, the Opone-Carare may
have been pushed through the southern foothills of
the Sierra onto the Magdalena River in Colombia by
the expanding Barí (the Magdalena flows fairly near
the foothills of the Sierra de Perijá in the north
Colombian Department of Magdalena).   The Opone-
Carare may then have proceeded down the Magdalena
to the tributaries where they were found historically.   Alternatively, the Opone-Carare may have
been pushed into Barí territory up the Catatumbo
River to its source in the present state of Norte
de Santander, which again is very close to the Magdalena.   There were probably other closely related
Carib groups in the general area who accompanied
the Opone-Carare.  Loukotka (1968: 220) lists several tribes in the same area whose names are drawn
from ethnohistorical sources for which there are no
linguistic data: Yariqui, Xinguan, Carate, Corbato,
Chinato, Zorca, Cariquera, Capacho.  He also lists
Hacaritama (once spoken around the modern city of

the same name in the Department of Santander) and Guane (once spoken in the Department of Santander at the sources of the Carare River). Our examination of the Hacaritama data reveals that it is probably a dialect of Guajiro; Guane is listed as having two recorded words, but we have never been able to locate them.

Nevertheless, Carib tribes must have been widespread at one time throughout northeastern Colombia and northwestern Venezuela, since we find some incontrovertible Carib influences upon Muzo, Colima, Pantagora, Panče, and Pijao, all languages of an unknown affiliation that extend downward through the present central Colombian departments of Santander, Cundinamarca, and Tolima. It had long been supposed that these unclassified languages were Carib, but we were able to demonstrate that the linguistic material included in prior discussion had not been sufficient to properly place them within this language family (Durbin and Seijas 1973b). Certainly the Pijao word list collected by Gerardo Reichel-Dolmatoff in 1943 (Ramirez-Sendoya 1952) substantiates our hypothesis that it is not Carib; thus all of these remain unclassified at the present time, though there seem to be Carib influences. It is quite possible that Opone-Carare and other now-extinct Carib groups displaced the above-mentioned groups. In summary, we believe that we can posit a close unity among the Venezuelan coastal groups, the groups in Sierra de Perijá, and the Opone-Carare. This would seem to represent a western migration across the plains into the Lake Ma-

racaibo area, then north into the Sierra de Perijá,
and also south through the foothills of the Sierra
and down the Magdalena.  An important point to keep
in mind is that the Carib languages of southeastern
Colombia do not fall into this same group.

## Areas South of the Amazon

Northern Brazilian Outliers.  In northern Brazil
the following Carib languages are found: Palmella,
Arara, Apiaka, Pariri, Aracaju, Aramayana, Yaruma,
and Txicão.  It is genuinely doubtful that Pimenteira (an eastern language in this general area,
now extinct) is Carib, since the only extant material contains more Tupi-Guarani than Carib.  Aracaju and Aramayana have counterparts north of the
Amazon in Brazilian Guiana and appear to have strayed into their present positions south of the Amazon.  It appears that Arara, Apiaka (not to be confused with Tupi Apiaca), Pariri, Yaruma, Palmella,
and Txicão have also strayed across the Amazon, because they closely resemble languages from the eastern Guiana areas, including eastern Brazilian Guiana, French Guiana, and Surinam.  The movement must
have been a concerted one, for Apiaka, Arara, Pariri, Yaruma, and Txicão closely resemble each other
more than any one resembles any other group or language.  They share the common trait of lacking a
fricative series, which is unusual in Carib languages.  As far as we know, the only other Carib language without a fricative series is Tamanaco,

though we do not postulate a close relation between Tamanaco and these languages.

Palmella, on the other hand, closely resembles a group we call the East-West Guiana Carib languages (see below). There are reports that Palmella society once had European whites as well as blacks in its midst. Although very little is known about Palmella, it is conceivable that it might have been one of several Pidgin or Creole languages frequently found in Guiana, and that its speakers might have been a band of racially mixed refugees who wandered as far south as the border between Brazil and Bolivia. Very small amounts of data have been available to us from Txicão and Yaruma, formerly located on the margins of the Upper Xingu Basin; for this reason the position of these languages is only tentative. Finally, a language called Yuma, for which no data exist, is posited by Loukotka (1968: 222) as being in this group.

Because Aramayana and Aracaju are found south of the Amazon and seem to have definitely emigrated from Brazilian Guiana (north of the Amazon), we have also placed the point of origin for Arara, Apiaka, Pariri, Yaruma, and Txicão approximately in this area. The majority of Arara, Apiaka, and Pariri speakers are reasonably close to this point of origin and most of them could have traveled from the point of origin to the nearby Amazon and down the Amazon to various tributaries. We would like to account for this migration by population pressures exerted in Brazilian Guiana (north of the

Amazon) by Tupi-speaking groups.    These Tupi groups
seem to have appeared in the area just before European contact and to have continued living there
throughout much of the colonial period.    If this
was indeed the case, then all of Brazilian Guiana
could at one time have been Carib (except for a few
old residue pockets of Arawak).

Xingu River Basin.    Bakairi and Nahukwa form a
group of languages in the Xingu Basin area.    Bakairi appears to have two main dialects, as does
Nahukwa.    Hermann Meyer gave the names Yanamakapë
and Akuku to the Nahukwa subdivisions, and he cre-
dited each with a large number of dialects (Krause
1936); however, the latter are mainly names for
village groups (Ellen B. Basso 1973: personal communication).    The Bakairi were made famous by von
den Steinen (1892) when he first demonstrated that
Proto-Carib *p developed into an intervocalic mani-
fested in the language of that Xingu Carib tribe.
This change has also occurred in Nahukwa.
    Von den Steinen also posited that the Lower Xin-
gu Basin was the homeland of the Caribs and that
Apiaka represented an intermediate group ("missing
link") left behind in the migration of the Guianan
Caribs to the north (1940: 226). If this were true,
Proto-Carib would have had to change a great deal
before migrating very far.    We have chosen to
explain Apiaka (along with Yaruma, Txicão, Arara,
Pariri, Palmella, and possibly Pimenteira) as extensions of Brazilian Guiana Carib languages that
crossed the Amazon sometime within the past 500

years. We have done this because they most closely
resemble these Brazilian Guiana languages, and because Bakairi and Nahukwa on the other hand more
closely resemble Hianacoto-Umaua-Carijona-Guaque
and languages in the southwestern and southern Guianas such as Ye'cuana, Ocomesiana, Wayumara, and
Hishkaryana, among others. In all these languages
Proto-Carib *p has undergone considerable changes,
whereas in the rest of the Guianan languages it has
remained intact.

The Guiana Land Mass. The next area we turn to is
the land mass of Guiana, where the largest geographical and numerical concentration of Carib languages is found. Carib speakers form one unbroken
group, with only two small islands separated from
the rest (one in northern Surinam and one on the
Atlantic coast of Brazil).

The region also contains what appear to be recent incursions into the area--Tupi from the south
(represented by Mutuan, which has been classified
as Carib but definitely is not, and Emerillon),
Coastal Carib in the form of Tamanaco, and Yanomamö
(an unclassified language, coming from the south).

There are other islands in the area that represent what we believe to be remnants of languages
that survived the original Carib expansion. In
French Guiana are Tocoyene (no data) and Palikur
(Arawakan); in Brazil are the language isolates
Taripio and Maracano, for which no data are available; in Venezuela we find Joti (Chikano and Yuana). It can thus be seen that except for recent

incursions into the area, the integrity of Carib in
the Guianas has been complete since contact time
and probably since much earlier.

We suspect that Carib occupied most of the Guiana area until recent incursions of Tupi and Yanomamö speakers from the south (in Brazil).  It would
seem almost certain that the Caribs replaced Arawaks, since we see the Guiana Carib languages boxed
in among Arawaks on all sides--north and south,
east and west.  Just as recent Tupi and Yanomamö
expansions began to dislodge Caribs from various
areas, we would hypothesize that the Caribs pushed
Arawaks north into the Antilles, to the west, and
deep into southern Brazil.  In line with this hypothesis, isolated northern language groups such as
the Warao, Sape, Arutani, Joti, Auake, Kaliana,
Guahibo, Yaruro, Otomac, Taparita, and possibly Yanomamö (among others) would have been the original
inhabitants of the Guianas before the Arawaks replaced them.

While we have not yet finished our analysis of
the data from the Guiana area, we can nevertheless
discern four main linguistic subdivisions.  The
first is that of <u>Galibi</u>, which starts in extreme
northern Brazil, covers the entire area of French
Guiana, small portions of Surinam, northern Guyana,
and northeastern Venezuela, and extends out of the
Guiana area into the coastal region of Venezuela.
Galibi is commonly called Carib or Carabisce in
English, Kribisi in English Creole of Surinam, Caribe in Spanish, Caraiben in Dutch and Galibi in
French and Portuguese (Hoff 1968:1); it has also

been called Cariniaco, as well as Cariña and Kaliña, in Venezuela. Of all the Carib languages, it
has the largest geographical spread and probably
had the largest number of speakers.

The second linguistic subdivision, which we have
called Western Guiana Carib, occurs in the extreme
western part of the Guiana Carib area in western
Venezuela, immediately below the Orinoco River.
The languages are Quaca, Pareca, Panare, Yabarana,
and Mapoyo. Quaca and Pareca are now extinct, with
very little data available; they are very aberrant
from most Carib languages and appear to have been
heavily influenced by outside languages.

The third linguistic subdivision we have chosen
to call Southern Guiana Carib. It consists, on the
one hand, of Kashuyana, Warikyana, Kahuyana, and
Ingarune (all dialects of the same language), and,
on the other, of Hishkaryana, Wayumara-Azumara, Parukoto, and Ye'cuana. In these languages several
sound shifts have taken place, the most prominent
of which is the change of Proto-Carib *p to Proto-
Southern Carib *h. In this respect the group is
more closely related to the Southeastern Colombian
group and to the Xingu River Basin groups (discussed above) than it is to any of the other Carib
languages in the Guiana area.

The fourth subdivision of the Guiana area contains the largest number of languages. These languages range from east to west, hence our term for
them, East-West Guiana Carib. Starting with Brazil, we have Aracaju, Pianakoto, Urukuyana, Wayana-
Aparai, Trio-Rangu, Cachuena, Sapara, Yauapery,

Pauxi, Wabui, Bonari, Crichana, Waimiri, Chikena,
Saluma, Paravilhana, and Pauxiana.  Roucouyene is
the name for Urukuyana in French Guiana.  In Surinam are Kumayena, Akuriyo, and Triometesen.  In
Guyana we find Makusi, Akawaio, and Patamona (Ingariko).  In eastern Venezuela we find Pemong (Taulipang, Kamarakoto), Arinagoto, and Purucoto.

CONCLUSIONS
I wish to repeat that our work is not complete
enough to lead us to a reconstruction of a basic
Proto-Carib lexicon.  We are at the state of reconstructing various internal subdivisions.  Nevertheless, we can state several conclusions with some
confidence.

   1.  Among the Carib there appears to be a basic
   north-south dichotomy that runs on an east-west
   axis.  We refer to these major divisions as
   Northern Carib and Southern Carib.  Each can
   be subdivided further, as outlined in Table 2.
   Northern Carib compromises what we have called
   (IA) Coastal Carib (with its Sierra de Perijá
   and Opone-Carare outliers), (IB) Western Guiana Carib, (IC) Galibi, (ID) the central
   East-West Guiana Carib languages running
   through the Guiana area, and (IE) their
   northern Brazilian outliers south of the Amazon.
   Southern Carib consists of (IIA) Southeastern Colombia Carib, (IIB) Xingu Basin Carib
   in central Brazil, and (IIC) what we have called Southern Guiana Carib, a group of Carib lan-

guages in the southern part of the Guiana Carib area north of the Amazon.

2. There appear to be approximately 50 to 55 Carib languages, though further research should reduce this number.

3. Although we are not sure how the division has come about, we do feel relatively sure that Coastal Carib, Western Guiana Carib, Galibi and East-West Guiana Carib (four of the five Northern Carib subdivisions) are closer to Proto-Carib than any of the Southern Carib languages are.

Throughout our work we have used the hypothesis that the more changed a language is from the proto-form, the farther it is likely to have traveled from its original homeland. For this reason we have excluded any Southern Carib languages or locations as being possibly close to the homeland of the original Caribs. We would tend to place the homeland of the Caribs in the Guiana area of Venezuela, Guyana, Surinam, or French Guiana, but probably not in Brazilian Guiana. When we have been able to reconstruct more Proto-Carib forms, we may be able to substantiate this hypothesis and perhaps even make the location more precise.

According to Layrisse and Wilbert's preliminary rough glottochronological counts, Proto-Carib began to break up about 4,500 years ago, when 30 percent of the separation occurred. About 3,400 to 2,400

TABLE 2. Internal Relations Among the Carib Languages
(Dialects Excluded)

I. Northern Carib
  A. Coastal Carib (mostly outside Guiana land mass)
    1. Venezuelan Coastal Carib
      a. Chayma $\alpha$
      b. Cumanagoto $\alpha$
      c. Yao $\alpha$
      d. Tamanaco (in Guiana land mass) $\alpha$
    2. Sierra de Perijá (border of northeastern Colombia and
      Venezuela)
      a. Japreria
      b. Yukpa
      c. Yuko (Colombian Yukpa)
    3. Opone-Carare (Central Colombia) $\alpha$
  B. Western Guiana Carib (Western Venezuela)
    1. Mapoyo
    2. Yabarana
    3. Panare
    4. Quaca $\alpha$
    5. Pareca $\alpha$
  C. Galibi (mostly along the Atlantic Coast from mouth of
    Amazon to Orinoco)
  D. East-West Guiana Carib (mostly in Brazilian Guiana with
    outliers in Surinam, Guyana, Venezuela, and French
    Guiana)
    1. Wayana-Aparaí
    2. Roucouyene (French-Guiana) $\alpha$
    3. Aracaju $\alpha$
    4. Trio-Rangu

5.  Wama (Akuriyo)(Surinam)
6.  Urukuyana
7.  Triometesen (Surinam)
8.  Kumayena (Surinam)
9.  Pianakoto
10. Saluma
11. Pauxiα
12. Cachuena
13. Chikena
14. Waiwai
15. Paravilhanaα
16. Wabui
17. Sapara
18. Yauapery
19. Waimiri
20. Crichana α
21. Pauxiana
22. Bonariα
23. Makusi (Guyana)
24. Purucoto (Venezuela)
25. Pemong (Taulipang)(Venezuela)
26. Patamona (Guyana)
27. Akawaio (Guyana)
28. Arinagoto (Venezuela)α

E. Northern Brazilian Outliers (south of the Amazon)

1. Palmellaα
2. Pimenteira?α
3. Yarumaα
4. Txicão
5. Paririα
6. Apiakaα
7. Araraα
8. Yumaα

TABLE 2. Internal Relations Among the Carib Languages (continued)

II. Southern Carib
    A. Southeastern Colombia Carib
        1. Hianacoto-Umaua $\alpha$
        2. Guaque $\alpha$
        3. Carijona
    B. Xingu Basin Carib (Brazil)
        1. Bakairi
        2. Nahukwa
    C. Southern Guiana Carib (mostly in southern Venezuela and Brazil)
        1. Ye'cuana (Venezuela)
        2. Wayumara-Azumara (Venezuela)
        3. Parukoto
        4. Hishkaryana
        5. Warikyana (Kashuyana-Kahuyana-Ingarune)

Key:
$\alpha$ extinct
{ possible subgroupings

years ago approximately 56 percent of the separation of Carib tribes occurred in a second phase,
and finally, about 2,300 to 1,000 years ago some 14
percent of the present diversity of the Carib
groups originated. Of course, since colonial contact a great deal of movement has occurred. Layrisse and Wilbert (1966: 105) correlate these glottochronological dates with an archaeological period
established by Cruxent and Rouse (1958-1959, 1:
238). From 4,500 to 3,000 years ago (Layrisse and
Wilbert's first stage), the Proto-Caribs are believed to have been agricultural hunters and gatherers, which would have accounted for approximately
30 percent of the total linguistic diversity we see
today. Stated in another way, the present-day diversity of approximately 50 languages would have
been roughly 15 languages about 3,000 years ago.
In the second stage (3,000-1,600 years ago) the
first traces of manioc cultivation are noted. Presumably this new subsistence technique would have
been successful enough to have brought about population increases, the possibility of greater density of population, and movements and migrations
out of the central homeland area. By the end of
the second stage there could have been approximately 45 languages. The third stage would have been
characterized by stability, with only a few diver-
gences being added until the time of contact. Layrisse and Wilbert (1966: 106) further suggest that
Bakairi represents the earliest split from Proto-
Carib; our data also suggest this, but we would add
to Bakairi the other Southern Carib languages, in-

cluding Hianakoto-Umaua-Carijona-Guaque, Nahukwa, Ye'cuana, Wayumara, Azumara, Hishkaryana, and Warikyana.

## ACKNOWLEDGEMENTS
I wish to thank Richard Meier and Ellen B. Basso for their comments on this paper, and Diane Fischer for preparing a preliminary version of the maps [editors note: for maps, see Durbin 1977]. This work was carried out through the generous assistance of the Department of Anthropology, Instituto Venezolano de Investigaciones Cientificas, Caracas, while I was a Visiting Researcher there in 1971-72. The results reported here are as much due to Dr. Haydee Seijas of IVIC as they are to me, since we jointly carried on the fieldwork and library research. The only portion of this paper that I have done alone is the writing.
[N.B. The editors of this volume gratefully acknowledge the kind permission of the University of Arizona Press and Mridula Adenwala Durbin to republish our late colleague's study.]

## NOTES
1. Gilij's classification gave rise to that of Hervás y Panduro (1800-1805). Specifically, the latter noted the following Carib languages: Carib(e) (Kaliña), Maquiritare (Ye'cuana), Pareca, Avaricoto, Tamanaco, Yabarana, Quaqua, Akerecoto, Mapoyo, Achirigotos, Cariabes Mansos, Caribes Huraños, Macuchis, Ocomesianas, Paudacotos, Purugotos, Uarinagoto, Pariacotos, Uokéari, Ua-

racá-pachilí, Uara-Múcuru, Mujeres Solas, Cumanacoto, Guanero, Areveriana, Guaikíri, Palenco,
and Oye. He also noted that Carib languages
were spoken on the Peninsula of Paria, near Caracas, and perhaps in other parts of Venezuela.
He further noted the similarity of Island Carib
to Carib languages. However, Gilij's classification was actually based upon Tamanaco, Pareca,
Uokéari, Mapoyo, Oye, Akerecoto, Avaricoto, Pa-
riacoto, Cumanacoto, Guanero, Guaikíri, Palenco,
Maquiritare (Ye'cuana), Areveriana, Uaracá-Pa-
chilí, Uara-Múcuru, Mujeres Solas, Payuro, Kiki-
rípa, and Carib (Gilij 1965, 3: 174). Of all
the languages mentioned by Gilij, only Carib,
Maquiritare (Ye'cuana), Yabarana, Mapoyo (all in
Venezuela), Macuchis (Guyana), and Okomesianas
(Brazil) still survive.
2.    See Lounsbury's review (1947) of this work.
3.    See Rowe (1951: 15) for an evaluation of Ri-
      vet's work with which we wholeheartedly agree.

REFERENCES
Adam, Lucien.    1893. Matériaux pour servir a l'é-
      tablissement d'une grammaire comparée des dia-
      lectes de la famille Caribe. Paris: Bibliothé-
      que Linguistique Américaine 17.
Adelung, Johann Christoph, and Johann Severin Va-
      ter.    1806-17. Mithridates, oder allgemeine
      Sprachenkunde, mit dem Vater Unser als Sprach-
      probe en beynahe fünf hundert Sprachen und
      Mundarten, vol.3 (of 4 vols.). Berlin.

Armellada, Cesareo de.  1972.  Pemonton Taremuru
(Invocaciones mágicas de los indios Pemon).
Caracas: Universidad Católica Andres Bello,
Instituto de Investigaciones Históricas, Centro
de Lenguas Indígenas.

Balbi, Adriano.  1826.  Atlas ethnographique du
globe, ou Classification des peuples anciens et
modernes d'après leurs langues, précédé d'un
discours sur l'utilité et  l'importance de l'é-
tude des langues appliquée à plusieurs branches
des connaissances humaines...avec environ de
sept cents vocabulaires des principaux idiomes
connus... Paris.

Brinton, Daniel G.  1891.  The American Race: A
Linguistic Classification and Ethnographic
Description of the Native Tribes of North and
South America.  New York: N.D.C. Hodges.

Chamberlain, Alexander F.  1903.  Indians, America.
In The [Encyclopedia] Americana, vol. 9. Revised in Encyclopedia Americana, 1941, vol. 15:
43-58.

------. 1913.  Linguistic Stocks of South American
Indians, with distribution map.  American Anthropologist 15: 236-47.

Cruxent, José M., and Irving Rouse.  1958-59.  An
Archeological Chronology of Venezuela. 2 vols.
Washington, D.C.: Pan American Union Social
Science Monographs 6.

Derbyshire, Desmond, 1961.  Hishkaryana (Carib)
Syntax Structure.  International Journal of
American Linguistics 27: 125-42.

D'Orbigny, Alcide D.  1839.  L'Homme américain de
l'Amérique méridionale considéré sous ses
rapports physiologiques et moraux.  Paris.

Durbin, Marshall.  1977. A Survey of the Carib Language Family.  In Carib-Speaking Indians: Culture, Society and Language, Ellen B. Basso, ed.,
pp. 23-38.  Anthropological Papers of the University of Arizona, 28.  Tucson: University of
Arizona Press.

Durbin, Marshall, and Haydée Seijas.  1973a.  A
Note on Opon-Carare.  Zeitschrift für Ethnologie
98 (2): 242-45.

------.  1973b.  A Note on Panche, Pijao, Pantagora
(Palenque), Colima and Muzo.  International
Journal of American Linguistics 39: 47-51.

------.  1973c.  Proto-Hianacoto: Guaque-Carijona-
Hianacoto Umaua.  International Journal of American Linguistics 39: 22-31.

------.  1973d.  Linguistic Interrelations Among the
Yukpa.  Paper read at the 1973 annual meeting of
the American Anthropological Association, New
Orleans.

------.  1975.  The Phonological Structure of the
Western Carib Languages of the Sierra de Perijá,
Venezuela.  In Atti del XL Congresso Internazionale degli Americanisti (Rome-Genoa, 1972), vol.
3: 69-77.

Gilij, Filippo Salvatore.  1965.  Ensayo de histo-
ria americana,  trans. Antonio Tovar.  3 vols.
Caracas: Biblioteca de la Academia Nacional de
Historia 71-73.  (Originally published 1782,
Rome.)

Goeje, Claudius H. de. 1910. Études linguistiques
    Caraïbes. Amsterdam: Verhandelingen van de Ko-
    ninklijke Akademie van Wetenschappen, Afdeeling
    letterkunde. n.r. 10 (3).
------. 1944. Études linguistiques Caraïbes. Am-
    sterdam: Verhandelingen van de Koninklijke Aka-
    demie van Wetenschappen, Afdeeling letterkunde.
    n.r. 49 (2).
Greenberg, Joseph H. 1959. The General Classifi-
    cation of Central and South American Languages.
    In Men and Cultures: Selected Papers of the 5th
    International Congress of Anthropological and
    Ethnological Sciences, A.F.C. Wallace, ed., pp.
    793-94. Philadelphia: U. of Penn. Press.
Grimes, Joseph, ed. 1972. Languages of the Gui-
    anas. Tlalpan, Mexico: Summer Institute of
    Linguistics.
Hawkins, Neil W. 1972. A fonologia da lingua
    Uaiuai. Faculdade de Filosofia, Ciências, e
    Letras, Universidade de São Paulo, Boletim 157,
    Etnografia e Língua Tupí-Guaraní 25.
Hervás y Panduro, Lorenzo. 1800. Catálogo de las
    lenguas de las naciones conocidas, y numeración,
    división, y clases de estas según la diversidad
    de sus idiomas y dialectos. Vol. 1: Lenguas y
    naciones americanos. Madrid.
Hoff, B.J. 1968. The Carib Language. The Hague:
    Martinus Nijhoff. Verhandelingen van het Konin-
    klijk Instituut voor Taal-, Land- en Volkenkunde
    55.
Jahn, Alfredo. 1927. Los aborígenes del occidente
    de Venezuela: Su historia, etnografía y afinida-

des linguisticas, vols. 1 and 2. Caracas: Lit.
y Tip. Comercio.

Koch-Grünberg, Theodor. 1928. Vom Roroima zum
Orinoco. Vol. 4: Sprachen. Stuttgart: Stre-
tcher und Schröder.

Krause, Fritz. 1936. Die Yarumá- und Arawine-In-
dianer Zentralbrasiliens. Baessler-Archiv Beiträge zur Völkerkunde 19: 32-44.

Layrisse, Miguel, and Johannes Wilbert. 1966.
Indian Societies of Venezuela: Their Blood Group
Types. Caracas: Editorial Sucre. Instituto Ca-
ribe de Antropología y Sociología, Fundación La
Salle de Ciencias Naturales, Monograph 13.

Loukotka, Čestmir. 1935. Clasificación de las
lenguas sudamericanas. Lingüística Sudamericana
1 (Prague).

------. 1941. Roztřídění jihoamerických jazyků.
Lingüística Sudamericana 3 (Prague).

------. 1944. Klassifikation der südamerikanischen
Sprachen. Zeitschrift für Ethnologie 74 (1-6):
1-69.

------. 1948. Sur la classification des langues
indigènes de l'Amérique de Sud. In Actes du
XXVIIIe Congrès International des Américanistes
(Paris, 1947), pp. 193-99.

------. 1968. Classification of South American Indian Languages. Los Angeles: Latin American
Center, UCLA, Reference Series 7.

Lounsbury, Floyd. 1947. Review of Études linguistiques Caribes [sic], vol. 2, by C.H. de Goeje.
Language 23: 308-11.

Ludewig. H.E. 1858. The Literature of American
Aboriginal Languages. London: Trubner.

Martius, Karl Friedrich Philipp von. 1867. Beiträge zur Ethnographie und Sprachenkunde Amerikas, zumal Brasiliens. 2 vols. Leipzig.

Mason, John A. 1950. The Languages of South Ame-
rican Indians. In Handbook of South American
Indians, Julian Steward, ed., vol. 6: 157-317.
U.S. Bureau of American Ethnology, Bulletin 143.
Washington: Government Printing Office.

McQuown, Norman A. 1955. The Indigenous Languages
of Latin America. American Anthropologist 57
(3):501-70.

Morison, Samuel Eliot. 1963. Journals and Other
Documents on the Life and and Voyages of Chris-
topher Columbus. New York: Heritage Press.

Ortiz, Sergio Elias. 1965. Lenguas y dialectos
indígenas de Colombia: Historia extensa de
Colombia, vol. 1, book 3. Bogota: Academia
Colombiana de Historia.

Ramirez-Sendoya, Pedro J. 1952. Diccionario indio
del Gran Tolima. Publicaciones del Ministerio
de Educación Nacional. Bogota: Editorial
Minerva.

Rey, José del. 1971. Aportes Jesuíticos a la
filologia colonial Venezolano. Caracas: Universidad Católica Andres Bello, Instituto de
Investigaciones Históricas, Seminario de Lenguas Indígenas.

Rivet, Paul. 1924. Langues américaines. II:
Langues de l'Amérique du Sud et des Antilles.

In Les langues du monde, ed. A. Meillet and
Marcel Cohen, pp. 639-712. Paris: La Société de
Linguistique de Paris, Collection Linguistique
XVI.
------. 1943a.  La influencia karib en Colombia.
Revista del Instituto Etnológico Nacional 1:
55-93, 283-95 (Bogota).
------. 1943b.  La lengua Chocó.  Revista del In-
stituto Etnológico Nacional 1: 131-96 (Bogota).
Rivet, Paul, and Čestmir Loukotka.  1952.  Langues
de l'Amérique du Sud et des Antilles.  In Les
Langues du monde (new ed.), A. Meillet and Mar-
cel Cohen, ed., pp. 1099-1160.  Paris: Centre
National de la Recherche Scientifique.
Rowe, John H.  1951.  Linguistic Classification
Problems in South America.  University of Cali-
fornia Publications in Linguistics 10: 13-26.
Schindler, Helmut.  1977.  Carijona and Manakïnï:
An Opposition in the Mythology of a Carib Tribe.
In Carib-Speaking Indians: Culture, Society and
Language, Ellen B. Basso, ed., pp. 66-75.  An-
thropological Papers of the University of Ari-
zona, 28.  Tucson: University of Arizona Press.
Steinen, Karl von den.  1892.  Die Bakaïri-Sprache.
Leipzig: K.F. Koehler's Antiquarium.
------. 1940.  Entre os aborígenes do Brasil Cen-
tral.  São Paulo: Departamento de Cultura. (Ori-
ginally published in Revista do Arquivo Munici-
pal [São Paulo] XXXIV-LVIII.)
Steward, Julian, and Louis Faron.  1959.  Native
Peoples of South America.  New York: McGraw-
Hill.

Swadesh, Morris.  1955.  Towards a Satisfactory Ge-
    netic Classification of Amerindian Languages.
    In Anais do XXXI Congresso International de
    Americanistas (São Paulo, 1954), pp. 1001-12.
------.  1959.  Mapas de clasificación lingüística
    de México y las Américas.  Mexico City: Cuader-
    nos del Instituto de Historia, Serie Antropoló-
    gica 8.
Tax, Sol.  1960.  Aboriginal Languages of Latin
    America.  Current Anthropology 1: 431-36.
Taylor, Douglas R.  1969.  Consonantal Correspon-
    dence and Loss in Northern Arawakan with Special
    Reference to Guajiro.  Word 25: 275-88.
Villamañan, Adolfo, ed.  1971-74.  Lingüística,
    antropologia, misionologia Bari-Yukpa-Xapreria.
    Hoja Semanal, pp. 1-140.  (Sirapta, Venezuela;
    mimeographed bulletin.)
Voegelin, Charles F., and Florence M. Voegelin.
    1965.  Languages of the World: Native America
    Fascicle Two.  Anthropological Linguistics 7
    (7), pt. I.
Wilbert, Johannes.  1968.  Loukotka's Classifica-
    tion of South American Indian Languages.  Pre-
    face to Classification of South American Indian
    Languages, by Cestmir Loukotka, pp.7-23.  Los
    Angeles: Latin American Center, UCLA, Reference
    Series 7.

# 9. Evidence for Tupi-Carib Relationships

## Aryon D. Rodrigues

The purpose of this paper is to present some evidence of prehistoric and historical relations between the languages of the Tupí stock and those of the Carib family.

I proposed the Tupí stock as comprising seven families--Tupí-Guaraní, Munduruku, Jurúna, Arikém, Tuparí, Mondé, and Ramaráma--and a linguistic isolate, Puruborá (Rodrigues 1958a), 1958b, 1964, 1970). There is thus far only sparse unelaborated lexical evidence for the affiliation of some of these families; for others, such as Tuparí, Munduruku, and Tupí-Guaraní, we have already worked out more extensive lexical and phonological correspondences (Rodrigues 1961, 1980). At the moment I believe that two languages previously included in the Tupí-Guaraní family, Awetí and Sataré, should be reclassified as two additional isolates (or one-member families) in the Tupí stock.

The geographical distribution of the Tupí stock has the following main features:

(a) It lies essentially south of the Amazon River (to the north of this boundary we find only the Tupí-Guaranían dialect group Wayapí-Emérillon, which reached the Oyapock river on the Brazil-French Guyana border in post-Colombian times (Métraux 1927:29-35), and the Amazonian Língua Geral or Nheengatú, a creolized dialect of Tupí-Guaranían

Tupinambá introduced in Amazonia by Portuguese colonization and missionary activity).

(b) It is found mainly in the Amazon Basin; the
only exception to this is the Tupí-Guaraní family,
which, although it has many languages in that Basin, also spreads over the Paraná Basin in the
south and along most of the length of the Brazilian
coast in the east.

(c) Five of the members of this stock--Tuparí,
Arikém, Mondé, Ramaráma, and Puruborá--are found in
the area between the Machado (Jiparaná) and the
Guaporé Rivers, in the highest part of the Madeira
Basin (in the Brazilian State of Rondônia), and a
sixth member, Sataré (Mawé), is spoken on the lower
Madeira.

The Carib languages constitute only one family,
which may be subdivided into genetically differentiated subgroups. These subgroups have not yet
been clearly defined.[1] However, the most likely
division is between languages spoken north and
south of the Amazon River. The latter group may be
further divided into two subgroups, with one com-
prised of Apiaká of the Tocantins, Arára and Pariri
of the lower Xingú, and Txikão of the upper Xingú.
The other would encompass Nahukwá-Kalapálo-Kuikúru
on the upper Xingú and Bakairí, the southernmost
Carib language on the upper Culiseu and Batoví
Rivers (Xingu Basin) and on the Teles Pires and
Novo Rivers (Tapajós Basin).

The northern Carib languages are numerous and
widespread, extending from north of the Amazon
mouth to the Orinoco River and further, along the

Venezuelan coast, in the past having reached the Antilles. After a geographical discontinuity, we find the westernmost and perhaps most divergent subgroup of Carib languages (Opone, Carare) in the Madalena Valley of Colombia. Another discontinuous subgroup, whose best known member is Hianákoto-Umáua, is located on the Caquetá and Apaporis Rivers (Yapurá Basin) in southern Colombia, but this is linguistically very close to the Makiritare (Yekuana) subgroup on the Ventuari River in Venezuela (which, in turn, is more akin to the languages of the Uraricuera, such as Wayumará).[2] Palmela, a Carib language once spoken on the Guaporé River, south of the Amazon, exhibits features typical of the North Amazonian languages and was probably displaced to that region in a very late migration (19th century) (cf. Fonseca and Almeida 1899:229-234). A Carib linguistic isolate is Pimenteira, a language which in the 18th and 19th centuries was spoken far from Amazonia, between the Gurguéia and the Piauí Rivers in the northeastern Brazilian State of Piauí, and by the end of the 17th century had been farther in western Pernambuco, near Cabrobó, on the left bank of the São Francisco River.[3]

Lexical similarities between Tupí and Carib languages were pointed out in the past by various scholars. As early as 1909 de Goeje said that "several words, which are not onomatopoetic, appear to pertain at once to the primitive (i.e. proto-) Carib language and to the primitive Tupi or to the primitive Aruak; would they be relics from a time, when these families were yet only one?"[4]

Our comparison of some languages of the Tupí
stock with languages of the Carib family led to the
establishment of regular phonological correspondences between both groups. These correspondences,
presented in Tables 1 and 2, are based on over 100
lexical equations covering such domains as kinship,
body and plant parts, nature, non-cultural and cultural items, qualities, actions and states, in addition to some grammatical morphemes, including
person markers. The equations, which are presented
in List A, are indicative of genetic relationship.

   In compiling Tables 1 and 2 only the Carib languages often recurring in List A were specified;
the other languages of the same family appearing in
that list behave in general similar to one of the
specified languages.

   For List A only some languages of each group
were used, selected from those for which more lexical and grammatical information was available to
me. For the Tupí stock, I took Tupinambá (16th and
17th century sources, especially Anonymous 1952-
1953, phonemicized after Rodrigues 1959 and 1981)
as a representative of the Tupí-Guaraní family
(words not attested for Tupinambá were taken from
Old Guaraní, Ruíz de Montoya 1639); Tuparí (Caspar
and Rodrigues ms.) as a member of the Tuparí family; and Mundurukú (Crofts 1973 and ms.) as a
member of the Mundurukú family. For the Carib
family, I took basically Waiwai (Hawkins 1952 and
1962), Hishkaryána (Derbyshire 1979 and ms.), and
Taulipang (Pemong) (Koch-Grünberg 1928) as representatives of the North Amazonian languages (but

words from some other languages were added, most of
them taken from de Goeje 1909 and 1946); and Bakairí (Steinen 1892 and Weatley ms.) as a representative of the South Amazonian languages (with a few
examples from Nahukwá after Steinen 1894 and de
Goeje 1909). By taking into account such languages
we reduce the possibility of including in List A
sets of correspondences valid only for a particular
subgroup of languages.

   List B consists of correspondences found only
between the Tupí-Guaraní family (excluding the
other Tupí families) and North Amazonian Carib languages.  To the Carib languages used in List A were
added Wayána (Coudreau 1892, de Goeje 1946) as well
as other North Amazonian languages (after de Goeje
1909 and Koch-Grünberg 1928). These correspondences include words for fauna, flora, and cultural
artifacts which are common to the whole Tupí-Guaraní family.  They probably reflect a contact either
between an ancestor of the present day Tupí-Guaraní
languages and an ancestor of the north Amazonian
Carib languages, or between one of the Tupí-Guaraní
languages and one of the North Amazonian Carib languages with subsequent diffusion within the respective family.  But these strictly Tupí-Guaraní/North
Amazonian Carib correspondences (which constitute
the bulk of the lexical similarities so far mentioned by previous authors) are surely not due to genetic relationship and should therefore be clearly
distinguished from the cognate sets represented in
List A.[5]  This point is mentioned here only in passing, but it deserves a more thorough examination

in the future, as we acquire better knowledge of a
larger number of Carib languages.   It should also
be taken into account that many lexical items
included in List B are to be found as well in some
North Amazonian Arawak languages.[6]

List C presents correspondences most probably
due to recent contacts.   Here I include loanwords
of several Carib languages taken either from Língua
Geral or from some other particular Tupí-Guaraní
language: C.1 - loanwords from Língua Geral (Tatevin 1910, Stradelli 1929) in North Amazonian Carib
languages; C.2 - loanwords from Wayapí (Coudreau
1892)[7] or Língua Geral in Wayána.   I add also a
list of Carib loanwords in a Tupí-Guaraní language:
C.3 - loanwords from Wayána in Wayapí.[8]

TABLE 1. Phonological Correspondences--Consonants
(Abbreviations and Numbers are those of List A)

---

Tb p, Tr p, c/#__i, pc/V__i, Mu p, Ø/__i,e; Ww p,
   h, Hk h, Tp, Gl, Wn p, Bk p, x: 7, 20, 29, 33,
   35, 38, 49, 55, 59, 70, 71, 93, 94, 95, 97, 98,
   114, 117
Tb p, Tr p', Ø/#__; Tp p, Ø/#__, Ww, Hk, Bk Ø/#__:
   29, 30, 31, 47.
Tb β, Tr p, Mu m; Ww, Hk, Gl, Wn w: 8, 82, 91, 114.
Tb β/__#, Tr, Mu p/__#; Ww, Hk m/__#: 21, 67, 69,
   92, 106.
Tb β/__#, Tr, Mu p/__#; Ww, Hk, Bk Ø (w): 25, 26,
   31, 73, 77, 107.
Tb, Tr t, Mu t, d; Ww, Hk, Tp, Gl, Wn, HU, Bk t:
   4, 15, 33, 36, 95, 103, 103a.
Tb s, Tr t, c/__i, Mu č; Ww t, š/__i, Hk t, c/__e,
   Tp, Wn t: 43, 52, 62, 63, 73, 79, 100, 102, 118.
Tb, Tr, Mu k; Ww, Hk, Tp, Gl, Wn k, Bk k, kx: 5,
   13, 19, 40, 41, 45, 54, 61, 68, 75, 76, 83, 85,
   93, 94, 98, 101, 111, 114, 115, 116, 117, 118,
   121.
Tb ?, Tr k, Mu ?; Ww, Hk, Tp, Gl, Wn, Bk k: 24, 49,
   50, 80, 108, 110.
Tb, Tr, Mu ?; Ww, Hk, Tp, Bk Ø: 17, 22, 35, 65, 67,
   74, 109.
Tb, Tr, Mu m; Ww, Hk, Gl, Wn m, Bk Ø: 6, 9, 14, 42,
   56, 63, 83, 88, 90, 103a, 116.

---

Table 1. Phonological Correspondences--Consonants
(Continued)

---

Tb m, Tr ?; Mk, Bk m: 46.

Tb, Tr n; Ww, Hk, Tp, Gl, Bk n: 16, 57, 58, 77, 84, 89.

Tb n, Tr Ø; Ww Ø: 81, 88.

Tb, Tr ŋ; Tp ŋ, Ww, Hk, Bk m: 20, 62, 74, 89, 119.

Tb r, Tr, Mu r, t/__#; Ww, Hk, Tp, Bk r Wn l: 12, 16, 17, 19, 30, 32, 37, 38, 45, 46, 49, 50, 54, 64, 87, 96, 99, 101, 106, 112, 113, 114, 120.

Tb r/__#, Tr, Mu t/__#; Ww, Hk, Bk Ø: 55, 72, 75, 87.

Tb r, Tr h; Ww, Hk, Tp y: 11, 56.

Tb, Tr, Mu y; Hk y: 22, 39, 97, 107.

Tb y, Tr, Mu w; Tp, Gl, Wn w, Ww, Hk kw: 65, 66, 113, 121.

Tb y/#__, Tr, Mu w/#__; Ww, Hk, Tp Ø: 10, 105, 106.

Tb Ṽ; Hk Vm: 22, 39, 57.

Metatheses: 9, 32, 33, 42, 50, 62, 68, 80, 83, 85, 87, 91, 94, 95, 96, 97, 110.

---

TABLE 2.    Phonological Correspondences--Vowels
(Abbreviations and Numbers are those of List A)

---

Tb, Tr, Mu i; Ww, Tp, Bk i, Hk e: 3, 57, 58, 81,
   83, 119.
Tb, Tr i; Ww, Hk i̇: 1, 5, 54.
Tb i̇, Tr, Mu i; Ww, Hk, Tp, Ap, Bk i̇: 18, 22, 23,
   32, 33, 34, 43, 52, 59, 66, 76, 80, 82, 99.
Tb i̇, Tr, Mu i; Hk, Tp, Bk a: 16, 19, 45, 76, 103a,
   115.
Tb i̇, Tr i; Ww, Hk, Tp e, Bk i: 17, 23, 24, 59, 60,
   79, 95.
Tb u: Tr o, Mu o, i̇; Ww, Hk i̇, Tp, Bk u: 21, 77,
   90.
Tb u, Tr, Mu o; Ww, Hk, Tp o: 39, 110, 113, 121.
Tb, Tr, Mu e; Ww, Hk, Tp, Bk e: 10, 16, 24, 30, 31,
   58, 59, 75, 76, 77, 78, 79, 106, 108, 115.
Tb, Tr e; Ww, Tp, Bk i/__#: 28, 55, 65, 87.
Tb, Tr, Mu e; Ww, Hk, Tp, Bk a: 2, 13, 20, 94, 106,
   108.
Tb, Tr, Mu a; Ww, Hk, Tp, Bk a: 14, 15, 25, 27, 33,
   35, 37, 38, 41, 42, 43, 44, 50, 52, 56, 60, 63,
   65, 67, 68, 70, 71, 72, 74, 75, 83, 84, 85, 86,
   88, 91, 92, 93, 94, 95, 111, 112, 114, 116, 117,
   120.
Tb, Mu a; Ww, Hk e: 45, 62, 73, 105.
Tb, Tr o, Mu i̇; Ww, Hk, o, u, Tp, Bk o: 1, 8, 9,
   15,    29, 58, 69, 71, 82, 89, 97, 100, 109, 118.
Tb, Tr o; Ww, Hk, Bk a: 26, 47, 68, 96, 101.
Tb, Tr Ṽ; Ww, Hk, Tp, Bk V: 14, 15, 32, 35, 51, 65,
   80, 82.

LIST A: Tupí-Carib Cognates

> Abbreviations:  Bk Bakairí, Gl Galibí (Kaliña, Karina), Hk Hishkaryána, IC Island Carib[9], Mk Makushí, Mu Mundurukú, Nk Nahukwá, Tb Tupinambá, Tp Taulipang (Pemong), TR Tuparí, Wn Wayána (Oyana), Ww Waiwai.

## Personal affixes

1. Tb wi-, Tr w-, o-, Mu we-, o- 1st singular;
   Ww wɨ-, w-, o-, oy-, Hk w-, ɨ-, Bk w-, u-,
   i-, Tp u-, uy-, y-.

2. Tb, Tr, Mu e- 2nd singular; Ww a-, Bk ə-, Tp
   a-, aw-, Hk a-, ay-, o-, ow-, oy-.

3. Tb, Tr, Mu i- 3rd non reflexive; Ww, Bk, Tp
   i-, Hk ɨ-, u-.

4. Tb t-, Mu t- 3rd non reflexive, Tr te-, t-
   3rd reflexive; Ww, Tp tɨ-, t-, Hk tɨ, tu-,
   t-, Bk tə- 3rd reflexive.

5. Tr ki-, k- 1st plural inclusive; Ww kɨ-, k-,
   Hk kɨ-, ku-, k- Bk ki-, ku-, k-.

## Case affixes

6. Tb -mo,-amo in the state of; Ww -me, Hk -me.

7. Tb -pe punctual locative, Tr -pe inessive,
   Mu -pe, -be locative; Hk -ho, Tp, Wn -po
   locative.

8. Tb -βo diffuse locative; Hk -wo at.

## Other affixes

9. Tb mo-, Tr m-, õ-, Mu mɨ- causative; Hk om-,
   on-, em-.

10. Tb ye-, Tr we-, Mu ǰe-we- reflexive; Tp, Hk

e-.

11. Tb r-, Mu d-, Tr h- relational; Ww, Hk, Tp
y-.

Grammatical particles and words

12. Tb ri 'for, on'; Ww re 'through', Hk rye
'through, along'.
13. Tb -ke (in oβa-ke 'in front of, lit. in
face of'); Hk ka 'to' (e.g. ompata-ka
'towards the face of').
14. Tb amõ 'another, some'; Gl, Wn, IC amu.

Kinship terms

15. Tb amõy 'grandfather', tamõy 'grandfather of
somebody'; Tp amo-ko 'grandfather', u-tamo
'my grandfather', Wn, Gl tamu, Hk tam-,
tamu- 'grandfather'.
16. Tb enɨr 'male's sister'; Bk -enaru-to, Gl
-enau-tik 'sister'.
17. Tb i?ɨr 'male's cross cousin'; Bk i·ri
'female's cousin'.
18. Tb ɨβɨr 'male's younger brother'; Apalaí
ɨpɨrɨ, Gl pi·ri, IC íbiri.
19. Tb ɨker 'female's older sister', ɨke-?-ɨr
'male's older brother', Tr ike 'male's older
brother', ike-it 'female's older sister';
Apalaí -akoro-ne, Tp akoŋ, akon-ũ 'brother',
Wn akon 'older brother'.
20. Tb peŋ 'female's cross nephew'; Ww pamo, Gl
pamu 'brother-in-law', Hk hamo 'cross
cousin', Bk pama 'male's brother-in-law'.
21. Tb uβ, Tr op 'father'; Ww Hk ɨm, Apalaí um

Gl umu, Tp uŋ, Bk ũe.

Body parts and parts of plants

22.  Tb a-?ĩy 'grain, seed'; Hk ɨyme 'nut'.

23.  Tb ɨpɨ 'tree stem'; Ww, Wn epu 'tree stem',
     Hk ehɨ, ohɨ 'standing tree'.

24.  [n.b. missing]

25.  Tb kaβ, Tr ?ap, Mu šep 'fat (noun)'; Wn
     kap-hak 'fat (adjective)', ka-t 'fat
     (noun)', Ww ka, Hk, Gl ka-tɨ 'fat (noun)'.

26.  Tb oβ, Tr ep, Mu ɨp 'leaf'; Ww, Hk, Bk a.

27.  Tb oβa, Mu opa 'face', Tr epa 'eye'; Ww
     epa-ta, Hk empa-ta, ompa-ta, Gl emba-ta, Tp
     empo-ta, empe-ta 'face'.

28.  Tb pe 'bark', Tr pe 'bark, skin', Mu i-be
     'bark'; Ww pɨ 'bark', Tp pi-pɨ 'skin, bark'.

29.  Tb pepo, Tr pep'o 'wing feather'; Tp pepo-ko
     'to take off the feathers' (ko 'to pull
     away', see no. 109).

30.  Tb pere 'milt'; Ww, Wn, Bk ere, Hk erye, Tp
     eri 'liver'.

31.  Tb pereβ 'wound, ulcer'; Ww ere, Hk erew 'to
     ache'.

32.  Tb pɨrũ 'to tread'; Hk ɨhro 'foot'.

33.  Tb pɨta 'heel', Tr cito 'foot', Mu ida
     'heel'; Hk ɨhta 'sole', ɨhta-kmarunu 'heel',
     Ww hta, Tp pɨta 'foot', Wn pta 'sole',
     pta-pu 'heel', Nk uta-pɨ 'sole'.

Elements of nature

34.  Tb ɨβɨ 'earth, ground', ɨβɨ-tɨr 'mountain',
     Mu ipi 'earth'; Hk ɨhɨ, Apalaí ɨpɨ, Bk ɨwɨ,

Nk uu, Wn ipɨi, Gl wɨ·pɨ, IC wébo.

35.  Tb ɨpa?ũ 'island'; Wn, Gl pau, IC ubáo.

36.  Tb ɨtu 'waterfall'; Trio itu-ru, Gl ito-ti,
     Bk təu.

37.  Tb kwar 'sun', Mu ka-ʃi 'sun'; Hk a-kwarɨ
     'sunlight'.

38.  Tb para 'large river'; Tp paru 'water,
     river', Apalaí paru 'river', Bk paru
     'water'.

39.  Tb yũ 'field'; Hk o-yomo.


Qualities

40.  Tb akɨm 'wet'; Wn te-ukuma-i, t-ekupa-i, Gl
     ekup-i.

41.  Tb akuβ, Tr akop, Mu aʃip 'hot'; Hk ak.

42.  Tb aman 'circle, surround', Tr amon-?a
     'round, spherical'; Hk amno- 'round' (see
     no. 83).

43.  Tb asɨ, Tr aci 'to be sick, to ache'; Hk
     atɨh 'to be rotten, bad'.

44.  Tb ay 'sour'; Ww ai 'to be hot (pepper)', Hk
     ayih 'to be hot like pepper'.

45.  Tb kɨra 'fat (adjective)'; Hk kare 'to make
     fat'.

46.  Tb mirĩ, Tr ?iri 'small'; Bk i-meri, Mk
     miri-kɨ.

47.  Tb por, Tr ot 'full'; Hk ar-ɨhto 'to fill',
     t-ar-ke 'full', Ww arɨ 'contents'.

48.  Tb posɨy, Tr poci, Mu poʃi 'heavy'; Tp pɨsi,
     Gl awo·siŋ.

49.  Tb puru?a 'pregnant'; Ww puruki 'to swell'.

50.  Tb ?ar 'upper part, top'; Hk kare 'high',

akre 'to lift'.

## Non cultural items

51.   Tb apwã 'point'; Ww epo 'point', Tp epo-te
      'extremity of the arrow head'.

52.   Tb asɨk 'piece'; Ww asik-wo 'to break into
      two pieces'.

53.   Tb ɨpɨ 'beginning', ɨpɨ-ruŋ 'to begin'; Hk
      ɨh-če 'to begin'.

54.   Tr kire 'people; Hk kɨrɨ, Tp kuray 'man', Bk
      kurə 'people'.

55.   Tb per, Tr i-pet 'woman'; Ww pi Hk he-če
      'wife'.

56.   Tb mara- 'bravery', maran 'war'; Ww maya
      'bravery, to be wild,' Hk mayan 'to be wild
      (animal)'.

## Cultural items

57.   Tb inĩ 'hammock'; Hk eñeme 'to sew'.

58.   Tb enimo, inimo (< inĩ 'hammock' + po
      'fiber') 'thread, rope'; Ww k-eñepu 'hammock
      rope', w-eñepu, Hk w-eñehu 'baby sling'.

59.   Tb epɨ, Tr epci 'payment'; Ww epe, Tp
      epe-pɨ, Hk ehe-thɨri 'payment', Hk ehe-ma,
      Wn epe-ma 'to pay', Bk epɨ 'to cost', epɨ-wa
      'to pay, to make a gift'.

60.   Tb ɨta 'house pole'; Tp e?ða 'small lateral
      poles in the house'.

61.   Tb okar, Tr čker 'village plaza'; Ww eken
      'place'.

62.   Tb posaŋ 'medicine'; Ww ehče 'cure,
      medicine', ehčem- 'to treat', Hk ehče, ohče

'vegetal medicine', ehčema 'to give
medicine'.

63.  Tb sam 'rope'; Hk o-tame 'thick rope',
     e-tam-če 'thick rope (possessed)'.

64.  Tb uru 'basket'; Hk uru-to 'small basket for
     cassava bread'.

65.  Tb ya?ẽ 'dish, pot' Tr wa?ẽ 'pot', Mu wa?e
     'calabash'; Tp wai 'calabash bottle'.

66.  Tb yɨ, Tr wi 'ax'; Gl wɨ•-wɨ, Wɨ•-rɨ, Wn
     Apalaí wɨ-wɨ, Bk pɨ.

## Actions and States

67.  Tb ?aβ 'to cut'; Ww, Hk ama 'to cut wood'.

68.  Tb akaso 'to move to a far place'; Hk e-taka
     'to move', oh-taka 'to change the place'.

69.  Tb a-oβ 'to wrap, clothes'; Ww w-omɨ
     'wrapper', Hk w-omu 'clothes', Wn y-om
     'wrapper', Gl w-oomo 'European clothes'.

70.  Tb apɨ 'to burn'; Tp api 'to set on fire'.

71.  Tr apok 'to sit down'; Ww apo. Hk aho-nɨ,
     aho-nano, Tp apo-no, apoŋ 'seat, bench', Gl
     apo-ni 'seat in a canoe'.

72.  Tb ar, yar 'to take, to receive', Tr at, Mu
     jat 'to take'; Ww a-rɨ, Hk a, Tp a-lɨ, Gl
     a-ro, Bk a 'to take, to carry'.

73.  Tb asaβ 'to pass, to cross'; Hk w-eto, Gl
     wɨ•to 'to pass by, to cross'.

74.  Tb a?aŋ 'to try'; Hk ame.

75.  Tb ekar 'to look for'; Bk eka-heni 'to look
     for, to gather', eka-una 'to gather'.

76.  Tb ekɨy, Tr aki 'to pull', Tr eki 'to
     stretch'; Ww akɨ 'to bring', Tp w-aka 'to

pull'.

77.   Tb enuβ 'to hear'; Ww enɨ, enw-, Hk, Wn ene,
      Gl e•ne 'to see'.

78.   Tb epɨy 'to sprinkle'; Wn epɨke-i, Bk iwike
      'to wet'.

79.   Tb esɨr 'to roast'; Hk ečе-rɨ 'to be
      cooked'.

80.   Tb e?ɨ̃y 'to scratch'; Ww ikɨ, Hk ɨke, Bk ike
      'to scrape'.

81.   Tb in 'to sit', Tr i-ap 'container (i.e.
      sitting place)'; Ww i-rɨ 'to set on the
      ground'.

82.   Tb ɨβõ 'to arrow'; Ww ɨwo, Hk wo 'to fire',
      Gl iwo 'to wound, to kill'.

83.   Guaraní kamik 'to squeeze, to tread'; Hk
      akmeke 'to tread'.

84.   Tb kane?õ 'tired'; Bk i-kana 'to rest'.

85.   Tb kay 'to burn (intr.)'; Ww akñi 'to burn
      (tr.)', Hk ake 'to burn (intr.)'.

86.   Tb ka?ẽ 'to roast on a platform'; Hk kan-ho.

87.   Tb ker, Tr ?et, Mu šet 'to sleep'; Ww akri
      'to lie down', Bk iki 'to sleep'.

88.   Tb man 'to go around, to fence', Tr ma- 'to
      roll up'; Ww ma 'to dance', Hk man-ho 'to
      dance', mam-ko 'to fence', mam u 'wall', Tp
      man-um 'to dance (see no. 38)'.

89.   Tb noɲ 'to put'; Hk nom, Tp noɲa 'to let
      stay'.

90.   Tr om, Mu ɨ̃m 'to give'; Ww, Hk ɨm, Apalaí
      um, Bk u.

91.   Tb paβ, Tr pap 'to end, to die', Mu apam 'to
      die (many people)'; Hk wah 'to die', Tp

pa?-nese 'dead'.

92. Tb paβ 'all'; Hk e-ham 'to have many'.

93. Tb pak 'to wake', mo-pak 'to cause to wake',
Tr e-pak 'to wake'; Ww paka, Tp paka-, Hk
haka 'to wake', om-paka 'to cause to wake'.

94. Tb peka, Tr peeka 'to open'; Ww ahka 'to
break'.

95. Tb pɨta 'to stay, to stop'; Ww ehčo 'to
stay', Tp pɨta 'to stay', pɨǰa 'harbour'.

96. Tb por 'to jump', Tr pot-?eki 'to jump',
õ-pot 'to pluck'; Ww ahro, Tp -puru- 'to
jump'.

97. Tb poy 'to feed', Mu pɨy-bit 'meal'; Hk
yho-hto 'to feed', yho-ta 'to have food'.

98. Tb puk 'to get pierced'; Gl e-puka, Wn, Trio
i-puka, Bk i-xoki 'to pierce', Ipurukotó
poka, IC i-buka, Mk poka-ki 'to kill with an
arrow'.

99. Tb rɨrɨy 'to tremble'; Hk rɨrɨn 'to
tremble', rɨrɨnɨ 'trembling'.

100. Tb so, Mu čɨ, Sataré, Awetí to 'to go'; Ww,
Hk to, Bk dǝ.

101. Tb sorok 'to tear'; IC t-atáraka, Bk saroɣe.

102. Tb su?u, Tr toko 'to bite'; Wn e-tuku,
o-tuku 'to eat'.

103. Tb tĩ 'to tie'; Trio tiñi, Hianákoto-Umáua
i-tena-ma-, Mk šeena.

103a. Tb tɨm 'to plant, to bury'; Hk e-nam 'to
plant, to bury', Bk e-ta 'to plant'.

104. Tb weβ 'to extinguish the fire'; Wn epu 'to
go out (fire)', epu-ka 'to extinguish the
fire', Kumanagoto ep-ka.

105.   Tb yay 'to mock', Mu way 'to laugh'; Ww ei
       'to scold'.

106.   Tb yereβ 'to return'; Hk, Trio erama, Gl
       eramo, Wn irama 'to turn, to return'.

107.   Tb yɨβ 'to be cooked', Tr õ-yip 'to roast on
       coals'; Hk yo 'to cook'.

108.   Tb ?e 'to say, to do', Tr ke 'to say', ka
       'to do', Mu ?e 'to say'; Ww Hk, Tp ka 'to
       say, to do', Bk ke 'to say, to speak'.

109.   Tb ?ok, Mu ?ɨk 'to pull away'; Hk oko 'to
       cut (meat)', Tp ka, ko 'to pull away'.

110.   Tb ?u, Tr ko, Mu ?o 'to eat, to drink'; Hk
       ok, Ww okɨ 'to eat (bread)', Tp eku 'to
       eat'.


Animals and plants

111.   Tb akuti 'agouti'; Tp, Mk, Nk akuri, Gl, Wn,
       Apalaí, Trio, Hianákoto-Umáua akuli.

112.   Tr arime 'species of monkey'; Wn, Apalaí,
       Trio alimi, Hinákoto-Umáua alim-ime (ime
       'big').

113.   Tb ayuru, Tr aoro, Mu aro 'parrot'; Tp
       woro-we 'parrot', Ww, Hk kworo 'species of
       macaw'.

114.   Tb kapi?iβar Hydorchoerus capybara; Wn
       kapiwala, Apalaí kapiara, Akawai kapiwa, Gl
       kapia, Bk pakia.

115.   Tb kɨse '(bamboo) knife', Tr kɨte 'bamboo';
       Tp kate 'bamboo'.

116.   Tb komana 'beans'; Gl kumata, Arekuna
       kumã•ta, Wayumará kuma•sa, Bk kuata.

117.   Tb pak Coelogenys paca; Gl pak C. paca, Bk

haki, aki 'agouti'; see Hk hak-ra 'pig',
Tp pak-ila 'wild pig'.

118. Tb soko 'a heron'; Wn toko Ibis infuscata.

119. Tb tiŋ, Tr niŋ 'timbó vine, a fish poison';
Hk čeme 'to poison the fish', Tp i-teg
'poisonous vine', Gl e-tim-ui, Mk i-teme,
Trio tiñe 'to inebriate'.

120. Tb urua, Guaraní uruwa 'snail'; Hk warwa,
Hianókoto-Umáua alúua 'snail', IC óra
'shell', Bk uru-ši 'shell used for smoothing
bows'.

121. Tb yaku, Tr wako, Mu wakõ Penelope sp.,
Cracidae; Gl, Trio woko, Wn wok, Hianákoto-
Umáua oko-ime (ime 'big') Crax sp., Cracidae.

List B: Loanwords common to Tupí-Guaraní and North
Amazonian Carib

   Abbreviations: Ap Apalaí, Ar Arekúna, Gl Galibí
   (Kaliña, Karina), Hk Hishkaryána, HU Hianákoto-
   Umáua, IC Island Carib[9], In Ingarikó, Ip
   Ipurukotó, Mk Makushi, Tb Tupinambá, Tp
   Taulipang, Wn Wayána (and Upurui), Ww Waiwai,
   Yb Yabarána.

Tb aβati 'corn'; Gl awasi, Ap, IC awaši.

Tb araβe 'cockroach'; Tp aráuɛ, Gl alawi, IC eléwe.

Tb arakwã 'a bird, Ortalis sp.'; Wn aragua.

Tb ɨsɨpo 'vine'; Gl simo.

Tb karawata 'Bromelia sp.'; Wn kulaiwata, Tamanaco
karuata.

Tb kupi?i 'termite'; Gl kupisa.

Tb kuremã 'a fish, <u>Mugil sp.</u>'; Gl kwerimaŋ.

Tb kurimata 'a fish, <u>Prochilodus sp.</u>, Characidae';
Gl kulimata '<u>Salmo curimata</u>, Characidae'.

Tb kwati 'honey-bear (coatimundi), <u>Nasua socialis</u>';
Gl kuasi, Tp koazi, Ip koadži.

Tb marakanã 'species of parrot'; Gl, Wn marakana,
Trio, HU malakana, Mk marakan, Tp marakaŋ, Ip
marakona.

Tb marakaya 'wild cat'; Gl, Wn marakaya, Tp
marakaǯa.

Tb marakuya, Guaraní <u>murukuya</u> 'passion flower'; Gl
marekuya, IC merekoya, Wn murukuya.

Tb nanã 'pineapple'; Ap, Gl, Wn, Trio nana.

Tb paku 'a fish, <u>Myleɩes sp.</u>'; Ap, Gl paku, HU
haku.

Tb paranã 'sea'; Gl, Wn parana, IC balánna 'sea',
Tp palana 'waves'.

Tb parawa 'a parrot'; Gl, Wn, Trio palawa, Ap
paraua.

Tb pirãy 'piranha, <u>Pygocentrus sp.</u> and <u>Serrasalmus</u>
<u>sp.</u>'; Gl pirai '<u>Pygocentrus sp</u>'.

Tb tamanuʔa 'anteater'; Gl, Trio tamanoa, Mk
tamanua.

Tb tapiukaβ 'a wasp'; Gl tapiuka 'bee'.

Tb tapɨy 'hut, shelter'; Ap tapɨy 'house', Tp tapɨy
'house, hut', tapuluka 'hut'.

Tb taya '<u>Xanthosoma sp.</u>'; Wn, Trio taya, IC táia,
Gl táier.

Tb tokay '(hunter's) hut'; Gl tokai 'shaman's small
house'.

Tb tuyuyu 'big stork, <u>Mycteria americana</u>'; Gl
tuyuyu.

Tb urapar, Guaraní wɨrapa 'bow'; Tp, In urapa, Gl
    ulaba, Wayumará uraha, Hk kuraha, Ww krapa.
Tb urukure?a 'an owl'; Gl ulukuleya.
Tb urupe 'mushroom'; Gl ulupi.
Tb wara 'a heron, <u>Ibis rubra</u>'; Gl uala '<u>Ibis
    rubra</u>', HU uala, Trio wara '<u>Ibis egretta</u>'.
Tb warawa 'manatee'; Gl yalawa.
Tb warinĩ 'war'; Yb ualini, Gl walimi.
Tb yakare 'alligator'; In yakalé, Ar yakalɛ́, Ap
    zakare, Tp ɟakare, Gl akare.
Tb yawar 'jaguar'; Hk awar-ko, Tp ɟawaira 'black
    jaguar'.
Tb yurara 'a turtle'; Gl walala, Yb uaraara, Hu
    alala.


LIST C.1: Borrowings from Língua Geral in North
Amazonian Carib languages[10]


LG wakawã '<u>Herpetotheres cachinnans</u>, a hawk that
    cries in the night'; Tp wakawa 'night bird with
    screaming cry'.
LG akayurána 'false cashew tree'; Gl akáyula 'wild
    cashew tree, <u>Curatella americana</u>'.
LG apukuitá 'oar'; Ap apakɨita, Gl abokuitya.
LG kɨseapára 'sickel'; Ww kacɨpara, Gl supara
    'knife'.
LG pašiɨwa 'a palm, <u>Itiartea exorrhiza</u>'; Gl pasiu.
LG yakamĩ '<u>Psophia crepitans</u>'; Tp yakami, Gl akami.
LG yan[d]iá 'a catfish'; Tp ɟandia.


LIST C.2: Borrowings from Wayapí (Oyampi) or from
Língua Geral in Wayána

Wn apukuita 'oar'; Wp ipɨkuita, LG apukuitá.

Wn ararawa 'macaw'; Wp, LG arára

Wn arua 'mirror'; Wn LG waruá.

Wn karana 'species of palm tree'; LG karaná.

Wn panamem 'butterfly'; Wp panama.

Wn tukurawa 'grasshopper'; LG tukúra.

Wn yakumanɘ 'pilot oar'; LG yakumã.


LIST C.3: Borrowings from Wayána in Wayapí


Wp pari 'grandchild'; Wn pari-psik (psik 'small').

Wp kaparu 'club'; Wn kaparu.

Wp kasuru 'beads'; Wn kašuru.

Wp kɨto 'a toad'; Wn kuto.

Wp kurupara 'gun powder'; Wn kurupara.

Wp kusiri 'sapajou-monkey'; Wn kusiri.

Wp kuakɨ 'manioc flour'; Wn kuake

Wp maria 'knife'; Wn maria.

Wp orori 'a lizard'; Wn orori 'iguana'.

Wp paira 'bow, wood for making bows'; Wn paira 'bow'.

Wp parapi, marapi 'dish'; Wn marapi 'dish of the white man'.

Wp piroto 'lead shot'; Wn piroto.

Wp saa 'machete'; Wn sapa.

Wp sautu 'salt'; Wn sautu.

Wp sawana 'savannah'; Wn sawanɘ.

Wp sirike 'Pleiades constellation'; Wn sirika 'star'.

Wp warapuru 'cocoa'; Wn warapuru 'cocoa-tree'.

COMMENTS AND CONCLUSIONS

Although a possible genetic relationship between
Tupí and Carib was conjectured at least as early as
1909 (by de Goeje), the general classifications of
South American Indian languages (e.g.  Rivet 1924,
Schmidt 1926, Rivet and Loukotka 1952, Swadesh
1959, Greenberg 1960, Loukotka 1968) have not taken
this possibility into account, not even for a long
range (phylum) relationship.  In the data just presented, not every set of similarities between Tupí
and Carib languages should be ascribed to a genetic
relationship; rather the most obvious lexical similarities between such languages appear to be the
result of borrowing, both recent (as between Wayampí and Wayána) and old (as between the whole Tupí-
Guaraní family and North Amazonian Carib).

There are, however, a sizable number of lexical
items that, although not so obviously similar, can
be shown to be cognates linked by regular phonological correspondences.  Most of these belong to semantic domains in which the intrusion of loanwords
is less likely to occur.  It is probable that not
every set in List A will stand as truly cognate after tighter scrutiny is made on the basis of more
complete knowledge of the internal relations of
both Tupí and Carib.  Given the present state of
Carib linguistics, it is not possible to estimate
the likelihood of the reconstruction of a lexical
item in a given language as a component of the
Proto-Carib lexicon.  For instance, in Taulipang
(Pemong) pepoko 'to take off the feathers' may be
analyzed as containing ko 'to pull away' and a mor-

pheme pepo, attested to only in this word and for
which we may provide the meaning 'feather', even
though the free form for the same meaning is another word (yapɨri).  The abstract morpheme pepo is
very similar to Tupinambá pepo and Tuparí pep'o,
both meaning 'wing, feather' (no.  29 of List A) as
well as to Mawé pepo 'wing', Jurúna peo- 'wing' and
Karitiána papɨ 'arrow feather', all leading to the
reconstruction of Proto-Tupí *pep'o.  However, we
lack any evidence of <u>pepoko</u> having cognates in
other Carib languages and we do not even know how
its meaning is conveyed in them.  Thus until we
have increased knowledge of a greater number of Carib languages, the possibility of <u>pepoko</u> being a
loanword cannot be discarded.

   Nevertheless it is likely that the hypothesis of
a common Tupí-Carib descent for a good part of List
A will be strengthened by greater knowledge of the
Carib languages.  This should of course also hold
true for our growing knowledge of the Tupí languages.  When the compared words are attested to in
several languages both in the Tupí and in the Carib
group the case is of course stronger, as in sets 1,
2, 3, 4, 21, 25, 26, 33, 34, 46, 59, 72, 88, 90,
91, 93, 96, 100, 108, 119. It is unlikely that
these instances could be due to borrowing between
single languages, for each of them involves more
than one family in the Tupí stock and more than one
subgroup in the Carib family.  Additionally, only
set 119 is culture/environment-bound.

   To these lexical correspondences we could add
some identical structural features of the phonolo-

gies and grammars of the Tupí and Carib languages,
such as: (a) a typical six-vowel vocalic system
with three high vowels and three non-high vowels (i
ɨ u e a o); (b) postpositions, genitive-noun phrases, and basically verb-final clauses; (c) prefixal
person markers in the noun and the verb, other inflections being suffixal; (d) possessor markers and
object markers are in general the same; (e) clear
distinction of reflexive and non-reflexive 3rd person, as well as of inclusive and exclusive 1st person; (f) verb morphology and syntax are predominantly ergative.

It should be noted that some of the words (or
morphemes) appearing in List A seem to belong to a
wider net of relations which encompasses the Macro-
Jê languages, besides Tupí and Carib. Taking Kaingáng (Jê) and Boróro as representatives of Macro-
Jê, we can exemplify this with, among others the
following correspondences: for set no. 21, which
could be derived from a common form *uŋ$^{w}$ 'father',
Kaingáng has yoŋ and Bororo has ogwa, both with the
same meaning; and for set no. 69, which analogous-
ly could stem from *oŋ$^{w}$ 'to wrap', Boróro has ogwa
(homonymous with the preceding word) 'to conceal'.
These two reconstructions have *ŋ$^{w}$ after a back vowel; after a front vowel *ŋ$^{w}$ could be reconstructed on the same basis of Tb -β = Carib -m in
*wereŋ$^{w}$ 'to (re)turn' (set no. 106). This is com-
parable to Boróro kirimi 'to return' and perhaps
also to Kaingáng wĩrĩn 'to turn' (for Boróro k as a
reflex of *w note also *woro 'parrot' for set no.
113 and Boróro korao 'parrot' and, in cases where

Carib is not involved, Proto-Tupí *wor 'neck' and
Boróro ko 'neck' korora 'bird neck'; Proto-Tupí
*wab 'to split' and Boróro kwa, ka 'split'). For
set no. 108 a possible proto-form is *k'e 'to say,
to do', which corresponds to Kaingáng ke with the
same meaning; and for set no. 110, with the ana-
logously postulated proto-form *k'u 'to eat', we
have both Kaingáng and Boróro with ko 'to eat'.
Set no. 47, for which *p'or 'full' is postulated
as a proto-form, appears to correspond to Kaingáng
ᵽɔr 'full' in the same way as set no. 96 with a
proto-form *por 'to jump' evokes Kaingáng ᵽor 'to
be thrown'. Perhaps W pɨ 'bark' does not correspond to Tb pc 'bark' (set no. 28), but rather to
Tb pir 'skin', which is matched by Kaingáng ᵽɨr and
Boróro biri, both meaning 'bark, skin'.

The whole set of person markers (especially
nos. 2-5 in List A): also belongs to this net of
relations. Compare for no. 2 Kaingáng ã, Shavante
(Jê family) a-, Boróro a-, Kipeá (Karirí family)
e-, Karajá a- '2nd person'; for no. 3 Shavante ĩ-,
Boróro, Kipeá, and Karajá i- 3rd person non reflexive'; for no. 4 Kaingáng ti '3rd person non reflexive', Shavante ti-, Boróro tu-, Kipeá d-, di-,
Karajá ta- '3rd person reflexive'; for no. 5 Kipeá
k-, ku- '1st person plural inclusive'.

A possible genetic relationship of Carib with
the Macro-Jê languages should not appear surprising
since Greenberg (1960) has already proposed a hypothetical Jê-Pano-Carib phylum. But although the
data above seem to substantiate some aspects of
Greenberg's hypothesis (evidence of Carib-Jê), they

also question other aspects of it.   No evidence has
so far been found of regular phonological correspondences between Pano or Pano-Takána and either Jê
or Carib.   If any genetic relationship would in the
future be discovered between them, it would probably be more remote than the possible relationship
between Jê and Carib, as well as the possible relationship between Carib (and Jê) and Tupí.   In other
words, Tupí and Carib (and Macro-Jê) are more likely candidates for a valid genetic grouping than Jê-
Pano-Carib as such.   But the grouping of Tupí with
Carib (and Macro-Jê) does not fit well within
Greenberg's hypothesis, because Tupí then would be
placed within another of the three major divisions
conceived of for South America--Macro-Chibchan,
Andean-Equatorial, and Jê-Pano-Carib.   As a supposed member of the Equatorial branch of Andean-Equatorial, Tupí would be related more closely to Arawak than to either Carib or Jê. Just the opposite
relationship is emerging from comparative work.
Greenberg has himself remarked that "the greatest
uncertainty exists in the case of the two new vast
groupings in South America, Andean-Equatorial and
Ge-Pano-Carib" (1960:791), and emphasizes that his
doubt pertains "to the correctness of these two
assemblages of languages as valid genetic groupings" (1960:792).   Indeed, the evidence being gathered, where phonologically controlled comparative
work may be attempted, suggests the likelihood of a
genetic group encompassing Carib and Macro-Jê as
well as Tupí.

NOTES

1.  After writing this paper I read Marshall Dur-
    bin's "A Survey of the Carib Language Family"
    (Durbin 1977, reprinted in this volume), in
    which the Carib languages are divided into Nor-
    thern Carib and Southern Carib, but with only
    partial coincidence with my guess on North and
    South Amazonian languages. Durbin's classifi-
    cation deserves greater consideration than I can
    possibly include here [editors' note: see also
    discussion by Migliazza and Davis in this
    volume].

2.  Cf. Koch-Grünberg (1928:258) on Wayumará:
    "(es) gehört zu der Karibengruppe Nord- und
    Nordostguayanas, wozu auch die Hianákoto und
    Verwandte des oberen Yapurá-Caquetá zu rechnen
    sind. Das Wayumará bildet sogar mit seiner Er-
    weichung des inlautenden und meistens auch an-
    lautenden p in h mit anderen Merkmalen das bis
    jetzt fehlende Bindeglied zwischen dem [sic]
    Yapurá-Kariben und ihren nahen Verwandten im
    fernen Osten: Trio, Galibi und anderen."

3.  Although the Carib affiliation of Pimenteira
    has been cast in doubt by some authors (e.g.
    Tovar 1961:112, Durbin 1977:27, 31), I believe
    this language is Carib.

4.  "Nous fixons l'attention sur ce fait, qu'il y a
    plusieurs mots qui semblent appartenir à la fois
    a la langue caraïbe primitive, et au Tupi ou à
    l'Arrouague primitif et qui cependant ne sont
    pas des onomatopées. Seraient-ce des restes

d'une époque où ces familles n'en faisaient en-
core qu'une seule?  Nous nous contentons pour le
moment de mettre en évidence ces concordances"
(de Goeje 1909:1-2).

5.  In some instances it is difficult to decide for
a given set between List A and List B.  In this
study we took the presence of a word also in the
South Amazonian Carib languages, e.g.  Bakairí
or Nahukwá, as indicative of its belonging to
List A (for instance, the word for 'beans', no.
116 of List A).  After I wrote the last draft of
this paper, I received a copy of B.J.  Hoff's
The Carib Language (The Hague: Nijhoff, 1968),
in which he comments (pp.  13-14) on borrowings
between Carib and Tupí and gives a list of 69
lexical correspondences based on Tatevin's Tupí,
which is a dialect of Língua Geral.  25 items of
Hoff's list appear in our Lists A, B, and C--6
in List A, 17 in List B, 2 in List C.  With one
exception (koko/koxko 'coconut', which Tatevin's
LG surely took from Portuguese, while Carib received it, directly or indirectly, from Spanish), the other more than 40 correspondences
found by Hoff should fall in some of the three
categories of Lists A, B, and C, as well as in a
fourth one of Carib loanwords in Língua Geral,
not excluding a further possibility of words
from a third Amazonian language entering Carib
and LG independently (see note 10).

6.  Theories about prehistoric migrations of Tupí-
Guaraní speaking peoples as well as about Carib
speaking ones must take into consideration loan-

words such as those in List B as important in-
dicators of possible moments of contact. It is
significant that most words in List B exceed the
average length of Tupí-Guaraní roots (which are
regularly mono- and disyllabic) and can not be
analyzed as consisting of more than one Tupí-
Guaraní morpheme. This marks them as highly
probable borrowings into Tupí-Guaraní.

7.  I am grateful to Cheryl J. Jensen for having
checked Coudreau's Wayapí words used here a-
gainst data of her own and Gary Olson's field
work. This permitted me to conclude that Coudreau's wordlist is very reliable in both semantic and phonological representation.

8.  It is also possible that South Amazonian Carib
languages have received Tupí words from languages within their more immediate reach, such as
Kamayurá and Awetí. The Bakairí word for 'carrying basket', mayaku, stems clearly from Awetí
mayãkú, typically with /y/ instead of Tupí-Guaraní /n/ (Tupinambá panakũ).

9.  Island Carib, as is now well known, is an Arawak language, not a Carib one. But it contains
a large number of Carib words due to the unusual
situation from which it evolved, namely the interaction of conquering Carib men with captured
Arawak women and children. Its Carib words are
included in Lists A and B because they indicate
the already existing presence of cognate words
in coastal Carib languages in the first half of
the 17th century. IC data was taken from de
Goeje (1909) and Taylor (1977).

10.  This short list includes only Língua Geral
words that are of certain Tupinambá descent.
Other LG words which are found also in North
Amazonian Carib languages are most likely loanwords in LG and may have their origin in other
(non-Tupí) Amazonian languages and possibly in
some Carib language.  So for some words it is
not at all clear now which was the direction of
the loan: i.e., LG > Carib or Carib > LG.  Some
examples are LG mukayá = Gl mokaya Acrocomia
sp., LG murumurú = Gl murumuru Astrocaryum murumuru, LG wasaí = Gl, Wn uasei Euterpe oleracea,
LG kušiú = Gl kesiu Pithecia satanas, LG ka-
rapanã = Gl kalápana 'mosquito').

REFERENCES
Anonymous.  1952-1953.  Vocabulário na língua bra-
sílica.  Universidade de São Paulo, Faculdade de
Filosofia, Ciências e Letras, Boletim 137, 164.
São Paulo.
Caspar, Franz and Aryon D.  Rodrigues.  n.d.  Die
Tuparí-Sprache.  ms.
Coudreau, H.  1892.  Vocabulaires méthodiques des
langues Ouayana, Aparaï, Oyampi, Emerillon.
Bibliothèque Linguistique Américaine XV.  Paris:
Maisonneuve.
Crofts, Marjorie.  1973.  Gramática munduruku.
Brasília: Summer Institute of Linguistics.
------.  n.d.  Munduruku field file.  Ms.
Derbyshire, Desmond.  1979.  Hixkaryana.  Lingua
Descriptive Studies 1.  Amsterdam: North
Holland.

------. Hixkaryana field file. ms.

Durbin, Marshall. 1977. A Survey of the Carib
    Language Family. In Carib Speaking Indians:
    Culture, Society and Language, Ellen B. Basso,
    ed., pp. 23-38. Tucson: University of Arizona
    Press.

Fonseca, João Severiano, and Pires de Almeida.
    1899. Voyage autour du Brésil (édition conden-
    sée). Rio de Janeiro: Lavignasse.

Goeje, C.H. de. 1906. Bijdrage tot de ethno-
    graphie der surinaamsche Indianen. Internationa-
    les Archiv für Ethnographie XVII (supplement).

------. 1909. Etudes linguistiques caraïbes. Ver-
    handlingen der Koninklijke Akademie van Weten-
    schappen te Amsterdam, Afdeeling Letterkunde,
    nieuwe reeks, deel X, n. 3.

------. 1946. Etudes linguistiques caraïbes, tome
    II. Verhandlingen der Koninklijke Nederlandsche
    Akademie van Wetenschappen, Afdeeling Letterkun-
    de, nieuwe reeks, deel IL, n. 2:1-274.

Hawkins, W. Neil. 1952. A fonologia da língua
    uaiuai. Universidade de São Paulo, Faculdade de
    Filosofia, Ciências e Letras, Boletim 157. São
    Paulo.

------. 1962. A morfologia do substantivo na lín-
    gua uaiuai. Rio de Janeiro: Museu Nacional.

Hawkins, W. Neil, and Robert Hawkins. 1953. Verb
    inflection in Waiwai (Carib). International
    Journal of American Linguistics 19:201-211.

Koch-Grünberg, Theodor. 1928. Vom Roroíma zum
    Orinoco, Vol. 4. Stuttgart: Strecker und
    Schröder.

Métraux, Alfred.  1927.  Migrations historiques des
    Tupi-Guarani.  Journal de la Société des Améri-
    canistes 19: 1-45.

Olson, Roberta.  1978.  Dicionário por tópicos nas
    línguas Oiampi (Wajapï)-Português.  Brasília:
    Summer Institute of Linguistics.

Rodrigues, Aryon D.  1958a.  Die Klassifikation des
    Tupi-Sprachstammes.  Proceedings of the 32nd
    International Congress of Americanists, pp.
    679-684.  Copenhague: Munskgaard.

------.  1958b.  Classification of Tupi-Guarani.
    International Journal of American Linguistics
    24: 231-234.

------.  1959.  Phonologie der Tupinambá-Sprache.
    Ph.D.  dissertation, Universität Hamburg.

------.  1961.  Tuparí e tupinambá: evidências de
    parentesco genético.  Paper read at the 5th mee-
    ting of the Brazilian Anthropological Associa-
    tion, Belo Horizonte.

------.  1964.  A classificação do tronco linguís-
    tico tupi.  Revista de Antropologia 12:99-104.
    São Paulo.

------.  1970.  Línguas ameríndias.  Grande Enci-
    clopédia Delta-Larousse: pp.  4034-4036.  Rio de
    Janeiro: Delta.

------.  1980.  Tupí-guaraní e munduruku: evidên-
    cias lexicais e fonológicas de parentesco gené-
    tico.  Estudos Linguísticos 3:194-209.  Arara-
    quara: Universidade Estadual Paulista.

------.  1981.  Fonologia e morfologia do Tupinam-
    bá.  Unpublished paper.

Ruiz de Montoya, A. 1639. Tesoro de la lengua
    guarani. Madrid: Juan Sanchez.
Steinen, Karl von den. 1892. Die Bakaírí-Sprache.
    Leipzig: K.F. Koehler's Antiquarium.
------. Unter den Naturvölkern Zentral-Brasiliens.
    Berlin: Dietrich Reimer.
Stradelli, E. 1929. Vocabularios da lingua geral
    portuguez-nheengatu e nheengatu-portuguez, pre-
    cedidos de um espoço de grammatica nheengatu-
    umbue-saua miri e seguido de contos em lingua
    geral nheengatu-poranduua. Revista do Instituto
    Historico e Geographico Brasileiro, t. 104, vol.
    158, pp. 9-768. Rio de Janeiro.
Tatevin, C. 1910. La langue tapíhíya dite tupí ou
    ñeéngatu (belle langue): grammaire, dictionnaire
    et textes. Schriften der Sprachenkommission II,
    Kaiserliche Akademie der Wissenschaften. Vien-
    na: Alfred Hölder.
Tovar, Antonio. 1961. Catálogo de las lenguas de
    América del Sur. Buenos Aires: Editorial
    Sudamericana.
Taylor, Douglas. 1977. Languages of the West In-
    dies. Baltimore: Johns Hopkins University
    Press.
Wheatley, James. n.d. Bakairí field file. ms.

# 10. The Present State of the Study of Brazilian Indian Languages

Aryon D. Rodrigues

INTRODUCTION

This essay presents a brief survey of current research on the indigenous languages of Brazil. It
will include a description of the individuals and
institutions participating in such research as well
as a schematic overview of studies either currently
being carried out, or having been recently completed, on the Indian languages of Brazil.

LANGUAGES

There are approximately 170 Indian languages spoken
today in Brazil. Most of these are found in the
northern and western states and territories, such
as Maranhão, Pará, Amapá, Amazonas, Roraima, Acre,
Rondônia, Mato Grosso, Goiás, and Mato Grosso do
Sul. But there are also a few Indian languages
spoken in the southern states of São Paulo, Paraná, Santa Catarina, and Rio Grande do Sul, as well
as two languages in Minas Gerais (Mashakalí and
Krenak-Nakrehé) and one in the northeastern state
of Pernambuco (Yathé or Fulniô).

Of a total population of 185,500 Indians around
30,500 are monolingual in Portuguese. The remaining 155,000 speakers of native languages are divided among 170 languages. Whereas we have higher

numbers of speakers for some languages (Tukúna with
18,000, Makushí with 14,500, Kaingáng and Guaraní
with about 10,000 each, Terena with over 8,000,
Guajajára with nearly 6,000, etc.), so also we have
very few speakers of other languages. According to
the most recent census, there are 36 Indian languages with fewer than 100 speakers and, among these,
14 languages with fewer than 50 speakers.

Two thirds of the indigenous languages of Brazil
are affiliated to one of the five larger linguistic
stocks identified in the country: Tupí, Macro-Jê,
Carib, Arawak, and Pano. The other third, about 60
languages, either belong to smaller linguistic families (Tukáno, Makú, Yanomámi, Katukína, Múra Cha-
pakúra, Nambikwára, Guaikurú), or are "isolated"
(which may simply mean they have not yet been
classified).

RESEARCHERS

Researchers from abroad
Currently most of the Indian languages being studied in Brazil are being recorded and analyzed by
people affiliated with the Summer Institute of
Linguistics/Wycliffe Bible translators. SIL activities started in Brazil in 1956 with institutional
support from the Department of Anthropology of the
Museu Nacional (Rio de Janeiro). In 1963 there was
an attempt at integrating the linguistic work of
SIL academically within the recently established
Universidade de Brasília. The purpose of this effort was to (a) provide training for Brazilian lin-

guists, (b) make accessible to Brazilian linguists
and anthropologists the results of SIL field work
and analyses, and (c) stimulate the most qualified
members of SIL to engage in research of scientific
significance. This experiment was interrupted in
1965 when federal authorities cut off funding for
further development of the Universidade de Brasília, thereby causing the exodus and dispersion of
its professors and graduate students. Shortly
thereafter SIL signed a contract with the Ministry
of the Interior and its agency for Indian affairs
(Fundação Nacional do Índio, FUNAI) which permitted
an expansion of its activities, but outside of an
academic setting. The number of members of SIL increased considerably, reaching in 1967 about 300
people, among whom nearly 90 were directly engaged
in linguistic field work on 40 languages.

    In 1977 the federal administration decided not
to renew the contract between the Ministry of the
Interior and SIL and to revoke the authorization
allowing SIL members to work in Indian areas.
Since then SIL's Brazil branch has lost some of its
field workers, so that the work on some languages
(e.g. Cinta-Larga, Mamaindé) has been completely
interrupted. For other languages, investigations
have continued on the basis of data and knowledge
accumulated previously. In some instances work
among Indian people had been made possible by special arrangements. In 1981 the Department of Anthropology of the Museu Nacional broke its 20 year
old relationship with SIL (the measure was effective as of January 1982). Presently the only aca-

demic contract that SIL has in Brazil is an agreement with UNICAMP (Universidade Estadual de Campinas) for scientific cooperation in the documentation and description of indigenous languages; this
contract has been in existence since October 1978.
Under this agreement and in connection with graduate studies at UNICAMP, five languages (Arara, Nadëb, Pirahã, Suruí, and Wayapí) are being studied
by Summer Institute of Linguistics members, among
them two Brazilians.

    Although many foreign anthropologists, European
and American, have chosen indigenous peoples of
Brazil for their research, the presence of foreign
non-missionary linguists on the Brazilian scene has
been a rarity.    Besides a few anthropologists with
linguistic interest and competence (like A. Monod
on Trumai, D. Price on Nambikwára, G. Urban on
Shokleng), there has been only one foreign student
of linguistics during the last 25 years who has
carried out systematic research on a Brazilian Indian language (D.    Moore on Gavião).    Perhaps the
reason for this lack of linguistic research is an
undue belief that SIL is in charge of the task of
working on all the indigenous languages of Brazil.
This is clearly not the case: (a) SIL teams have
worked on no more than one third of the native languages spoken today in Brazil, (b) the aims of SIL
research coincide only in part with those of other
linguists, and (c) only certain members of SIL
teams have high level research interests and competence, since their basic motivation is a practical
and clearly limited one.

In addition to SIL, other religious organizations have missionaries with some linguistic training (usually of the kind offered by SIL courses)
among the Indians of Brazilian Amazonia.  Such is
the case, for instance, of the New Tribes Mission
(Missão Novas Tribos do Brasil), Unevangelized
Fields Mission (Missão Cristã Evangélica do Brasil), and the Evangelical Mission of Amazonia (Missão Evangélica da Amazônia).  In general very little is known about the linguistic work of these
missionaries.

### Brazilian researchers

Two Brazilian institutions presently further research on Indian languages: the Museu Nacional in
Rio de Janeiro and the State University of Campinas
(UNICAMP) in the State of São Paulo.  The Museu Nacional has a linguistic section in its Department
of Anthropology which represents the longest tradition of institutional commitment to the scientific
study of Indian languages in the country.  Its linguistic staff includes Yonne F. Leite (Ph.D.),
Charlotte Emmerich (M.A.), Ruth M.F. Monserrat
(M.A.), Marília L.C. Facó Soares (M.A.), and Bruna
Franchetto.  Field work has been carried out on Tapirapé, Aweti, Txikão, Kuikúru.  In addition, researchers from other institutions have had thesis
supervision by Yonne F. Leite, viz.  on Kashuyána
by Ruth Wallace (Museu do Índio, Rio de Janeiro)
and on Gavião (Pukobye) by Leopoldina Araujo (Federal University of Pará, Belém).  The Museum itself
does not offer courses in linguistics, although be-

tween 1967 and 1972 it had the best graduate program in linguistics of the country.

The Department of Linguistics of the Instituto
de Estudos da Linguagem of UNICAMP began the study
of indigenous languages in 1977 and has ever since
stimulated fieldwork and linguistic analysis by
graduate students. [The Department also encourages
visiting scholars interested in Amerindian languages to participate in its seminars]. Members of
the staff who are particularly involved in research
or in supervision of theses on Indian languages
include Aryon D. Rodrigues (Dr.   Phil.), Lucy Seki
(Dr.   Phil.), Maurizio Gnerre (Dr.), Frank R.
Brandon (Ph.D.), Maria Bernadete Abaurre-Gnerre
(Ph.D.), Charlotte Chambelland (Dr.), Daniel L.
Everett (Dr.   Sc.) Márcio F. Silva (M.A.).

One doctoral degree and eight master's degrees
have been awarded on the basis of research on
Indian languages: Old Guaraní, Pirahã, Kamayurá,
Kadiwéu, Mundurukú, Suruí, Mbyá, Wayampí, Nadëb.
Graduate students at the Ph.D.   level are working
on four languages: Guató, Kaingáng of São Paulo,
Tukúna, and Bakairí (and a fifth one on Kawki in
Peru).   Students at the M.A. level are working on
six languages: Arara (Carib), Apurinã, Guajá,
Kaingáng of Nonoai, Katukína (Pano), Parakanã.
Other languages being analyzed by faculty members
of the department are: Guaraní, Kamayurá, Krenak-
Nakrehé, Pakaá-nova, Pirahã, Quechua (the Huanca
dialect of Peru), Shuar (of Ecuador), Tupinambá,
and Xetá.

## DESCRIPTIVE LINGUISTICS

### Languages Being Studied in Brazil

Of the approximately 170 native languages spoken in Brazil, about a third are being studied locally, either by national or by foreign linguists. The number of languages studied by SIL has decreased since 1977; some projects have been interrupted while others have been considered finished (this is the case of Hishkaryána, Kaingáng, and Mundurukú). However, work on two new languages has been initiated, so that today SIL is working descriptively on 39 languages. At UNICAMP 16 living languages of Brazilian Indians are objects of research and of these only five coincide with languages studied by SIL; at the Museu Nacional six languages have been studied in recent years. At least four languages are being investigated by individuals who are not affiliated with any of the three institutions just mentioned. Although I have no precise information on languages being analyzed by members of missionary organizations other than SIL, I estimate their number to be around ten. Therefore about 70 languages are now undergoing some kind of descriptive study in Brazil.

### Languages Studied Outside of Brazil

A number of Amerindian languages are spoken on both sides of the border separating Brazil and neighboring countries, such as Argentina, Paraguay, Bolivia, Peru, Colombia, Venezuela, and the Guyanas.

More than 20 of these languages are being analyzed,
most of them by missionary organizations: ten in
Colombia (Barasano, Désano, Karapaná, Kobéwa, Makú-
na, Siriáno, Tukáno, Tuyúka, Wanáno, Yurutí), 9 in
Peru (Amawáka, Kampa, Kapanáwa, Kulína, Mayorúna,
Piro, Sharanáwa, Tukúna, Witóto), two in Suriname
(Tirió, Wayána), and one each in French Guyana (Wayampí), Guyana (Wapishána) and Venezuela (Sanumá).
As a result, the total of Indian languages spoken
in Brazil and being studied one way or another numbers approximately 100.

Results

The variety of indigenous languages in Brazil is as
great as that of Mexico and the United States combined. That more than a half of the number of extant languages is already being studied is in itself a positive indication of the progress being
made in our knowledge of these languages and of the
people who speak them. But some qualification must
be made as to the nature and the accessibility of
the linguistic knowledge emerging from these studies:

(a) About three fourths of the nearly 100 languages being studied are the object of religiously
oriented work whose main goal is the translation of
the Bible and the indoctrination of Indian people
into some form of Christianity. This objective de-
termines certain emphases and preferences and leaves a number of untouched areas in the knowledge of
each language. To the missionaries, linguistic
analyses are a means of speeding up a practical

command of the language as well as assuring their technical control of native helpers.

(b) Among the missionary organizations that carry out linguistic analyses, only the largest one, SIL, uses a scientific interest in analysis as a means of increasing its institutional prestige and promoting its own ends. Other missionary organizations do not represent themselves as linguistic institutions. This makes a big difference in the diffusion of knowledge: SIL publishes its research, whereas the other organizations do not show the results of their analyses. Rather they are given the character of internal documents, thus making it extremely difficult to gain access to information even about their very existence..

(c) Even in an organization like SIL there are pronounced differences in the elaboration and publication of data from one "national" branch to another, as well as within the same branch, and from one language team to another. In some cases, one member of a team is a "linguist by vocation" and writes on diverse aspects of the language, and incorporates into his or her analysis sophisticated theories, while the other members of the team are largely concerned with practical tasks. Consequently, the analytical contribution of SIL linguists is rather fragmentary and the accumulation of published or simply archived data available to outsiders is relatively slow.

(d) Due to other factors, particularly the early stage of development of pertinent institutions, lay or academic linguists in Brazil publish little and

in a fragmentary way. Lack of adequate financing,
an excess of bureaucratic difficulties in carrying
out field work in indigenous areas, and insufficient linguistic training reduce the potentiality
and weaken the motivation not only of students, but
also of full fledged researchers.

(e) Improper understanding of the goals of linguistic analysis after the advent of generative
grammar, statistically oriented sociolinguistics,
and content-oriented discourse analysis leads
students of linguistics (and some of their instructors) to undervalue the need for training in pho-
netics, basic phonological and morphological analysis, extensive field work, and so on.

If we take published works (and unpublished
dissertations or theses) as an indication of the
accumulation of knowledge in this area during the
last 30 years, the result is not very impressive:
nevertheless, it is more than what is generally
recognized:

(a) eighteen grammars: Iranshe (Moura 1960,
Meader 1967), Tembé (Boudin 1963, 1978), Tukáno
(Giacone 1965, Silva 1966), Yathê (Lapenda 1968),
Guajajára (Bendor-Samuel 1972), Kaingáng (Wiesemann 1972), Mundurukú (Crofts 1973), Asuriní
(Harrison 1975), Urubú (Kakumasu 1976), Hixkaryána (Derbyshire 1979), Tapirapé (Almeida et al.
1983); unpublished are Apinayé (Callow 1962), Kipeá (Azevedo 1965), Boróro (Crowell 1979), Hishkaryána (Derbyshire 1979b), Karitiána (Landin
1980), Makushí (Carson 1981), Pirahã (Everett
1983).

(b) more than fifty papers on grammatical de-
tails of Apinayé, Apurinã, Awetí, Bakairí, Boróro,
Dení, Guaraní Mbyá, Hishkaryána, Hupda, Kadiwéu,
Kamayurá, Karajá, Kayabí, Kayapó, Krahó, Máku, Ma-
kushí, Mamaindé, Mashakalí, Munduruku, Nadëb, Nam-
bikwára, Ofayé, Palikúr, Paumarí, Pirahã, Sanumá,
Teréna, Tirió, Trumai, Tupinambá, Central Waiká,
Waurá, Wayampí, Waiwái and unpublished theses on
Munduruku and Nadëb.

(c) nearly thirty phonological descriptions:
Waiwái (Hawkins 1952), Kaiwá (Bridgeman 1961),
Shiriána (Migliazza and Grimes 1961), Pirahã (Hein-
richs 1964), Máku (Migliazza 1965), Munduruku
(Braun and Crofts 1965), Aikamteli (Tracy 1966),
Paresí (Rowan 1967), Apalaí (Koehn and Koehn 1971),
Parintintín (Pease and Betts 1971), Awetí (Emmerich
and Monserrat 1972), Kaingáng (Wiesemann 1972),
Guajajára (Bendor-Samuel 1972), Sherente (Mattos
1973), Shavante (McLeod 1974a), Kadiwéu (Griffiths
and Griffiths 1976), Nambikwára (Price 1976), Kashuyána (Paula 1980), Txikão (Emmerich 1980); unpublished: Tupinambá (Rodrigues 1959), Apinayé
(Callow 1962), Kamayurá (Ferreira 1973, Silva
1981), Old Guaraní (Rodrigues 1974), Pirahã (Everett 1980), Kadiwéu (Braggio 1981), Makuxí (Carson
1981), Suruí (van der Meer 1982), and Guaraní Mbyá
(Guedes 1983).

(d) about thirty papers on phonological details:
Apinayé, Asuriní, Aikamteli, Boróro, Kaingáng, Kaiwá, Kamayurá, Karajá, Kashuyána, Mashakalí, Makushí, Nambikwára, Mawé (Sateré), Pirahã, Suruí, Tapirapé, Teréna, Tirió, Shavante.

(e) nine pedagogical grammars: Tupinambá (Barbosa 1956), Yanomám (Ramos 1975), Shavante (McLeod
and Mitchell 1977), Asuriní (Nicholson 1978), Rikbaktsá (Boswood 1978), Teréna (Ekdahl and Butler
1979), Apinayé (Ham et al. 1979), Nambikwára (B.
Kroeker 1980) Makushí (Pira and Amodio 1983).

(f) about twenty papers on discourse: Apinayé,
Bakairí, Boróro, Hishkaryána, Hupda, Jamamadí, Kaiwá, Kamayurá, Kayapó, Mamaindé, Mundurukú, Nambikwára, Palikúr, Paresí, Rikbaktsá, Waurá.

(g) nine dictionaries: Tupinambá (Barbosa 1955,
1970), Boróro (Albisetti and Venturelli 1962), Tukáno (Giacone 1965), Tembé (Boudin 1966, 1978),
Kaingáng (Wiesemann 1971), Paresí (Rowan and Rowan
1978), Parintintín (Betts 1981), Guaraní Mbyá (Dooley 1982), Karitiána (Landin 1983); and some smaller vocabularies: Tariána (Giacone 1962), Mundurukú
(Crofts et al. 1977), Wayampí (Olson 1978), Bakairí (Taukane 1978).

(h) seven collections of texts: Hishkaryána
(Derbyshire 1965), Kaiwá (Taylor and Taylor 1966),
Parintintín (Betts and Pease 1966), Boróro (Albi-
setti and Venturelli 1969), Mundurukú (Burum 1977-
1979), Canela (Popjes 1982), Kayapó (Thomson 1982),
Paresí (Rowan 1983).

COMPARATIVE LINGUISTICS
The progress of comparative linguistic studies
depends of course on the development of phono-
logical, grammatical, and lexical descriptions.
The extreme scarcity of dictionaries for Brazilian
Indian languages precludes the undertaking of any

wide range comparative studies. This notwithstan-
ding, some comparative and even reconstructive work
has been done, most of it on the basis of restricted data.

Recent essays based on new data which either ex-
plore or demonstrate genetic relationships are the
following: Tupí stock (Rodrigues 1955b, 1958a,
1958b), Yanomámi (Rodrigues 1960, Migliazza 1978),
Hishkaryána-Kashuyána-Waiwái (Derbyshire 1961c),
Umutína-Boróro (Rodrigues 1962), Jê (Davis 1966),
Mondé (Rodrigues 1966), Macro-Jê (Davis 1968), Ofa-
yé-Jê (Gudschinsky 1971), Tupí-Guaraní (Lemle 1971,
Rodrigues 1984), Rikbaktsá-Jê (Boswood 1973), Nambikwára (Price 1978), Kaingáng (Wiesemann 1978),
Tupí-Jê (Rodrigues 1978b), Tupí-Caríb (Rodrigues
1978c), Xetá-Guaraní (Rodrigues 1979), Tupí-Guaraní
and Munduruků (Rodrigues 1980).

Among others the following are some interesting
points resulting from this comparative work:

(a) the demonstration of the internal consistency of families such as Tupí-Guaraní, Jê, Yanomámi,
and Nambikwára, as well as the first attempts at
reconstructing phonological properties of the respective proto-languages.

(b) the demonstration of the consistency of the
close relationship between Shokléng and the Kaingáng dialect cluster inside the Jê family.

(c) the hypothesis of a relationship above the
family level for explaining the affinity of Tupí-
Guaraní with other families or languages such as
Munduruků, Jurúna, Arikém, Tuparí, Mondé, Ramaráma,
Puruborá.

(d) the presentation of evidence for three kinds of affinities between Tupí and Carib languages due to genetic relationship, remote contact, and recent contact.

(e) the presentation (by Davis) of some phonological and lexical evidence for the hypothesis of a Macro-Jê linguistic stock, including Jê, Mashakalí, and Karajá. I hypothesize that Ofayé and Rikbaktsá should be added to these as members of a stock coordinate with the Jê family. I do not believe they should be classified as members of this family itself (other probable members of the stock are Boróro and Yathé [Fulniô]). As hypothesized by Davis, as well as according to my own research, Kariri, Kamakã, Botocudo, Coroado, and Guató should also be included with Macro-Jê.

(f) the possible genetic relationship between Jê and Tupí, for which Davis gave a few hints, has received more substantial support from the comparison of the Kaingáng language with Tupí-Guaranían Tupinambá and some other Tupí languages.

More recently we have had some typological comparative studies dealing with phonological and grammatical features of Brazilian Indian languages. The main issues have been word order (Lemle and Peixoto 1981), Derbyshire and Pullum 1981, Carson 1981, Derbyshire 1982) and nasalization (Rodrigues 1981, 1983·).

CONCLUSION
The study of the indigenous languages of Brazil has advanced in recent years due to the study by lin-

guistically trained people of a considerable number of languages. However, only a relatively few languages have been treated to a comprehensive analysis and for many languages substantial data bases are still lacking. The intensification and speeding up of research, badly called for as a result of the precarious conditions of survival for many languages, can only be achieved by means of institutional programs capable of overcoming the chronic lack of funds for linguistic research and by increasing the number of well trained researchers undertaking work in the documentation and analysis of the many Brazilian Indian languages still lacking investigation.

A BIBLIOGRAPHY OF RECENT STUDIES ON BRAZILIAN INDIAN LANGUAGES

Abbreviations: AL Anthropological Linguistics, EL Estudos Linguisticos, IJAL International Journal of American Linguistics, SIL Summer Institute of Linguistics, SL Série Linguística.

Abbott, Miriam. 1976. Estrutura oracional da língua Makúxi. SL 5: 231-66. Brasília: SIL.
Albisetti, César and Ângelo Jayme Venturelli. 1962. Enciclopédia Bororo, vol. I. Campo Grande: Museu Regional D. Bosco.
------. 1969. Enciclopédia Bororo, Vol. II. Campo Grande: Museu Regional D. Bosco.
Albright, Sue. 1965. Aykamteli higher-level phonology. AL 7.7, Part II: 16-22.

Almeida, Antônio, et al. 1983. A língua Tapirapé. Biblioteca Reprográfica Xerox. Rio de Janeiro: Xerox.

Azevedo, Gilda Maria Corrêa de. 1965. Língua Kiriri: descrição do dialeto Kipeá. Unpublished master's thesis, Universidade de Brasília.

Barbosa, A. Lemos. 1955. Pequeno vocabulário Tupi-Português. Rio de Janeiro: Livraria São José.

------. 1956. Curso de Tupi antigo. Rio de Janeiro: Livraria São José.

------. 1970. Pequeno vocabulário Português-Tupi. Rio de Janeiro: Livraria São José.

Bendor-Samuel, David. 1972. Hierarchical structures in Guajajára. Norman: Summer Institute of Linguistics.

Bendor-Samuel, David (ed.). 1971. Tupí studies I. Norman: SIL.

Bendor-Samuel, John T. 1960. Some problems of segmentation in the phonological analysis of Tereno. Word 16:348-55.

------. 1963a. A structure-function description of Terena phrases. Canadian Journal of Linguistics 8:59-70.

------. 1963b. Stress in Terena. Transactions of the Philological Society for 1962. Oxford.

------. 1966. Some prosodic features in Terena. In In memory of J.R. Firth, C.E. Bazell et al., eds., 30-39. London: Longmans.

Betts, LaVera D. 1981. Dicionário Parintintín-Português, Português-Parintintín. Brasília: SIL.

(Betts, LaVera D., and Helen Pease). 1966. Moro-
ğita: lendas dos Parintintín. Rio de Janeiro:
SIL.

Borgman, Donald M. 1974. Deep and Surface Case in
Sanuma. Linguistics 132: 5-18.

Borgman, Donald M. and Sandra L. Cue. 1963.
Sentence and Clause Types in Central Waica
(Shiriana). IJAL 29:222-49.

Boswood, Joan. 1973. Evidências para a inclusão
do Aripaktsá no filo Macro-Jê. SL 1:67-78.
Brasília: SIL.

------. 1974a. Algumas funções de participante
nas orações Rikbaktsa. SL 3:7-33. Brasília:
SIL.

------. 1974b. Citações no discurso narrativo da
língua Rikbaktsa. SL 3:99-129. Brasília: SIL.

------. 1978. Quer falar a língua dos Canoeiros?
Rikbaktsa em 26 lições. Brasília: Summer Institute of Linguistics.

Boudin, M.H. 1963. O simbolismo verbal primitivo:
análise estrutural de um dialeto Tupi-Guarani.
Presidente Prudente: Faculdade de Filosofia,
Ciências e Letras de Presidente Prudente.

------. 1966. Dicionário de Tupi moderno (dialeto
tembé-ténêtéhar do alto rio Gurupi). São Paulo:
Faculdade de Filosofia, Ciências e Letras de
Presidente Prudente [Tembé-Port.].

------. 1978. Dicionário de Tupi moderno (dialeto
tembé-ténêtéhar do alto rio Gurupi). 2 vols.
São Paulo: Conselho Estadual de Artes e Ciências
Humanas [Vol. I: Tembé-Portuguese, Vol. II:
Portuguese-Tembé and summary of grammar].

Braggio, Sílvia Lúcia Bigonjal. 1981. Aspectos
   fonológicos e morfológicos do Kadiwéu. Unpublished master's thesis, Universidade Estadual de
   Campinas.

Brandon, Frank R. and Lucy Seki. 1981a. Interrogativos e complementizadores em línguas Tupí.
   EL 5:107-14. São Paulo.

------. 1981b. A Note on COMP as a universal.
   Linguistic Inquiry 12:659-65.

Braun, Ilse and Marjorie Crofts. 1965. Munduruku
   phonology. AL 7.7, Part II:23-39.

Bridgeman, Loraine I. 1961. Kaiwá (Guaraní) phonology. IJAL 27:329-34.

------. 1981. O parágrafo no fala dos Kaiwá-Gua-
   raní. Brasília: SIL.

Burgess, Eunice. 1971. Duas análises das sílabas
   do Xavánte. Estudos sobre Línguas e Culturas
   Indígenas 96-102. Brasília: SIL.

Burgess, Eunice and Patricia Ham. 1968. Multilevel conditioning of phoneme variants in Apinayé. Linguistics 41:5-18.

Burum, Martinho (ed.). 1977-1979. Aypapayũ'ũm'ũm
   ekawẽn: lendas mundurukús. 3 vols. Brasília:
   SIL.

Butler, Nancy. 1977. Derivação verbal na língua
   Terêna. Série Lingüística 7:73-100. Brasília:
   SIL.

------. 1978. Modo, expressão temporal, tempo
   verbal e relevância contrastiva na língua Terêna. Ensaios Lingüísticos n° 1. Brasília: SIL.

Callow, John C. 1962. The Apinayé Language: Phonology and Grammar. Ph.D. diss., London Univ.

Campbell, Robert. 1977. Marcadores de fontes de
informação na língua Jamamadí. SL 7:117-26.
Brasília: SIL.

Carson, Neusa Martins. 1981a. Macuxi (Caribe) e
os universais de Greenberg. Revista do Centro
de Artes e Letras 3.1:66-70. Santa Maria.

------. 1981b. Phonology and morphosyntax of
Macuxi (Carib). Unpublished Ph.D. dissertation,
University of Kansas.

Chapman, Shirley. 1976. Significado e função de
margens verbais na língua Paumarí. SL 5:199-
230.

Comodo, Cristina Helena Rohweder. 1981a. Concordância nominal em Mundurukú. EL 4:265-72. Araraquara.

------. 1981b. Concordância em Mundurukú. Unpublished master's thesis, Universidade Estadual de
Campinas.

Crofts, Marjorie. 1967. Notas sobre dois dialetos
do Mundurukú. Atas do Simpósio sobre a Biota
Amazônica 2:85-91. Rio de Janeiro: Conselho Nacional de Pesquisas.

------. 1971. Repeated Morphs in Mundurukú. Estudos sobre Línguas e Culturas Indígenas 60-80.
Brasília: SIL.

------. 1973. Gramática Mundurukú. SL 2. Brasília: SIL.

Crofts, Marjorie, et al. 1977. Dicionário bilín-
güe em Português e Mundurukú. Brasília: Summer
Institute of Linguistics.

Crowell, Thomas H. 1973. Cohesion in Bororo discourse. Linguistics 104:15-27.

------. 1977. The Phonology of the Bororo Verb,
Postposition and Noun Paradigms. Arquivos de
Anatomia e Antropologia 2:157-78. Rio de Ja-
neiro.

------. 1979. A grammar of Bororo. Unpublished
Ph.D. dissertation, Cornell University.

Davis, Irvine. 1966. Comparative Jê phonology. EL
1.2:10-24. São Paulo.

------. 1968. Some Macro-Jê relationships. IJAL
34:42-47.

Derbyshire, Desmond C. 1961a. Hishkaryana (Carib)
Syntax Structure I: Word. IJAL 27:125-42.

------. 1961b. Hishkaryana (Carib) Syntax Structure II. IJAL 27: 226-36.

------. 1961c. Notas comparativas sobre três dialetos Karibe. Boletim do Museu Paraense Emílio
Goeldi, n.s., Antropologia 14:1-10. Belém.

------. 1965. Textos Hixkaryâna. Publicações
Avulsas 3. Belém: Museu Paraense Emílio Goeldi.

------. 1977. Discourse redundancy in Hixkaryána.
IJAL 43:176-88.

------. 1979a. Hixkaryana. Lingua Descriptive
Studies I. Amsterdam: North Holland.

------. 1979b. Hishkaryána syntax. Unpublished
Ph.D. dissertation, University of London.

------. 1982. Arawakan (Brazil) morphosyntax.
1982 Work Papers of the Summer Institute of
Linguistics, University of North Dakota Session,
vol. 26:1-81. Huntington Beach: Summer Institute of Linguistics.

Derbyshire, Desmond C. and G.K. Pullum. 1981.
Object-initial languages. IJAL 47:192-214.

Dobson, Rose.  1973.  Notas sobre substantivos do
    Kayabí.  SL 1:30-56.  Brasília: SIL.
------.  1976.  Repetição em Kayabí.  SL 5:83-106.
    Brasília: SIL.
Dooley, Robert A.  1977.  A Constituent Boundary
    Marker in Guaraní.  Arquivos de Anatomia e
    Antropologia 2:145-55.  Rio de Janeiro.
------.  1982a.  Vocabulário do Guaraní.  Brasília:
    SIL.
------.  1982b.  Options on the Pragmatic Structu-
    ring of Guaraní Sentences.  Language 58:307-31.
------.  1983.  Spatial Deixis in Guarani.  Ciência
    e Cultura 35.9:1243-50.  São Paulo.
Dooley, Robert A.  and Harold G.  Green.  1977.
    Aspectos verbais e categorias discursivas na
    língua Palikur.  SL 7:7-28.  Brasília: SIL.
Ekdahl, Muriel and Joseph E.  Grimes.  1964.  Tere-
    na verb inflection.  IJAL 30:261-68.
Edkahl, Muriel and Nancy E.  Butler.  1979a.
    Aprenda Terena, vol.  1.  Brasília: Summer In-
    stitute of Linguistics.
------.  1979b.  Aprenda Terena, vol.  2.  Bra-
    sília: SIL (xeroxed).
Emmerich, Charlotte.  1980.  A fonologia segmental
    da língua Txikão: um exercício de análise.  Lin-
    güística X.  Rio de Janeiro: Museu Nacional.
Emmerich, Charlotte, and Ruth M.F.  Monserrat.
    1972.  Sôbre a fonologia da língua Aweti (Tupi).
    Boletim do Museu Nacional, n.s., Antropologia
    25.  Rio de Janeiro.
Emiri, Loretta.  1981.  Gramática pedagógica da
    língua Yãnomamè.  Boa Vista: Missão Catrimâni.

Everett, Daniel L.  1979.  Aspectos da fonologia do
Pirahã.  Unpublished master's thesis, Universidade Estadual de Campinas.

------.  1981.  Acentuação, tom e silabificação no
Pirahã.  EL 5:115-27.

------.  1982.  Phonetic rarities in Pirahã.  Journal of the International Phonetic Association,
December 1982:94-97.

------.  1983.  A língua Pirahã e a teoria da sin-
taxe: descrição, perspectivas e teoria.  Unpublished Ph.D. dissertation, Universidade Estadual de Campinas.

Ferreira, Lucy Soares (see also Lucy Seki).  1973.
Jazyk Kamajura: fonetika i fonologija, kratkie
svedenija o grammatike.  Unpublished Ph.D.
dissertation, Universitet Druzhby Narodov imeni
Patrisa Lumumby.

Fortune, David L.  1973.  Gramática Karajá: um
estudo preliminar em forma transformacional.  SL
1:101-61.  Brasília: Summer Institute of Linguistics.

Fortune, David L.  and Gretchen Fortune.  1975.
Karajá Men's-Women's Speech Differences with
Social Correlates.  Arquivos de Anatomia e
Antropologia 1:109-24.  Rio de Janeiro.

Giacone, Antônio.  1962.  Pequena gramática e
dicionário da língua "Taliáseri ou Tariano".
Salvador, Bahia: Escola Tipográfica Salesiana.

------.  1965.  Gramática, dicionários e fraseo-
logia da língua Dahceié ou Tucano.  Belém.

Graham, Albert, and Sue Graham.  1978.  Assinala-
mento fonológico das unidades gramaticais em

Sateré. Arquivos de Anatomia e Antropologia
3:219-31. Rio de Janeiro.

Griffiths, Glyn. 1975. Numerals and Demonstra-
tives in Kadiwéu. Arquivos de Anatomia e
Antropologia 1:63-77. Rio de Janeiro.

Griffiths, Glyn and Cynthia Griffiths. 1976. Aspectos da língua Kadiwéu. SL 6. Brasília: SIL.

Gudschinsky, Sarah C. 1971. Ofaié-Xavante, a Jê
Language. Estudos sobre Línguas e Culturas
Indígenas 1-16. Brasília: SIL.

------. 1973. Sistemas contrastivos de marcadores
de pessoa em duas línguas Carib: Apalaí e Hixkaryána. SL 1:57-62. Brasília: SIL.

------. 1974. Fragmentos de Ofaié: a descrição de
uma língua extinta. SL 3:177-249. Brasília:
SIL.

Gudschinsky, Sarah C., and Waldo M. Aaron. 1971.
Some Relational Post-positionals of Guaraní.
Estudos sobre Línguas e Culturas Indígenas
81-95. Brasília: SIL.

Gudschinsky, Sarah C., Harold and Frances Popovich.
1970. Native Reaction and Phonetic Similarity
in Maxakalí Phonology. Language 46:77-88.

Guedes, Marymarcia. 1983. Subsídios para uma análise fonológica de Mbïá. Unpublished master's
thesis, Universidade Estadual de Campinas.

Hall, Joan. 1979. Os sistemas fonológicos e grá-
ficos Xavánte e Português (análise contrastiva).
Ensaios Linguísticos 4. Brasília: SIL.

Ham, Patricia. 1965. Multilevel influence on
Apinayé multidimensional clause structure.
Linguistics 15:5-32.

428    *Aryon D. Rodrigues*

------. 1967. Morfofonêmica Apinayé. Atas do Simpósio sobre a Biota Amazônica 2:123-26. Rio de Janeiro: Conselho Nacional de Pesquisas.

Ham, Patricia, Helen Waller, and Linda Koopman. 1979. Aspectos da língua Apinayé. Brasília: SIL.

Harrison, Carl H. 1971. The Morphophonology of Asuriní Words. Tupí Studies (D. Bendor-Samuel, ed.) 21-71. Norman: SIL.

------. 1975. Gramática Asuriní. SL 4. Brasília: SIL.

------. 1977. A forma lingüística de uma teoria folclórica dos Kamaiurás. Arquivos de Anatomia e Antropologia 2:81-98. Rio de Janeiro.

Harrison, Carl H., and John M. Taylor. 1971. Nasalization in Kaiwá. Tupí Studies I. (D. Bendor-Samuel, ed.) 15-20. Norman: Summer Institute of Linguistics.

Hawkins, W. Neil. 1952. A fonologia da língua Uaiuái. Boletim da Faculdade de Filosofia, Ciências e Letras 157 (Etnografia e Tupi-Guarani 25). São Paulo: Universidade de São Paulo.

------. 1962. A morfologia do substantivo na língua Waiwai. Rio de Janeiro: Museu Nacional.

Hawkins, W. Neil, and Robert E. Hawkins. 1953. Verb inflections in Waiwai (Carib). IJAL 19: 201-11.

Heinrichs, Arlo. 1964. Os fonemas do Mura-Pirahã. Boletim do Museu Paraense Emílio Goeldi, n.s., Antropologia 21:1-9.

------. 1967. Notas preliminares sobre núcleos oracionais contrastivos em Mura-Pirahã. Atas do

Simposio sobre a Biota Amazonica 2:127-31. Rio de Janeiro: Conselho Nacional de Pesquisas.

Hodsdon, Cathy Ann. 1976. Análise de cláusulas semânticas na língua Makúsi. SL 5:267-300. Brasília: SIL.

Huestis, George. 1963. Bororo clause structure. IJAL 29:230-238.

Jackson, Evelyn. 1977. Discurso processual em Waurá. Arquivos de Anatomia e Antropologia 2:179-97. Rio de Janeiro.

Jensen, Cheryl. 1978. Um estudo de frases não verbais em Oiampí. Arquivos· de Anatomia e Antropologia 3:263-83. Rio de Janeiro.

------. 1983. Algumas conseqüências morfológicas do desenvolvimento fonológico da língua Wayapí (Oyampí). EL 7:16-25. São Paulo.

Kakumasu, James. 1976. Gramática gerativa preli- minar da língua Urubú. SL 5: 171-98. Brasília: SIL.

Kingston, Peter. 1973. Repetition as a feature of discourse structure in Mamaindé. Notes on translation 50:12-33. Dallas: SIL.

------. 1976. Sufixos referenciais e o elemento nominal na língua Mamaindé. SL 5:31-82. Brasí- lia: SIL.

Koehn, Edward and Sally Koehn. 1971. Fonologia da língua Apalaí. Estudos sôbre Línguas e Culturas Indígenas 17-28. Brasília: SIL.

Koopman, Linda. 1976. Cláusulas semânticas na língua Apinajé. SL 5:301-20. Brasília: SIL.

Kroeker, Barbara J. 1972. Morphophonemics of Nam- biquara. AL 14:19-22.

------. 1980. Aspectos da língua Nambikuára.
Brasília: SIL.

Kroeker, Menno H. 1972. Thematic Linkage in Nambiquara Narrative. In The Thread of Discourse,
J.E. Grimes, ed., pp. 351-62. Ithaca: Cornell
University (Reprinted 1975, Janua Linguarum, series minor, 207:361-68. The Hague: Mouton).

------. 1976. Condicionamento múltiplo de vogais
na língua Nambikuára. SL 5:107-30. Brasília:
SIL.

------. 1977. The role of tone in Nambikuára.
Arquivos de Anatomia e Antropologia 2:119-43.
Rio de Janeiro.

Landin, David J. 1980. An Outline of the Syntactic Structure of Karitiana Sentences. Unpublished master's thesis, University College,
London.

------. 1983. Dicionário e léxico Karitiána-
Português. Brasília: SIL.

Lapenda, Geraldo. 1968. Estrutura da língua Iatê.
Recife: Universidade Federal de Pernambuco, Imprensa Universitária.

Leite, Yonne de Freitas. 1977. Aspectos da fonologia e morfofonologia Tapirapé. Lingüística
VIII. Rio de Janeiro: Museu Nacional.

Lemle, Miriam. 1971. Internal classification of
the Tupi-Guarani linguistic family. Tupí Studies I (D. Bendor-Samuel, ed.), 107-29. Norman: SIL.

Lemle, Miriam and Sylvia H.T. Peixoto. 1981.
Classificação tipológica das línguas indígenas
brasileiras. Anais do V Encontro Nacional de

Lingüística 349-82.  Rio de Janeiro:  Pontifíca
Universidade Católica do Rio de Janeiro.

Lowe, Ivan.  1972.  On the relation of formal to
sememic matrices with illustrations from Nambiquara.  Foundations of Language 8:360-390.

------.  1975.  Estrutura do tema verbal Nambiquara.  PILEI, Actas del Simposio de Montevideo,
enero de 1966:223-30.  México.

Mattos, Rinaldo de.  1973.  Fonêmica Xerente.  SL
1:79-100.  Brasília: SIL.

McLeod, Ruth.  1974a.  Fonemas Xavánte.  SL 3:
131-52.  Brasília: SIL.

------.  1974b.  Paragraph, Aspect and Participant
in Xavante.  Linguistics 132:51-74.

McLeod, Ruth and Valerie Mitchell.  1977.  Aspectos
da língua Xavánte.  Brasília: SIL.

Meader, Robert E.  1967.  Iranxe: notas gramaticais
e lista vocabular.  Lingüística 2.  Rio de
Janeiro:  Museu Nacional.

Meer, Tine H. van der.  1981.  A nasalização em
limite de palavra no Suruí.  EL 4:282-87.  Araraquara.

------.  1982.  Fonologia da língua Suruí.  Unpublished master's thesis, UNICAMP.

------.  1983.  Ideofones e palavras onomatopaicas
em Suruí.  EL 7:10-15.  São Paulo.

Migliazza, Ernesto.  1965a.  Fonologia Máku.  Boletim do Museu Paraense Emílio Goeldi, n.s.,
Antropologia 25.  Belém.

------.  1965b.  Notas fonológicas da língua Tiriyó.  Boletim do Museu Paraense Emílio Goeldi,
n.s., Antropologia 29.  Belém.

------. 1966. Esboço sintático de um corpus da
língua Máku. Boletim do Museu Paraense Emílio
Goeldi, n.s., Antropologia 32. Belém.

------. 1974. Yanomama grammar and intelligibility. Unpublished Ph.D. dissertation, Indiana
University.

Migliazza, Ernest and Joseph E. Grimes. 1961.
Shiriana phonology. AL 3.6:31-41.

Monod-Becquelin, Aurore. 1975. La pratique linguistique des indiens Trumai. Paris: SELAF.

------. 1976. Classes verbales et construction
ergative en Trumai. Amérindia 1:117-43. Paris.

Monserrat, Ruth M.F. 1976. Prefixos pessoais em
Aweti. Lingüística III. Rio de Janeiro: Museu
Nacional.

Moore, Barbara. 1977. Some discourse features of
Hupda Macú. In Discourse grammar: Studies in
indigenous languages of Colombia, Panama and
Ecuador, Robert E. Longacre, ed., Part 2, pp.
25-42. Dallas: SIL.

Moore, Barbara and Gail Franklin. 1979. Breves
notícias da língua Makú-Hupda. Ensaios Lingüísticos 6. Brasília: SIL.

Moran, Paul and Dorothy Moran. 1977. Notas sobre
morfologia verbal Dení. SL 7:29-72. Brasília:
SIL.

Moura, José de. 1960. Os Münkü: segunda contri-
buição ao estudo da tribo iranche. Pesquisas,
Antropologia 10. Porto Alegre: Instituto An-
chietano de Pesquisas.

Nicholson, Velda. 1978. Aspectos da língua Assu-
riní. Brasília: SIL.

------. 1982. Breve estudo da língua Asuriní do
Xingu. Ensaios Lingüísticos 5. Brasília: SIL.

Odmark, Mary Ann. 1977. Dois conetivos contras-
tantes da língua Paumarí. SL 7:111-16. Brasília: SIL.

Olson, Gary. 1978. Descrição preliminar de orações Wajapí. Ensaios Lingüísticos 3. Brasília:
SIL.

Olson, Roberta. 1978. Dicionário por tópicos nas
línguas Oiampí (Wajapí)-Português. Ensaios Lingüísticos 2. Brasília: SIL.

Palácio, Adair Pimentel. 1984. Flexão pessoal do
verbo em Guató: um sistema tripartido. Comuni-
cação ao XXVII Seminário do Grupo de Estudos
Lingüísticos do Estado de São Paulo. Assis.

Paula, Ruth Wallace Garcia de. 1980a. Língua
Kaxuyana: fonologia segmental e afixos. Lingüística IX. Rio de Janeiro: Museu Nacional.

------. 1980b. Notas verbais da língua Tiriyó.
Boletim do Museu do Índio, Série Lingüística, 1.
Rio de Janeiro.

Pease, Helen, and LaVera Betts. 1971. Parintintin
Phonology. Tupí studies I (D. Bendor-Samuel,
ed.), 1-14. Norman: SIL.

Pickering, Wilbur. 1977a. Interrogativos Apurinã.
Arquivos de Anatomia e Antropologia 2.2:99-117.
Rio de Janeiro.

------. 1977b. Relativização em Apurinã. SL 7:
127-40. Brasília: SIL.

------. 1978. Negação no Apurinã. Arquivos de
Anatomia e Antropologia 3:233-61. Rio de
Janeiro.

Pira, Vicente, and Emanuele Amodio. 1983. Makuxi maimu: guia para a aprendizagem e dicionário da língua Makuxi. Boa Vista: Centro de Documentação das Culturas Indígenas de Roraima.

(Popjes, Jack D., ed.). 1982. Lendas e contos Canela-Krahô. 6 vols. Brasília: SIL.

Popovich, Harold. 1967. Large Grammatical Units and the Space-Time Setting in Maxakalí. Atas do Simpósio sôbre a Biota Amazônica 2:195-99. Rio de Janeiro: Conselho Nacional de Pesquisas.

------. 1971. The sun and the Moon, a Maxakalí text. Estudos sobre Línguas e Culturas Indígenas 29-59. Brasília: SIL.

Price, P. David. 1976. Southern Nambiquara Phonology. IJAL 42: 338-48.

------. 1978. The Nambiquara linguistic family. AL 20.1:14-37.

Ramos, Alcida Rita. 1975. Manual para treinamento na língua Yanomam. Brasília: Univ. de Brasília.

Richards, Joan. 1973. Dificuldades na análise da possessão nominal na língua Waurá. SL 1:11-29. Brasília: SIL.

------. 1977. Oracoes em Waura. SL 7:141-84. Brasília: SIL.

Rodrigues, Aryon Dall'Igna. 1953. Morfologia do verbo tupi. Letras 1:121-52. Curitiba.

------. 1955a. Morphologische Erscheinungen einer Indianersprache. Münchener Studien zur Sprachwissenschaft 7:79-88.

------. 1955b. As línguas "impuras" da família Tupi-Guarani. Anais do XXXI Congresso Internacional de Americanistas 1055-71. São Paulo.

------. 1958a. Die Klassifikation des Tupi-
Sprachstammes Proceedings of the 32nd International Congress of Americanists 679-84. Copenhagen.

------. 1958b. Classification of Tupi-Guarani.
IJAL 24:231-34.

------. 1959. Phonologie der Tupinambá-Sprache.
Unpublished Ph.D. dissertation, Universität
Hamburg.

------. 1960. Über die Sprache der Surára und Pakidái. Mitteilungen aus dem Museum für Völkerkunde in Hamburg 26:134-38.

------. 1962. (Comparação das línguas Umutína e
Boróro). In Informações etnográficas sôbre os
Umutína, Harald Schultz, ed. Revista do Museu
Paulista, n.s., 13: 75-313 (see pp. 100-05).

------. 1966. Classificação da língua dos Cinta-
Larga. Revista de Antropologia 14:27-30. São
Paulo.

------. 1970. Línguas ameríndias. Grande Enciclopédia Delta-Larousse: pp. 4034-4036. Rio de
Janeiro: Delta.

------. 1978a. O sistema pessoal do Tupinambá.
Ensaios de Lingüística 1:167-73. Belo Hori-
zonte.

------. (1978b). Evidences for Tupi-Carib Relationships. 72nd Annual Meeting of the American
Anthropological Association, Los Angeles (an
updated version is published in this volume).

------. (1978c). Kaingáng e Tupinambá: Evidências
de relações genéticas Jê-Tupí? XI Reunião Brasileira de Antropologia, Recife (Unpublished).

------. 1979. A língua dos Índios Xetá como dialeto Guaraní. Cadernos e Estudos Linguísticos 1:7-11. São Paulo.

------. 1980. Tupinambá e munduruku: evidências fonológicas e lexicais de parentesco genético. EL 3:194-209. Araraquara.

------. 1981a. Abertura e ressonância. EL 4:324-33. Araraquara.

------. 1981b. Nasalização e fronteira de palavra em Maxakalí. Anais do V Encontro Nacional de Linguística 2:305-11.

------. 1983a. Typological parallelism due to social contact: Guató and Kadiwéu. Proceedings of the Ninth Annual Meeting of the Berkeley Linguistics Society 218-22. Berkeley.

------. (1983b). Silêncio, pausa e nasalização. VIII Encontro Nacional de Linguística, Rio de Janeiro (Unpublished).

Rodrigues, Aryon D., and Marita Porto Cavalcante. 1982. Assimilação intrassegmental em Kaingáng. 34a. Reunião Anual da SBPC, Campinas.

Rodrigues, Daniele Marcelle Grannier. 1974. Fonologia do Guaraní antigo. Unpublished master's thesis, Universidade Estadual de Campinas, Campinas.

Rowan, Orland. 1967. Phonology of Paresí (Arawakan). Acta Linguistica Hafniensia 10.2: 201-10.

------. 1972. Some features of Paresí discourse structure. AL 14.4:131-46.

------. 1983. Textos em Haliti (Parecis) I. Cuiabá: SIL.

Rowan, Orland and Phyllis Rowan. 1977. Estrutura
discursiva Parecis. SL 7:101-10. Brasília:
SIL.

------. 1978. Dicionário Parecis-Português e
Português-Parecis. Brasília: SIL.

Saelzer, Meinke. 1976. Fonologia provisória da
língua Kamayurá. SL 5:131-70.

Seki, Lucy (see also Lucy Soares Ferreira). 1976.
O Kamaiurá: língua de estrutura ativa. Língua e
Literatura 5:217-27. São Paulo: Universidade de
São Paulo.

Sheffler, Margaret. 1978. Munduruku Discourse.
In Papers on Discourse, Joseph E. Grimes, ed.,
pp. 119-42. Dallas: Summer Institute of Linguistics.

Sheldon, Steven N. Some Morphophonemic and Tone
Perturbation Rules in Mura-Pirahã. IJAL 40:
279-82.

Shell, Olive. 1960. Grammatical Outline of Kraho
(Ge family). IJAL 18:115-29.

Silva, Alcionílio Brüzzi Alves da. 1961. Discoteca
etno-linguístico-musical das tribos dos rios
Uaupés, Içana e Cauaburi. São Paulo. (With 12
LP records).

------. 1966. Observações gramaticais da língua
Daxseyé ou Tukano. Centro de Pesquisas de Iaua-
retê (Amazonas), s. l.

Silva, Márcio Ferreira da. 1981. A fonologia segmental Kamayurá. Unpublished master's thesis,
Universidade Estadual de Campinas.

Stout, Mickey and Ruth Thomson. 1971. Kayapó narrative. IJAL 37:250-56.

------. 1974a. Fonêmica Txukuhamẽi (Kayapó). SL
3:153-76. Brasília: SIL.

------. 1974b. Modalidade em Kayapó. SL 3:69-97.
Brasília: SIL.

Taukane, Estêvão Carlos (ed.). 1978. Vocabulário
Bakairí-Português, Português-Bakairí. Brasília:
SIL.

Taylor, John and Audrey Taylor. 1966. Nove contos
contados pelos Kaiwás e Guaranis. Revista de
Antropologia 14:81-104. São Paulo.

Thomson, Ruth R. G. 1982. Me bakukamã-re?ã
ujarẽnh-neja: lendas Kayapó. Brasília: SIL.

Thomson, Ruth and Mickey Stout. 1974. Elementos
proposicionais em orações Kayapó. SL 3:35-68.
Brasília: SIL.

Tracy, Frances V. 1966. The Phonology and Outline
Grammar of the Aikamtheli Dialect of Shiriana,
with Notes on Other Dialects. Unpublished master's thesis, University of Pennsylvania.

Wallace, Ruth (see also Ruth Wallace Garcia de
Paula). 1970. Notas fonológicas da língua
Kaxuyana. Boletim do Museu Paraense Emílio
Goeldi, n.s., Antropologia 43. Belém.

Waller, Helen. 1976. A conjunção nhũm na nar-
rativa Apinajé. SL 5:7-29. Brasília: SIL.

Weir, E.M. Helen. 1980. Um caso de OSV: a língua
Nadëb. XII Reunião Brasileira de Antropologia,
Rio de Janeiro.

------. 1981a. Desenvolvimento diacrônico de cer-
tos prefixos verbais na língua Nadëb. EL 5:
128-41. São Paulo.

------. 1981b. Análise de uma construção negativa no Nadëb. EL 4:273:81. Araraquara.

Wheatley, James. 1969. Bakairi verb structure. Linguistics 47:80-100.

------. 1973. Pronouns and Nominal Elements in Bacairi Discourse. Linguistics 104:105-15.

Wiesemann, Ursula. 1964. Phonological syllables and words in Kaingáng. Beiträge zur Völkerkunde Südamerikas: Festgabe für Herbert Baldus zum 65. Geburtstag (Hans Becher, ed.) 307-13. Hannover: Münstermann-Druck.

------. 1971. Dicionário Kaingáng-Português, Português-Kaingáng. Rio de Janeiro: SIL.

------. 1972. Die phonologische und grammatische Struktur der Kaingáng-Sprache. The Hague: Mouton.

------. 1974. Time distinctions in Kaingáng. Zeitschrift für Ethnologie 99:120-30.

------.1978. Os dialetos da língua Kaingang e o Xokléng. Arquivos de Anatomia e Antropologia 3:197-217. Rio de Janeiro.

------. 1980. Events and Non-Events in Kaingang Discourse. Wege zur Universalienforschung: sprachwissenschaftlie Beiträge zum 60. Geburtstag von Hansjakob Seiler (Gunter Brettschneider and Christian Lehmann, eds.) 419-33. Tübingen: Narr.

Wise, Mary Ruth and Harold G. Green. 1971. Compound Propositions and Surface Structure Sentences in Palikur (Arawakan). Lingua 26:252-80.

# PART II
# Indigenous Languages of the Andes

# 11. Ecuadorian Highland Quechua: History and Current Status

## Louisa R. Stark

INTRODUCTION

Of the multitude of languages which probably existed in the Ecuadorian highlands, the only extant
language is Quichua,[1] which extends from the areas
of Mariano Acosta and Pimampiro (Imbabura) in the
north to the parroquias of San Lucas and Saraguro
(Loja) in the south. It has close to 610,000 speakers.[2]

HISTORY

Traditionally it was always believed that the Quechua language was spread throughout western South
America as part of the conquest of this area by the
Incas (1321-1533). However, two well known Quechua
specialists, Alfredo Torero of Peru and Gary Parker
of the United States, working independently of one
another, have come to the conclusion that the history of the Quechua language is somewhat different
from that which had previously been postulated
(Torero 1964; Parker 1963).

Using recently acquired data for the dialects of
Quechua in north central Peru, Torero and Parker
came to the conclusion that Quechua originated in
northern Peru. At around 800 A.D. the speakers of
Quechua of this area divided into two groups. One

group stayed in the north central part of Peru in
what today are the provinces of Ancash, Huánuco,
Pasco, Lima and Junin.  They spoke a form of Quechua which is called Quechua I by Torero, and Quechua B by Parker.  The other group emigrated to the
South, to the Cuzco area.  The Incas descended from
this group and later extended the dialect of Quechua that they spoke (called Quechua II by Torero
and Quechua A by Parker) to Bolivia and subsequently, it is said, to Ecuador.  (For a more detailed
account of Quechua dialect history, see the article
by Bruce Mannheim in this volume.)

Let us now turn to the history of Quichua in
Ecuador.  In general there are two hypotheses about
the origin of Quichua in Ecuador.  The first, and
most general, is that Quichua spread to Ecuador during the period of Inca conquest (1487) and that
before this date Quichua was not spoken in the
area.  The second hypothesis asserts that Quichua
was spoken in Ecuador before the arrival of the
Incas.  Those who adhere to the second hypothesis
refer to the history of Ecuador written by Padre
Juan de Velasco where one reads that the language
encountered by the Incas when they conquered the
kingdom of Quito was:

...un dialecto del mismo idioma de los
Incas del Peru.  O más bien el mismo di-
versamente pronunciado y mezclado ya con
otros.  Esta circunstancia, que no se ha-
bía observado entre tantos países inter-
medios, causó a Huaynacápac tanta mara-

villa en Quito, que conoció y confesó
(segun es fama constante) el que ambas
monarquías habían tenido un mismo origen
(Velasco 1841:121).

Velasco's assumption was accepted by the 19th
century Italian scholar Hervás (1800:275-276) as
well as by von Tschudi, who noted that Quichua
originated in:

> ...las cercanías de Quito, los Andes y el
> alto Marañón, de donde habrían ido a Hua-
> raz y de allá al Sur, hasta las orillas
> de Titicaca, fundadosa para tal opinión,
> en lo que se imaginan formas arcaicas
> (von Tschudi 1953:16-17).

More recently Orr and Longacre, using linguistic
data, have come to the conclusion that:

> Since Quechua seems to be well entrenched
> in Ecuador and in Santiago de Estero (Ar-
> gentina), it may well be that the lin-
> guistic penetration of Quechua into these
> regions was actually under way before the
> main period of Inca domination (Orr and
> Longacre 1968:546).

And Guevara, arguing that Quichua existed in
Ecuador before the arrival of the Incas, states
that:

> ...no es posible creer que el Quichua que
> impusieron los Incas en el lapso de 46

años, haya tenido tanto poder para resis-
tir a las circunstancias adversas y con-
servarse vivo hasta ahora en los exdomi-
nios del extinto Tahuantinsuyo (Guevara
1972:17).

Finally, Parker has concluded that:

Cuando los incas llegaron al centro y
norte del Peru, y al Ecuador, el quechua
ya era hablado por la mayoría de esas
áreas (Parker 1972:115).

Even with the arguments that have been advanced
for the existence of Quichua in Ecuador before the
advent of the Incas, the majority of archaeologists
and historians have believed, and still believe,
that Quichua was introduced into Ecuador only after
the conquest by the Incas (Jijón y Caamaño 1952:67;
Porras G. 1973: Apendice II: iii-iv). These scholars base their evidence on ethnohistoric sources,
especially early Spanish chroniclers such as Cieza
de Leon and El Inca Garcilaso who mention that Quichua was introduced into Ecuador by the Incas. But
one should remember that Garcilaso probably never
visited Ecuador, and that Cieza only passed through
the area briefly.

What linguistic evidence do we have for the existence of Quichua in Ecuador before the arrival of
the Incas? If we examine the dialects of Quichua
that are spoken in Ecuador today, we find that they
can be divided into two groups. The first group,
which we will call Ecuadorian A, consists of the

dialects spoken in Pichincha, Cotopaxi and Tungurahua provinces. This group differs from the group
which we will call Ecuadorian B which is spoken in
Imbabura, Cañar, Azuay and Loja province.

Note that the dialects of Group A tend to share
certain similarities in suffixes which are not
found in Group B. Where Group B has an /a/ (low
vowel) before a velar fricative stop, or nasal,
Group A has an /i/ or /u/ (high vowels).[4] Based on
these differences, the dialects of the Ecuadorian
Sierra are divided into two groups -- those spoken
in the north central part of the Sierra, or in the
provinces of Pichincha, Cotopaxi and Tungurahua --
and those spoken in the extreme north and in the
south -- in the provinces of Imbabura, Chimborazo,
Canar, Azuay and Loja.

There are various insights that this grouping
can provide about the history of Quichua in Ecuador. The first is that the suffixes encountered in
the dialects that make up Group A represent forms
that are older than those in Group B. This is especially evident in the suffixes that indicate possession, the locatives 'to' and 'from', and the independent suffixes that indicate emphasis. All of
these suffixes from Group A represent forms which
are more similar to Quechua proto-forms than their
corresponding suffixes in Group B.

The reader will notice that the reconstructions
of proto-Quechua differ somewhat from those that
have been presented elsewhere by Parker (1969:123-
147). For although Parker has done an excellent job
in reconstructing proto-Quechua, his recon-

TABLE 1. Morphological Differences within Ecuadorian Quichua: Groups A and B

| | Group A | | Group B |
|---|---|---|---|
| **Possession/Benefactive[3]** | | | |
| | PI, TU$_2$: | -bug/-buj | IM: | -paj/-pag/-baj/-bag |
| | TU$_1$: | -bu/-pu | CA, CH: | -paj/-pag |
| | CO: | -bu | AZ: | -baj/-paj |
| | | | LO: | -paj |
| **Locatives** | | | |
| (1) 'to' | | | |
| | PI, TU$_2$: | -mun | IM, CH, CA, AZ: | -man |
| | CO, TU$_1$: | -mu | LO: | -m |
| (2) 'from' | | | |
| | PI: | -munta | IM: | -manda |
| | CO, TU$_1$, TU$_2$: | -munda | CH, CA, AZ, LO: | -manta |

TABLE 1. Morphological Differences within Ecuadorian Quichua: Groups A and B (continued)

Gerundive

PI, TU₁:          -sha        IM, CH, CA, LO:    -shpa

CO, TU₂:          -sh(a)      AZ:               -sh(pa)

Independent Suffixes

(1)  emphasis

            PI:        -tug/-tuj    IM:       -taj/-tag/-daj/-dag

     CO, TU₂:          -di          CH:       -taj/-tag

        TU₁:           -ti          CA, AZ, LO:    -taj

(2)  'still, yet'

            PI:        -rug/-ruj    IM, CH:   -raj/-rag

     CO, TU₁:          -ri          CA, AZ, LO:    -raj

        TU₂:           -rij

TABLE 2. Similarities between Ecuadorian Quichua and Proto-Quechua

| | Proto-Form | Ecuadorian A | Ecuadorian B |
|---|---|---|---|
| Possession/ Benefactive | *puq | -(bug)/-(buj))/-bu/-pu | -paj/-pag/-baj/-bag |
| Locatives | | | |
| (1) 'to' | *mun | -mu(n) | -man |
| (2) 'from' | *munta | -munta/-munda | -manta/-manda |
| Independent Suffixes | | | |
| (1) emphasis | *tiq | -tug/-tuj/-di/-ti | -taj/-tag/-daj/-dag |
| (2) 'still, yet' | *riq | -rug/-ruj/-ri/-rij | -raj/-rag |

structions are done purely through the comparative
method. If we take Parker's reconstructions one
step further, and analyze them through the method
of internal reconstruction, we arrive at earlier
forms of proto-Quechua than those he has postulated.

Our hypothesis is that proto-Quechua was originally an analytic language, rather than highly synthetic as it is today. This would follow the theory that through time analytic languages generally
evolve into synthetic ones, and vice-versa (Hodge
1970). This hypothesis also concurs with Solá's
that certain of the suffixes within the Quechua
modal system were originally verb stems (Solá
1967). However, we will take this one step further
and, in discussing the independent suffixes, state
that they originally consisted of a verb root plus
the derivational (substantivizing) suffix *-q.
Thus *riq 'still, yet' consists of the verb root
*ri- 'go' plus *-q. And *tiq emphasis ('so, then,
next') consists of the verb root *ti- 'exist' plus
*-q. The same phenomena seem to occur with the
suffix which indicates possession/benefactive.
Here *puq consists of the verb root *pu- 'perform
action away from the speaker' (this same root has a
reflex in the verb suffix -pu- in many Quechua dialects indicating action performed for the benefit
of someone other than the speaker) plus *-q.

Turning to the locatives, Parker has stated that
"most modern case suffixes...are recorded as noun
stems in the early grammars and dictionaries (1969:
135). Thus -mun 'to, towards' would have consisted
of the verb root *mu- 'perform action towards the

speaker' (this same root has a reflex in the verb
suffix -mu- which occurs in the modal system in
most Quechua dialects indicating direction or inception of an action in the direction of the speaker) plus the derivational (substantivizer) suffix
*-na (the 'a' was later dropped) which indicates
the instrument or place of an action.  The form
munta 'from' then consists of the form *mun(a) plus
*-ta accusative.[5]

    Besides the data mentioned above, another reason
for assuming that the Quichua A dialects are older
than those of Quichua B is that the A area demon-
strates much more diversity than the B area (especially the Pichincha dialect) which would tend to
imply that Quichua originated in that area of Ecuador (Sapir 1916; Muysken and Stark 1976). This
provides additional evidence for our hypothesis
that Quichua was spoken in that area before its
conquest by the Incas.

    If we examine what is known of the prehistory of
the provinces in which Quichua A is still spoken
(Pichincha, Cotopaxi, Tungurahua, Northern Chimborazo and Guaranda) we see that from around 600 A.D.
until the arrival of the Incas in 1487 these areas
formed a cultural complex called Panzaleo.  The exact coincidence between linguistic and archaeological evidence is too strong to dismiss as non-rele-
vant, and leads to the conclusion that Quichua was
introduced into the Ecuadorian Sierra soon after
600 A.D., after which period it spread throughout
the provinces in which the Quichua A dialects are
currently found.

Furthermore, there are enough similarities between Panzaleo and Cosanga ceramics from the Oriente
(400 B.C.-600 A.D.) to presume that the two are
related, with the Cosanga pottery of a period somewhat earlier than the Panzaleo ceramics (Porras
1975). If this is the case then perhaps we can assume, as did von Tschudi, that early speakers of
Quichua entered Ecuador from the East, and after
settling there a group split off and traveled
South. This group probably traveled along the
coast, settling on the north central coast of Peru
sometime before the 9th century (Torero 1972:82).
In fact, the Quechua of this area shares certain
phonological characteristics with the Quichua of
Ecuador which are not found in other Quechua speaking areas. These include the lack of post-velar
stops, lack of aspiration and glottalization in the
stop series, and the voicing of stops after nasals
(Parker 1970:167).

From the north central coast Quechua began its
spread throughout Peru. And through successive expansions, a group of Quechua speakers eventually
migrated to the Cuzco area where they formed the
cultural group which was eventually to become the
Incas. The Incas later began to expand territo-
rially until they reached Ecuador in the fifteenth
century. With them, and through their mitimaes,
they brought the dialects of Quechua that were spoken in the southern highlands of Peru, and in Bolivia. (The dialects spoken in Bolivia had been introduced earlier through Inca conquest.) These im-
ported dialects were introduced in their purest

forms into the provinces of Loja, Azuay, Cañar,
Chimborazo, and Imbabura, where Quichua had not
previously been spoken.  They also formed a kind of
superstratum of foreign influence in the central
provinces of Pichincha, Cotopaxi, and Tungurahua
where Quichua was already spoken.

Phonologically the Quechua which was brought by
the Incas was distinguished by a series of plain,
aspirated and glottalized stops.  Although the series of glottalized stops may have been introduced
through lexical items, it never seems to have taken
hold in Ecuadorian Quichua.  However the feature of
aspiration has been maintained, to a limited extent, in the lexicon of the southern Quichua dialects.  But as Parker has noted, "the stop manners
of Ecuadorian and Cuzco-Bolivian do not correspond
with the regularity we would expect" (Parker 1970:
159).  In fact, there is little or no correspondence between aspirated stops in the two dialect
areas, lending more evidence to the theory that
such aspiration was a borrowed, rather than a genetic feature, in the Quichua of Ecuador.

Beyond the introduction of aspirated stops, the
suffixes that occur in the Quichua B dialects of
the northern and southern Sierra provinces of Ecuador, and which set them off from the Quichua A dialects spoken in the central Sierra provinces arrived with the Cuzco-Bolivian Quechua introduced at
the time of the Inca conquest.

Note that where there are high vowels in the
Quichua A dialects, both the Ecuadorian Quichua B
dialects and the Cuzco dialect have low vowels.

TABLE 3. Similarities between Cuzco Quechua and Ecuadorian B Suffixes

|  | Cuzco | Ecuadorian B | Ecuadorian A |
|---|---|---|---|
| Possession/<br>Benefactive | -paq | -paj/-pag/-baj/-bag | -bug/-buj/-bu/-pu |
| Locatives<br>(1) 'to' | -man | -man | -mu(n) |
| (2) 'from' | -manta | -manta/-manda | -munta/-munda |
| Independent<br>Suffixes |  |  |  |
| (1) emphasis | -taq | -taj/-tag/-daj/-dag | -tug/-tuj/-di/-ti |
| (2) 'still,<br>yet' | -raq | -raj/-rag | -rug/-ruj/-ri/-rij |

If we can hypothesize, then, that Quichua ente-
red Ecuador in two waves -- an early wave from the
East, and a later one that was introduced by the
Incas -- what can we say about the Quichua which is
spoken in the Oriente today? Does it represent a
very old variant of pre-Panzaleo Quichua? Or was
Quichua introduced more recently into the Oriente?
Linguistically the answer seems to be the latter.
For the Quichua of the Oriente is more like the
Quichua introduced by the Incas into the Quichua B
area of the Sierra than it is like that encountered
in the older Quichua A speaking area of the highlands.

Note that the independent suffix which is translated 'still, yet' in the Sierra dialects originally consisted of cha(i) 'that' plus the suffix -ra
'still, yet' in the Oriente. Today it is the fro-
zen form chaira or chara. However, this form indicates that the original suffix in the Oriente had
the same low vowel as corresponding suffixes in the
Quichua B area. And with the other suffixes listed
in Table 4 showing the same similarities, we can
hypothesize that the Quichua which is spoken today
in the Ecuadorian Oriente, because of its similarity to the Quichua introduced by the Incas into the
southern and northern Sierra (Quichua B), represents a late introduction of Quichua into the jungle area, during the Inca period or afterward.

To conclude, there is evidence that Quichua was
originally introduced into the central Ecuadorian
Sierra during the Panzaleo period, probably having
come from the Oriente. A second variety of Quichua

TABLE 4. Comparison of Oriente Quichua with Sierra Quichua[b]

| | Oriente Quichua | Quichua B | Quichua A |
|---|---|---|---|
| Possession/ Benefactive | B, T: -wa/-pa/-ba<br>L: -pa/-ba | -paj/-pag/-baj/-bag | -bug/-buj/-bu/-pu |
| Locatives | | | |
| (1) 'to' | B,T,L: -ma | -man | -mu(n) |
| (2) 'from' | B,T,L: -manda | -manta/-manda | -munta/-munda |
| Independent Suffixes | | | |
| (1) emphasis | B, L: -ta<br>T: -da/-ra | -taj/-tag/-daj/-dag | -tug/-tuj/-di/-ti |
| (2) 'still, yet' | B, T: chara<br>L: chaira | -raj/-rag | -rug/-ruj/-ri/-rij |

is also evident in the Ecuadorian Sierra, introduced by the Incas as part of their conquest of the
country. This Quichua is found today in the northern and southern provinces of the Sierra. And it
is this latter variety which later made its way into the Ecuadorian Oriente.

PRESENT-DAY SITUATION
Today the Quichua of the Ecuadorian highlands is as
varied in its use as in its linguistic features.
Aside from dialectal variation within the language,
the various sub-dialects have been influenced in
differing degrees by their contact with the Spanish
language. This has been particularly evident in
the borrowing of Spanish vocabulary, which ranges
between 8.26% and 30.0% in the speech of male speakers, and 5.5% and 14.2% in the speech of female
speakers of Quichua (Schultz 1968). However, although Sierra Quichua has borrowed a good deal of
vocabulary from Spanish, one cannot overlook the
fact that the Spanish spoken in the Ecuadorian
highlands has also been greatly influenced by Quichua, more than anything in its grammatical constructions, but to an extent in its vocabulary as
well (Moya 1972).
    The following is a province-by-province survey
of the status of Quichua in the Ecuadorian highlands.

Imbabura
There are approximately 115,000 native speakers of
Quichua in the province of Imbabura (Stark and Dil-

worth 1973) of which approximately 60% are monolinguals. Geographically there are several sub-dialects spoken within the province (Stark et al.
1974:i-ii) as well as a few social dialects that
cut across community lines. The Indians of this
province are among the wealthiest in Ecuador, ear-
ning their living from agriculture and textiles.
Those whose economy is based primarily on agriculture are clustered along the eastern flanks of
Mounts Cotacachi and Imbabura. Living in relative
isolation, the majority of these Indians, adults
and children, are monolingual speakers of Quichua.
However, younger people are rapidly becoming bilingual as they travel outside of the area in order to
engage in wage labor. Increased educational opportunities are also leading to a rise in the knowledge of Spanish on the part of children and young
adults (Pereira 1979:122).

The western slopes of Mount Imbabura serve as
the homeland for the Otavaleño Indians whose income
comes primarily from the production of textiles.
In this part of Imbabura women and young children
are generally monolingual whereas the average adult
male is bilingual in Quichua and Spanish. Many of
the men are commerciantes who travel throughout
Ecuador and other Latin American countries selling
textiles. Their success in such sales is greatly
based on their appearance and cultural identity,
including language. In other words, in many sections of Ecuador and Latin America in general, textiles which have been made by, and are sold by, an
Indian from the area around Otavalo are thought to

have more value and to be of better quality than
those made and sold by a non-Indian.  Thus it is
financially valuable for an Otavaleño to maintain
his distinctive dress, as well as his language.
The latter is particularly useful for dealing with
Quichua-speaking Indians from other areas, as well
as for carrying out negotiations in secret in front
of monolingual Spanish-speaking customers.

## Pichincha

There are approximately 20,000 speakers of Quichua
in the province of Pichincha of which perhaps 10%
are monolinguals (Stark and Dilworth 1973).

As recently as fifty years ago Quichua was spoken in the valleys of Tumbaco, Los Chillos, and Machachi.  However, within the past two generations
typical indigenous dress, especially that worn by
men, has disappeared, as has the Quichua spoken in
these areas.  In the cases of Tumbaco and Los Chillos, Quito's residential suburbs are rapidly spreading into these valleys, displacing the small farmers who once lived there.  And in the Machachi
area the industrial section of southern Quito has
replaced farms and haciendas with factories and
other industrial plants.  Thus the only area of
Pichincha in which Quichua still seems to have a
foothold is in the northern part of the province,
in communities such as Calderón, Llano Grande, Santa Mariana de Jesus, and San Miguel de Calderón.
Here land is generally poor and dry so that most
men, and a few women, have to find work in Quito in
order to support themselves; since these communi-

ties are close to the city, however, those working
in Quito can come home nightly.  As a result of
their contacts with the capital, men are bilingual
and women are either bilingual (those who work in
Quito) or monolingual in Quichua.  With increased
contact with the city, and with no perceived reason
to continue using Quichua, families are generally
sending their children to the schools that are readily available in each community in order that they
learn Spanish.  Adults also encourage children to
speak Spanish at any opportunity, and thus the next
generation of children will in all probability be
monolingual speakers of Spanish.

Cotopaxi

There are currently an estimated 100,000 speakers
of Quichua in the province of Cotopaxi (Stark and
Dilworth 1973) of which approximately 65% are monolinguals.

The central part of this province consists of a
large valley, and it is on the east and west sides
of this valley that there are native speakers of
Quichua.  On the western side the number is small,
and those who speak Quichua are generally monolinguals who live on the upper slopes of the valley
towards the páramo.  The poverty and isolation of
this part of the province is such that Quichua will
probably continue to be spoken monolingually here
for at least a few more generations.

On the eastern side of the valley, there are
many more Indians, and thus more Quichua is spoken.  This side of the valley has traditionally

been one of haciendas and Indian c̲a̲c̲e̲r̲í̲a̲s̲.  It is a
fairly isolated zone which has had little contact
with the other parts of the province.  Adult Indian
men may have learned some Spanish on the haciendas
whereas women and children are mostly monolingual
speakers of Quichua.  However, a road built through
this part of the province connects it with the Oriente.  And with such a convenience there are Indians from this area who are moving out and coloni-
zing land in the lowlands.  The effect that these
migrations will have on their language situation
has yet to be determined.

T̲u̲n̲g̲u̲r̲a̲h̲u̲a̲
There are currently an estimated 54,000 speakers of
Quichua in the province of Tungurahua (Stark and
Dilworth 1973) of which approximately 50% are monolinguals.  These are divided among three distinct
ethnic groups.  Two of these groups are the Salasaca and Chibuleo; the third group we will call "Platillos."[7]  All three groups speak dialects of Quichua A which are mutually intelligible.  However,
within each dialect there are a large number of
minor variations.

S̲a̲l̲a̲s̲a̲c̲a̲.  There are 12,00 Salasacas, all of whom
are native speakers of Quichua.  Of this group an
estimated 60% are bilingual, the rest monolingual
speakers of Quichua.
    The Salasaca live. in the eastern part of the
province of Tungurahua in small communities scattered around the canton of Pelileo.  Until recently

the group maintained a very isolated existence and had little contact with outsiders, Indian or white. However, over the last few decades they have sold much of their land to those very outsiders that they once avoided, and as a result their economy has changed from one which relied almost completely on agriculture to one that places a heavy emphasis on the manufacture and sale of "tapestries." These "tapestries" are made solely for outside consumption and, in developing markets for them, the Salasaca have begun to have more contact than previously with the Spanish-speaking world. Thus the majority of younger men are now bilingual in both Quichua and Spanish, whereas the older generations, many women, and most young children are still monolingual speakers of Quichua. Therefore Quichua still has a very strong position among the Salasaca and this, coupled with a strong ethnic identity, makes it seem certain that the language will continue to thrive in this part of eastern Tungurahua.

Chibuleo. There are approximately 12,000 Chibuleo, all of whom are native speakers of Quichua. Of this group an estimated 40% are bilingual, the majority of them adult men and children. However, as more and more women are gaining exposure to Spanish, they too are beginning to become bilingual in Quichua and Spanish.

The Chibuleo live to the southwest of the city of Ambato, in villages scattered throughout the parroquias of Juan Benigno Vela and Pilahuín. Until recently the Chibuleo were small-scale agriculturalists, raising garlic and onions to sell in the market in Ambato. However, with the failure of their own crops several years ago, the Chibuleo began to buy onions and garlic from white and mestizo farmers to sell throughout the Ecuadorian highlands. At first only men traveled, passing from house to house selling their products. But in recent years many have had their wives join them in setting up stalls in most of the markets in the Ecuadorian Sierra. As a result women, who generally would not have had much contact with Spanish as a part of traditional home life, are now learning the language in their market dealings. And their younger children who generally accompany them are also learning the language. This, coupled with the founding of a new colegio indígena in Cuatro Esquinas, may well mean the end of any monolingualism among the Chibuleo. However, it seems certain that the Indian population wishes to maintain a distinct ethnic identity. The question now is whether they will retain Quichua as a language associated with their ethnicity, or whether they may well become like the Saragurans who have retained their ethnic identity while losing the language.

"Platillos". There are approximately 30,000 "Platillos" living primarily in communities to the north and west of Ambato, and along the northern slopes of Mount Chimborazo. All are native speakers of Quichua with an estimated 50% who are bilingual in Spanish and Quichua.

Those Indians living to the northwest of Ambato have a great deal of contact with areas outside of their immediate communities. Many work as <u>carga-</u><u>dores</u> in the market in Ambato, while others may work seasonally on the coast. Thus most men are bilingual as are children who have learned Spanish in school. However women and older men are still mostly monolingual speakers of Quichua. Increased seasonal migrations to the coast, more formal education in Spanish, and a tendency for younger people to identify with a mestizo rather than an Indian culture are among the factors that will probably bring about the demise of Quichua in this area in a generation or two.

The "Platillos" living on the northern slopes of Mount Chimborazo have an economy based on herding and some subsistence agriculture, in particular root crops. A few men are functionally bilingual although the majority, because of the isolation in which they live, are monolingual Quichua speakers. There are few Spanish speakers in the area, and little in the way of public facilities such as schools, health centers, and churches. This makes contact with the outside world even more limited. And, with the economically depressed nature of the area, there is no reason to believe that such facilities will be available in the near future. Thus it seems quite certain that as long as the "Platillos" stay in the very inhospitable area which they currently inhabit, their language and culture will remain intact.

## Bolivar

There are approximately 30,000 speakers of Quichua in the province of Bolivar centered around the parroquias of San Simón, Guanujo, Salinas, and Simiátug. Perhaps 50% are monolingual speakers of Quichua (Stark and Dilworth 1973).

The Quichua spoken in the parroquias north of Guaranda is linguistically very much like that of the "Platillos" of Tungurahua, whereas the Quichua spoken in the parroquia of San Simón is very much like that spoken in northwestern Chimborazo. The latter is not surprising since a large number of Bolivar Quichua speakers are immigrants from that area. As a result of their recent migration from Chimborazo, they have left many of their Indian cultural traditions behind them and have become quite mestizoed in culture and dress. Their children generally grow up speaking Spanish, although Quichua may be used between husband and wife in the home. Thus it is quite probable that within the next few generations the speaking of Quichua as a native language will cease to exist in the parroquia of San Simón. On the other hand, Indians in the parroquias of Guanujo, Salinas, and Simiátug live in more isolated areas of the province, and are generally monolingual speakers of Quichua. Therefore the prognosis for the survival of the language in this part of the province is excellent

## Chimborazo

The largest concentration of Quichua speakers in the Ecuadorian Sierra is found in the province of

Chimborazo and numbers almost 200,000 (Stark and
Dilworth 1973). Of these perhaps 70% are monolingual speakers of Quichua. The majority of those
who can also speak Spanish are adult men.

From a purely linguistic point of view the province is divided into several dialect zones. To
the north of Guano the Quichua spoken in Chimborazo
is very much like that of Tungurahua with affinities towards Quichua A. Between Guano and Tixan
there is a mixture of speakers of Quichua A and B.
Here older people tend to maintain the A dialect
that was originally spoken in this area while younger speakers mix elements of the traditional language with elements of Quichua B which they are
learning from radio programs broadcast from Quito,
Riobamba, and Colta. Beyond this, the valley between Guano and Guamote is divided between Catholics
and Protestants, the latter who are part of a nati-
vistic movement in which Protestantism is being
equated with a sense of Indian ethnicity and pride,
much of which is tied in with the speaking of Quichua (Muratorio 1981:520). On the other hand, the
Catholic Indians, with the encouragement of the
current archbishop of Riobamba, have also begun to
take great pride in their ethnic identity. As part
of this religious schism there are occasions when
each group asserts that the other speaks a somewhat
"different" Quichua. In turn, the language spoken
by both of these groups has been more influenced by
Spanish than has been the Quichua spoken in more
isolated communities towards the páramo. This has
been because Indians living in the valley have had

a great deal of contact with Spanish-speaking outsiders, both religious and secular. They have also
had ready access to schools which has facilitated
their learning of Spanish.

Within the valley the normal economic basis is´
subsistence agriculture and the occasional production of artisan goods. The one exception is the
community of San Antonio near Lake Colta where the
majority of the community is involved, in one way
or another, with the marketing of contraband Colombian household goods. Both men and women spend
large amounts of time traveling from market to market selling these products. However, because the
products that they market have no indigenous background, there is apparently no need to maintain
Quichua in the handling of them. Thus it is quite
probable that within the next few generations San
Antonio will become a totally bilingual community
and later will become monolingual in Spanish. For
the rest of the central part of the province, the
building of schools, some of them bilingual, will
be certain to bring about more bilingualism in Spanish and Quichua. However, the ideological split
between Protestants and Catholics, a split which is
strongly rooted in ethnic pride and which assumes
Quichua language maintenance, may well insure the
general survival of the language in this area of
Chimborazo.

The Quichua spoken to the south of Tixan is analogous to that of Cañar, even though the Indians of
this area are ethnically very different from their
Cañari neighbors. The Indians of southern Chimbo-

razo are primarily subsistence farmers who live in
rather isolated areas. They have little recourse
to the educational, health, and other public facilities, which emanate from Riobamba. And, outside
of market day in Alausí, they have little contact
with speakers of Spanish. Thus, there are very few
even functionally bilingual Indians in this zone.

What may well bring about an increased knowledge
of Spanish among the Indians of Chimborazo is the
adult education program which has been developed by
the Unidad para el Desarrollo de la Educación of
Chimborazo. The program, which teaches adults to
read and write in Quechua while at the same time
they learn Spanish, has had a great impact on the
Indian communities of Chimborazo as well as of
neighboring Bolivar. The program has also offered
training to Indian promotores from other Quechua
speaking areas. Today, there are over 1,200 Quechua speaking promotores who are conducting classes
in adult literacy throughout Chimborazo. Their
work goes somewhat further than simply teaching the
rudiments of reading, writing and Spanish. They
are also in charge of community development programs that are designed to help the Indians of the
region avoid the economic exploitation that they
have suffered for centuries at the hands of their
non-Indian neighbors. At the same time the promotores are furthering a sense of ethnic pride among
the residents of their villages (Stark 1982). The
program has been immensely successful, and has been
considered for wide-scale adoption in other parts
of the country, as well as in Bolivia.

## Cañar

There are approximately 70,000 speakers of Quichua
B living in the province of Cañar (Stark and Dilworth 1973). Of these probably 60% are monolingual
speakers of the language.

Of all the Indians of the Ecuadorian Sierra, the
Cañari have been most noted for their ethnic
pride.  Traditionally they have been extremely hostile to non-Indians, preferring to live in virtual
isolation from the mainstream of Ecuadorian life.
Starting almost two decades ago, several development groups began to work intensively in the province to provide increased opportunities in health
and education for the Cañaris.  Some of their hostilities have been modified as these Indians have
begun to have contact with the non-Indian world.
Beyond this, with the advent of land reform, many
of the Cañari have taken advantage of forming agricultural cooperatives which have benefited them
economically.  The cooperatives have also brought
them into contact with the Spanish-speaking world,
both from the point of view of the actual marketing
situation as well as by maintaining contact with
Ecuadorian governmental organizations concerned
with agriculture.  There are also a number of Cañari men who find seasonal employment on the coast
and learn Spanish accordingly.

Thus the Cañari are moving in the direction of
more bilingualism.  However, with their very intense ethnic pride, it is doubtful that they will
ever replace Quichua with Spanish totally.

Azuay

Although Azuay may be said to have approximately
80,000 Indians, only 50% can be said to be native
speakers of Quechua, of which perhaps 1/2 are monolinguals (Stark and Dilworth 1973). The heaviest
concentrations of Quichua speakers are in the Tarqui area just to the south of Cuenca, in the areas
around Sigsig and Quingeo to the east of Cuenca,
and in the Nabon and Shina areas in the southern
part of the province.  The economy in all three regions is based primarily on subsistence agriculture
plus the production of some crafts.  In Tarqui men
may supplement their income from farming and wea-
ving by working as cargadores in the markets in
Cuenca.  As a result of geographical proximity to
Cuenca, work in the city, and new schools in the
area, the speaking of Quichua in the Tarqui area is
rapidly disappearing.  The same is true in the Sig-
sig-Quingeo region where increased contacts with
the provincial capital combined with new schools
and health centers are bringing the area into rapid
contact with the Spanish-speaking world.  Thus,
with the exception of a few very isolated agricultural regions up towards the páramo, the majority
of Indian residents in this area are bilingual,
with many school-age children speaking only Spanish

     In the Nabon and Shina areas Quichua still main-
tains a strong position.  Since there is little
contact between the Indians of that region and Spanish-speakers, there is little incentive to learn
Spanish.  However, ethnic identity as an Indian and

the speaking of Quichua is fairly tenuous in this
area.   Therefore if schools and other outside a-
gents of linguistic change were to be introduced,
there would probably be a rapid assimilation towards Spanish.

## Loja

There are approximately 30,000 Indians living in
the province of Loja.   They are located chiefly in
the parroquias of Saraguro and San Lucas.   Probably
75% are bilingual in Spanish and Quichua with perhaps 25%, mostly older women, monolingual speakers
of Quichua (Stark and Dilworth 1973).

Ethnically the Indians of Loja are called Saragurans.   Although they have been traditionally subsistence agriculturalists and artisans, in recent
years many Saragurans have gone into cattle-raising
because of the market for contraband beef in Peru.
However, since land is scarce in Saraguro and San
Lucas, the Indians usually pasture their cattle
either high on the páramos, or in the jungles of
the southern Oriente.   In either case, children often work as herders and thus do not attend school.
But even though Saraguran children may not be learning Spanish in the schools, Spanish is often spoken in the homes.   Thus many children, whether at-
tending school or not, are monolingual speakers of
Spanish.   Saraguran adults seem to be divided in
their opinions concerning the lack of knowledge of
Quichua on the part of their children.   There are
those who feel that the more rapidly Quichua disappears and the group becomes monolingual Spanish-

speakers, the better the social and economic life of the people will be. On the other hand, there are those who are concerned over the loss of the language and wish to see some sort of revitalization movement within the group. Without such a program, it is quite certain that future generations of Saragurans will not speak any Quichua.

What is interesting about the Saraguran situation is that the people as a whole have a very positive attitude towards their own ethnic identity. Their culture and style of dress are very distinctive, and those who give it up to acculturate and become laychos are greatly disdained. However, language does not seem to fit into their self-conceived cultural identity so that it makes no difference whether one speaks Quichua, Quichua and Spanish, or only Spanish -- one maintains one's identity as an Indian through dress and custom. In fact, to be a monolingual speaker of Spanish is to be admired. Thus, although the Saragurans will probably continue as a cultural entity for many years to come, their language may well disappear in the very near future.

CONCLUSION
In the Ecuadorian highlands, Quichua is spoken by enough people so as to preclude its immediate replacement by Spanish. However its eventual survival or extinction will be determined in good part by its identification with "Indian-ness." There are several ways in which Quichua is correlated with Indian self-identity, both positively and ne-

gatively.  (1) There are groups who are turning
from Quichua to Spanish in the process of replacing
their Indian culture with a Mestizo one.  These
include many of the indigenous peoples of Pichincha, Cotopaxi, Azuay, and parts of Bolivar.  (2)
There are groups which are maintaining both their
indigenous language and culture.  These include
groups that live in very isolated areas and thus
have little contact with the national language and
culture, such as Indians living in the more remote
areas of Tungurahua, Bolivar, and Chimborazo.
There are also Indians found in less isolated areas
of the highlands who are consciously determined to
maintain their traditional language and culture.
This may be for religious reasons, as among certain
groups in Chimborazo, or it may be tied into an
identification of ethnicity with certain economic
activities defined as "Indian," such as the manufacture of textiles among the Otavaleños and Salasacas.  (3) In addition, there are groups who are
losing their native language while maintaining a
strong ethnic identity.  Such groups include the
Indians of Saraguro, and of San Antonio in Chimborazo.  In this case there may be a relationship
between language loss and new economic bases which
are not identified as traditional, or "Indian," by
the groups themselves.  This is presented in the
paradigm on the following page.
    Thus it appears in Highland Ecuador that iden-
tification of one's basis of economic subsistence
as "Indian" or "non-Indian" may have more of a bea-

ring on the maintenance of Quichua, or a change to Spanish, than ethnic identification as an "Indian". Whether indeed this continues to be the case in Ecuador, or occurs in other areas of Latin America, remains for further study.

| Economic Activity Identified as "Indian" | Ethnic Self- Identification as "Indian" | |
|---|---|---|
| + | + | = Maintenance of Quichua |
| − | + | = Loss of Quichua |
| − | − | = Loss of Quichua |

NOTES

1. When we are referring to the language as it pertains to Ecuador, we will use the word Quichua. However, when the language is referred to in a Pan-Andean context, the word Quechua is used.

2. This population figure, as well as others included in the text, refers to the number of speakers encountered in rural parts of the Highlands. Not included are Highland Quichua speaking migrants living in Quito, on the Coast, or in the Oriente.

3. Abbreviations are the following:  IM: Imbabura;
   PI: Pichincha; CO: Cotopaxi; $TU_1$: Tungurahua
   (Chibuleo); $TU_2$:  Tungurahua (Salasaca); CH:
   Chimborazo; CA: Cañar; AZ: Azuay; LO: Loja.
   (Data from Stark 1975.)

4. Note that this correspondence occurs only in
   suffixes, and not in the general lexicon of the
   dialects.

5. In this and in our analysis of the possessive/
   benefactive suffix we are assuming that the
   correlation between a- and u- forms in seven
   of the modal position classes (Parker 1969:129)
   did not exist in proto-Quechua.  Rather we will
   assume, at least as regards the contemporary
   -pu-/-pa- and -mu-/-ma- correlation, that the
   u form was the original form, with the a form
   coming later.  This is supported by the fact
   that in almost all the dialects today there are
   verb roots which correlate with the -pu- and
   -mu- forms, but none for the -pa- and -ma-
   forms.  Thus, these two forms would have begun
   as u- verb roots which became suffixes.  And
   it would have been from these suffixes that a
   forms later evolved.

6. Abbreviations are the following:  B: Puyo-Bobo-
   naza; T: Tena; L: Limoncocha. (Data from Orr and
   Wrisley 1965.)

7. Indians who are ethnically neither Salasaca nor
   Chibuleo are generally called "Platillos" by the
   campesinos of rural Tungurahua.  The word
   "Platillo" derives from the saucer-like shape of
   their traditional hats.

REFERENCES

Guevara, Darío. 1972. El castellano y el quichua
   en el Ecuador. Quito: Editorial Casa de la Cul-
   tura Ecuatoriana.
Hervás, Lorenzo. 1800. Catálogo de las lenguas de
   naciones conocidas. Tomo I. Madrid.
Hodge, C.T. 1970. The Linguistic Cycle. Language
   Sciences. 13:1-17. (Bloomington, Indiana)
Jijón y Caamaño, Jacinto. 1952. Antropología pre-
   hispánica del Ecuador. Quito.
Moya, Ruth. 1972. Influencia del Quichua en el
   Español de Quito. M.A. Thesis, University of
   Ottawa.
Muratorio, Blanca. 1981. Protestantism, Ethnici-
   ty, and Class in Chimborazo. In Cultural Trans-
   formations and Ethnicity in Modern Ecuador, Nor-
   man E. Whitten, ed., pp. 506-534. Urbana,
   Illinois: University of Illinois Press.
Muysken, Pieter and Louisa Stark. 1976. Dialect
   Variations in the Quichua of the Provinces of
   Pichincha, Cotopaxi, and Tungurahua, Ecuador.
   manuscript.
Orr, Carolyn and Robert Longacre. 1968. Proto-
   Quechumaran. Language, 44: 528-555).
Orr, Carolyn and Betsy Wrisley. 1965. Vocabulario
   Quichua del Oriente. Quito.
Parker, Gary J. 1963. Clasificación genética de
   los dialectos quechuas. Revista del Museo Na-
   cional, 32: 241-252 (Lima).
------. 1969. Comparative Quechua Phonology and
   Grammar II: Proto-Quechua Phonology and Morpho-

logy. University of Hawaii - Working Papers in
Linguistics, 1/2.

------. 1970. Comparative Quichua Phonology and
Grammar IV: The Evolution of Quechua A. University of Hawaii-Working Papers in Linguistics, 9.

------. 1972. Falacias y verdades acerca del quechua. In El Reto del multilingüismo en el
Perú, Alberto Escobar, ed., pp. 107-122. Lima,
Peru: Instituto de Estudios Peruanos (Serie Peru, Problema no. 9).

Pereira V., Jose. 1979. Algunas factores del bi-
lingüismo quichua-castellano. In Lengua y
cultura en el Ecuador, Ileana Almeida, ed., pp.
95-126. Otavalo, Ecuador: Instituto Otavaleño
de Antropología.

Porras, G., Pedro I. 1973. Breves notas sobre arqueología del Ecuador. Quito.

------. 1975. Fase Cosanga. Quito, Ecuador:
Universidad Católica del Ecuador.

Sapir, Edward. 1916. Time Perspective in Aboriginal American Culture, A Study in Method. Department of Mines, no. 13. Anthropological Series,
Memoir 90. Ottawa, Canada: Government Printing
Bureau.

Schultz, Gunter. 1968. Dialekt Unterschiede.
Manuscript.

Solá, Donald F. 1967. Gramatica del Quechua de
Huánuco, Plan de Fomento Lingüístico. Lima,
Peru: Universidad Nacional Mayor de San Marcos.

Stark, Louisa R. 1975. El quichua de la sierra
ecuatoriana. Otavalo: Instituto Interandino de
Desarrollo.

-----. 1982. Music, Bread and Tapestries. Report
to the Inter American Foundation, Rosslyn, Va.

Stark, Louisa R., with Lawrence K. Carpenter, Miguel Anrango Concha and Carlos A. Conterón Cordoba. 1974. El Quichua de Imbabura: Una Gramática Pedagógica. Otavalo, Ecuador: Instituto
Inter Andino de Desarrollo.

Stark, Louisa R. and Donald W. Dilworth. 1973.
Report to AID/Ecuador (November). Manuscript.

Torero, Alfredo. 1964. Los dialectos quechuas.
Anales Científicos de la Universidad Agraria
2:446-478 (Lima).

------. 1972. Lingüística e historia de los Andes
del Perú y Bolivia. In El reto del multilingüismo en el Peru, Alberto Escobar, ed., pp. 51-
106. Lima, Peru: Instituto de Estudios Peruanos
(Serie Perú, Problema no. 9).

Velasco, Juan De. 1841. Historia del Reino de
Quito. Tomo I. Quito.

von Tschudi, J. 1884. Organismus der Quechua
Sprache. Leipzig.

------. 1953. Die Quechua Sprache. Tomo I.
Wien.

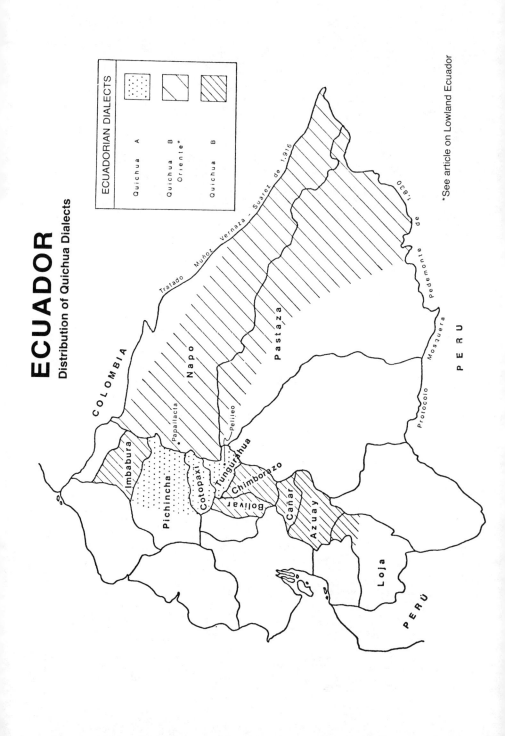

# ECUADOR
## Distribution of Quichua Dialects

ECUADORIAN DIALECTS

Quichua A

Quichua B
Oriente*

Quichua B

*See article on Lowland Ecuador

COLOMBIA

PERU

PERÚ

Tratado Muñoz Vernaza – Suárez de 1.916

Pedemonte de 1.830

Protocolo Mosquera

Imbabura

Pichincha

Cotopaxi

Tungurahua

Bolívar

Chimborazo

Cañar

Azuay

Loja

Napo

Pastaza

Papallacta

Pelileo

# 12. Southern Peruvian Quechua

## Bruce Mannheim

INTRODUCTION

Southern Peruvian Quechua is spoken by approximately two million inhabitants of, and urban migrants
from, the contiguous highland departments of Apurimac, Arequipa, Ayacucho, Cuzco, Huancavelica and
Puno. Although there are fairly striking differences in phonology and lexicon between polar varieties spoken in Cuzco and Ayacucho, in broad terms
the Quechua spoken in the southern highlands of
Peru was melded in a single crucible and should, as
Alfredo Torero suggested, be considered a single
unit for language planning in the region (1974:
43-60). If the label 'language' can appropriately
designate a discrete unit in the absence of a stan-
dardization movement, then Southern Peruvian Quechua, as it will be referred to here, is such a
unit. The present article is intended as an introduction to its genetic affiliation, dialectology,
geographic and demographic contexts, and its present status.

THE ECOLOGY OF A NAME

At the time of the European invasion (1532) Southern Peruvian Quechua was the koiné and administrative language of the Inka state, Tawantinsuyu,
and was called by the Spaniards the "lengua general del Inca." The label Quechua, as the Spanish

designation of the language, was already in use by
the mid-sixteenth century, as evidenced by its appearance in the Lexicon and Grammática of Domingo
de Santo Tomas (both 1560). The designation apparently arose when the Spaniards mistook the word
for 'valley'(in the dialectal designation qheswa
simi 'valley speech') for the name of the language.

Since the mid-sixteenth century, qheswa, as Quechua (from the sixteenth century form *qhechwa),
has been something of a standard label, so much so
that over much of the Quechua-speaking area the
word has been reborrowed (as kichwa, kichuwa, kech-
wa and the like) as the name for the language.[1]
Strictly speaking, the name of the language is Runa
simi 'human speech'; any regional form may be designated by the place name followed by the word simi, for example Qosqo simi, 'the speech of Cuzco'.
While for convenience's sake the now international-
ly accepted designation 'Quechua' will be used for
the language, the self-designation Runa 'human'
will be used for its first-language speakers.[2]


THE GEOGRAPHIC DOMAIN OF SOUTHERN PERUVIAN QUECHUA
The demarcation of the external geographic boundaries of Southern Peruvian Quechua cannot yet be
stated with precision.  This lack seriously under-
cuts any attempt to ascertain the historical dynamic of expansion or contraction of the Southern Peruvian Quechua linguistic community vis-a-vis
neighboring ones, although it is clear that the
Quechua linguistic community has historically ex-

panded toward the lowlands by way of migration from
Quechua-speaking highland communities and to the
south against Aymara by community-wide shifts of
linguistic allegiance (see Mannheim, this volume).
Synthesizing the reports of Cusihuamán (1976a:
30f.), Parker (1969b:7) and Torero (1974:35), we
may sketch the geographic provenience of Southern
Peruvian Quechua as follows: the highland portion[3]
of the Department of Ayacucho; the Department of
Huancavelica up to its northwestern border (excluding a small portion of Tayacaja province), where
it is contiguous with Huanca Quechua, spoken in Junín (Cerrón-Palomino, 1976:30);[4] the Department of
Apurímac; the highland portion of the Department of
Cuzco and the jungle portion up to the Yavero River
and the border with the Department of Madre de
Dios; the highland portions of the Department of
Arequipa (largely in the provinces of La Unión,
Condesuyos, Castilla and Cailloma) along with about
84,000 Quechua-speaking migrants mostly from Puno
and Cuzco in the city of Arequipa itself (Adams,
1976, 1979); the northwest highland portion of the
department of Puno, particularly the provinces of
Carabaya, Melgar, Lampa and western Sandia. Southern Peruvian Quechua is spoken in the city of
Puno itself, along with Aymara.

POPULATION
The several estimates which have been made of Quechua speakers were based on national census reports. The last three censuses in Peru (1940,
1961, and 1972) have all included questions concer-

ning language.  For several reasons such reports
must be interpreted with great caution.  Apart from
the expected undercount when a politically and socially dominated group is surveyed by the dominant
one, censuses in Peru have been associated with ta-
xation since the beginning of European domination
(cf.  Kubler 1952 and Mayer 1972).

Recent censuses have been conducted in Spanish:
it is not clear how they were administered to non-
Spanish speakers.  The language questions of the
two earlier censuses were explicitly biased toward
Spanish in that they were oriented toward showing
"the extent to which Spanish has spread" and "the
degree of linguistic unity in the nation" (Rowe
1947:209f.; Myers 1967:21-7).  However, a tabulation of the extent of bilingualism which reported
only those who admitted to a language other than
Spanish as their first tongue was eliminated in the
most recent census report.  This census has fairly
often been used alongside the incommensurate 1941
figures allegedly to 'demonstrate' the expansion of
bilingualism during the 1940s and 1950s. Among
other problems with such figures -- and with similar surveys of 'bilingualism' in the Andes -- is
the lack of meaningful and explicit criteria for
what constitutes a 'bilingual' in the first place.

According to the Peruvian national census of
1972 there are approximately two million speakers
of Southern Peruvian Quechua.  The figures for the
departments in which Southern Peruvian Quechua is
spoken which appear in Table 1 are based on a census question asking for the 'mother tongue' of res-

TABLE 1. Population 5 years and older by 'mother tongue' for the six Southern Peruvian Quechua-speaking departments. Total figure for Southern Peruvian Quechua includes the Constitutional Province of Callao and urban portions of the Department of Lima, projected from the Quechua total for both.

| Department | Quechua | Other Indigenous$^a$ | Spanish | Population Censused |
|---|---|---|---|---|
| Huancavelica | 236,020 | 771 | 33,732 | 272,469 |
| Ayacucho | 339,729 | 1,126 | 35,333 | 378,388 |
| Apurimac | 233,093 | 850 | 19,320 | 254,979 |
| Cuzco | 485,603 | 4,927 | 102,332 | 597,571 |
| Arequipa | 124,612 | 11,499$^b$ | 310,421 | 450,630 |
| Puno | 324,300 | 268,009$^c$ | 51,155 | 647,506 |
| TOTAL (Six Southern Departments) | 1,743,357 | 287,282 | 552,293 | 2,601,543 |
| Lima/Callao | 248,078 (Estimated) | | | |
| SPQ TOTAL | 1,991,435 (Estimated) | | | |

a   Includes Aymara and the census category 'otro autóctono'.
b   Includes 10,784 Aymara speakers.
c   Includes 267,209 Aymara speakers.

Sources: República del Perú, Dirección de Estadística, Censo Nacional de 1972, 4:304; 4:309; 5:390; 5:396; 6:81; 10:450; 18:394; 18:400; 19:360; 19:366; 20:481; 20:487; 22:294; 22:299.

pondents of five years of age or older. It should
be kept in mind that the choice of response among
languages of extremely different state prestige was
made in the context of governmental interviews.
Certain simplifying assumptions were made in elabo-
rating the tables. First, it was assumed that all
Quechua respondents in the six departments speak
some variety of Southern Peruvian Quechua, rather
than an exogenous Quechua variety. This is based
on the further assumption that migration within the
rural areas is fairly limited, and that speakers of
other Quechuan languages are more likely to migrate
to regional centers in their own region and capital, rather than to other provincial centers.
Since there is no cross-tabulation available of the
language question with place of birth, one cannot
be certain that this is in fact the case. Second,
as a rule the borders of Southern Peruvian Quechua
are coterminous with department borders, and so the
few exceptions noted earlier were overlooked.

The figure for urban Lima and Callao represents
an extrapolation from the proportion of Southern
Peruvian speakers to Quechua speakers nationwide.
This figure presumes that Southern Peruvian speakers are represented among migrants to Lima roughly
in the same measure as they are represented among
speakers of all Quechua languages nationwide.
These simplifications are made necessary by the
fact that the census did not distinguish among the
several Quechua languages. In at least one case
speakers of a non-Southern Peruvian Quechuan language were even classified as 'other autochtho-

nous,' the rubric that was applied to the numerous lowland languages in the tabulation (Cerrón-Palomino 1976:35). No figures are available for a dialectal breakdown <u>within</u> Southern Peruvian Quechua.

The percentages of first language speakers of Quechua, other indigenous languages (including Aymara), and Spanish for the six departments appear in Table 2. In the Department of Arequipa, Quechua speakers are concentrated in the highland provinces (chiefly Cailloma and La Unión) in roughly the same proportion as in the first four departments.  In Puno there is, of course, a sizeable Aymara-speaking population.

Since 1961 the percentage of first-language Quechua respondents has decreased between 1.69% (for Puno) and 7.64% (for Cuzco), while in absolute terms, their number has increased.  The disproportionately large increase in Arequipa may reflect local migration to the city of Arequipa itself, and thus might partly condition the relative decline in neighboring departments.

On the whole the population of Quechua first-language speakers responding to the census has been remarkably stable demographically between the two censuses of 1961 and 1972. And at least as of the most recent census (1972), the linguistic domination of the southern highlands of Peru by Quechua speakers (save for a large concentration of Aymara speakers in Puno) continues to be pervasive.

TABLE 2. Percentages of the population 5 years and older by 'mother tongue' for the six Southern Peruvian Quechua speaking departments, 1972.

| DEPARTMENT | QUECHUA | OTHER INDIGENOUS[a] | SPANISH |
|---|---|---|---|
| Huancavelica | 86.62 | .28 | 12.38 |
| Ayacucho | 89.78 | .30 | 9.34 |
| Apurímac | 91.42 | .33 | 7.58 |
| Cuzco | 81.26 | .82[b] | 17.12 |
| Arequipa | 27.65 | 2.55[b] | 68.89 |
| Puno | 50.08 | 41.39[c] | 7.90 |
| All Six Southern Departments | 67.01 | 11.04 | 21.23 |

a   Includes Aymara and the census category 'otro autóctono'.
b   Aymara responses constitute 2.39% of the censused total.
c   Aymara responses constitute 41.27% of the censused total.

Source: TABLE 1.

THE PLACE OF SOUTHERN PERUVIAN QUECHUA IN THE
QUECHUA FAMILY

Although subgrouping of the Quechua family is still
embryonic, scholars of the Quechua languages posit
an initial division into two major branches. Central Quechua (Gary Parker's 'Quechua B', Alfredo
Torero's 'Quechua I' and 'Waywash') is represented
by the present-day varieties spoken in the central
Peruvian highlands, particularly in the Departments
of Huaylas, Huanuco and Jauja. Peripheral Quechua
(Parker's 'Quechua A' and Torero's 'Quechua II' and
'Wampuy') flanks Central Quechua both to the north
and south. It is represented to the north by Quichua (spoken in Ecuador), Inga (spoken in Colombia)
and the Peruvian varieties of Cajamarca, Lambayeque
and San Martín, and to the south by the Bolivian
and Argentinian varieties, along with Southern Peruvian Quechua. This view of Quechua subgrouping,
now widely accepted by Quechua historical scholars,
represents a radical departure from the traditional
assumption that all extant varieties of Quechua
were descended from the Inka koiné, with Cuzco as
its center of dispersion.[5] The earlier position
rested on the further unsound assumption that the
colonial expression "lengua general del ynga" was
extensionally equivalent to what we today term
'Quechua languages', and was facilitated by an
unawareness of the extent of diversity within the
Quechua family in general and of the existence of
Central varieties in particular.

The place of Southern Peruvian Quechua in the
family may be schematized as in Table 3, which is

TABLE 3: Place of Southern Peruvian Quechua within Quechua family

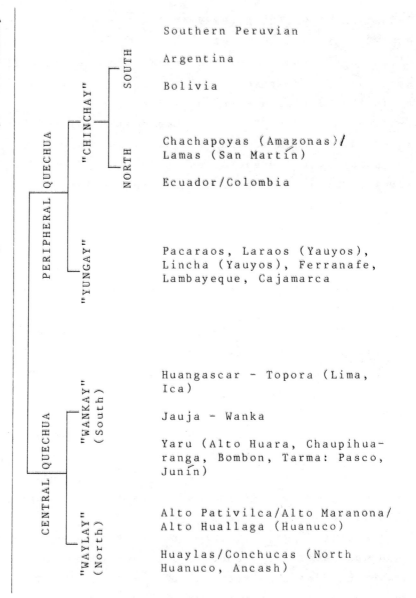

Southern Peruvian

Argentina

Bolivia

Chachapoyas (Amazonas)/
Lamas (San Martín)

Ecuador/Colombia

Pacaraos, Laraos (Yauyos),
Lincha (Yauyos), Ferranafe,
Lambayeque, Cajamarca

Huangascar - Topora (Lima,
Ica)

Jauja - Wanka

Yaru (Alto Huara, Chaupihua-
ranga, Bombon, Tarma: Pasco,
Junín)

Alto Pativilca/Alto Maranona/
Alto Huallaga (Huanuco)

Huaylas/Conchucas (North
Huanuco, Ancash)

based loosely on Alfredo Torero's 1974 classification. Varieties of Southern Peruvian Quechua are
mutually intelligible. In general, intelligibility
decreases drastically as one moves from node to
node of Table 3. Torero conducted intelligibility
tests to demonstrate that Southern Peruvian Quechua
and Central Quechua are <u>not</u> mutually intelligible,
and my own experience with Cuzqueño reactions to
Central Quechua songs accords with his findings
(1974:36-51). This observation must be tempered by
recalling that intelligibility is as much a social
fact as a linguistic one, as Cerrón-Palomino's description of asymmetric intelligibility between Ayacucho (Southern Peruvian Quechua) and Wanka (Central) demonstrated (1969:3). Nevertheless, claims
that speakers of one Quechua variety can recognize
any other variety as kindred are unfounded.[6]

THE MAJOR INTERNAL DIVISION: AYACUCHO AND CUZCO
QUECHUA
The primary dialectal break within southern Peruvian Quechua may be most clearly observed by contrasting the sound system of the Cuzco variety with
that spoken in Ayacucho. The segmental inventory
of the Ayacucho variety is seen in Table 4.

Notice that the Cuzco variety, in contrast, opposes three stop series, an ejective (or 'glottalized') and an aspirate series, in addition to one
which, as in Ayacucho, is neither (see Table 5).

Ejectivity and aspiration are restricted to the
initial stop in a word and may occur only in syllable initial position. At the ends of syllables,

TABLE 4. Segmental inventory of Ayacucho-type varieties of Southern Peruvian Quechua.

CONSONANTS

| | labial | alveolar | palatal | velar | uvular | laryngeal |
|---|---|---|---|---|---|---|
| stop | p | t | ch | k | q | |
| spirant | | s | | | | |
| (retroflex) tap/spirant | | r | | | | |
| nasal | m | n | ñ | | | |
| lateral | | l | ll | | | |
| glide | w | | y | | | h |

VOWELS

| | front | back |
|---|---|---|
| high | i | u |
| low | | a |

TABLE 5.  Segmental inventory of Cuzco-type varieties of Southern
Peruvian Quechua.  Bracketed segments are dialectally distinctive.

CONSONANTS

| | labial | alveolar | palatal | velar | uvular | laryngeal |
|---|---|---|---|---|---|---|
| stop | p | t | ch | k | q | |
| ejective | p' | t' | ch' | k' | q' | |
| aspirate | pʰ | tʰ | chʰ | kʰ | qʰ | |
| spirant | [φ] | s | [sh] | [x] | [x̣] | |
| (retroflex) tap/spirant | | r | | | | |
| nasal | m | n | ñ | | | |
| lateral | | l | ll | | | |
| glide | w | | y | | | h |

VOWELS

| | front | back |
|---|---|---|
| high | i | u |
| low | | a |

Cuzco Quechua has been undergoing a series of spi-
rantizations of stops and outright mergers at least
since the conquest (Mannheim 1983:121ff; 267ff.).

At present, Ayacucho 'plain' stops correspond to
Cuzco 'plain' or ejective or aspirated stops in
syllable-initial position, e.g.:


        Aya.  pacha 'world, clothing'
        Cuz.  pacha 'world', p'acha 'clothing'


        Aya.  chaki 'dry, leg'
        Cuz.  chaki 'leg', ch'aki 'dry'


        Aya.  qasa 'frozen, freezing; notch,
                        ravine'
        Cuz.  qasa 'frozen, frost', q'asa 'ravine,
                        something removed'


and to Cuzco spirants in syllable-final position,
e.g.:


        Aya.  llipta
                 'ash lime chewed with coca'
        Cuz.  lliφt'a ~ lli$^{w}$xt'a ~ llixt'a


        Aya.  utqay
                 'to hurry'
        Cuz.  usqhay


        Aya.  achka
                 'many, much'
        Cuz.  ashka ~ askha

Moreover, Ayacucho q̲ spirantized to [x̣] in all
positions (Parker, 1969b: 17 and 19; 1965: 12 and
14). Hence reflexes of final q̲ are identical in the
two varieties.

The nasals, laterals and glides of Cuzco Quechua
show a reduced inventory when compared to Ayacucho
Quechua. Of the nasals, m̲ and n̲ are opposed syllable-finally in Ayacucho; they are merged in
Cuzco, e.g.:

        Aya. <u>kimsa</u>

                  'three'

        Cuz. <u>kinsa</u>

The opposition between the Ayacucho laterals <u>ll</u>
and <u>l</u> is neutralized before t̲, where the <u>l</u> appears
and before k̲ and <u>ch</u> where the <u>ll</u> appears. Cuzco
laterals have the same distribution before all den-
tal, palatal and velar stops. Additionally, <u>ll</u> and
<u>l</u> have merged to <u>l</u> before uvulars in Cuzco, e.g.:

        Aya. <u>allqo</u>

               'dog'

        Cuz. <u>alqo</u>

Vowel-glide combinations in the Department of
Cuzco are dialectally in the process of reduction:
<u>ay</u>>e̲:>i̲; <u>uy</u>>i̲, under dialectally variable condi-
tioning. Also, in Cuzco, syllable-final w̲ has
become y̲ under dialectally and lexically variable
conditioning, e.g.:

Aya.  punchaw

                  'day'

Cuz.  p'unchay

In summary, the Cuzco type of Southern Peruvian Quechua opposes ejectivity and aspiration to the lack thereof on the first stop of the word, and evidences erosion of syllable finals. The Ayacucho type has a single stop series which lacks glottalization and aspiration and maintains the finals of syllables intact. Cuzco-type varieties are spoken in the departments of Cuzco, Puno, and Arequipa. Ayacucho-type varieties are spoken in the Departments of Ayacucho and Huancavelica. Both varieties are attested in the Department of Apurimac along with transitional varieties. In the province of Aymaraes, for example, a lexically and grammatically Ayacucho-type variant weakly incorporates ejectives and aspirates but does not lenite finals, apparently as a result of a relatively recent switch of cultural and linguistic allegiance from Ayacucho to Cuzco. In the area of Abancay, on the other hand, aspiration but not glottalization is present in the stop system and finals are conservatively lenited in what is otherwise a Cuzco-type variant. Within the Department of Cuzco phonological variation results largely from (1) variable acquisition of glottalization and aspiration and implementation of restrictions on these features; (2) dialectally variable rates of implementation of syllable final lenitions and mergers; (3) creation of new, low-yield phonemes (especially φ, x and sh;

bracketed in Table 5) from one of the lenition out-
puts via local, lexically sporadic shifts and metatheses. A major Department-wide variation pattern
involves the sibilants s and sh. To the north of
Cuzco and to the east of the Vilcanota River, the
two sibilants (the latter the output of a ch>sh
spirantization) tend to merge as s. To the south
of Cuzco, they tend to converge on sh by means of
phonologically conditioned, lexically diffused
shifts of s to sh.

SOUTHERN PERUVIAN QUECHUA PRACTICAL ORTHOGRAPHY
A single, standardized alphabet for the Quechua
languages spoken in Peru was officially adopted by
the Peruvian government in 1975 (Resolución Minis-
terial 4023-75-ED, 16-x-75). It is appropriate to
most practical purposes, including literature, pe-
dagogy, and cultural description, and reasonably
approximates the inner structures of Southern Peruvian Quechua sound systems. Of the many orthographic systems proposed over the years, it stands the
best chance of achieving widespread acceptance and
therefore offers the best possibility of ending the
sterile and pointless orthographic disputes which
have served only to impede the development and pro-
motion of Quechua written discourse.
    In Cuzco-type varieties, the official orthogra-
phy under-differentiates a dialectally variable
phonological opposition of extremely low producti-
vity, namely the difference between the velar spirant /x/ and the uvular spirant /x̣/ between vowels,
rendering both as h. In those cases the phonic

value of h is usually clear from the context. Vowel orthography is over-differentiated in order to
approximate use of the alphabet by bilinguals who
often associate lowered alternates of the high vowels with Spanish mid vowels.

Vowels and glides are presented in Table 6. The
letters appear in the left-most column, followed by
the underlying segment they represent (between sla-
shes). Examples of each appear in the columns on
the right. Consonants are presented in Table 7. As
we have seen earlier in this work, the consonant
systems of Ayacucho-type varieties and Cuzco-type
varieties are quite divergent in both inventory and
privileges of occurrence of most of the consonants. The presentation of the consonants letters
therefore includes (from the left to right) the
letter, the most important phonetic alternates (between square brackets) and examples of each in syllable-initial and syllable-final position for both
Cuzco-type and Ayacucho-type varieties. Where the
segment is not found in syllable-final position (in
Cuzco) or at all (in Ayacucho) an asterisk appears
in the appropriate column. For a detailed description of Cuzco segmental phonology, see Mannheim
1983, chapter 5. Unassimilated loanwords from Spanish are written with Spanish orthography. Finally, for more details on the official orthography
and examples of its use, see Cusihuamán, 1976a and
1976b, and Soto, 1976a and 1976b.[7]

TABLE 5. Practical Orthography: Vowels and Glides

___

                        Vowels

a       /a/            pampa        'plane'
                       ima          'what'

e[B]    /i/            reqsiy       'to know a person'
                       seqe         'straight line'

i       /i/            kiki         'oneself'
                       wasi         'house'

o[B]    /u/            qoy          'to give'
                       sonqo        'heart, essence'

u       /u/            tuta         'darkness, night'
                       tukuy        'to finish, to change
                                    form'

                        Glides

h       /h/            huq          'one'

y       /i/            yachay       'to know, to learn'
                       may          'where'

w       /u/            wasi         'house'
                       chawpi       'center'
___

TABLE 7.  Practical Orthography: Consonants

| | Cuzco | | | Ayacucho | | |
|---|---|---|---|---|---|---|
| p | [p] / [ɣ]¹⁰ | tupu llipt'a | 'clothing' | [p] [p] | tupu llipta | 'measure of land' 'paste chewed with coca' |
| p' | [p'] | p'acha | 'clothing' | *ʔ | | |
| ph | [pʰ] | phaway | 'to run, to fly' | *ʔ | | |
| t | [t] / *¹¹ | tapuy | | [t] [t] | tapuy utqay | 'to ask' 'to hurry' |
| t' | [t'] | t'anta | 'bread' | *ʔ | | |
| th | [tʰ] | thanta | 'rag, worn out' | *ʔ | | |
| ch | [č] / *¹¹ | chaki | | [č] [č] | chaki uchpa | 'foot' 'ash' |
| ch' | [č'] | ch'aki | 'dry' | *ʔ | | |
| chh | [čʰ] | chhachu | 'baby donkey' | *ʔ | | |

TABLE 7. Practical Orthography: Consonants (continued)

| | Cuzco | | | Ayacucho | | |
|---|---|---|---|---|---|---|
| k | [k] | kusi | | [k] | kusi | 'happy' |
| | [x] | wakcha | | [k] | wakcha | 'poor, orphan' |
| k' | [k'] | k'uychi | 'rainbow' | *ꟼ | | |
| kh | [kʰ~x] | khuru | 'insect, worm' | *ꟼ | | |
| q | [q] | qosa | | [x] | qosa | 'husband' |
| | [x̣] | llaqta | | [x̣] | llaqta | 'home place, village' |
| q' | [q'] | q'ero | 'ritual drinking vessel' | *ꟼ | | |
| qh | [qʰ] | qhata | 'incline' | *ꟼ | | |
| r | [ɾ] | kiru | | [ɾ] | kiru | 'tooth' |
| | [ɻ] | yawar | | [ɻ] | yawar | 'blood' |

TABLE 7. Practical Orthography: Consonants (concluded)

| | | Cuzco | | | | Ayacucho | |
|---|---|---|---|---|---|---|---|
| m | [m] | warmi | | [m] | warmi | 'woman' |
| n | [n] | nina | | [n] | nina | 'fire' |
| ñ | [ñ] | wañuy | | [ñ] | wañuy | 'to die' |
| l | [l] | layqa | | [l] | layqa | 'witch' |
| ll | [ʎ] | killa | | [ʎ] | killa | 'moon' |
| s | [s] | sapa | | [s] | sapa | 'each' |
| sh[12] | [ʃ] | ashka | 'many' | | | |
| h | [x][13] | aha | 'chicha' | | | |
| | [x][14] | uhu | 'inside' | | | |

WHY RUNA SIMI?

The demographic pervasiveness of Southern Peruvian
Quechua in the six highland departments contrasts
with its stigmatization in interethnic interaction
and at a national level. Southern Peruvian Quechua
is an 'oppressed language' (Albó, 1973; Cerrón-Palomino, 1975; Bareiro, 1975) in that its functional
development has, since the European invasion, been
the political, economic, and ideological preroga-
tive of people and institutions foreign to its
speakers (see Mannheim 1984a). Southern Peruvian
Quechua speakers, Runa, have incorporated both language maintenance and multilingualism into a complex and often ambiguous set of responses to domination by Spanish Peru.

   Throughout Southern Peru, Quechua speakers treat
the boundary between Quechua- and Spanish-speakers
as of primordial importance in their social uni-
verse. To be Runa is to be a human being, to speak
Runa simi ('Quechua'), to be of a place, to live
under the rule of reciprocity, ayni, and its atten-
dant etiquette. To be otherwise is to be q'ara,
'naked', 'uncultured', 'uncivilized' (cf. Núñez
del Prado, 1972; B.J. Isbell, 1978: 70ff.; Wagner,
1978:147; Allen, 1981). Ayni is understood by Runa,
not merely as an abstract principle governing social interaction, but as the fundamental organizing
basis of the material world.

   The continued viability of Southern Peruvian
Quechua, then, is not only a case of 'language loyalty' in the limited sense of this expression, but
reflects a comprehensive loyalty to a way of life

with an exclusionary view of social interaction.
Put another way, 'language loyalty' in the contemporary agrarian communities of Southern Peru is
bound up in a most profound way with loyalty to
being Runa. To insist, along with Southern Peruvian Quechua speakers, that the language itself is
properly called Runa simi 'Runa speech, human
speech' is to accede to their identification of the
language with both the natural and social order.

I do not wish to imply that the stance of Southern Peruvian Quechua speakers toward Spanish is
one of outright rejection, or even that there is a
stance. Since the institution of Spanish rule, access to Spanish language has been a necessary resource for Runa communities. A community's access
to productive resources and very survival may be
called into question within the framework of administrative and legal systems in which all of the
moves are made in Spanish. Bureaucratic control
over the affairs of rural communities has grown
considerably over the last decade, and with it the
need for speakers who control Spanish at a sufficient level to negotiate the paperwork. The Spanish language is, moreover, a resource for individuals, particularly the unmarried youth who attempt
to find temporary urban wage labor. Finally, there
is to some extent an internalization of the national society's evaluation of the two languages: parents are often anxious that their children learn
Spanish in the vague expectation that it will be
useful to their household and ultimately to their
children.

Runa, then, have the same ambivalence toward Spanish as they do toward q'ara institutions in general.  In this context, language is emblematic of an intrusive social system whose values contradict the very order of the world.  Recognition by Runa of the reality of national domination by Spanish-language institutions is tempered by an ethnocentrically-tinted anger.  On the model of Runa simi 'human speech', the Southern Peruvian Quechua name for their own language, Runa sometimes, with bitter humor, refer to Spanish as alqo simi, 'dog speech'.

It would be presumptuous to offer a prognosis for Southern Peruvian Quechua in view of the social and political complexity of the language situation.  The present vigorous predominance of Runa simi in rural areas of the six southeastern departments of Peru suggests that reports of its imminent demise are premature, to say the least.  But only an inccurable romantic would deny the considerable institutional and political pressures applied to the language and its speakers in the context of a Spanish-speaking nation-state.  The survival of Southern Peruvian Quechua over the long term is bound up with the survival of the Runa nation.

ACKNOWLEDGEMENTS

The support of portions of this work by the Organization of American States, the National Science Foundation and the Wenner-Gren Foundation for Anthropological Research is herewith acknowledged. I also wish to thank Martha Anders, Diane E.

Hopkins and Madeline Newfield, whose helpful
suggestions materially improved the paper. The
final draft was typed by Esor Groulx.


NOTES

1.  Variation in the back-borrowed term has to do
    with orthography and local differences in the
    sound systems.
2.  Another possibility, proposed by Markham (1871:
    300) and adopted by a handful of North American
    scholars, has been to use the label 'Inka' for
    both the language and its speakers as a reminder
    of the great Runa cultural past. While this
    would be feasible for Southern Peruvian Quechua,
    the former Inka koiné which during the vice-
    royalty was often called the "lengua general del
    ynga" it is unappealing for other Quechua lan-
    guages (such as Wanka and Ancash) which histori-
    cally are not descended from the Inka koiné and
    whose speakers maintain a cultural tradition of
    regarding the Inkas as foreign oppressors.
3.  The extent of migration to the lowlands of Aya-
    cucho by Quechua speakers is not reported.
4.  The geographic status of Southern Peruvian Que-
    chua relative to the borders of Huancavelica
    with Ica and Lima is not known.
5.  Ferrario's 1956 classification was the first
    major break from the older viewpoint. Since
    then, the major contributions to Quechua sub-
    grouping have come from Alfredo Torero (1964,
    1968, 1970 and 1974) and Gary J. Parker (1963,
    1969-1971 and 1969c). Several attempts have

been made at relating dispersions of the Quechua
family to ethnohistoric and archeological evidence, most notably by Zuidema (1973), Torero
(1974), W.H.  Isbell (1974), and Bird et al.
(1979).  The allusion I made to the 'embryonic'
nature of Quechua classification should be kept
in mind in any attempt to relate it to non-lin-
guistic material.  A classification or a reconstruction are not static objects, but rather
constantly change to reflect the descriptive and
historical state-of-the-art.  Quechua studies
have grown quite rapidly in the decade that has
elapsed since the bulk of the classificatory
work of Torero and Parker, and with it the number of new facts to be accounted for has also
grown, particularly for the varieties spoken in
central and northern Peru and in Ecuador, and
especially in the area of syntax.  The consensus
of support for the Torero-Parker classification
has grown progressively brittle over recent
years due to more detailed study of the linguistic histories of individual Quechua languages.
Landerman (1978), Cerrón-Palomino (1979), and
Adelaar (1984) have challenged the division of
the Northern Peripheral from the Central languages on morphological grounds; Mannheim (1984b)
reconstructed Common Southern Peruvian phonology
to the point of homologous correspondences with
the Central language, Wanka.  Suffice to say
that a major revision of Quechua subclassifica-
tion reflecting the recent growth in detailed
descriptive material is well overdue.

6.   On this point, see Torero's counter-evidence
     (1974:36ff.) to Wölck's assertion.

7.   Several excellent book-length reference gram-
     mars have been published on the Southern Peru-
     vian Quechua language: Cusihuamán (1976a) on
     the Cuzco variety, and Parker (1969b) and Soto
     (1976a) on the Ayacucho variety. All three con-
     centrate on description of the complex morpho-
     syntax, particularly on word-internal processes.
     Companion basic stem-lexicons have been publi-
     shed for the Cusihuamán and Soto grammars (Cusi-
     huamán, 1976b; Soto, 1976b; a briefer stem lexi-
     con is included in the Parker volume). Hornber-
     ger and Hornberger (1978) have published a use-
     ful trilingual stem lexicon of Cuzco Quechua,
     with entries in English and Spanish. Cerrón-Pa-
     lomino and Mannheim each have volumes in press
     on the Quechua linguistic history. Cerrón-Palo-
     mino's Linguistica Andina is a language family-
     wide survey. Mannheim's The Language of the
     Inka since the Conquest specifically treats of
     the history of Cuzco Quechua since the conquest.
     Soto's (1979) pedagogical grammar is an excel-
     lent practical introduction to the Ayacucho
     variety; Morato Peña (1981) is very helpful for
     those who wish to learn Cuzco Quechua.

8.   The sounds represented by e and o are combi-
     natory variants of i and u, respectively. The
     high vowels i and u are always lowered adja-
     cent to a uvular. (Additionally, certain seg-
     ments may intervene before a uvular. For an
     exact formulation, see Mannheim, 1983: 157ff.)

High vowels also tend to be lowered and centra-
lized toward the end of a word by a variable
prosodic rule.  In either of these cases they
are written as mid vowels (e, o) in the official orthography since to the Spanish ear they
correspond to the Spanish mid-vowels provided
that this does not lead to orthographic alterna-
tions of a word or suffix (e.g.  takiq 'singer'
from taki+q is not written *takeq).  Quechua
first-language speakers often use e and o to
represent the lax alternates of the high vowels
and i and u the tense alternates, respectively.

9.   Ejective and aspirate stops do not exist in
     Ayacucho Quechua.

10.  Bilabial spirant alternates [Φ] may also be
     written f.

11.  Spirantizes syllable-finally and merges with
     another segment in Cuzco Quechua.

12.  sh is a geographically-circumscribed, dialec-
     tally distinctive sound of low-yield in Cuzco.
     Both examples also have variants without sh in
     other areas.

13.  In Ayacucho-type varieties [x̣] is represented
     only by q.  In Cuzco-type varieties [x̣] is
     dialectally distinctive intervocalically and
     represented by h.

14.  [x] is dialectally distinctive in Cuzco.  In
     syllable-initial position it may, along with
     [x̣], be represented by the h graph.

510    *Bruce Mannheim*

REFERENCES

Adams, Stewart I.   1976.   The emergence of a Quechua subculture in the city of Arequipa as a result of the phenomenon of internal migration
from rural areas within Peru.   Center for Latin
American Studies, University of Saint Andrews,
Working Paper 5.

------.   1979.   Los urbanizadores de Arequipa.
Doctoral dissertation in Latin American Linguistic Studies, University of St. Andrews.

Adelaar, Willem F.H.   1984.   The significance of
grammatical processes involving vowel lengthening for the classification of Quechua dialects.
IJAL   50:25-47.

Albó, Javier.   1973.   El futuro de los idiomas
oprimidos en los Andes.   La Paz:   Centro de
Investigación y Promoción del Campesinado.

Allen, Catherine J.   1981.   To be Quechua:   The
symbolism of coca chewing in highland Peru.
American Ethnologist 8: 157-71.

Bareiro Saquier, Rubén.   1975.   Expresión de grupo
dominante y dominado en el bilinguismo paraguayo.   Actas del 39 Congreso Internacional de Americanistas, 5: 289-95.

Bird, Robert McK., David L.   Browman, and Marshall
Durbin.   1979.   Quechua and maize:   Mirrors of
Andean culture history.   Manuscript.

Cerrón-Palomino, Rodolfo M.   1969.   Wanka Kechua
morphology.   Master's thesis in linguistics,
Cornell University.

------.   1975.   La 'motosidad' y sus implicancias
en el enseñanza del Castellano.   In Aportes para

la enseñanza del lenguaje, M. Quintana Ch. and
D. Sanchez, eds., pp. 125-65. Lima: Retablo
de Papel.

------. 1976. Gramática Quechua: Junin-Huanca.
Lima: Instituto de Estudios Peruanos.

------. 1979. La primera persona posesora-actora
del protoquechua. Lexis (Lima) 3: 1-40.

------. in press. Lingüistica andina. Lima:
Instituto de Estudios Peruanos.

Cusihuamán Gutiérrez, Antonio. 1976a. Gramática
Quechua: Cuzco-Collao. Lima: Instituto de
Estudios Peruanos.

------. 1976b. Diccionario Quechua: Cuzco-Collao.
Lima: Instituto de Estudios Peruanos. (Both are
available from IEP, Horacio Urteaga 694, Lima
11, Peru.)

Ferrario, B. 1956. La dialettologia ed i problemi
interni della Runa-simi (vulgo Quéchua). Orbis
5: 131-40.

Hornberger, Stephen and Nancy Hornberger. 1978.
Diccionario tri-lingüe, Quechua de Cusco: Que-
chua English, Castellano (1983 reprint), La Paz.
(Published by the authors, 307 E. Eagle Heights,
Madison, WI 53705.)

Isbell, Billie Jean. 1978. To defend ourselves.
Austin: University of Texas Press.

Isbell, William H. 1974. Ecología de le expansión
de los quechua hablantes. Revista del Museo
Nacional (Lima) 40: 141-55.

Kubler, George. 1952. The Indian caste of Peru,
1795-1940. Washington: Smithsonian Institution.

Landerman, Peter. 1978. The Proto-quechua first person marker and the classification of Quechua dialects. Paper presented to the Workshop on Andean Linguistics, Urbana.

Mannheim, Bruce. 1983. Structural change and the structure of change: the linguistic history of Cuzco Quechua in relation to its social history. Doctoral dissertation in anthropology and linguistics, University of Chicago.

------. 1984a. 'Una nación acorralada': Southern Peruvian Quechua language planning and politics in historical perspective. Language in Society 13(3):291-309.

------. 1984b. New evidence on the sibilants of Colonial Southern Peruvian Quechua: Toward Andean philology.

------. Ms. The Language of the Inka since the conquest.

Markham, Clements. 1871. On the geographical positions of the tribes which formed the empire of the Yncas, with an appendix on the name 'Aymara'. Journal of the Royal Geographical Society (London) 41: 281-338.

Mayer, Enrique. 1972. Censos insensatos. In Visita de la Provincia de León de Huánuco en 1562, John V. Murra, ed., 2:339-65. Huanuco: Universidad Nacional Hermilio Valdizán.

Morato Peña, Luis. 1981. Runasimi basico Qosqo-Qollaw. Cusco: Instituto Pastoral Andina (Apartado 1018, Cusco).

Myers, Sarah K. 1967. The distribution of languages in Peru: A critical analysis of the cen-

sus of 1961. Master's thesis in geography, the
University of Chicago.
Núñez del Prado Bejar, Daisy I. 1972. La recipro-
cidad como ethos de la cultura indígena. Bache-
lor's thesis in anthropology, Universidad Nacional San Antonio Abad del Cuzco.
Parker, Gary J. 1963. La classificación genética
de los dialectos quechuas. Revista del Museo
Nacional (Lima) 32:241-52.
------. 1965. Gramática del quechua ayacuchano.
Lima: Universidad Nacional de San Marcos. (Spanish language version of the grammatical portion
of Parker, 1969b.)
------. 1969-71. Comparative Quechua phonology
and grammar. University of Hawaii Working Papers in Linguistics I: 1(1): 65-88; II: 1(2):
123-47; III: 1(4): 1-61; IV: 1(9): 149-204; V:
3(3): 45-109.
------. 1969b. Ayacucho Quechua grammar and dictionary. The Hague: Mouton.
------. 1969c. Bosquejo de una teoría de la evolución del Quechua A. Programa Interamericano
de Lingüística y Enseñanza de Idiomas, El Simposio de México, 270-81. Mexico: Universidad Nacional Autónoma de México.
Rowe, John Howland. 1947. The distribution of
Indians and Indian languages in Peru. The
Geographical Review 37: 202-15.
------. 1950. Sound patterns in three Inca dialects. IJAL 16:137-48.
Santo Tomás, Domingo de. 1560a. Gramática o arte
de la lengua general de los indios de los reynos

del Perú.  Valladolid: Fernández de Cordova.
Facsimile edition, Lima:  Universidad Nacional
San Marcos, 1951.

------.  1560b.  Lexicon o vocabulario de la lengua
general.  Valladolid:  Fernández de Cordova.
Facsimile edition, Lima: Universidad Nacional de
San Marcos, 1951.

Soto Ruiz, Clodoaldo.  1976a.  Gramatica quechua:
Ayacucho-Chanca.  Lima:  Instituto de Estudios
Peruanos.

------.  1976b.  Diccionario quechua: Ayacucho-
Chanca.  Lima: Instituto de Estudios Peruanos.

------.  1979.  Quechua:  Manual de enseñanza.
Lima: Instituto de Estudios Peruanos.  (All
three are available from IEP, Horacio Urteaga
694, Lima 11, Peru.)

Torero Fernández de Cordova, Alfredo.  1964.  Los
dialectos quechuas.  Anales Cientificos de la
Universidad Agraria 2:446-78.

------.  1968.  Procedencia geografica de los
dialectos quechuas de Ferrenafe y Cajamarca.
Anales Científicos de la Universidad Agraria 6:
168-97.

------.  1970.  Lingüística e historia de la sociedad andina.  Anales Científicos de la Universidad Agraria 8: 231-64.  Reprinted in El reto del
multilingüismo en el Perú, Alberto Escobar, ed.,
pp. 46-106.  Lima:  Instituto de Estudios Peruanos, 1972, and Actas del 39 Congreso Internacional de Americanistas 5: 221-59, 1975.

------.  1974.  El quechua y la historia social
andina.  Lima: Universidad Ricardo Palma.

Wagner, Catherine Allen. 1978. Coca, chica, and
    trago. Doctoral dissertation in anthropology,
    University of Illinois. (Available from Univer-
    sity Microfilms, 300 North Zeeb Road, Ann Arbor,
    MI, 48103.)
Wölck, Wolfgang. 1977. Un problema ficticio: len-
    gua o dialecto quechua? Lexis (Lima) 1: 151-62.
Zuidema, R. Tom. 1973. The origin of the Inca Em-
    pire. Les grandes empires, Recueils de la Soci-
    été Jean Bodin pour l'Histoire Comparative des
    Institutions 31: 733-57.

# 13. The Quechua Language in Bolivia
## Louisa R. Stark

INTRODUCTION

The purpose of this study will be to present a
brief account of the history and distribution of
the Quechua language in Bolivia, including a discussion of its derivative, Machaj Juyai.

Speakers of Quechua consist of an estimated two
million, or 35% of the population of Bolivia (Albó
1973:15). They are concentrated in two separate,
discontinuous areas: the central part of the department of La Paz, and the highland area extending
southward from Oruro to Villazón on the Argentine
border. The language is also spoken in certain
areas in the Bolivian lowlands, where it has been
introduced relatively recently through the migration of Quechua-speaking highlanders.

The Quechua of Bolivia is divided into dialect
areas which coincide with the two discontinuous regions in which the language is spoken. One dialect, that spoken in the provinces of Muñecas, Bautista Saavedra, Franz Tamayo (formerly Caupolicán)
in the department of La Paz will be designated as
Northern (Bolivian) Quechua (NQ). The other dialect is spoken in the area which extends southward
from Oruro as far as Villazón on the Argentine border and includes concentrations of speakers in the
departments of Oruro, Cochabamba, Chuquisaca, and
Potosí. It is also the dialect which has been in-

troduced into lowland Bolivia, especially in the
department of Santa Cruz, through the migration of
Quechua-speaking colonists from the highlands.   We
will designate this variant Southern (Bolivian)
Quechua (SQ).   Variation within SQ is greater than
that found in NQ, which is more uniform in phonology, grammar, and lexicon.

Table 1 is a comparison of some of the differences between NQ and SQ.  NQ examples are from the
Quechua spoken in Apolo, province of Franz Tamayo,
department of La Paz (Stark 1972b), with SQ examples from the Quechua spoken in Cabezas, province
of Yamparaez, department of Chuquisaca (Stark, et
al.  1971).

NORTHERN BOLIVIAN QUECHUA (NQ)
There are an estimated 16,500 native speakers of NQ
living in the provinces of Muñecas and Bautista
Saavedra, plus an additional 11,500 to be found in
Franz Tamayo (estimates are based on Albó 1980:
92-93).  There are additional concentrations of NQ
speakers in the northern part of the province of
Larecaja in the regions around Consata and Mapiri
(Albó 1980:93).

History

Bautista Saavedra and Muñecas.  The following linguistic history can be hypothesized for the areas
of Bautista Saavedra and Muñecas in which NQ is
currently spoken.   It appears that one of the earliest languages spoken in the region was Pukina

TABLE 1. Differences between Northern and Southern Bolivian Quechua

| APOLO (NQ) | CABEZAS (SQ) |
|---|---|

**PHONOLOGY:**

(1) /p/, /t/, /č/ occur syllable final. (E.g. /lipt'a/ 'ash for chewing with coca'; /mutk"iy/ 'to smell'; /p"ičqa/ 'five')

(1) /p/, /t/, /č/ have assimilated to /x/, /s/, and /š/ respectively syllable final. (E.g. /lixt'a/ 'ash for chewing with coca'; /musk"iy/ 'to smell'; /piška/ 'five')

(2) /m/ may occur syllable final. (E.g. /kimsa/ 'three')

(2) /m/ does not occur syllable final. (Example: /kinsa/ 'three')

**GRAMMAR:**

(3) /-pas/ 'also'

(3) /-pis/ 'also'

(4) Noun plural marker is /-kuna/ in all environments. (E.g. /wasikuna/ 'houses'; /nankuna/ 'roads')

(4) Noun plural marker is /-s/ after V, /-kuna/ after C. (E.g. /wasis/ 'houses'; /nankuna/ 'roads')

(5) Noun plural marker follows a pronominal suffix. (E.g. /nanniykukuna/ 'our (excl.) roads')

(5) Noun plural marker precedes a pronominal suffix. (E.g. /nankunayku/ 'our (excl.) roads')

TABLE 1. Differences between Northern and Southern Bolivian Quechua
(continued)

| APOLO (NQ) | CABEZAS (SQ) |
|---|---|
| (6) /-rqan/ third person singular past tense. (E.g. /parlarqan/ 'he spoke') | /-rqa/ third person singular past tense. (E.g. /parlarqa/ 'he spoke') |
| (7) /-nqaku/ third person plural future tense. (E.g. /wilanqaku/ 'they'll tell') | /-nqanku/ third person plural future tense. (E.g. /wilanqanku/ 'they'll tell') |
| (8)[1] /-čka-/ continuous action. (E.g. /wilačkani/ 'I'm telling (it)') | /-sa-/ continuous action. (E.g. /wilašani/ 'I'm telling (it)') |
| (9) /-čis/ plural of pronouns. (E.g. /xamusunčis/ 'we'll (incl.) come') | /-čex/ plural of pronouns. (E.g. /xamusunčex/ 'we'll (incl.) come') |
| (10)[2] Genitive is /-pax/. (E.g. /wawapax misin/ 'the child's cat'; /supaypax wasin/ 'the devil's house') | Genitive is /-x/ after V, /-pa/ after C. (E.g. /wawax misin/ 'the child's cat'; /supaypa wasin/ 'the devil's house') |

(now extinct). Aymara-speaking people then entered
the region, probably beginning in the early thir-
teenth century, and formed part of the Tiahuanaco-
derived Mollo culture (Ibarra Grasso 1973:215-221),
which was later absorbed into the Aymara nation
(Bastian 1978:xxi-xxii). Pukina continued to be
spoken, co-existing with Aymara. Later the region
was conquered by the Incas during the reign of the
emperor Pachacuti Inca (1438-1463) (Mesa and Gisbert 1973:45). It was then that the Quechua language was introduced into this area of northern
Bolivia (Bastian 1978:xxii, 23), quite probably
brought by Quechua-speaking mitimaes, or colonists, from southern Peru (Bouysse-Cassagne 1975:
319). This is supported linguistically by the fact
that Northern Bolivian Quechua and Southern Peruvian Quechua share both aspirated and glottalized
stops. Both features are found only in the Quechua
of southern Peru, Bolivia, and parts of northwest
Argentina.

The new Quechua-speaking arrivals took over the
more fertile, lower lands of the region, pushing
the Aymara speakers up into the higher, less agri-
culturally productive regions where they turned to
herding. Aymara is still spoken in these areas today (Bastian 1973:7). Pukina also continued to be
spoken, at least in the Charazani region of Bautista Saavedra, until the first half of the seventeenth century (Stark 1972a:1) when it became extinct. However, there are still vestiges of Pukina found in Machaj Juyai, the secret language of
the Callahuaya (Qollawaya) curers.

Since the introduction of Quechua from Peru into northern Bolivia, there has been continued contact between the two areas. For example, in 1928 there was a new migration of Quechua-speaking Peruvians into the Charazani region (Bastian 1978:12, 117). Even today there is a good deal of interaction between the two areas, especially between Quechua speakers of the northernmost province of Franz Tamayo and those of neighboring Peru (Stark 1972b).

Franz Tamayo. The linguistic history of Franz Tamayo differs from that of the rest of the NQ area. Oral tradition asserts that Quechua was introduced into the Apolo region by Indians who migrated there from the Cuzco Valley 100 years ago. They are said to have replaced the Leco-speaking Indians who were the original inhabitants of most of the province (Stark 1972b). Actually, from what we can construct of the linguistic history of Franz Tamayo, Leco has indeed been replaced by Quechua, but the process has been a much longer one than what is popularly believed.

When the Spaniards first arrived in the area now designated as the province of Franz Tamayo, they discovered that most of the region was inhabited by speakers of Leco, who occupied most of the area bounded by the Rio Tuichi in the north, the Rio Tipuani in the south, and the Rio Beni to the east (Armentia 1905:93-98). They do not appear to have extended further west than the present-day towns of Apolo, Aten, and Mapiri. (Mapiri is currently located in the province of Larecaja.) In 1621, a

priest who visited Apolo and Aten noted that the
Leco men that he encountered were able to communicate with him in Quechua (Anónimo 1903:13). Quite
probably the Lecos had learned Quechua in order to
communicate with the Indians of Charazani with whom
they traded lowland products, including coca, for
those produced at higher altitudes (Anónimo 1903:
111-112).

During the late 17th and early 18th centuries,
Franciscan priests began to congregate the Lecos in
the missions that they had constructed at Apolo,
Aten, and Mapiri, along the westernmost edge of the
territory then occupied by the Indians. Quechua
appears to have been used as a lingua franca in the
missions (Armentia 1905:15), which probably helped
to spread its use among the Indians. After the
Lecos, who had always been considered a somewhat
bellicose group (Armentia 1905:93), had been "paci-
fied" by the Franciscans, large groups of Quechua
speakers began to migrate into the region around
Apolo (Anónimo 1903:56), probably attracted by the
possibilities that the area offered for the cultivation of coca. Little by little Quechua began to
make inroads until Leco all but disappeared. Today
there are perhaps a total of 200 Leco speakers (ILV
1975), most of whom live near the town of Mapiri
(Stark 1972b).

Although the linguistic history of Franz Tamayo
differs from that of Bautista Saavedra and Muñecas,
the Quechua spoken in both areas is nearly identical phonologically, grammatically, and lexically.
This may be attributable to a variety of factors.

Historically, the Lecos probably first learned Quechua through trading with the Indians of Bautista
Saavedra and Muñecas. More recently there have
been migrations of families from Canisaya, in Bautista Saavedra, to Apolo in order to cultivate coca
there (Bastian 1978:127-128). Although these are
the only recent migrations that have been noted in
the anthropological literature, they may simply reflect the continuation of the close contact between
the two areas which has resulted in the lack of
linguistic variation in the Quechua spoken in northern Bolivia.

Current Status

The largest concentration of Quechua speakers is
found in Bautista Saavedra where in 1976 some 78%
of the total population spoke the language in the
home, as compared with 17% who spoke Aymara (Albó
1980:93). The largest concentration of Quechua
speakers within that province is located in its
northern part (Albó 1980:108). In 1976, 70% of the
population in Franz Tamayo spoke Quechua as their
first language as compared with 13% who were Aymara
speakers (Albó 1980:93). Most Quechua speakers live
in the eastern part of the province (Albó 1980:
108). Finally, in the southernmost of the three
provinces, Muñecas, only 39% of the total population spoke Quechua as the language of the home.
This compared with 54% who spoke Aymara (Albó 1980:
92). In Muñecas, most Quechua speakers are found in
the northern and eastern areas of the province
(Albó 1980:108).

Quechua and Aymara speakers inhabit the rural
areas of the provinces. Where there is communication between speakers of the two languages, it is
described as bi-aural. A speaker of Quechua can
understand a speaker of Aymara, yet is unable to
communicate in the other language (Bastian 1978:
xxi). The same holds true of Aymara speakers vis-
a-vis Quechua.

Spanish speakers tend to be concentrated in the
provincial capitals where they own small stores and
trucks which provide local and long-distance transportation. In Apolo most native speakers of Spanish command very little Quechua. They rely on bilingual employees when they wish to communicate
with Quechua-speaking clients.

There is little social stratification among
speakers of Quechua in this area of Bolivia. As a
result, the language does not possess the sociolinguistic variation that has been demonstrated for SQ
(Albó 1970, 1974). Beyond this, the possibility of
the incursion of Spanish on Quechua, as is so prevalent in other parts of the Andes, does not appear
to be a great threat in the area under discussion.

In Franz Tamayo there seems to be little reason
for learning Spanish. The area is very isolated
with little direct influence from the larger Spanish-speaking Bolivian society. The only contact
between Apolo and the outside world is through air
travel, which is hardly within the realm of possibility for the average campesino, or by walking
seven days to Charazani. From Charazani one can
then take a truck to La Paz, which involves a trip

of between one and three days.  What the average
campesino from Franz Tamayo knows about the world
outside of his or her community is based on occasional shopping trips to the town of Apolo.

Most schools in Franz Tamayo are located in, or
close to, the provincial capital of Apolo.  School
teachers fly in from La Paz at the beginning of the
school year, leaving only for vacations.  They are
generally urban, monolingual Spanish speakers.
Those who are "unlucky" enough to be assigned to
one of the few rural schools complain bitterly that
their students enter without knowing a word of Spanish, that they "have no interest in schooling."
As evidence, they point to the high drop-out rate,
and the fact that most students must repeat the
first grade until they learn enough of the national
language so as to be able to continue with their
schooling.  This, of course, mirrors the educational situation in many other parts of rural Latin
America.  However, in contrast to other areas of
Latin America, it appears that campesino parents in
Franz Tamayo do not necessarily view as important
the role that the school might have in teaching
their children the national language; few of them
feel it is essential that they or their children
learn Spanish.  The area is isolated from the national culture, and there is little need to learn
Spanish so as to communicate with speakers of that
language.  Beyond this, there is enough land, and
it is rich enough, so that the average campesino
need not contemplate having to migrate to another
(perhaps Spanish-speaking) area to look for land or

work.    Thus, the majority of <u>campesinos</u> in Franz
Tamayo are monolingual Quechua speakers.    If Spanish is spoken by anyone in rural Franz Tamayo it
is by adult males.    Women and young children are
almost all monolingual speakers of Quechua (Stark
1970).

The situation in Bautista Saavedra is both similar and different.    Here the social situation is
similar to that of Franz Tamayo, as is the availability of land.    However, Charazani, the capital of
Bautista Saavedra, is connected to La Paz by a
road.    And although travel between the two areas is
long and arduous, the people of Charazani have direct contact with the nation's capital.    This has
resulted in increased military service by young
men.    There has also been some migration to La Paz,
including a few young women who have gone there to
work as maids.    Moreover, there are now <u>campesinos</u>
who travel to La Paz to buy and sell, as well as
occasionally to participate in such government-
sponsored events as musical festivals.

Although a few men have learned some Spanish as
a result of their trips to the capital, it has been
fairly negligible.    Most of the people with whom
they have commercial dealings in La Paz either
speak Quechua or have access to bilingual assis-
tants who aid them in their business transactions.
Knowledge of Spanish is more important for use in
dealing with monolingual bureaucrats in government
offices.    There are always a few <u>campesino</u> men in
every area who know enough Spanish to serve as
interpreters when a delegation must make an offi-

cial visit.  Or, at times, a bilingual Mestizo will
accompany the group, serving as interpreter for his
compadres.

Others who speak Spanish are the entrepreneurs
from Charazani who are involved in the coca trade,
buying coca in Apolo and transporting it for sale
in La Paz.  For these individuals knowing Spanish
is a necessity, since they must communicate with
the owners and pilots of the DC3's that they char-
ter for their transportation.  Although many of
these entrepreneurs now live in La Paz, they appear
to be intent upon maintaining their command of Quechua.  This is partly because it is with Quechua
speakers they must negotiate in the buying of
coca.  But beyond this, Quechua plays in important
role in their self esteem as Callahuayas (Bastian
1973:296).

In Bautista Saavedra there are professional curers who travel all over Bolivia, as well as to
other areas of Latin America, where they ply their
trade as professional herbalists and curers.  They
administer to other Indians as well as to Mestizos
who today appear to be using the services of herbalists more than ever before (Grollig 1978).  As a
result of professional dealings with speakers of a
variety of languages, most of the traveling curanderos have mastery of four languages: Quechua, Aymara, Spanish, and their secret curing language,
Machaj Juyai.  However, the language of the home is
Quechua.  As with the entrepreneurs who deal in
coca, the curanderos maintain their Quechua because (1) it has a commercial value in dealing with

Quechua-speaking patients, and (2) they consider
the speaking of Quechua to be intimately tied into
their ethnic self-identity as Callahuayas, in which
they have great pride.

Although some of the residents of Bautista Saavedra learn Spanish through contact with speakers
of the national language outside of the province, a
few learn the language through formal schooling.
There are schools in the various cantones in Bautista Saavedra; however, most parents do not want
to send their children to these institutions. This
is partly because they need their labor, and partly
because they feel that the national educational
system belittles their native culture. There also
appears to be the feeling that the school, by teaching their children Spanish, prepares them to emi-
grate from the community, as has happened with
those who thus far have learned the rudiments of
the national language (Bastian 1973:82).

On the other hand, there appears to be little
chance that those who are currently bilingual in
Spanish and Quechua would want their children to
grow up monolingual in Spanish. The speaking of
Quechua is simply too important for economic reasons, and as a part of their ethnic self-identity,
to allow it to disappear. Thus for the moment the
prognosis for the survival of Quechua in northern
Bolivia is good.

## Machaj Juyai

Machaj Juyai is spoken by Callahuaya curers living
in the region of Charazani, province of Bautista

Saavedra. It is used only by men, and is passed on from father to son; as a result women and children do not understand or speak the language. Because its use is limited to men within a specific and closed profession, Machaj Juyai has been called a "secret language" (Oblitas Poblete 1968) and, indeed, it functions in this way. It is used to insure secrecy from speakers of Spanish, Quechua, and Aymara, and at times other languages, for whom curing ceremonies are performed. Structurally, Machaj Juyai is most like a pidgin, consisting of a mixture of Pukina, the original but now extinct language spoken in the area, and Quechua. More specifically, the phonology of Machaj Juyai shows a combination of Pukina and Quechua sound systems, its grammar is Quechua, and its lexicon, which is highly reduced, is predominantly Pukina (Stark 1972a:23). As such, Machaj Juyai is clearly a mixed language and not a sister to Pukina as has previously been postulated.

## SOUTHERN BOLIVIAN QUECHUA (SQ)

As has been noted before, SQ extends southward from Oruro as far as Villazón on the frontier with Argentina. There are Quechua-speaking settlements along the eastern and southern borders of the department of Oruro, as well as Quechua-speaking residents living in the town by that name. Large concentrations of Quechua speakers are found in the eastern part of the department of Cochabamba, in rural areas, provincial towns, and the department capital. Quechua is spoken throughout the depart-

530 Louisa R. Stark

ments of Chuquisaca and Potosi.

## History

It has traditionally been believed that SQ was introduced into Bolivia through Inca conquest in the
fifteenth century. However, it was probably introduced into this region later than it was introduced
into northern Bolivia. This is because there are
certain phonological and morphological features
which are shared by Cuzco and SQ, but which do not
occur in NQ and Proto-Quechua. For a comparison,
see Table 2. NQ is that spoken in Apolo (Stark
1972b), SQ that spoken in Cabezas (Stark, et al.
1971), and Cuzco Quechua that spoken in Chincheros,
province of Urubamba, department of Cuzco, Peru
(Cusihuaman 1976). Proto-Quechua forms are from
Parker (1969a, 1969b) and Stark (1974).

In each of the examples in Table 2, the NQ form
represents a more archaic variant of Quechua than
the SQ and Cuzco forms. This would indicate that
Quechua was introduced into northern Bolivia at an
earlier period than in southern Bolivia. This also
appears to coincide with the archaeological record
in which it is hypothesized that the Incas conquered northern Bolivia during the reign of Pachacuti
Inca between 1438 and 1463, but that the conquest
of southern Bolivia took place during the rule of
the emperor Topa Inca at some point after 1470
(Mesa and Gisbert 1973:45). If we accept a period
of at least fifty years between the conquest of
northern and southern Bolivia, then we must posit
that Cuzco Quechua underwent certain changes within

TABLE 2. Comparison of Proto, NQ, SQ, and Cuzco Quechua

| PROTO-QUECHUA | APOLO(NQ) | CABEZAS (SQ) | CHINCHEROS (CUZCO) |
|---|---|---|---|
| **PHONOLOGY:** | | | |
| (1) */p/, */t/, */č/ occur syllable final. (E.g.: *lipta 'ash for chewing with coca'; *mutkiy 'to smell'; *pičqa 'five') | /p/, /t/, /č/ occur syllable final. (E.g.: /lipt'a/ 'ash for chewing with coca'; /mutk"iy/ 'to smell'; /p"ičqa/ 'five') | /p/, /t/, /č/ have assimilated to /x/, /s/, and /š/ respectively. (E.g.: /lixt'a/ 'ash for chewing with coca'; /musk"iy/ 'to smell'; /pišqa/ 'five') | /p/, /t/, /č/ have assimilated to /x/, /s/, and /š/ respectively. (E.g.: /lixt'a/ 'ash for chewing with coca'; /musk"iy/ 'to smell'; /pišqa/ 'five') |
| (2) */m/ may occur syllable final. (E.g.: *kimsa 'three') | /m/ may occur syllable final. (E.g.: /kimsa/ 'three') | /m/ does not occur final. (E.g.: /kinsa/ 'three') | /m/ does not final. (E.g.: /kinsa/ 'three') |

TABLE 2. Comparison of Proto, NQ, SQ, and Cuzco Quechua (continued)

| PROTO-QUECHUA | APOLO(NQ) | CABEZAS (SQ) | CHINCHEROS (CUZCO) |
|---|---|---|---|
| **GRAMMAR:** | | | |
| (3) *-rqan third person singular past tense. (E.g. *wilarqan 'he told (it)') | /-rqan/ third person singular past tense. (E.g. /wilarqan/ 'he told (it)') | /-rqa/ third person singular past tense. (E.g. /wilarqa/ 'he told (it)') | /-rqa/ third person singular past tense. (E.g. /wilarqa/ 'he told (it)') |
| (4) *-čka- continuous action. (E.g. *wilačkani 'I'm telling (it)') | /-čka-/ continuous action.(E.g. /wilačkani/ 'I'm telling (it)') | /-ša-/ continuous action. (E.g. /wilašani/ I'm telling (it)') | /-ša/ continuous action. (E.g. /wilašani/ I'm telling (it)') |
| (5) Genitive is *-paq. (E.g.: *supaypaq wasin 'the devil's house'; *wawapaq maman 'the child's mother') | Genitive is /-pax/. (E.g.: /supaypax wasin/ 'the devil's house'; /wawapax maman/ 'the child's mother') | Genitive is /-pa/ after C, /-x/ after V, (E.g. /supaypa wasin/ 'the devil's house'; /wawax maman/ 'the child's mother') | Genitive is /-pa/ after C, /-x/ after V. (E.g.: /supaypa wasin/ 'the devil's house'; /wawax maman/ 'the child's mother') |

the fifty years between the time that it was introduced in each region. As Parker (1969c:174) has noted, the sound changes common to Cuzco and Southern Bolivian Quechua probably took place during the imperial period. The language of Cuzco appears to have been changing rapidly during the short period of Inca expansion which started under the emperor Pachacuti Inca and ended with the arrival of the Spaniards in 1532. As such the language was probably reflecting the political and social turmoil of the times.

Current Status

Unlike NQ, which is spoken primarily by rural campesinos in northern Bolivia, SQ is spoken along a much wider social spectrum. In a very general outline, this includes the following:

(1) At one end of the social spectrum are the older members of the upper class who, before the peasant uprisings and agrarian reform of the 1950's, were the owners and children of owners of haciendas. Although such individuals rarely lived on the haciendas that they owned, they often spent extended periods of time on their properties. In this way, while still young they learned Quechua through playing with local children. Such individuals also learned the language from their nurses and other household servants who were employed not only on their haciendas, but also in their homes in the cities. Even today upper class women may learn some Quechua in order to communicate with monolingual servants. However, their fluency is never

equal to that of earlier generations, who had the
opportunity to learn the language when young.    It
is also among this social group that one encounters
an "appreciation" of the language.    This is mani-
fested through such activities as the recitation
and writing of Quechua poetry and prose.

(2) Middle class Quechua speakers include the
upper strata of those living in the small towns in
SQ-speaking areas, as well as those occupying the
middle strata in the larger cities.    Such individuals are often bilingual in Quechua and Spanish.
Some have grown up with Spanish as their first
language, but have learned Quechua in order to
communicate with the Quechua-speaking population.
The most common example is the small town business
person who has learned Quechua in order to communicate with campesino clients.    Such an individual is
generally not ashamed of speaking the language.    It
simply makes good business sense!    It follows the
generalized rule that: "One can buy in any language.    But to be successful in business one must sell
in the language of the buyer."

Another situation is one in which the speaker
grew up speaking Quechua and later learned Spanish
primarily for business purposes.    Such individuals
would include, for example, truck drivers and traders living in small communities, especially along
the main roads to larger cities.    Traders that
serve the small communities generally work as middlemen (or women), buying up local produce and re-
selling it in local metropolitan centers, often to
Spanish-speaking urbanites.    They may also operate

small stores in their own communities, dealing in
manufactured goods bought from Spanish-speaking
merchants in metropolitan areas. For such traders
knowledge of Spanish is a necessity. These rural
merchants often own their own trucks, or they may
rely on others to transport their goods. The latter, too, are generally rural Quechua speakers who
have learned Spanish in order to form a bridge between rural Quechua-speaking areas and predominantly
Spanish-speaking cities, between which they travel
with trucks loaded with passengers and produce.

(3) At the bottom of the social structure are
the Quechua-speaking campesinos. For them Quechua
is the language of everyday life. In many areas
they are cut off from the national society and have
little opportunity to learn Spanish. In other
areas, such as the Cochabamba Valley, bilingualism
among campesinos has increased due to travel, military service, and formal schooling (Albó 1970:78).

There are, of course, exceptions to all of the
generalizations presented above. If we examine the
specific linguistic situation in each of the departments in which SQ is spoken, we find the following
variations on the generalized theme.

Oruro. The major language of the department is Aymara. But there are small communities of Quechua
speakers found along its eastern and southern fron-
tiers, as well as within the city of Oruro. However, Quechua appears to be losing ground to Aymara. In some communities older people speak only
Quechua, children are bilingual in Quechua and Ay-

mara, and grandchildren are monolingual in Aymara
or perhaps bilingual in Aymara and Spanish. If
this situation continues, and there are no new in-
fluxes of Quechua speakers, the language may disappear completely, being replaced by Aymara and
Spanish (Albó 1972).

Cochabamba. After the peasant uprisings of the
1950's, the collapse of the hacienda system, and
ensuing agrarian reform, peasant organizations have
become political forces to be reckoned with. For
such groups Quechua plays an important role in
their self-identity which, in turn, has raised the
prestige of the language. The result has been that
"agents from the city, politicians, sellers,
priests, etc., are aware of the fact and are ready
to use Quechua to reach and win this sector for
their product" (Albó 1970:78). Here we again encounter a situation in which the seller is learning
the language of the buyer -- albeit in order to
market a political or spiritual product rather than
a strictly commercial one.

Chuquisaca. Quechua-speaking campesinos in Chuquisaca and Potosí have never evolved into the political force that their compatriots have in Cochabamba. As a result the benefits of the national society have been less accessible. Subsequently in
some areas of Chuquisaca campesinos have been migrating to Argentina where they work in the agricultural areas of the north, or settle in the city
of Buenos Aires. A common pattern is for men to go

to Argentina, leaving their wives and younger children behind.  Later whole families will go for
short periods of time, leaving an older relative to
take care of agricultural tasks at home.  And
finally, after the family has spent some time in
Argentina, there may be the decision made to stay
there permanently.  Thus there is a steadily increasing out-migration of campesinos from Chuquisaca which, in turn, is lowering somewhat the
number of rural Quechua speakers in the department.

Potosí.  The department of Potosí has perhaps the
largest concentration of Quechua speakers in Bolivia.  They are to be found in both urban and rural
environments where Quechua is the principal language of the home, as well as of commerce.  In the
city of Potosí merchants are generally bilingual,
speaking Spanish as a first language but dominating
Quechua so as to better communicate with their
campesino clients.

    There are also many miners living in the city of
Potosí.  They generally speak some Spanish but prefer to speak Quechua both within the home and without.  The miners are highly organized politically,
and their linguistic preference for Quechua is taken into account by politicians and priests who
deal with them.

    Finally, because of geographical isolation and
lack of formal education, the great number of campesinos living in the department are monolingual in
Quechua.  However, since almost the whole non-

campesino population can speak Quechua, there is
little need to learn Spanish in order to deal with
representatives of the national society and economy
outside of the community. This does not mean that
the campesinos are unaware of the exploitation they
often suffer at the hands of those who are bilingual. They realize that were they to know Spanish
they would have better access to the goods and benefits of the national Spanish-speaking society.
But, because of geographical and social isolation,
there appears to be little that they can currently
do to change their linguistic situation.

BOLIVIAN LINGUISTIC SITUATION
In reviewing the linguistic situation in Bolivia,
one can come to the general conclusion that unlike
other Andean countries where Quechua is only spoken
by campesinos defined ethnically as "Indian," in
southern Bolivia the language is spoken by many
strata of the society. This has resulted in certain linguistic variation within SQ which has social correlates. For example, in the Cochabamba
region, Albó (1970, 1974) has found correlates between the social background of a speaker and certain phonological and grammatical variables.
    Although Albó deals only with the Quechua of Co-
chabamba, most of his phonological and lexical variables can be used in discussing the sociolinguistic situation in other areas of southern Bolivia.
Grammatically the use of Spanish loan diminutives,
the presence of the direct object marker -ta, and
the degree of suffix density serve as general so-

ciolinguistic variables for most SQ. There may also be other grammatical variables that are correlated with social differences in the departments of
Chuquisaca and Potosí. For Potosí: (1) the choice
of plural marker (-s, -skuna (+V); -es, -kuna,
-kunas (+C)); (2) the choice of first person future
pronominal marker (-sqayku vs.   -sayku vs.
-sahku).   For Chuquisaca: (1) the choice of second
person conditional (-wax vs.   -nkiman); (2) the
choice of first person plural inclusive conditional
(-sunman vs.   -nčexman); (3) the use of possessive
form (-pa or -pata (+C); -x or -xpa (+V)). These
are among the linguistic variables that warrant a
sociolinguistic study.

In more general terms, if we were to correlate
variation in the utilization of SQ with the prestige accorded to language function by the national
society, we would find correspondences between language use and social strata. (See Table 3. In
drawing this table, we are proposing that the rural
population of the Cochabamba Valley, for whom the
speaking of Quechua is prestigious, is an exception
rather than the rule.) Use of Quechua is also correlated with an urban-rural continuum, as well as
the prestige continuum. But perhaps most impor-
tantly, what is seen as linguistically advantageous
is to be either monolingual in Spanish, or bilingual in Quechua and Spanish. Those who are monolingual speakers of Quechua realize that without
being able to dominate Spanish, they are at a ter-
rible disadvantage socially and economically in a
national society which has generally refused to

TABLE 3. LANGUAGE USE AND SOCIAL STRATA

| VALUE<br>ASSIGNED<br>QUECHUA | HIGH<------------------------------------------------->LOW | | |
|---|---|---|---|
| LANGUAGE<br>USE: | 1st language<br>Spanish:<br>Quechua used<br>"aesthetically!" | 1st language<br>Spanish:<br>Quechua used<br>as commercial<br>language | 1st language<br>Quechua:<br>Spanish used<br>as commercial<br>language | Quechua<br>only<br>language<br>of<br>speaker |
| SOCIAL<br>STRATA: | UPPER STRATA<br>of society | MIDDLE STRATA<br>of society | LOWEST STRATA<br>of society |
| LOCATION: | URBAN <------------------------------------------------>RURAL | | |

recognize officially the linguistic background of, in this case, 35% of its population.

CONCLUSION

To conclude, we have found that Bolivian Quechua consists of two dialect areas, those of NQ and SQ. They differ from one another in their history, degree of geographical isolation, and sociolinguistic variation. But there are certain commonalties shared by both NQ and SQ. In particular, wherever it is spoken in Bolivia, Quechua is an "idioma oprimido" (Albó 1973). That is, in Bolivia the dominant minority speaks only Spanish, while the majority that they dominate speak only Quechua, with a few bilingual mediators in between. The future in Bolivia does not appear to be one in which there may be any fear that the Quechua language may subside and disappear. Far from it! It appears that the population in the rural areas is growing, and that through migration Quechua speakers are moving into new urban and rural areas, bringing their language and its accompanying problems with them.

In order to solve these problems, the government of Bolivia is beginning to recognize that policies of (1) attempting to force the replacement of Quechua and Aymara with Spanish (Albó 1974:228) or (2) ignoring the current linguistic situation and its concomitant social problems (Albó 1974:230) are bound to lead to even more severe social and economic problems, both for the government and for the people that it governs. Rather, Bolivia is star-

ting to acknowledge that, aside from Spanish, there
are two other major languages in the country --
Quechua and Aymara.  As a result the government is
launching a massive literacy program, using a bilingual approach, which will educate its adult population, allowing them to retain their own languages and cultures, while at the same time providing
the opportunity to learn Spanish.  In this way
Bolivia, by giving its inhabitants equal access to
all of its languages, plus the goods and services
that are associated with them, may be better able
to bring about the social changes promised by its
Revolution of 1952.

NOTES

1.  Albó (1970:245-248) has pointed out in his so-
    ciolinguistic study of the Quechua of Cochabamba
    that suffixes denoting continuous action (8) and
    plurality of pronouns (9) show a certain amount
    of variation, with choice of form used correla-
    ted with specific social variables.  Since the
    data presented in this table is based on the
    speech of informants of the same age, sex, and
    socio-economic background, it should be conside-
    red comparable.  But it should be noted also
    that some younger Apolo Quechua speakers are be-
    ginning to use /-ska/, /-ška/, or /-ša-/ vari-
    ants of the suffix indicating continuous action
    which probably shows influence from the Quechua
    of southern Bolivia or of neighboring Peru.

2.  /-pax/ may be realized as /-x/ after the first
    person pronoun /noqa/ when it modifies a noun.

Example: /noqax wasiy/ 'my house,' but /noqapax/
'It's mine.'  /-pax/ may also be realized as
/-x/ after the plural suffix /-kuna/ as in /mana
wawaykunaxču/ 'It isn't my children's.' Otherwise /-pax/ occurs in all environments, except
among certain younger Quechua speakers where
/-pax/ occurs after consonants and /-x/ after
vowels.  Examples: /supaypax nannin/ 'the
devil's road'; /alqox čupan/ 'the dog's tail'.
Again, as with the variants of /-čka-/, this
probably indicates influence from the Quechua of
southern Bolivia or of neighboring Peru.

REFERENCES

Albó, Xavier. 1970. Social Constraints on Cochabamba Quechua.  PhD dissertation, Cornell University (Ithaca, New York).
------. 1972. Personal Communication, November 15,
1972 (La Paz).
------. 1973.  El futuro de los idiomas oprimidos
en los Andes. Cochabamba: Centro Pedagógico y
Cultural de Portales.
------. 1974.  Los mil rostros del Quechua. Lima:
Instituto de Estudios Peruanos.
------. 1980.  Lengua y Sociedad en Bolivia, 1976.
La Paz:  Proyecto INE-Naciones Unidas.
Anónimo.  1903.  Relación Histórica de Las Misiones
Franciscanas de Apolobamba por otro Nombre Frontera de Caupolicán.  La Paz: Imprenta del Estado
Yanacocha.
Armentia, Nicolás.  1905.  Descripción del Territo-
rio de las Misiones Franciscanas de Apolobamba

por otro Nombre Frontera de Caupolican.. La Paz: Tip. Artistica.

Bastian, Joseph William.  1973.  Qollahuaya Rituals: An Ethnographic Account of the Symbolic Relations of Man and Land in an Andean Village. Ph.D. dissertation, Cornell University (Ithaca, New York).

------.  1978.  Mountain of the Condor. Monograph 64. The American Ethnological Society (St. Paul, Minnesota).

Bouysse-Cassagne, Therese.  1975.  Pertenencia Étnica, Status Económico y Lenguas en Charcas a fines del Siglo XVI.  In Tasa de la Visita de Francisco de Toledo, N.D. Cook, ed. Lima: Universidad Nacional de San Marcos.

Cusihuaman, Antonio.  1976.. Gramática Quechua Cuzco-Collao. Lima: Ministerio de Educación.

Grollig, Francis X.  1978.  Medicine and the Occult in Peru and Bolivia. Paper presented at the 77th Annual Meeting, American Anthropological Association, November 16, 1978 (Los Angeles).

Ibarra Grasso, Dick Edgar.  1973.  Prehistoria de Bolivia.  La Paz: Editorial "Los Amigos del Libro" [2nd edition].

ILV (Instituto Lingüístico de Verano).  1975.  Lenguas y Étnias Orientales Según el Instituto Lingüístico de Verano (Map).  Riberalta, Beni, Bolivia.

Mesa, Jose dé and Teresa Gisbert.  1973.  Los Incas de Bolivia.  Historia y Cultura 1:15-50.  La Paz: Instituto de Estudios Bolivianos.

Oblitas Poblete, Enrique. 1968. La Lengua Secreta de los Incas. La Paz: Editorial "Los Amigos del Libro".

Parker, Gary J. 1969a. Comparative Quechua Phonology and Grammar II: Proto-Quechua Phonology and Morphology. Working Papers in Linguistics, University of Hawaii, March 1969. 2:123-147 (Honolulu, Hawaii).

------. 1969b. Comparative Quechua Phonology and Grammar III: Proto-Quechua Lexicon. Working Papers in Linguistics. University of Hawaii, May 1969. 4:1-61 (Honolulu, Hawaii).

------. 1969c. Comparative Quechua Phonology and Grammar IV: The Evolution of Quechua A. Working Papers in Linguistics, University of Hawaii, October 1969. 9:149-204 (Honolulu, Hawaii).

Stark, Louisa R. 1970. Field Notes. Apolo, Bolivia.

------. 1972a. Machaj-Juyai: Secret Language of the Callahuayas. Papers in Andean Linguistics, 1(2):199-227 (Madison, Wisconsin).

------. 1972b. Notes on the Quechua of Apolo. Unpublished manuscript.

------. 1974. A Reconstruction of Case and Enclitic Suffixes in Proto-Quechua. Unpublished manuscript.

Stark, Louisa R., Manuel Segovia Bayo, and Felicia Segovia Polo. 1971. Sucre Quechua: A Pedagogical Grammar. Madison, Wisconsin: Department of Anthropology, University of Wisconsin.

# 14. A Critical Survey of the Literature on the Aymara Language

## Lucy Therina Briggs

INTRODUCTION

Spoken on the high Andean plains of Peru and Bolivia from Lake Titicaca to the salt flats south of
Lake Poopó, and in northern Chile, Aymara is the
most widespread member of the Jaqi language family
whose sole other remnants, spoken in Yauyos, department of Lima, Peru, are the nearly extinct Kawki
and the still vigorous Jaqaru.[1] Aymara is estimated to have over a million and a half speakers in
Bolivia, roughly 350,000 in Peru, 25,000 in Chile,
and an unspecified number in Argentina, bringing
the total to at least two million.

The two major bibliographical sources for Aymara
and its sister languages are the Bibliografía de
las lenguas quechua y aymará by José Toribio Medina (1930) and the monumental four-volume Bibliographie des langues Aymará et Kičua by Paul Rivet
and Georges de Créqui-Montfort (1951-1956). A few
references to recent works on Aymara and one on Jaqaru are contained in a bibliography entitled Languages of North, Central, and South America (1976)
published by the Center for Applied Linguistics,
and a bibliography of recent books on South American Indian languages by Eduardo Lozano (1977) contains 12 entries for Aymara. Typological surveys
that include references to Aymara are The langua-

ges of South American Indians (1950) by John Alden
Mason, Catálogo de las lenguas de America del Sur
(1961) by Antonio Tovar, and Classification of
South American Indian Languages (1968) by Čestmir
Loukotka. Until the present, however, there has
been no critical survey of works on the Jaqi languages in the light of contemporary linguistic
scholarship. The present study attempts to provide such a survey of works on Aymara.

Apart from the aforementioned bibliographies,
works on the Aymara language may be divided into
two basic groups: traditional studies written without benefit of the techniques of modern linguistic
scholarship, and studies reflecting contemporary
linguistic theory and practice. The first group
may be referred to as prelinguistic and the second,
as linguistic studies.

PRELINGUISTIC STUDIES

Colonial period (16th to early 19th centuries)
As is well known, the Spanish found no written materials in the languages of the Inca Empire. In
the 16th and early 17th centuries all works published in or on Aymara were written for the purpose
of spreading the Christian faith by missionaries
assisted by unnamed Aymara converts bilingual in
Aymara and Spanish. Such works consisted of cate-
chisms and other religious tracts, grammars, and
dictionaries or 'vocabularies'. The earliest published work known to contain Aymara is the anonymous Doctrina christiana, y catecismo para la in-

strucción de los Indios published in Lima in 1584 (Rivet & Créqui-Montfort 1951:4-9).

The first attempts at complete grammars of Aymara were those of the Jesuit missionaries Ludovico Bertonio and Diego de Torres Rubio, both of whom wrote on the Aymara of Juli in what is now the department of Puno, Peru. Bertonio was the more prolific, producing three grammars, a dictionary, and several religious works. In 1603 two of his grammars appeared, Arte breve de la lengua aymara (1603a) and Arte y grammatica muy copiosa de la lengua aymara (1603b). A facsimile edition of the latter was published in Leipzig in 1879 by Julio Platzmann (Rivet & Créqui-Montfort 1953:35).[2] In 1612 Bertonio published a dictionary, the Vocabulario de la lengua aymara, which has since appeared in several facsimile editions, most recently in La Paz in 1956. Torres Rubio's Arte de la lengua aymara appeared in 1616.[3] In 1967 Mario Franco Inojosa published a modern version of it in Peru, giving the original spellings followed by transcriptions in the official Peruvian alphabet for Aymara adopted in 1946.

Although distorted by their Latinate structure and unsystematic spelling, the Bertonio and Torres Rubio grammars provide a wealth of information on the Aymara of the period. Many suffixes attested are in general use today, others are found in only one or a few present-day Aymara dialects, while still others are not attested in modern Aymara but are extant in other Jaqi languages (see Briggs 1976a and 1976b). Nevertheless, the 17th century texts need careful reinterpretation in the light of contemporary linguistic scholarship and recent discoveries concerning Aymara language and culture. According to two present-day native speakers who are bilingual in Spanish and Aymara, many Aymara terms and sentences given as examples are more or less awkward translations of Spanish rather than native words and expressions.[4] This is not surprising, as Bertonio himself indicated in the introduction to his Vocabulario that he took his entries from translations of religious texts into Aymara. In any event, the early grammars became models for later descriptions and laid the basis for Aymara usages that persist today among native speakers and other persons associated with missionaries; such usages are referred to by certain other native speakers as Missionary Aymara.[5]

After the mid 17th century the fervor of missionary zeal abated, and the use of Aymara as a general language gradually gave way to Quechua (Tovar 1961:186-194). According to Rivet and Créqui-Montfort, for the next hundred years little was published in Aymara except occasional sermons, few of which have survived. The European philologists Hervas, Vater, Adelung, Pott, and Jehan, writing in the late 18th and early 19th centuries, included in their encyclopedic works Aymara examples taken from earlier sources.

Post-Colonial period (19th and 20th centuries)
In the second decade of the 19th century some political speeches and documents relating to the inde-

pendence movements in South America were published
in Aymara, as in other native languages. The first
Protestant materials in Aymara appeared in 1826,
followed by a resurgence of Catholic materials,
mostly by Bolivian priests. Late 19th century accounts by European scholar-adventurers of their
travels on the altiplano included Aymara grammatical sketches or word lists like those found in
David Forbes' On the Aymara Indians of Bolivia and
Peru (1870).

Forbes gave Aymara names for objects, activities, and the like, most of which, although defor-
med by an inadequate transcription, are recognizable today. His grammatical analysis of Aymara is
brief but accurate so far as it goes. Appendix C
of his book is a vocabulary of Aymara words, including kinship terms, with English translations.
Forbes cast light on the status of Aymara studies
at the time in remarking on his fruitless efforts
while in Bolivia to obtain a copy of a 17th century
Aymara grammar or dictionary, even though he had
advertised in the papers that he would pay "the
high sum of 50 dollars" for it (274,fn.).

In 1891 the German philologist Ernst Middendorf
published an Aymara grammar, Die Aimará-Sprache, as
the fifth volume of his study of aboriginal languages of Peru (Rivet & Créqui-Montfort 1952:558).
The introduction to this grammar was translated
into Spanish by the Bolivian scholar Franz Tamayo
and published in 1910 in La Paz (Rivet and Créqui-
Montfort 1952:558). Later, the Peruvian scholar
Estuardo Núñez, working from an incomplete copy of

the Tamayo translation, revised and added some
notes to it and published it in a volume entitled
Las lenguas aborígenes del Perú prepared under the
auspices of the Universidad Mayor de San Marcos in
Lima to commemorate the 50th anniversary of Middendorf's death.  The following summary is taken from
the Núñez book (1959:96-102), which I was able to
examine.

Middendorf indicated that his grammar was based
on Bertonio's and on the dialect then spoken in La
Paz.  He stated that while both whites and mestizos
in that city spoke Aymara, it was in most cases
only to communicate with Aymara servants or market
vendors, and that he could find only a few persons
with enough knowledge to teach him the language.
Finally, with the help of some lawyers who had
lived among rural Aymara, he reviewed his copy of a
Bertonio grammar, comparing forms then in use with
earlier ones, noting both, and using them to draw
up rules of sentence formation.  In the introduction to the Middendorf grammar there are several
paragraphs devoted to vowel-dropping (a common morphophonemic process in Aymara), with examples of
inflected verbs and comments on verbs of going and
carrying.  It is to be hoped that Middendorf's
grammar may some day be translated into Spanish (or
Aymara), preferably by a linguist competent in German, Aymara, and Spanish.

In 1917 another Aymara grammar based largely on
Bertonio's appeared, by Juan Antonio García, a Bolivian priest.  Subsequently, etymologies and word
lists proliferated on such topics as kinship terms,

place names, and musical instruments.  A number of
stories, poems, and legends were published by self-
styled Aymara scholars (aymarólogos) in unsystematic transcriptions and in Aymara that is perceived
by certain native speakers today as distorted from
Aymara reality.  Because of its association with
the patrón (landholding) class, such Aymara is referred to by those native speakers as Patrón Aymara.[6]

The characteristics of Patrón Aymara are seen in
the many virtually identical trilingual handbooks
or catalogues of common expressions in Aymara, Quechua, and Spanish published and republished in Bolivia, Peru, and Chile from the middle of the 19th
century to the present.  In the catalogues individual words may be correctly translated, but Spanish
phrases are glossed word for word into an Aymara
that some native speakers find discourteous if not
downright insulting, and often grammatically incorrect.  Moreover, chaotic spelling reflects a very
inadequate grasp of Aymara phonology.

A variation on the catalogue is Gramática del
kechua y del aymara (1942) by Germán G. Villamor,
containing short grammatical descriptions of Quechua and Aymara, a brief three-way dictionary of
words from those languages and Spanish, and sections on history, myths, and superstitions.  Inso-
far as the Aymara language is concerned (I cannot
speak for the Quechua) the book is deficient, with
incorrect material poorly arranged.  Another variation on the catalogue is Vocablos aymaras en el
habla popular paceña (1963) by Antonio Paredes Can-

dia, containing Aymara words alleged to occur in colloquial La Paz speech. According to a native speaker from La Paz who reviewed the book with me, the context is not culturally Aymara; the tone is often insulting, many of the Aymara forms are incorrectly translated, and they are in any case terms used by whites and mestizos rather than by rural Aymara. The book may usefully serve, however, as a source of white and mestizo usages and interpretations of Aymara borrowings into Spanish.

Two works that contain more accurate translations are a short Spanish-Aymara dictionary by Mario Franco Inojosa citing forms used in Puno (1965) and a more complete dictionary by Pedro Miranda for forms used in La Paz (1970). These two books employ, respectively, the official Peruvian Quechua/Aymara alphabet of 1946 and the official Bolivian Quechua/Aymara alphabet of 1954. Used by Catholic missionaries, the two alphabets are identical and are phonemic except for representing the three Aymara vowel phonemes by the five Spanish vowel letters.

Protestant missionaries employ the similar CALA alphabet (for Comisión de Alfabetización y Literatura Aymara) which was adopted by official Bolivian decree in 1968, apparently without rescinding official support of the 1954 alphabet. The only difference between the Catholic and Protestant alphabets is that the former uses k and q for the velar and postvelar occlusives (following International Phonetic Alphabet practice), while the CALA (Protestant) alphabet uses c and qu for the velar and k

for the postvelar. Both use j for velar fricative
and jj for postvelar fricative, which leads to
spelling ambiguities since the phonemes frequently
occur in clusters with each other as well as with
other consonants.

By far the best Aymara grammar modeled on Bertonio's is that of Juan Enrique Ebbing (1965). Although it too reflects missionary and patrón usages, it shows an understanding of aspects of Aymara
usually overlooked, such as the role of sentence
suffixes. On the other hand, the nadir in such
grammars is Suma lajjra aymara parlaña by Erasmo
Tarifa Ascarrunz (1969). Although it contains a
wealth of material, it is very badly analyzed, organized, and presented. Interestingly, in the book
the Spanish translations of the Aymara (or Spanish
sentences from which the Aymara was translated?)
are in popular Andean Spanish that reflects Aymara
structure to a considerable extent. As Laprade has
shown (1976 and 1981) such evidence of Aymara grammatical interference appears even in the speech of
monolingual Spanish speakers in La Paz. The Aymara-Spanish contact situation merits further investigation in the light of recent research on pidginization and creolization in other parts of the
world.

In a special category of prelinguistic studies
are the three typological surveys mentioned in the
introduction. Mason (1950) contains a short section on the Aymara language, but it is full of inaccuracies, not only with respect to the supposed
relationship of Aymara to other languages but also

to identification of Aymara-speaking areas and dialects. Tovar (1961) represents a slight improvement in the information provided, but the work is still incomplete and inaccurate, and the brief grammatical description of Aymara is inadequate. Loukotka (1968) lists traditional names of Aymara regional dialects and identifies a few sources of data for some of them.

LINGUISTIC STUDIES

Synchronic studies
Turning now to linguistic studies--those with pretensions to being considered within the pale of scientific linguistic theory and scholarship--it appears that the first linguist to state in print that Aymara has a three-vowel rather than a five-vowel phonemic system was Bertil Malmberg (1947-1948), although Kenneth Pike included an Aymara problem in his Phonemics (1947:153) implying a three vowel system.

      The first texts of Aymara to be published in phonetically reliable (though not completely phonemic) transcriptions are 1) the folktales told by monolingual speakers from Chucuito (Puno, Peru) as recorded by Harry Tschopik (1948) and 2) the folktale told by a speaker of the Pacasa dialect (north of Tiahuanaco, Bolivia), as recorded by Weston La-Barre (1950). Given with English translations, though without grammatical analysis, these texts are significant as the first published native free texts known to exist for Aymara. They are also im-

portant as a basis for comparison with present-day
renditions of folktales from the same and other
Aymara-speaking areas.

The first published morphological analysis of
Aymara is that of Thomas Sebeok (1951a). Based on
an Aymara version of <u>Little Red Ridinghood</u> told by
"a highly urbanized native speaker of Aymara...from
La Paz," the text is an example of Patrón Aymara.
Sebeok also collected material for an Aymara dictionary (1951b), using data from Tschopik, LaBarre,
Villamor, Pike, and Floyd Lounsbury as well as his
own research.   Each entry consists of a set of Aymara words sharing the same root morphemes, with
English or Spanish translations.

<u>Missionary grammars and associated studies</u>
At about the time that the studies referred to
above were appearing, Protestant missionary linguists were turning their attention to the analysis
of Aymara.   The first attempt at a fairly complete
grammatical description of Aymara by a contemporary
linguist was <u>Rudimentos de gramática aymara</u> by
Ellen M. Ross, published by the Canadian Baptist
Mission in La Paz in 1953, and again in 1963 for
the use of American Peace Corps Volunteers.

Three native speakers of Aymara collaborated
with Ross in producing the grammar, a trilingual
textbook for English-speaking missionaries and
Spanish speakers based on the Aymara spoken in
Huatajata, department of La Paz.   Making use of
aural/oral language-teaching techniques, the book
presents graded Aymara dialogues and drills with

translations into Spanish and grammatical explanations in Spanish and English. The grammar includes
helpful cultural notes such as a comment on the importance of greetings among the Aymara. While it
has an index of grammatical forms and topics (in
Spanish), it lacks a table of contents and thus
cannot easily be used as a reference grammar. The
drawbacks of the CALA alphabet used in the book
have already been noted above.

Although more recent research has revealed
numerous inaccuracies in the grammatical analysis,
when viewed in the context of the state of research
on Aymara at the time it was published, Rudimentos de gramática aymara represents a creditable
achievement, and a tremendous improvement over
previous Aymara grammars. Nevertheless it must be
noted that, as in the case of the earlier grammars,
the Aymara examples it contains are perceived as
distorted or non-native by certain native speakers.

In 1958 Ross published a (mimeographed) Aymara-
Spanish dictionary, Diccionario aymara-castellano, castellano-aymara; it was reprinted (also in
mimeograph) in 1973 by CALA, but was not seen for
this research.

Ross later wrote a reference grammar for native
speakers of Aymara, Manual aymara para los aymaristas (n.d.--considerably after Ross 1953). Its
stated purpose was to enable Aymara speakers already bilingual and literate in Spanish ("who appreciate the great value of their linguistic heritage and wish to study it formally"--Preface, page

4) to learn to read and write Aymara and to become
aware of differences between Aymara and Spanish
structure which may create difficulties for Aymara
monolinguals wishing to learn Spanish.    In effect,
the Manual is a contrastive study of Spanish and
(Missionary) Aymara, often describing Aymara in
terms of Spanish and prescribing correct usages,
for example in punctuation (see Lesson IX). The
grammatical analysis is lacking in some important
respects; for instance, the person system is not
completely understood.    The obligatory semantic
distinction of personal and nonpersonal knowledge
is recognized, however, for the first time.    The
grammatical importance of vowel length and vowel
dropping is also grasped and the reader is urged to
write words as they are pronounced, although this
injunction is not always followed in the examples
given in the text.    The role of sentence suffixes
(called enclitics) is well covered.

But while the Manual has its strengths, nevertheless according to native speakers from Puno and
La Paz who have reviewed the book with me, the mes-
sage it conveys is that learning to read and write
in Aymara is primarily a means toward learning to
be fully literate in Spanish, rather than an end in
itself.    Illustrative of this attitude is use of
the five Spanish vowels to write Aymara, which has
only three vowel phonemes, and the advice to the
reader who wishes to write in a more involved Aymara style ("un estilo mas enredado") to consult a
good Spanish grammar or to observe the style of
writers in that language (p.   121).[7]

Two subsequent teaching grammars of Aymara owe much to Ross. Paul Wexler and his associates attempted in Beginning Aymara: A course for English speakers (1967) to write a linguistically-sound pedagogical grammar of Aymara specifically for English speakers. Intended for Peace Corps Volunteers, this grammar was based on research carried out in Bolivia by three American field workers who spent a short time there aided by three Aymara native speakers from La Paz who were bilingual in Spanish. While the book is carefully organized into graded dialogues and drills on topics usually relevant to altiplano life, according to some native speakers the Aymara in it again often sounds translated from Spanish, with missionary and/or patrón terminology that is culturally and linguistically unacceptable. Wexler recognized that the Aymara of the book probably was heavily influenced by Spanish, and he did recommend further research with monolingual speakers.

The second Aymara grammar owing much to Ross, and the best of the missionary grammars to date, is Lecciones de aymara (1971-72) by Joaquín Herrero, Daniel Cotari, and Jaime Mejía, based on a dialect from roughly the same area as that of the Ross grammars. Herrero is a native of Spain; Cotari and Mejía are Bolivian Aymara speakers bilingual in Spanish. Developed for teaching the language at the Maryknoll Instituto de Idiomas in Cochabamba, this grammar is superior to its predecessors in grammatical analysis, but has some of the same characteristics perceived by certain native speakers

as non-Aymara or distorted. An innovation useful
for students of Spanish dialects is the provision
of two translations of each Aymara dialogue, one in
Andean Spanish and the other in peninsular Spanish.

The phonology section of Lecciones de aymara
includes numerous minimal triplets illustrating
plain, aspirated, and glottalized occlusives (the
plain forms written as p, t, k, and q). The importance of grammatical vowel dropping is clearly
grasped and suffixes are designated as weak (retai-
ning preceding vowel) and strong (causing preceding
vowel to drop) when they are first introduced, helping the learner to produce correct forms from the
beginning. The book presents the person system accurately, avoiding Ross' error, repeated by Wexler
et al., of designating the inclusive person (speaker plus addressee) as dual. (More than two persons may be involved.) Full verbal inflectional
paradigms with affirmative and negative examples
are presented in the body of the text.[8]

A much shorter, less complete grammar by a Catholic missionary is Método de aymara (1973) by
Marcelo Grondin. Published in Oruro, the book mentions certain forms as different from those occurring in La Paz, but fails to note the velar nasal
phoneme occurring in Carangas province of the department of Oruro (see Briggs 1976a and 1976b). The
Aymara person system is clearly grasped, vowel-
dropping is understood, and the role of sentence
suffixes noted, but the Aymara is presented in
short dialogues that once again are perceived as

non-native by some Aymara speakers. The translations of the dialogues are in Andean Spanish.

Aymara-centered studies

Aymara-centered studies focus on the language as
spoken in traditional Aymara cultural contexts by
monolingual speakers and by bilingual speakers concerned with preserving linguistic and cultural traditions. Such studies are largely the outgrowth of
research begun by M.J. Hardman in Jaqaru and Kawki. Hardman's Jaqaru: Outline of phonological and
morphological structure (1966) was the first descriptive reference grammar of a Jaqi language,
written by a linguist for linguists. Two reviews
of it are Lastra (1968) and Solá (1971). A revised
edition of it, in Spanish translation, is entitled
Jaqaru: Compendio de estructura fonológica y morfológica (1983).[9]

While in Bolivia as a Fulbright professor in
1965, Hardman founded the Instituto Nacional de Estudios Lingüísticos (INEL) with Julia Elena Fortún
of the Bolivian Ministry of Education. Under INEL
auspices, Hardman taught linguistics and conducted
field work in the department of La Paz with the aid
of students including Aymara native speakers such
as Juan de Dios Yapita, author of the first (and so
far, only) phonemic alphabet of Aymara produced by
a native speaker of the language, and the one used
by Hardman and associates ever since; its use among
Aymara native speakers is now also widespread.[10]
The first published result of research by a Hardman
student was Bosquejo de estructura de la lengua ay-

mara (1969) by the Argentine linguist Herminia Eusebia Martín.  Based on the Aymara spoken in Irpa
Chico, province of Ingavi, La Paz, the Bosquejo is
important as the first published description of
Aymara by a linguist for linguists, combining both
adequate theory and competent field investigation.
It is, however, merely a sketch, as its title indicates.

On the basis of Aymara research undertaken by
Hardman and associates in Bolivia, the Aymara Language Materials Project began at the University of
Florida in 1969 with support from the U.S. Office
of Education (DHEW).  The goal of the project was
to produce teaching and reference grammars of Aymara reflecting linguistic and cultural realities of
the language from the point of view of native speakers.  The materials were prepared by a team consisting of Hardman, three Bolivian native speakers
of Aymara trained in anthropological linguistics
(Yapita and Vásquez, later assisted by Pedro Copana); and three graduate students in anthropology
and linguistics who assisted with the analysis and
pilot-tested the teaching materials in Aymara language classes.  A number of other students and native speakers of Aymara collaborated in the study,
which was based on data provided by 17 Bolivian
native speakers (in addition to Vásquez and
Yapita), many of them monolingual.[11]

The primary result of the project was a three-
volume work by Hardman, Vásquez, and Yapita with
individual chapters contributed by the three graduate students, entitled Aymar ar yatiqañataki (To

learn Aymara) which appeared first in 1973 and in a
revised edition in 1975. [12] Volume I is a course in
Aymara for English and Spanish speakers, consisting
of graded dialogues based on rural Aymara life,
with drills and translations into English and Spanish, and accompanied by tape recordings with English translations. Volume II is a teacher's manual keyed to the course, with cultural and grammatical explanations. Volume III, entitled Aymara
grammatical sketch in the first edition and Outline of Aymara phonological and grammatical structure in the second, is a detailed reference grammar that may stand alone. It incorporates master's
theses by Laura Martin-Barber on phonology and Nora
Clearman England on verbal derivational suffixes,
and my chapter on the structure of the noun system. The project also produced a computerized con-
cordance glossary of words, roots, and suffixes.
        The three volumes of the Florida Aymara grammar
have been translated into Spanish by Edgard Chávez
Cuentas, under the direction of Hardman. Volume
III, the reference grammar, entitled in Spanish
Compendio de estructura fonológica y gramatical del
idioma aymara, is undergoing final revisions prior
to publication.
        Secondary results of the project include nume-
rous papers by students at the University of Florida, some of which were published in 1981 in The
Aymara Language in its Social and Cultural Context, edited by Hardman (see for example 1981 references for Briggs, England, Gallaher, Laprade, Maidana, Miracle, Sharpe, and Tate). This book has

been reviewed by Albó (1983) and Brody (1983).
Other results of the Aymara project are two M.A.
theses, Sylvia Boynton's on contrastive analysis of
Spanish and Aymara phonology (1974) and Richard
Laprade's on dialect features of La Paz Spanish
(1976) containing evidence of an Aymara grammatical
substratum, and two doctoral dissertations, Andrew
Miracle's on the effects of cultural perception on
the education of Aymara children (1976) and mine on
regional dialectal variation in the Aymara language
(1976a). Supporting his argument with linguistic
evidence, Miracle attributes the failure of Bolivian educational programs for the Aymara to conflict between Aymara and Hispanic cultural perceptions in the realms of social identification, social ethic, spatial domain, and the bases (sources)
of knowledge.

Published articles resulting from the Aymara
Project include Hardman's on Jaqi linguistic postulates (1972a and 1979a) and the reconstruction of
the Proto-Jaqi person system (1975, 1978a, and
1978b), Pedro Copana's recommendations concerning
the education of rural Aymara children (1973 and
1981), and numerous articles by Yapita (see References). Two carefully researched articles focusing on the Aymara of Puno, Peru are Collins (1983)
on affinal kinship terms and Painter (1983) on Spanish-Aymara bilingualism in the region.

Increasing numbers of materials in the Aymara
language itself, written in the Yapita alphabet,
have appeared as a result of the project. The
Aymara Newsletter has been published at the Uni-

versity of Florida since 1970, under the successive editorships of Yapita, Juana Vásquez, Justino Llanque Chana, and Yolanda López, Aymara instructors there. In Bolivia Yapita has been among the most prolific writers, producing under INEL and ILCA auspices mimeographed literary journals, introductory readers, and Spanish-English-Aymara vocabularies. In 1981 he published a textbook for teaching Aymara as a second language, Enseñanza del idioma aymara como segundo idioma.[13]

Former students of Yapita in Bolivia have also produced materials in Aymara. Representative are articles by Vitaliano Wanka (also spelled Huanca describing his Aymara literacy program in Tiahuanaco (1973a and 1973b); an Aymara primer for adults by Francisco Calle P. (1974) of which a first edition of 17,000 was printed, according to Chaski, a La Paz publication;[14] and a bilingual manual on medicinal plants and herbs by Gavino Kispi (1974). Domingo Choque Quispe and Martirián Benavides Rodríguez wrote Cursado de fonología aymara for use in Oruro (1970). Choque Quispe is also the author of Aymara yatiqañani, an Aymara literacy text for native speakers published in 1976 by INEL.

Independently of the Aymara Project at the University of Florida, the anthropologist John T. Cole discovered the primacy of the inclusive over the exclusive in the Aymara world view, a primacy which Hardman (1972a and b) and Dell Hymes (1972) noted is reflected in the Aymara person system. In his dissertation, Cole characterized the Aymara concept of the soul as fundamentally mutual rather than in-

dividual and indicated that "the emphasis on mutuality as more fundamental than individuality forms
a theme that runs through Aymara culture accounting
for a number of otherwise inexplicable details of
Aymara custom (Cole 1969, abstract)."

In other words, Cole sees mutuality as what
Hardman would call a linguistic postulate (and Miracle, a cultural perception) of Aymara. Hardman
has pointed out that in the Aymara language this
mutuality is not only expressed overtly in the inclusive fourth grammatical person (speaker plus
addressee), but is also signalled by overmarking of
the second person in verbs (see Hardman et al.
1975:3.33).

## Sociolinguistic studies

The thrust of much of the new research on Aymara is
sociolinguistic, focusing on such concerns as language attitudes and dialect variation.[15]

Language attitudes.  Yapita, who teaches Aymara at
the Universidad Nacional de San Andrés in La Paz
and conducts research in Aymara ethno- and socio-
linguistics, lectures extensively on Aymara language and culture and bilingual education, and is
training his students, many of whom are bilingual
in Spanish and Aymara, to do research in the linguistic correlates of social discrimination, some
preliminary results of which are found in his article Discriminación y lingüística y conflicto social (1977).  In 1973 and 1974, Yapita and Pedro
Plaza, then director of INEL in La Paz, conducted

with support from the Ford Foundation and the Centro Pedagógico y Cultural de Portales in Cochabamba
sociolinguistic surveys of Aymara and Quechua speakers in Bolivia, using methods developed by Wolfgang Wölck for Quechua in Peru (Wölck 1972 and
1973).

The Portales Center in Cochabamba, which is supported by the Patiño Foundation, published during
1973-74 a series of materials in Spanish, such as
an article by Javier Albó on the future of Aymara
and Quechua (which he considered to be "oppressed
languages"), the Yapita phonemic alphabet, a summary of Hardman's article (1972a) on linguistic
postulates of Aymara, and my article on the Aymara
person system. The Centro de Investigación y Promoción del Campesinado (CIPCA) has also published
several studies in Spanish and Aymara dealing with
Aymara society and culture.[16]

A valid contribution to knowledge of the Aymara-
speaking population of northern Potosí department
in Bolivia is an article by the British anthropologist Olivia Harris (1974) giving indications of
apparent Aymara-Quechua diglossia.

In Peru, where the government inaugurated a policy of bilingual education in 1972, so far as I am
aware there has been only one sociolinguistic survey of Aymara speakers: a 1973 survey of 85 high
school students in the town of Chucuito near Puno
by Justino Llanque Chana (1974). The survey revealed negative attitudes toward Aymara language and
culture which the author interpreted as confirming
the alienating effects of an educational system

that stressed acquisition of Spanish skills while
banning (in theory if not in strict practice) the
use of vernacular languages.

In 1973 Domingo Llanque Chana, a Peruvian Aymara
who is a Catholic priest, published in Spanish
translation an interview he had conducted in Aymara
with a 56-year-old man from a rural community near
Lake Titicaca. To my knowledge this is the first
time the topic of social interaction among the Aymara has been discussed in print by an Aymara.
(The topic has since been taken up by Yapita and
others.) The author observed that the basic element of Aymara interaction is mutual respect (a-
gain, the focus on mutuality) expressed primarily
through courteous speech as exemplified in greetings.

Dialect variation. Reference has been made above
to missionary and patrón usages that appear in
published sources. As for regional dialect variation, although it has been known to exist since
colonial times, very little attention has been paid
to describing it systematically. My field work in
1972-74 (described in Briggs 1976a and b; see the
next article in this volume) shows the existence of
two major dialect areas, north and south, with an
intermediate area sharing features of both; of certain features linking noncontiguous dialects; and
of innovations spreading outward from La Paz to
more conservative peripheral areas. These findings
have implications for reconstruction of Proto-Jaqi,
as Hardman has noted (1975), and also for determi-

nation of past population movements and present
social trends.

A useful phonological description of the Aymara
of the Chilean altiplano (department of Tarapacá,
districts of Los Condores and Cariquima) is that of
Christos Clair-Vasiliades (1976; reviewed by Eric
Hamp in IJAL 43:3.255). On the basis of his description, the Chilean dialect may be classed as
southern, with the similar nearby dialects of Carangas and Salinas de Garci Mendoza in Oruro, Bolivia (Briggs 1976a and b). Like the Carangas dialect, the Chilean has a velar nasal phoneme, and
like Salinas, occlusive voicing rules. The only
weakness in the analysis (which would have been
eliminated with a larger corpus) are the failure to
note phonemic vowel length and failure to distinguish the vowels /i/ and /u/ from the consonantal
glides /y/ and /w/. (Examples proving this distinction may be found in Martin-Barber 1975.) On
the whole the study is a very welcome addition to
the sparse published literature on Aymara regional
dialects.[17]

A linguistic analysis of the Aymara spoken in
Chucuito (Puno, Peru) is done by Porterie-Gutiérrez
1981. (The same author treats Aymara case in Porterie-Gutiérrez 1980.)

Historical studies
As for historical studies, the most detailed to
date, based on glottochronological calculations, is
that of Alfredo Torero (1972), although the results
of my research on Aymara regional variation suggest

Torero's theory of a gradual north-to-south expansion of Aymara needs further refinement. Hardman is now engaged in reconstruction of Proto-Jaqi on the basis of data from existing Aymara dialects as well as from present-day Jaqaru and Kawki.

The relationship of the Jaqi languages and Quechua, the other major language family of the Andean area, has long been debated. Mason (1950:196) proposed Kechumaran as a term "to designate the yet unproved but highly probable subphylum consisting of Quechua and Aymara." Subsequently, James Loriot (1964) and Louisa Stark (1965) included a few references dealing with the supposed relationship in their brief bibliographies of Aymara and Quechua under the heading Quechumaran. Also supporting a fairly close relationship between Quechua and Aymara are Carolyn Orr and Robert E. Longacre (1968) and Lastra (1970). On the other hand, Hardman (1979b) marshals impressive evidence of important differences in grammatical structure that have not hitherto been taken into account, to show that similarities in lexicon, phonology, and semantic categories, where they exist, must be ascribed to geographic proximity and borrowing rather than to a genetic relationship (see her article in this volume). Stark (1970) has provided phonological data that support Hardman's position, and more recently, further support has been forthcoming from Davidson (1977), based on a careful comparison of morphological data from Cuzco Quechua and Bolivian Aymara (data for the latter primarily from Hardman et al. 1973).

CONCLUSIONS AND SUGGESTIONS FOR FURTHER RESEARCH
This survey has shown that almost all published
works and research on the Aymara language have until very recently been written or directed by non-
Aymara. It is only now that, after centuries of
cultural isolation, Aymara native speakers are beginning to undertake research in their language and
culture and bringing the results to public attention via the spoken and written word. Recent wri-
tings by native speakers reaffirm Aymara cultural
and linguistic values that, together with regional
and social variation, should be taken into account
in the development of materials for literacy and
bilingual education, if the conflict between Spanish and Aymara norms noted by Miracle (1976) is to
be resolved.

Further research is needed on the social correlates of Missionary and Patrón Aymara. In particular, the extent to which native speakers themselves
use them, and in what circumstances, needs to be
clarified. That is, do native speakers use missionary and patrón forms primarily or solely when
speaking with non-Aymara who use those forms and/or
represent certain social groups? Or, do certain
native speakers regularly use Missionary and Patrón
Aymara among themselves, and if so, in what contexts?[18] Does a kind of bidialectalism or diglossia exist with respect to their use?

In the future, searches for other Jaqi languages
possibly surviving along the ancient Andean high-
ways should be undertaken, and the Aymara spoken in
Bolivia, Peru, and Chile investigated further, with

the eventual aim of compiling a linguistic atlas of
the entire Jaqi area.  To be fully effective, such
studies should be carried out by native speakers
trained in anthropological and sociolinguistic
field methods, in conjunction with similar studies
of Quechua and Andean Spanish.[19]

ACKNOWLEDGEMENTS

This article, dedicated to my father, is an updated
version of one with the same title that appeared in
Latin American Research Review 14.3 (1979).  I gratefully acknowledge LARR's permission to republish
it.  An earlier version of this article was read at
the 76th Annual Meeting of the American Anthropological Association at Houston in December 1977.  Some
of the research on which the article is based was
funded by graduate fellowships from the National
Science Foundation and the University of Florida,
which I acknowledge with appreciation.  I wish also
to acknowledge the facilitation provided me by the
Instituto Nacional de Investigación y Desarrollo de
la Educación (INIDE) in Peru, and by the Instituto
Nacional de Estudios Lingüísticos (INEL) and the
Instituto de Lengua y Cultura Aymara (ILCA) in
Bolivia.  Acknowledgements to native speakers of
Aymara who assisted me with this study are given in
footnote 5.

NOTES

1.  M.J.  Hardman instituted the use of the term
    Jaqi, which means 'person, human being' in all
    the member languages, to designate the language

family.    (N.B.    Present-day usage usually omits
a final accent mark on the word Aymara, as it
is pronounced by native speakers with the stress
on the second syllable.)

2.    A photocopy of a volume belonging to Juan de
Dios Yapita, containing the first 14 pages of
the Arte breve bound together with pages 19
through 348 of the Arte y grammatica muy copiosa (missing the title pages, a section entitled Al lector, and pages 207 and 208) is in
the University of Florida Library.   (Photostatic
copies of the missing pages were obtained for
that library from the John Carter Brown Library
of Brown University, which owns a complete copy
of the Arte y grammatica muy copiosa.)

3.    A photocopy, the original of which belongs to
ILCA in La Paz, Bolivia, is also in the University of Florida Library.   It lacks leaves 65
through 68 and 72 through 77 but contains, following the grammar itself, the complete Catecismo en la lengua española y aymara del Piru
originally published in Sevilla in 1604 on the
basis of materials dating from a provincial
council in Lima in 1583.

4.    The native speakers are Juana Vásquez of INEL
(Casilla 7846, La Paz, Bolivia) and Juan de Dios
Yapita, Director of ILCA (Casilla 2681, La Paz)
whose generous help made this study possible.
The pre-linguistic Aymara grammars and other
works were exhaustively analyzed and retranscri-
bed with their assistance, and their comments
were sought on later grammars as well.   Mr.   Ya-

pita is from Compi and La Paz, and Ms. Vásquez
is from Tiahuanaco and La Paz. Although determination of the exact extent to which their
views are shared by other Aymara speakers must
await further research, all indications are that
they speak for a considerable sector of the Aymara community. Other native speakers of Aymara
whose views on Aymara language and culture also
reflect concern for the preservation of traditional speech forms and social values are Domingo Choque Quispe and Martirián Benavides Rodríguez of ILCA Oruro (Casilla 812, Oruro, Bolivia); the Reverend Domingo Llanque Chana of
Socca, Puno, Peru; and persons associated with
ILCA in La Paz (see footnote 13).

5.  It should be noted that this term is applied to
the speech of certain native speakers of Aymara,
not primarily to that of missionaries. Examples
of Missionary Aymara may be found in Briggs
1976a, Chapter 9 and Briggs 1981b.

6.  Examples of Patrón Aymara are given in Briggs
1976a, Chapter 9 and in Briggs 1981b.

7.  Readers' interested in obtaining an up-to-date
catalogue of CALA publications in and on Aymara
may write to the Comisión de Alfabetización y
Literatura Aymara, Cajón 2724, La Paz, Bolivia.

8.  Further information about Maryknoll-sponsored
publications may be obtained by writing to the
Instituto de Idiomas Padres de Maryknoll, Casil-
la 550, Cochabamba, Bolivia. An Aymara-Spanish,
Spanish-Aymara dictionary was published by the
Instituto in 1978. In 1983 the Instituto pub-

lished a revised Aymara textbook described as
"totally new" and planned to publish a second
volume to accompany it. In Puno, the Maryknoll-
operated Instituto de Estudios Aymaras (IDEA)
has published research bulletins on Aymara cultural life. The address of IDEA is Casilla 295,
Puno, Peru.

9.  Pre-Hardman sources for the study of Jaqaru and
    Kawki are J.M.B. Farfán (1955) and José Matos
    Mar (1956), not read for this study.

10.  The phonemic alphabet developed by Yapita is
     provided in Table 1.

11.  Their names are given on page ii (Credits) of
     Outline of Aymara Phonological and Grammatical
     Structure, Part 1.

12.  Since I was a participant in the University of
     Florida Aymara Project, my account of its re-
     sults will be descriptive rather than evalua-
     tive.

13.  Others writing in ILCA publications in recent
     years are Basilia Copana Yapita, Francisco Calle
     Parra, Jorge Chambi Siñani, Celia Yapita de Lau-
     ra, Petrona Apaza, Félix Layme Payrumani (author
     of a 1980 historical study of the development of
     the Aymara alphabet), and Bertha Villanueva (a
     collector of folktales; see Yapita and Briggs
     1980).

14.  Chaski del Servicio Ecuménico de Documenta-
     ción, No. 2, July 1974.

15.  Research on Aymara child language acquisition
     has also been reported by Terry Jacobsen, a gra-
     duate student in Psychology at the University of

TABLE 1. Yapita Phonemic Alphabet

---

VOWELS:

    i    a    u              Vowel length:    "    or    :

CONSONANTS:

|  |  | Alveolar |  | Velar |  |
|---|---|---|---|---|---|
|  | Bilabial |  | Palatal |  | Postvelar |

Occlusives
|  | Bilabial | Alveolar | Palatal | Velar | Postvelar |
|---|---|---|---|---|---|
| Plain | p | t |  | k | q |
| Aspirated | p" | t" |  | k" | q" |
| Glottalized | p' | t' |  | k' | q' |

Affricates
| Plain |  |  | ch |  |  |
|---|---|---|---|---|---|
| Aspirated |  |  | ch" |  |  |
| Glottalized |  |  | ch' |  |  |

| Fricatives |  | s |  | j | x |
|---|---|---|---|---|---|

| Laterals |  | l | ll |  |  |
|---|---|---|---|---|---|

| Nasals | m |  | n | ñ | (nh)[a] |
|---|---|---|---|---|---|

| Glides | w |  |  | y |  |
|---|---|---|---|---|---|

| Flap |  | r |  |  |  |
|---|---|---|---|---|---|

---

[a] The digraph "nh" is used for the velar nasal phoneme that occurs in the Aymara of Tarata (Peru), Carangas (Oruro, Bolivia), and Chile.

California (Berkeley). The research took place
from August 1975 to September 1977 in small nur-
sery schools near Chucuito and Acora near the
city of Puno, Peru. As of early 1978 the researcher planned to begin an extensive analysis
of the data in the summer (Jacobsen, personal
communication).

16. As of mid-1980 a list of CIPCA publications
could be obtained by writing to that organization at Casilla 5854, La Paz, Bolivia.

17. Additional information about the Aymara of
Chile may be obtained from Professor Manuel
Mamani, who teaches the language at the Univer-
sidad del Norte in Arica and has written an
Aymara course outline (1973).

18. The Reverend Domingo Llanque Chana indicates
that according to his observations, the use of
Patrón and Missionary Aymara is socially and
contextually determined. That is, Patrón Aymara
is used by persons who identify with the Patrón
class, which may now include native speakers of
Aymara, even though such usages are stigmatized
as rude; while Missionary Aymara is used in religious circumstances when doctrinal matters are
treated, such as in sermons or Bible study.

19. Sociolinguistic field work has been conducted
in trilingual Aymara-Quechua-Spanish areas in
northern Potosí department and in Muñecas province of the department of La Paz, by Koomei
Hosokawa, Juan Carvajal Carvajal, and Juana
Vásquez, all associated with INEL. Published
reports of their research include Hosokawa

1979a, 1979b, and 1980, and Carvajal 1979.
Carvajal, Vásquez, and Vitaliano Huanca Torrez
collaborated on an Aymara-Spanish dictionary
(1978) and on a collection of Aymara folktales
in a bilingual Aymara-Spanish edition (1980).
(For the address of INEL see footnote 4.) A
landmark work in Bolivian sociolinguistics is
Lengua y sociedad en Bolivia 1976, by Javier
Albó (1980). Based on data from the Bolivian
national census of 1976 and that of 1950, the
study contains detailed analyses of language
developments in rural and urban areas, the
influence of age and sex, and the relationships
among language, education, and occupation.
There are numerous charts, maps, and figures.

REFERENCES

Albó, Javier. 1973. El futuro de los idiomas op-
    rimidos en los Andes. Cochabamba: Centro Peda-
    gógico y Cultural de Portales.
------. 1980. Lengua y sociedad en Bolivia 1976.
    La Paz: Instituto Nacional de Estadística, Mini-
    sterio de Planeamiento y Coordinación.
------. 1983. Review of the Aymara language in
    its social and cultural context, ed. by M.J.
    Hardman. LAIL 7:1.52-57.
Bertonio, Ludovico. 1603a. Arte breve de la len-
    gua aymara. Rome: Luis Zannetti.
------. 1603b. Arte y grammatica muy copiosa de
    la lengua aymara. Rome: Luis Zannetti.
------. 1612. Vocabulario de la lengua aymara.
    Juli: Francisco del Canto.

Boynton, Sylvia. 1974. A contrastive analysis of
    Spanish and Aymara phonology: Spanish as a goal
    language. Master's thesis, University of Flo-
    rida.

------. 1980. Análisis contrastivo de la fonología
    del aymara y del castellano. (Translated by Ped-
    ro Plaza Martinez from A contrastive analysis of
    Spanish and Aymara phonology: Spanish as a goal
    language). La Paz: Instituto Nacional de Estu-
    dios Lingüísticos.

------. 1981. A phonemic analysis of monolingual
    Andean (Bolivian) Spanish. In The Aymara lan-
    guage in its social and cultural context, M.J.
    Hardman, ed. Gainesville: University of Florida
    Press.

Briggs, Lucy Therina. 1973. The Aymara four-per-
    son system. Papers in Andean Linguistics
    2:1.1-3.

------. 1974a. Las cuatro personas gramaticales
    del aymara. (Documentos No. 9, Depto. Lingüísti-
    ca). Cochabamba: Centro Pedagógico y Cultural
    de Portales.

------. 1974b. Algunos rasgos dialectales del
    aymara de Bolivia y del Perú. Paper read at
    41st International Congress of Americanists,
    Mexico City.

------. 1975. Structure of the substantive system.
    Ch. 8, Aymar ar yatiqañataki, 2nd ed., vol.
    3, by Hardman et al. Ann Arbor: University
    Microfilms International (Research Abstracts).

------. 1976a. Dialectal variation in the Aymara
    language of Bolivia and Peru. Ph.D. disserta-

tion, University of Florida. Ann Arbor: University Microfilms International.

------. 1976b. Dialectal variation in Aymara. Latinamericanist 12:1, December 1976.

------. 1978. Mururata: An Aymara text. Latin American Indian Literatures 2:1.

------. 1979. A critical survey of the literature on the Aymara language. Latin American Research Review 14.3.

------. 1981a. Aymarization, an example of language change. In The Aymara language in its social and cultural context, M.J. Hardman, ed. Gainesville: University of Florida Press.

------. 1981b. Missionary, patrón, and radio Aymara. In The Aymara language in its social and cultural context, M.J. Hardman, ed. Gainesville: University of Florida Press.

------. 1981c. Politeness in Aymara language and culture. In The Aymara language in its social and cultural context, M.J. Hardman, ed. Gainesville: University of Florida Press.

Briggs, Lucy Therina and Nora C. England. 1973. Education and anthropological linguistics. New Voices in Education 3:1.21-22.

Briggs, Lucy Therina and Domingo Llanque Chana. 1979. Humor in Aymara oral narrative. Latin American Indian Literatures 3.1.

Brody, Jill. 1983. Review of the Aymara language in its social and cultural context. American Anthropologist 85:486.

Calle, P., Francisco. 1974. Aymarat liyt'apxaña:n qillqt'apxaña:ni. Tiahuanaco: Centro de Promo-

ción Cultural Tiwanaku-Taraco, Jesús y San Andrés de Machaca, Bolivia.

Carvajal Carvajal, Juan.  1979.  Esbozo de un análisis lingüístico del aymara del Norte de Potosí.  Notas y Noticias Lingüísticas 2:3 (Instituto Nacional de Estudios Lingüísticos, La Paz).

------.  (ed.)  1980.  Wiñay arunaka (Cuentos andinos).  La Paz: Instituto Nacional de Estudios
Lingüísticos.

------, Vitaliano Huanca Torrez and Juana Vásquez.
1978.  Diccionario aymara castellano.  La Paz:
Instituto Nacional de Estudios Lingüísticos.

Catálogo de las voces usuales del aymara con la
correspondencia en castellano y quechua.  1953,
1963, 1971.  La Paz, Gisbert.

Center for Applied Linguistics.  1976.  Languages
of North, Central, and South America.  Arlington, Va.

Choque Quispe, Domingo.  1976.  Aymara yatiqañani.
La Paz: Instituto Nacional de Estudios Lingüísticos.

------ and Martirián Benavides Rodríguez.  1970.
Cursado de fonología aymara.  Oruro: Departamen-
to de Extensión Cultural, Universidad Técnica de
Oruro.

Clair-Vasiliades, Christos.  1976.  Esquisse phono-
logique de l'aymara parle au Chili.  La Lingüis-
tique 12.2.143-152.

Cole, John Tafel.  1969.  The human soul in the
Aymara culture of Pumasara.  Ph.D. disserta-
tion, University of Pennsylvania.  Ann Arbor:
University Microfilms International.

Collins, Jane. 1983. Translation traditions and the organization of productive activity: The case of Aymara affinal kinship terms. In Bilingualism: Social Issues and policy implications, Andrew W. Miracle, Jr., ed. Athens, Ga: The University of Georgia Press.

Copana Yapita Pedro. 1973. Linguistics and education in rural schools among the Aymara. New Voices in Education 3:1.26-27. Reprinted in The Aymara language in its social and cultural context, M.J. Hardman, ed. 1981. Gainesville: University of Florida Press.

Cotari, Daniel, Jaime Mejía and Victor Carrasco. 1978. Diccionario aymara-castellano castellano-aymara. Cochabamba: Instituto de Idiomas Padres de Maryknoll.

Davidson, Joseph O. 1977. A contrastive study of the grammatical structures of Aymara and Cuzco Quechua. Ph.D. dissertation, University of California, Berkeley. Ann Arbor: University Microfilms International.

Ebbing, Juan Enrique. 1965. Gramática y diccionario aymara. La Paz: Don Bosco.

England, Nora Clearman. 1975. Verbal derivational suffixes. Ch. 6, Aymar ar yatiqañataki, 2nd ed., vol. 3, by Hardman et al. Ann Arbor: University Microfilms International (Research Abstracts).

------ and Lucy Therina Briggs. 1981. Linguistics and foreign aid. In The Aymara language in its social and cultural context, M.J. Hardman, ed. Gainesville: University of Florida Press.

Escobar, Alberto (ed.)  1972.  El reto del multilinguismo en el Perú.  Lima: Instituto de Estudios Peruanos.

Farfán, J.M.B.  1955.  Estudio de un vocabulario de
las lenguas quechua, aymara y jaqe-aru.  Revista
del Museo Nacional 24.81 (Lima).

Forbes, David.  1870.  On the Aymara Indians of Bolivia and Peru.  Journal of the Ethnological Society of London, n.s. 2:13.193-305.

Franco Inojosa, Mario.  1965.  Breve vocabulario
castellano aymara.  Puno: Departamento de Inte-
gración Cultural de la CORPUNO.

------.  1967.  Arte de la lengua aymara de Diego
de Torres Rubio [1616].  Actualización de Mario
Franco Inojosa [1966].  Lima: LYRSA.

Gallaher, Rhea.  1981.  Cross-cultural conversation: Time as a variable and paralinguistic
cues for persuasion.  In The Aymara language
in its social and cultural context, Martha J.
Hardman, ed.  Gainesville: University of Florida
Press.

García, Juan Antonio.  1917.  Gramática aymara -
sobre la base de una edición antigua.  La Paz:
Imprenta y Litografía Artística.

Grondin N., Marcelo.  1973.  Método de aymara.
Oruro: Rodríguez-Muriel.

Hardman, M.J.  1966.  Jaqaru: Outline of phonological and morphological structure.  The Hague:
Mouton.

------.  1969.  Computerized archive and dictionary
of the Jaqimara languages of South America.
Papers in Linguistics 1.606-617.

------. 1972a. Postulados lingüísticos del idioma aymara. In El reto del multilingüismo en el Perú, Alberto Escobar, ed., pp. 35-46. Lima: Instituto de Estudios Peruanos.

------. 1972b. Early use of inclusive/exclusive. IJAL 38.145-146.

------. 1975. Proto-jaqi: Reconstrucción del sistema de personas gramaticales. Revista del Museo Nacional 41.433-456 (Lima).

------. 1978a. Jaqi: The linguistic family. IJAL 44:2.146-150.

------. 1978b. Familia lingüística andina jaqi: Jaqaru, kawki, aymara. VICUS Cuadernos, Lingüística 2.5-28.

------. 1979a. Linguistic postulates and applied anthropological linguistics. Papers on Linguistics and Child Language. Ruth Hirsch Weir Memorial Volume, M.J. Hardman and Vladimir Honsa, eds. The Hague: Mouton.

------. 1979b. Quechua y aymara: lenguas en contacto. Antropología (Revista del Museo de Etnografía y Folklore) 1.1, La Paz, Bolivia.

------. (in press). Jaqaru. Compendio de la estructura fonológica y morfológica. Lima: Instituto de Estudios Peruanos.

Hardman, M.J. (ed.). 1981. The Aymara language in its social and cultural context. Gainesville: University of Florida Press.

Hardman, M.J., Juana Vásquez, and Juan de Dios Yapita, with Laura Martin-Barber, Lucy Therina Briggs, and Nora Clearman England. 1973. Aymar ar yatiqañataki. 3 vols.: 1, Aymar ar

yatiqañataki; 2, Teachers' Manual to accompany
Aymar ar yatiqañataki; 3, Aymara grammatical
sketch. Washington D.C.: ERIC.

------. 1975. Aymar ar yatiqañataki, 2nd ed.
(Vols. 1 and 2 have same titles as first ed.;
Vol. 3 is entitled Outline of Aymara phonolo-
gical and grammatical structure.) Ann Arbor:
University Microfilms International (Research
Abstracts).

Harris, Olivia. 1974. Los laymis y machas del
Norte de Potosí. La Paz: Semana - Ultima Hora,
11 October 1974.

Herrero, Joaquín, Daniel Cotari, and Jaime Mejía.
1971-72. Lecciones de aymara, 2nd ed., 2 vols.
Cochabamba: Instituto de Idiomas, Padres de
Maryknoll.

Hosokawa, Koomei. 1979a. Perfiles de la situación
trilingüe de Panacachi, Norte de Potosí. Notas
y Noticias 2.2 (Instituto Nacional de Estudios
Lingüísticos, La Paz).

------. 1979b. Esbozo de la red de comunicación
socio-económica como factor del trilingüismo en
Titicachi, Provincia Muñecas, norte del Departamento de La Paz. Notas y Noticias Lingüísticas
2.4 (Instituto Nacional de Estudios Lingüísticos, La Paz).

------. 1980. Diagnóstico sociolingüístico de la
región Norte de Potosí. La Paz: Instituto
Nacional de Estudios Lingüísticos.

Huanca Torrez, Vitaliano. 1973a. Kunkrisutak
q"ana chawi. Cochabamba: Centro Pedagógico y
Cultural de Portales.

------. 1973b. La promoción de la lengua aymara
en el área rural. Tiahuanaco: Comisión para la
Promoción de la Lengua Aymara (COPLA).

Hymes, Dell. 1972. On personal pronouns: 'Fourth
'person and phonesthematic aspects. In Studies
in honor of George L. Trager, M. Estellie
Smith, ed. The Hague/Paris: Mouton.

Kispi H., Gabino. 1974. Aymaranakan q"ichwanakan
qullapa. Plantas, yerbas medicinales en nues-
tros campos. Tiahuanaco: Comisión para la Promoción de la Lengua Aymara (COPLA) y Centro de
Servicio Cultural de Tiwanaku.

LaBarre, Weston. 1950. Aymara folktales. IJAL
16.40-45.

Laprade, Richard A. 1976. Some salient dialectal
features of La Paz Spanish. Master's thesis,
University of Florida.

------. 1981. Some cases of Aymara influence on
La Paz Spanish. In The Aymara language in its
social and cultural context, M.J. Hardman, ed.
Gainesville: University of Florida Press.

Lastra de Suárez, Yolanda. 1968. Review of Jaqaru: Outline of phonological and morphological
structure. Lg. 44.652-654.

------. 1970. Categorías posicionales en quechua
y aymara. Anales de Antropología 7.263-284.

Layme P., Félix. 1980. Desarrollo del alfabeto
aymara. La Paz: Instituto de Lengua y Cultura
Aymara.

Llanque Chana, Domingo. 1973. El trato social
entre los aymaras. Allpanchis (Revista del
Instituto Pastoral Andino, Cusco) 5.19-32.

Llanque Chana, Justino.  1974.  Educación y lengua
    aymara.  Thesis presented to Escuela Normal
    Superior de Varones San Juan Bosco, Salcedo,
    Puno, Peru.  Mimeo.
Loriot, James.  1964.  A selected bibliography of
    comparative American Indian linguistics.  IJAL
    30:1.77-78.
Loukotka, Čestmir.  1968.  Classification of South
    American Indian languages.  Los Angeles: Univer-
    sity of California (Latin American Center).
Lozano, Eduardo.  1977.  Bibliography - Recent
    books on South American Indian Languages.  Latin
    American Indian Literatures 1:2.
Maidana, Juan.  1981.  Consequences of direct
    "alphabetization" in Spanish on Aymara children.
    In The Aymara language in its social and cultu-
    ral context, M.J.  Hardman, ed.  Gainesville:
    University of Florida Press.
Malmberg, Bertil.  1947-1948.  L'espagnol dans le
    nouveau monde. Problème de linguistique géné-
    rale.  Studia Linguistica vols.  1.79-116,
    2.1-36.
Mamani, Manuel.  1973.  Aymara.  Arica (Chile):
    Universidad del Norte, Sección Idiomas (mimeo-
    graphed course outline).
Martín, Eusebia Herminia.  1969.  Bosquejo de
    estructura de la lengua aymara.  (Colección de
    Estudios Indigenistas 2, Instituto de Filología
    y Literaturas Hispánicas.)  Buenos Aires: Uni-
    versidad de Buenos Aires.
Martin-Barber, Laura.  1975.  Phonology.  Ch. 3,
    Aymar ar yatiqañataki, 2nd ed., vol. 3, by

588     *Lucy Therina Briggs*

Hardman et. al.    Ann Arbor: University Microfilms International (Research Abstracts).

Mason, John Alden.  1950.  The languages of South
American Indians. In Handbook of South American
Indians 6.157-317.

Matos Mar, José.  1956.  Yauyos, Tupe y el idioma
Kauke.  Lima: Instituto de Etnología y Arqueología.

Medina, José Toribio.  1930.  Bibliografía de las
lenguas quechua y aymará.  New York: Museum of
the American Indian.

Middendorf, Ernst W.  1891.  Die Aimará-Sprache.
Die enheimischen Sprachen Perus, vol. 5.
Leipzig: F.A. Brockhaus.

------.  1910.  Introducción a la gramática aymara
(tr. from the German by Franz Tamayo).  La Paz:
Boletin de la Oficina  Nacional de Estadística
5.517-560.

------.  1959.  Las lenguas aborígenes del Perú
(Proemios e introducciones al quechua, al aimará
y al mochica).  Part II, El aimará (tr.  by
Franz Tamayo, revised by Estuardo Núñez).  Instituto de Literatura de la Facultad de Letras
No. 8, 56-102.  Lima: Universidad Nacional Mayor
de San Marcos.

Miracle, Andrew.  1976.  The effects of cultural
perception on Aymara schooling.  Ph.D. dissertation, University of Florida.  Ann Arbor: University Microfilms International.

Miracle, Andrew, ed.  1983.  Bilingualism: Social
Issues and Policy Implications. Athens, Ga.: The
University of Georgia Press.

Miracle, Andrew with Juana Vásquez. 1981. Jama, t"axa, and p"uru: Three categories of feces in Aymara. In The Aymara language in its social and cultural context, M.J. Hardman, ed. Gainesville: University of Florida Press.

Miracle, Andrew with Juan de Dios Yapita. 1981. Time and space in Aymara. In The Aymara language in its social and cultural context, M.J. Hardman, ed. Gainesville: University of Florida Press.

Miranda, Pedro. 1970. Diccionario breve castellano-aymara aymara-castellano. La Paz: El Siglo.

Orr, Carolyn and Robert E. Longacre. 1968. Proto-Quechumaran. Lg. 44.528-555.

Painter, Michael. 1983. Aymara and Spanish in southern Peru: The relationship of language to economic class and social identity. In Bilingualism: Social issues and policy implications, ed. by Andrew W. Miracle, Jr. Athens, Ga.: The University of Georgia Press.

Paredes Candia, Antonio. 1963. Vocablos aymaras en el habla popular paceña. La Paz: Ediciones Isla.

Pike, Kenneth L. 1947. Phonemics. Ann Arbor: University of Michigan Press.

Porterie-Gutiérrez, Liliane. 1980. Les relations actancielles en aymara. Amerindia 5. 7-29.

------. 1981. El ratón y el zorro: Cuento aymara de Chucuito (Puno, Perú). Amérindia 6. 97-125.

Pyle, Ransford Comstock. 1981. Aymara kinship, real and spiritual. In The Aymara language in

its social and cultural context, M.J. Hardman,
ed. Gainesville, University of Florida Press.

Rivet, Paul and George de Créqui-Montfort. 1951-
56. Bibliographie des langues Aymará et Kičua.
4 vols. Paris: Institut d'Ethnologie.

Ross, Ellen M. 1953. Rudimentos de gramática
aymara. La Paz: Canadian Baptist Mission.

------. 1958. Diccionario aymara-castellano, castellano-aymara. La Paz: Misión Cristiana Pro-Al-
fabetización. Mimeo. (Reprinted 1973 by Comisión de Alfabetización y Literatura Aymara,
CALA).

------. 1963. Rudimentos de gramática aymara, 2nd
ed. La Paz: Canadian Baptist Mission.

------. n.d. Manuel aymara para los aymaristas.
La Paz: Sociedades Bíblicas.

Sebeok, Thomas A. 1951a. Aymara 'Little Red Ri-
ding-hood' with morphological analysis. Archi-
vum Linguisticum 3.53-69.

------. 1951b. Materials for an Aymara dictionary. Journal de la Société des Américanistes
n.s. 40.89-151.

Sharpe, Pamela J. 1981. Spanish borrowing into
Aymara clothing vocabulary. In The Aymara lan-
guage in its social and cultural context, M.J.
Hardman, ed. Gainesville: University of Florida
Press.

Solá, Donald. 1971. Review of Jaqaru: Outline of
phonological and morphological structure. IJAL
37.208-9.

Stark, Louisa. 1965. Further bibliography on Quechumaran. IJAL 31:2.192-193.

------. 1970. A reconsideration of Proto-Quechua phonology. Paper read at 39th International Congress of Americanists, Lima.

Stearman, Allyn MacLean. 1981. Language as a mechanism for social discrimination and class distinction: Lowland Bolivia. In The Aymara language in its social and cultural context, M.J. Hardman. Gainesville: University of Florida Press.

Tarifa Ascarrunz, Erasmo. 1969. Suma lajjra aymara parlaña. Gramática de la lengua aymara. La Paz: Don Bosco.

Tate, Norman. 1981. An ethno-semantic study of Aymara "to carry". In The Aymara language in its social and cultural context, M.J. Hardman, ed. Gainesville: University of Florida Press.

Torero, Alfredo. 1972. Lingüística e historia de los Andes del Perú y Bolivia. In El reto del multilingüismo en el Perú, A. Escobar, ed., pp. 47-106. Lima: Instituto de Estudios Peruanos.

Torres Rubio, Diego de. 1616. Arte de la lengua aymara. Lima: Francisco del Canto. (Reprinted with commentary by Mario Franco Inojosa, ed. Lima: LYRSA, 1967.)

Tovar, Antonio. 1961. Catálogo de las lenguas de América del Sur. Buenos Aires: Sudamericana.

Tschopik, Harry. 1948. Aymara texts: Lupaca dialect. International Journal of American Linguistics 14.108-114.

Vásquez, Juana. 1970. Primera cartilla de aymara. La Paz. Mimeo.

------. 1971. Newsletter nos. 8-15. Gainesville:
University of Florida (Center for Latin American
Studies).

Vásquez, Juana and Juan de Dios Yapita. 1969.
Sistema YAVA aymar liyiñ qillqañ yatiqañataki.
Gainesville: University of Florida (Center for
Latin American Studies).

Villamor, Germán G. 1942. Gramática del kechua y
del aymar. La Paz: Editorial Popular.

Wexler, Paul (ed.) 1967. Beginning Aymara: A
course for English speakers. Seattle: University of Washington.

Wölck, Wolfgang. 1972. Las lenguas mayores del
Perú y sus hablantes. In El reto del multilingüismo en el Perú, Alberto Escobar, ed., pp.
189-216. Lima: Instituto de Estudios Peruanos.

------. 1973. Attitudes toward Spanish and Quechua
in bilingual Peru. In Language attitudes: Current trends and prospects, Roger W. Shuy and
Ralph W. Fasold, eds., pp. 129-147. Washington
D.C.: Georgetown University Press.

Yapita, Juan de Dios. 1968. Lecciones de aymara.
La Paz. Mimeo.

------. 1968-69. Textos de aymara, nos. 1, 2, 3.
La Paz: Departamento de Idiomas de la Universidad Mayor de San Andrés.

------. 1969. Noticias culturales. (Four issues).
La Paz: Instituto Nacional de Estudios Lingüísticos.

------. 1973a. Alfabeto fonemico del aymara.
Gainesville: University of Florida (Center for
Latin American Studies).

Yapita, Juan de Dios.  1973b.  Linguistics in
    Bolivia.  New Voices in Education 3:1.23-25.
------.  1973c.  Alfabeto fónemico aymara.  Manuales
    Departamento Lingüística No. 1.  Cochabamba:
    Centro Pedagógico y Cultural de Portales.
------.  1974.  Vocabulario castellano-inglés-
    aymara.  Oruro: INDICEP.
------.  1975.  Brief description of local Aymara
    life.  Gainesville: University of Florida (Center
    for Latin American Studies).
------.  1976.  Aymara married life.  Diálogo.
    Gainesville: University of Florida (Center for
    Latin American Studies).
------.  1977a.  Discriminación y lingüística y
    conflicto social.  La Paz: Museo Nacional de
    Etnografía y Folklore.
------.  1977b.  Los onomásticos en el mundo aymara.
    La Paz: El Diario, 24 April 1977.
------.  1977c.  Etnosemántica de 'reír' en aymara.
    La Paz: El  Diario, 4 May 1977.
------.  1977d.  Pautas para una educación bilingüe.
    La Paz: Presencia, 17 September 1977.
------.  1977e.  Labores de lingüística aplicada del
    aymara realizadas en la Universidad del Norte de
    Arica, 1977. Paris: UNESCO.
------.  1978.  Kunjamarakchiniya (Cómo será el
    futuro).  La Paz: El Diario, 26 August 1978.
------.  1981a.  Enseñanza del idioma aymara como
    segundo idioma. La Paz: Difusión Ltda.
------.  1981b.  The Aymara alphabet: Linguistics
    for indigenous communities.  In The Aymara
    language in its social and cultural context,

M.J. Hardman, ed.   Gainesville: University of
Florida Press.

Yapita, Juan de Dios, ed.   1970a.   Yatiñasawa.
Gainesville: University of Florida (Center for
Latin American Studies).

------.   1970b.   Aymara Newsletter nos. 1-7.
Gainesville: University of Florida (Center for
Latin American Studies).

------.   1970c.   Boletín Ji:pi de Qumpi.   Compi,
Bolivia.   Mimeo.

------.   1972-73.   Literatura aymara, nos. 1-3.   La
Paz.   Mimeo.

------.   1978.   Yatiñasawa.   Boletín 15 (febrero),
16 (marzo), 17 (abril-mayo), 18 (agosto).   La
Paz.   Mimeo.

Yapita, Juan de Dios and Lucy T. Briggs.   1980.
The origin of the charango: An Aymara tale (as
told by Berta Villanueva).   Latin American
Indian Literatures 4.2.

# 15. Dialectical Variation in Aymara
## Lucy Therina Briggs

INTRODUCTION

Aymara is spoken by some two million inhabitants of
the high Andean plains of Peru and Bolivia, from
the northern tip of Lake Titicaca to the Uyuni salt
flats south of Lake Poopó and in some of the valleys that descend from the altiplano to the east
and west. There are also some speakers in northern
Chile and Argentina (see map). In Bolivia alone
there may be well over a million and a half speakers (Hardman et al. 1975:3.2) constituting almost
a third of the total Bolivian population, which was
estimated at 5.75 million in 1981 (U.S. Dept. of
State 1983). In contrast, Aymara speakers in Peru
were reckoned in 1972 at no more than 332,595 or
only about 3 percent of the population (República
del Peru 1974: 2.646). The number of speakers in
Chile has been estimated at 25,000 (Martínez Soto-
Aguilar 1981: 37). Figures are not available for
the number of Aymara in Argentina.

Hardman (1972) has identified Aymara as a member
of the Jaqi language family which includes the
still vigorous Jaqaru and the nearly extinct Kawki,
both spoken in remote communities in the department
of Lima, Peru. In Jaqi languages the processes of
suffixing and of vowel-dropping and -lengthening
perform almost all grammatical functions. Accumulation of many suffixes on a stem is common. Suf-

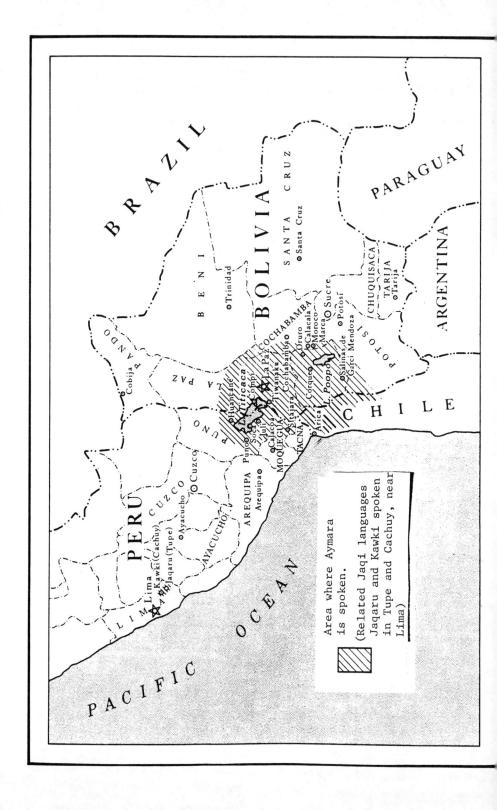

BRAZIL

PARAGUAY

ARGENTINA

BOLIVIA

BENI

SANTA CRUZ
○Santa Cruz

○Trinidad

CHUQUISACA

TARIJA
○Tarija

PANDO

○Cobija

LA PAZ

COCHABAMBA
○Sucre
Calacala○Moroco
Marca○Potosí
○Oruro Corqueo
Corqueo○ Poopó
○Salinas de
Garci Mendoza

La Paz
Tiwanaku
Cochabamba○

POTOSI

CHILE

PERÚ

PUNO

Titicaca
Huancane
○Juli
Copi
Soca
Calacoa

Juli○
Calacoa○
Acora○

MOQUEGUA

TACNA

Arica

CUZCO
○Cuzco

AREQUIPA
Puno○
Arequipa○

AYACUCHO
○Ayacucho

LIMA
★Lima ♣Kawki(Cachuy)
⚡Jaqaru(Tupe)

PACIFIC OCEAN

Area where Aymara
is spoken.

(Related Jaqi languages
Jaqaru and Kawki spoken
in Tupe and Cachuy, near
Lima)

fix order and word order within a phrase are usually fixed, but word order is otherwise quite free.
As Hardman has pointed out, the Jaqi languages also
share certain semantic categories or linguistic
postulates that are marked throughout their structure: a system of four grammatical persons,[1] a
distinction of human and non-human, and a distinction of direct (i.e. personally experienced) and
indirect knowledge. The phonemes of Aymara are
three vowels, vowel length, and 26 (or 27) consonants, including plain, aspirated, and glottalized
stops and affricates, as well as fricatives, nasals, laterals, glides, and a flap or trill. Table
1 gives the phonemic alphabet of Aymara devised by
the Aymara linguist Juan de Dios Yapita.

Although regional dialectal variation in the Aymara language has been known to exist since colonial times, systematic published descriptions of
the variations are lacking. My own interest in Aymara dialects was sparked in 1972 when I found in
the province of Carangas, department of Oruro, Bolivia, a phoneme not occurring in the Aymara of La
Paz, although it does occur in Jaqaru: the velar
nasal symbolized by nh. Having worked on a reference grammar of La Paz Aymara (Hardman et al.
1975:3), I decided to sample selectively the Aymara
spoken over a wide area (approximately 40,000
square miles) in ten communities in Peru and Bolivia, to determine dialectal features and identify
regional dialect groups, if any existed. Apart
from their usefulness in historical reconstructions
of proto-Jaqi (Hardman 1975), descriptions of vari-

TABLE 1.  Yapita Phonemic Alphabet

---

VOWELS:

i   a   u           Vowel length:   "   or   :

CONSONANTS:

|  | Bilabial | Alveolar | Palatal | Velar | Postvelar |
|---|---|---|---|---|---|
| Occlusives |  |  |  |  |  |
| Plain | p | t |  | k | q |
| Aspirated | p" | t" |  | k" | q" |
| Glottalized | p' | t' |  | k' | q' |
| Affricates |  |  |  |  |  |
| Plain |  |  | ch |  |  |
| Aspirated |  |  | ch" |  |  |
| Glottalized |  |  | ch' |  |  |
| Fricatives |  | s |  | j | x |
| Laterals |  | l | ll |  |  |
| Nasals | m | n | ñ | (nh)[a] |  |
| Glides | w |  | y |  |  |
| Flap |  | r |  |  |  |

---

[a]The digraph "nh" is used for the velar nasal phoneme that occurs in the Aymara of Tarata (Peru), Carangas (Oruro, Bolivia), and Chile.

ations in Aymara have practical applications outside linguistics. Descriptions of areal features
in conjunction with information in colonial documents may enable historians to reconstruct past
population movements and relationships among areas
(Murra 1970:20). Bilingual education programs in
Peru and Bolivia (see Briggs 1983 and in press)
require detailed descriptions of Aymara language
and culture for their successful implementation.

My field work took place in July and August 1972
and from March 1973 to January 1974. With the
speakers' permission, I recorded stories and conversations on tape and obtained Aymara translations
of Andean Spanish words and phrases selected to
elicit Aymara forms found to vary locally as research progressed. Several hundred hours were
spent transcribing the tapes with the help of native speakers. Transcriptions were then exhaustively analyzed with respect to phonology, morphology, morphophonemics, syntax, and semantics. Typed
transcripts of some stories have been provided to
the tellers, a few have been published in Aymara
newsletters in Bolivia, and it is hoped that more
may be published there in the future.

Choice of sites and sources was random and se-
rendipitous, owing much to contacts provided by
Juan de Dios Yapita. Attempts were made to obtain
data from widely separated communities and from
men, women, and children representing different
occupations and levels of education. An average of
six native speakers from each major site participated. The majority were under 45 years old and bi-

lingual in Aymara and Spanish. After returning to
the U.S., I consulted all available published sources on Aymara, incorporating data from colonial and
later publications into my field work materials.

RESEARCH RESULTS
As has always been supposed, Aymara is clearly one
language. Regional variation does not significant-
ly affect intelligibility except when certain utte-
rances are taken out of context, primarily because
the inventory of phonemes is uniform except for the
velar nasal, and secondarily because all dialects
share a basic core of morphemes (roots and suffixes) with the same or very similar meanings and
similar phonological shapes. Nevertheless, on the
basis of regional patterning of certain morphemes
by incidence, meaning, and shape of allomorphs,
Aymara dialects fall into the following groups: a
northern (N) group located on or near Lake Titicaca and including Juli, Socca, and Huancané (department of Puno) and La Paz (city and department),
and a southern (S) group in the departments of Oruro and Potosí, Bolivia: Corque, Jopoqueri, and Salinas de Garci Mendoza in Oruro; and Morocomarca
and Calacala in Potosí. The intermediate (I) dialects of Calacoa (province of Mariscal Nieto, department of Moquegua) and Sitajara (province of Tarata, department of Tacna) in southern Peru southwest of Lake Titicaca share some features with the
northern and some with the southern group. Apart
from the north/south division, there is a distinction between a central (C) group of dialects near

La Paz and those on the periphery (P) of La Paz
influence, whether to the north, south, or west.
For example, Huancané, a northern dialect sharing a
number of features with La Paz, is also peripheral
in sharing certain non-La Paz attributes with the
southern and intermediate dialects.  There are also
certain features that cut across north/south and
center/periphery lines.

Some of the features on the basis of which regional groupings may be made are given below, arranged according to whether they involve phonological shapes, morphophonemics, incidence of morphemes, or semantics.

NORTHERN (N) VS. SOUTHERN (S) DIALECTS
Phonological Shapes of Morphemes
Noun Suffixes.
First person possessive suffix 'my, our but not
    your'. N: /-ja/, /-xa/.  S: /-ña/ Salinas,
    Morocomarca, Calacala; /-nha/ Jopoqueri, also
    Sitajara.
-mpi ~ -nti 'with'.  N: /-mpi/.  S: /-nti/ Sali-
        2
    nas;  both allomorphs elsewhere.


Verbs and verb suffixes.
Presence or absence of initial /si-/ or /ji-/ on
        3
    the verb sa.ña 'to say', when inflected.  N:
    optional /si/ or /ji/.  S: no /si/ or /ji/.
'to eat'.  N and Jopoqueri: /manq'a.ña/.  S
    except Jopoqueri: /maq'a.ña/.
Distancer verbal derivational suffix.  N: /-wa-/
    Juli, Socca, Huancané, also Calacoa; /-waya-/,

/-wa:/ La Paz.  S: /-wi-/, /-wiya-/.
Incompletive verbal derivational suffix.  N:
/-ka-/.  S: /-ja-/ as sole allomorph or alternating with /-ka-/ by morphophonemic rule.
-sina subordinator suffix.  N: /-sina/ or /-sna/.
S except Salinas: /-sana/.

Nonfinal and final suffixes.
Independent nonfinal 'just, only'.  N plus Jopoqueri: /-ki/.  S except Jopoqueri: /-ki/, /-ji/.
Final suffix, reiterator of known information.  N:
/-pi/.  S: /-pu/ Jopoqueri, Salinas, also Sitajara.

Incidence of morphemes
Temporal noun arumant"i 'tomorrow'.  N plus Calacoa; does not occur in S.
Incidence of completive or incompletive suffixes on
verbs.  N plus Calacoa and Sitajara: verbs in
negative sentences usually have a completive or
incompletive suffix.  S: verbs in negative sentences usually do not.

Semantics. Verb roots and stems.
Examples from the three dialects are presented in
Table 2.

CENTRAL (C) VS. PERIPHERAL (P) DIALECTS
Phonological shapes of morphemes
Nouns and noun suffixes.
Demonstrative '(that) way over yonder'.  C: /k"a/,
/k"a:/, /k"aya/.  P: /k"u/, /k"u:/,/k"uyu/ (N:

TABLE 2. Semantics. Verb roots and stems

| NORTHERN | INTERMEDIATE | SOUTHERN |
|---|---|---|
| ati.ña 'to block a door with small stones' (La Paz) | ati.ña 'to send water through a canal' (Sitajara) | ati.ña 'to be able' |
| puyri.ña 'to be able' < Sp. poder | | |
| chuk.t'a.si.ña 'to squat' | | chuk.t'a.si.ña 'to sit down' |
| qun.ta.si.ña 'to sit' | | |
| jala.ña 'to run' | wala.ña 'to fly' (Calacoa) | jala.ña 'to fly' |
| tuyu.ña 'to fly, to swim' | | tani.ña 'to run' |
| suya.ña 'to wait for someone' | | wanqi.ña 'to wait for someone' |
| k'iya.ña 'to grind red peppers with a small round stone' | | k'iya.ña 'to grind corn with a rocking stone' (Salinas) |

Huancané [also has /k"uri/]; S: Salinas, Morocomarca).

Noun suffix -t"a~-ta 'from, of'. C: /-ta/. P:
/-t"a/ and /-ta/ (N: both variants [Juli,
Huancané]; S: /-t"a/ only [Salinas, Moroco-
marca]; both variants [Jopoqueri]).

Verb suffixes.

2→3, 3→2, and 2→1 future tense suffixes.[4] C:
Initial or medial long vowel. P: Initial or
medial alveolar, palatal, or velar nasals (N:
/n/ [Huancané]; I: /nh/ [Sitajara]; S: /nh/
[Jopoqueri], /ñ/ [Salinas]).

Nonfinal and final suffixes.

-raki~-raji nonfinal independent suffix. C:
/-raki/ only. P: both variants (N: Huancané;
I: Sitajara; S: Salinas, Morocomarca, Calacala).

-lla~-ya politive final suffix. C: /-ya-/ only. P: /-lla/ only (N: Juli, Socca; I: Calacoa, Sitajara; S: Jopoqueri, Salinas, Calacala).

Morphophonemics

Voicing of prevocalic stops after homorganic nasals, e.g. /ampara/ [ambara] 'hand, arm'. C:
rule does not apply. P: rule applies (N: Huancané, optional; I: Sitajara, optional; S: Salinas, obligatory within morphemes, optional
otherwise; Corque, optional).

Morphophonemics of -na possessive/locational noun

suffix. C: always requires a preceding vowel.
P: variable (N: Juli, Socca; I: Calacoa).
Morphophonemics of personal possessive suffixes. C:
always require a preceding vowel. P: some dialects require a preceding vowel, some a preceding consonant, and others have variable rules.

Incidence of morphemes

Nouns and Noun Suffixes.

Temporal noun q'alta∼q"alt'i 'morning, tomorrow'. C: does not occur. P:N: /q'alta/ (Socca);
I: /q'alta/;  S: /q"alt'i/.

Noun suffix -chapi∼-ch"api 'the one which'.  C:
does not occur. P: N: Huancané; I: Sitajara; S:
Jopoqueri.

Diminutive noun suffix -lla. C: does not occur.  P:
N: Huancané; I: Sitajara; S: Corque, Jopoqueri,
Salinas.

Verb subordinating suffixes.

C: -ipana used when subjects of main verb and subordinate verb are different; sometimes replaced
by subordinators -sa and -sina (otherwise used
when subjects of main and subordinate verbs are
the same); most commonly used subordinator is
the topic marker final suffix -xa. P: full paradigm of four subordinators of which -ipana is
third person, used when subjects of main and
subordinate verbs are different; -sa and -sina
used only when subjects of main and subordinate
verbs are the same; final suffix -xa not the
most commonly used subordinator.

Semantics

The first and fourth grammatical persons are always distinguished in C dialects but are fal-
ling together in certain verbal inflections in
P dialects. N: Huancané; I: Sitajara (also in
personal possessive suffixes); S: Morocomarca.

Peripheral features of limited occurrence

There are certain features found in only a few peripheral dialects and having identical or similar reflexes in present-day Jaqaru. Such features are 1) the velar nasal phoneme /nh/ which in
Aymara has been found to occur in Tarata (Perú)
and Carangas (Bolivia); 2) the Aymara diminutive
noun suffix -cha, which corresponds to the Jaqaru limitative and occurs only in Huancané and
Calacoa; and 3) the 4->3 future tense allomorph
/-tana/ which is the sole form of the suffix in
Calacoa and also occurs in S. dialects but not
in N. ones.

Certain Aymara forms cited by the Jesuit missionary
Bertonio (1603) as occurring in Juli, I found only
in Sitajara, e.g., /mimilla/ 'girl', /marmi/ 'woman', /-itta/ 2→1 simple tense suffix, and ama:.ña
'to want'. (Elsewhere the equivalents today are
/imilla/, /warmi/, /-ista/, and muna.ña.) Bertonio listed two full paradigms each for the two
tenses now referred to as Desiderative and Remonstrator. In all Aymara dialects studied, these two
tenses consist of two partially merged paradigms

each, one having forms with /sa/, the other having
forms with /iri/. The incidence of these forms
varies regionally. The present-day dialect having
the greatest number of /sa/ and /iri/ forms for the
two tenses (some of them different from the forms
cited by Bertonio) is Salinas, which also has other
features that mark it as one of the most distinctive Aymara dialects.

CROSS-REGIONAL FEATURES
Phonological shapes
4→3 future tense suffix. N: /-ñani/ (Huancané,
    Juli, Socca, La Paz). I: /-tana/ and variants
    (Calacoa), /-ñani/ (Sitajara). S: /-ñani/
    (Jopoqueri), /-ñani/ and /-tana/ and variants
    (Salinas, Morocomarca, Calacala).
1→2 future tense suffix -mama∽-:ma. N except
    La Paz: both allomorphs. S plus La Paz: /-:ma/
    only.
Desiderative and Remonstrator tense suffixes. N
    plus Calacoa and Morocomarca: preponderance of
    /sa/ forms, and /iri/ forms with /k(s)/ or
    /s(k)/. S (except Morocomarca) plus Sitajara:
    shared or very similar allomorphs of the two
    tenses, with a preponderance of /iri/ over /sa/
    forms; /iri/ forms have /j/, not /k/.
Final suffix -xa∽-: topic marker, attenuator, C:
    /-xa/ only. P: /-xa/ and /-:/ (vowel length);
    N: Juli; I: Sitajara, Calacoa; S: Salinas,
    Morocomarca). P: /-xa/ only (N: Socca; S:
    Jopoqueri).

Morphophonemics. Morphophonemics of 2→3 impera-
tive suffix -m[a]
Always requiring a preceding vowel. N: La Paz.  I:
  Calacoa, Sitajara.  S: Jopoqueri, Salinas.
Requiring a preceding consonant after /-ka-/ incom-
  pletive, otherwise a preceding vowel.  N: Juli,
  Socca, Huancané.  S: Morocomarca.

INTERPRETATION OF RESEARCH RESULTS
In the absence of archaeological or historical evidence concerning population movements and trade
routes or of a more complete knowledge of existing
Aymara dialects, interpretations of my data are
still tentative. The evidence of a division into
northern and southern dialects does not disprove
the theory advanced by Torero (1972) of a gradual
north to south expansion of Aymara, since such an
expansion might have taken place before the division occurred, but a simple southward expansion
does not explain the dialectal complexities revealed by the present study, such as 1) certain similar features in noncontiguous areas like Tarata,
Perú and Carangas, Bolivia, 2) features linking
peripheral and central dialects or crossing north-
south, center-periphery lines, or 3) features shared by certain Aymara dialects with contemporary
Jaqaru or surviving as apparent relics from earlier
times.
    These complexities may be linguistic reflections
of population movements associated with what Murra
(1968, 1972) calls the pan-Andean preoccupation
with controlling different ecological floors.  Po-

pulations speaking different dialects might have
been linked in one vertical archipelago, e.g., the
16th century Lupaca Aymara kingdom in Juli (Murra
1968). Present-day differences among the dialects
of Calacoa, Sitajara, and Juli may reflect distinctions existing in ancient times, with processes of
internal change accounting for certain idiosyncra-
tic allomorphs found in only one dialect.

On the other hand, similarities in noncontiguous
dialects may reflect descent from one community,
some of whose members moved away voluntarily or as
the result of conquest (Murra 1968). The fact that
today Aymara speakers in Tarata and Carangas are
apparently unaware that their dialects share certain unique features, and the nature of these similarities, suggest that any separation must have occurred long before the Spanish conquest.

Another explanation may account for some similarities among dialects distant from La Paz. Most of
the features that distinguish peripheral dialects
from those of La Paz are conservative in terms of
the latter. That is, peripheral features represent
a survival of forms or of morphophonemic processes
that La Paz probably once had but has now lost.
This hypothesis is supported by the existence in La
Paz Aymara of certain relics like Tayk.s Mariya
'Our Mother Mary', Na.nak.n Awki 'Our Father', and
s.ipna 'having said' which follow vowel-dropping
rules that do not normally occur in La Paz today.
The loss of such rules may be partly attributable
to Spanish influence, always stronger in the Bolivian capital and areas accessible to it than in re-

moter monolingual areas. La Paz dialects conform
more closely to Spanish sound patterning than do
the peripheral dialects.

Not all innovations fostered by La Paz can be
attributed to Spanish influence, however. An example of a usage that is on the way out because of
internal pressures within Aymara is the 4→3 future
allomorph /-tana/ (see above), which is homophonous
with allomorphs of two other verb tenses and has
been replaced by /-ñani/ in most dialects. It
should be noted that the types of changes emanating
from La Paz mainly affect phonology and lexicon,
relatively superficial levels of Aymara grammar.
Changes in linguistic postulates are rare, except
in the usages of missionaries, their followers, and
the patrón class.[5] The distinction of first and
fourth grammatical persons appears to be eroding in
some peripheral dialects but is still very strong
elsewhere, especially in La Paz.

That the dialects of La Paz should be influen-
cing others, rather than vice versa, is the logical
result of the economic, social, and political power
concentrated in and near the Bolivian capital and
the fact that the prestige of La Paz Aymara predis-
poses most Aymara speakers to adopt La Paz usages.
Although La Paz Aymara is taking in Spanish loanwords at an accelerating rate, speakers revert to
less Hispanicized usages when talking to monolinguals, and it appears that positive attitudes toward Aymara originating in La Paz (and, more recently, in Puno) may encourage a revival of Aymara lo-
calisms, thereby engendering a conservative coun-

ter-trend.   Certain  educated  Aymara  speakers  who
are  literate  in  both  Spanish  and  Aymara  are  now
articulating  their  cultural  heritage  and  seeking
out  its  guardians  in  order  to  reformulate  it  and
bring  it  to  public  attention.[6]

DIRECTIONS  FOR  FUTURE  RESEARCH
Future  research  into  Aymara  dialects  should  aim  toward  the  compilation  of  a  linguistic  atlas  for  the
entire  Aymara-speaking  area.   A  special  effort
should  be  made  to  obtain  more  data  from  monolinguals  and  to  determine  whether  monolingual  communities,  or  communities  bilingual  in  Quechua  and  Aymara  but  without  knowledge  of  Spanish,  exist.   To  do
this  will  require  the  training  of  more  field  workers  who  are  native  speakers  of  Aymara  and  Quechua.   In  addition  to  the  collection  of  field  data,
written  sources  in  libraries  and  private  collections  should  be  consulted  in  Bolivia,  Perú,  and
elsewhere.

Apart  from  continuation  of  the  kinds  of  investigation  undertaken  for  this  study,  additional  inquiry  might  be  made  into  matters  of  style  in  the  narrative,  oratory,  prayer,  and  poetry  and  the  uses  of
politeness,  irony,  and  metaphor.   Studies  of  the
speech  of  different  groups  (e.g.,  women,  men,  young
people,  the  elderly,  members  of  religious  sects),
of  bilingualism  and  multilingualism,  of  language
acquisition,  and  all  the  proliferating  subfields  of
contemporary  linguistics  may  also  be  undertaken.

Whether  or  not  such  studies  as  these  get  underway  in  the  foreseeable  future  depends  on  many  in-

terrelated factors, such as the priorities set by
governments and scholarly institutions, the extent
to which linguists participate in the setting of
such priorities, and most important, the interest
of Aymara speakers themselves in fostering the use
of Aymara as a vehicle of written literature and
education.

## ACKNOWLEDGEMENTS

This work originally appeared in Latinamericanist
12:1 (December 1976), a publication of the Center
for Latin American Studies of the University of
Florida. I gratefully acknowledge their kind permission to republish. In this version, the statis-
tics in the first paragraph have been updated.

My acceptance in the communities I visited was
largely the result of my preparation in field methods and in Aymara language and culture under
Professor Hardman and my two Aymara teachers, Yapita and Juana Vásquez, of La Paz, Bolivia. To
them and to the many other Aymara speakers who
helped me in the analysis go my deepest appreciation. I wish also to acknowledge grant support
from the National Science Foundation and the University of Florida and the facilitation afforded by
the Instituto Nacional de Investigación y Desarrollo de la Educación (INIDE) in Peru, and the
Instituto Nacional de Estudios Lingüísticos (INEL)
and the Instituto de Lengua and Cultura Aymara
(ILCA) in Bolivia.

NOTES

1.  The four grammatical persons of Aymara, which
    have neither number nor gender, may be transla-
    ted as follows:

$$
1p \left.\begin{array}{l} \text{'I} \\ \\ \text{'We} \end{array}\right\} \text{excluding you'}
$$

2p  'you'

3p  'he, she, they'

$$
4p \text{ 'you and } \left\{\begin{array}{l} \text{I'} \\ \\ \text{we'} \end{array}\right.
$$

2.  Phonological shapes of a few morphemes found in
    southern Aymara dialects are identical to those
    of morphemes in the Quechua spoken in the area,
    for example /-nti/ 'with', but such shared items
    are of minor significance, given the fact that
    similar shapes of the morphemes are pan-Andean
    (see Hardman, this volume).  The present evi-
    dence is that the Aymara spoken by Aymara-Que-
    chua bilinguals in areas where Quechua has the
    greater prestige (for example, in northern Poto-
    sí) remains remarkably free of Quechua admix-
    ture.

3.  Periods shown in Aymara examples indicate mor-
    pheme boundaries.

4. Aymara verb tense suffixes denote both the subject person and object person; hence, 2→3 means
'second person subject, third person object.'
5. In addition to the regional dialect features
discussed in this article, my research turned up
certain usages whereby speakers are identified
as being associated with missionaries and their
followers, or as talking like landowners (patrones). See Briggs 1981.
6. See, for example, the work of Juan de Dios Yapita, Juana Vásquez, Felix Layme, and others in
Bolivia, and of Domingo and Justino Llanque Chana in Peru.

REFERENCES
Bertonio, Ludovico. 1603. Arte y grammatica muy
copiosa de la lengua aymara. Rome: Luis Zan-
netti.
Briggs, Lucy T. 1981. Missionary, patrón, and radio Aymara. In The Aymara language in its social and cultural context, M.J. Hardman, ed.
Gainesville: University Presses of Florida.
------. 1983. Bilingual education in Bolivia. In
Bilingualism: Social issues and policy implications, Andrew W. Miracle, Jr., ed. Athens,
Georgia: The University of Georgia Press.
------. (in press) Bilingual education in Peru
and Bolivia. In Language of inequality, Nes-
sa Wolfson and Joan Manes, eds. The Hague:
Mouton.
Hardman, M.J. 1972. Postulados lingüísticos del
idioma aymara. In El reto del multilingüismo en

el Perú, Alberto Escobar, ed. Lima: Instituto de Estudios Peruanos.

------. 1975. Proto-jaqi: Reconstrucción del sistema de personas gramaticales. Lima: Revista del Museo Nacional 41. 433-456.

Hardman, M.J., Juana Vásquez, and Juan de Dios Yapita, with Laura Martin-Barber, Lucy Therina Briggs, and Nora Clearman England. 1975. Aymar ar yatiqañataki, 2nd ed., 3 vols. Ann Arbor: University Microfilms International.

Martínez Soto-Aguilar, Gabriel. 1981. Los Aymaras chilenos. Acerca de la historia y el universo aymara. Lima: Centro de Información, Estudios y Documentación.

Murra, John V. 1968. An Aymara kingdom in 1567. Ethnohistory 15: 115-151.

------. 1970. Current research and prospects in Andean ethnohistory. Latin American Research Review 5.3-36.

------. 1972. El 'control vertical' de un máximo de pisos ecológicos en la economía de las sociedades andinas. Visita de la provincia de León de Huanuco (1562), Iñigo Ortiz de Zuñiga, visitador, vol. 2. Huanuco, Peru: Universidad Hermilio Valdizan.

República del Perú. Oficina Nacional de Estadística y Censos. 1974. Censos Nacionales VII de Población, II de Vivienda, 4 de junio de 1972.

Torero, Alfredo. 1972. Lingüística e historia de los Andes del Perú y Bolivia. In El reto del multilingüismo en el Peru, Alberto Escobar, ed. Lima: Instituto de Estudios Peruanos.

U.S.   Department of State.   1983.   Background notes
    [on] Bolivia.   Washington D.C.   October.

# 16. Aymara and Quechua: Languages in Contact

## M. J. Hardman

When the Spaniards conquered Peru -- the Great Peru
which was the Inca Empire extending from Pasto in
Colombia to Argentina and from the Pacific Ocean to
the borders of the Amazon jungle, they were met
with innumerable languages -- the chroniclers comment again and again that "every town has its language". It was, however, usually possible to get
along with the "general language" of the Incas, if
not with the people themselves, then at least with
the governors and priests. This language came to
be called Quechua, which means "of the temperate
valleys". This term, in time, applied to all members of the Quechua family, including those very
distinct from each other and from the Cuzco variety, such as those of Huancayo and Ecuador, although
these varieties were not originally included in the
meaning of "lengua general".

As commonly happens in human history, political
forces resulted in conferring prestige on one particular form of language fortuitously linked with
military and/or political power. Thus the Quechua
of Cuzco came to be held to be the "most pure",
"most ancient", "most correct", "most expressive"
form of Quechua, and indeed, "mother of all languages" (of the Andes) simply by having been, at the
moment of the arrival of the Spaniards, the language the Incas were using for conquest purposes. To

complete the irony, the Spaniards continued using
this language for the same purpose, but it was now
the European conquest that spread the Imperial Language of the Incas. The Quechua language under the
aegis of the Spaniards spread further than had ever
been the case under the Incas, and in the process
caused the disappearance of numerous languages spoken by small groups. The particular form of Quechua that was spread (after some initial play with
the Chinchay variety) was Cuzco Quechua.

The beliefs about the relative purity, age, ele-
gance, etc., of Cuzco Quechua were, of course, political fictions with no basis in linguistic reality.[1] Rather, by becoming a language of conquest,
it was more exposed to outside influences, and,
upon being adopted by peoples with another mother
tongue, it would inevitably suffer even further
innovations through interference. Cuzco Quechua
shows strong evidence of precisely these processes:
within the Quechua linguistic family it is the most
innovative and shows the largest number of adaptations traceable to influences of other languages
(Torero 1975).

The political position of Cuzco Quechua has led
to endless speculation concerning its relationship
to the other languages of the Andes. Of particular
interest for political reasons, is the relationship
of Quechua to the Aymara language.[2] The same political interplay which led to the spread of Cuzco
Quechua left the Aymara language in the shadows,
leading the majority of the people who have written
about Aymara, and the populace in general, to con-

sider it some sort of derivative of Quechua. Although Cuzco Quechua is, indeed, the member of its
family most influenced by Aymara, and Aymara in its
turn, is the member of its family most influenced
by Quechua, they are not, as we will show here, related in the linguistic sense. Contrary to many
proposals of common origin, Aymara and Quechua
could not have derived from a single mother tongue,
certainly not within the last 50,000 years and not
in the Andes.

     Since the issue of contact vs. common origin is
not an issue to be taken lightly, we will first argue against the proposals of common origin and then
argue for the significance of language contact.

     The authors most known in the linguistic world
for the proposal of common origin are Orr and Longacre (1968). I contend here, as I have done elsewhere (Hardman 1966b, 1978a, 1979) that inadequate
data, poorly collected and insufficiently analyzed
has led these authors to a faulty conclusion. For
example, the data chosen for comparison by Orr and
Longacre came precisely from Cuzco Quechua and Aymara, with little regard for other Quechua languages and no data at all from the sister languages of
Aymara. This should not have occurred because Torero (1964) had already published materials relevant to Quechua, and Hardman (1966a) had already
published a grammar of Jaqaru. Unpublished materials were also offered, but rejected by the authors as not useful.[3]

     The article of Orr and Longacre and its hypothe-
sis of the proto-language *Quechuamaran is based on

a list of 531 words of which 253 are presumed Que-
chua/Aymara cognates, that is 47 percent. This figure presumes the separation of the languages in
the Andes where they are still spoken even today
and where, during the entire period, they have lived in continuous interaction. This 47 percent
comes from a list chosen purposely to include as
many cognates as possible for these two languages
living side by side or even, in some places, together. It is very difficult to believe so small a
percentage for two languages descended from the
same mother tongue differentiating in the very area
where they are still spoken. Language change does
not work that way in any normal circumstances.

Even more critically, of the 253 that are clai-
med to be cognates, 25 percent (63 items) must be
eliminated from consideration because they are either non-existent forms, incorrectly stated forms,
or complex forms poorly analyzed. Thus there remain 190 forms where there would appear to be some
genuine similarity between Aymara and Quechua -- 35
percent of the original list.

Of these 190 words, 46 percent have a phonological structure that points to borrowing from Jaqi
into Quechua rather than historical correspondence. This high percentage should have been an a-
lert signal for consideration of borrowing. Twen-
ty-six percent are pan-Andean words, some of which
also occur even in jungle languages, and thus do
not really serve to prove anything one way or the
other at this point, but could be used as evidence
of widespread trade. Twenty percent are terms sha-

red only by Cuzco Quechua and Aymara, that is, they
are characteristic of the Southern Andes, rather
than of the respective language families, and,
again, would seem to point to cultural interaction
accompanied by linguistic borrowing rather than
language divergence. Five percent are clearly borrowings from Quechua to Aymara, mostly fairly recent ones. Thus we have a remainder of two percent, that is, four items, which could indeed be
put forth as "proof" of the common genetic origin
of Quechua and Aymara. For that percentage one
could as easily invoke chance correspondence.

For languages that have a very long history of
mutual contact and cultural interaction, it is to
be expected that there would exist some sets of
adapted borrowings which would mimic sound correspondence sets, probably going both ways, e.g.,
-ceive in English and -bol in Spanish from Romance
and English respectively. Simple sound correspondences in especially selected sets, even if well
done, cannot be used in these cases to prove common
origin -- only mutual influence. Overall structure
and patterning, phonological and grammatical, must
also be brought to bear, as Rask (1932-5) pointed
out long ago.

The major point of debate is, and always has
been, the question of aspiration and glottalization
of the occlusive consonants. Aymara and Cuzco Quechua do indeed have the same phonemic inventory,
that is, five occlusive consonants in three series,
simple, aspirate, and glottal.[4]

```
p      t      ch     k      q

p"     t"     ch"    k"     q"

p'     t'     ch'    k'     q'
```

This system does not occur in the other Quechua languages (Torero 1972, 1975; Carpenter 1982) with the exception of the Ayacucho-Cuzco and Cuzco-Collao varieties.  The Quechua of Ayacucho-Chanca, for example, is almost like that of Cuzco, but without aspiration and glottalization.  Even within Cuzco Quechua the functional load of aspiration and glottalization is very light.  The result is that, in spite of being <u>the</u> distinguishing feature of Cuzco Quechua, there are very few, if any, sentences which are distinguished only by aspiration and glottalization.  There are, furthermore, extreme phonological limitations in terms of permitted environments:

1) they may only occur in roots, never in suffixes;
2) they always occur on the first occlusive consonant of the word;
3) they never occur more than one to a word (with some exceptions of reduplicative onomatopoeia) as if one of these very strange sounds were enough to mark the word itself.

In the other Quechua languages <u>ch</u> functions rather as part of the sibilant and/or fricative systems, not as part of the occlusive system (Torero

1975), and the occlusive system is limited to p̲
t̲ k̲ (q̲).

The Aymara system, although with the same inventory, is nevertheless very different.  None of the
noted restrictions apply.  Aspiration and glottalization occur in suffixes and roots alike and may
occur on any occlusive in the word -- there is no
theoretical limit on the number, selection or order
in any given word.  Note the following Aymara forms
from Suqa, Peru:

taq"aña            'to look for'

taq"t'aña          'to look for once'

taq"t't"a          'I just look for (x)'

This aspect of Jaqi structure is even more evident in the consonantally conservative sister languages of Jaqaru and Kawki.  The occlusive inventory for these languages is:[5]

p     t     tx    tz    ch    cx    k     q

p"    t"    tx"   tz"   ch"   cx"   k"    q"

p'    t'    tx'   tz'   ch'   cx'   k'    q'

Examples of multiple occurrences of glottalization and aspiration in both roots and words are
frequent, e.g.

q"acx"a                       'grumpy'

tx"ap"a                       'blind'

q'aq'a                        'throw in a blanket'

sijcx'k"q"kt"rk"a             'I tear paper again'

ach't'q"asp"a                 'it would be nice to
                              add a bit of earth
                              (to a mound)'

jayt'awq"t"sk"a               'I left it again'

In spite of the identical inventory, it should
now be clear that the phonological systems of Cuzco
Quechua and Aymara are not the same. It is my thesis that the glottalization and aspiration that today mark Cuzco Quechua came first through massive
borrowings from (proto-)Jaqi and more recently from
Aymara itself (Hardman 1964a,b). The distributional information already presented is direct evidence of this. Additional confirming data may be
seen in Stark (1975) where she shows that, dealing
with words with aspiration and glottalization there
is a 67 percent similarity rate between Aymara and
Cuzco Quechua; the rate for words without these
features is only 20 percent. Furthermore, of the
apparently non-similar words left, 22 percent of
those with aspiration and glottalization were judged by native speakers to be onomatopoetic, but
only two percent of those without were so judged.

Thus, in forms with glottalization and aspiration, only 11 percent appear not to be similar, while in all other forms the non-similar rate is 78 per-cent.[6]

Thus, the data would lead to the conclusion that Jaqi is primarily responsible for glottalization and aspiration in Cuzco Quechua. Once such a fea-ture is borrowed into a language, of course, these new phonological elements may extend beyond borro-wed words -- in this case primarily into the realm of onomatopoeia.

An additional criticism which needs to be remar-ked on relative to all of the various lists used to prove the common origin hypothesis, is that the items selected are <u>not</u> what are usually conside-red to be the 'basic' terms, in e.g. the way Swa-desh used the concept. Basic terms split quite clearly on family grounds. For example, the num-bers 1 and 2 are not cognate, although higher num-bers sometimes appear to be; also 'black' and 'white' show no similarity, although some of the other colors sometimes do -- both circumstances re-flect quite clearly market interchange. The num-bers especially tend to be pan-Andean and colors are much influenced by dyes, among other exchange patterns.

The specific form that a borrowing takes may permit us to establish the period in which it was borrowed: for example, the Aymara word <u>iwisa</u> 'sheep' was borrowed from Spanish while the Spanish language still had <u>sh</u> where today it has <u>j</u>. At times one hears <u>uwija</u>, which shows a reborrowing from a more modern period. Another example of the same type is from Jaqaru, <u>shupuna</u> 'jacket' from when the Spanish still used <u>jubones</u>, cognate with modern French <u>jupe</u> 'skirt', and also before the consonant shift, that is, during approximately the first century after the conquest. This last example makes us appreciate another possibility -- that a borrowing can remain alive in the language that does the borrowing and die out in the language that does the lending. Another example of that is <u>parlar</u> which is no longer a Spanish word but which was borrowed into Aymara and continues in regular use in that language today as <u>parlaña</u> 'to talk'.

In the above argumentation, I have shown that the evidence produced to support the hypothesis of common origin for Quechua and Aymara is faulty and that adequate proof for the hypothesis is not available. I have also indicated that a far more likely explanation for the strong similarities, which in some respects do exist between the two languages, is the long and persistent linguistic and cultural contact.

I would like to propose a possible linguistic history of the Andes, as a speculation that would incorporate the linguistic evidence as it currently stands without in any way contradicting the archaeological, indeed incorporating it in many respects. The following outline owes a great deal to the work of Alfredo Torero (1964, 1968, 1972, 1975).

The original language of the Tiwanaku builders was most likely Puquina, but this was not the lan-

guage used for commercial expansion. The lingua
franca of the Tiwanaku-Wari expansion period was
that of proto-Jaqi. Toponymics, among other evidence, support this hypothesis. When the founders
of Tiwanaku crossed Lake Titicaca and settled in
Cuzco, it may be presumed that they brought their
home language with them -- certainly Cuzco itself
was trilingual at the time of the conquest. When
these people, by then known as the Incas, began
their own expansion, they reserved the Puquina language for the royal family only (i.e. the original
conquering group) and used the readily available
lingua franca, Jaqi, for expansionist purposes, until they met up with the powerful Pachacamac expansion. One might recall the great honors paid the
Lord of Pachacamac even at Cajamarca. The people
of Pachacamac were Quechua speaking, of the Chinchay variety, and dominated the coastal area
through domination of the sea. They had apparently
already expanded as far as Ecuador as much as a
half millennium earlier (Carpenter 1982). Thus,
apparently, it seemed to be to the advantage of the
Incas to switch the lingua franca. (Also, Wayna
Capac was in love with a woman from Pachacamac, be
it noted.) Politically, such a switch was possible
to legislate -- the court had no great personal loyalty to any conquest language per se. It might be
remembered that the Spanish repeated, or carried
on, the same pattern in expanding the use of Quechua themselves, to which they certainly felt no
loyalty. Thus, only some 100 years before the European conquest, the Cuzco administrator adopted a

new language. This reconstruction of events would clearly explain the enormous similarities between Aymara and Cuzco Quechua -- the entire Inca court would for a while be trilingual and all administrators drawn from conquered peoples minimally bilingual -- a situation designed for ready language interference, as well as for the convergence that is common when languages even of different families live long in interactive situations, as has also happened, e.g. in India (Emeneau 1964).

The double expansion of the Inca and the Chinchay Quechua left the Jaqi languages isolated and fragmented, particularly those closest to the Chinchay, in what is today the Department of Lima. But the remnants of the intensive and extensive contacts are still evident in the multiple borrowings.

From Jaqi to Quechua I propose two waves of massive borrowing: 1) during the commercial and cultural dominance of Wari, from proto-Jaqi specifically, during a period approximately 1500 to 1000 years ago; 2) during the first years of Inca expansion, while Jaqi was the official language; these borrowings would then have been from the language that is today Aymara, already separated from the sister languages closer to the coast. These borrowings would have been considerably later, for example, 400 to 700 years ago.

The major wave of borrowing from Quechua into Jaqi would have come from the last years of the Empire, from the extensive use of Quechua during the virreinato, and even continuing through to today, sometimes via Spanish.

Reconstruction of the proto-Jaqi languages has led us to postulate an occlusive system no less complex than that of Jaqaru today, although doubt-[7]less differing in phonetic details. The largest difference between the system of Jaqaru/Kawki and that of Aymara is that the latter lacks the occlusive series t x  t z  c x. The modern reflexes of these are t  ch  t respectively. The result is that the modern t of Aymara comes from three sources, *tx, *cx, or *t. For example,

| Jaqaru: | shutxi | qucxa | katu |
| Aymara: | suti | quta | katu- |
| | 'name' | 'lake' | 'grab' |

The modern Aymara ch comes from two sources, *tz or *ch.

| Jaqaru: | tz'iqa | ichu |
| Aymara: | ch'iqa | ichu- |
| | 'left (hand)' | 'carry something rather heavy without a handle' |

Therefore, words with t or ch only in the modern languages do not directly give us evidence of whether they originated in the Jaqi or the Quechua family. However, when glottalization or aspiration is present, it is clearly strong evidence that these terms originated in the Jaqi languages, and that they arrived into Quechua from Jaqi. The actual shape of the words in Quechua today can indicate the approximate period of the borrowing. So, for example, the commercial expansion of Wari is[8] reflected in the borrowings of numerals.

| Jaqaru: | cxunhka | pacxaka |
|---------|---------|---------|
| Aymara: | tunka | pataka |
| Quechua: | chunka | pachak |
| | '10' | '100' |

Quechua has <u>ch</u> where proto-Jaqi had *cx, which is just what would be expected of those which had no <u>cx</u> as part of their occlusive system and thus did not hear the distinction. Even today, <u>cx</u> in modern Jaqaru words is perceived by Quechua speakers as <u>ch</u>. Other words of this early period show the same adaptation, for example:

| Jaqaru: | qucxa |
|---------|-------|
| Aymara: | quta |
| Quechua: | qucha |
| | 'lake'[9] |

In the later period -- and to a lesser extent than the first wave, during the direct impingement of Aymara on the early Incas -- there are direct borrowings from Aymara, when Aymara had already experienced the change from *cx to t. Thus, upon borrowing a form, Quechua borrowed it with t, and Quechua has t in those items today, for example:

| Jaqaru:  | jamp'acxa | k"icx"i |
|----------|-----------|---------|
| Aymara:  | jamp'atu  | k"it"u [10] |
| Quechua: | jamp'atu  | k"itu |
|          | 'frog'    | 'scrape, e.g., wood' |

To complete the picture, during the modern period we have the third wave, with Southern Quechua returning to Aymara words from the early period, with the *cx (re)borrowing resulting in ch, without, of course, any consequence being felt by the northern languages, for example:

| Jaqaru:  | ancxacxi | micx'a  | qincxa  |
|----------|----------|---------|---------|
| Aymara:  | ancha    | mich'a  | qincha  |
| Quechua: | ancha    | mich'a  | qincha  |
|          | 'much'   | 'miser' | 'fence' |

Thus from the history of one sound we can glimpse the history of a region.  The process can be seen also with *tx, where Quechua took <u>ch</u> in the first wave, but Aymara continued its own way in the development of <u>t</u>; later borrowings from Aymara went into Quechua with <u>t</u>.  An example of the first is:

| | |
|---|---|
| Jaqaru: | yatxi |
| Aymara: | yati |
| Quechua: | yacha |
| | 'to know' |

and of the second:

| | | |
|---|---|---|
| Jaqaru | shutxi | tx'impu |
| Aymara: | suti | t'impu |
| Quechua: | suti | t'impu |
| | 'name' | 'boil' |

Some words, of course, have their own individually unique history.  Let us look at:

| | |
|---|---|
| Kawki: | intxi |
| Jaqaru: | inti |
| Aymara: | inti |
| Quechua: | inti |
| | 'sun (astral body only)' |

Given the evidence of Kawki, we would be led to postulate a Jaqi origin for this word which is so identified with the Inca empire.  The <u>t</u> in Jaqaru does not fit regular sound change; let us look at the socio-cultural situations. Kawki is the most consonantly conservative of the Jaqi languages. In contrast, of the two, Jaqaru is the most innovative. Furthermore, Tupe, where Jaqaru is spoken, was for a long period, lasting up to about 25 years ago, the cultural center of the area. Early in this century Tupe had a most distinguished educational center and peoples from all around, including Quechua and Spanish speakers as well as Jaqi speakers, went to school in Tupe on a boarding basis. Inti is a common word in Peruvian schoolbooks. It is, actually, used more in the schoolroom than in common conversation, which is more concerned with sunlight and warmth (nup'i in Jaqaru) than the star itself. Thus, inti in Jaqaru appears to be a reborrowing from Quechua through Spanish back into a Jaqi language. The same did not occur in Kawki because there was no schooling while the language was still the dominant language for the children.

These examples show the impact of socio-economic and historical factors on languages as well as the dangers of proposing genetic relationships between somewhat similar languages without giving importance to either the grammatical structure or the cultural situation. As is now clear, after two millennia of intimate contact, massive borrowing was inevitable. Making lists of correspondences in these cases is not a viable method of establishing common language origin without a concomitant recourse to the grammar.

Both language families are suffixing languages; however, since suffixation is the most common morphological process in language, the above constitutes a typological statement, not a comparative one. There is a major difference in the way suffixation is handled in the two languages. Quechua suffixes are loosely tacked on, easily peeled off, in the manner that has been called 'agglutinating'. Morphophonemic rules are almost non-existent -- for most of the Quechua languages one rule only suffices. In other words, morphological structure is transparent.

The Jaqi languages, on the other hand, are of the type that has been called 'inflective'; the suffixes are complex, there is a great deal of complex morphophonemic modification and suffixes are certainly not easily separable from each other. As one example, the form <u>mamshqa</u> 'with our mother' from Jaqaru <u>mama</u> 'mother' plus <u>-sa</u> 'fourth person possessive' plus <u>-wshqa</u> 'subject coordinate' requires a number of complex morphophonemic rules involving both morphological and phonological conditioning to account for the surface form. Quechua has nothing like this type of morphophonemics anywhere.

The Jaqi languages are based on a system of four persons, without number mark, where the distinctive features are presence or absence of first/second person. The proto-forms as currently reconstructed are:

```
*naya        first person 'I, we, but not you'

*juma        second person 'you'

*jup"a       third person 'she, they, he;
             neither you nor I, but human'
*jiwasa      fourth person, 'we, you and I'
```

This system is reflected throughout the grammar, noun and verb systems alike (Hardman 1975a,b,c).

```
Jaqaru       Aymara
utnha        utaxa        'our/my house, but not
                          yours'
utma         utma         'your house'

utp"a        utapa        'her, their, his house'

utsa         utasa        'our house, yours and
                          mine'
```

Quechua, on the other hand, works with a system of three persons with (usually) number mark. Cuzco Quechua (but not all Quechua languages) has two plural suffixes which allow the language to mark the distinction between inclusive and exclusive.

```
ñuqa     'I'              ñuqayku    'we, not
                                      you'
qan      'you (sg.)'      ñuqanchis  'we, with
                                      you'
pay      'she, he'
```

In Ecuador and some other places this contrast
is nonexistent.  This is evidence of convergence --
when a distinction so important to one's neighbors
that it cannot be ignored is finally incorporated
into one's own system (Hardman 1972; 1978a,b; 1983
a,b).  Thus Quechua speakers came to be able to
translate what they understand to be the distinction between Jaqi first and fourth persons, and, in
Cuzco Quechua at least, it now forms part of that
system.

The verbal person systems in each language family are congruent with the nominal person systems.
In the case of Jaqi the basic four person system is
developed into a verbal person system such that
each suffix which marks person is interactive --
that is, subject and object are merged into the
single inflective suffix, giving a paradigm of ten
inflected persons in Jaqaru and Kawki and nine in
Aymara.  In the case of Quechua, in contrast -- in
Cuzco at least -- the system is one of three persons and two numbers, allowing for the two-way contrast in first person plural for a total of seven
persons, no objects included.  Other varieties of
Quechua have fewer persons, in some cases with little or no number (Carpenter 1982). In Quechua there
are a few suffixes which may refer to objects and
which may be included within the verb, but they are
primarily extensions of directional suffixes and
occupy a rather different position within the
overall structure.

At the syntactic level, an important point of
distinction is that within the Jaqi languages the

sentence is defined through the use of a particular
set of suffixes which we call sentence suffixes.
There are some signs of this type of system within
Cuzco Quechua, but without the obligatoriness and
pervasiveness characteristic of the Jaqi system,
nor does this use constitute the definition of the
sentence within Quechua.

In summary, taking careful consideration of a
body of data, including grammatical and phonological structure as well as correspondence lists, together with socio-cultural history and circumstances, the only viable conclusion is that there are,
indeed, at least two great language families extant
in the Andes: Jaqi and Quechua. The apparent similarities between the languages of these two families are best explained by mutual borrowings and
influences, which are easily accounted for by the
type and extent of contact that has occurred
through the centuries. It is therefore impossible
to maintain any vestige of the notion of a common
origin with differentiation in the Andes, and even
more absurd to hold that Cuzco Quechua be considered a relatively conservative language. Rather,
Aymara and Quechua can be for us an example of the
innovations and adaptations that can and do occur
when languages and cultures meet.

NOTES

1.  Also see Mannheim's "Contact and Quechua-Exter-
    nal Genetic Relationships" in this volume.
2.  The Aymara language is a member of the Jaqi fa-
    mily of languages: Aymara, spoken today by up-

wards of three million people including one-
third of the population of Bolivia, a large portion of the population of southern Peru, and in
northern Chile and Argentina; Jaqaru, spoken by
approximately five thousand in Tupe, Yauyos, and
in immigrant communities in the cities of Huancayo, Chincha, Cañete, Lima, Peru; and Kawki, a
dying language with a few speakers left in Cachuy, Peru.

3.  Curiously enough, a recent dissertation (Davidson 1977) manages to <u>disprove</u> the Longacre/Orr
hypothesis using, by claim of the author, only
Cuzco Quechua and Aymara. Davidson's conclusion
corroborates mine, but is not genuinely independent, although the author believes it to be so,
and his work was unknown to me at the time he
was doing it. The grammars on which he based
his work were: 1) the Aymara grammar done at the
University of Florida (Hardman, Yapita, & Vásquez 1975); 2) my Jaqaru grammar (Hardman 1966a
[1983a]); 3) the Cuzco Quechua grammar on which
I was working when I first came to the conclusion that Jaqaru and Cuzco Quechua were not related (Sola and Cusihuaman 1967).

4.  All examples from the Andean languages are presented in the practical (phonemic) alphabets.
The Aymara alphabet was developed by a linguist
native speaker of Aymara (Yapita 1981). For further details on this alphabet see the two articles by Briggs in this volume.

|     |     |      |     |      |
|-----|-----|------|-----|------|
| p   | t   | c h  | k   | q    |
| p " | t " | c h "| k " | q "  |
| p ' | t ' | c h '| k ' | q '  |
| m   | n   | ñ    |     |      |
|     | l   | l l  |     |      |
|     | s   |      | j   | x    |
| w   | r   | y    |     |      |
|     |     |      |     |      |
| a   |     | i    |     | u    |
| ̈a  |     | ̈i   |     | ̈u   |

c̲h̲, alveopalatal fricative, functions structurally as a stop.

The k̲ series is velar; the q̲ series is post-velar.

Aspiration is represented by "; glottalization by '.

j̲ represents a pharyngeal fricative; x̲ a post-velar
   fricative.

The rest of the letters have the conventional values
   of English and/or Spanish.

5.  For Jaqaru and Kawki the Aymara alphabet is
   compatible, except that x̲ does not function as
   a separate letter and there are no long vowels
   (Hardman 1983b). The following characters are
   added for consonants not present in Aymara:

|      |      |      |
|------|------|------|
| t x  | t z  | c x  |
| t x "| t z "| c x "|
| t x '| t z '| c x '|
|      |      | n h  |
|      |      | s h  |
| `a  | `i  | `u  |

tx represents an alveopalatal stop; tz a pre-
palatal affricate; cx a palatal retroflex
stop/affricate. All function within the same
stop/affricate series as the five set in Aymara.
nh represents a velar nasal.
sh represents a palatal sibilant.
\ represents short vowels.
Because Cuzco Quechua phonology is so similar to
    that of Aymara, it is possible to present exam-
    ples with the compatible Aymara alphabet.
6.   If we take into account also the Jaqaru/Kawki
    data, the number of items with glottalization/
    aspiration with no similar form in Jaqi is redu-
    ced - apparently Aymara lost some of the forms
    after "loaning" them to Quechua.
7.   Part of the reconstruction work has been repor-
    ted in Hardman (1975b). Work continues on the
    reconstruction of proto-Jaqi; with primacy given
    to the reconstruction of grammatical paradigms.
    Lists of general vocabulary correspondences have
    not yet been published.
8.   The most common morphophonemic variation in the
    Jaqi languages is vowel dropping; in any syntac-
    tic position and in any complex number, '100'
    would occur without the final vowel. Quechua
    permits final consonants, and therefore would be
    expected to borrow the word without the final
    vowel given that they would most certainly rare-
    ly if ever have heard the word uttered with the
    final vowel.
9.   This borrowing may reflect the fact that the
    Jaqi languages were mountain languages, where

the lakes are, while Quechua was clearly a coastal one.

10. There is a process of aspiration loss in Aymara, so that the form k"itu 'scrape' is also attested in some areas.


REFERENCES

Carpenter, Lawrence K.  1982.  Ecuadorian Quichua:
    Descriptive Sketch and Variation.  Doctoral
    Dissertation, University of Gainesville.

Davidson, Joseph Orville, Jr.  1977.  A Contrastive
    Study of the Grammatical Structures of Aymara
    and Cuzco Kechua.  Doctoral Dissertation,
    University of California, Berkeley.

Emeneau, Murray B.  1964.  India as a linguistic
    area.  In Language in Culture and Society,
    Dell Hymes, ed., pp. 642-653.  New York:
    Harper and Row.

Escobar, Alberto (ed.).  1972.  Reto del Multi-
    lingüismo en el Peru.  Lima: Institute de Estu-
    dios Peruanos.

Hardman, M.J.  1964a.  Sistema fonémico del jaqa-
    ru.  Revista del Museo Nacional.  Tomo XXXII.
    Lima, Peru.

------.  1964b.  Discussion of paper by Lanham.
    p. 690.  Proceedings of the Ninth International
    Congress of Linguists.  The Hague: Mouton.

------.  1966a.  Jaqaru: Outline of Phonological
    and Morphological Structure.  The Hague: Mouton.

------.  1966b.  El Jaqaru, el Kawki, y el Aymara.
    Primer Congreso Interamericano de Lingüística.
    Montevideo, Uruguay, January 1966.

------. 1972. Postulado lingüístico del idioma
aymara. In Reto del Multilinguismo en el Peru,
Alberto Escobar, ed. Lima: Instituto de Estudios Peruanos.

------. 1975a. El Jaqaru, el Kawki, y el Aymara.
Simposio de Montevideo. Mexico: PILEI.

------. 1975b. Reconstrucción del sistema personal verbal de Proto-Jaqi. Revista del Museo
Nacional. Tomo XLI.

------. 1975c. La familia lingüística Jaqi. Revista Yauyos. Vol. 4, Nos. 15-16, 17 (Aug-
Sept-Oct 1975 and Jan-Feb 1976).

------. 1978a. Jaqi: the linguistic family. International Journal of American Linguistics.
44.2 (April), 146-153.

------. 1978b. Linguistic postulates and applied
anthropological linguistics. In Papers on Linguistics and Child Language, V. Honsa and M.J.
Hardman-de-Bautista, eds. The Hague: Mouton.

------. 1979. Quechua y Aymara: lenguas en contacto. Antropologia 1.1, 69-84. La Paz: Instituto Nacional de Antropologia.

------. 1983a. Jaqaru: Compendio de Estructura
Fonologica y Morfologica. Lima: Instituto de
Estudios Peruanos/Instituto Indigenista Inter-
americano.

------. 1983b. Jaqaru short vowel. IJAL 49:203.

Hardman, M.J., Juan de Dios Yapita Moya, and Juana
Vásquez. 1975. Aymar ar Yatiqañataki. (Three
volumes). Gainesville: University of Florida.

Orr, Caroline and William A. Longacre. 1968.
Proto-Quechumaran. Language 44:528-555.

Rask, Rasmus. 1932-5. Udvalgte Afhandlinger, Louis Hjelmslev, ed. Three volumes. Copenhagen: Levin & Munksgaard.

Sola, Donald F. and Antonio Cusihuaman G. 1967. The Structure of Cuzco Kechua. Ithaca: Cornell University Quechua Language Materials Project.

Stark, Louisa R. 1975. A Reconsideration of Proto-Quechua phonology. In Linguistica e Indigenismo en America. Lima: Instituto de Estudios Peruanos.

Torero, Alfredo. 1964. Los dialectos quechuas. Anales Cientificos de la Universidad Nacional Agraria. Vol. 11, No. 4. Lima.

------. 1968. Procedencia geográfica de los dialectos quechuas de Ferrenafe y Cajamarca. Anales Cientificos de la Universidad Nacional Agraria. Vol. VI, No. 3-4. Lima.

------. 1972. Lingüística e historia de la sociedad andina. In Reto del Multilinguismo en el Peru Alberto Escobar, ed. Lima: Instituto de Estudios Peruanos.

------. 1975. Quechua y la Historia Social de la Region Andina. Lima: Universidad Ricardo Palma.

Valcarcel, Luis E. 1964. Historia del Peru Antiguo (3 tomos). Lima: Editorial Juan Mejia Baca.

Yapita Moya, Juan de Dios. 1981. The Aymara alphabet: linguistics for indigenous communities. In The Aymara Language in its Social and Cultural Context, M.J. Hardman, ed. Gainesville: University of Florida Press.

# 17. Contact and Quechua-External Genetic Relationships

## Bruce Mannheim

INTRODUCTION

Over the years numerous genetic relationships have
been suggested involving Quechuan languages, most
often Southern Peruvian Quechua. Once we pass the
neogrammarian watershed of the late nineteenth century, really the first point at which we can, in
contemporary terms, speak of a 'proof' of genetic
relationship, it becomes clear that the inclination
to proclaim exogamous genetic relationships is inversely related to the extent to which the author
is willing to stake such a claim on systematic comparison of morphology and lexicon and postulation
of sound correspondences, which is to say the extent to which it is being posited in an explicit
and falsifiable way. The criteria for a genetic
relationship are quite strict. In effect, a proof
requires the reconstruction of a parent language
and a set of falsifiable hypotheses about the evolution of each of the daughter languages, including
the postulation of sound laws, morphological and
restructuring processes (Kuryłowicz, 1973), and
lexical and grammatical etymologies. None of the
set is conceivable without the others and all are
indispensable parts of the whole, prospective reconstruction (Saussure, 1971 [1915]: 291ff.). And

mere resemblances between lexicon do not approximate any of the set.

Inclination to proclaim an exogamous genetic relationship also varies inversely with the degree to which the internal diversity in the Quechua family is understood. Recognition of the multiformity of the Quechuan languages and focus of attention on reconstruction of the process of diversification is recent. That reorientation, less than two decades old, is probably the signal accomplishment of the growth of interest in Quechuan linguistics in this period. Only a small portion of its potential, especially the portent of contribution to theoretical work on the processes of morpho-syntactic restructuring, has yet been realized. The considerable time-depth involved should likewise prove of importance to culture historians, particularly as detailed knowledge of the processes of phonological and morpho-syntactic change permits reconstruction of the lexicon. The reorientation should put a brake on efforts to 'show' genetic affiliation based on evidence from one language in the family only (usually Southern Peruvian Quechua) or one branch only (Peripheral), or based on forms taken indiscriminately from among the Quechuan languages or even - as has been the case in the more long distance hypotheses - indiscriminately from Quechua and a neighboring language family, Jaqi (Harrington, 1943; Swadesh, 1969).

The most persistent allegations of genetic relationship have of course been with Aymara, a language which borders on Southern Peruvian Quechua. Ay-

mara has now been shown with considerable certainty
to be a member of the more inclusive Jaqi family,
along with the two non-adjacent Peruvian languages,
Jaqaru and Kawki (Hardman-de-Bautista, 1966b, 1976,
1978). Likewise, from the Quechua side, the claims
most always have drawn evidence from the Southern
Peruvian and Bolivian languages, precisely those
which have been in closest contact with Jaqi languages. This article evaluates the extent to which
such allegations of a genetic relationship are war-
ranted, examines ideographic historical evidence
which permits more careful forming of the rival
contact hypothesis and suggests that there is good
linguistic evidence which actually precludes the
genetic hypothesis. (A complementary evaluation of
the problem by Hardman-de-Bautista appears elsewhere in this volume.)

QUECHUA AND AYMARA, GENETIC VERSUS AREAL
Bernabe Cobo struck a theme in 1653 when he wrote
that,

> the two languages, Quechua and Aymara
> ... belonging to two neighboring and co-
> terminous peoples, have such a similarity
> in vocabulary and construction, that even
> someone who knows as little of them as I
> do could hardly deny that both have ori-
> ginated from a single forerunner, in the
> fashion with which Spanish and Italian
> were born from Latin (1956 [1653]:XI,ix,
> 19).[1]

This position, endorsed by such renowned Andean scholars as Clements Markham, J.J. von Tschudi, Heymann Steinthal and Jacinto Jijón y Caamaño, was largely based on an observed parallel in the phonological inventories of Cuzco Quechua and Aymara and approximately 20% identical or resemblant vocabulary.[2]  Recent proponents of a genetic relationship include J.M.B. Farfán, Catherine Orr, Robert Longacre, and Yolanda Lastra de Suárez.  Farfán (1954) merely assumed a genetic relationship and attempted to "date" it using lexicostatistics.  Orr and Longacre's proposed "Proto-Quechuamaran" (1968) is the only work to date to support a genetic relationship based on anything remotely resembling comparative method.  Their use of data, however, was tilted toward support for the hypothesis.  Of the nine witnesses used to reconstruct "proto-Quechua" only one is from Central Quechua (see the subgrouping diagram in Mannheim, this volume).  Of the remaining eight, three border directly on Aymara-speaking areas and four are presumed descendents of a direct forebear of one of the first three.[3]  From the language family of which Aymara is a member, Jaqi (Hardman-de-Bautista, 1966a, 1978), Aymara was the only language considered, and the Jaqi languages which are structurally the most remote from Quechua and hence more problematic for the Orr-Longacre hypothesis, Jaqaru and Kawki, were ignored.[4]  Only lexical items present in all nine Quechua varieties were used.  This tended to favor the vocabulary strata associated with the political hegemony of Cuzco-based Tawantinsuyu.[5]  Louisa Stark

(1975:214) pointed out that, "in a more randomly
selected set of examples, systematic correspondences simply do not occur" (at a pan-Quechua-Jaqi
level), and presented counter examples to a good
number of Orr and Longacre's putative correspondences, all crucially involving ejectivity and
aspiration.

Lastra (1970) compared positional classes and
grammatical categories of Aymara and Ayacucho Quechua and noted a similarity in relative order of
suffixes and an overlap in the grammatical categories signified by them (cf.  Hymes, 1955). She
inferred a genetic relationship from the position
class match and concluded that this might provide
sufficient evidence to reconstruct positional categories of a proto-language.  Yet such a match-up is
neither sufficient nor necessary to demonstrate a
genetic relation.  In fact, the match-up of relative order is precisely what one would expect in a
tightly knit long-term language contact situation
(cf.  Gumperz, 1967; Gumperz and Wilson, 1971).
Moreover, both languages are typologically extremely consistent verb-final languages.  Thus both are
exclusively suffixing and agglutinative, although
Quechua languages are transparently so, while Aymara and all of the Jaqi languages exhibit complex
sandhi.  In the Quechua case at least, the relative
order of suffixes is semantically iconic in a way
that accords with the other typological facts
(Mannheim, 1981), and is therefore of as little use
in attesting to a genetic relationship as onomatopoeia.  Finally, the labels applied to the gramma-

tical categories are so vague as to constitute virtual analytic universals.[6]

The opposing position -- that the resemblances between the languages are the result of long-term contact rather than common origin -- has been sustained by Max Uhle, Benigno Ferrario, Gary Parker, Alfredo Torero and Martha J. Hardman-de-Bautista. From the Quechua side, arguments have revolved around claims as to the source of the ejective and aspirated stops in the Cuzco-type varieties of Southern Peruvian Quechua and the closely related Bolivian varieties. Those who sustained the genetic position have either assumed or argued that both features are inherited, largely on the basis of their presence in the numerically predominant Cuzco and Bolivian varieties. Opponents of a genetic relationship (that is, supporters of the contact position) have pointed to the fact that there are no known reflexes of either feature in the Central languages situated in the Quechua homeland and that glottalization and aspiration are restricted to those varieties which have been in contact with Jaqi languages or are contemporary descendants of such contact varieties in order to support their claim that the features are areal and not reconstructable to proto-Quechua.

HISTORICAL EVIDENCE FOR THE AREAL POSITION
Indeed, for Southern Peruvian Quechua the contact position is less historically hypothetical than it appears at first blush because there is quite good colonial evidence that a Jaqi language, Aymara, was

spoken over much of the area in which Cuzco-type varieties of Southern Peruvian Quechua are presently spoken, including the provincias altas of the Department of Cuzco (Canas, Canchis, Chumbivilcas and Espinar) (Tercer Concilio Provincial, 1584: f.78r.; Bertonio, 1603:10; 1612:f.A3). This point has been ruthlessly pursued or rejected according to the authors' ideological commitment to one or another of the languages or their position with respect to the genetic relationship debate itself. Given the unusual quantity of conjecture on this point which has entered the Andean literature, and in order to avoid such circularity, a careful review of the colonial sources is in order here.[7]

The best sources on the linguistic situation in colonial highland Peru are local reports from priests and colonial administrators. In general, one does not find specific and reliable enough material in the chronicle overviews of colonial and preconquest history and geography. Another potential source, trial records in which local people appeared as witnesses usually does not bear up data; here the local language is most often referred to as 'lengua indica' and so forth.

Francisco de Acuña, the corregidor of Chumbivilcas reported of Lluso and Quinota in 1586 that "some...speak the Aymara language and others the lengua general of the Inka, Quechua."[8] In the same year a report on the province of the Collaguas described a local system of two ethnic groups with distinctive dress and distinct origin myths in which one group, the Collaguas, spoke Aymara, and

the other, the Cavana, spoke Quechua ("la lengua
general del Cuzco corruta y muy avillanada") (Duran, 1586:328f.). In 1620 the Bishop of Arequipa
warned of the necessity of teaching Spanish as a
prerequisite to Catholic indoctrination because of
the linguistic diversity of the parishioners: "...
Cuzco...tiene pueblos de indios quichuas, aymaraes
y puquinas, la cual diversidad se halla tambien en
este obispado de Arequipa...⁹" This was still the
case for the partido of Condesuyos (Arequipa) at
the beginning of the nineteenth century, where a
priest reported that while the lengua general was
Quechua, other languages -- Aymara, Coli, Isapi,
and Chinchaysuyo (Northern Quechua?) -- were spoken (Almonte, 1813: 307). Of Andagua (Condesuyos),
Frank Salomon (1984:25) has encountered eighteenth
century evidence that Aymara was used as a sacred
language alongside Quechua as the most widespread
secular language. A number of the reports of 1586
which were later edited into the Relaciones geogra-
ficas de Indias (abbreviated RGI) attest to the
multilingualism of the region (in particular areas
around Anta, Cotahuasi, and again, Condesuyos.)¹⁰
In addition each of the reports from the present-
day provinces of Chumbivilcas, Espinar and Grau
inform us of the existence of a "Chumbivilcan language" which was spoken there alongside the Inka
koiné, Quechua.¹¹ Rivet (1924:652) conjectured that
"Chumbivilcan" was an Aymara-related language (or,
as we would now say, a Jaqi language). As a final
reference on Jaqi in Cuzco, a Censo de Indios (tax)
of 1633 to 1641 lists a number of communities in

the present day departments of Cuzco and Apurimac, often including Aymara ethnic names or the desig-[12] nation "Aymara" next to community names.

The Ayacucho region presents quite a distinct problem with respect to interpretation of histori- cal reports on languages spoken in particular set- tlements. According to both (ethno-) historical sources and oral tradition, the region -- particu- larly the area around Vilcashuamán -- was evacuated by the Inkas and resettled with mitmaq colonists from the other regions of Tawantinsuyu, who main- tained their own ethnic identity, marriage ties to their homelands, and language. Moreover, rather than settle the mitmaq in geographically contiguous regions according to ethnic polity of origin, the settlements were interspersed with those of mitmaq of distinct ethnic origin and language (Zuidema, 1966:69-71, 1968: 504, 1970: 154-5; Isbell, 1978: 63-5; Salas, 1979: 17-30).[13]

In such a situation, apart from the mitmaq brought from the immediate vicinity of Cuzco, the Inka koiné apparently served as a medium of inter- communication between linguistically distinct mit- maq settlers. Thus, Ribera y Chaves (1965[1586]: 187-8) reported on the area around the modern day city of Ayacucho that, "they have different langua- ges because each community speaks its distinct lan- guage although all speak the lingua franca of Cuz- co, as the Inkas ordered them to speak. And out of necessity they have continued their use of the Que- chua koiné, using their own language among them- selves."[14]  Likewise, Carabajal (1965[1586]:206)

reported that although Quechua was in general use
around Vilcashuamán, the <u>mitmaq</u> continued to speak
the tongues of their places of origin.[15] In light
of such a clear description of the linguistic ecology of Vilcashuamán and the remainder of the modern day departments of Ayacucho and Huancavelica
one must ask whether the reports that in many loca-
lities Aymara was spoken alongside Quechua are not
to be interpreted as the result of Inkaic <u>mitmaq</u>-
resettlement policies rather than the persistence
of an autochthonous Aymara-speaking population
stratum. It appears that the cultural valuations
applied to the respective languages, Quechua as the
stereotypic valley (<u>qheswa</u>) language, Aymara as the
stereotypic high plateau (<u>puna</u>) language, determined at least in part the pattern of <u>mitmaq</u> resettlement of the region.[16] I suggest that the question of the historical genesis of the Ayacucho-type
varieties of Southern Peruvian Quechua and their
relationship to Cuzco-type varieties be re-examined
linguistically in close consort with historical investigation into the social ecology of language in
sixteenth century Ayacucho and Huancavelica.


PUQUINA

In general, one must hope that working Andean
(ethno-)historians become sufficiently aware of the
need for concrete, contextualized information on
the linguistic situation in Southern Peru during
the first century or so after the conquest so as to
supplement the presently sparse material which has
been at the root of much conjecture and controversy

over the years.  As a case in point, consider the
seventeenth century village of Andahuaylillas located about thirty kilometers southeast of Cuzco, of
which a seemingly straightforward piece of evidence
appeared conclusively to indicate Quechua-Aymara-
Puquina trilingualism.  There, a baptistry has an
inscription in the three languages, plus Latin and
Spanish which reads, Ñocam baptizayqui Yayap Churip
Espiritu Sanctop Sutinpi.  Amen: 'I baptize you in
the name of the Father, of the Son and of the Holy
Spirit.  Amen.'[17]  Torero (1972[1970]:63) took this
as evidence that Aymara and Puquina were spoken
alongside Quechua in the seventeenth century village.  Yet a fairly extensive search for documentation of colonial Andahuaylillas (Hopkins, 1983)
did not turn up evidence of Puquina speakers.  The
parish priest in the early seventeenth century was
Pérez Bocanegra, famous for his Quechua doctrinal
manual of 1631 based on his experiences in Andahuaylillas.[18]  The Jesuits were covetous of Pérez
Bocanegra's successful parish and argued that it
would be an ideal language-training parish for
Quechua missionary work parallel to the Aymara
training parish they had established in Juli.
Their detractors argued that they really wanted it
as a base from which to oversee their nearby haciendas.

   The Jesuits actually gained control of the parish from 1628 to 1636, and much of the artwork in
the church dates from that period.  The morphology
of the Quechua inscription precludes its being from

much later than the periods in which Pérez Bocanegra or the Jesuits controlled the parish.[19] Apart
from the inscription itself, there is no evidence
that either Aymara or Puquina was spoken in Andahuaylillas. The parish is unusually well-documen-
ted linguistically, and all evidence points to Quechua as the parish language. Given the status of
Andahuaylillas as a center of mission-oriented linguistic work in the 1620s and 1630s, the very period during which the church was completed, it appears that the multilingual inscription on the baptistry was emblematic of that orientation. One
cannot be certain whether the inscription was done
under the curacy of Pérez Bocanegra or of the Jesuits, but in the latter case, it could represent a
reaffirmation of the Jesuit dedication to work with
the three languages begun by Barzana and Acosta in
the late sixteenth century.[20]

    There is evidence, however, that Puquina was
spoken elsewhere within the present geographic domain of Southern Peruvian Quechua into the seventeenth century. The Cuzco synod of 1591 required
the use of Puquina along with Quechua and Aymara in
the Bishopric of Cuzco, and the Arequipa synod of
1631 likewise ordered indoctrination in all three
languages in the latter bishopric. In addition the
Bishop of Arequipa, Pedro de Villagomez, assigned a
Puquina translation of the Catechism of the Tercer
Concilio to two priests, Alvara Mogrovejo of Caru-
mas and Miguel de Azana of Ilabaya and Locumba
(Vargas, 1953:50). Whatever became of the project?

INTERPRETING HISTORICAL EVIDENCE
A greater awareness of the social ecology and cultural meaning of language (and dialect) difference
during the colonial period would lay the basis for
a "diachronically slanted socio-linguistics" (to
borrow a felicitous phrase from Malkiel 1966:28) in
the Andes and in terms of Andean patterns and vistas. At this stage in Andean studies, there are
two related eurocentric procrustean tendencies
which must be avoided.[21] First, there is a tendency to interpret the domain of linguistic communities in uniformitarian and geographically contiguous terms. Geographic contiguity appears not to
have been a criterion for language distribution in
the South-central Andes until imposed as conscious
policy by the colonial administration (Mannheim,
1984a). As we have already seen, Southern Peru was
extremely complex linguistically during the immediate post-conquest period, and this diversity extended to social settings as well. They ranged
from the fragmented mitmaq colonist situation of
Vilcashuamán to the symbiotic Collaguas and Cavana,
who spoke Aymara and Quechua, respectively. Murra's influential work has demonstrated the importance of non-contiguous 'archipelagos' as a pre-
colombian Andean organizational principle (1972),
and this may turn out also to be a major factor in
language distribution. Santa Cruz Pachacuti Yamqui's intriguing statement (c. 1613) that Manqo
Qhapaq "ordered that the dress and clothing of each
people be different, along with speech,"[22] mythi-

cally tying speech to a major cultural index of and for ethnic differentiation -- as an assigned rather than acquired status marker -- points out a direction for the cultural interpretation of both inter- and intra-lingual variation in pre-conquest Peru. Zuidema (1973) pointed out that preconquest ethnicity often coded social hierarchy, and this has been shown to be precisely the case for sixteenth century Aymara speakers and Uru in southernmost Peru and Bolivia by Bouysse-Cassagne (1975) and Klein (1973).

Second, along with the tendency to treat linguistic communities as uniform and geographically contiguous there is a mind-set of positing otherwise unevidenced population migrations as 'explanations' of linguistic discontinuities, including discontinuities of dialectical isogloss and of language shift. We have already seen that the social conditioning of discontinuity is far more subtle. The southward expansion of Southern Peruvian Quechua against Aymara over the years along with the linguistic homogenization of Southern Peru noted above speaks for the opposite interpretation: languages, in a sense, move over populations. Notice also that this way of looking at the problem is the more productive in that it requires specification of the historical and social conditions for such movement. 'Migrations,' on the other hand, at least in practice tend to be circular: the evidence is the very material which was to be explained.

Bruce Mannheim

LINGUISTIC EVIDENCE FOR THE AREAL POSITION
As we pointed out earlier, the issue of whether
ejective and aspirate stops arc genetic (in Quechua) or areal has been deemed crucial to claims as
to whether Quechua and Aymara/Jaqi are genetically
related. Louisa Stark presented several arguments
that the features are areal and hence against hypotheses of genetic relation as they have up to now
been construed. First, Southern Peruvian Quechua
lexical stems containing ejective or aspirated
stops show a disproportionate number of lexical
stems which are resemblant in both form and meaning
in Aymara: 67% as opposed to 20% without either
(Stark 1975:212f). Were the features genetic, one
would expect a more equal distribution of putative
cognates. Given that the features ejectivity and
aspiration have a far more restricted distribution
in the Quechua varieties which use those features
than in the Jaqi languages, in very many cases the
direction of the loan process -- from the Jaqi languages to the Quechua -- is fairly clear (cf.
Hardman-de-Bautista 1964). A claim of the opposite
loan direction forces the analyst to claim that
subsequent ejective or aspirated stops in the Jaqi
stem in question are acquired entirely arbitrarily
whereas from the Quechua side there is an independently motivated explanation for the loss of ejectivity and aspiration from stops which follow the
first stop in the word.[23]
　　Second, comparison of cognate lexical stems from
Southern Peruvian Quechua (Cuzco) and Bolivian Quechua (Cochabamba and Sucre) show the presence of e-

jectivity and aspiration to be highly variable, so much so that reconstruction of the two features even at the lowest taxonomic nodes in Quechua sub-groupings (up to 'Common Southern Peruvian - Bolivian' is quite problematic (Stark 1975:214ff.)[24] This is also true even within the Cuzco variety of Southern Peruvian Quechua, though to a lesser extent. Presence of glottalization and aspiration on particular lexical items (e.g. irqi ∼ hirq'i 'child'; allpa ∼ hallp'a 'ground'; haqay ∼ haquay and chaqay ∼ chhaqay 'that, there (deictic of situation)') is one of the few phonological variables which is consciously perceived by speakers.[25]

Third, there is evidence that, apart from the loan-word core discussed above, ejectivity and aspiration further diffused through the lexicon via contamination, the features spreading across lexical domains (Parker 1969-1971, I:85; Proulx 1972: 143f.; Mannheim and Newfield 1982). Note the a-greement of ejectivity and aspiration in the following lexical sets: 'to become flat': p'aqpakuy, p'arpakuy, last'ayukuy, p'altayukuy, t'aslayakuy; 'foam': phusuqu, phuqpu, phullpu; 'curved, bend': q'iwiy, p'akiy; 'curved, crooked': q'iwi, wist'u, t'iksu; 'worn out': thanta, mullpha; 'limp': wist'uy, hank'ay, wiqruy (glottalization blocked on the last); 'narrow space': k'iski, t'iqi, q'iqi; 'narrow object': k'ikllu, p'iti; 'dusk': arkhiyay, laquayay, rasphiyay.[26] The contamination process was still alive after the conquest as Spanish loan-words which likewise acquired the features attest: khuchi 'pig' <Sp. cochina; phustullu 'blister'

<Sp. pústulla (modern pústula); mut'uy 'mutilate'
<Sp. mutilar (cf. Stark 1975:212). Sound symbo-
lism (which Jakobson and Waugh [1979:178] term "an
inmost, natural similarity association between
sound and meaning") also motivated the spread of
ejectives through the lexicon. Again, Spanish loan
words are valuable witnesses: hach'a 'ax' <Sp.
hacha; hasut'i 'whip' <Sp. azote; hich'ay 'throw
out' <Sp. echar (Stark 1975:212). The 'narrow'
sets above are also sound symbolic, in the ejective
feature and the vowels.

Another possible source for contemporary Southern Quechua ejectives was pointed out by Alfredo
Torero (1964) who observed that a high proportion
of stems which -- on the evidence of Central Quechua cognates -- etymologically possessed apical
palatal affricates *č̌ are presently attested with
ejectives. In cases in which the palatal appears
in a position other than first oral stop, it is the
first oral stop which carries ejectivity. His suggestion is supported by evidence that in minimal
pairs for the now-disappeared colonial opposition
between dorsal and apical sibilants, the apical
stem has the regular reflex of ejectivity on its
first oral stop (Mannheim 1984d:52).

It appears, then, that apart from ejective reflexes of the former apicals, lexical stems containing ejectivity and aspiration divide into a sizable common core in which the features are consistent throughout the varieties of Quechua which use
them plus a periphery through which the features
diffused somewhat less systematically via paradig-

matic similarity and sound symbolism (Mannheim
1983:247-262).

The directionality of historical change in the
Southern Peruvian Quechua varieties which possess
ejectivity and aspiration is an additional argument
in favor of the acquired (rather than genetic) status of these features and therefore also for the
areal (rather than genetic) position.  Possession
of these features in the stop system is in fact the
major dialectal rupture within Southern Peruvian
Quechua.  Varieties spoken within the Peruvian Departments of Ayacucho and Huancavelica and part of
Apurimac (let's call them the 'Ayacucho type') lack
ejectivity and aspiration in their stop systems.
They also retain the finals of syllables intact.
The varieties spoken in the Departments of Cuzco,
Puno, Arequipa and the remainder of Apurimac ('Cuzco-type varieties') on the other hand have a three-
way opposition in the stop system between ejectives, aspirates, and 'plain' stops, and have merged
the syllable finals.  (For examples of Cuzco-Aya-
cucho correspondences, see Mannheim, this volume).
The fact that the Cuzco-type varieties are innovative in their mergers (rather than the Ayacucho
type in, say, merging the three-way stop distinction and splitting the finals) is very strongly
supported by considerations of internal reconstruction of Cuzco Quechua and independently attested by
a philological record which spans four centuries[28]
(Mannheim 1983, chapters five and six).

I suspect that it is no accident that the Cuzco-
type with a three-way opposition of occlusives in

syllable-initial position has systematically merged
its finals (Mannheim 1983:191-247). I suggest that
the occurrence of lenitions and mergers with the
presence of ejectives and aspirates could be given
an information theoretic interpretation. Because
of the three-way opposition the consonant-vowel
combination in the Cuzco-type varieties has a mean
frequency (the inverse of information load) of
.0133, whereas for the Ayacucho-type varieties the
same combination has a mean frequency of .0256. In
other words, almost twice as much information is
carried in the selection of a consonant-vowel combination in Cuzco as in Ayacucho. If we now compare canonical consonant-vowel combinations for the
Ayacucho type and a fairly common modern Cuzco variety -- one which has undergone a good number of
the syllable-final mergers -- we find that they
carry informational loads of a similar scale. The
CV(C) combination in Ayacucho has a mean frequency
of .00216 and in Cuzco of .00222.[29] In other words,
it appears that the erosion of syllable-finals in
the Cuzco variety represents a kind of compensation
for the addition of glottalization and aspiration
to the phonological system, an informational read-
justment in the sound pattern relative to a fairly
constant morpho-semantic system. Given an incre-
ment in the significative power of the perceptually
stronger syllable onset, the significative role of
the perceptually weaker syllable finals has gradually though systematically been eliminated.[30] In
short, the changes which the Cuzco-type varieties
have undergone over several centuries become intel-

ligible if ejectivity and aspiration were acquired,
rather than inherited features.   And this in turn
contributes to the areal position.

   An intriguing recent effort by Lyle Campbell
(1976:83) to reopen the question of the source of
the Southern Quechua ejectives and aspirates is em-
bedded in the general claim that borrowed segments
(or features) tend to lose distributional restrictions in the course of borrowing.[31]   Notice that
there are in fact <u>more</u> restrictions on the distribution of ejectives and aspirates in Southern Quechua than in the Jaqi languages even though by the
areal hypothesis the direction of borrowing was
from the Jaqi languages to Southern Quechua (Campbell 1976:191-2).  By Campbell's hypothesis, though,
one would expect Southern Quechua to show <u>fewer</u> restrictions on the distribution of ejectives and
aspirates.   Campbell concludes that,

   If the hypothesis that diffused segments
   lack distributional restrictions of the
   donor language should survive investigation, then the question of whether Quechua owes the origin of its glottalization and aspiration to Aymara would receive a negative answer, and the question of Quechua - Aymara affinity would
   need to be investigated from a new perspective (1976:191-2).

Several points of a methodological as well as ideographic nature need be raised with respect to Camp-

bell's proposal.  An obvious red herring must be
disposed of first.  If a Jaqi areal source for e-
jectives and aspirates is precluded by the general
principle, are we to assume that they are genetic
to the Quechua family and reflexes of a common Quechua-Jaqi inheritance?  The answer, quite plainly,
is that we cannot do so (as Campbell concurs in a
letter) without the evidence of careful, systematic
comparative reconstruction within each of the families.  Should the general hypothesis (that distributional restrictions are generalized or lost in
the process of borrowing) prove to be well-formed,
it can only take its place alongside the standard
canons of genetic proof; it could never supplant
them.

    The confrontation of general principles with the
specifics of the case need not yield the conclusion
which Campbell draws.  It may well be the case that
the hypothesis is a useful "rule of thumb" but not
valid in a hard and fast way.  As we have seen,
there is evidence in this case to suggest (contrary
to the hypothesis) the preferential borrowing of
stems with ejectives and aspirates with subsequent
diffusion of these features through the Quechua lexicon.  The iconic mechanisms for such spread continued to be operative after the European invasion
to the point that there are Spanish loans which
have acquired the features (cf.  Mannheim and Newfield, 1982).  Or it may be that the hypothesis is
correct in its essentials but vague in its domain
of application.  What exactly is it that is generalized: the sequential distribution, the rule(s) go-

verning the sequential distribution, or a functional property of the phonological opposition in
question? In this particular case, it appears to
be the last of these, in two senses. First, ejectivity at least (if not aspiration also) performs a
culminative function (Jakobson and Halle, 1956:20)
in the phonological system of the Cuzco-type varieties of Quechua as well as the sense-discriminative function it has in common with the remaining
phonological features. In their culminative role,
ejectives signal the word as a phonological unit as
well as the hierarchy of sub-lexical elements which
make up the word, from the latter point of view
marking lexical stems, which potentially may carry
ejectivity and aspiration as against suffixes,
which under no circumstances may carry those features. Ejectivity quite commonly has a culminative
function in the world's languages, that is, marking
the word as a unit (Greenberg 1970). Notice though
that at the same time as ejectivity acquires a culminative function, its systematic integration from
the sense-discriminative standpoint is weakened.

Second, the 'once per word' restriction on both
features is in a way a generalization of the sense-
discriminative function of the features to its most
simple form: words are distinguished by the presence or absence of a feature (ejectivity, aspiration) whose position in the word is nearly predic-
table, and whose domain is the entire word. In
short, granted the hypothesis that restrictions on
distribution are generalized or lost in the process
of borrowing, its relevance to the problem of the

source of ejectives and aspirates in Cuzco-type varieties of Southern Peruvian Quechua is equivocal.
Although the <u>formal</u> distribution of ejectives and
aspirates is indeed more restricted in Southern
Quechua than in Aymara, from a functional point of
view, the Quechua distribution is more general.
The hypothesis of generalization of distribution in
the process of borrowing can therefore speak neither to the source of Southern Peruvian Quechua e-
jectives and aspirates nor to the question of whether Quechua and Aymara are genetically related.

EVALUATING THE DEBATE
If debate about, and pronouncements upon, genetic
relationships between languages appear unusually
slippery and elusive to non-specialists, it is
perhaps due to the notion of 'genetic relationship'
itself.  As William Bright (1970) observed, one
cannot demonstrate nonrelatedness between two languages; rather, the notion of 'common ancestry'
rests entirely on positive evidence.  On the other
hand, 'non-relatedness' takes on a different meaning within the limited chronological horizons with
which culture historians usually work, in spite of
the fact that the same methodological restrictions
apply as for an unlimited horizon.  Under such circumstances we are bound to require proof positive
(in the form of phonological correspondences and
well-argued etyma) as the criterion of genetic relationship and not presume to pronounce upon a relationship without such proof.  The frequent and
often unsupported allegations of genetic relation-

ship or lack thereof which often appear in the literature on Andean prehistory are symptomatic of general confusion about the meaning of 'genetic relationship' and the scholarly impulse to classify that which resists more concrete investigation. A proof of common ancestry between languages -- or, as is the case here, between language families -- requires first a detailed, accurate and reasonably thorough command of the relevant data, and second, in Thieme's (1964:585) words, that it be "demonstrably evident that there is no other hypothesis that would serve the purpose better or as well". As we have already observed, attempts to demonstrate a genetic tie between Quechua and Aymara have not met the evidential criterion of such a proof. Indeed, the manner in which the problem itself has often been posed -- assuming a direct correspondence between Southern Peruvian Quechua, perhaps along with its closest consociates from the Quechua languages, and Aymara from the Jaqi languages, that is, precisely the members of each family most influenced by the other -- has precluded meeting such standards. Faith in the eventual demonstrability of a genetic relationship between the respective language families is, of course, no substitute for a proof thereof. The first requirement has not been met; that is to say, no genetic relationship has been demonstrated.

Turning to the second requirement -- "that no other hypothesis...would serve the purpose better or as well" -- several investigators have now presented at least a partial case that the resemblances between the languages are explicable more parsimoniously as resulting from contact and massive borrowing than common inheritance (Torero, 1970; Stark, 1975; Hardman-de-Bautista, this volume). The success with which this position can be developed depends in part on progress in dialectology and detailed historical reconstruction within the two families.[32] Moreover, precise investigation of the linguistic, social and cultural aspects of the present-day contact situation between Quechua and Aymara: on the processes of structural accommodation between these languages in contact, on the motivation for change on the part of the speakers, and on the speakers' own evaluation of the situation would certainly shed light on parallel processes in the past. Given the present state of our knowledge of linguistic prehistory in the Andes we must attribute lexical and typological similarities between Southern Peruvian Quechua and Aymara to long-term contact between the two languages. Hypotheses of 'genetic relationship' between the Quechua and Jaqi families have simply not borne fruit. We would do well not to continue to expend limited research resources on this issue.[33]

In a more positive vein, the search for Quechua-external genetic relationships is a long term desideratum of historical linguists and students of South American prehistory. In order for this long range goal to be realized, we need to focus our more immediate attention on accounting historically for internal grammatical and phonological diversity within the Quechua family. It is likely that de-

tailed attention to the linguistic histories of the
Quechua languages will radically reshape our reconstruction of proto-Quechua.  This would in turn allow us to cast our genetic net in other, potentially more fruitful directions.

ACKNOWLEDGEMENTS
This article is based on ongoing investigation carried out since 1976 into Southern Peruvian Quechua
history, dialectology, philology, and culture, several components of which have been supported by
the Organization of American States, the National
Science Foundation, the Wenner-Gren Foundation for
Anthropological Research, and the Tinker Foundation
through a grant to the Center for Latin American
Studies of the University of Arizona.  I am also
indebted to Martha Anders, Rodolfo Cerrón-Palomino,
Paul Friedrich, Martha J. Hardman-de-Bautista,
Diane E. Hopkins, Madeleine Newfield and R. Tom
Zuidema for their comments and suggestions and particularly to Lyle Campbell for a detailed critique
from the field.  I am likely to regret not having
followed their kind comments and sagacious criti-
cisms more closely.  The final draft was typed by
Esor Groulx.

NOTES
1.  "...las dos lenguas quichua y aimara...por ser
    de dos naciones vecinas y coterminas tienen tan-
    ta similitud en los vocablos y construcción, que
    cualquiera que supiese lo poco que yo dellas, no
    podra negar haberse originado ambas de un prin-

670    *Bruce Mannheim*

cipio, al modo que la española e italiana nacie-
ron de la latina."
2.  Neither fact, of course, says anything one way
    or another about a genetic relationship.  A ca-
    talogue of proponents of a genetic relationship
    is actually quite vast and largely composed of
    historically and methodologically baseless, bia-
    sed statements such as, 'Quechua is a derived
    subordinate dialect of the primitive (in the
    sense of 'primary') language, Aymara' or vice
    versa (e.g. Valcarcel, Lira, Villar, and von
    Buchwald).  It should be kept in mind that the
    common grouping of the two families in biblio-
    graphic overview works on South America is real-
    ly not a stand on genetic relationship at all,
    but a convenient classificatory device.
3.  Particularly serious questions have been raised
    as to whether the Ecuadorian varieties, which
    figured quite prominently in the Orr-Longacre
    work, are in fact witnesses of Proto-Quechua in-
    dependently of the Inka koiné.  (For a carefully
    documented discussion of this problem, see Hart-
    mann, 1979.)  Gary Parker (1969-1971:158ff.) has
    pointed out the "irregularity" of Ecuadorian
    manner correspondences as another thorn in the
    Orr-Longacre attempt to reconstruct the stop
    system of Southern Peruvian Quechua at a much
    earlier stage in Quechua history.
4.  Note that the Orr-Longacre study (1968) was
    published well after the pioneer Quechua classi-
    fications by Parker (1963) and Torero (1964).
    On the Jaqi side, preliminary work on Kawki had

already appeared (Matos 1956); M.J. Hardman-de-
Bautista had already published her important Jaqaru grammar and lexicon (1966a). In her rebut-
tal of "Proto-Quechuamaran" (this volume) she
reported offering the authors additional material on Kawki and Jaqaru. See also Parker 1969-
1971 II:145-146.

5. On the influence on other Quechua languages by
the Inka koiné (classical Cuzco Quechua) see
Parker 1969-1971 I:72.

6. A more extensive study along the lines of Lastra's has since been undertaken by Joseph Davidson (1977, 1979) who concluded that, "a detailed
analysis of the suffix inventories has revealed
no evidence of a decisive nature that would
prove descent from a common source." (1979:11)

7. In writing this article I have reviewed most
major discussions of this point since the nineteenth century and followed up their references,
eliminating those which turned out not to be directly relevant to the question under discussion, but were brought in to prop up conjecture.
Second, I eliminated references which were quite
obviously calques on older, more specific reports (e.g. the Decadas of Antonio de Herrera
on some of the reports later included in the Relaciones Geográficas de Indias). Third, 'autho-
ritative' conjectures were eliminated. And
fourth, I carefully endeavored to disambiguate
each use of the name 'Aymara' in colonial texts.
It designated a pre-Colombian local polity located in present-day Apurimac, mitmaq who hailed

from there, as well as the language. It appears that the language name resulted from a Spanish error (see Markham [1871] among the many to observe this) and has nothing whatever to do with the province or its people. This left the residue which is reported here. For the area to the south of that considered here, see Espinoza 1983.

Torero's survey of evidence on the colonial geographic domain of Jaqi languages is excellent (1972 [1970]:66-75). Some differences in interpretation of some of this material should be evident in the text.

8.   "...hablan algunos dellos la lengua aymará y otros la lengua general del inga..."

9.   Archivo General de Indias (Seville), Lima 309, cited by Millones 1971: 303. Almonte 1813: 307.

10.  See the reports for Anta (RGI 2:17) and Cotahuasi (RGI 2:310).

11.  See the reports for Alccavitoria (RGI 2:313), Capamarca (RGI 2:318), Santo Tomás and Colquemarca (RGI 2:320), Velille (RGI 2:322), and Livitaca (RGI 2:324).

12.  Archivo Departmental del Cuzco, Archivo del Ilustre Cabildo del Cuzco, Top. 14, Sig. 3-31, Caja 9.

13.  The late sixteenth century RGI reports on the region collated by Jiménez de la Espada are particularly important sources here.

14.  "Tienen diferentes lenguas, porque cada parcialidad habla su lengua diferente, aunque todos hablan la general del Cuzco, que les mandaron

hablar generalamente los Ingas, y se han quedado
en este uso, que es muy necesario, usando la suya y la natural entre si."

15.  Also see Monzón 1586a:220; 1586b:228; 1586c:
239 and for Huancavelica, de Cantos 1586:307.

16.  See Mannheim, this volume. A related observation was made by Kubler 1946:332f.

17.  Photographs appear in Keleman (1967 [1951] II:
113) and Macera (1975:84).

18.  Note the reference on page 619. For a discussion of the Ritual Formulario...see Mannheim,
1983:214-5 and 1984b.

19.  The doubt raised by Macera (1975:70) as to
this point can therefore be laid to rest.

20.  For detailed information on the parish of
Andahuayillas under Spanish control, see
Hopkins 1983.

21.  A third euro-centric imposition is the attri-
bution of linguistic expansion to the action of
'traders'. For an able critique, see Rojas
1980.

22.  " ... mandó que los bestidos y traxes de cada
pueblo fuessen diferentes, como en hablar, para
conocer, porque en este tiempo no echaven de ver
y conoscer a los indios que nación o pueblo eran
... "

23.  Carenko (1972) provides a first approximation
of the constraints. The diachronic processes
involved are stated in Mannheim 1983:262-7. The
synchronic grammar of Cuzco Quechua contains a
word structure constraint which restricts glottalization and aspiration to the first stop in

the word, and by other rules it must also be
syllable-initial. For a formal statement and
discussion of the synchronic constraint see
Mannheim 1983:157-60.

24.  Examples are presented on pages 214-17 (coun-
ter-examples to the Orr-Longacre statements 1,
2, 4-10 and the table on page 217). For a more
detailed discussion of these and related aspects
of the incorporation of ejectivity and aspiration into the Cuzco Quechua sound system, see
Mannheim and Newfield 1982.

25.  cf. Stark 1975:217f. on Cochabamba.

26.  Parker <u>et</u> <u>al</u>. 1964:35, 45, 54, 56, 81, 90,
93. In the 'flat' set <u>t'aslay</u> is likely from
<u>last'ay</u>.

27.  Cerrón-Palomino has pointed out to me, though,
that SPQ <u>hich'ay</u> has regular cognates in Wanka
<u>hitray</u> [hičay] ~ <u>sitray</u> [sičay]; this would pre-
sumably allow us to reconstruct a proto-Quechua
source for these forms and obviate the case as a
loan example. But the evidence is not unequivo-
cal; correspondences of this kind may arise by
means of loans across dialectal shibboleths, as
Leonard Bloomfield's (1946:107) famous reconstruction of the proto-Algonquin compound for
'whiskey' showed.

28.  By this, I do not wish to imply that the Ayacucho-type varieties did not at one time -- however briefly, and certainly to lesser extent
than the modern Cuzco-type -- have ejectives and
aspirates. Both Rowe (1950) and Parker (1969-
1971;1969b) assumed that they did and subse-

quently lost them, but do not present a single
shred of evidence for this belief. Arguments
might take shape around the status of a small
set of lexical stems which appear to have undergone h̲-prothesis in Cuzco Quechua because of
glottalization elsewhere in the word and likewise have initial h̲ in Ayacucho. Are they
loans from Cuzco, or do they evidence an earlier
stage of Ayacucho Quechua with ejectives?

29.    Roughly this is the variety described in Mannheim, 1983, chapter five.

30.    For a discussion of functional motivation in
phonological change see Campbell and Ringen
1982, and Mannheim 1984c.

31.    For the record, one of his restrictions, "if
the root begins with h̲, the next stop in the
root must be glottalized," (191) is incorrect as
there are numerous roots with initial h̲ in
which the following stop is not an ejective.
The relationship he alludes to is a diachronic
process of h̲ prothesis, $\emptyset$>h / # __ VT', in
which prothesis is not the only historical
source of initial h̲. Synchronically, the pro-
thetic h̲ prevents the occurrence of a predic-
table glottal catch which would violate a constraint that prohibits the occurrence of two
glottalized segments in a word (Mannheim 1983:
157 ff.)

32.    On the Jaqi family, see Hardman-de Bautista
1966, 1976, 1978; Briggs 1976, and this volume.
On the Quechua family, see Torero 1964, 1968,
1970, 1974; Parker 1969-1971; Hartmann 1972;

Landerman 1978;   Adelaar 1979, 1984;   Cerron-
Palomino 1979, 1980.

33.  After completing the final version of this essay, I received Cerrón-Palomino's article on the
present state of the Quechua-Jaqi problem (published in 1984 in a delayed issue of Lexis).
Cerrón-Palomino concurs with the present article
that, "the attempts to establish a genetic relationship between the [Quechua and Jaqi] linguistic families do not resist a serious confronta-
tion with empirical data and appear to be vitia-
ted from the beginning because of their unilate-
ral selection of testimony languages within the
families...In view of the fact that the hypothesis of common origin has proven unproductive,
convergence remains the more probable theory at
least until deeper synchronic and diachronic
study of both language families permits proof to
the contrary (1982:238, my translation)." Apart
from criticism of the Orr and Longacre (1968)
and Lastra (1970) proposals, Cerrón-Palomino
responds to details of Davidson (1977) and Hardman-de-Bautista (this volume, in an earlier
draft). (The references therein to Mannheim
1981, are to an earlier draft of the present
essay.)

REFERENCES
Acuña, Francisco de.   1586.   Relación fecha por el
corregidor de los Chunbibilcas Don Francisco de
Acuña por mandado de su Ex.ᵃ   del Señor Don
Fernando de Torres y Portugal, Vissorey destos

Reynos, por la discrepción de las Indias que Su
Magestad manda hacer. RGI 2:310-25.

Adelaar, Willem F. H. 1979. De Dialectologie van
het Quechua. Forum der Lettern 20:477-96.

------. 1984. The significance of grammatical
processes involving vowel lengthening for the
classification of Quechua dialects. IJAL 50(1):
25-47.

Almonte, Clemento. 1813. Respuestas al interroga-
torio al cura de Andahua (partido de Condesuyos)
sobre las costumbres y organización de los pob-
lados de su jurisdicción. Archivo General de
Indias, Lima 1598. Transcription published by
Luis Millones (1971).

Bertonio, Ludovico. 1603. Arte y grammatica muy
copiosa de la lengua aymara. Rome: Luis Zannet-
ti. (Facsimile edition, Leipzig, 1879).

------. 1612. Vocabulario de la lengua aymara.
Juli: Francisco del Canto. (Facsimile edition,
La Paz: Don Bosco, 1956).

Bloomfield, Leonard. 1946. Algonquin. In Linguistic Structures of Native America, Harry
Hoijer, ed., pp. 85-129. Viking Fund Publications in Anthropology 6.

Bouysse-Cassagne, Thérese. 1977. Pertenencia
étnica, status económico y lenguas en Charcas a
fines del siglo xvii. In Tasa de la Visita
General de Francisco de Toledo, N. David Cook,
ed., pp. 312-28. Lima: Universidad Nacional de
San Marcos.

Briggs, Lucy. 1976. Dialectal variation in the
Aymara language of Bolivia and Peru. Doctoral

dissertation in anthropology, University of
Florida, Gainesville.

Bright, William. 1970. On linguistic unrelated-
ness. IJAL 36:288-90.

Campbell, Lyle. 1976. Language contact and sound
change. In Current Progress in Historical Linguistics, William Christie, ed., pp. 181-94,
Amsterdam: North Holland.

Campbell, Lyle and Jon Ringen. 1982. Teleology
and the explanation of sound change. In Phono-
logica 1980, Wolfgang U. Dressler, Oskar E.
Pfeiffer and John R. Rennison, eds. pp. 57-68.
Innsbruck.

Cantos de Andrada, Rodrigo de, Garci Núñez Vela,
Gaspar de Contreras and Francisco Caballero.
1586. Relación de la Villa Rica de Oropesa y
minas de Guancavelica. RGI 2:303-9.

Carabajal, Pedro. 1586. Descripción fecha de la
Provincia de Vilcas Guaman por el illustre señor
don Pedro de Carabajal, corregidor y justica mayor della. RGI I:205-19.

Carenko, E.I. 1972. O laringalizačii u jazyke
kečua. Voprosy jazykoznanija (1):97-103. (English translation: On laryngealization in Quechua. Linguistics 146:5-14. [1975]).

Cerrón-Palomino, Rodolfo M. 1979. La primera persona posesora-actora del protoquechua. Lexis
(Lima) 3(1):1-40.

------. 1980. El quechua: una mirada de conjunto.
Universidad Nacional de San Marcos. Centro de
Investigación de Lingüística Aplicada. Documen-
to de Trabajo No. 42.

------. 1982. El problema de la relación Quechua-
Aru: Estado actual. Lexis (Lima) 6(2):213-42.
Cobo, Bernabe. 1956 [1656]. Historia del nuevo
mundo. In Obras del P. Bernabe Cobo, vol. 2,
F. Mateos, ed. Biblioteca de Autores Espanoles
92. Madrid: Atlas. Also published in 1892 under
the editorship of M. Jimenez de la Espada. Seville: Rasca and Tuvera.
Davidson, Joseph O. Jr. 1977. A Contrastive Study
of the Grammatical Structures of Aymara and Cuzco Quechua. Doctoral dissertation, University
of California, Berkeley.
------. 1979. On the genetic relationship of Aymara and Quechua. Unpublished paper presented
to the 43rd International Congress of Americanists.
Duran, Juan (escribano). 1586. Relación de la
provincia de los Collaguas para la discrepción
de las Yndias que Su Magestad manda hacer. RGI
2:326-33.
Espinoza Soriano, Waldemar. 1983. Los fundamentos
lingüísticos de la etnohistoria andina y comen-
tarios en torno al anonimo de Charcas de 1604.
In Aula quechua, Rodolfo Cerrón-Palomino,
ed., pp. 163-202. Lima: Signo Universita-
rio.
Farfán, J.M.B. 1954. Cronología Quechua - Aymará
según el cálculo estadístico. Revista del Museo
Nacional (Lima) 23:50-5.
Ferrario, B. 1956. La dialettologia ed i problemi
interni della Runa-simi (vulgo Quéchua). Orbis
5:131-40.

Greenberg, Joseph.  1970.  The role of typology in
the development of a scientific linguistics.
In Theoretical Problems of Typology and the
Northern Eurasian Languages, L. Dezső and P.
Hajdú, eds., pp. 11-24.  Budapest: Akadémiai
Kiadó.

Gumperz, John.  1967.  On the linguistic markers of
bilingual communication.  Journal of Social Issues.  23(2):48-57.

Gumperz, John and Robert Wilson.  1971.  Convergence and creolization.  In Pidginization and
Creolization of Languages, Dell Hymes, ed., pp.
151-67.  Cambridge: University Press.

Hardman-de-Bautista, Martha J.  1964.  Discussion.
In Proceedings of the Ninth International Congress of Linguists, p. 391.

------.  1966a.  Jaqaru: Outline of Phonological
and Morphological Structure.  The Hague: Mouton.

------.  1966b.  El Jaqaru, el Kawki y el Aymara.
El simposio de Montevideo - ALFAL 1: 186-92
(appeared in 1975).

------.  1976.  Proto-Jaqi: Reconstrucción del sistema de personas gramaticales.  Revista de Museo
Nacional (Lima) 41:433-56.

------.  1978.  Jaqi: The Linguistic family.  IJAL
44(2):146-53.

Harrington, John P.  1943.  Hokan Discovered in
South America. Journal of the Washington Academy
of Sciences.  33(11):334-44.

Hartmann, Roswith.  1972.  Linguistik im Andenge-
biet: Geschichte und Stand der Quechuaforshung.
Zeitschrift für Lateinamerika Wien 4:97-131.

------. 1979. ¿'Quechuismo preincaico' en Ecuador? Ibero-Amerikanisches Archiv (n.s.) 5(3):267-99.

Hopkins, Diane E. 1983. The colonial history of the hacienda system in a southern Peruvian high-land district. Doctoral dissertation in development sociology, Cornell University.

Hymes, Dell. 1955. Positional analysis of categories: a frame for reconstruction. Word 11:10-23

Isbell, Billie Jean. 1978. To defend ourselves: Ecology and ritual in an Andean village. Austin: University of Texas Press.

Jakobson, Roman and Morris Halle. 1956. Fundamentals of language. The Hague: Mouton.

Jakobson, Roman and Linda R. Waugh. 1979. The sound shape of language. Bloomington: Indiana University Press.

Jijón y Caamaño, Jacinto. 1941-1947. El Ecuador interandino y occidental antes de la conquista castellana (4 volumes). Quito: Editorial Ecuatoriana.

Keleman, Pál. 1967 [1951]. Baroque and rococo in Latin America. Second edition, 2 volumes. New York: Dover.

Klein, Harriet E. Manelis. 1973. Los uros: extra-ño pueblo del Altiplano. Estudios Andinos 7, III(1):129-150.

Kubler, George. 1946. The Quechua in the colonial world. Handbook of South American Indians 2: 331-410. Washington: Smithsonian Institution, Bureau of American Ethnology Bulletin 143.

Kuryłowicz, Jerzy. 1973. Internal reconstruction. Current Trends in Linguistics 11:63-92.

Landerman, Peter. 1978. The Proto-Quechua first
person marker and the classification of Quechua
dialects. Unpublished paper presented to the
Workshop on Andean Linguistics, Urbana,
Illinois.

Lastra de Suárez, Yolanda. 1970. Categorías posicionales en Quechua y Aymara. Anales de Antropología (México, D.F.) 7:263-84.

Lira, Jorge A. 1944. Diccionario Kkéchuwa-Espa-
ñol. Tucumán (Argentina): Universidad Nacional
de Tucumán.

Longacre, Robert. 1968a. Comparative reconstruction of indigenous languages. In Current Trends
in Linguistics 4:320-60.

------. 1968b. Proto-Quechuamaran: An ethnolinguistic note. Ethnohistory 15:403-14.

Macera, Pablo. 1975. El arte mural cuzqueño, siglos xvi-xx. Apuntes (Lima) 4:59-112.

Malkiel, Yakov. 1966. The inflectional paradigm
as an occasional determinant of sound change. In
Directions for Historical Linguistics, Winifred
P. Lehmann and Yakov Malkiel, eds. pp. 21-64.
Austin: University of Texas Press.

Mannheim, Bruce. 1981. Quechua internal syntax.
Unpublished paper presented to the New York
State Council on Linguistics Workshop on Iconi-
city and Arbitrariness, Ithaca, New York, April.

------. 1983. Structural change and the structure
of change: The linguistic history of Cuzco Quechua in relation to its social history. Doctoral dissertation in anthropology and in linguistics, University of Chicago.

------. 1984a. 'Una nación acorralada': Southern Peruvian Quechua language planning and politics in historical perspective. Language in Society 13(3):291-309.

------. 1984b. A semiotic of Andean dreams. In Dreaming in cross-cultural perspective, Barbara Tedlock, ed. Albuquerque: University of New Mexico Press, in press.

------. 1984c. '...A current of its own making': Functional targets in historical phonology. Ms. Department of Anthropology, University of Michigan.

------. 1984d. New evidence on the sibilants of colonial Southern Peruvian Quechua: Toward Andean philology. Ms. Department of Anthropology, University of Michigan.

Mannheim, Bruce and Madeleine Newfield. 1982. Iconicity in phonological change. In Papers from the Fifth International Conference on Historical Linguistics, Anders Ahlqvist, ed., pp. 211-22. Amsterdam: John Benjamins.

Markham, Clements. 1871. On the geographical positions of the tribes which formed the Empire of the Yncas, with an appendix on the name 'Aymara'. Journal of the Royal Geographical Society (London) 41:281-338.

Matos Mar, José. 1956. Yauyos, Tupe y el idioma Kauke. Revista del Museo Nacional (Lima) 25: 140-83.

Millones Gadea, Luis. 1971. Pastores y tejedores de los Condesuyos de Arequipa: Un informe etnológico al Consejo de Regencia. Quinto Congreso Internacional de Historia de América 3: 302-17.

Monzón, Luis de. 1586a. Descripción de la tierra del repartimiento de Atunsora... RGI 1:220-5.

------. 1586b. Descripción de la tierra del repartimiento de San Francisco de Atunrucana y Laramati... RGI 1:226-36.

------. 1586c. Descripción de la tierra del repartimiento de los Rucanas Antamarcas... RGI 1: 237-48.

Murra, John Victor. 1972. El control vertical de un máximo de pisos ecológicos en la economía de las sociedades andinas. In Visita de la Provincia de León de Huánuco en 1562, vol. 2:429-76. Huánuco: Universidad Nacional Hermilio Validizán.

Orr, Carolyn and Robert E. Longacre. 1968. Proto-Quechuamaran. Language 44:528-55.

Pachachuti Yamqui (see Santa Cruz Pachuchuti Yamqui)

Parker, Gary J. 1963. La clasificación genética de los dialectos quechuas. Revista del Museo Nacional (Lima) 32:241-52.

------. 1965. Gramática del quechua ayacuchano. Lima: Universidad Nacional de San Marcos (Spanish language version of the grammatical portion of Parker, 1969c).

------. 1969a/1971. Comparative Quechua phonology and grammar. University of Hawaii Working Papers in Linguistics I:1(1) 65-88; II:1(2) 123-47; III:1(4) 1-61; IV:1(9) 149-204; V:3(3) 45-109.

------. 1969b. Bosquejo de una teoría de la evolución del Quechua A. Programa Interamericano del Lingüística y Enseñanza de idiomas, El Simposio de México, pp. 270-81. México: Universidad Nacional Autónoma de México.

------. 1969c. Ayacucho Quechua grammar and dictionary. The Hague: Mouton.

Parker, Gary J., Antonio Cusihuamán, Gloria Escobar, Alicia Ibañez, Yolanda Lastra, Alfredo Olarte, and Donald Solá. 1964. English-Quechua Dictionary: Cuzco, Ayacucho, Cochabamba. Ithaca, New York: Cornell University Quechua Language Materials Project (Available from ERIC, P.O. Box 190, Arlington, VA. 22210.

Pérez de Bocanegra, Joan de. 1631. Ritual formulario e institución de Curas para administrar a los naturales de este Reyno los Santos Sacramentos...por el Bachiller J.P.B., presbíterio, en la lengua Quechua general. Lima.

Proulx, Paul. 1972. Proto-quechua /ph/. IJAL 38(2):142-5.

Relaciones geográficas de Indians (RGI). 1965 [1881-1897]. Marcos Jiménez de la Espada, ed., 4 vols. in 3. Biblioteca de Autores Españoles. vol. 183-5. Madrid: Atlas.

Ribera, Pedro de. 1586. Relación de la Ciudad de Guamanga y sus terminos. RGI 1:181-204.

Rivet, Paul. 1924. Langues américaines. In Les langues du monde, Antoine Meillet and Marcel Cohen, eds., pp. 596-707. Paris: Champion.

Rojas Rojas, Ibico. 1979. Expansión del quechua. Lima: Ediciones Signo.

Rowe, John Holland. 1950. Sound patterns in three
Inca dialects. IJAL 16:137-48.

Salas de Coloma, Miriam. 1979. De los obrajes de
Canaria y Chincheros a las comunidades indígenas
de Vilcashuamán, siglo xvi. Lima: Sesator.

Salomon, Frank. 1984. El culto a los ancestros y
la resistencia al estado en un pueblo arequipe-
ño, 174(8?) - 1754. Manuscript presented to
the seminar on "Resistance and Rebellion in the
Andean World," University of Wisconsin, Madison,
26 April.

Santa Cruz Pachacuti Yamqi, Joan de. c. 1613. Relación de antigüedades deste reyno del Pirú.
Manuscript 3169, ff. 132-169, Biblioteca Nacional, Madrid.

Saussure, Ferdinand de. 1971 [1915]. Cours de
linguistique générale. Posthumously edited by
C. Bally and A. Sechehaye, with A. Reidlinger.
Paris: Payot.

Stark, Louisa A. 1975. A reconstruction of Proto-
quechua phonology. Actas del 39 Congreso Internacional de Americanistas 5:209-19.

Steinthal, Haymann. 1890. Das verhältniss, das
zwishen dem Keschua und Aymara besteht. 7 Congrès Internacional des Americanistes (Berlin,
1888), 462-5.

Swadesh, Morris (Mauricio). 1969. Un nexo pre-
histórico entre Quechua y Tarasco. Anales del
Instituto Nacional de Antropología e Historia
(México, D.F.) 7:127-38.

Tercer Concilio Provincial. 1584. Doctrina Christiana y catecismo para instrucción de los Indi-

os, y las demás personas que han de ser enseña-
dos en nuestra sancta fe. Los Reyes (Lima): Antonio Ricardo.

Thieme, Paul. 1964. The comparative method for
reconstruction on linguistics. In Language in
culture and society, Dell Hymes, ed., pp.
585-598. New York: Harper and Row.

Torero Fernández de Cordova, Alfredo. 1964. Los
dialectos quechuas. Anales Científicos de la
Universidad Agraria 2:446-78.

------. 1968. Procedencia geográfica de los dialectos quechuas de Ferreñafe y Cajamarca. Anales Científicos de la Universidad Agraria 6:
168-97.

------. 1970. Lingüística e historia de la sociedad andina. Anales Científicos de la Universidad
Agraria 8:231-64. (Reprinted in El reto del
multilingüismo en el Perú, Alberto Escobar,
ed., pp. 46-106. Lima: Instituto de Estudios
Peruanos (1972), and Actas del 39 Congreso Internacional de Americanistas 5:221-59 (1975).)

------. 1974. El quechua y la historia social
andina. Lima: Universidad Ricardo Palma.

Uhle, Max. 1912. Los origines de las Incas.
Actas del 17 Congreso Internacional de Americanistas (Sesión de Buenos Aires), 301-53.

Valcarcel, Luis E. 1936-1941. Mirador Indio, 2
vols. Lima. Reprinted (1958), Cuzco: Primer
Festival del Libro Sur-peruano.

Vargas Ugarte, Ruben. 1953. Historia de la
Iglesia en el Perú. Lima: Imprenta Santa
Maria.

Villar, Leonardo.   1890.   Lingüística nacional,
Estudios sobre la Keshua. Lima: El Comercio.

Zuidema, R. Tom.   1966.   Algunos problemas etno-
históricos del departamento de Ayacucho.   Wamani
(Ayucucho) 1:68-75.

------.   1968.   El estudio arqueológico, etnohis-
tórico y antropológico social en unas comunidades del Rio Pampas. Verhandlungen des 38 In-
ternationalen Amerikanistenkongressen 2:503-5.

------.   1970.   Social versus structural change in
Quechua society of southern Peru.   In Anniver-
sary Contributions to Anthropology, 153-8.
Leiden: E.J. Brill.

------.   1973.   The Origin of the Inca Empire.   Les
grandes empires, Recueils de la Société Jean
Bodin pour l'Histoire Comparative des Institutions 31:733-57.

# PART III
# Indigenous Languages of Southern
# and Eastern South America

# 18. Current Status of Argentine Indigenous Languages

## Harriet E. Manelis Klein

INTRODUCTION

Most Argentines know very little about the 100,000-
150,000 Indians living in their country. Part of
the reason for this is that the Indian accounts for
less than one per cent of the nation's population.
By contrast, when the Spanish conquistadores arrived there in the 1500's, there were an estimated
300,000-500,000 Indians divided into at least 20
distinct tribes. Despite long opposition to their
conquest and subjugation, by the end of the 19th
century the aboriginal population had been pushed
into the marginal lands of the new nation of Argentina and were confined to the northeastern, northwestern and southern territories.

Of the total indigenous population today, about
half is to be found in the provinces of the Northeast (Formosa, Chaco, Misiones). Some of these Indians are still monolingual indigenous speakers and
a few still follow a semi-nomadic style of life,
not that different in structure from the pre-conquest period. In the Andean and Piedmont provinces
of the Northwest (Salta, Jujuy, Santiago del Esterro and Tucuman), several large groups are to be
found. It has been estimated that about half of
these northwestern Indians are bilingual speakers
who participate in Argentine culture. Together
these two northern regions contain by far the lar-

gest number of indigenous languages -- nine languages belonging to six language families: Guaykurú,
Mataco, Jaqí, Quechua, Lule-Vilela and Guaraní.

Immediately south of these provinces is an area
where indigenous languages are generally not spoken. Here lies the core region of Argentina, the
most fertile part of the country, where agriculture
and cattle raising are the primary industries and
which was the center of Spanish and European settlement. The provinces of Santa Fé, Entre Rios,
Cordoba and Buenos Aires form one of the wealthiest
zones of non-Indian settlement in all the continent. Because of that wealth, however, small pockets of Amerindians have been drawn to the central
cities, some of these of non-Argentine origin.[1] But
given their marginality and their small numbers in
each city, these Indians have not formed cohesive
indigenous communities.

In the southern provinces of La Pampa, Río Negro, Neuquén, Chubut, Santa Cruz and Tierra del Fuego, another clustering of Indian groups can be
found. The largest of these, the Araucanians, are
located in the more northern of the provinces (La
Pampa, Río Negro and Neuquén). Further south, primarily in Tierra del Fuego, are three different
tribal and language groups, all of whom are on the
verge of extinction.

In the organization of this chapter, I have divided the languages into the nine linguistic families which are spoken within Argentina. I have on
the whole accepted the broad linguistic classifica-

tions established by Loukotka (1968), Tovar (1961) and Voegelin and Voegelin (1977), but have indicated points of disagreement. After a discussion of each linguistic family, the individual members of that family are noted along with the name of the language as it is commonly called in Argentina, as well as the auto-designation and the name or names by which other ethnic groups refer to it. Population estimates are based on data gathered while in the field, from discussions with indigenous leaders, missionaries, church and government officials, and other field anthropologists, as well as from published sources and privately circulated unpublished manuscripts.

For each section, I have cited works that have been published either about the language or in the language. In some instances, studies on languages which are extinct are also included because of the recent resurgence of interest in their study and the significance that these investigations have for understanding the related contemporary languages. Following the tradition of the rest of the papers in this volume, I have included only those bibliographical references which were published after O'Leary's (1963) Ethnographic Bibliography of South America. Finally, wherever possible, prognoses for the future of the language and the culture are provided. This is done so as to encourage investigators to concern themselves with immediate efforts to carry out research, especially on those languages which are so close to extinction.

GUAYKURU FAMILY
    1. Toba
    2. Mocoví
    3. Pilagá
    4. Abipon
    5. Mbayá-Guaykurú

Toba, Mocoví and Abipon have been classified as languages pertaining to the Guaicurú stock by Lou-kotka (1968:48-52), to the Guaikurú family by Tovar (1961:42-43), while Pilagá is listed by both as a dialect of Toba, and Caduveo (or Kadiueo) as a dialect of the now extinct Guaicurú or Mbayá language. Voegelin and Voegelin (1977:149) classify four languages in the Guaycurú grouping: two of which are extinct - Abipon and Mbayá-Guaycurú - and the other two - Mocoví and Toba. Mbayá and Abipon were both spoken by large numbers of Indians who roamed the Gran Chaco from north of Asunción to Corrientes during late pre-historic and early colonial times. Although these languages are no longer spoken, there is some recent literature about them, using eighteenth and nineteenth century linguistic materials for analysis. Abipon is extinct, that is, there is no modern version of the language; however, Caduveo, presently spoken in Brazil, is considered by most classifiers to be a contemporary dialect of Mbayá. Klein (1980), having done linguistic fieldwork among the Caduveo, argues against the classification of Caduveo with these other Guaykuruan languages.

Mocoví, Toba and Pilagá are still spoken in Argentina (Tomasini 1978). There are many Mocoví
speakers to be found in the southern part of the
Chaco province, especially in the area of Villa
Angela and Napalpí (Miranda 1968). Toba is spoken
throughout the Chaco province and in parts of eastern Formosa. The relationship between Toba and
Mocoví seems fairly close. However, no time depth
of separation can be determined, for there has not
been any systematic work done on Mocoví. According
to Toba speakers, there are some initial difficulties in understanding Mocoví speech, but these are
readily overcome (Klein 1973). Pilagá, although
classified as a dialect of Toba, is considered by
fieldworkers in Argentina to be another Guaykurú
language (Bruno and Najlis 1965).

1. Toba.   The Toba call themselves and their language namqom.   It is spoken by the Toba Indians of
Argentina and Paraguay.   In 1968, the 17,602 Argentine Toba were to be found in 74 communities located in the provinces of Chaco (13,455), Formosa
(3,207), and Salta (400) (Boucherie 1968). The Toba are the largest indigenous group in the northeastern region, and the ones with the greatest influence both among the Indian and the non-Indian
regional population.   Another 600-700 Toba are
found in the Chaco region of Paraguay (for the Paraguayan Toba situation, see Klein and Stark in
this volume).   Recent immigration has led to the
settlement of about 500 speakers in the Gran Buenos

Aires area and about the same number in several cities of the province of Santa Fé.

In both the Chaco and Formosa provinces, the
linguistic situation is different for the urban
than for the rural speakers. In the urban environment a number of young Toba no longer speak the
language. However, those Toba who are over 50 (no
more than 8% of the population) are almost always
monolingual speakers. Those between the ages of 35
and 49 (about 16%) are principally Toba speakers,
but also speak some Spanish. Most Toba between 18
and 34, both urban and non-urban, speak both languages, the degree of fluency in Spanish being determined by education and economic activity. In
the non-urban areas of the Chaco, those under 18
tend to speak better Toba than Spanish, but generally some of both. Urban pre-school children also
tend to speak both languages.

The fact that their children are losing command
of their language is both a source of pride and of
distress to their parents. It adds self-respect to
those parents who place great emphasis on the children's ability to acquire correct Spanish speech
habits, for they view such a qualification as a
means to progress in the Argentine world. Thus,
they mistakenly equate the loss of their native
speech with a loss of the provincial accent, believing that only the urban dialects will lead to
advancement. While some are eager for linguistic
acculturation, other Toba view its results with
fear. Their concern for their language and their

customs is great and is reflected in the recent growth of numerous pro-indigenous organizations and committees. For the vast majority of Toba, loss of language by their children seems to be the ultimate fate of the group. The urban barrios are closely linked with other poor Indian as well as non-Indian populations and Toba children are in contact with only Spanish speakers both in and out of school. The result is that urban Toba children use Spanish both at play and in school and retain Toba only for home use. Even in such well-known districts as the Barrio Toba in Resistencia, numbers of non-Toba families have moved in and have even inter-married with the Toba. Since there are ever-increasing numbers of non-Toba speakers, for example, in the Barrio Toba, some of the younger children are not even speaking Toba at home. In the cities outside of the Chaco, the more scattered families of Toba speakers find retention of language and customs among their children even more difficult.

The prognosis for Toba is mixed. An ever larger percentage of the Toba are now becoming urban dwellers and since Spanish is clearly preferred in the work situation, school situation, and in numerous cases of criollo inter-marriage, for these Toba the language will soon disappear. In some of the smaller towns where there is some attempt at bilingual education (for example, in Castelli), the prognosis is much better. Children are learning to read and write in their native language, and greater pride in language maintenance is found. Finally, in the

very rural areas, monolingual speakers of all ages
may still be found, thus the prognosis there is excellent.

The linguistic work on Argentina Toba has recently been increasing quite considerably.  In addition to Klein's analyses of Toba (1973, 1978, 1979,
1980, 1981, forthcoming a and b), there is a lexical index based on semantic domains (Vellard 1969),
a comparative Toba-Pilagá study (Bruno and Najlis
1965), a phonological statement on Resistencia Toba
(Martireña de Gasquet 1977), and work on Paraguayan
Toba (Susnik 1962, 1971/73; Sanchez Labrador 1972;
Gómez-Perasso 1979).  There are also a number of
ethnolinguistic studies, including Elmer Miller's
studies on kin terms (1966, 1973), an ethnobotanic
comparative statement by Martínez-Crovetto (1971).
Toba mythology and folklore have been studied by
Cordeu (1969/70), Fernandez G. and Bigot de Perez
(1983), Martínez-Crovetto (1975), E. Palavecino
(1969/70), M. de Palavecino (1983), and Wilbert and
Simoneau (1983).

2. Mocoví.  The Mocoví call themselves and their
language Mocoví.  Unlike the Toba, the Mocoví have
been poorly studied.  The National Aboriginal Census of 1968 (hereafter cited as CIN) lists a population of 2,900, found in 22 groups within the southern part of the Chaco province, especially in
Villa Angela and Napalpí; Mary Key (1979:114) cites
their number as 5,718. The majority of Mocoví are
fluent speakers of their own language, even though
they are frequently found working side by side with

the Toba either as small-scale cotton farmers or as salaried employees of large cotton plantations.

The only recent linguistic materials on the Mocoví are some references in the ethnobotanical study of Martínez-Crovetto (1971), some myths provided only in Spanish and analyzed by Rivera de Bianchi (1973), and an edited volume of Florian Paucke's letters written between 1762-64 (Furlong 1972), which include many details on the Mocoví language.

Since most of the Mocoví are primarily speakers of their own language, the prognosis for the survival of the language is excellent. Furthermore, because of the paucity of studies, the Mocoví language and culture is an excellent area for study.

3. Pilagá.    The Pilagá call themselves and their language Pilagá, or Toba-Pilagá, as does the non-indigenous Argentine population.   They are to be found in Pampa del Indio, Pampa Chica, Fortín Lavalle--all in the Chaco province--and in some small groups in the Province of Formosa.   Population estimates range from 500-1350 (Martínez-Crovetto 1971, Newbury 1973, CIN 1968, Key 1979). The Pilagá live in eight scattered communities consisting of about 100-250 people in each.   They intermarry with Tobas, Matacos, and local economically, socially and educationally similar non-Indians.

In the last sixteen years, the only study done of the Pilagá language is a comparative work based on the vocabularies of Toba and Pilagá (Bruno and Najlis 1965). There is some indication that with

further study it can be determined whether Pilagá
is a dialect of Toba rather than a separate language, but that issue has still not been resolved.
Due to constant contact with the Toba, the fact
that the differences between the languages are less
than between the other languages in the Guaykurú
family, the fact that the Toba have greater prestige in the region, a shift to Toba is certainly
possible.

One article (Newbury 1973), which deals with Pilagá folklore, is the only other source for Pilagá
studies. Therefore, since there is practically no
work done on this language, and since the population is quite small, a study of the language should
be undertaken soon.

4. Abipon. Although Abipon is one of the extinct
languages of Argentina, it is being included in
this survey because in recent years several scholars interested in historical reconstruction have
based their analyses on several of the 18th century
ethnographies and linguistic descriptions written
about this language and culture.

Based on Dobrizhoffer (1967/70 [original
1783/84]) and Brigniel's works (1896), Elena Najlis
(1966) has done a study which consists of both a
grammar and a lexicon in two volumes. More recently (1970), she has written a simplified version of
the grammar, stating morphophonemic rules in a generative framework. Utilizing Dobrizhoffer's work,
Sherzer (1970) has analyzed this late 18th century
ethnography in terms of the social and cultural

factors that were involved in the Abipon's use of
language.  Balmorí also refers to Dobrizhoffer's
work in his various articles on differences in
male-female speech (1967).

Further research on this language will of necessity require comparative analyses, but for this
language with the admirable quantity of material
available, this should prove relatively easy to
accomplish.

5. <u>Mbayá-Guaykurú (Eyiguayegi-Mbayá)</u>.  The sole
survivors of this once most-feared group, are the
Caduveo or Kadiueo, 600 in number, no longer found
in the Argentine Chaco, but rather in Mato Grosso
do Sul in Brazil.  They therefore fall outside the
scope of this article.

Because the Mbayá language had been widely spoken in northern Argentina in early colonial times,
there was considerable material collected by the
early missionaries.  It is on the basis of these
works, and comments by Dobrizhoffer in his work on
the Abipones, that Balmorí (1967) analyzed the co-
occurrence of grammatical gender historically in
the language and dealt with the differentiation
that Mbayá made between male and female speech.  A
potential help in reconstructing the language is
Susnik's recently edited version (1971/73) of San-
chez-Labrador's 18th century dictionary of Eyiguayegi-Mbayá, a Mbayá dialect, as well as Susnik's
structural analysis of the Eyiguayegi-Mbayá verb.
Klein's (1979b, 1980) preliminary studies of Caduveo further add to the increased interest in the

genetic and typological relationship of Caduveo
with other Chaco languages.

MATACO/MATAGUAYO FAMILY
    6. Chorotí (Yófuaha, Moyanek)
    7. Mataco (Vejos)

The Mataco/Mataguayo language family consists of
seven languages in all.  However, only two are presently to be found in Argentina: Mataco, which has
by far the larger number of speakers, and Chorotí.
Although the National Aboriginal Census of 1968
(CIN), indicates that there were 526 Chulupí (or
Ashlushlay or Chunupí) in the province of Salta,
more recent materials do not indicate they still
are located there.  The Chulupí originally came
from Paraguay in the 1930's looking for work on
sugar plantations, but with the severe and harsh
work conditions, many had already returned to Paraguay even before the 1968 census was taken.
    Mataco, Chorotí and Chulupí are classified as
pertaining to the Mataco stock by Loukotka; as part
of the Mataco family and Mataco branch by Voegelin
and Voegelin (1977:223-224); and part of the Mata-
co-Mataguayo family by Tovar (1961:35-39).  Chorotí
and Chulupí are grouped together, while Mataco is
placed in a separate branch of the family by Loukotka.  Tovar and Voegelin and Voegelin group each
language separately.
    Antonio Tovar has done the greatest amount of
research and fieldwork on this family.  He argues
that Mataco/Mataguayo represents the oldest lan-

guage family in the region, and that both the Guaraní and Guaykurú families should be considered as
innovators in the region.  He also notes that there
is very little borrowing from Spanish in Mataco/Ma-
taguayo, but some slight borrowing from Quechua,
which therefore provides an example of the post-
conquest spread of Quechua (1964a).  Also worth
mentioning here is Tovar's work on the relations
between the various Mataco languages in which he
provides a comparative list of the vocabulary of
four languages: Mataco, Chorotí, Chunupí (or Chulupí or Ashlushlay), and Macá (or Enimaga) (1964a);
as well as his lexico-statistical comparison of
Mataco with other languages of South America
(1964b, 1966a). Adding to this comparative and
historical perspective is a 1984 study of proto-
Mataco phonology by Elena L. Najlis.

In several volumes of <u>Latin American Indian Li-
teratures</u>, essays on Mataco folklore and mythology
have appeared (see for example, Palavecino 1979;
Alvarsson, L. Martínez and Perez Diaz 1983). Wilbert and Simoneau also edited a volume of folk literature of the Mataco Indians (1982).   Materials
including bibliographic references on the other Ma-
taco/Mataguayo languages spoken in Paraguay are
discussed in Klein and Stark in this volume.

6. <u>Chorotí</u>.   There are a small number of Chorotí or
<u>yofúaha</u>, as they call themselves, in the region of
the Pilcomayo River.   They are also called <u>moya-
nek</u>.   Tovar in 1966 noted that the Argentine Chorotí numbered about 1,000 (1966b).   Wilmar Stahl, a

Paraguayan anthropologist, in a recent communication, indicated that in the Argentine Mision de La
Paz there were 120 Chorotí (Stahl 1977).

The only linguistic material available for Chorotí in Argentina, besides the field notes of Tovar
(1966b), which include both a phonological statement and the long Swadesh word list, and his comparative work (1964) mentioned above, are two recent
works of Gerzenstein (1978 and 1983).

7. Mataco. There are three dialects of Mataco, all
of which are mutually intelligible and which reflect the geographic distribution of this group.
The northern Mataco, the least acculturated group,
are the Nocten; the western group, the Vejos; and
the Guisnay, the eastern group. The largest dialect group is the Vejos, although the estimates of
their total numbers vary considerably. Niels Fock
(1967) noted there were about 20,000 Mataco, while
Elena Najlis (1971b) stated that there were more
than 10,000. The 1968 CIN figures indicated that
10,022 Mataco were found in 111 groups, some of
whom were in permanent, some in isolated, and some
in irregular contact. Bartolomé (1972) noted that
if some groups the census missed were included, the
total might reach 12,000. In 1979, Barabas and
Bartolomé estimated 12,000 Mataco in the provinces
of Formosa and Salta, not including those in the
province of Chaco.

The linguistic situation of and the prognosis
for the Mataco is better than for most of the other
Chaco languages. There has been a long tradition

of missionary concern for the Mataco, especially on the part of the Anglican missionaries (Tovar 1972a). They have taught the Mataco to read and write in their own language and have acted on their behalf in assuring their civil rights. They have established schools run by the Mataco themselves who teach in their own language. Although their knowledge of Spanish is limited and unemployment among them is severe, because of their strong tra- ditionalism, their sense of tribal identity and monolinguistic patterns, the future of the Mataco language looks bright.

Research on the Mataco language is also better than for many of the other languages under discus- sion here. There is a two volume linguistic des- cription (Viñas Urquiza 1974) as well as a grammar of Mataco which accompanies a discourse analysis (Tovar 1981); several good phonological statements (Najlis 1968, 1971; Viñas Urquiza 1970; Tovar 1972b, 1975), on comparative Mataco (Tovar 1964a, 1964b), Male-Female speech dealing with the diffe- rences in pronouns used by males and females (Bal- morí 1967), and on mythology by Arancibia (1973) and Barabas and Bartolomé (1979).

JAQI FAMILY
        8. Aymara (Colla)

Aymara or Colla is considered a stock by Loukotka (1968:268-69), a family by Tovar (1961:49-52), a language within the Quechumaran phylum by Voegelin and Voegelin, and a language within the Jaqi family

by Hardman (1978:146-53). Its relationship with
other Jaqí and Andean languages are discussed in
this volume in the papers by Hardman and Briggs.

Aymara is spoken in Argentina in the provinces
of Salta and Jujuy. It is also spoken by a large
number of immigrant Bolivians in the <u>villas misé-</u>
<u>rias</u> that border the city of Buenos Aires. It is
difficult to estimate the Aymara speaking population in both sectors for different reasons. Those
who are found around Buenos Aires are often illegal
immigrants who are reluctant to provide any information about themselves. The Salta and Jujuy Aymara, on the other hand, have no such reluctance but
are aggregated in the indigenous census with other
groups in those provinces and so more precise counting is difficult. The combined number of Aymara
and Quechua for those two provinces is 20,000 (CIN
1968).

On the basis of a review of the linguistic literature, the work by Fidalgo (1965) peripherally notes the influence of Aymara on the Spanish of Jujuy. Other than this study it is impossible to
find any recent material on the status of either
the speakers or research on the Argentine Aymara.
This is clearly an important area for future research.

QUECHUA FAMILY
        9. Quichua

Quechua is classified by Loukotka (1968:263-68) as
a stock, containing 18 modern or post-Colombian

dialects, including Catamarca and Santiagueño or Panpa-simi spoken in Argentina. Tovar (1963:52-60) list Quechua as a language, with many dialects, not identifying any Argentine ones, while Voegelin and Voegelin (1977:21) classify Quechua as a language within the Quechumaran phylum, noting names and locations of its many dialects. Gary Parker (Longacre 1979) notes that Argentine Quechua should be classified as Quechua B. Louisa Stark, in the most recent work on this subject, notes that the Argentine Quichua language is divided into three dialects, with the Santiago dialect having the majority of speakers (60,000). For a compete statement of the current linguistic situation and a full bibliography, see L. Stark's essay on the history of the Quichua of Santiago de Esterro in this volume.


LULE-VILELA FAMILY
        10. Vilela

Loukotka, in his classification, lists Vilela as a stock (1968:53) in the Chaco Division, with a number of languages, all of which are considered extinct; Lule as a stock in the Southern division, also containing a variety of languages, all of which are presently extinct; and Charrua as a stock belonging to the Central Brazilian division, with a number of extinct languages. Tovar lists the Lule-Tonocote as one family and the Vilela as another (1963:32-35), but he notes that the connections between the two are probably strong. He urges work

be done to clarify the relationship of these various languages, which he calls languages in transition between an Andean type, and a Chaco type.  He
does not cite Charrua in connection with either
Lule or Vilela.  Voegelin and Voegelin (1977:212)
classify a Lule-Vilela-Charrua family as extinct,
stating that there is inadequate data available to
assign a grouping or determine if there was more
than one language.  Balmorí (1967) and Lozano
(1977) have most recently and seriously explored
and defined the relationship of the Lule-Vilela
family.  These latter scholars have also shown that
Vilela is not extinct.

Vilela, which is also called Chulupí and Chunupí, and is not to be confused with the Mataco languages of the same name, is spoken in Argentina in
the Chaco Province.  It had been assumed for years
to have been extinct; however, in the late 1960's,
at least five families were discovered in Napalpí,
and a couple of speakers in Resistencia.  Their total population now is less than ten, and only two
Vilela actually speak the language.

This language consisted of several dialects, but
the remaining speakers all speak the Ocol dialect.
The Vilela informants whom Lozano cites (1977) indicated that there was considerable inter-marriage
with other Chaco groups, but that the language was
passed through the paternal line so that there were
still some speakers to be found.  The prognosis,
nevertheless, is pessimistic.

The work that has been done on Vilela has primarily been done by Elena Lozano, who has published a

phonology with grammatical notes (1963/64), a text
with notes on the Vilela verb (1970a), and a translation of a Vilela story (1970b).  She also notes
that by comparing the word lists of Machoni on the
Lule language with her own data, one is able to establish a strong relationship between the two languages (1977).  Balmori (1967) also wrote a significant essay on comparative Lule-Vilela, in which
he noted that the differences between male speech
and female speech are demonstrated by third person
possessive markers.  Vilela is also frequently mentioned in the research being done on Charrua, an
extinct language, of disputed classification.  Rona
(1964), especially, argues that Charrua is probably
related to Vilela, and Balmori (1967) classifies it
in the subfamily Lule-Vilela.

TUPI-GUARANI FAMILY
    11. Guarani-Mbya
    12. Chiriguano-Chane

There are two Tupi-Guaranian languages that are
spoken in the northern part of Argentina: one in
Misiones and the other in Jujuy and Salta.[2]  The
language spoken in Misiones is sometimes called
Caingua, sometimes Mbya, and sometimes Guarani-
Mbya.  The language spoken in the western part is
called Chiriguano-Chane.
    Historically, there were other parts of the
country where Tupi-Guarani languages were spoken.
Ongoing interest in toponomy (Buffa 1966) provides
us with evidence of the spread in Entre Rios of one

of the languages of that family. For folklorists, Muniagurria (1966) has written in Spanish about the legends of the Correntinos of Guaraní origin.

Tovar (1961:85-86) labels Guaraní-Mbyá and Chiriguano-Chané as Tupi-Guaranian; Loukotka (1968: 105-118) places Guaraní-Mbyá (Caingua) in the Guaraní group and Chiriguano in the Chiriguano group of his Tupi stock, and Voegelin and Voegelin (1977: 338) list both languages as part of the Tupi subgroup. For a more detailed discussion on this subject, see the work by Rodrigues in this volume.

11. <u>Guaraní-Mbyá</u> (Caingua, Kaiwa). For this language, there is minimal linguistic, ethnographic and population information. According to the National Aboriginal Census (CIN), there were between 500 and 625 Mbyás in Misiones located in 28 communities. Bartolomé (1972) argues that they must number more than 1,000, while Martínez-Crovetto (1971) provides an estimate of 2,000. For this group, little linguistic material is available. Martínez-Crovetto's (1971) ethnobotanic study lists some terms in the language, but provides no other language data. Bartolomé notes in passing that most Mbyá speak <u>yopara</u>, a popular dialect of Guaraní spoken primarily in Paraguay, with non-Mbyá speakers.

12. <u>Chiriguano-Chané</u>. The Chiriguano-Chané are both of Amazonian origin: the Chiriguano speaking a Tupi-Guaraní language, and the Chané an Arawakan language. Since the middle of the 15th century,

the Chané, who had been found in the westernmost
region of the Chaco, have been in constant contact
with the Chiriguano, often as slaves.  As a result,
they adopted the Chiriguano language.  It is for
this reason that the two groups are referred to as
one, with a combined total population of 14,800
(CIN 1968).  They are taken as a cultural community
and possess a common language.  However, in spite
of the linguistic and, to a large extent, cultural
blending, the Chiriguano and Chané continue to
identify themselves as either Chiriguano or Chané
and occupy different municipalities.

Because of this interesting linguistic and cultural adaptation, this would be a good group to
study.  Except for the article by Dietrich (1977)
in which, for his analysis of Guarani languages, he
utilizes Chiriguano verbal morphology, no linguistic work has appeared.

There is considerable disagreement over the prognosis for survival of the group.  Metraux (1932)
announced that the group would disappear during the
1930's, which obviously has not occurred.  Manuel
Maria Rocca (1973) argues that Chiriguano is not
spoken with pride.  Cipoletti (1978), on the other
hand, argues that the presence and strength of Chiriguano story-telling and knowledge of mythology
indicates just the reverse.  Finally, Oñativia and
Reyes Donoso in an article on bilingual education
(1977), note that most Chiriguano children have no
competence in Spanish when they enter primary
school.  Thus, it would seem that if children are
still speaking the indigenous language at age 6-7,

712    *Harriet E. Manelis Klein*

the prognosis for the survival of the language is good.

ARAUCANIAN FAMILY

13. Araucanian

The Araucanians are known as Araucano or Mapuche, although they prefer being called Mapuche ("people of the earth"). They call their language mapudungu ("language of the earth"). The various dialects of the language are very similar and are still spoken by a large portion of the indigenous population in both Argentina and Chile. For more details, see the article by Croese in this volume.

Loukotka (1968:273-75) identifies Araucano or Mapuche as a language, with a number of dialects, which belongs to the Mapuche stock. Tovar (1963: 22-24) calls the language family Araucano and says there are several dialects spoken in Chile and several in Argentina. He also notes that the relationship of some of these languages is problematic. Voegelin and Voegelin group Araucanian within a Penutian phylum, arguing that it is distantly related to a grouping of languages and language families extending along the western coast of both North and South America. It is interesting to note that in spite of the fact that it has been known and studied for almost four centuries, the relationship of Araucanian with other South American Indian languages is still unknown.

In Chile, the Mapuche form the dominant indigenous group, having an estimated population of be-

tween 400,000 and 500,000 (International Review of
Mission 1973; Stuchlik and Salas 1974). Other
sources cited by Croese (this volume) provide a
considerably lower figure. In Argentina, they consist of a smaller number, estimated between a low
of 8,000 (Tovar 1963:23) and a high of 50,000 (CIN
1968). This higher figure may include other groups
(e.g., Tehuelche), who have become "araucanized."
The mapudungu speakers are concentrated primarily
in the province of Neuquén, but also live in the
provinces of Río Negro, La Pampa, Chubut and Santa
Cruz.

Recently, there has been considerable research
done on Araucanian. Especially interesting is the
work on its linguistic affiliation--on correspondences between Mayan and Araucanian (Stark 1970;
Hamp 1971), on Araucanian comparative linguistics
(Key 1978b), and on Araucanian genetic relationships (Key 1978a). Molina and Burruat de Bun (1967)
have studied the relationship of various Araucanian
dialects spoken in Argentina. Casullo (1963, 1964)
has studied the influence of that language on the
Spanish of Argentina and Chile. Fontanella (1967)
has done a componential analysis of personal suffixes, while Garay and Goluscio (1978) have analyzed
an aspect of Araucanian discourse. Folklore of
Neuquén speakers has been written about by Koessler-Ilg (1963). Ritual language spoken in the Lu-
kutun, an annual ceremony is discussed by Robertson-DeCarbo (1977). A phonological transcription,
a translation and an analysis of a traditional
Araucanian tale has been done by Golbert de Goodbar

(1975). Casamiquela, in an etymological analysis,
has also noted that Araucanian sacred places have
been heavily influenced by Tehuelche (1977). Clairis (1977, 1983) and Croese (this volume) provide
important details on the current situation and distribution of Araucanian speakers. Other areas of
linguistic studies involve comparative phonologies
of Chilean dialects, and dictionaries and grammars,
some of which have been reissued because of increased interest in Araucanian in both Chile and Argentina (Augusta Feliz 1966; P. Ernesto Wilhelm de
Moesbach 1978).

YAGAN FAMILY
    14. Yagan (Yámana)

According to the CIN (1968), inčikut ("speech of
the Indians") was spoken by less than 12 speakers
in the extreme south of the Island of Tierra del
Fuego. Ortiz-Troncoso (1973) concurs with this
number, but states that there are only 8 pure Yámana remaining, without possible descendents.
Clairis (1977) notes that in 1972 there were still
two good speakers of the language; however, both
had died by 1975. The group is definitely on the
point of disappearing (Clairis 1981a and this volume).

    Loukotka (1968:43) lists Yámana as an isolated
language, Voegelin and Voegelin (1977:22) as a single language within the Andean division, while Tovar (1963:15-17) classifies Yámana as a language
with up to five dialects.[3]

Golbert de Goodbar (1977, 1978) has published an
analysis of both the nominal morphology and of the
sentence structure, while Wilbert (1977) has published some Yámana texts which contain useful appendices.  Guyot (1968) has compared Yámana myths with
Selknam myths.  A lexicon of Yámana toponymy is
provided by Molina (1974).  Clairis (1977, 1981b,
1983) discusses Yámana and its relationship to
other southern Amerindian languages, and Chapman
and Clairis (1981) present phonological and typological material in a comparative context.

CHON FAMILY
    15. Ona (Šelknam)
    16. Tehuelche

In the major classifications of these final two
languages, there is total disagreement by scholars
on the grouping of these languages, the names by
which they are and have been known, and the origin
of the family name.  These languages, which extended historically from Tierra del Fuego up to Buenos
Aires, have had little serious or comparative study, and until recently were of interest more to
folklorists and historians than to linguists.

    As a result, it is no surprise to note that Lou-
kotka (1968:44-46) classifies Ona or Šelknam in the
languages of the island group and Tehuelche in the
Patagonian group, and both as part of the Patagonia
or Tschon stock; he also lists Gennaken (or Puelche
or Pampa or Gununa-kune) as belonging to another
isolated language.  Voegelin and Voegelin (1977:21)

classify both Ona and Tehuelche as part of the Ona-
Chon family, and list Puelche as a single language.[4] Tovar (1963:17-20) on the other hand groups
Ona, Tehuelche and Puelche together in the Tsoneka-
Selknam family, noting that gününa-küne was the old
name for more modern Tehuelche. Suarez (1973) also
adds Moseten to this grouping of languages, and
Stark (1970) adds these languages to the Penutian
phylum. Gerzenstein (1968) agrees with Loukotka's
contention that gününa-küne is a separate language. With the appearance of Casamiquela's work on
gününa-küne (1981) and with Clairis' work on Patagonian and Fuegian languages, it seems that we will
be able to clear up some of the confusion. Clairis
classifies gününa-küne as the language spoken by
the northern branch of Tehuelche, who were to the
south of Neuquen, and further notes that the only
"true" Tehuelche is that spoken today by the southernmost branch of the Tehuelche (Clairis 1981b,
1983 and this volume).

15. Ona. The Ona call themselves and their language šelknam. It is spoken in Tierra del Fuego in
Argentina and Chile. In 1968, there were 12 Ona
listed in the CIN, but as of 1977, there remained
but one Ona and 4 mestizos. In 1980, three aged
speakers remained (Clairis 1981b). In 1981, Chapman wrote "there is only one person who speaks
Selknam more or less fluently...and another man
knows some Selknam" (personal communication).
Thus, the linguistic prognosis for this group is
hopeless.

Considering that the Ona have been a relatively
small group for such a long time, there has been
much research on the language and culture. The
best linguistic materials are the works of Najlis
(1971a, 1973, 1975). Chapman, in addition to her
ethnographic studies of the Ona, has together with
Delia Suardíaz gathered linguistic data on Ona
which was utilized by Suarez in his publication of
1973; has analyzed Ona myths and rituals (1973);
has produced a film, "The Ona People: Life and
Death in Tierra del Fuego" (1976), which contains
large segments of spoken Selknam; and has co-authored with Clairis (1981) a linguistic and ethnographic study of proper names in Selknam. Wilbert
has edited Martin Gusinde's Selknam texts (1975),
which, together with Guyot's (1968) study of Selknam and Yámana myths and Pereira La Hitte's (1977)
study of Selknam myths, are useful for comparative
analyses. Key and Clairis (1978) have also compared Selknam with other Fuegian and Central South
American Indian languages.

16. Tehuelche. Although this language is also on
the verge of extinction, it was spoken until very
recent times by people who called themselves tso-
neka and who lived in southern Patagonia in the
province of Santa Cruz. They have also been called
the Patagonians or the aonikenke by scholars working on the subject. Data from 1913-14 indicated
that there were about 110 speakers. From a 1960
census we have aggregate data including the Tehuelche with the Araucanians, and the same situation

has occurred with CIN (1968), so it is unclear how many actually existed. Although many contemporary sources claim that the Tehuelche are extinct, Casamiquela (1973) and Key (1979) list their number as 52, while Barabas and Bartolomé (1979) note a few dozen still do remain. Clairis (1981c) claims that there are between 50-100 Tehuelche; however, there are less than ten fluent speakers of the language.

Interest in this Patagonian group remains strong, and Tehuelche has been recently studied by several linguists. We have a good phonological analysis of the language based on data collected by Rodolfo Casamiquela in 1951-56 (Gerzenstein 1968), dialect descriptions by Molina (1963), and several studies on the phonology, semantics and linguistic classification of Tehuelche by Suarez (1971, 1973). Juan Adolfo Vazquez has added to the folkloric literature in his analysis of a Tehuelche myth (1976). Most recently, the language has been studied by Clairis (1977, 1981b) and continues to be studied by a group of students under his direction (personal communication, 1984).

NOTES

1.  It has been estimated that there are about 60,000 indigenous peoples scattered in northern Santa Fe, Misiones, Corrientes and belts of misery around Buenos Aires (Rubio Orbe 1973:643).
2.  Although I have not listed yopara, the Guaraní dialect spoken in Paraguay, as a Tupi-Guaraní language, there are many speakers of yopara, especially in rural Argentina.

3.  Most authors have preferred the Yámana to Yagan
    or Yahgan (coined by Bridges and not a native
    term) in referring to this southernmost group;
    however, recently several female members of the
    group objected to the use of Yámana since it
    means "man, male" and they have requested the
    return to the neutral term Yagan (Clairis 1981b,
    1981c).

4.  They also state that another name for Tehuelche
    is Chon, but do not refer to Puelche as gününa-
    küne.

REFERENCES

Alvarsson, J.A.  1983.  Mataco.  Latin American In-
    dian Literatures 7.2:167-69.
Arancibia, Ubén Gerardo.  1973.  Vida y mitos del
    mundo mataco.  Serie conducta y communicación 4,
    Buenos Aires: Ediciones Depalma.
Augusta Feliz, Fr. José de.  1966.  Diccionario
    araucano-español y español-araucano, tomo I,
    Chile: Padre Las Casas (re-edición de 1916).
Balmorí, Cl. H.  1967.  Estudios de área lingüís-
    tica indígena.  Buenos Aires: Centro de Estudios
    Lingüísticos.
Barabas, Alicia and Bartolomé, Miguel A.  1979.  Un
    Testimonio mítico de los Mataco. Journal de la
    Société des Américanistes (Paris) 66:125-132.
Bartolomé, Miguel A.  1972.  The Situation of the
    Indians in the Argentine: The Chaco area and Mi-
    siones Province.  In The Situation of the In-
    dian in South America, pp. 218-251.  Genève: L'
    Université de Berne.

Borruat de Bun, M. 1967. El nillatun en la tribu Linares, una comunidad Mapuche del Sur de Neuquén. Runa 10:406-421.

Boucherie, Jorge C. 1968. Los Indios Tobas del Chaco Argentino. Separata del Tomo II del Censo Indígena Nacional. Buenos Aires.

Brigniel, Joseph. 1896. Vocabulario castellano-abipón con frases y verbos y Oraciones y doctrina cristiana, edited by Samuel Lafone Quevedo. Boletin de la Academia Nacional de Ciencias XV: 185-253.

Bruno, L.N. and Najlis, E.L. 1965. Estudio comparativo de vocabulario Tobas y Pilagás. Buenos Aires. Facultad de Filosofia y Letras, Centro de Estudios Lingüisticos, Universidad de Buenos Aires.

Buffa, J.L. 1966. Toponimia aborigen de Entre Rios. La Plata.

Casamiquela, Rodolfo. 1973. Alacalufes, Canoeros Occidentales y Pueblos Marginales o Metamórficos, Relaciones de la Sociedad Argentina de Antropologia (Buenos Aires) n.s. 7:125-143.

------. 1977. Posibles raíces patagónicas en creencias araucanas, I. Las Piedras sagradas 'con ojos'. Relaciones de la Sociedad Argentina de Antropología n.s. 9:107-114.

------. 1981. Grammaire inédite de gününa këna. C.N.R.S., Paris.

Casullo, Fernando Hugo. 1963. Voces de Supervivencia Indígena (de Origen Araucano), Boletin de la Academia Argentina de Letras, Buenos Aires, XXVIII:121-129.

------.  1963/1964.  Voces indígenas en el idioma
español.  Buenos Aires.  Compañía Argentina de
Editores.

Censo Indígena Nacional (CIN).  1968.  Ministerio
del Interior, República de Argentina, Buenos
Aires, vols. II.

Chapman, Anne M.  1973.  Ensayo sobre algunos mitos
y ritos de los Selk'nam (Ona).  Karukinka
6:2-11.

------.  1976.  The Ona People: Life and Death in
Tierra del Fuego (a film).

Chapman, Anne and Christos Clairis.  1981.  Observaciones Etnológicas y Lingüísticas acerca de
Antropónimos Selk'nam.  Estudios Filológicos 16:
7-33 (Valdivia).

Cipoletti, Maria Susana.  1978.  Mitología chiri-
guana en Los Grupos Aborigenes del Limite del
Gran Chaco.  Cuadernos Franciscanos 49:47-66
(Salta).

Clairis, Christos.  1977.  Lingüística fueguina.
Boletín de Filologia, Universidad de Chile 28:
29-47.

------.  1981a.  José Emperaire et Les Qawasqar:
Notes Linguistiques Inedites sur Les "Nomades de
la Mer".  Journal de la Société des Américanistes, juillet.

------.  1981b.  "Préface" de la Grammaire Inédite
de gününa këna de Rodolfo Casamiquela, C.N.R.S.
(Paris).

------.  1983.  Las Lenguas de la Patagonia.  In
América Latina en sus lenguas indígenas, B. Pottier, ed.  Caracas: UNESCO/Monte Avila Editores.

Cordeu, Edgardo J.    1969/70.    Aproximación al hori-
zonte mítico de los tobas.    Runa 12(1/2):67-176.

Dobrizhoffer, Martin.    1783 (original version).
Geschichte der Abiponer, einer berittenen und
kriegerischen Nation in Paraguay, 3 vols.    Wien:
Joseph Edlen von Kurzbet.

------.    1967-1970.    Historia de los abipones, Tra-
ducción de E.    Wernicke y Clara V.    de Guillen,
Advertencia de Ernesto J.A.    Maeder, Noticia
bio-bibliografica de Guillermo Furlong, 3 vols
(Resistencia).

Ernesto Wilhelm de Moesbach, P.    1978.    Diccionario español-mapuche, Siringa Libros.

Fernandez G., German M.S.    and M.    Bigot de Peréz.
1983.    Those who come from the sky.    A Toba myth
about the origin of women and the humanization
of men.    Latin American Indian Literatures 7.2:
123-133.

Fidalgo, Andrés.    1965.    Breves toponimía y vocabulario jujeños, Buenos Aires.

Fock, Niels.    1967.    Mataco Indians in their Argentine setting.    Folk 8-9:89-104 (KØbenhavn).

Fontanella, M.B.    1967.    Componential Analysis of
personal affixes in Araucanian.    IJAL 33:305-
308.

Furlong, Guillermo.    1972.    Florián Paucke, S.I.    y
sus cartas al visitador Contucci (1762-1764).
Buenos Aires: Casa Pardo.

Garay, Ana Fernandez and Goluscio, Lucía.    1978.
Rogativas araucanas. Vicus II.

Gerzenstein, A.    1968.    Fonología de la lengua Gününa-këna.    Cuadernos de lingüística indígena,

5. Buenos Aires: Facultad de Filosofía y Letras, Universidad de Buenos Aires.
------. 1978. Lengua Chorote, I. Instituto de
Lingüística, Universidad de Buenos Aires.
------. 1983. Lengua Chorote, II. Estudio des-
criptivo, comparativo y vocabulario. Buenos
Aires: Universidad de Buenos Aires/Instituto de
lingüística.
Golbert de Goodbar, Perla. 1975. Epu peñiwen (los
dos hermanos): cuento tradicional araucano.
Buenos Aires: Centro de Investigaciones en Cien-
cias de la Educación, Sección Lenguas Indígenas.
------. 1977. Yagán I: Las partes de la oración.
Vicus I.
------. 1978. Yágan II: Morfología nominal.
Vicus II.
Gómez-Perasso, José Antonio. 1979. Estudios Kom-
lyk. Etnografía paraguaya 2.1. Asunción:
Centro Paraguayo de Estudios Antropológicos.
Guyot, M. 1968. Les Mythes chez les Selk'nam et
les Yamana de la Terre de Feu, 156-159.
Hamp, E.P. 1971. On Mayan-Araucanian Comparative
Phonology. IJAL 37.3:156-159.
Hardman-de-Bautista, M.J. 1978. Jaqí: The Lin-
guistic Family. IJAL 44.4:146-153.
International Review of Mission. 1973. South
American Indians: The Barbados Discussion.
International Review of Mission 62:261-345.
Key, Mary R. 1978a. Araucanian Genetic Relation-
ships. IJAL 44.4:280-293.
------. 1978b. Linguistica comparativa araucana,
Vicus II.

_____. 1979. The grouping of South American In-
dian languages. Ars linguistica 2. Tübingen:
Narr.

Key, Mary R. and Christos Clairis. 1978. Fuegian
and Central South American Language Relationships. Actes du XLII International Congress of
Americanists (1976) Paris 4:635-645.

Klein, Harriet E. Manelis. 1973. A grammar of
Argentine Toba: verbal and nominal morphology
(Columbia University), doctoral dissertation.

------. 1978. Una Gramática de la Lengua Toba:
Morfología Verbal y Nominal. Montevideo: Facul-
tad de Humanidades y Ciencias, Universidad de la
Republica.

------. 1979a. Noun Classifiers in Toba. Ethno-
linguistics: Boas, Sapir and Whorf Revisited, M.
Mathiot, ed., pp. 85-95. The Hague: Mouton.

------. 1979b. Comparative Toba-Caduveo Semantics, Paper presented at the Linguistic Society
of America, December.

------. 1980. Deixis as a Semantic Category in
Chaco Indian Languages: An Example of Areal
Linguistics. Paper presented at the American
Anthropological Association, December.

------. 1981. Location and Direction in Toba:
Verbal Morphology. IJAL 47.3:227-235.

------. forthcoming a. Styles of Toba Discourse:
Oratory and Narrative.

------. forthcoming b. Toba, A Grammar. Croom
Helm Descriptive Grammar Series. Kent: Croom
Helm Ltd.

Klein, Harriet E. Manelis and Louisa Stark. 1977. Indian Languages of the Paraguayan Chaco. Anthropological Linguistics 19.8:378-401 (Reprinted in this volume).

Koessler-Ilg, Bertha. 1963. Tradiciones Araucanas, Supplement I to Rhesis, Revista Filologia y Lingüística, Universidad Nacional de la Plata, Buenos Aires.

Latin American Indian Literatures.

Longacre, Robert E. 1969. Comparative reconstruction of indigenous languages. In Current Trends in Linguistics 4, T.A. Sebeok, ed., pp. 320-360. The Hague: Mouton.

Loukotka, Čestmír. 1968. Classification of South American Indian Languages, Reference Series vol. 7. Los Angeles: Latin American Center, University of California.

Lozano, Elena. 1963/64. Estudios sobre el Vilela. Boletin de Filologia 10(61-62-63):15-157 (Montevideo).

------. 1970a. Textos Vilelas, Consejo Nacional de Investigaciones Científicas y Tecnicas, La Plata.

------. 1970b. La mujer infiel. Anales del Instituto de Lingüística, Universidad Nacional de Cuyo 10:97-100 (Mendoza).

------. 1977. Cuentos secretos vilela: La mujer tigre. Vicus I.

Machoni de Cerdeña, P. Antonio. 1732. Arte y vocabulario de la lengua Lule y Tonocoté compuestos con facultad de sus superiores....Madrid.

Maria Rocca, Manuel. 1973. Los chiriguano-chané. America Indígena 33:3-149.

Martínez, L., S.J. 1983. Mataco. Latin American Indian Literatures 7.2:200-201.

Martínez-Crovetto, Raúl. 1971. Introducción a la etno-botánica aborigen del Nordeste argentino, Congrés International des Américanistes 38.3: 91-97.

------. 1975. Folklore Toba oriental: Relatos fantásticos de origen chamánico. Suplemento Antropológico X(1-2):177-205 (Asunción).

Martireña de Gasquet, Ana María. 1977. Fonologia de la lengua toba. Vicus I.

Metraux, Alfred. 1932. Mitos y cuentos de los indios Chiriguano. Revista del Museo de la Plata XXXIII:119-184 (La Plata).

Miller, Elmer S. 1966. Toba Kin terms, Ethnology 5.2:194-201.

------. 1973. The Linguistic and Ecological Basis of Toba Kin Categories, International Congress of Ethnological and Anthropological Sciences (Chicago).

Miranda, Guido A., ed. 1968. Aportes para la Historia del Chaco. Resistencia: Biblioteca "El Territorio".

Molina, Manuel J. 1963. Un antiguo idioma patagónico: el "Inajet". Los Mapuches argentinos. Historia IX.31:46-59 (Buenos Aires).

------. 1974. Toponimia indígena fueguina. Karukinka 8:2-10.

Muniagurria, Saturnino. 1966. Yboti Rogue (Petales de Flores). Santa Fe: Editorial Castellvi.

Najlis, Elena L. 1966. Lengua abipona. Buenos Aires: Centro de Estudios Lingüísticos, vol. 2.

------. 1968. Dialectos del Mataco. Universidad del Salvador, Anales 4:1-14 (Buenos Aires).

------. 1970. Morfemas de persona en abipón. Universidad del Salvador, Buenos Aires.

------. 1971a. Disambiguation in Selknam. IJAL 37.1:46-47.

------. 1971b. Premataco phonology. IJAL 37.2: 128-130.

------. 1973. Lengua Selknam. Universidad del Salvador, Buenos Aires.

------. 1975. Diccionario Selknam. Universidad del Salvador, Buenos Aires.

------. 1984. Fonologia de la protolengua mataguaya. Buenos Aires: Universidad de Buenos Aires/Instituto de Linguistica.

Newbury, Sara Josefina. 1973. Los Pilagá: su religión y sus mitos de origen. America Indígena 33.

O'Leary, Timothy J. 1963. Ethnographic Bibliography of South America. New Haven: Human Relations Area Files.

Oñativia, Oscar V. and Maria Alejandra Reyes Donoso. 1977. Basic Issues in Establishing a Bilingual Method. The Reading Teacher 30.7:727-734.

Ortiz-Troncoso, Omar R. 1973. Los Yámana, veinticinco años después de la misión Lipschutz. Anales del Instituto de la Patagonia IV.1-3:77-105.

Palavecino, Enrique. 1969/70. Mitos de los indios tobas. Runa 12.1/2:177-197.

------. 1979. The Magic World of the Mataco (trans. by J.A. Vazquez). Latin American Indian Literatures 3.2:61-75.

Palavecino, M.D.M. de. 1983. Toba. Latin American Indian Literatures 7.2:170-71.

Pereira LaHitte, C.T. 1977. Aportes de un sabio francoargentino al conocimiento de la mitologia ona. Karukinka 19-20:58-64.

Perez Diaz, Andres A. 1983. Mataco Myths. Latin American Indian Literatures 7.2:134-166.

Republica de Argentina (see Censo Indígena Nacional).

Rivera de Bianchi, Mabel. 1973. Mitología de los pueblos del Chaco, según visión de los autores de los siglos XVII y XVIII. America Indígena 33.3:695-733.

Robertson-DeCarbo, Carol E. 1977. Lukutún: Text and Context in Mapuche Rogations. Latin American Indian Literatures, 2.1.:67-78.

Rona, J.P. 1964. Nuevos elementos acerca de la Lengua Charrua. Montevideo.

Rubio Orbe, Gonzalo. 1973. Argentina Indígena. America Indígena 33.3:643-654.

Sanchez Labrador, José (see Susnik, Branislava, 1971-73).

Sherzer, Joel. 1970. La parole chez les Abipone: pour une ethnographie de la parole. L'Homme 10.1:40-76.

Stahl, Wilmar. 1977. Personal communication.

Stark, Louisa R. 1970. Mayan affinities with Araucanian. Chicago Linguistic Society 6:57-69.

Stuchlik, Milan and Adalberto Salas. 1974. Rasgos de la sociedad mapuche contemporanea. Modo, persona y número en el verbo mapuche. Universidad de Chile, 136pp.

Suarez, Jorge A. 1970. Clasificación interna de la familia lingüística Chon, Anales del Instituto de Lingüística. Universidad Nacional de Cuyo 10:29-59.

------. 1971. A Case of absolute synonyms. IJAL 37:192-195.

------. 1973. Macro-Pano-Tacanan. IJAL 39.3:137-154.

Sušnik, Branislava (Branka). 1962. Estudios emoktoba: I. Boletin de la Sociedad Científica del Paraguay VII:1-214.

------. 1971-73. Familia Guaykurú, Lenguas Chaqueñas, vols. 1-3. Asunción: Museo Etnográfico.

Tomasini, Alfredo. 1978. Contribución al estudio de la conquista y colonización del Chaco. Cuadernos Franciscanos 49:7-20 (Salta).

Tovar, Antonio. 1961. Catálogo de las lenguas de América del Sur: enumeración, con indicaciones tipológicas bibliografía y mapas. Buenos Aires: Editorial Sudamericana.

------. 1962. Los préstamos en mataco: contacto de español y lenguas indígenas. Acta Salmanticensia 16:461-468.

------. 1964a. Relación entre las lenguas del grupo mataco. Homenaje a Fernando Márquez-Miranda, 370-377 (Madrid).

------. 1964b. El grupo mataco y su relación con otras lenguas de América del Sur. Actas y Memo-

rias, XXXV Congreso International de Americanistas II:439-452.

------. 1966a. Genealogía, lexico-estadística y
tipología en la comparación de lenguas americanas. Proceedings of the XXXVI International
Congress of Americanists II:229-238.

------. 1966b. Notas de campo sobre el idioma
Chorote. Proceedings of the XXXVI International
Congress of Americanists II:221-227.

------. 1972a. Report on Mataco. IJAL 38:208.

------. 1972b. Sobre el material lingüístico Mataco. International Congress of Americanists
395:99-103.

------. 1975. Estudiando una lengua indígena: el
Mataco. Estudios Sobre Política Indigenista Española en America 1:247-255.

------. 1981. Relatos y Dialogos de los Matacos.
Madrid: Ediciones Culturas Hispanicas.

Vázquez, Juan Adolfo. 1976. Nacimiento e infancia
de Elal: mitoanálisis de un texto tehuelche meridional. Revista Iberoamericana 42.95:210-216.

Vellard, J.A. 1969. Vocabulario toba. Cuadernos
de Lingüística Indígena. Centro de Estudios
Lingüísticos 6:1-49.

Viñas Urquiza, María Teresa. 1970. Fonología de
la lengua Mataco. Cuadernos de Lingüística Indígena. Centro de Estudios Lingüísticos 7:1-82.

------. 1974. Lengua Mataca, I-II. Buenos Aires.
Centro de Estudios Lingüísticos.

Voegelin, C.F. and F.M. Voegelin. 1977. Classification and Index of the World's Languages.
Amsterdam: Elsevier.

Wilbert, Johannes.  1975.  Folk Literature of the
    Selknam Indians.  Los Angeles: Latin American
    Center, University of California.
------.  1977.  Folk Literature of the Yamana In-
    dians.  Berkeley: University of California.
Wilbert, Johannes and Karin Simoneau, eds.  1982.
    Folk Literature of the Mataco Indians.  Los
    Angeles: University of California Press.
------.  1983.  Folk Literature of the Toba In-
    dians, I. Los Angeles: University of Califor-
    nia Press.
Wolf, Dietrich.  1977.  Las categorias verbales,
    partes de la oración, en tupí-guaraní.  Indiana
    4:245-261 (Berlin).

# 19. History of the Quichua of Santiago del Estero

## Louisa R. Stark

INTRODUCTION

The purpose of this paper is twofold. First, using
linguistic data it attempts to contribute to our
understanding of the history of northwestern Argentina. Secondly, and more specifically, it seeks to
resolve several problems pertaining to the history[1]
of the Quichua spoken in Santiago del Estero. The
paper itself is based on fieldwork carried out in
Argentina during the Spring of 1978, as well as on
published and unpublished sources.

DIALECTS OF QUICHUA SPOKEN IN NORTHWESTERN
ARGENTINA

The area of northwestern Argentina where Quichua
has traditionally been spoken is a mountainous region extending from Bolivia in the north to Mendoza
in the south, and from the Chilean border in the
west to the Argentinean Chaco in the east. In
terms of modern political divisions it encompasses
the provinces of Jujuy, Salta, Catamarca, La Rioja,
Tucumán, and parts of Santiago del Estero, Córdoba,
San Juan, and Mendoza. This region forms a valid
culture area in itself which stands in contrast to
the rest of the country (Bennett, Bleiler and Sommer 1948:15).

Based on phonological, morphological and lexical data, the Quichua of northwestern Argentina is divided into three principal dialects (Stark 1978). A Northern dialect is spoken in the province of Jujuy, and probably extends to the east into the mountainous region of the province of Salta. The Sierra de Chani, which forms the southern boundary of Jujuy, also serves as the southernmost boundary of this dialect of Quichua. A central dialect was traditionally spoken in today's provinces of Salta, Tucumán, Catamarca, La Rioja, Córdoba, and northern Mendoza. There may also have been speakers of this dialect in the northeast corner of today's province of the Chaco. Finally, an eastern dialect is spoken in Santiago del Estero. It is this dialect, hereafter referred to as SE Quichua, which will serve as the focus of the following discussion.

THE QUICHUA OF SANTIAGO DEL ESTERO

Geographical Location
Today there are approximately 60,000 speakers of Quichua (Bravo 1975:xiii) located in the northern and central parts of the provinces of Santiago del Estero in the departments of Capital, Banda, Figueroa, Matará, Sarmiento, Robles, Loreto, San Martín, Salavina, Avellaneda, and some parts of Copo, Alberdi, Pellegrini, and General Toabada (Christensen 1970:34). The area extends to the west into the Andean foothills, to the south into a group of salt flats on the pampas, and to the northeast and east into the true Chaco.

## History of SE Quichua

*Theories As To The History of SE Quichua.* With a
few exceptions (Christensen 1970; Gargaro 1953;
Santucho 1954), it is popularly believed that Quichua was introduced into Santiago del Estero after
its conquest by the Spaniards in the sixteenth century (Bravo 1965:11; Larrouy 1914:29; Ledesma Medina 1946:29). The belief that the language did not
exist in this area before the arrival of the Spaniards is based on the following criteria: (1) that
archaeologically there are no Inca remains in the
area, and (2) that the early Spaniards did not note
having encountered Quichua speakers when they entered the region. The hypothesis that Quichua was
introduced after Spanish contact is also based on
the assumption that the Spaniards brought many Quechua speakers with them from Peru when they colonized the area. However, there is no historical evidence that this was actually the case (Levillier
1927:37). But beyond this, newly discovered archaeological and ethnohistorical evidence points to
the probability that Quichua was spoken in Santiago
del Estero *before* the arrival of the Spaniards.

## The Linguistic Prehistory of SE Quichua

*Archaeological Evidence.* As mentioned above, one
of the criterion used for believing that Quichua
was not spoken in Santiago del Estero before the
arrival of the Spaniards comes from the lack of archaeological evidence pointing to Inca occupation

of the area.  Certainly there is little that has
been uncovered that has been analyzed as Inca.[2]
However, the archaeological research that has been
carried out in Santiago del Estero has concentrated
on the southcentral and southern parts of the province, with little in the way of investigations occurring in the northern area where Quichua has traditionally been spoken.  Recent surveys carried out
in that part of the province, however, have uncovered evidence of Inca occupation (Toga 1978) which
could form a basis for the belief that Quichua was
introduced into this region before the arrival of
the Spaniards.

Ethnohistorical Evidence.  Early Spanish visitors
noted the presence of an Inca road in the vicinity
of Santiago del Estero.  In a letter to the King of
Spain written in 1566, Juan de Matienzo reports:

> De allí (Tambos de la Cienaga), dice, se
> aparta el camino del Inca para la ciudad
> de Londres y de allí para Chile por la
> cordillera de Almargo que dizen sobre· la
> mano derecha y sobre la izquierda se to-
> ma el camino para Cañete y Santiago del
> Estero que es mediendose hacía los llanos
> del Rio de la Plata (Christensen 1970:38)

And in 1613, several residents of Santiago del Estero mention an Inca road which connected their
homeland with Santiago de Chile (Gargaro 1953:
9-12).

There is also ethnohistorical evidence for the
construction of Inca buildings in Santiago del Estero.    In 1566, Juan de Matienzo writes of "Tambe-
rias del Ynga" which were found on the old Inca
road to Santiago del Estero, as well as in Santiago
del Estero itself, and which were staffed by Quichua-speaking Chichas (Christensen 1970:38). And in
1613 an inhabitant of Santiago del Estero mentions
"paredones viejos de la casa del Inca" near the
ancient Inca road that ran through the area (Gargaro 1953:10).

Upon their arrival in Santiago del Estero, the
Spaniards encountered speakers of Quichua and Jurie.[3]    The Jurie were a peaceful, sedentary tribe
which occupied the area between the Salado and Dul-
ce Rivers, in more or less the exact geographical
area in which Quichua is now spoken.    They seem to
have been co-existing peacefully with the Quichua
when the Spaniards first arrived in 1550. Although
they could not communicate directly with the Jurie,
the Spaniards noted with surprise that the Peruvian
Indians who accompanied them could communicate with
them in Quechua (Levillier 1919: 92, 104, 115, 119;
Nardi 1962:263; von Hauenschild 1943:118).

Beyond specific references to the speaking of
Quichua, the early Spaniards noted upon their arrival the presence of "Peruvians" (Sotelo Narváez
1965:391), Chichas (Christensen 1970:38), and Incas
(Sotelo Narváez 1965:392), all of whom were presumably speakers of Quichua.

Based on archaeological and ethnohistorical data, we conclude that Quichua was spoken in Santiago

del Estero before the arrival of the Spaniards.   It
was probably introduced at some time after 1471,
during the reign of Topa Inca.   At this time the
Incas were already exploiting the mines of northwestern Argentina (Stark 1978:6-11) and the Chaco
tribes, wanting the minerals that they produced,
had already launched their first attack on this
part of the Empire (Metraux 1945:465). Since Santiago del Estero was located at a strategic point
geographically, on the only natural pass that connected the Paraná and the Chaco tribes in the east
with the Andean foothills and their mines in the
west, the Incas quite probably set up military outposts in this area.   These would have been manned
by a combination of soldiers and <u>mitimae</u> (colonists), a practice which had been followed in other
parts of Argentina (Fock 1961). After the Spaniards arrived, they also populated the area with
garrisons in an attempt to control continuous invasions by the Chaco tribes (Figueroa 1949:61-65; Jolis 1789:560; Archivo de Santiago del Estero 1925b:
100).

## The Spanish Conquest and the Colonial Period

Soon after the Spaniards arrived in Santiago del
Estero they began to follow the practice of their
compatriots throughout the rest of South America in
dividing up the Indians that they encountered into
encomiendas.[4]   Thus Indian groups which before had
lived in scattered settlements were brought together into towns (Archivo de Santiago del Estero
1925b:77) so as to be more accessible for the exac-

tion of tribute and labor services by the Spaniards. In the area in which Quichua is still spoken, the first groups which came under the encomienda system were local speakers of Quichua and
Jurie; later they were joined by members of other
tribal groups, including speakers of Lule, Diagui-
ta, Sanavirone-Indama, and Comechingone. These Indians, finding themselves concentrated in settlements with Jurie and Quichua speakers, first seem
to have spoken Jurie (Tonocote) as a second language, and then later replaced Jurie with Quichua.[5]
There is, for example, a report made during the
early Colonial Period by P. Pedro Lozano who describes a group of native speakers of Lule. Among
them the older people understood Tonocote (Jurie)
while the younger ones commonly spoke Quichua
(Santucho 1954:5).

Had the Spaniards chosen the Jurie to serve as
their middlemen, perhaps Jurie would have become
the dominant language in Santiago del Estero. Instead they appear to have chosen local Quichua
speakers,[6] which they drew from among the original
mitimaes or from among the few "Peruvians" that had
accompanied them, to serve as their mandanes (Figueroa 1948, 1949; Archivo de Santiago del Estero
1924:130, 1925a:110, 1925b:77).[7] This occurred,
quite probably, because the Spaniards had known
Quechua speakers in Peru, and considered them to be
more "civilized" than members of the other Indian
groups and thus capable of filling positions of responsibility. The Indians who served under the
Quichua speakers learned the language from them,

using it during the early Colonial Period as a lingua franca among themselves, and later as their
first language. Thus the local native languages
began to decline. This process was also fostered
by a natural enemy, disease, which took its toll of
the concentrations of Indians newly assembled in
the towns. However, disease quite probably had
less of an effect on the Quichua-speaking native
leaders who were less over-worked and better fed
than the peoples that they governed (Bolton 1978).[8]

The mita also had an effect on the linguistic
situation, with many Indians being sent away to Potosí to work in the mines.[9] Although mention is
made of large numbers of Juries being sent to Bolivia (Levillier 1927:37), the Quichuas of the area,
perhaps because of their favored status, do not
seem to have suffered this fate. Thus there seems
to have been a rapid depletion of non-Quichua speakers since few of the Juries sent to Potosí ever
returned. Those who did return, if they had not
already learned Quichua in Santiago del Estero, had
probably become fluent in this language in Potosí.
Quichua was not only spoken in the city, but also
served as a lingua franca among the workers sent
there from all parts of the Spanish Empire.

The combination of disease and the mita caused a
rapid decline in the Indian population of Santiago del Estero. Between 1553 and 1609 the population had decreased by almost 50%; in 1553 there
were 48 Spaniards and 12,000 Indians in the area as
compared to 1609 when there were 100 Spaniards and
6,729 Indians (Carrizo 1937:119). Linguistically,

the decline was probably greatest among non-Quichua
speakers. For example, the Sanavirones-Indamas who
appear to have been a fairly sizable group at the
time of Spanish contact, are described in 1594 as:

> ...poca gente y tan hábil, que todos han
> aprendido la lengua de Cuzco (Quechua)
> como todos los indios que sirven a Santi-
> ago...(Baranza 1965:79).

It was probably in good part due to the drastic decline in the non-Quichua-speaking population that
the Spaniards themselves began to adopt Quichua as
a lingua franca in order to communicate with the
various Indian groups. This was nowhere more evident than in the policy of the Church, which was
made official in 1579 at the first synod celebrated
in Santiago del Estero. There it was decided that
the Indians of the area should be taught the doctrina and catecismo "en lengua del Cuzco" (Cuzco
Quechua) because a large number of Indians already
knew how to pray in that language, and because the
other Indian languages spoken in the province were
too many, and too small, to make it worthwhile to
learn and evangelize in all of them. Priests who
were to work with Indians had to be able to speak
the "lengua general del Cuzco."

Unlike other areas of northwest Argentina, this
did not seem to be too difficult. In fact, most
Criollos born in Santiago del Estero seem to have
spoken Quichua as is noted in a report of 1592-1593
when witnesses in the provincial capital state that

a Criollo priest spoke Quichua well simply from having been born there (Nardi 1962:264-265).[10]    And in
1635 the bishop of the area complained that:

> ...poco hablan los índios y españoles en
> castellano porque está más connaturali-
> zada la lengua general de los índios
> (Quichua)...(Bravo 1965:19).

Again, in 1734 it was noted that:

> ...en las ciudades de esta provincia no
> obstante de la comunicación y asisten-
> cia de sus obispos, parrocos y Goberna-
> dores, vecinos y comerciantes, es mas
> generalmente hablada entre la gente co-
> mun la dicha lengua (Quichua)...(Nardi
> 1962:267).

By the end of the Colonial Period, we find that the
original languages of Santiago del Estero had disappeared, having been replaced by Quichua which
had progressed from functioning as a lingua franca to serving as the first language of Indians and
Criollos alike.  The adoption of the Indian language as their first language by the Criollos seems to
have been the result of their small numbers, in
relationship to the Indian population, as well as
their isolation from the Spanish-speaking centers
of the country.

    To summarize, Quichua seems to have begun its
ascendancy in Santiago del Estero during the early
Colonial Period, with the depletion of speakers of

other Indian languages through disease and forced
labor in the mita. This was then reinforced by the
clergy who found it useful to use Cuzco Quichua as
a lingua franca in their work with the Indians.[11]
Their use of the Cuzco dialect probably had some
influence on the Quichua spoken during the Colonial
Period, and also up until today. In particular
this can be noted in the first person inclusive
pronominal suffix /-nčis/. Beyond this, Spanish-
speaking Criollos seem to have left their mark on
the language. This is particularly noticeable in
word order, where adjectives follow nouns, rather
than precede them, as is common in the Quechua spoken throughout the rest of South America.

The Nineteenth and Twentieth Centuries
By the middle of the nineteenth century, the Indian
population of Santiago del Estero had all but disappeared. As a French visitor noted during his
stay sometime between 1841 and 1859:

> ...el grueso de la población de la Pro-
> vincia de Santiago del Estero está com-
> puesta de mestizos provenientes de ín-
> dios de raza Quichua...se habla el qui-
> chua en toda la Provincia de Santiago,
> como se habla el Guaraní en el Paraguay
> ...(Santucho 1954:15).

What appears to have happened is that over time the
Indians of the province had become assimilated into
its "Mestizo," or Criollo, population. However,

Quichua, which had long been spoken by both groups, was maintained but identified as a non-Indian Cri-ollo language. As such it continued to flourish in Santiago del Estero. In the 1860s, an English traveler wrote of Bracho:

> The population here numbers about three thousand souls, of whom only three or four know Castilian--the remainder spea-king the Quichua (Hutchinson 1865:162).

Bracho, it should be noted, lies within a few kilo-meters of the provincial capital of Santiago del Estero.

And during the first decades of the twentieth century:

> ...en la misma capital de Santiago era todavía frecuente oir a caballeros y matronas de los más altos linajes pat-ricios y de la más elevada cultura, emplear el quichua con la misma fluidez y desenvoltura con que también hablaban el castellano (Christensen 1970:89).

However, more recently, inroads have been made into the language.  To begin with, Santiago del Estero, which for so long had existed in almost total iso-lation, has become integrated into the rest of Spa-nish-speaking Argentina.  Thus Quichua has all but disappeared among the urbanites, as well as among rural middle and upper classes; all of these indi-viduals have better means of communication with the

rest of the country, whether through transportation
to other parts of Argentina, or by means of Spanish-language radio, television, newspapers, and
magazines.  And, unlike the situation in Paraguay
where to speak Guaraní reinforces one's identity as
a Paraguayan, whatever one's class or geographical
background, such has not been the case in Santiago
del Estero.

Where Quichua remains is in the rural areas
where it is still spoken by the campesinos of the
province.  However, even there inroads are beginning to be made into the language, especially with
compulsory education of Quichua-speaking children
in Spanish-language schools.  Beyond this, men are
conscripted into the army, and younger members of
the rural population are leaving their communities
to look for work in urban areas, as close as the
provincial capital or as far away as Buenos Aires
(Hadis 1975). As a result there is beginning to be
a stigma attached to the speaking of Quichua.  For
in speaking the language, one admits that one is a
lower class rural rustic (D.  Bravo 1978; Christensen 1970:90), something that one hates to be in a
society which emphasizes so greatly the glories of
middle class urban life.  Worse yet, one can be ac-
cused of being an Indian, since outside of Santiago
del Estero Quichua is considered an "Indian" language.[12]  In a country which has been noted for its
"racismo antiindigenista" (Martínez 1972:46), being
identified in any way as an Indian is an insult indeed.[13]  As a result, the double stigma of ethnicity and class associated with its usage has caused a

decline in the speaking of Quichua. But with a population of some 60,000 speakers, a few of them
still monolinguals, the language is nowhere yet on
the verge of extinction.

CONCLUSION

In conclusion, we find that the Quichua of Santiago
del Estero is still fairly vigorous, especially in
comparison to the state of the language in the rest
of northwest Argentina where it is on the verge of
extinction (Stark 1978). To what do we attribute
this factor? The feature that appears to have contributed most to the survival of SE Quichua after
the sixteenth century is the fact that it has never
been thought of as an Indian language in Santiago
del Estero. In a country such as Argentina which,
like the United States, spent a good part of the
nineteenth century attempting to exterminate its
Indian population,Indian-ness, whether linguistic
or cultural, has been barely tolerated. Thus it is
not surprising that during the nineteenth century
Quichua disappeared in those parts of Argentina
where it has always been regarded as a Indian language; its speakers appear to have decided consciously to eradicate that aspect of their culture
that identified them most obviously as Indian
(Stark 1978). However, Quichua has not suffered the
same fate in Santiago del Estero, where it has long
been conceptualized as a "lengua criolla" (Bravo
1965:98). A good part of this belief is tied to the
historical interpretation that Quichua was brought
to Santiago del Estero by the Spaniards. This as-

sumption, while not based on historical fact, has
served to disassociate the language from its Indian
past.   And in so doing, it has probably contributed
to the survival of the language in Santiago del
Estero, a feat which has not been possible for the
majority of the Indian languages of Argentina.

ACKNOWLEDGEMENTS
This work was originally presented to the Symposium
on Andean Linguistics, XLIII International Congress
of Americanists, Vancouver, August 10-17, 1979. I
wish to thank Donald Dilworth and Pam Hunte for
commenting on earlier versions of this paper.   I
have also profited from discussions with Rodrigo
Bravo of Cafayete while I was in Argentina which
led to the development of some of the ideas about
the Indian and non-Indian nature of Argentine Quichua which are included in this paper.

NOTES
1.  When referring to the language as it pertains
    to Argentina, the term "Quichua" will be used.
    However, when reference is made to the language
    in its pan-Andean context, it will referred to
    as "Quechua."
2.  There is the possibility that some of the ar-
    chaeological materials uncovered in Santiago del
    Estero are actually Inca, although not labeled
    as such by investigators.   In particular this
    might apply to stone masonry and metal objects
    found at Icaño and published by Reichlen (1940).

3.   It is interesting to note that Jurie means "os-
     trich" in Quechua, and probably referred to the
     ostrich feather clothing worn by this group.

4.   In the early Colonial Period the encomienda was
     a royal grant by which a number of Indian fami-
     lies were entrusted to a Spaniard who was enti-
     tled to extract their tribute and labor services

5.   I am assuming, as does Metraux (1944:228), that
     Jurie and Tonocote are different names for the
     same tribal group.

6.   At times additional Quichua speakers from High-
     land Argentina were brought by the Spaniards to
     work as carpenters and cartwrights.   They, too,
     lived in the Indian towns (Junta Conservadora
     del Archivo Historico de Tucumán 1941:23; Acade-
     mia Nacional de la Historia 1941:469-470).

7.   A mandán was an Indian administrator appoin-
     ted by the Spaniards.

8.   Actually disease seems to have had an even
     greater effect on the Indians gathered together
     in missions.   However, in Santiago del Estero
     there were only two missions, both of which ap-
     pear to have been quite small (Lascano 1973:34).

9.   The mita was a labor system during the Coloni-
     al Period in which Indians were forced to spend
     a certain amount of time working on projects
     which would benefit the Crown.

10.  A Criollo was a person of Spanish parentage
     born in Latin America.

11.  See Bravo (1956:96) for a copy of The Lord's
     Prayer in Cuzco Quechua which was used by the
     clergy in Santiago del Estero.

12.  Outside of Santiago del Estero, Quichua is
     still considered an "Indian" language by the
     inhabitants of northwestern Argentina.  In fact,
     when asked if there are still Quichua speakers
     in such areas as Salta, Tucumán, and Jujuy, the
     usual response is that since there are no Indi-
     ans in the area there are no speakers of Qui-
     chua, and that if one is interested in the lan-
     guage one should go to Bolivia where "there are
     many Indians."

13.  This anti-Indian feeling is visible in the mu-
     rals found on public buildings throughout north-
     western Argentina.  Among them there is always
     one section or more that glorifies the "salva-
     tion" of Argentina from the "barbarian" Indian.
     Such depictions inevitably show a Gaucho killing
     an Indian either from horseback or in hand-to-
     hand combat.

## REFERENCES

Academia Nacional de la Historia.  1941.  Actas Ca-
     pitulares de Santiago del Estero, I, Años 1554-
     1747.  Buenos Aires.

Archivo de Santiago del Estero.  1924.  Revista del
     Archivo de Santiago del Estero.  Volume I, Num-
     ber 2.  Santiago del Estero.

------.  1925a.  Revista del Archivo de Santiago
     del Estero.  Volume II, Number 3.  Santiago del
     Estero.

------.  1925b.  Revista del Archivo de Santiago
     del Estero.  Volume II, Number 4.  Santiago del
     Estero.

Baranza, P. Alonzo de. 1965. Carta del P. Alon-
zo de Baranza, de la Companía de Jesús, al P.
Juan Sebastián, su Provincial. Fecha en la
Asunción del Paraguay a 8 de Setiembre de 1594.
RGIP, Biblioteca de Autores Españoles, Vol.
184:78-85. Madrid.

Bennett, Wendell C., Everett F. Bleiler, and Frank
H. Sommer. 1948. Northwest Argentine Archaeology. New Haven: Yale University Press.

Bolton, Ralph. 1978. Health and Wealth in a Peasant Community. Paper Delivered at the 77th Annual Meetings of the American Anthropological
Association, Los Angeles.

Bravo, Domingo A. 1956. El Quichua Santiagueño.
Tucumán: Instituto de Letras, Universidad de
Tucumán.

------. 1965. Estado Actual del Quichua Santiagueño. Tucumán: Universidad Nacional de Tucumán.

------. 1975. Diccionario Quichua Santiagueño -
Castellano. Segunda Edición. Buenos Aires:
Editorial Universitaria de Buenos Aires.

------. 1978. Personal Communication, La Banda
(May 19, 1978).

Bravo, Rodrigo. 1978. Personal Communication,
Cafayete (May 16, 1978).

Carrizo, Juan Alfonso. 1937. Cancionero Popular
de Tucumán, Vol. I. Universidad Nacional de
Tucumán.

Christensen, Emilio A. 1970. El Quichua Santiagueño, Buenos Aires: Ministerio de Cultura y
Educación.

Figueroa, Andres A.   1948.   Los Antiguos Pueblos de
    Indios de Santiago de Estero.   Revista de la
    Junta de Estudios Historicos de Santiago del
    Estero (RJEHSE), Año VI, Nos. 19-22 (Enero -
    Diciembre), pp. 19-22.   Santiago del Estero.
------.   1949.   Los Antiguos Pueblos de Indios de
    Santiago del Estero.   RJEHSE, Año VII, Nos. 23-
    26 (Enero-Diciembre), pp.   58-69.   Santiago del
    Estero.
Fock, Niels.   1961.   Inca Imperialism in North-West
    Argentina and Chaco Burial Forms.   Folk 3: 67-90
    (Copenhagen).
Gargaro, Maria Luisa G.   de.   1953.   La Lengua Qui-
    chua en Santiago del Estero.   Santiago del
    Estero.
Hadis, Benjamin F.   1975.   La Estructura Ocupacio-
    nal y la Emigración en Santiago del Estero.   De-
    partamento de Ciencias Sociales de la Fundación
    Bariloche, San Carlos de Bariloche, Rio Negro.
Hutchinson, Thomas J.   1865.   Buenos Ayres and Ar-
    gentine Gleanings: With Extracts From A Diary of
    Salado Exploration in 1862 and 1863.   London:
    Edward Stanford.
Jolis, D.   Giuseppe.   1789.   Saggio sulla Storia
    Naturale della Provincia del Gran Chaco.   Faenza.
Junta Conservadora del Archivo Historico de Tucu-
    mán.   1941.   Documentos Coloniales Relativos a
    San Miguel de Tucumán y a la Gobernación de Tu-
    cumán, Siglo XVII, Serie I, Vol. IV, Tucumán.
Larrouy, P.A.   1914.   Los Indios del Valle de Cata-
    marca: Estudio Histórico.   Revista de la Univer-
    sidad de Buenos Aires XXVII:155 ff.

Lascano, Luis C. Alen. 1973. Desarrollo Históri-
co Socioeconómico de la Provincia de Santiago de
Estero. Departamento de Sociología, Fundación
Bariloche, San Carlos de Bariloche, Rio Negro.

Ledesma Medina, Luis A. 1946. La Lengua Quechua y
su Difusión en el Territorio del Antiguo Virreinato del Peru. RJEHSE, Año 4, Nos. 11-13
(Setiembre), pp. 20-29. Santiago del Estero.

Levillier, Robert. 1919. Gobernación del Tucumán;
Probanzas de Meritos y Servicios de los Conquistadores; Documentos del Archivo de Indias, Vol I
(1548-1583). Madrid: Colección de Publicaciones
Históricas de la Biblioteca del Congreso Argentino (CPHBCA).

------. 1927. Nueva Crónica de la Conquista del
Tucumán. Vol. I (1542-1563). Madrid: Suceso-
res de Rivadeneyra.

Martínez, Pedro S. 1972. La Asimilación de los
Indios Sometidos (1880-1890). Mendoza.

Metraux, Alfred. 1944. Ethnography of the Gran
Chaco. HSAI, Vol. I, Bureau of American Ethno-
logy, Bulletin 143, pp. 197-245. Washington,
D.C.

------. 1945. Tribes of the Eastern Slopes of the
Bolivian Andes. HSAI, Vol. II, Bureau of American Ethnology, Bulletin 143, pp. 465-506. Washington, D.C.

Nardi, Ricardo L.J. 1962. El Quichua de Catamarca
y La Rioja. CINA, Vol. III, pp. 189-285.
Buenos Aires.

Reichlen, H. 1940. Recherches archeologiques dans
la province de Santiago del Estero (Rep. Argen-

tine).   Journal de la Société des Americanistes,
n.s.   Vol. 32, pp. 133-225.   París.

Santucho, Francisco René.   1954.   El Indio en la
Provincia de Santiago del Estero.   Santiago del
Estero: Librería Aymará.

Sotelo, Narváez, Pedro.   1965.   Relación de las
Provincias de Tucumán que Dio Pedro Sotelo
Narváez, Vecino de Aquellas Provincias, al muy
Illustre Señor Licenciado Cepeda, Presidente
desta Real Audiencia de la Plata.   RGIP, Biblioteca de Autores Españoles, Vol. 183, pp. 390-
401. Madrid.

Stark, Louisa R.   1978.   History and Distribution
of the Quichua Spoken in Northwestern Argentina.
Paper Presented at the 77th Annual Meeting of
the American Anthropological Association, Los
Angeles.

Toga, Jose.   1978.   Personal Communication, La
Banda (May 19, 1978).

von Hauenschild, Jorge.   1943.   Los Aborígenes de
Santiago del Estero.   RJEHSE, Año I, No. 2
(Diciembre), pp. 116-137. Santiago del Estero.

# 20. Indigenous Languages of Tierra del Fuego

## Christos Clairis

"According to our thinking the language of these
people barely merits classification as an articula-
ted language."[1]  Thus, the great English naturalist
Charles Darwin, in his diary dated December 17,
1832, described his first contact with the Fuegians.  Darwin's reaction is characteristic of the
attitude, generally negative, shown towards Fuegian
languages.  Most important is the fact that Darwin
considered himself authorized to formulate such a
decisive opinion about the language, even though he
had no professional background on the subject.
Surprisingly such an attitude towards a language
can readily be discovered even in our own times;
the assumption being that since all individuals are
able to speak, all people should consider themselves capable of pronouncing judgments about speech.
Although it would be difficult to find a linguist
who promotes a theory of physics or of biology,
etc., the opposite occurs frequently.  Even today
one can encounter individuals who believe that indigenous people are unable to communicate with
words and are convinced that these people produce
only inarticulate grunts, similar to those of animals.  These same critics also bestow upon themselves the right to civilize, christianize, kill,

enforce labor, etc. This is indeed a peculiar attitude on the part of the white man!

With these comments about attitudes, both past and present, as a background, we are now going to focus on Amerindian languages spoken in that part of South America which is south of the Southern latitude of 40°. This is, in effect, the area in which the Fuegian languages are spoken. The term Fuegian linguistics, suggested by André Martinet, is a broad term that includes the languages spoken on the Island of Tierra del Fuego, as well as those spoken in the territories adjacent to Patagonia.

Today in this vast territory of some 800,000 square kilometers, no more than several dozen survivors of the old autochthonous inhabitants remain. Of these, those who live to the west, by the Magellan Channel, belonged to the group called Canoe Nomads, while those who live to the east, on the Argentine Pampas, were Pedestrian Nomads.

Throughout the history of the region, there has been considerable confusion between the identification of specific indigenous groups and the languages attributed to them. For example, people have discussed the Chono language -- and still do so today -- even though there is not a single linguistic fact available about this putative language.[2] Whether or not the Chono existed as an ethnic entity may be an historic and/or an ethnological problem; but to posit the existence of a language for which there is no data is almost a logical contradiction -- unless one is dealing with linguistic reconstructions or protolanguages.

The proliferation of several terms to designate
the same linguistic realities derives in large part
from this initial methodological confusion, and is
tied furthermore to the lack of work done by bona-
fide linguists.[3]  By using materials that refer only to the Qawasqar language, the confusion which
reigns in nomenclature can best be illustrated.  In
the following citation, three names are attributed
to the same entity:

> Olivier van Noort, who in 1599 had a
> bloody encounter with those Indians, took
> away several captives, with whose assis-
> tance he obtained the various names of
> tribes, places and animals.  Different
> authors suppose that the Enoo, which is
> what these natives call themselves, were
> the Alakaluf of the group named Pesherai
> in the eighteenth century (Hammerly Dupuy
> 1952:140).

We are now sufficiently advanced in our research to
understand the reason for these three different
terms.  First, the Dutch traveler, van Noort, whom
the Indians must have asked for things, uttered the
expression xeno "give it to me" repeatedly; therefore van Noort considered it appropriate to give
them the name Enoo.  Later Bougainville became im-
pressed by the cries pescewe pescewe "stranger"
made by the same group, and therefore called them
Pesherai.  Fitz-Roy, in turn, first called a coastal promontory Alakaluf and subsequently, by exten-

sion, gave the people who lived around it the same name (1839). As to the origin of the term <u>Alaka-luf</u>, Speggazini, towards the end of the 19th century, maintained that it derived from a Yahgan expression meaning "clam eaters," which the Indians attributed to their neighbors to the north.[4]  Many other designations have been utilized to name this group of canoe people, but the use of the term created by Fitz-Roy predominates.

In his 1952 work, Hammerly Dupuy also suggested that a group "Kaueskar" existed, which spoke a language called "aksanas," a language which not only differed from, but was located further south than Alakaluf.[5]  Hammerly "discovered" the "Kaueskar" by comparing 50 words of a vocabulary collected in 1698 by the French pirate Jean de la Guilbaudière with a vocabulary that he himself had collected (Marcel 1982a,b). The "proof" which he offers us is that he has judged these two vocabularies to be different.  It is sufficient to examine just the first word of this comparative list in order to get an idea of the inevitable errors of this type of "method."  Taking the word "water" for which la Guilbaudière noted <u>arret</u>, Hammerly listed <u>c̆afalai</u>. Here, one is dealing with an error made by la Guilbaudière.  He showed the Qawasqar a bucket of water so as to obtain the equivalent in their language and did not notice that their response was to the receptacle and not to the content.  Thus, <u>aret</u> means "container of liquid."

It would not be necessary in this essay to comment on Hammerly if he had not had an important

supporter. Čestmir Loukotka, who apparently never
visited the area, trusted Hammerly's analysis and
thereby perpetuated the myth of the existence of
the aksanas language by regarding it as an isolated
language different from Alakaluf (1962, 1963,
1968). The right of groups to choose their own name
led me to propose to the VI Congress of Chilean Archaeology, in October 1971, that the name Qawasqar
be used for the group as well as its language and
that the term alakaluf, which is nothing more than
a bibliographic fiction, be avoided.[6]

Languages which, in one way or another, are attested to in the territory located south of the 40°
parallel are the following: Qawasqar or Alakaluf,
Yahgan or Yamana, Selk'nam or Ona, Haush or Mane-
kenk, Tehuelche or Patagon or Aonikenke, Teushen or
Tehues, Gununa Kune or Gennaken or Pampa. One may
also cite, although it is outside the category of
Fuegian languages, MapuƟuŋu (the language of the
Mapuche), which is spoken further north in Chilean
territory, in the region called "La Frontera" between the Bio-Bio and Toltén Rivers. (See also the
article by Croese in this volume.) Due to a historical phenomenon, which took place in the 17th century, known by the term "araucanization" and which
consisted of a Mapuche migration towards the southeast, we have today several thousand Mapuche located in Patagonia, especially in the region of
Neuquén (in Argentina). This migration also has
had linguistic consequences to the extent that the
Mapuche language pushed back the Tehuelche language.

We will try now to provide some details about the geographic location of the languages we have cited. The publications on Fuegian languages are to be found in the extensive bibliography, which is located at the end of this essay.

Qawasqar: The habitat of these speakers extends from the Gulf of Penas to the Straits of Magellan and the coastal islands of Chile. As of 1972 the last 47 Qawasqar had regrouped at the small bay of Puerto Eden (49°08'S, 74°26'0) on the east coast of Wellington Island. There they inhabit a location where the only access is by sea, at a distance of more than one day's sailing from the nearest town. The best known designation of this group is alaka-luf. A modern study on the Qawasqar has not yet appeared; however, a description by this author has been completed and is soon to be published (see Clairis 1982).

Yahgan: It is the southernmost language of the world. Its traditional territory included the southern coast of the Island of Tierra del Fuego, the Hoste, Navarino, Picton, and Wollaston Islands, and extends to Cape Horn. Today no more than 6-8 individuals, who have maintained their language, remain on Navarino Island.

One of our informants protested recently against the term yamana, usually used to designate that language, arguing that yamana means "man" in that language and that women speak it also. It is, therefore, preferable to use the term yahgan which was proposed by the missionary Thomas Bridges based on a toponym. There is no an indigenous term to designate the language or the people in question. The compound word inčikut, which speakers sometimes use, has as its first element the English word "Indian"; the second element, from Yahgan, means "speech, to speak," from which is derived "speech of the Indians."

The people who spoke Qawasqar and Yahgan can be differentiated from other Fuegian people by their physique and life style. Those belonging to the groups in question are of small physical stature. They live in their canoes and practice maritime nomadism. By contrast, the other peoples of the region are known for their great height, a fact which, very likely, is the origin of the term Patagon; their natural setting is no longer the sea, but the pampas, where they are nomadic hunters. Selk'nam: This language was spoken in the largest part of Tierra del Fuego, especially in the northwest part of the Island. One aged speaker can still speak the language, but there is not a single person left who speaks Haush, which was once spoken at the extreme southeast of the same island. Patagonian languages: Three languages are found in continental Patagonia. Before designating them with a specific name, it would be perhaps a good idea to recall that from an ethnological point of view, the group of inhabitants of this territory, from the Rio Negro to the Straits of Magellan, have been referred to frequently by means of the generic term of Patagonians or Tehuelches. Parallel to other cases already cited, an infinity of other terms have been utilized in order to characterize

some even smaller groups. We cite, as an example,
the term aonikenke which means "people.of the
south" and by extension the language spoken by
them. It is obvious that this term which is opposed to peenkenke "people of the north" never has
the same referent, given the fact that its meaning
depends on the geographic position of the person
using it.

We owe the attempt at classification of the inhabitants of continental Patagonia shown in Table 1
to Rodolfo Casamiquela. Of the four ethnic groups
defined, the Septentrional Boreal Tehuelche (SBT)
disappeared towards the middle of the last century
without leaving any trace of their language. Of
the three other groups, the only one still extant
is that of the Meridional Austral Tehuelche (MAT).
The linguistic data available for these three ethnic groups, however, permit us to maintain that
each group constituted a distinct community, speaking a language completely different from the
others.

The language spoken by the Septentrional Austral
Tehuelche (SAT), has been termed gününa küne, gennaken or pampa, while the language spoken by the
Meridional Boreal Tehuelche (MBT) is referred to as
teushen or tehues and disappeared during the last
ten years.

I have left for last the language of the Meridional Austral Tehuelche, which is the only one known
by the name of Tehuelche. Among the other names by
which it is called we still have patagon and aonikenke. Therefore each time the term tehuelche is

TABLE 1.   Classification of Patagonian Inhabitants

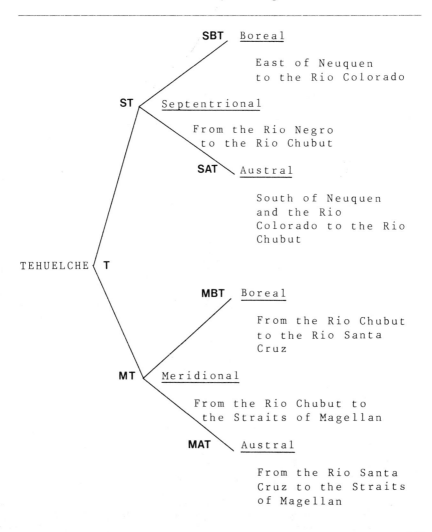

**SBT**  <u>Boreal</u>

East of Neuquen
to the Rio Colorado

**ST**  <u>Septentrional</u>

From the Rio Negro
to the Rio Chubut

**SAT**  <u>Austral</u>

South of Neuquen
and the Rio
Colorado to the Rio
Chubut

TEHUELCHE  **T**

**MBT**  <u>Boreal</u>

From the Rio Chubut
to the Rio Santa
Cruz

**MT**  <u>Meridional</u>

From the Rio Chubut to
the Straits of Magellan

**MAT**  <u>Austral</u>

From the Rio Santa
Cruz to the Straits
of Magellan

used, we must determine whether what is being discussed is the language of the Meridional Austral
Tehuelche or rather the people who inhabited continental Patagonia from one end to the other and
spoke at least three different languages. Today
there are only a few dozen surviving Meridional
Austral Tehuelche dispersed throughout the Argentine province of Santa Cruz. Among them only a minority recall some tehuelche and of these there are
about ten who would be able to serve as informants. These are the speakers we discovered in a
field trip undertaken in the area (December 1980).

Given the state of work on Fuegian languages, it
is difficult to make decisions on family relationships among them and other groups. Lehmann-Nitsche
proposed in 1913 a regrouping of tehuelche (the
language of the MAT), teushen (the language of the
MBT), and selk'nam and haush into the same linguistic family, which he proposed be called chon. Suarez in 1970 attempted to confirm this hypothesis
when he examined the linguistic data more closely.
By comparing and contrasting vocabularies, he arrived at the following chart based on the similarities of 88 terms:

|          | Haush   | Selk'nam | Tehuelche |
|----------|---------|----------|-----------|
| Teushen  | 22.72%  | 27.27%   | 55.68%    |
| Tehuelche| 28.18%  | 29.54%   |           |
| Selk'nam | 35.22%  |          |           |

Using 145 comparable items from gününa küne (material taken from the grammar of Casamiquela) and
from tehuelche (material gathered by us), we are
able to recognize 10.27% of related words, which is
not greater than the other languages (see chart),
but which seems proportional to the geographic distance between the languages in question.

Together with Mary R. Key, in 1976, we formula-
ted an hypothesis -- which we still have to test --
regarding the relationship between Qawasqar and the
languages of the Chon family. We think, however,
that more time is needed to define the small language families before comparative work can reach a
more satisfactory level.

More recently, Mary R. Key presented a hypothesis, about possible affinities between the Uto-Aztecan languages of North America and Mexico, on the
one hand, and Quechua, Aymara, Mapuche, Moseten
(Bolivia), Tacanan (Bolivia), Panoan (Bolivia and
Peru) and the Fuegian languages on the other
(1981a). This hypothesis will provide new perspectives for study and discussion.

NOTES

1. Cited by Lipschutz and Mostny (1950:25).

2. The only "evidence" for this language consists
   of the three words collected by Fitz-Roy and the
   "chono or wayteka" vocabulary of 95 words, published by Samitier (1967) which consists of an
   unspecified mixture of first-hand data gathered
   by him in a hospital of the Regiment of Comodoro

Rivadavia in 1937, from one -- according to him
-- chon informant.  This individual spoke the
"wurk-wur-we"! language.  Samitier added to
these forms "a few rare words noted by former
travelers, because it was not possible to find a
chon vocabulary anywhere" (1967:165).  We simply
can not take this seriously.

3.  These issues are discussed in greater detail in
Clairis (1977b, 1982, in press).

4.  This hypothesis is probably correct, because in
the work of the French Scientific Mission we
found oualo "to eat sea urchins or anything
else which must be cracked" and arhoup "a type
of mussel, the most common found on the beach."
We encountered this same arhoup, listed as
aruf, in Thomas Bridges' Yamana-English Dictionary (1933) translated as "mussels generally; specially that sort which are usually
gathered on the shores, being let by the tide."

5.  Aksanas in Qawasqar means "man (as an anto-
nym of woman)".  Hammerly arbitrarily proposed
to designate the language in this way, perhaps
believing he was applying by analogy a concept
which occurs in other Amerindian languages.  The
reality is, however, that the Qawasqar not only
call themselves Qawasqar, but also refer to
their language by the same term.

6.  I have chosen to spell the word according to
the phonological notation.

7.  This chapter was translated from the original
French by Harriet E. Manelis Klein.

BIBLIOGRAPHY

Adam, Lucien. 1884-1885. Grammaire de la lãngue jagane. Revue de linguistique et de philologie comparée. 17/18: 295-322/10-26 & 160-173 (Paris).

Arnaud, Patrick M. 1972. Ressources marines des Terres de Magellan, leur utilisation par les Yamana et les Alakaluf. Objets et Mondes 12.2: 107-116 (Paris).

Beauvoir, José María. 1915. Los Shelknam, indígenas de la Tierra del Fuego, sus tradiciones, costumbres y lengua. Buenos Aires.

Bird, Junius. 1946. The Alacaluf. Bulletin of the Bureau of American Ethnology, no. 143, Handbook of South American Indians 1: 55-79. Washington, D.C.

Borgatello, Maggiorino. 1921. Le Nozze d'Argento. Torino.

------. 1928a. Alcune notizie grammaticali della lingua Alakaluf. In CIA 22 (1926), 2:422-458. Rome.

------. 1928b. Notizie grammaticali e glossario della lingua degli indi Alakaluf abitanti dei canali magellanici della Terra del Fuoco. Torino.

------. (After 1914 and probably before 1928). Nella Terra del Fuoco, Memorie di un missionario salesiano. Torino.

Bormida, Marcelo and Rodolfo Casamiquela. 1958-59. Etnografía gününa-kena. Testimónio del último de los tehuelches septentrionales. Runa IX. 1-2: 153-193.

Bridges, Lucas B. 1948. Uttermost Part of the Earth. London. (Spanish translation by Elena Cruz de Schwelm. 1952. Buenos Aires.

Bridges, Thomas. 1933. Yamana-English: A Dictionary of the Speech of Tierra del Fuego, D. Hestermann and M. Gusinde, editors. Mödling, Austria.

Casamiquela, Rodolfo. 1956. Sobre el parentesco de las lenguas patagónicas. Runa VII.2:195-202 (Buenos Aires).

------. 1958. Canciones totémicas araucanas y gününa-këna (Tehuelches septentrionales). Revista del Museo de la Plata IV, Antr. 22:293-314.

------. 1965. Rectificaciones y ratificaciones hacia una interpretación definitiva del panorama etnológico de la Patagonia y area septentrional adyacente. Cuadernos del Sur. Bahia Blanca: Universidad Nacional del Sur.

------. 1969. Un nuevo panorama etnológico del area pan-pampeana y patagónica adyacente. Pruebas etnohistóricas de la filiación tehuelche septentrional de los Querandíes. Santiago de Chile.

------. 1973. Alacalufes, canoeros occidentales y pueblos marginales o metamórficos. Relaciones VII:125-143 (Buenos Aires).

------. 1983. Nociones de gramática del gününa küne. Présentation de la langue des Tehuelche septentrionaux australs (Patagonie continentale). Preface by Christos Clairis. Paris: Editions du CNRS.

Ceballos, Rita. 1972. Les habitants de la Patago-
    nie continentale argentine. Objets et Mondes
    12.2:117-126 (Paris).
Censo Indígena Nacional, I-IV. 1967-68. Buenos
    Aires: Ministerio del Interior.
Chamberlain, Alexander F. 1911a. The Present Sta-
    te of Our Knowledge Concerning the Three Lin-
    guistic Stocks of the Region of Tierra del
    Fuego, South America. American Anthropologist
    13.1:89-98.
------. 1911b. On the Puelchean and Tsonekan (Te-
    huelchean), the Atacameñan (Atacaman) and Chono-
    an, and the Charruan Linguistic Stocks of South
    America. American Anthropologist 13:458-471.
------. 1913. Linguistic Stocks of South American
    Indians, with a Distribution-Map. American An-
    thropologist 15:236-247.
Chapman, Anne M. 1972. Lune en Terre de Feu: My-
    thes et rites des Selk'nam. Objets et Mondes
    12.2:145-58 (Paris).
------. 1973. Ensayo sobre algunos mitos y ritos
    de los Selk'nam (Onas). Karukinka: Cuaderno
    Fueguino 6:2-11 (Buenos Aires).
------. 1977. Economía de los Selk'nam de Tierra
    del Fuego. JSA 64:135-148 (Paris).
Chapman, Anne M. and Alan Lomax. 1972. Selk'nam
    Chants of Tierra del Fuego, Argentina. Folkways
    Records, FE 4176. New York (Ethnological record
    with introductory text).
Chapman, Anne M. and Thomas R. Hester. 1973.
    New Data on the Archaeology of the Haush: Tierra
    del Fuego. JSA 62:185-210 (Paris).

Clairis, Christos. 1972a. Les Alakalufs de Puerto Edén (1971). Objets et Mondes 12.2:197-200 (Paris).

------. 1972b. Qawasqar: una investigación etnolingüística en el Pacífico. Revista de Estudios del Pacífico 5:7-26 (Valparaiso).

------. 1976a. Los Qawasqar. Expedición a Chile 22:48-49 (Santiago).

------. 1976b. Estado actual de los estudios sobre lenguas indígenas de Chile. Expedición a Chile 23:74-75 (Santiago).

------. 1977a. Première approche du qawasqar. Identification et phonologie. La Linguistique 13.1:145-152.

------. 1977b. Lingüística fuegina. Boletín de Filología 28:29-48 (Universidad de Chile)

------. 1978. La lengua qawasqar (alakaluf). Vicus 2:29-44 (Amsterdam).

------. 1979. Les grands traits de la syntax qawasqar (alakaluf). In Linguistique Fonctionnelle, Morteza Mahmoudian, ed., pp. 203-211. Paris: PUF.

------. 1980-81. José Emperaire et les Qawasqar, Notes linguistiques inédites sur les Nomades de la Mer. JSA LXVII:359-80 (Paris).

------. 1981. La fluctuation des phonèmes. Dilbilim VI:99-100 (Istanbul).

------. 1982. Linguistique fuégienne: Le qawasqar. Unpublished dissertation (Thèse d'Etat), 2 vols. Paris: Sorbonne.

------. 1983. Le genitif en qawasqar. In Estudios lingüísticos en memoria de Gaston Carrillo

Herrera, Leopoldo Saez-Godoy, ed., pp. 57-66.
Bonn.

------. in press. Report on the Symposium "Linguistique fuégienne" organized by C. Clairis
for the 44th International Congress of Americanists at Manchester (1982).

Clairis, Christos, Rodrigo Medina, Adalberto Salas
and Mirka Stratigopoulou. 1975. Amerindian Music of Chile: Aymara, Qawasqar, Mapuche. Folk-
ways Records, FE 4054. New York (Ethnological
record with an introductory text).

Clairis, Christos and Anne Chapman. 1981. Observaciones etnológicas y lingüísticas acerca de
antropónimos Selk'nam. Estudios Filológicos
16:7-33 (Valdivia).

Cojazzi, Antonio. 1914. Los Indios del Archipié-
lago Fueguino. Revista chilena de historia y
geografía 9:288-352; 10:5-51.

Cooper, John Montgomery. 1917a. Analytical and
Critical Bibliography of the Tribes of Tierra
del Fuego and Adjacent Territory. Washington,
D.C.: Bulletin of the Bureau of American Ethno-
logy, Number 63. Reprinted by Johnson Reprint
Corporation, New York, 1967. Also reprinted in
Anthropology. 1967. Netherlands: Anthropologi-
cal Publications.

------. 1917b. Fuegian and Chonoan - Tribal Relations. In CIA 19 (1915), pp. 445-453.
Washington, D.C.

------. 1925. Culture Diffusion and Culture Areas
in Southern South America. In CIA 21 (1924),
pp. 406-421. Göteborg.

------. 1946a. The Yahgan. Bulletin of the Bureau of American Ethnology, Number 143. Handbook of South American Indians, 1:81-106. Washington, D.C.

------. 1946b. The Ona. Bulletin of the Bureau of American Ethnology, Number 143. Handbook of South American Indians 1:107-125. Wash.,D.C.

------. 1946c. The Patagonian and Pampean Hunters. Bulletin of the Bureau of American Ethnology, Number 143. Handbook of South American Indians, 1:127-168.

Cousteau, Jacques-Yves and Yves Paccalet. 1979. La vie au bout du Monde, Patagonie, Terre de Feu, Archipel Magellanique. Paris: Flammarion.

Damianovic, Juan. 1948. Realidad sanitaria de la población indígena de la zona austral antartica. Revista chilena de higiene y medicina preventiva 10:1-15 (Santiago).

Darwin, Charles Robert. 1839. Journal and Remarks, 1832-1836. London.

Delaborde, Jean. 1981. Patagonia. Paris: Robert Laffont.

Emperaire, José. 1950a. Due anni fra gli indiani Alakaluf. Le vie del mundo 12.8:814-32.

------. 1950b. Evolution démographique des indiens alakaluf: Mission de L. Robin et J. Emperaire 1946-1948. Journal de la Société des Américanistes 39:187-218 (Paris).

------. 1950-51. Archipels de Magellan et Terre de Feu, 2 ans avec les derniers indiens alakaluf. Les Cahiers de La Pléiade, pp. 181-98 (Paris).

------. 1955a. Survivors from the Stone Age in the Magellan Archipelagos. Antiquity and Survival 2:123-37 (The Hague).

------. 1955b. Les nomades de la mer. Paris.

------. 1972. Alakaluf 1946-47. Objets et Mondes 12.2:185-96 (Paris).

Emperaire, José and Annette Laming. 1954. La disparition des derniers Fuégiens. Diogène 8:48-81 (Paris).

Escalada, Federico. 1949. El complejo "Tehuelche". Estudios de etnografía patagónica. Buenos Aires.

Ferrario, Benigno. 1939. El idioma de los Chonos y de los Caucáues. Physis (Revista de la Sociedad Argentina de Ciencias Naturales) XVI:379-88.

------. 1942. Revisión gramatical y la lengua tsóneca. In CIA 27 (1939), 2:41-46. Lima.

------. 1952. El problema lingüístico de la Patagonia. Su estado actual. Folia lingüística americana I.1:3-9 (Buenos Aires).

------. 1956. Tres textos en lengua tsóneca. Montevideo (Reviewed in 1958 by Aryon D. Rodrigues in Kratylos III.2:188-89 [Wiesbaden]).

Fitz-Roy, Robert. 1839. Narrative of the Surveying Voyages of His Majesty's Ships Adventure and Beagle..., 2 vols. London.

Fontanella, María Beatriz. 1967. Componential analysis of personal affixes in Araucanian. IJAL 33.4:305-308.

Gerzenstein, Ana. 1968. Fonología de la lengua gününa-këna. Cuadernos de lingüística indígena 5. Buenos Aires.

Golbert, Perla.  1977.  Yagan I.  Las partes de la
    oración.  Vicus I:5-60 (Amsterdam).

------.  1978.  Yagan II.  Morfología nominal.  Vi-
    cus II:87-101 (Amsterdam).

Greenberg, Joseph H.  1960.  The General Classifi-
    cation of Central and South American Languages.
    In Selected Papers of the 7th International
    Congress of Anthropological and Ethnological
    Sciences, 1956, pp.  791-94.  Philadelphia.

Gusinde, Martin.  1926.  Das Lautsystem der feuer-
    ländischen Sprachen.  Anthropos 21:1000-1024.

------.  1931.  Die feuerland Indianer, Band I Die
    Selk'nam.  Mödling bei Wien.

------.  1937.  Die feuerland Indianer, Band II Die
    Yamana.  Mödling bei Wien.

------.  1939.  Die feuerland Indianer, Band III.
    Anthropologie.  Mödling bei Wien.

------.  1951.  Hombres primitivos en la Tierra del
    Fuego (De investigador a compañero de tribu).
    Translated from the German by Diego Bermudez
    Camacho.  Seville.

------.  1974.  Die feuerland Indianer, Band III.
    Die Halakwulup.  Mödling bei Wien.

Guyot, Mireille.  1968.  Les mythes chez les Sel-
    k'nam et les Yamana de la Terre de Feu.  Paris.

Hammerly Dupuy, Daniel.  1947.  Clasificación del
    nuevo grupo lingüístico Aksánas de la Patagonia
    occidental.  Ciencia e Investigación 3.12:492-
    501 (Buenos Aires).

------.  1947.  Redescubrimiento de una tribu de
    indios canoeros del sur de Chile.  Revista Geo-
    gráfica Americana XXVIII.168:117-22 (Argentina).

------. 1952. Los pueblos canoeros de Fuegopatagonia y los límites del habitat Alakalúf. Runa
5.1-2:134-70 (Buenos Aires).

Harrington, Tomás. 1941-1946. Contribución al
estudio del indio Gününa Küne. Revista del
Museo de La Plata, Antr. 2:237-76.

Haudricourt, André. 1952. Yamana. Les langues du
monde, nouvelle édition, pp. 1196-98 (Paris).

Hestermann-Hamburg, Ferd. 1929. Das Pronomen im
Yamana, Feuerland. IJAL 5.2-4:150-79.

Holmer, Nils M. 1953-54. Apuntes comparados sobre
la lengua de los Yaganes (Tierra del Fuego).
Revista de la Facultad de Humanidades y Ciencias
10:193-223; 11:121-42 (Montevideo).

Imbelloni, José. 1931. Toki: La primera cadena
isoglosemática establecida entre las islas del
Océano Pacífico y el Continente Americano.
Abstract from the Revista de la Sociedad "Amigos
de la Arqueología," V. Reprinted by the Museo
Nacional de Historia Natural de Buenos Aires,
1932. Montevideo.

------. 1936. Culturas indígenas de la Tierra del
Fuego. Historia de la Nación Argentina I:647-92.

Key, Mary Ritchie. 1968a. Phonemic patterns and
phoneme fluctuation in Bolivian Chama (Tacanan).
La Linguistique 2:35-48 (Paris).

------. 1968b. Comparative Tacanan Phonology:
With Cavineña Phonology and Notes on Pano-Tacanan Relationships. The Hague: Mouton.

------. 1976. La fluctuación de fonemas en la
teoria fonológica. Signos 9.1:137-43 (Universidad Católica de Valparaiso).

------. 1978. Araucanian Genetic Relationships. IJAL 44.4:280-93.

------. 1979a. The Grouping of South American Indian Languages. Tübingen.

------. 1979b. Phoneme Fluctuation and Minimal Pairs in Language Change. In Linguistique fonctionelle - Debáts et perspectives, Mortéza Mahmoudian, ed., pp. 305-310. Paris: PUF.

------. 1981a. North and South American Linguistic Connections. La Linguistique 17.1:3-18.

------. 1981b. Quechumaran and Affinities. Scripta Ethnologica VI:93-97 (Buenos Aires).

Key, Mary Ritchie and Christos Clairis. 1976. Fuegian and Central South American Language Relationships. In CIA 42 (1974), IV:635-45. Paris.

Koppers, Wilhelm. 1924. Unter Feuerland-Indianern. Eine forschungreise zu den südlichsten bewohnern der Erde mit M. Gusinde. Stuttgart.

------. 1927. Die fünf Dialekte in der Sprache der Yamana auf Feuerland. Anthropos 22:466-76 (Wien).

La Grasserie, Raoul de. 1902. Contribution à l'étude des langues de la Patagonie. Vocabulaire Pehuelche. In CIA 12 (1900), pp. 339-54. Paris.

------. 1906. De la langue tehuelche. In CIA 14 (1904), II:611-47. Stuttgart.

Laming-Emperaire, Annette. 1954. Tout au bout du monde. Paris (Spanish translation by José Zañartu. 1957. En la Patagonia, Confín del Mundo. Santiago de Chile).

------. 1972. Pecheurs des archipels et chasseurs
    des pampas. Objets et Mondes 12.2:167-84.
Larrucea de Tovar, Consuelo. 1972. Suplemento al
    catálogo de las lenguas de América del Sur.
    Firenze.
Lehmann-Nitsche, Robert. 1912. Las obras lingüís-
    ticas de Theophilus Schmid sobre el idioma pata-
    gón ó tehuelche, recién publicadas. In CIA 17
    (1910), pp. 224-25. Buenos Aires.
------. 1913. El grupo lingüístico Tshon de los
    territorios magallánicos. Revista del Museo de
    La Plata 22:217-76.
------. 1919. El grupo lingüístico alakaluf de
    los canales magallánicos. Revista del Museo de
    La Plata 25:15-69 (Buenos Aires).
------. 1922. El grupo lingüístico "Het" de la
    Pampa argentina. Revista del Museo de La Plata
    27:10-85 (Buenos Aires).
------. 1925. Das Chechehet, eine isolierte und
    ausgestorbene bisher unbekannte Sprache der
    argentinischen Pampa. In CIA 21 (1924), pp.
    581-83. Göteborg.
------. 1930. El idioma Chechehet (Pampa bonae-
    rense), Nombres propios. Revista del Museo de
    La Plata 32:277-91 (Buenos Aires).
Lenz, Rodolfo. 1895-1897. Estudios araucanos.
    Santiago de Chile.
Lipschutz, Alejandro. 1948. Results of a recent
    expedition to Tierra del Fuego. Man 48:7-8.
------. 1950. On the Reliability of Some Written
    Sources of the Seventeenth and Eighteenth Centu-
    ries. American Anthropologist 52:123-26.

------. 1962. Los últimos fueguinos: transculturación y desculturación, extinción y extermina-
ción. Genus 18.1-4:3-29 (Rome).

------. 1968. Perfil de Indoamérica de nuestro
tiempo. Santiago de Chile.

------. 1971. Martin Gusinde y los fueguinos.
Mapocho, pp. 23-32. Santiago de Chile:
Biblioteca Nacional.

Lipschutz, Alejandro and Grete Mostny. 1950.
Cuatro conferencias sobre los indios fueguinos.
Revista Geográfica de Chile. Santiago.

Lipschutz, Alejandro, Grete Mostny, and Louis
Robin. 1946. The Bearing of Ethnic and Genetic
Conditions on the Blood Groups of Three Fuegian
Tribes. American Journal of Physical Anthropo-
logy, n.s. 4.3:301-321.

Lipschutz, Alejandro et al. 1947. Physical Characteristics of Fuegians. American Journal of
Physical Anthropology, n.s. 5.3:295-321.

Lista, Ramón. 1894. Los indios Tehuelches. Una
raza que desaparece. Buenos Aires.

------. 1896. Lenguas argentinas. Los Tehuelches
de la Patagonia. Anales de la Sociedad Científica Argentina 42:35-43.

Lothrop, Samuel Kirkland. 1928. The Indians of
Tierra del Fuego. New York.

Loukotka, Čestmír. 1962. Dringende Forschungsauf-
gaben in Nordost-Brasilien, Paraguay und Chile.
In CIA 34 (1960), pp. 137-38 (Vienna).

------. 1963. Documents et vocabulaires inédits
de langues et de dialectes sud-américains. JSA
52:7-60.

------. 1967. Annals Map Supplement Number Eight.
Ethnolinguistic Distribution of South American
Indians. Annals of the Association of American
Geographers 57.2:437-38.

------. 1968. Classification of South American
Indian Languages. Los Angeles.

Marcel, Gabriel. 1892a. Vocabulaire des Fuégiens
a la fin du XVIIe siècle. In CIA 8 (1890), pp.
463-66 (Paris).

------. 1892b. Les fuegiéns à la fin du XVIIe siècle d'après des documents francais inédits. In
CIA 8 (1890), pp. 485-96 (Paris).

Mason, Alden J. The Languages of South American
Indians. Bulletin of the Bureau of American
Ethnology, number 143. Handbook of South Ame-
rican Indians 6, pp. 157-317 (Washington,
D.C.)

Matijevic, Nicolas and Olga H. Matijevic. 1973/
1978. Bibliografia patagónica y de las tierras
australes, vols I and II. Bahía Blanca: Centro
de Documentación Patagónica.

McQuown, Norman A. 1955. The Indigenous Languages
of Latin America. American Anthropologist 57.3:
501-70.

Mitre, Bartolomé. 1894. Lenguas americanas. Estudio bibliográfico-lingüístico de las obras del
P. Luis de Valdivia sobre el araucano y el al-
lentiak, con un vocabulario razonado del allen-
tiak. La Plata.

Molina, Manuel J. 1969-70. El idioma "aksanas" de
los canoeros de los canales patagónicos occidentales: una crítica a D. Hammerly Dupuy. Anales

de Arqueología y Etnología 24-25:251-54
(Mendoza).

Moorehead, Alan. 1971. Darwin and the Beagle.
London: Penguin Books.

Musters, George Chaworth. 1969. At Home with the
Patagonians. A Years Wanderings... New York
(original publication 1897, London: John Murray;
Spanish translation by Arturo Costa Alvarez
1964, Buenos Aires).

Najlis, Elena L. 1971. Disambiguation in Selk'-
nam. IJAL 37.1:46-47.

------. 1973. Lengua selknam. Buenos Aires.

------. 1975. Diccionario selknam. Buenos Aires.

Orbigny, Alcide d'. 1835-1847. Voyage dans l'Amérique Méridionale, exécuté dans le cours des
années 1826, 1827, 1828, 1829, 1830, 1831, 1832
et 1833, 11 volumes. Paris.

------. 1836. Voyage pittoresque dans les deux
Amériques. Paris.

------. 1839. L'homme américan (De l'Amérique
méridionale) considéré sous ses rapports physiologiques et moraux, 2 vols. Paris.

Ortiz Troncoso, Omar R. 1973. Los Yamana, veinticinco años después de la misión Lipschütz. Anales del Instituto de la Patagonia IV.1-3:77-105
(Punta Arenas).

------. 1975. La navegación indígena en el confín
austral de América. Revista General de Marina
(Junio) pp. 601-611 (Madrid).

Outes, Félix F. 1913a. Vocabularios inéditos del
patagón antiguo con introducción. Revista de la
Universidad de Buenos Aires XXI-XXII:474-94.

------. 1913b. Sobre las lenguas indígenas rio-
platenses. Materiales para su estudio. Revista
de la Universidad de Buenos Aires XXIV:231-37.

------. 1914. Un texto y un vocabulario en dialecto pehuenche de fines del siglo XVIII con
introducción y notas. Revista de la Universidad
de Buenos Aires XXV:68-73.

------. 1926a. Sobre el idioma de los Yamana de
Wulaia (Isla Navarino). Materiales reunidos por
el misionero Rau con anterioridad a 1866. Revista del Museo de la Plata XXX:1-47 (Buenos
Aires).

------. 1926b. Datos sobre la ergología y el
idioma de los Yamana de Wulaia (Isla Navarino),
reunidos por el misionero R.R. Rau, con anterioridad a 1866 y anotados por don Jorge Claraz.
Revista del Museo de La Plata XXX:49-77.

------. 1928a. Vocabulario y fraseario genakenn
(puelche) reunidos por Juan Federico Hunziker en
1864. Revista del Museo de La Plata XXXI:261-
294 (Buenos Aires).

------. 1928b. Versiones al aônükün'k (patagón
meridional) de la oración dominical y del ver-
sículo 8° del salmo II adaptadas por Teófilo
Schmid en 1863. Revista del Museo de La Plata
XXX:299-333 (Buenos Aires).

------. 1928c. Un texto aônükün'k (patagón meri-
dional) para incitar a la caza, obtenido por
Juan Federico Hunziker en 1861. Revista del
Museo de La Plata XXX:353-369 (Buenos Aires).

------. 1928d. Las variantes del vocabulario patagón reunido por Antonio Pigafetta en 1520.

Revista del Museo de La Plata XXX:371-80 (Buenos Aires).

------. 1935. Un ejemplar único de nuestra bibliografía lingüística indígena. Publicaciones del Museo Antropológico y Etnográfico de la Facultad de Filosofía y Letras, serie A, III: 93-97 (Buenos Aires).

Pereira da Silva, M.A. 1974. Les dermatoglyphes digito-palmaires des indiens alakaluf des archipels de Patagonie occidentale. Bulletin et Mémoire de la Société d'Anthropologie de Paris 1.13:85-108.

Platzmann, Julius. 1903. Der Sprachstoff der Patagonischen Grammatik des Theophilus Schmid, Mit einer Karte des südlichen Südamerika. Leipzig.

Pottier, Bernard. 1962. Sur la description des systèmes temporels des langues amérindiennes. In CIA 34 (1960), pp. 763-76. Vienna.

Rivet, Paul. 1925. Les australiens en Amérique (abstract from the Bulletin de la Société de la Linguistique de Paris XXVI). Paris.

Rouget, Gilbert with the collaboration of Jean Schwarz. 1976. Chant fuégien, consonance, mélodie de voyelles. Revue de Musicologie 62.1:5-24.

Salas, Adalberto. 1970a. Notas sobre el verbo en el mapuche de Chile (I). Segunda Semana Indigenista, Colección de "Documentos de la Frontera" 2:59-95 (Temuco).

------. 1970b. Notas sobre el verbo en el mapuche de Chile (II). Stylo 10:119-34 (Temuco).

------. 1971a. Notas sobre el verbo en el mapuche de Chile (III). Boletín de Filología XXII:99-116 (Universidad de Chile).

------. 1971b. Notas sobre el verbo en el mapuche de Chile (IV). Revista de Lingüística Teórica y Aplicada 9:75-101 (Concepción, Chile).

------. 1976. Esbozo fonológico del mapudungu, lengua de los Mapuče o Araucanos de Chile central. Estudios Filológicos II:143-53 (Universidad Austral de Chile, Valdivia).

------. 1980. La lingüística mapuche en Chile. Revista de lingüística teórica y aplicada 18:23-57 (Concepción, Chile).

Samitier, Llaras. 1967. El grupo chono o wayteka y los demás pueblos fuegopatagonia. Runa 10. 1-2:123-94 (Buenos Aires).

Schmid, Theophilus. 1910. Two Linguistic Treatises on the Patagonian or Tehuelche Language, edited with an Introduction by Robert Lehmann-Nitsche. Buenos Aires.

------. 1964. Misionando por Patagonia Austral, 1858-1865. Usos y costumbres de los indios Patagones. Buenos Aires.

Schmidt, Wilhelm. 1926. Die Sprachfamilien und Sprachenkreise der Erde. Heidelberg.

Skottsberg, Carl. 1913. Observations on the Natives of the Patagonian Channel Region. American Anthropologist 15:578-616.

Stratigopoulou, Mirka. 1980-1981. Etude sur la musique des Qawasqar (Alakaluf). JSA LXVII:385-403 (Paris).

Stuchlik, Milan and Adalberto Salas. 1974. Rasgos de la sociedad mapuche contemporanea. Modo, persona y número en el verbo mapuche. Universidad Católica de Chile.

Suarez, Jorge A. 1959. The Phonemes of an Araucanian Dialect. IJAL 25:177-81.

------. 1970. Clasificación interna de la familia lingüística chon. Anales del Instituto de Linguistica 10:29-59 (Mendoza).

------. 1974. South American Indian Languages. In Encyclopedia Britannica.

Swadesh, Morris. 1955. Towards a Satisfactory Genetic Classification of Amerindian Languages. In CIA 31 (1954), II:1001-1012. Sao Paolo.

------. 1961. Los supuestos australianos en América. In Homenaje a Pablo Martinez del Río, en el XXV aniversario de la edición de los Origenes Americanos, pp. 147-161. Mexico.

------. 1962. Afinidades de las lenguas amerindias. In CIA 34 (1960), pp. 729-38. Vienna.

Tax, Sol. 1960. Aboriginal Languages of Latin America. Current Anthropology I (Sept-Nov), pp. 430-46.

Tonelli, Antonio. 1926. Grammatica e glossario della lingua degli Ona-Selknam. Torino.

Tovar, Antonio. 1961. Catálogo de las lenguas de América del Sur. Buenos Aires.

Valory, Dale. 1968. Notas sobre la antropología de las tribus fueguinas. América Indígena XXVIII.3:653-74 (Mexico).

Vignati, Milciades Alejo. 1939a. Los Indios Poyas. Contribución al conocimiento etnográfico

de los antiguos habitantes de Patagonia. Notas
del Museo de La Plata IV, Antr. 12:211-244
(Buenos Aires).

------. 1939b. Apuntes bioiconográficos del caci-
que tuelche Casimiro. Notas del Museo de La
Plata IV, Antr. 13:251-58 (Buenos Aires).

------. 1940a. Materiales para la lingüística patagona. El vocabulario de Elizalde. Boletín de
la Academia Argentina de Letras 8.30:159-202.

------. 1940b. Glosario yamana de fines del siglo
XVIII. Boletín de la Academia Argentina de
Letras 8.30:637-663.

Weddell, James. 1825. A Voyage towards the South
Pole, Performed in the Years 1822-1824...and a
Visit to Tierra del Fuego.... London (A second
edition was published in 1827 which also included his second trip to Tierra del Fuego.).

Zapater, Horacio. 1973. Los aborígenes chilenos a
través de cronistas y viajeros. Santiago de
Chile.

# 21. Mapuche Dialect Survey

## Robert A. Croese

INTRODUCTION

In this work we shall describe the results of a re-
cently-conducted dialect survey among the Mapuche
people of the eighth, ninth and tenth regions of
Chile.[1] This area has also been referred to as the
Frontera or the Araucanía of Chile. The Spanish
conquistadores called the Mapuches Araucanians, a
term with connotations of brave, valiant or fierce
warrior. Reference is made in the literature to
subgroups of Mapuches, i.e. Lafquenches, Pehuen-
ches, Huilliches, Picunches, Puelches, Moluches,
etc.; however, since all of these people tend to
call themselves Mapuche we shall here employ the
term Mapuche as a generic denominator for the whole
group surveyed. Later in this chapter we shall
utilize the subgroup denominations to explain certain dialect manifestations and possible migration
patterns. The Mapuches refer to their native language as mapudungun which is a short form for ma-
puche-dungun 'the words of the Mapuches'.

The area surveyed comprises the entire width of
(continental) Chile basically between the 37° and
41° Latitude South, an area of 370 km. long and an
average of 200 km. wide for a total of approximately 74,000 km[2]. Though we recognize that there
are Mapuches living outside of this area, their
numbers are relatively few and the active use of

the Mapuche language is greatly diminished, if not totally gone in some areas. We have not had an opportunity to study the dialect situation across the border in Argentina. Also we have not taken into account the many Mapuches who have emigrated to Santiago and other urban centers during the past few decades.

The actual population count of Mapuches in Chile is an issue with some rather divergent answers. Luis Faron (1961), a noted anthropologist, estimated a population of 200,000 Mapuches living on 2,000 small reservations. He does not say anything about the number of Mapuches not living on reservations. Milan Stuchlik (1974) simply states that there are 500,000 Mapuches, who comprise 5% of the Chilean population. In a recent newspaper article, Manuel Cheuque Huenulaf, Director of the Centro Cultural Mapuche de la Novena Región, estimated that there are 90,000 Mapuches in Chile, of whom 25% live in urban areas of the country (Diario Austral, January 25, 1979). M.R. Key states that "estimates of the Araucanian population in Chile range from 200,000 to 400,000" (1978:280).

The name Mapuche (mapu 'land', che 'people') provides an important clue toward understanding the history of Mapuche society - and consequently, their language. At the time of the arrival of the first Spanish conquistadores, at about the year 1550, there was apparently enough land under cultivation and small animal husbandry among the Mapuches to cause them forcefully to resist Spanish colonialization until Chilean troops subdued them

in the last Rebellion of 1880-1882. Subsequently,
the Mapuches were restricted to small family-sized
reserves, where most of them have remained sedentary until the present.

Mapuche society continues to function as it has
for many years with its own traditional religious
observances, social structure and language. Though
there exists a surface socio-economic integration
with Chilean society and widespread bilingualism,
most of the Mapuches on reservations are by no
means bi-cultural.

One of the most striking, and somewhat puzzling,
observations we have made is that of linguistic
unity in the Mapuche language. There is almost
complete mutual intelligibility throughout the
whole region surveyed, despite sharply marked topo-
graphical divisions, such as major rivers and mountain ranges. It appears from present-day linguistic evidence that the Mapuches have maintained a
high degree of social and linguistic interaction,
at least during pre-reservation times. And now,
after almost one hundred years of reservation life
there still exists a great amount of linguistic
uniformity. However, some dialect variations can
be readily observed and dialect groupings can be
posited on the basis of phonetic, lexical and grammatical differentiators.


PURPOSE
Although there exists a relatively good sized bibliography on the Mapuche language, there is nothing available in print, other than some vague

hints, about Mapuche dialectal variations and distributions. One could consult the grammars, dictionaries and text materials by such authors as:
Valdivia (1606), Febrés (1764), Havestadt (1777),
Lenz (1895-97), Augusta (1903, 1916 and 1934), Erize (1960) etc., and glean dialectal information
from them. However, since the above authors used
different phonetic transcriptions, it is difficult
to determine whether variant entries between authors actually represent dialectal variations or
merely a difference in writing. This problem has
been observed in Loukotka's Classification of South
American Indian Languages (1968), where the following pairs were used to show differences between
dialects of the Mapuche language. Actually, they
are most likely the result of having consulted different authors with different transcription techniques:

|  |  |  |
|---|---|---|
| 'head' | longko | lonko |
| 'sun' | antu | antü |
| 'moon' | kuyen | küyen |
| 'dog' | thehua | thewa |
| 'jaguar' | nahuel | nawel |

Therefore, since it is almost impossible to get
a clear picture of the dialect situation from a
historical perspective, something needs to be done
to get, minimally, a better idea of present-day
dialectal differences. The purpose of this essay,
then, is to present the variations that exist in
the language as it is spoken today.

There exists among contemporary scholars and educators, who are interested in the study of the Mapuche language, a wide variety of opinions about where the Mapuches speak differently and what these differences are. The Mapuches themselves have some ideas of where people speak differently but are generally unable to express what the differences really are. They usually say that the "tone" differs or that others speak more rapidly than they do. And when native speakers are asked if they have ever encountered a Mapuche speaker whom they could not understand, they will almost always say, no! The Mapuches except for the Huilliche seem always to be able to understand each other, even though there may be some initial difficulty.

PROCEDURES
The survey consisted of two interrelated parts: (1) transcribing and recording phonetic, lexical and grammatical data and (2) gathering culture-related linguistic information (socio-linguistics). In this paper, however, we discuss only a summary of the findings of the former part, not the latter (see Note 1 and Croese 1980).

For the recording of the linguistic data we used a 176 item word list, which was a compilation of pre-determined known differentiators. An attempt was made to include all phonemes – both the stable and unstable ones. Special attention was given to include minimal pairs for testing the (inter)dental sounds: t', l', and n' vs. their alveolar counterparts: t, l, and n.[2]

For the lexical items we concentrated mainly on
known variables in order to find the precise boundary lines. We also purposely included regional
ecological items to see how far they spread, for
example, snow, volcano, fish, seaweed, shell fish,
canoe, mountain lion, pampa, etc. We also included
some of the most common items, such as: greetings,
food items, colors, body parts, kinship terms, animal names, meteorological items, etc. A few known
Spanish loans were also included, i.e.: bed, soft,
plow, ox, barn yard animal, and sheep.

To record the grammatical differentiators we included some basic phrases obtained from previously
gathered data in order to check pronouns, subject/
object transitions, negation, verbs of wish, command, condition, ambience, etc. Our first test locations were near Temuco, the geographic, socio-political, demographic and institutional center of
the Mapuche territory. From there we worked out
into different directions, first for one-day trips
and later for longer durations working larger areas
in circular fashion.

RESULTS

Mapuche phonemes can be divided into two categories: stable and unstable segments. Stable phonemes do not generally manifest any fluctuations or
dialectal variations. These are: /i, e, a, u; p,
t, k, m, n, ñ, ŋ, l, y, w, ƛ/. The unstable phonemes are the following: /o, ï, ṭ, t͛ʳ, č, λ, f, θ,
s, ṛ, ṇ, ḻ/. Thus, all (inter)dentals, all fricatives and affricates, all alveopalatals (less ñ),

and all high back vowels, are considered unstable
segments.

The <u>results</u> of the word list fall into five categories:

1.    Stable items which show no variation
throughout all eight divisions of the Mapuche territory (see Map).

2.    Stable items which show no variation
throughout the whole territory, excluding subgroup
VIII (Huilliche dialect).

3.    Unstable items which show dialectal variations in geographic patterns.

4.    Unstable items which show no geographic patterns.

5.    Items which proved difficult to elicit, such
as geographically restricted ecological items,
items that were too generic and needed further specification, and items that had diminished usage.

When we combine the results of categories 1, 2,
and 3, which conveniently totals 100 items, and
count the phonetically identical entries that each
of the eight subgroups has in common with each
other, we can posit Table 1.

By way of example, subgroups II and VI intersect
at 54 identical common items. (Since the total
possible is 100, the 54 common items represent
54%). The numbers outlined by a broken line point
up the fact that subgroups I and II, and subgroup
VIII to a higher degree, are less closely related
to the central five subgroups than these five

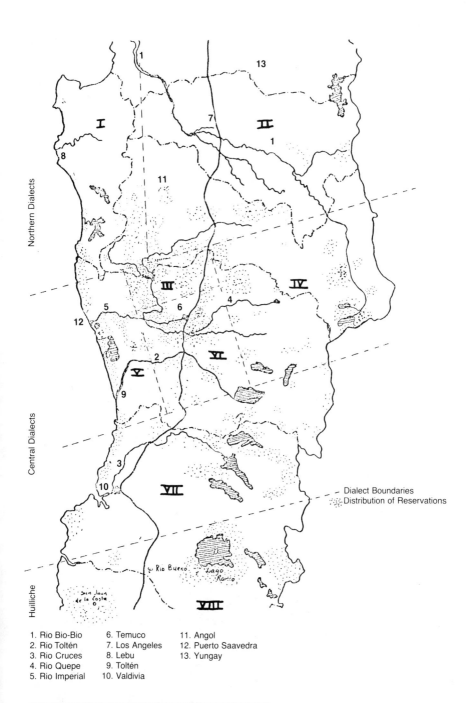

1. Rio Bio-Bio   6. Temuco        11. Angol
2. Rio Toltén    7. Los Angeles   12. Puerto Saavedra
3. Rio Cruces    8. Lebu          13. Yungay
4. Rio Quepe     9. Toltén
5. Rio Imperial  10. Valdivia

**MAP OF MAPUCHE DIALECT SUBGROUP BOUNDARIES**

TABLE 1.    Intersection of 100 Phonetically
Identical Entries of Categories 1, 2 and 3

|        | I  | II | III | IV | V  | VI | VII | VIII |
|--------|----|----|-----|----|----|----|-----|------|
| I      |    | 81 | 74  | 66 | 59 | 58 | 54  | 46   |
| II     | 81 |    | 72  | 64 | 57 | 54 | 52  | 41   |
| III    | 74 | 72 |     | 78 | 79 | 74 | 74  | 41   |
| IV     | 66 | 64 | 78  |    | 74 | 74 | 76  | 42   |
| V      | 59 | 57 | 79  | 74 |    | 84 | 87  | 40   |
| VI     | 58 | 54 | 74  | 74 | 84 |    | 93  | 39   |
| VII    | 54 | 52 | 74  | 76 | 87 | 93 |     | 48   |
| VIII   | 46 | 41 | 41  | 42 | 40 | 39 | 48  |      |

groups are related to one another. Coincidentally, among the central groups, areas III, V and VI are by far the most heavily populated with Mapuche speakers.

Going one step further, a tree diagram (Table 2) can be posited to show the interrelatedness of the various subgroups - this is not to be confused with a theory for historical development of the Mapuche language and dialects, although this tree may well coincide with such a study.

Now that we have shown <u>what</u> the dialectal differences are and <u>where</u> they occur, it remains yet to state something about <u>mutual intelligibility</u>. From the test results, the subjective information from the native Mapuche survey team member, and our knowledge of the Mapuche language, it appears that:

1. Subgroup VIII (Huilliche) is not mutually intelligible to the other subgroups.

2. Subgroups I and II (the northern branch), besides being mutually intelligible to each other, appear to be mutually intelligible to the 5 central subgroups, though not without some initial difficulty in understanding and communication.[3]

3. The central subgroups are all mutually intelligible to each other; however, the variant rhythm and intonation patterns may cause slight initial difficulty in communication.

After the dialect survey was completed, and the geographical-linguistic sub-groupings had been posited, we checked our results against the theory of

TABLE 2.    Interrelatedness of Mapuche Subgroups

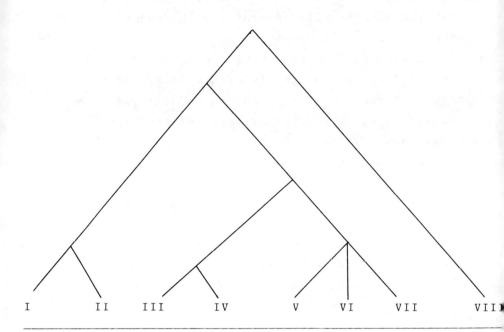

I            II    III        IV        V      VI    VII          VIII

historical migration outlined in Ricardo E. Latcham's book on Mapuche social organization and religious beliefs (1924).[4] Interestingly, our dialect
findings coincide closely with Latcham's theory.
Latcham (1924: Chapter 1) states that from archaeological evidence it is apparent that Southern Chile (including the area under investigation in this
paper) was originally inhabited by native <u>fishermen</u>
along the coastal areas and by another physical-
type of people (whom he calls <u>Araucanos</u>) in the
fertile central plains. The mountain area along
the eastern border of Chile was inhabited by nomadic hunters who extended into the high plains of
western Argentina; these people are the <u>Pehuenches</u>
'gatherers of pine-nuts'. Latcham goes on to say
that this population distribution was disrupted by
a group of invaders from the <u>pampas</u> of Argentina
called <u>Moluches</u> 'war people'. The Moluches, moving
into the central valleys and coastal areas of Chile, especially between the Bío-Bío and Toltén rivers, pushed the original inhabitants of these
lands to the south and to the north, or mixed with
them in the central territory. Latcham calls this
new amalgamation <u>Mapuches</u>. This fusion was completed by the time the Spanish arrived. These Mapuches called the people to the south <u>Huilliches</u>
and the people to the north <u>Picunches</u>.

About the language, Latcham comes to the
conclusion that:

...la forma pura y a la vez más arcaica
de la lengua será la hablada por los in-

dios huilliches de Valdivia al sur, que
sufrieron menos por los cambios introdu-
cidos en la pronunciación por los inva-
sores moluches (1924:23,24).

And Rodolfo Lenz stated that: "El dialecto de los
picunches es el que ha conservado con mayor fideli-
dad el estado fonético primitivo de idioma" (1895:
Tomo 91:196).

Latcham's information indicates that our own
dialect groupings coincide with his theory. We see
that our subgroup VIII belongs to the Huilliche de-
nomination and could well be an older dialect of
Mapuche stock. Our subgroupings I and II, in the
North, could be an older dialect form which has
been less influenced by the Moluche invasion than
the central dialects. Furthermore, it is especially significant to note that some of the same distinctive dialectal features, i.e. voicing of fricatives, greater occurrence of grooved fricatives,
etc., occur in the South, the North and in the extreme Eastern part of our subgroup IV leaving the
central dialects - Moluche influenced - free of
these features. Thus, since the marginal groups
show common linguistic elements, Latcham's theory
that an invader group drove the original inhabitants apart is very well possible.

DIALECTAL VARIATIONS AND GEOGRAPHIC LOCATION
Besides the influences of possible migrations and
fusions, geographic location seems to have played
an important part in Mapuche language variation.

The degree of isolation almost always contributes
to the formation of varying dialects. Social, economic, religious and political contact, or the lack
of it, tends to influence language variation. Another factor of isolation is brought about by the
topography of the terrain. Mountain ranges, large
rivers, swamps, etc. all contribute to linguistic
isolation and dialect formation. We find these
factors in the Mapuche territory. For example:

1. The border that separates our subgroup I
follows the ridge of the coastal mountain range:
Nahuelbuta.

2. The southern borders of subgroups IV, V, and
VI follow generally the east-west mountain range of
Mahuidanche (la cuesta de Lastarria).

3. The river Bío-Bío, though we do not know
that area very well, seems to form the border for
some divergent northern dialect differences.

Socio-economic differentiators also coincide
with the dialectal variation found in Mapuche.

1. Subgroups I and V are mainly engaged in fishing and gathering cochayuyo (marine algae), manufacturing charcoal, and herding sheep and goats.

2. Subgroups III and VI are farmers and merchants who are in constant contact with the non-
Mapuche population.

3. Subgroup IV are farmers in the Western part
and pine-nut gatherers in the eastern mountain
slopes.

4. Subgroup VII is mainly involved in animal husbandry and timber.

5. The Huilliches, subgroup VIII, are involved in farming and sheep herding.

## CONCLUSION

We feel that we now have a better general picture of the Mapuche dialect situation in the area described in this presentation. More detailed survey work, however, could still be done in the central heart-land where the vast majority of Mapuches live, as well as in the extreme north (Santa Barbara) and south, perhaps as far as the island of Chiloe. It would also be most interesting to compare the Mapuche language of the Argentine pampas with our findings in Chile. We therefore hope that this essay will stimulate the linguistic appetites of our colleagues and cause them to elaborate on this study. Much remains to be investigated, especially in the areas of stress, length, intonation, fluctuation, discourse phonology, as well as a more precise test for mutual intelligibility.

## NOTES

1. This dialect survey was conducted under the auspices of a Mapuche linguistic investigation contract signed between the Universidad Austral de Chile and the Summer Institute of Linguistics. An earlier and expanded Spanish version, including the data upon which the generalizations in this chapter are based, appeared in Estudios Filológicos in 1980.

2.   The choice of word list items came from Augusta's Diccionaric (1916), suggestions from Dr. Adalberto Salas and Gastón Sepúlveda, and from personal acquaintance with and study of the language.
3.   Our survey did not include the northern Mapuche groups around Santa Barbara and the so-called Trapa-Trapa area which, according to personal communication with Father Eugene Theisen, speak "very differently". These groups would appear to belong to the group traditionally known as Pehuenche.
4.   We are indebted to Mr. Gastón Sepúlveda for bringing this book to our attention.

REFERENCES
Augusta, Felix José. 1903. Gramática Araucana. Valdivia: Imprenta Central, J. Lampert.
------. 1916. Diccionario Araucano-Español y Español-Araucano. Santiago: Imprenta Universitaria.
------. 1934. Lecturas Araucanas, segunda edición. Padre Las Casas: Imprenta y editorial "San Francisco".
Croese, Robert A. 1980. Estudio dialectológico del mapuche. Estudios Filológicos 15:7-38. Universidad Austral de Chile, Valdivia.
------. 1983. Algunos resultados de un trabajo de campo sobre las actitudes de los mapuches frente a su lengua materna. Revista de Lingüística Teórica y Aplicada 21:23-34 (Universidad de Concepción, Chile).

Erize, Esteban. 1960. Diccionario comentado mapuche-español. Cuadernos del Sur. Buenos Aires:
Universidad Nacional del Sur.

Faron, L.C. 1961. Mapuche Social Structure, Institutional Reintegration in a Patrilineal Society of Central Chile. Illinois Studies in Anthropology, No. 1. Urbana: The University of
Illinois Press.

Febrés, Andrés. 1764. Arte de la lengua general
del Reino de Chile. Lima.

Havestadt, Bernardo. 1777. Chilidungu sive tractatus lingae chilensis.

Key, Mary Ritchie. 1978. Araucanian genetic relationships. International Journal of American
Linguistics 44:280-293.

Latcham, Ricardo E. 1924. La organización social
y las creencias religiosas de los antiguos araucanos. Santiago: Imprenta Cervantes.

Lenz, Rodolfo. 1895-1897. Estudios Araucanos. 17
articles in Anales de la Universidad de Chile,
Santiago. Vols. 90-98.

Loukotka, Cestmir. 1968. Classification of South
American Indian Languages, Johannes Wilbert, ed.
Reference Series, Vol. 7. Los Angeles: University of California.

Payne, David L. and Robert A. Croese. ms. On
Mapudungun Linguistic Affiliations: An Evaluation of Previous Proposals and Evidence for an
Arawakan Relationship. Instituto Lingüístico de
Verano, Perú and Universidad de la Frontera,
Chile.

Stuchlik, Milan.  1974.  Rasgos de la sociedad ma-
    puche contemporánea.  Santiago: Ediciones Nueva
    Universidad.
Valdivia, Luis.  1606.  Arte y gramática general de
    la lengua que corre en todo el Reino de Chile.
    Lima.

# 22. Indian Languages of the Paraguayan Chaco

## Harriet E. Manelis Klein and Louisa R. Stark

INTRODUCTION

Paraguay is divided into two geographical zones:
the Oriental or eastern part of the country, and
the western part or Chaco.  The latter, consisting
of 60% of the land mass of Paraguay, is inhabited
by 3% of the country's population.  It is also the
area which is home to the largest number of Paraguayan Indians, representing thirteen languages and
five linguistic families.

The purpose of this essay is to describe the
present linguistic situation of the Indians of the
Paraguayan Chaco.  Such a survey requires a description of the geographic and demographic distribution of these peoples as well as a discussion of
the distinctive socio-linguistic features of their
languages.  Both are best described in the light of
a series of migrations.

Generally the Indians of the Chaco have gone
from hunting or fishing and gathering to a cash
economy.  Even groups such as the Ayoreo, Chamakoko, and Chorotí which have been most tied to their
traditional ways have participated marginally in
the national economy by selling the skins of the
animals that they have hunted.  However, as more
and more of their former territories have been

turned into ranches, wild game has been dimini-
shing.   This in turn has prompted the Paraguayan
government, as a conservation measure, to ban the
sale of animal skins.   Thus with their hunting
lands disappearing and no market for their skins,
Indians such as those mentioned above have begun to
look for work as laborers on neighboring ranches
and military bases, or have been migrating to the
central Chaco to find work in the Mennonite colonies there.

Other Indian groups have been involved in a cash
economy for up to three or four generations.   In
the late nineteenth and early twentieth centuries
many of the Mascoian Indians migrated to towns
along the Paraguay River that offered employment in
their tannin factories.   However, with the recent
demise of most of these factories, there has been a
shift of Indian groups away from the river and towards the central Chaco where they, too, have gone
to search for work as agricultural laborers in the
Mennonite colonies.

Another set of migrations has taken place from
the southern Chaco.   After the Chaco War (1932-
1935) that area began to be opened for ranching.
This resulted in a need for large quantities of un-
skilled labor for clearing and fencing fields, most
of which was supplied by the Indians of Chaco.
However, once this stage of agricultural development was terminated, large numbers of Indians became unemployed.   And, like the other Indians of
the Chaco, possessing neither skills nor land, they
too have been migrating to the Mennonite colonies

where in 1976 the Indian population was estimated
at 10,316 (Stahl 1977:8).

These recent population shifts in the Paraguayan
Chaco have led to concomitant linguistic changes.
For as Indian groups separate and move to new areas
they are bound to have contact with other groups,
both Indian and non-Indian. These contacts necessarily bring about language change as well as changes in their self-conceptualizations as ethnic
groups, and in so doing in the value that they
place on the maintenance or loss of their native
languages.

In the organization of this paper we have divided the Chaco languages into five linguistic families. In order to do this we collected lexical and
grammatical data on each language, compared it with
data collected from other languages, and determined
our linguistic classification accordingly.

After a discussion of a particular linguistic
family we turn to its individual members. In each
case we have designated the language with the name
which is most commonly used to refer to it in Paraguay. We have also indicated what the particular
ethnic group under discussion calls itself and its
language.

Our population estimates are based on data gathered in the field and from discussions with indigenous leaders, church and mission officials, factory managers, field anthropologists, and in a few
cases recently published reports. We have not included in our figures the number of Indians in any
location which totalled less than five, nor did we

include those few acculturated Indians to be found in Asunción.  We also omitted the occasional Indian migrant from Bolivia or Argentina who does not speak a Paraguayan Chaco language.  And although we attempted to be as thorough as possible in gathering our data, we are certain that there are Indians working on ranches and farms in isolated areas whose numbers and locations are simply unknown to us.  The inclusion of these groups might raise our population estimates, but by no more than five percent.

In addition to population estimates, we also estimate the actual number of the speakers of each language.  For example, in those instances where children also speak the language, and there are at least three generations of speakers, the estimated number of speakers is the same as the population estimate.  However, in many cases where only the oldest generation (out of three) speaks the language, we have calculated the number of speakers to be approximately 20% of the estimated population.

We have also cited in each section recent linguistic works.  However, for the sake of brevity we have generally included only those bibliographical references which were published after, or not included in, O'Leary's bibliography of 1963.

Our primary motivation in undertaking this study has been to pinpoint the linguistic areas that are desperately in need of study.  As will become apparent, the prognosis for the survival of some of the indigenous languages is excellent; for others it is very poor.  It is hoped that, as a result of this article, speedy linguistic and anthropological work can be carried out in those Chaco Indian languages closest to extinction, and that maintenance factors such as bilingual education programs can be started, or in some cases continued, so as to assure the continued existence of those languages whose prognosis for survival is still good.

ZAMUCO FAMILY
     1.  Ayoreo (Moro)
     2.  Chamakoko

Ayoreo (Moro) and Chamakoko have been classified as members of a Zamuco stock (Loukotka 1968:58-59), a Zamucoan family (Voegelin and Voegelin 1977:132), or a family called Zamuco-Chamakoko (Tovar 1961: 46-47). In every case each language is placed on a different branch of the family or stock.

Loukotka also classifies Ayoré (Ayoreo), spoken in Paraguay, as a different language from Moro, which he places in Bolivia. He also classifies Chamakoko and Chamakoko Bravo as two different languages. From our own investigations, however, we have come to the conclusion that Ayoreo and Moro are names which refer to the same language spoken in both Paraguay and Bolivia with minor, mostly phonological, dialect differences between the two areas. This is also true for the distinctions between Chamakoko and Chamakoko Bravo which, although greater than those found within Ayoreo (Moro), still do not warrant being classified as two different languages.

1. Ayoreo. The Ayoreo call themselves and their
language Ayoreo, Ayoweo, or Ayoeo, although both
tribe and language are called Moro by the non-
Indians of Paraguay.

Location and Population Estimate. Ayoreo are found
in the following locations: the territory stretch-
ing from Cerro Leon in the northeast up to the Bolivian border (150); Faro Moro in the northcentral
Chaco (550); María Auxiliadora on the Paraguay River (400). Total: 1,000.

General Linguistic Situation. Culturally the Ayoreo are divided into two groups. One is composed
of hunters and gathers who wander seasonally from
Cerro Leon in the northern Chaco along a northwes-
terly course up to and across the Bolivian border.
As can be expected, linguistically this group is
composed of monolingual speakers of Ayoreo.

The other group of Ayoreo has become sedentary
and has settled at Faro Moro and María Auxiliadora. At Faro Moro the Ayoreo have gardens and occasionally hunt. However, since they can no longer
sell the skins of the animals that they have
caught, small groups are beginning to migrate to
the Mennonite colonies in search of work as agricultural laborers. Of the fifty or so Indians that
have gone to the Mennonite colonies, a few of the
men have picked up some words of Spanish. The
Indians that have stayed at Faro Moro are monolinguals. The New Tribes Mission is currently planning a program in bilingual education in Ayoreo and
Spanish so that the Indians at Faro Moro can eventually become proficient in both languages.

In María Auxiliadora the Salesian missionaries
are teaching the Ayoreo the technology of cattle
raising with the hope that they will eventually be
able to support themselves with this occupation.
The Indians at María Auxiliadora all speak Ayoreo
and until recently were mostly monolingual in that
language. However the Salesians have started a
pre-school program of teaching Ayoreo children the
rudiments of Spanish before they enter the first
grade; thus the children are learning Spanish
through school attendance.

Estimate of Number of Speakers of Ayoreo.    From
Cerro Leon to the Bolivian border ( 150); Faro Moro
(550); María Auxiliadora (400).    Total: 1100

Prognosis.    Since of 100% of tribal members speak
Ayoreo the prognosis for the survival of the language is excellent.

Recommendations.    Although there have been a fair
number of recent studies of Ayoreo (Briggs 1973;
Kelm 1964; Sušnik 1972, 1973), they included neither a complete grammar nor a dictionary of the
language.    These should be undertaken before there
is too much contact with Spanish and Ayoreo begins
to be influenced considerably by that language.


2. Chamakoko.    The Chamakoko self-designation is
 öshörö /isiri/.    They are called Chamakoko by most
other people.

Location and Population Estimates.    Chamakoko are
found in the following locations: Puerto Diana and
surrounding area (800); Fuerte Olimpo ( 100-150);
along the railroad line westwards from Puerto Casa-

do, presently at about Kilometer 90 (100).   Total:
1000 or 1050.

General Linguistic Situation.   Most Chamakoko today are bilingual in Spanish and Chamakoko, although women appear to be less fluent than men.
Some Chamakoko, especially men, also speak Guaraní.   The explanation for their greater skill in
Spanish is derived from the history of the exploitation of palo santo by the Argentines in the northern part of the Rio Paraguay.   Since the Argentines spoke only Spanish, the Chamakoko working for
these firms learned Spanish.   Since then the palo
santo has run out, and the Chamakokos have needed
to look elsewhere for work.   Their labor on ranches
required communication in Guaraní and at Puerto Diana, for example, their proximity to a military
base, and the conscription of some of the Chamakoko
males, has further added to increased knowledge of
Guaraní.   Women, however, frequently state that
Guaraní is too difficult to learn, and seem to
speak it less in public.   At present, Chamakoko living at the missions are more comfortable speaking
in Spanish, while those who live on ranches are
more comfortable with Guaraní.

There appears to be some slight influence of
Spanish on Chamakoko, especially in words that
refer to food goods; Guaraní seems to have had
little impact on the language.

Because Chamakoko is spoken at home, and children are monolingual speakers of Chamakoko, in the
past parents wanted their children to learn only
Spanish in school.   Therefore no programs in bi-

lingual education were offered. Presently, there is an increased desire for bilingual programs and increased instruction in Chamakoko.

In addition to the Chamakoko just discussed, there is another group of Chamakoko, called the Chamakoko Bravo, who originally came from Puerto Sastre. This group speaks another dialect of Chamakoko, and has little to no contact with the northern group.

Estimate of Number of Speakers of Chamakoko. General area of Puerto Diana (800); Fuerte Olimpo (100-150); west of Puerto Casado (100). Total: 1000 to 1050.

Prognosis. The prognosis for Chamakoko is excellent. The language is spoken at home between parents and between parents and children. Chamakoko is also usually spoken at play. Given the increased interest in bilingual education, and the recent opening of an Indian school by the Ministry of Education in Puerto Diana, there is every indication that Chamakoko will continue to be spoken as the first language of this group.

Recommendations. There are a relatively large number of recent studies that have been written on Chamakoko (Ceccarelli 1965; Kelm 1964; Sušnik 1957, 1970, 1972) which can be added to the body of literature already written by renowned scholars. There remain, however, many unanswered questions about the language. Dialect differences, language change, and sociolinguistic distinctions are examples of issues that would be most important to pursue.

MASCOI FAMILY
   3.  Angaité
   4.  Guaná
   5.  Lengua
   6.  Sanapaná
   7.  Toba (Mascoi)

Angaité, Guaná, Lengua, and Sanapaná are classified
as languages pertaining to the mascoi family by Tovar (1961:40) and as dialects of the Mascoy family
by Voegelin and Voegelin (1977:284). Loukotka
(1968:56-57) adds Toba (Kilyetwaiwa or Kilmaharats)
and classifies all five of the languages as members
of his Lengua stock.

   Toba (Mascoi) should not be confused with Toba
(Guaykurú) which has frequently been called Emok-
Toba in Paraguay and classified as a Guaykurúan
language. On the basis of the linguistic data that
we have collected, plus already available material,
discussions with field linguists in Paraguay and
native speakers, we have determined that those
languages which are called Toba in Paraguay are actually two languages, Mascoian Toba and Guaykurúan
Toba.[1]

3. Angaité. The Angaité call themselves and their
language Enlhit.
Location and Population Estimates. Angaité are
found in the following locations: Puerto Casado
(100); Estancias of Guajó, Cerrito, San Pedro, Tuparandá (400); San Carlos (250); Colonia 3 (40);
Juan de Salazar (20); Makthlawaiya-Anglican Mission

(50); area administered by the Anglican Mission (600). Total: 1460.

General Linguistic Situation.  There have been Angaité working in the tannin factories along the Paraguay River for two or three generations.  These factories have also attracted Indians from a variety of other Mascoi speaking groups which has led to a large amount of intermarriage.  And although there is a fair amount of intelligibility between these languages, husbands and wives of different linguistic groups prefer to speak Guaraní with one another, as well as with their children.  In the few cases in which a husband and wife are both speakers of Angaité, they will speak Angaité with one another, but Guaraní with their children.  Thus in Puerto Casado, Angaité children are monolingual speakers of Guaraní before they begin to learn Spanish in school.

There are also Angaité working with cattle on the Guajó, Cerrito, San Pedro, and Tuparandá ranches to the southwest of Puerto Casado.  Although they consider the speaking of Guaraní to be prestigious, adult women are still pretty much monolingual speakers of Angaité, and their children speak that language until they are old enough to be exposed to the Guaraní spoken by Paraguayans also working on the ranches.

In 1971 the New Tribes Mission brought a group of Angaité from Tuparandá to San Carlos on the Paraguayan River.  There they are receiving land and are being taught agricultural techniques by the Mission.  At San Carlos, Angaité is spoken in the home and children speak only that language until they begin formal schooling. Thus the New Tribes Mission is planning to begin educational programs in Angaité, Guaraní, and Spanish for the children at San Carlos.

At Colonia 3 (Gnadenheim) at Colonia Fernheim the Angaité are employed as agricultural laborers on neighboring Mennonite farms. This group of Angaité probably migrated to the area from the ranch at San Juan de Salazar, or from Puerto Casado. Among them Guaraní is spoken between husbands and wives, and to their children. Since the children are growing up as monolingual speakers of Guaraní, their parents have asked that they be enrolled in bilingual educational programs in Guaraní and Spanish.

At the Juan de Salazar Ranch, at the Anglican Mission, and in the area administered by that mission, there is a gradual eroding away of Angaité. Here the Angaité feel that it is better to speak Guaraní than their tribal language. Thus whenever an Angaité woman is fluent enough in Guaraní she and her husband will communicate in that language between themselves, and with their children. Therefore in many cases Angaité children are growing up as monolingual speakers of Guaraní.

Estimate of Number of Speakers of Angaité. Puerto Casado (20); ranches at Guajó, Cerrito, San Pedro, Tuparandá (400); San Carlos (250); Colonia 3 (15); Juan de Salazar (5); Makthlawaiya-Anglican Mission (10); area administered by the Anglican Mission (150). Total: 850.

Prognosis.  Although there are still many adults
that speak Angaité, their general assumption that
it is of little value, and that Guaraní should be
spoken by their children, makes it seem quite probable that the number of speakers of Angaité will
diminish rapidly over the next two generations.  In
Puerto Casado Angaité will soon disappear because
of the increased use of Guaraní within the family
and between ethnic groups.  On the other hand the
prognosis for the language is probably best at San
Carlos where its value will be emphasized through
use in bilingual education programs.
Recommendations.  There are no grammars or other
linguistic materials available on Angaité.  Thus it
is strongly recommended that Angaité soon receive
the attention of linguists.

4. Guaná.  The Guaná call themselves and their language Enlhit.
Location and Population Estimates.  Guaná are found
in the following locations along the Paraguay River: Puerto Sastre (6/ one family); María Casilda
(150); Puerto Casado (250).  Total: 406.
General Linguistic Situation.  Among tribal groups
in Paraguay, the Guaná have probably had the most
negative contact with the white world and yet they
are considered to be the most traditional of the
Mascoi groups, maintaining their customary ceremonies and patterns of leadership.  The Guaná for
many years have worked in the tannin factories
along the Paraguay River, and today there are second, third, and fourth generation Guaná who have

been born and raised in factory towns. These towns
have attracted Indians from a variety of tribes,
which has inevitably led to a large amount of intermarriage between the members of the various
groups. In the case of the Guaná at Puerto Casado,
this has been with speakers of Angaité, Sanapaná,
Lengua, and Toba (Mascoi). And although there is a
fair amount of mutual intelligibility between all
of these languages, especially between Guaná and
Sanapaná, husbands and wives of two linguistic entities (and today even those who are both Guaná)
prefer to speak Guaraní with one another as well as
with their children. Thus in Puerto Casado there
are one or two old people who are monolingual speakers of Guaná, adults who prefer to speak Guaraní
both in and outside of the home, and children who
are monolingual speakers of Guaraní before they begin learning Spanish at school. In María Casilda
and Puerto Sastre there is little or no marriage
outside of the tribe, yet adults in both areas prefer to speak Guaraní among themselves and to their
children whose linguistic situation is the same as
in Puerto Casado. In María Casilda, Guaná men are
commuting daily across the river to Valle-mi where
they work in the cement factory, thus reinforcing
their use of Guaraní.
Estimate of Number of Speakers of Guaná. Puerto
Sastre (2); María Casilda (20); Puerto Casado
(33). Total: 55.
Prognosis. Guaná will disappear most rapidly in
Puerto Sastre where there are currently only two
speakers who remember any of the language. In

Puerto Casado there are several reasons why the language will probably not survive for much longer. (1) Because of the intermarriage of Guaná with other ethnic groups, Guaraní has become the lingua franca between adults. (2) The younger generation no longer speaks the tribal language. (3) There is a lack of interest on the part of the missionaries in charge of educating the Indians in Puerto Casado in maintaining the languages (perhaps because of the multilingual situation they have on their hands). (4) There is the general belief among the Guaná themselves that it is better to speak Guaraní than Guaná. Thus the prognosis for the survival of Guaná beyond the current generation of adults over 40 years of age is poor indeed.

Recommendations. Since there is only one published report on this language, a 23-page word list (Boggiani 1896), it is strongly recommended that Guaná be studied thoroughly before it disappears altogether.

5. Lengua. Like the Angaité, the Lengua call themselves and their language Enlhit.

Location and Population Estimate. Lengua are found in the following locations: Puerto Casado (100). In the following locations associated with the Mennonite Colony: Yalve Sanga (975); Campo Largo (485); Pozo Amarillo (515); La Esperanza (170); Fernheim Colony (150); Nord Menno (670); Sud Menno (720). In the Makthlawaiya Anglican Mission (900); area administered by the Anglican Mission (3,800). Total: 8485.

<u>General Linguistic Situation</u>.  The language is di-
vided into two dialects called North and South Lengua.  North Lengua is generally spoken in the central Chaco from around 150 km. north of the town
of Filadelfia to 130 km. to the south of that center.  South Lengua is spoken in the area administered by the Anglican Mission, running from the Paraguay River in the east to the Trans Chaco Highway
in the west, and from the San Carlos River in the
north to the Monte Linda River in the south.  From
this area Lengua speakers have migrated as far as
Puerto Casado to work in the tannin factories
there.  The original division between the two dialects seemed to have been based on ecological factors; the North Lengua seem to have had an economy
based on hunting and gathering in the higher lands
of the central Chaco while the South Lengua were
involved in a lowland river economy based on fishing.
    Today the majority of North Lengua live in the
Mennonite Colonies where they are employed as agricultural workers on neighboring Mennonite farms, or
in the tannin factory at Yalve Sanga.  All of these
Lengua speak their language among themselves and
with their children.  Adult men over 30 years of
age may have learned some Platt Deutsch from their
employers whereas those under 30 may have learned
Spanish in the same way.  In a recent study of Spanish language competency among adult Lengua men, 4%
were found to speak Spanish well, 32% spoke it more
or less well, 48% spoke a little Spanish, and 16%
spoke no Spanish at all.  Among the adult women,

20% spoke a little Spanish and 80% spoke no Spanish
at all (Stahl n.d.:14). Children are monolingual
speakers of Lengua until they begin their education
in bilingual programs (Lengua and Spanish) in the
Indian schools in their communities. Until recently there was no desire on the part of Lengua speakers to learn, or to have their children learn, either Spanish or Guaraní; both languages are associated with the Paraguayans who killed many of their
relatives during the Chaco War. However today the
Lengua believe that a 'modern' Lengua, complete
with Spanish and Guaraní borrowings, should be used
in textbooks and in the Mennonite Colony's daily
broadcasts in that language.

The Lengua in the northern part of the areas administered by the Anglican Mission speak South Lengua. They are also fluent in Guaraní, which they
consider to be the more prestigious of the two languages. In fact, many of the Lengua children in
this area are growing up as monolingual speakers of
Guaraní. To the south of this area Lengua is being
better retained with adult Lengua speakers communicating in that language with one another and with
their children. However, most adult men are fluent
in Guaraní as well. On the Anglican Mission itself
women are usually monolingual Lengua speakers while
men are bilingual in Guaraní and Lengua or may know
some Spanish. Children are also monolingual in
Lengua before they enter the school system on the
Mission. There they spend a pre-school year learning to speak Guaraní after which they continue
their education in that language while making a

transition into Spanish. For adults the Mission
has literacy classes in Lengua.

Lengua have worked for many years in the tannin
factories along the Paraguay River where they have
intermarried with other Mascoian-speaking Indians.
In the case of Puerto Casado this has been with
speakers of Guaná, Angaité, Sanapaná, and Toba
(Mascoi). And although there is a fair degree of
intelligibility between these languages, spouses of
different linguistic groups prefer to speak Guaraní
with one another and with their children. And even
in the cases where husband and wife are Lengua
speakers, and communicate in that language with one
another, they will tend to speak Guaraní with their
children. Thus in Puerto Casado Lengua children
are monolingual speakers of Guaraní before they begin to learn Spanish in the schools.

Estimate of Number of Speakers of Lengua. Puerto
Casado (20). In the following locations associated
with the Mennonite Colony: Yalve Sanga (975); Campo
Largo (485); Pozo Amarillo (515); La Esperanza
(170); Fernheim Colony (150); Nord Menno (670); Sud
Menno (720). In the Makthlawaiya Anglican Mission
(900); area administered by the Anglican Mission
(3000). Total: 6705.

Prognosis. With the exception of the Lengua spoken
at Puerto Casado, which will probably die out in
another generation or two, the language seems to be
in a very healthy state. On the Mennonite Colony
its use is being reinforced in bilingual education
programs and radio broadcasts. And on the Anglican
Mission there is the strong possibility of future

education programs in which Lengua children will be taught to read and write in their own language, as well as in Guaraní and Spanish.

Recommendations. There are a relatively large number of linguistic studies on Lengua (Coryn n.d.; Ferrario 1947; Lowes 1954; Susnik 1958). There remain, however, many unanswered questions about the language. A precise account of dialect differences, or studies of language change and sociolinguistic distinctions, for example, are issues that would be most important to pursue.

6. Sanapaná. The Sanapaná call themselves and their language Sa'apan or Enenlhit.

Location and Population Estimate. Administrative area of the Anglican Mission (600); San Juan de Salazar (280); Puerto Casado (100); Kilometer 11/West of Puerto Casado (50); La Esperanza (250); Pozo Amarillo (25); Nord Menno/Heuboden (25); Sud Menno/Nueva Vida (29). Total: 1359.

General Linguistic Situation. In the administrative area of the Anglican Mission, most Sanapaná parents speak Guaraní to each other and to their children. There is also some intermarriage with Angaité and Lengua speakers. The result is that Sanapaná children here are monolingual in Guaraní.

In San Juan de Salazar, most of the men have worked on nearby ranches. As a result, they are quite bilingual in Sanapaná and Guaraní. When the children go to school, they learn Spanish but continue to speak Sanapaná. The women remain essentially monolingual Sanapaná speakers.

In Puerto Casado, a multi-Mascoian language situation exists. Besides Sanapaná, one finds Angaité, Guaná, Lengua, and Toba (Mascoi) speakers. Although there is a fair amount of mutual intelligibility in this language family, the result of the
multilingual situation has been a levelling of language difference by substituting Guaraní as the
language of communication. Since there is frequent
intermarriage between the various linguistic
groups, and spouses speak to each other in Guaraní,
very little Sanapaná is spoken. There are also no
educational programs in the indigenous language to
reinforce the learning of such, and so most children do not speak Sanapaná. It is only people over
the age of 50 and a few younger women who still
speak the language.

West of Puerto Casado at Kilometer 11, the small
group of Sanapaná continue to speak the language
regularly. The older people are monolingual in Sanapaná, whereas the younger ones are bilingual with
Guaraní.

In the area administered by the Mennonites, that
is La Esperanza, Pozo Amarillo, and North and South
Menno, the women and older men prefer to speak Sanapaná. However, males of 35 and under prefer
speaking Spanish and Guaraní. Although there is a
Sanapaná teacher in La Esperanza, she does not know
the language, and until recently felt that the teaching of the language was unnecessary. Although
there has been a change of attitude and a greater
emphasis is placed on the tribal language, there
are no Sanapaná textbooks for any of the schools.

Estimate of Number of Speakers of Sanapaná. Area administered by the Anglican Mission (150); San Juan de Salazar (280); Puerto Casado (20); Kilometer 11 (50); La Esperanza (250); Pozo Amarillo (25); Nord Menno (25); Sud Menno (29). Total: 829. Prognosis. In both the Anglican mission area and in Puerto Casado, the prognosis for the survival of Sanapaná is quite poor. Since Guaraní is spoken in most situations, since intermarriage with other groups is constantly occurring, and since no education programs exist in the language, it seems clear that in another generation or two there will be no more Sanapaná speakers in these locations. On the other hand, in those areas where the women and children still speak primarily Sanapaná, and where there is an increased awareness of the importance of the tribal language, the prognosis seems quite positive.

Recommendations. Since there are no grammars, vocabularies, or even elementary school primers on Sanapaná, it is most urgent that linguists undertake an analysis of the language with utmost speed.

7. Toba (Mascoi). Like the Guaná and Sanapaná, the Toba (Mascoi) call themselves and their language Enenlhit. They are not to be confused with the Toba (Guaykurú) who call themselves Namqom and speak a very different language.

Location and Population Estimate. Puerto Casado (100); Kilometer 83 and northward along the new road (400); Estancia Palo Santo (18); Pozo Amarillo

(288); Colonia Fernheim (145); Loma Plata (242);
Nueva Vida (10). Total: 1203.

General Linguistic Situation. In Puerto Casado,
most of the adult Toba are bilingual in Toba and
Guaraní. They are working in the tannin factories
at Puerto Casado or on neighboring ranches in that
area. As a result of these work contacts all the
males have learned to speak Guaraní. The women,
because of the multi-Mascoi language environment at
Puerto Casado, have also learned to communicate
with each other in Guaraní. Adults tend to speak
Guaraní most of the time, even though some speak
Toba at home. Most children play with other Mascoian-speaking children and although they can understand the Indian language, have no desire to
speak it. The school, run by the Salesian Order,
does not have a program for bilingual education in
the indigenous languages.

At Kilometer 83 and north on the new road which
leads to the quebracho forests, the Toba laborers
and their families are all bilingual speakers of
Toba and Guaraní. The same situation holds true
for the Toba on Estancia Palo Santo.

In the area under Mennonite administration, the
Toba speak their own language in the home. Most of
the women are monolingual speakers of Toba, while
the men speak a little Spanish or low German. In
the schools, children are first taught by Toba teachers who are using Lengua materials modified for
Toba use. Because of the similarities between the
two languages, this is not an impossible task.
Spanish is introduced as a new language after the

first two grades in the indigenous schools are completed. Because of the large number of Toba speakers it has been suggested that separate Toba texts
be developed instead of relying on the Lengua materials.

Estimate of Number of Speakers of Toba(Mascoi).
Puerto Casado (20); Kilometer 83 and north (400);
Estancia Palo Santo (18); Pozo Amarillo (288);
Colonia Fernheim (145); Loma Plata (242); Nueva
Vida (10).    Total: 1123.

Prognosis.    In Puerto Casado, the prognosis for
survival of the language is quite negative.    There
is no reinforcement of the native language at home,
in the community, or at school.    In all other areas
the prognosis is quite good.    In each of these places children and women speak Toba more fluently
than Guaraní, Spanish, or German.    Since the language is spoken at home and, in the Mennonite area,
at school, it seems quite probable that the language will continue to be spoken for at least another
two generations.

Recommendations.    Since there is no vocabulary,
grammar, or any other linguistic analysis of Toba
(Mascoi), such a study should be undertaken.    Especially important is the determination of the status
of the language in terms of its relationship to
other Mascoian languages.

MATACO/MATAGUAYO FAMILY
        8.    Chorotí
        9.    Chulupí
       10.    Mac'á

Chorotí, Chulupí, and Mac'á are classified as pertaining to the Mataco stock by Loukotka (1968:53-
55), and as part of the Mataco family by Voegelin
and Voegelin (1977:223-224). In each case Chorotí
and Chulupí are found together in one branch of the
family or stock, while Mac'á is found in another.
All three languages are classified separately by
Tovar (1961:38-39) and included in his grouping of
Chaco languages. Our own investigations indicate
that perhaps Chorotí and Chulupí are somewhat more
closely related to one another than either is to
Mac'á. But for the moment our data is not conclusive enough to warrant placing Chorotí and Chulupí
together in one branch of the Mataco/Mataguayo family as opposed to Mac'á in another.

8. Chorotí. The Chorotí call themselves and their
language Yofuasha, although they are usually called
Chorotí or Manjuy by others.

Location and Population Estimate. Chorotí are
found in the following locations: the area surrounding Prats Gil (150); Santa Rosa (150); Colonia 22
at Colonia Fernheim (50); the ranch at Hernandarius
(30). Total: 380.

General Linguistic Situation. The Chorotí who have
settled around Prats Gil are generally employed on
the military base there as well as on the ranches
in the area. There are still those who support
themselves by hunting, but with the market for animal hides drying up, they are having to search for
more sedentary activities in order to support themselves. All of this group speaks Chorotí, although

those who are working on the military base are
learning some Guaraní from the soldiers there,
while those who work on the ranches are learning
some Spanish.

At Santa Rosa the New Tribes Missionaries are
attempting to teach the Chorotí the techniques of
agriculture.  As there is ample water here, the
Chorotí have small gardens and are raising goats.
A number of them are also involved in hunting and
trapping.  However, since there is now virtually no
market for animal hides, many Chorotí have had to
turn to work on neighboring ranches so as to gain a
livelihood.  For those who remain at Santa Rosa the
New Tribes Mission is setting up a bilingual education program in Chorotí and Spanish.

At the ranch at Hernandarius there are five families of Chorotí who have come from Santa Rosa to
work.  And at Colonia 22 in Colonia Fernheim the
Chorotí have also come from Santa Rosa, but by way
of Mariscal Estigarribia.  Since the population of
this colony is primarily Chulupí, some of the Chorotí speak Chulupí while some have picked up a few
words of Spanish from their Mennonite employers.
Estimate of Number of Speakers of Chorotí.  Area
surrounding Prats Gil (150); Santa Rosa (150); Colonia 22 (50); Hernandarius (30).  Total: 380.
Prognosis.  Since 100% of tribal members speak Chorotí, the prognosis for the survival of the language at the moment appears good.  However, the total number of speakers of Chorotí is small, and
those inroads made by Spanish or Guaraní will seriously threaten the stability of the language.

Recommendations.  Since there are only two recent
publications on this language (Susnik 1962; Tovar
1966), it is recommended that a thorough study of
the grammar of Chorotí, plus a dictionary, be prepared as soon as possible.

9. Chulupí.  The Chulupí call themselves Niwakle
and their language Niwakle Lhi'ish.
Location and Population Estimate.  Chulupí are
found in the following locations administered by
the Oblate Mission: Esteros (409), Laguna Escalante
(784), Pedro P. Peña (168), Mariscal Estigarribia
and Santa Teresita (283), Matarife (21), Yichinachat (423), Loma Pyta (181), Rancho Minona (57),
Est. Santa Emilia (62); and in the following locations administered by the Mennonite Mission: Filadelfia (316), Colonia 6 (30), Colonia 8 (185), Colonia 10 (185), Colonia 22 (82), Yalve Sanga
(1242), Campo Alegre (831), Colonia 14 (12), Toledo
(22), Sandhorst (116), Cayin (506).  Total: 5915.
General Linguistic Situation.  It is felt that the
Chulupí are the proudest tribe in the Chaco as far
as language and culture are concerned.  The language consists of two main dialects which correspond
to historical and geographical differences.  The
inland or 'bush' Chulupí, who considered their language as purer because they lived in the center of
the Chaco, had a culture which was very similar to
the Lengua.  The more numerous river Chulupí, who
were fishermen, also had slight sub-dialectical
differences depending on whether they were up, mid,
or down stream Chulupí.  However, present-day dif-

ferences between these dialects is minimal. Chulupí, though they have been exposed to Spanish for
over forty years, still speak that language poorly. There is a slight bit more influence of Spanish on the language in Mariscal Estigarribia than
there is in the Mennonite colonies (Central Chaco)
but there is very little mixing of Chulupí with
Guaraní. When the Chulupí are found in contact
with other Mataguayo speakers, even though the languages are quite different, great efforts are made
to understand each other.

In Esteros, Laguna Escalante, Mariscal Estigarribia, Yichinachat, Loma Pyta, Rancho Minona, and
Est. Santa Emilia, where the Oblate Mission is the
administrative unit, there are bilingual Spanish-
Chulupí programs available for children in the indigenous schools. In Santa Teresita, where more
than one indigenous language group is located, most
children are bilingual in Chulupí and Guaraní before they get to school. The educational program
there is excellent and it is considered to be the
best place for Indians to learn Spanish. The language at home, however, remains Chulupí. In Pedro
P. Peña bilingual education programs have still not
begun, and there is no school at all in Matarife.

In the area administered by the Central Mennonite Committee, the Chulupí are monolingual in their
own language until the age of seven. In the
schools where there are Chulupí and Spanish bilingual programs, pre-school and first grade are
taught in Chulupí only. In the second grade Spa-

nish is introduced as a foreign language. In Filadelfia, Colonia 6, 8, 10, and 22, the Oblates su-
pervise the Chulupí education program using their
own materials. In the other locations, classes are
taught using Chulupí materials developed by the
Mennonites. Generally in the colonies the Chulupí
are encouraged to learn Spanish so that they can
communicate with other Indians groups; some have
also learned a little Platt Deutsch. At home the
language spoken is Chulupí. Since, however, there
is considerable movement among the Chulupí from colony to colony and from ranch to ranch, those who
are more nomadic tend to speak some Guaraní; those
who have lived most of the time in the colony or
who have migrated from the Pilcomayo region may
speak some Spanish or German. Among women and older people, however, there are also some monolingual speakers of Chulupí.

Estimate of Number of Speakers of Chulupí. Esteros (409); Laguna Escalante (784); Pedro P. Peña
(168); Mariscal Estigarribia and Santa Teresita
(283); Matarife (21); Yichinachat (423); Loma Pyta
(181); Rancho Minona (57); Est. Santa Emilia (62);
Filadelfia (316); Colonia 6 (30); Colonia 8 ( 185);
Colonia 10 (185); Colonia 22 (82); Yalve Sanga
(1242); Campo Alegre (831); Colonia 14 (12); Toledo
(22); Sandhorst (116); Cayin (506). Total: 5915.

Prognosis. The prognosis for the survival of Chulupí is excellent. Not only is Chulupí spoken at
home and taught in a large number of schools, but
the importance of the language is reinforced by radio programs in Chulupí in the Mennonite colonies.

In Filadelfia, for example, the Indians have even
requested that all Spanish loan words be removed
from radio programming in Chulupí, including the
news, so that listeners will hear only the 'pure'
language.

Recommendations. The Chulupí language has received considerable attention recently (Junker, Wilkskamp, and Seelwische 1975; Susnik 1968; Wicke and
Chase-Sardi 1969); however there are many areas of
language change and sociolinguistics that could
well be studied.

10. Mac'á. The Mac'á call themselves and their
language Mac'á.

Location and Population Estimate. The Mac'á are
found at the colony of Fray Bartolomé de las Casas
on the west bank of the Paraguay River across from
the Botanical Gardens in Asunción (800).

General Linguistic Situation. In the early 1940s a
group of Mac'á was brought to this area from the
interior of the Chaco where their traditional hunting lands were disappearing as a result of the development of that area after the Chaco War. After
a group had been settled at the colony they were
joined little by little by those still living in
the interior. Today the Mac'á still make journeys
into the interior where they hunt, but then return
to the colony which they consider their home. A
few of the Mac'á have garden plots, but because of
flooding by the river they do not produce much in
the way of food supplies. Thus without either a
hunting and gathering or agricultural base with

which to supply their needs, the Mac'á have turned
to a cash economy. This has taken the form of selling Indian artifacts to tourists and Paraguayan
nationals alike.

Because the Mac'á are tied into this kind of
economy, one would expect that they would be learning to speak Guaraní and Spanish so as to better
their commercial relations. But such has not been
the case. A few older men who had contact with
Guaraní speakers when they still lived in the Chaco
may remember a bit of that language, but the majority of younger adults do not speak Guaraní. Nor
do men in general speak much Spanish, except for
the few words and phrases which they may have acquired in selling tourist goods in Asunción. Women also sell their products in Asunción, and are
also basically monolingual in Mac'á, except for the
Spanish vocabulary they have picked up in their business dealings with tourists and shop owners.

Until recently the New Tribes Mission had an
education program at the colony in which children
were taught bilingually in Mac'á and Spanish; this
has recently been discontinued. However there are
a few Mac'á children who are being educated by the
missionaries in Asunción and, as a result, are
learning Spanish.

Number of Speakers of Mac'á. 800.

Prognosis. With 100% of the Mac'á speaking their
native language, the prognosis for its survival
appears to be good.

Recommendations. There is still the need of an
adequate grammar of Mac'á plus a dictionary of the

language.  What might also be of interest would be
a sociolinguistic study treating the phenomenon of
a linguistic group located in the suburbs of the
capital of a South American country, working within
the national economy, but knowing neither of the
nation's major languages.

GUAYKURÚ FAMILY
        11.  Toba

Toba has been classified as pertaining to the Guaycurú stock by Loukotka (1968:48-50) and to the
Guaycurú family by Voegelin and Voegelin (1977:
149).  Tovar (1961:42-43) classifies Toba as part of
the Guaycurú family, but mentions it as being spoken only in Argentina.

    In Paraguay the language is most frequently cal-
led Emok-Toba.  However our data shows that what
has generally been called Toba in Paraguay is in
reality two languages: Guaykuruan Toba and Mascoian
Toba.  The former is similar to the Guaykuruan Toba
spoken in Argentina and shares 90% or more of its
lexicon with that language.  See also 2 on the Mascoian languages, plus footnote 1 to this paper for
comparative lists of Toba (Guaykurú), Toba (Mascoi), and Lengua, another Mascoian language.

11.  Toba (Guaykurú).  The Toba call themselves Toba
and their language Namqom.  They have traditionally
been called Emok by various authors; however, this
is neither what they call themselves nor what other
indigenous groups call them.

Location and Population Estimate. Cerrito (Mision San Francisco de Asis) (600); Villa del Rosario (20); Fray Bartolomé de las Casas (Asunción)
(12). Total: 632.

General Linguistic Situation. The general linguistic situation for the Toba has been one of considerable change. The group which is presently found
in Cerrito has come together from a variety of different locations in the past seven years. Before
this influx, a large number of the Toba worked on
ranches in the Rosario area and became quite fluent
Guaraní speakers. Their children went to schools
where Guaraní was spoken, and it was felt that it
was important to be a good speaker of Guaraní.
Now, however, they are settled in Cerrito and speak
Toba among themselves and Toba to their children,
and feel that their own language is the one to be
fluent in. Less and less Guaraní is spoken at
home, so that this year for the first time it was
impossible to have beginning school classes in Guaraní because the children of six and seven did not
speak it. At present some of the men from Cerrito
find work on the estancias along the Trans-Chaco,
but they maintain a home base at the mission, and
families generally remain there. In Cerrito the
first two school years are taught in Toba. New
materials are being organized because the old Toba-
Guaraní primers are not considered adequate. Children are also learning some Spanish, but they are
not obliged to speak it.

In Rosario, where there are only four families,
the children speak both Toba and Guaraní. There is

considerable visiting, however, between Cerrito and
Rosario and while those from Rosario are at the
mission they also speak Toba.

   In Bartolomé de las Casas both Toba and Guaraní
are spoken.  There is no separate Toba school for
these children and they are taught in the same
schools as the Mac'á.

Estimate of Number of Speakers of Toba (Guaykurú).
Cerrito (600); Rosario (13); Bartolomé de las Casas
(6).  Total: 619.

Prognosis.  For Cerrito the prognosis for survival
is excellent.  In Rosario and Bartolomé de las Casas the prognosis is far less positive, since the
children are much more exposed to non-Toba language
situations.

Recommendations.  There have been a fair number of
linguistic studies of Toba written which are based
on the dialects spoken in Argentina.  Since there
is some slight variation lexically, it would be very useful to have a more complete study of the dialectical differences between Argentine and Paraguayan Toba.  This would be especially helpful in
adapting Argentine Toba pedagogical materials for
use in the Cerrito school program.


TUPI-GUARANÍ FAMILY
       12.  Guarayo
       13.  Tapieté

Guarayo and Tapieté are Tupi-Guaranian languages.
Tovar (1961:85) labels them Tupi-Guaranian 'in the
strict sense of the word', Loukotka (1968:118) pla-

ces them in the Chiriguano branch of his Tupi
stock, and Voegelin and Voegelin (1977:338) locate
them in the Tupi branch of the Tupi-Guarani family
of languages.


12. Guarayo. The Guarayo call themselves Guaraní
and their language Guaraní-eté or Ñañañe'.
Location and Population Estimate. Santa Teresita
(256); Mariscal Estigarribia (169); Muñeca (35);
Matarife (93); Filadelfia (180); Cayin o Clim
(Colonia Neuland) (13); Loma Plata (Colonia Nord
Menno) (10); Pedro P. Peña (250). Total: 1006.
General Linguistic Situation. In Santa Teresita
the Guarayo are agriculturalists, whereas in Mariscal Estigarribia the majority work in the military
installations. In each location a few of the older
people are believed to still be able to communicate
with one another in Guaraní-eté, but the majority
of adults and children have lost the older language
and now speak Paraguayan Guaraní. However, there
is also a high degree of fluency in Spanish in these areas because of the availability of good school
facilities. Thus all men between 15 and 45 years
of age are bilingual in Guaraní and Spanish. And
among women of the same age group some 80% are
bilingual in Guaraní and Spanish.
    In Matarife and Muñeca the Guaraní are agricul-
turalists. With the exception of perhaps a few older people who may still speak the tribal language,
both adults and children are native speakers of Paraguayan Guaraní. Since there are no schools in
these communities, Spanish is not acquired through

the educational system and the majority of Indians, both adults and children, have remained monolingual speakers of Paraguayan Guaraní.

In Filadelfia, on the Mennonite Colony, the Guaraní work in local factories or for neighboring Mennonite farmers. With the exception of a few older people who may occasionally communicate with one another in Guaraní-eté, the majority of adults and children speak some Platt Deutsch which they have picked up from their employers, whereas others have learned Spanish in the same way. Guaraní-speaking children in Filadelfia are taught bilingually at the Indian school in Paraguayan Guaraní and Spanish. There are also religious radio programs emanating from Filadelfia in Paraguayan Guaraní.

In Cayin and in Loma Plata the Guaraní work as agricultural laborers for neighboring Mennonite farmers. It is doubtful whether there are any speakers of tribal Guaraní in these communities, as both adults and children appear to be native speakers of Paraguayan Guaraní. However, adult men have also learned some Spanish from their employers

In Pedro P. Peña the Guaraní are also agriculturalists, although at times they engage in seasonal agricultural work on neighboring estancias in Paraguay and Argentina. Because they have has little contact with Paraguayan Guaraní most young people as well as adults still speak their traditional tribal language. Spanish is learned by children in schools and by adults through seasonal employment away from the community.

Estimate of Number of Speakers of Guarayo. Santa
Teresita (12); Mariscal Estigarribia (8); Muñeca
(2); Matarife (4); Filadelfia (8); Cayin o Clim
(0); Loma Plata (0); Pedro P. Peña (270). Total:
304.

Prognosis. Guarayo, with approximately 304 speakers, is on the verge of extinction in all areas
except Pedro P. Peña. The rapid rate of extinction of Guarayo has come about partly because Guarayo and Paraguayan Guaraní, both members of the
Tupi-Guaraní family of languages, are mutually
intelligible. Thus it has been very easy for speakers of Guarayo to make a transfer from their tribal language to Paraguayan Guaraní in the areas in
which that language is spoken.

Recommendations. Except for a short word list of
Guarayo (Chiriguano) published by Schmidt in 1938,
nothing else has been printed about Guarayo. Thus
it is urgent that the language be studied thoroughly before it disappears altogether.


13. Tapieté. The Tapieté call themselves Guaraní,
Ñanaigua, or Avá and call their language Guaraní'
eté or Ñanaikú.

Location and Population Estimate. Santa Teresita
(50); Matarife (10); Cauce 5 (95); Campo'i (41); on
Colonia Fernheim at the following Colonias: 1 (17);
3 (84); 5 (173); 11 (43). Total: 513.

General Linguistic Situation. In Santa Teresita
the Tapieté are agriculturalists. Whereas a few of
the older people are believed to communicate with
one another in Tapieté, they are also fluent in Pa-

raguayan Guaraní. Younger adults may understand some Tapieté but speak Guaraní as their first language. And children are monolingual speakers of Guaraní until they began formal schooling in Spanish. There is also a high degree of fluency in Spanish among the Tapieté in Santa Teresita. All men between 15 and 45 years of age are bilingual in Guaraní and Spanish as are 80% of the women of that age group (Grünberg and Grünberg 1974:45). The reason for this seems to be the emphasis placed on Spanish by the missionaries at Santa Teresita as well as the contacts that some of the Tapieté have had with army officers at the neighboring military base of Mariscal Estigarribia.

At Matarife and Cauce 5 the Tapieté work as seasonal laborers on neighboring ranches, and at Campo'i they are agriculturalists. As in Santa Teresita there are believed to be a few older people who communicate with one another in Tapieté. However, they are also fluent in Guaraní, as are younger adults who speak Guaraní as their first language but who may understand some Tapieté. Children are monolingual speakers of Guaraní.

Colonia 1 in Colonia Fernheim is an encampment whereas at Colonias 3,5, and 11 the Tapieté have received parcels of land on which to settle more permanently. At Colonia 5 many of the Tapieté work at a nearby brick factory whereas at the Colonias they work as agricultural laborers on neighboring Mennonite farms. Here there are a few older people who still remember some Tapieté. But they also speak Paraguayan Guaraní, as do the rest of the Ta-

pieté on the Colonias who consider it their first
language. Adult men have also picked up some Spanish through contact with their Mennonite employers.

Estimate of Number of Speakers of Tapieté. Santa
Teresita (6); Matarife (2); Cauce 5 (10); Campo'i
(5); Colonia Fernheim (10). Total: 33.

Prognosis. Tapieté, with approximately 33 speakers all over the age of fifty, is clearly on the
verge of extinction. This has partly come about
because Tapieté and Guaraní, both members of the
Tupi-Guaraní family of languages, are mutually intelligible. Thus it has been very easy for speakers of Tapieté to make a transfer from their tribal language to Paraguayan Guaraní.

Recommendations. Except for a short word list of
Tapieté published by Schmidt in 1937, nothing else
has been printed about the language. Thus it is
urgent that the language be studied before it disappears altogether.

ACKNOWLEDGEMENTS
This chapter is a slightly revised version of one
with the same title which appeared in Anthropological Linguistics 19.8 (1977). We gratefully acknowledge AL's permission to republish it.

We would also like to thank the many people in
Paraguay who in some measure helped us in our re-
search. Among those who contributed basic linguis-
tic data were the following: A. Alosa, F. Aquino
Bogarín, C. Caballero, B. Colonga, J. Fletes, P.
Flores, S. Flores, N. Jara, R. Lisamón, A. Lopez,

C. Lopez, M. Lopez Fletes, M. Maciél, L. Mencía, A. Morejuán, S. Rojas, R. Saldivár, E. Segundo, P. Souza, G. Vega, E. Villaba, and L. Villara.

We have also profited from discussions with Padre J. Ballín, J. Beechy, J. Bell, Hermano A. Benz, M. Chase-Sardi, R. Clark, D. Dilworth, P. Faulkner, G. Hein, W. Jones, R. Kerr, D. Lepp, E. Nelson, R. and F. Sammons, Col. A. Sanmaniego, Sor Julia and the sisters of the Salesian Order (Misión Livio Farina, Puerto Casado), and W. Stahl.

Finally we would like to thank the following for their help in the logistics of carrying out this study: D. Dilworth, J. Gant, P. Hunte, J. and L. Laird, D. Leon Casado, Mons. F. Lucas, Col. P. Ortiz Molina, A. Peña, Padre J. Schöber, W. Stahl, and C. Walde.

## NOTES

1. The following lexical lists (Table 1) indicate the differences between the two Toba languages, as well as the similarities between Toba (Mascoi) and Lengua, another of the Mascoian languages.

## REFERENCES

Binda, Ricardo, and Antonio Tovar. 1959. Algunas notas sobre un idioma de Chaco: El Chulupí. Quaderni dell' Instituto de Glottologia dell' Université di Bologna IV:55-58.

Boggiani, Guido. 1896. Vocabulario dell'idioma Guaná, Parte I. Atti della R. Academia de Licel Memorie, Vol. 3:57-80.

Table 1. Lexical Lists of Three Chaco Languages

| Gloss | Lengua | Toba (Mascoi) | Toba (Guaykurú) |
|---|---|---|---|
| ashes | mes̆Lima | tahap | mala' |
| blood | e'ema' | ema' | netago' |
| bone | aS̆Lapok | askapok | nopinek |
| dog | semheŋ | simhen | pi'oq |
| ear | eŋhayko' | enhaykok | ltela |
| earth | sLapop | sepop | alwa |
| eat | sekto | antota | halyik |
| eye | akta'ak | enaktek | na'ayete |
| fire | ta'asLa | tasLa | novik |
| fish | kelasma' | kilasma | qote |
| foot | e'emenek | emenek | napia' |
| hand | e'emek | emek | lvaq |
| heart | yiphempak | enhekhek | lɏjaqte |
| leaf | yantaw'a | yametawa | epaqlavi |
| mouth | ahatoŋ | eheton | halame' |
| night | aLta'a | petsasep | pe |

Table 1. Lexical Lists of Three Chaco Languages (cont.)

| | | | |
|---|---|---|---|
| nose | awahek | enwahek | lmik |
| rain | mamey'a | momaya | hawot |
| root | ankepminak | hapokmenak | epaɡlopa' |
| skin | empehek | eŋempehek | lo'oq |
| sky | ne'eten | neten | pigem |
| smoke | e'eten | eten | nodek lomala' |
| star | yow'a | yaw'a | woqahñi |
| sun | mayahet | mahat | nala' |
| tail | eta'la' | enyetek | lqote' |
| tongue | ahaskok | enlaskok | naĉaɡat |
| tooth | eŋma'ak | ema'ak | nowi |
| tree | ya'amet | yamek | epaq |
| water | yiŋmen | yemen | etaɡat |
| woman | kelana | ikenwana | alo |
| breast | eŋkeñek | ininek | ltovi |
| moon | pelten | pelten | ka'awoɡoyk |

*L=voiceless alveolar lateral

Briggs, Janet R.  1973.  Ayoreo Narrative Analysis.
International Journal of American Linguistics
39:155-63.

Ceccarelli, L.  1965.  I Caduveo e i Chamacoco, Archive per L'antropologia e la etnologia 95:145-
215 (Firenze).

Coryn, Alfredo.  n.d.  Los Indios Lenguas, sus Costumbres y su Idioma, con Compendio de Gramática
y Vocabulario.  Annuario Sociedad Científica
Argentina 93:221-82.

Ferrario, B.  1947.  Contribución al Conocimiento
del idioma 'Lengua'.  Actas y Trabajos Científicos del XXVII^e Congreso Internacional de Americanistas: Sessión de Mexico II:377-82.

Grünberg, Georg, and Friedl Grünberg.  1974.  Los
Chiriguanos (Guaraní occidentales) del Chaco
Central Paraguayo.  Supplemento Antropologico
IX. 1-2:7-109.

Junker, P., J. Wilkskamp, and J. Seelwische.
1968.  Manual de la Gramática Chulupí.  Supplemento Antropológico III. 1-2:159-248.

Kelm, Heinz.  1964.  Das Zamuco - Eine Lebende
Sprache.  Anthropos LIX:457-516/770-842
(Freiburg in der Schweiz).

Loukotka, Čestmir.  1968.  Classification of South
American Indian Languages.  Los Angeles: Reference Series, v. 7, Latin American Center, University of California.

Lowes, R.H.G.  1954.  Alphabetical List of Lengua
Indian Words With English Equivalents.  Journal
de la Société des Americanistes 43:85-109
(Paris).

O'Leary, Timothy J.   1963.   Ethnographic Bibliography of South America.   New Haven: Human Relations Area Files.

Schmidt, Max.   1937.   Los Tapietés.   Revista de la Sociedad Científica del Paraguay 4.2:36-67 (Asunción).

------.   1938.   Los Chiriguanos e Izozós.   Revista de la Sociedad Científica del Paraguay 4.3:1-115

Seelwische, José.   1975.   Na Lhasinonash napi Nivacle: Gramática Nivacle.   Asunción.

Stahl, Wilmar, ed.   1977.   Informe general de trabajo del Comité Asesor Indígena: Correspondiente al año 1976.   Filadelfia, Paraguay: Asociación de Cooperación Indígena Mennonita.

Stahl, Wilmar.   n.d.   Towards Bilingualism in Lengua Schools: A Socio-Linguistic Study of Indigenous Schools in the Paraguayan Chaco, Filadelfia.

Sušnik, B.   1957.   Estructura de la lengua chamacoco-ebitoso.   Boletín de la Sociedad Científica del Paraguay y del Museo Andrés Barbero: Etnolingüística I. 1-86.

------.   1958.   Estructura grammatical de los Lenguas Maskoys, Boletín de la Sociedad Científica del Paraguay y Museo Etnográfico Andrés Barbero: Etnolingüística II.

------.   1962.   Vocabularios inéditos de los idiomas Emok-Toba y Chorotí recogidos por el doctor Max Schmidt.   Boletín de la Sociedad Científica del Paraguay y del Museo Andrés Barbero VI.3.

------.   1968.   Chulupí: Esbozo gramatical analítico.   Asunción.

------. 1970. Chamacocos II: Diccionario etnográfico. Asunción: Museo etnográfico A. Barbero.

------. 1971. Los patrones estructurales de la
lengua Toba. Guaykurú (Lenguas Chaqueñas I/1),
Asunción: Museo etnográfico A. Barbero.

------. 1972. Familia zamuko: čamakoko-ayoweo
(Lenguas Chaqueñas II). Asunción: Museo etnográfico A. Barbero.

------. 1973. La lengua de los ayoweos-moros:
estructura gramatical y fraseario etnográfico,
2nd ed. Asunción: Museo Etnográfico Andrés
Barbero.

Tovar, Antonio. 1961. Catálogo de las lenguas de
América del Sur: enumeración, con indicaciones
tipológicas, bibliografía y mapas. Buenos
Aires: Editorial Sudamericana.

------. 1966. Notas de campo sobre el idioma Chorote, Proceedings of the XXXVI International
Congress of Americanists II:221-227 (Geneva).

Voegelin, C.F., and F.M. Voegelin. 1977. Classification and Index of the World's Languages.
Amsterdam.

Wicke, C.R., and M. Chase-Sardi. 1969. Componential Analysis of Chulupí (Ashluslay) Kinship
Terminology. Ethnology 8:484-93.

# Index

This index contains names of languages and language groups that occur in the introduction and in the text, but not those that occur in the tables or reference sections.

Quechuamaran, 619
Quechumaran, 181-184
Quechumaran, 570, 705, 707
Quichua, 7, 157, 164, 169, 170, 171, 173, 174, 175, 180, 181-184, 187, 669, 706-707, 732-752. See also Quechua
Quichua, Ecuadorian, 443-480
Quirixaná. See Waimiri

Ramaráma, 371, 372, 417
Rangu. See Trio-Rangu
Resígaro, 216
Rikbaktsá, 416, 418
Rikbaktsá-Jê, 417
Rionegriño, 347
Roucouyene, 330, 356
Runa-simi, 503, 504, 505

SE Quichua, 732-752
Sa'apan. See Sanapana
Sabanê, 308, 309, 310, 312, 316, 318, 319
Sabela (= Ssabela), 171. See also Huaorani
Sainawa, 225
Sakaka. See Hishkaryána
Saliban (= Salivan), 21, 41-45 passim
Saluma, 332, 356
Samathari, 36
San Genaro, 347
Sanapaná, 811, 815, 819, 820-822
Sanavirone-Indama, 738, 740
Saníma (=Tsaníma), 25, 28, 38-41

Sanumá, 76, 77, 78, 412, 415. See also Yanomama
Sapara, 67, 68, 120, 333, 355. See also Makushí
Sapé, 33, 46, 49, 51-52, 82, 354
Sararé, 310
Sataré (= Satere), 371, 372, 415. See also Mawé
Secoya, 157, 164-167 passim, 214
Sekaka. See Hishkaryána
Selk'nam, 757, 759, 762. See also Ona
Selknam, 715, 716, 717. See also Ona
Septentrional Austral Tehuelche, 760
Septentrional Boreal Tehuelche, 760
Shamathari, 36
Shaparru, 347
Shapra, 216
Sharanahua, 213, 225, 227, 251-253, 265
Sharanáwa, 412
Shavante, 396, 415, 416
Shawanahua, 282
Shebayo. See Arawakan
Sherente, 415
Shereu (= Chereu, Djereu, Sereu, Tchereu), 62 98, 100
Shikana. See Hoti
Shimigae, 184, 185
Shipibo, 214, 227, 245, 253-265, 268, 269, 283. See also Conibo
Shiriána, 414. See also Yanam
Shirianan, 25